THE DEATH OF EAST PRUSSIA

War and Revenge in Germany's Easternmost Province

THE DEATH OF EAST PRUSSIA

War and Revenge in Germany's
Easternmost Province

PETER B. CLARK

ANDOVER
PRESS

Cover design by Liz Trovato
Andover Press and the Andover Press colophon
are registered trademarks of Vantage Press, Inc.

FIRST EDITION
5503 Montgomery Street
Chevy Chase, MD 20815
DeathofEastPrussia@gmail.com

Published by Andover Press

 Manufactured in the United States of America
ISBN: 978-1-481935-75-3

Library of Congress Catalog Card No: 2012936102

0 9 8 7 6 5 4 3 2 1

Excerpts from PRUSSIAN NIGHTS: A POEM by Alexander Solzhenitsyn, translated by
Robert Conquest. Translation copyright © 1977 by Robert Conquest. Reprinted by
permission of Farrar, Straus and Giroux

Wieck, Michael. A CHILDHOOD UNDER HITLER AND STALIN. © 2003 by the
Board of Regents of the University of Wisconsin System. Reprinted by permission of The
University of Wisconsin Press.

To my wife

CONTENTS

ACKNOWLEDGMENTS

Without my wife, Heide-Hede Könitzer Clark, this book could not have been written. Her East Prussian background and that of her family provided the motivation for this book. She painstakingly edited each draft of the text and her extremely high standards and insistence on clarity vastly improved the manuscript. Moreover, she made innumerable suggestions regarding the tone and organization of the book that I incorporated in the text. I am most grateful for her sound advice and unstinting support throughout all phases of the creation of *The Death of East Prussia*.

I wish to acknowledge the generous support and very helpful assistance from other close family members. My daughter, Vanessa J. H. Clark, a keen student of the English language, carefully read the manuscript and made many suggestions of style and substance that significantly improved the text. In addition, I appreciate very much her encouragement to persist with the publication of the book. My son, Barton B. Clark, made many insightful comments on the manuscript, and with his background and knowledge of history, he helped to clarify some of the threads of the narrative. He also provided invaluable assistance and advice regarding the publishing process.

I wish to thank my brother-in-law, Burkhard Könitzer. With a strong interest in German history, he encouraged me from the outset of my research and gave me twenty-five pages of detailed comments and suggestions after reading an entire draft. He corrected a number of errors I had made concerning

German history and proposed the inclusion of additional historical detail that fleshed out the exposition. Unfortunately, he did not live to see the published copy that incorporates many of his suggestions.

Early on in my research I had the good fortune to interview Michael Wieck. Growing up in Königsberg and being half-Jewish, he barely escaped being killed by the Nazis but then nearly perished under the Russian occupation. His memoir, *A Childhood under Hitler and Stalin – Memoirs of a "Certified Jew,"* is one of my main sources; it describes his incredible struggle to survive under the harsh conditions of post-war Königsberg. Herr Wieck read the entire manuscript and made a number of suggestions that improved the text. I also thank him for his efforts to have the book published in Germany. While I was researching, writing, and polishing my manuscript, he was a constant source of inspiration and support, and I deeply appreciate his encouragement to persevere in the publication process.

I would like to express my thanks to Lorenz Grimoni, head of the Museum Stadt Königsberg in Duisburg, Germany. He graciously welcomed my wife, brother-in-law, and me to his office where he shared his extensive knowledge of the demise of Königsberg. On these visits he gave me several books and other publications of considerable relevance for my research, and he also sent me a number of photographs of Königsberg for which I am most grateful.

I would also like to thank Michael Röskau for his careful reading of the manuscript and pointing out a number of errors. In addition, I greatly value his gift of a book by his grandfather, Erich Göttgen, *Der Wiederaufbau Ostpreussens (The Reconstruction of East Prussia)*, which describes the reconstruction of East Prussia following the Russian invasion in World War I. I benefited from discussions with Charles McCain, author of *An Honorable German,* particularly concerning the German Navy in World War II. After he read the manuscript, he provided key references on Operation Hannibal, the evacuation via the Baltic of German civilians and soldiers from East Prussia. He also went out of his way to help me find a literary agent.

Rita Warnock kindly sent me a detailed account of how she survived the end of the war in Stettin under Russian and then Polish occupation, and on her treks east and then finally west, for which I wish to thank her. I would in addition like to mention Iris Rörup, my wife's second cousin. As a young girl she experienced firsthand the Russian occupation of Königsberg which she described in her book, *Also Sprach Vielliebchen,* and also conveyed to me in an interview and several conversations. My book, which draws on her vivid accounts and that of many other East Prussians, bears witness to their fate.

While doing research for my book in Germany, I visited the Bundesarchiv in Koblenz and wish to thank Klaus-Dieter Postupa and Barbara Sander for their assistance in locating relevant documents and other material. I am also grateful to Dr. Ernst Gierlich at the Kulturstiftung der deutschen Vertriebenen (Cultural Foundation of German Expellees) in Bonn for a lengthy interview and for providing me with vivid eyewitness accounts of the fate of women in Königsberg under Russian rule. In the United States most of my research was conducted at the European Reading Room in the Library of Congress in Washington, DC. The staff was unfailingly cordial and helpful in guiding me to the vast collection of material at the Library of Congress related to my topic. I would like to thank in particular Grant Harris, Harold Leich and Predrag Pajic, and especially Regina Frackowiak for her assistance in locating Polish sources and translating a number of passages from Polish into English. While researching at the European Reading Room I met Steve Grant and Chalmers Hood, and I am indebted to them for steering me to some especially relevant references.

Others read all or parts of the manuscript and provided helpful suggestions, including which publishers might be attracted to the topic. These are John Buntin, Prof. Donald Horowitz, Prof. Jerome Stein, and Chris Ward. I would also like to thank Matt Fullerty for implementing some important improvements in the arrangement of the text. Finally, I was most grateful to have Fiona Hallowell as my editor at Andover Press. Her patience and cheerfullness were very much appreciated. I also wish to thank my copy editor, Grace Morsberger, who significantly helped improve the text, and Richard Rothschild for facilitating the final production.

CONCORDANCE OF
PLACE NAMES

The towns and cities in East Prussia mentioned in the text are referred to by their German names, given that the province was German territory during most the time period covered by the book. They are now in Poland, Russia, and Lithuania, and their contemporary names are provided below following their German names.

German Name	Contemporary Name
Allenburg	Druzhba
Allenstein	Olsztyn
Balga	Wesjolnoje
Bartenstein	Bartoszyce
Brandenburg	Uschakowo
Braunsberg	Braniewo
Bromberg	Bydgoszcz
Cranz	Zelenogradsk
Danzig	Gdansk

Darkehmen/Angerapp	Ozyorsk
Deutsch Eylau	Ilawa
Dirschau	Tczew
Ebenrode/Stallupönen	Nesterow
Elbing	Elblag
Eydtkuhnen/Eydtkau	Chernyshevskoye
Fischhausen	Primorsk
Frauenburg	Frombork
Friedland	Pravdinsk
Friedrichstein	Kamenka
Gdingen/Gotenhafen	Gdynia
Georgenburg	Mayovka
Gerdauen	Shelesodororoshnyi
Gilgenburg	Dabrowno
Goldap	Goldap
Gotenhafen	Gdynia
Graudenz	Grudziadz
Gumbinnen	Gusev
Heilsberg	Lidzbark Warminski
Hela	Hel
Heiligenbeil	Mamonovo
Heydekrug	Silute
Insterburg	Chernyakhovsk
Johannisburg	Pisz
Juditten	Mendeleevo

Kahlberg	Krynica Morska
Karthaus	Kartuzy
Katowitz	Kattowitz
Königsberg	Kaliningrad
Kulm	Chelmno
Küstrin	Kostrzyn
Labiau	Polessk
Landsberg	Gorowo
Lemberg	Lwow
Libau	Liepaja
Lötzen	Gizycko
Lyck	Elk
Marienwerder	Kwidzyn
Marienburg	Malbork
Memel	Klaipeda
Metgethen	Lesnoye
Mohrungen	Morag
Neidenburg	Nidzica
Nemmersdorf	Mayakovskoye
Neukrug	Nowa Karczma
Neukuhren	Pionersky
Nidden	Nida
Ortelsburg	Szczytno
Osterode	Ostroda
Palmnicken	Yantarny
Pillkallen/Schlossberg	Dobrovolsk
Pillau	Baltiysk

Posen	Poznan
Preussisch Eylau	Bagrationovsk
Preussisch Holland	Paslek
Ragnit	Neman
Rastenburg	Ketrzyn
Rauschen	Svetlogorsk
Rosenberg	Susz
Rossitten	Rybachy
Rössel	Reszel
Schlossberg/Pillkallen	Dobrovolsk
Schneidemühl	Pila
Schwirwindt	Kutusowo
Sensburg	Mragowo
Soldau	Dzialdowo
Stallupönen/Ebenrode	Nesterov
Strasburg	Brodnica
Stettin	Szczecin
Stuhm	Sztum
Stutthof	Sztutowo
Suwalki	Suwalki
Tannenberg	Stebark
Tapiau	Gvardeysk
Tauroggen	Taurage
Thorn	Torun
Tilsit	Sovetsk
Tolkemit	Tolkmicko
Trakehnen	Yasnaya Polyana
Wartenburg	Barczewo
Wehlau	Znamensk
Wilna	Vilnius
Wormditt	Orneta

LIST OF MAPS

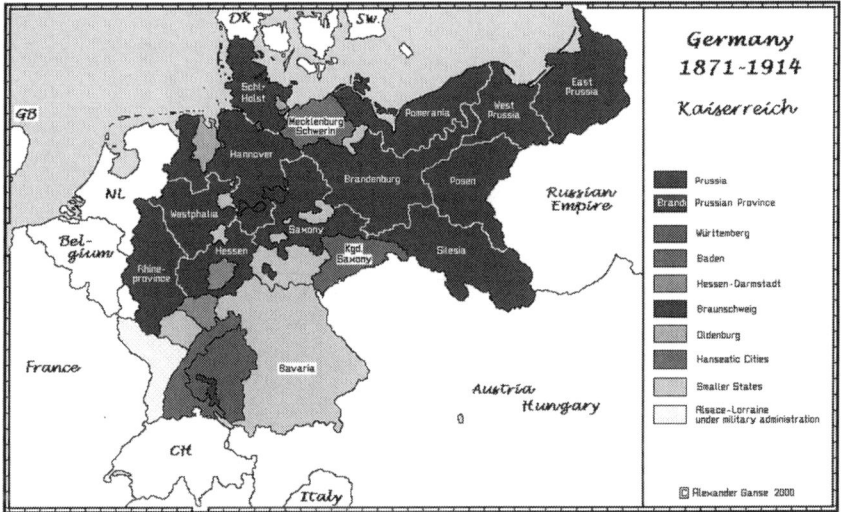

Map 1. Germany before World War I.

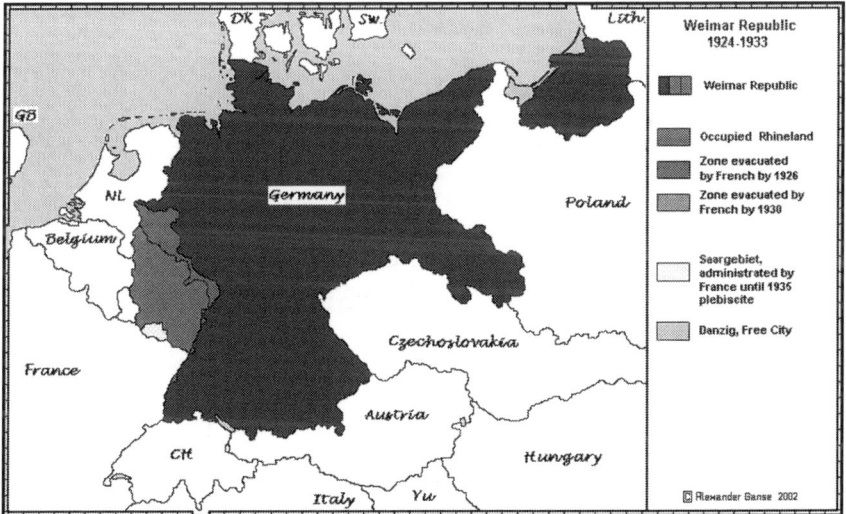

Map 2. Germany after World War I with Polish Corridor.

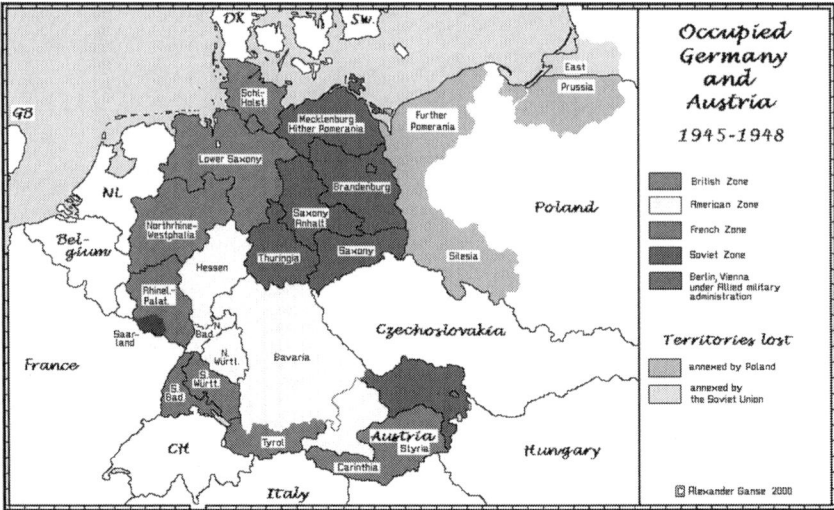

Map 3. Germany after World War II.

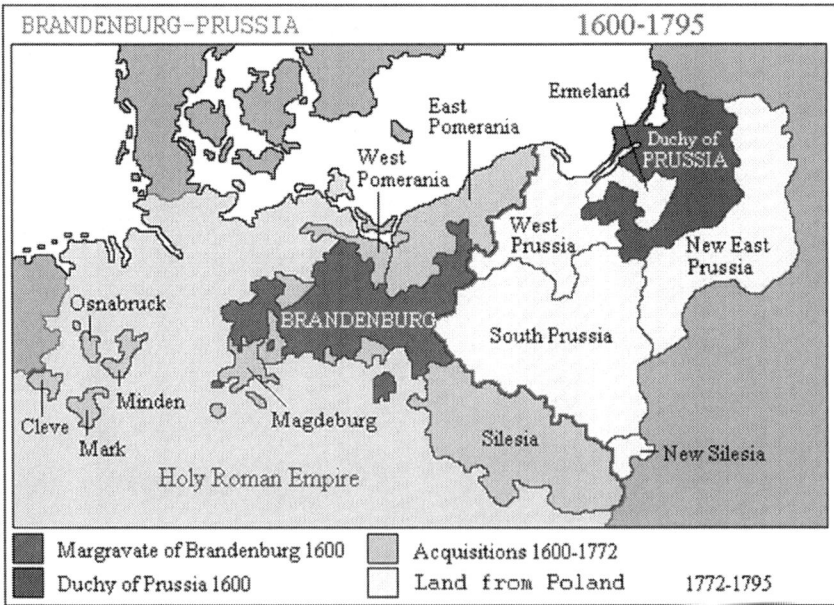

Map 4. Union of the Duchy of Prussia and Brandenburg.

Map 5. East Prussia 1923–1939.

Fischhausen
16. 4.

Peyss

H.-Gr. Nord

Neuhäuser

Pillau 25. 4.

OST-SEE

Neutief

0   5   10 km

FRISCHES HAFF

4.

19. 3.
Kahlholz

Wolitta

Balga 18. 3.

Wolittnick

Follendorf
17. 3.

Pr. Lütjen
18. 3.

Gr Hoppenbruch

Straubwort

Rosenberg
17. 3.

18. 3.
Bladiau   Lank

Dtsch Bahnau

Steindorf

Königsdorf

Narmeln

Karben

Schirten
24. 3.
Heiligenbeil

18. 3.

Leysuhnen

Jürkendorf

Pr Bahnou

Bahnau

Thomsdorf
20. 3.

Jarft

Alt-
Ruhnenberg

Wermten
18. 3.

Neu-Passarge

Rossen

Birkenau

Rehfeld 18. 3.

Waltersdorf
18. 3.

XX.

Hammersdorf

Eisenberg
17. 3.

VI.

Fuchs-Berg

Braunsberg
20. 3.

Hohenwalde
11. 3.

14.

349.

Passarge

Bahnau-Mühle

61.

541.

Frauenburg
8. 3.

24. Pz.

131.

Breitlinde
14. 3.

Bahnau

48.

3.

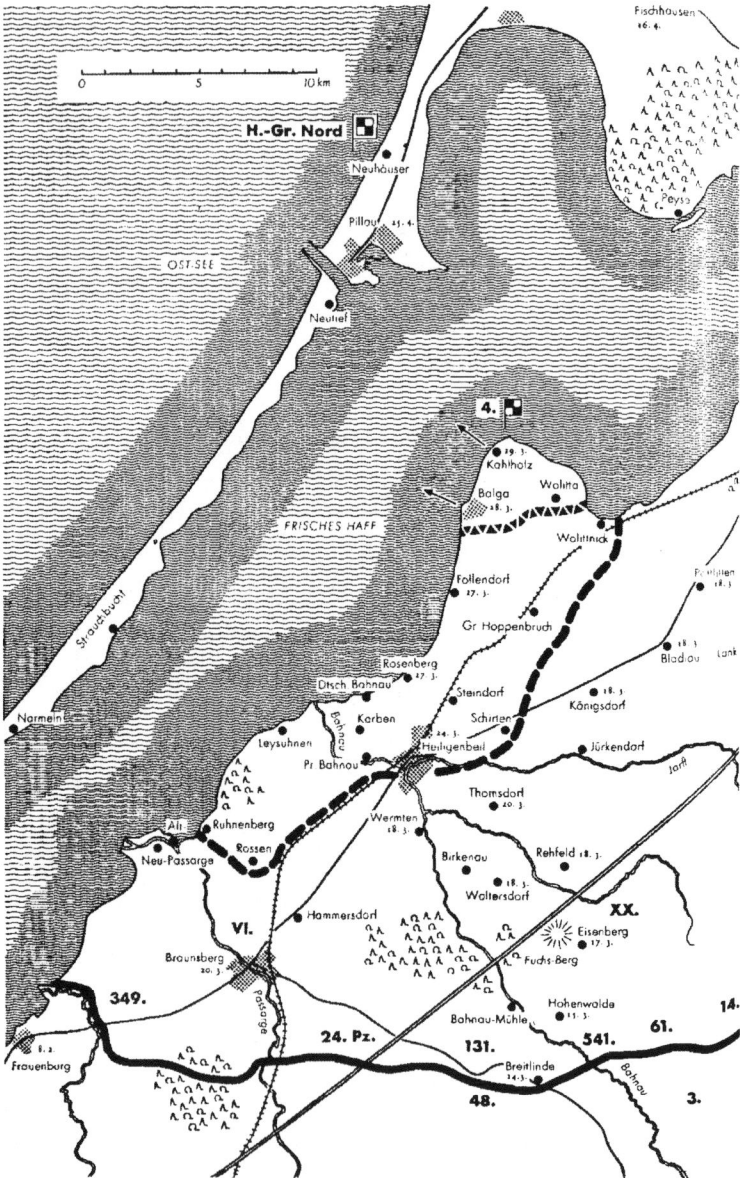

Map 6. The Heiligenbeil Cauldron.

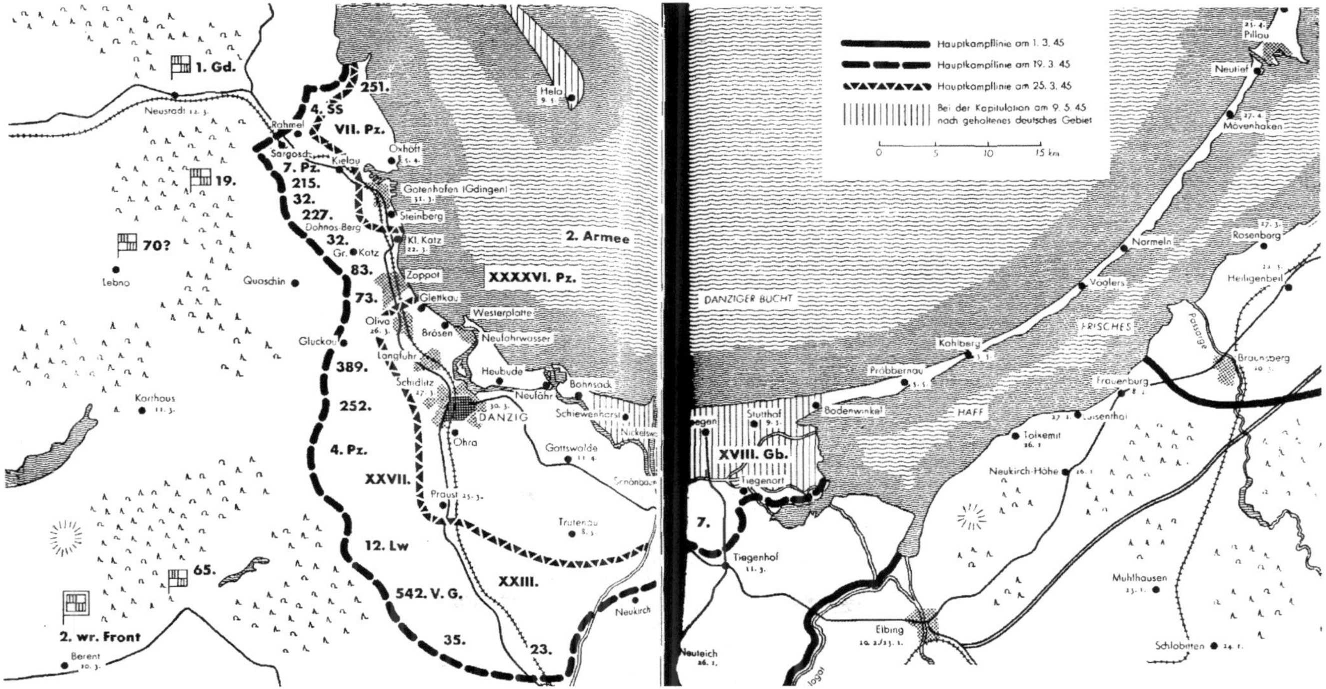

Map 7. Towns on the Bay of Danzig.

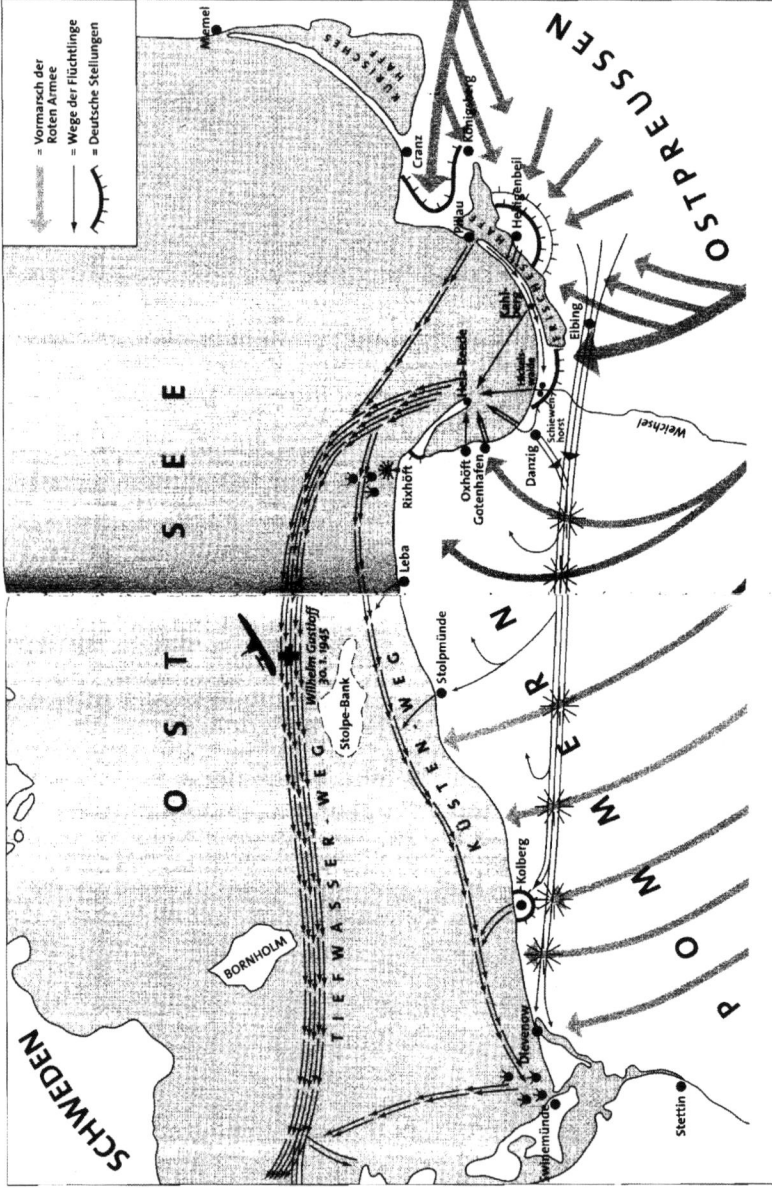

Map 8. Last Voyage of the *Wilhelm Gustloff*.

Map 9. Westward Shift of Poland's Borders.

POLAND: EASTERN FRONTIER

LEGEND

- National boundaries
- Line of Russian occupation, June 1941
- Boundaries of the Ukraine and White Russia
- Voivodship boundaries
- Curzon Line
- Railroads
- Line "A"
- Line "B"
- Line "C"
- Line "D"
- Line "E"
- Line "F"

Scale 1:3,700,000

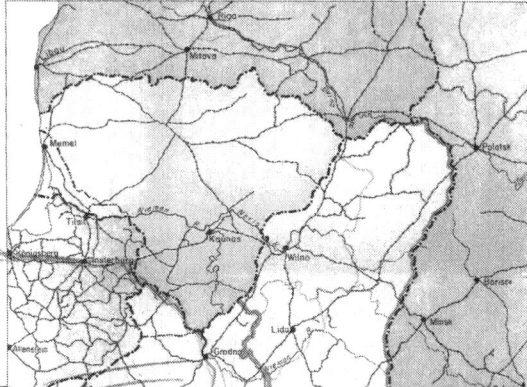

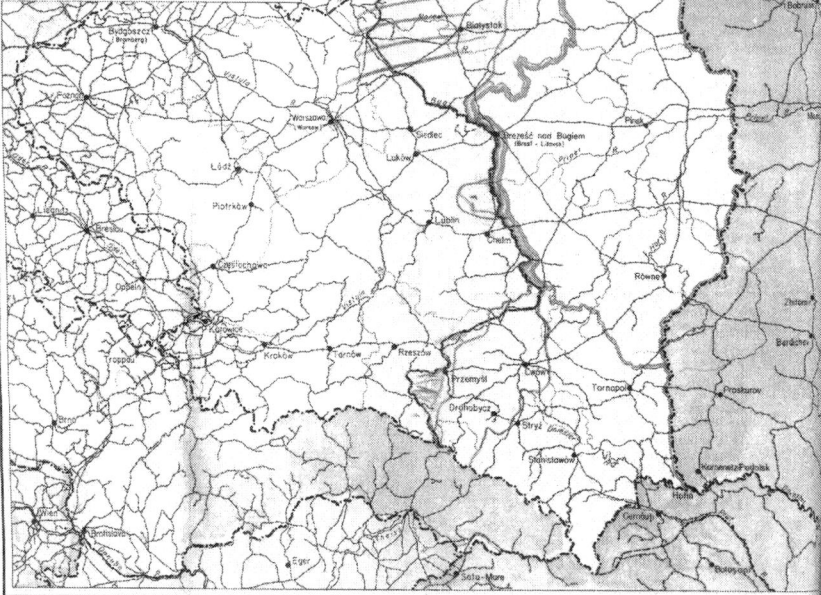

Compiled and drawn in Ge, Nov. 26, 1942

Original classification [Secret]

Map 10. Poland: Eastern Frontier with Stalin's Red Line.

The Oder-Neisse Line and Germany's postwar territorial losses

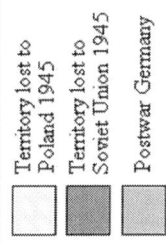

Territory lost to Poland 1945

Territory lost to Soviet Union 1945

Postwar Germany

1. The Border Mark included those parts of the former Prussian districts of Posen and West Prussia which were not lost to Poland in 1918, apart from the area of West Prussia around Elbing.

2. All the areas of Germany on this map apart from Saxony were part of the prewar State of Prussia.

3. Danzig was a Free City administered by the League of Nations 1919-39.

4. Stettin and the surrounding area were annexed by Poland despite being west of the Oder-Neisse Line.

5. This map uses the English forms of the German names of the cities and regions annexed by Poland in 1945. This does not imply any position on the "correct" form of these names.

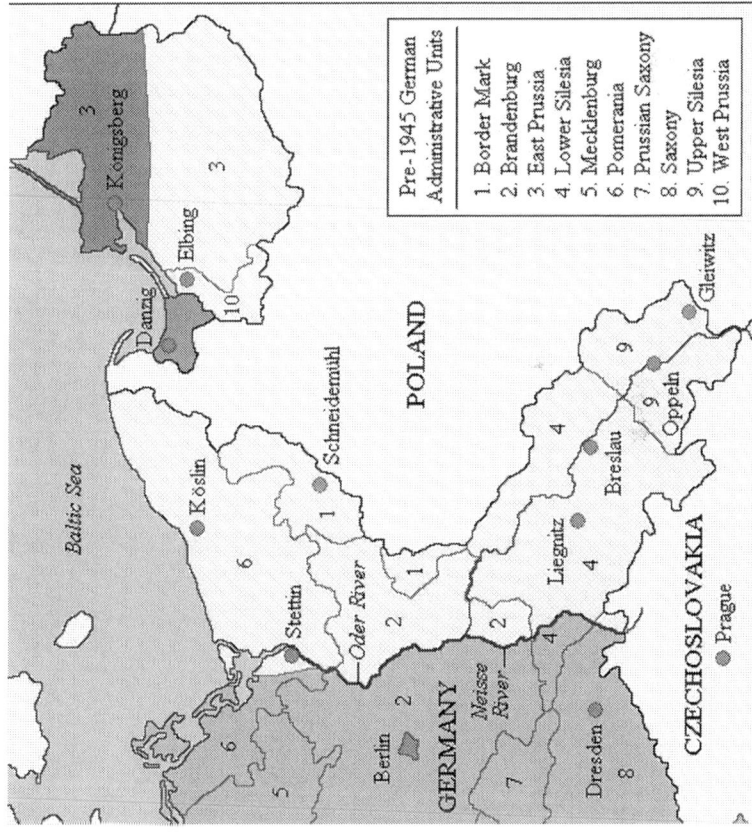

Pre-1945 German Administrative Units

1. Border Mark
2. Brandenburg
3. East Prussia
4. Lower Silesia
5. Mecklenburg
6. Pomerania
7. Prussian Saxony
8. Saxony
9. Upper Silesia
10. West Prussia

Map 11. The Oder-Neisse Line.

LIST OF ILLUSTRATIONS
(Located between Chapters IV and V)

INTRODUCTION

East Prussia was the easternmost province of Germany when World War II broke out in September 1939. Founded by the Teutonic Knights in the thirteenth century, it contributed significantly to the economy of Germany as the country's breadbasket and to its intellectual and cultural life. Probably the best-known native of East Prussia is the eighteenth-century philosopher, Immanuel Kant. Born and educated in the capital, Königsberg, Kant spent his entire academic career at the Albertina University, where he wrote his pathbreaking contributions to philosophy. Anyone wishing to make a pilgrimage to the birthplace and home of Kant would find a memorial erected in his honor, but would also discover that the splendors of the German Königsberg are gone and have been replaced by what is now the Russian city of Kaliningrad. The German province of East Prussia has vanished as well. As a consequence of World War II, the northern third of this once-thriving German province was taken over by Russia and the southern two-thirds by Poland. Why did this happen? It will be seen that geography, revenge, and political callousness and calculation all contributed to the end of East Prussia.

This book also describes the fate of East Prussians during World War II and afterward, when their homeland was expunged from Germany, as this story of the war's collateral damage to civilians is largely unknown in the United States. East Prussia bore the brunt of the Red Army's invasion in late 1944 and early 1945 when Soviet soldiers were bent on revenge for the atrocities committed by the Nazis in their country. Hundreds of thousands of German refugees tried to escape the advancing Soviet forces in the frigid winter of 1945; many died of exhaustion and starvation on the trek or drowned when their ships were attacked in the Baltic. The East Prussians who stayed behind or were overtaken by the rapidly invading Soviet Army faced rape, murder, assault, and plunder by rampaging Soviet soldiers. Those who survived the war became virtual slave laborers for the Russians and the Poles who had become their new masters as a result of the Allies' decision to allocate East Prussia to the Soviet Union and Poland. The East Prussians either succumbed to starvation and disease or were expelled from their homeland in the late 1940s.

While this book focuses on what happened in East Prussia in World War II and afterward, some historical background is needed to understand the causes of the elimination of Germany's easternmost province. Chapter I provides a brief history of East Prussia from its founding in the thirteenth century by the Order of the Teutonic Knights up to the eve of World War II. From the very beginning, geography was important as this province was an outpost situated far from the heartland of Germany (see Map 1. Germany before World War I). It was subject to incursions from nearby countries—Lithuania, Poland, Russia, and Sweden—and over the centuries was in danger of being absorbed by them. The chapter highlights East Prussia's vulnerability to these invaders and shows that from its founding, its fate was inextricably linked to its eastern neighbor, Poland. This historical background is needed to explain why for centuries Poland had what it regarded as well-justified claims to East Prussia, claims that were eventually realized in the twentieth century.

After World War I, East Prussia's precarious geographic position was exacerbated when it was separated from the rest of Germany by the Polish Corridor as a result of the Versailles Treaty (see Map 2. Germany after World War I with Polish Corridor). The province might have survived this isolation had Hitler not unleashed World War II by attacking Poland in September 1939 and invading the Soviet Union in June 1941. Chapter II describes in some detail the vicious campaign of total war waged by the German armed forces which wreaked death and destruction on Poland and the Soviet Union and sowed the seeds for revenge. This chapter also shows that East Prussia remained an island of relative calm largely unscathed by the war, in contrast to the rest of Germany, which was subjected to air raids of increasing severity. Yet a look at daily life in the province in the early 1940s reveals that the civilian population experienced considerable hardship due to the scarcity of food and coal, as well as tension caused by the presence of large numbers of Berliners and Germans from other cities who had been evacuated to what was considered "safe" East Prussia. In addition, Chapter II describes the Kristallnacht in Königsberg and the transport to their deaths of the remaining Jews in the city. Only in late August 1944, did the war come home in earnest to Königsberg when it was severely damaged by British Royal Air Force bombers during two night-time raids.

Chapter III covers the invasion of East Prussia and the flight of its inhabitants from the Red Army. The annihilation of the German Army Group Center in Belorussia in 1944 was the beginning of the end. The stage was thus set for the Red Army to make its first incursions onto German soil in October and November of 1944 when East Prussian civilians experienced firsthand the horrors of a ground war. The atrocities in Nemmersdorf are described as is the controversy that still surrounds the extent of the cruelties committed there by Soviet forces. The chapter cites eyewitness reports that describe the Red Army's brutal treatment of East Prussian civilians when the Soviets launched their full-scale invasion of East Prussia in mid-January 1945. Some civilians were shot on the spot, many women were raped, some repeatedly, and whole villages were burned down. As word spread that atrocities had been committed during the invasion, the flight from the rapidly advancing Red Army took on epic proportions. Wagons were hastily loaded with food, bedding, and hay for horses and oxen, and thousands of women and children and a few men—sometimes POWs working on East Prussian farms—made their way westward in the bitter cold toward the German interior in a desperate effort to outrun the oncoming Soviet forces.

Making painfully slow progress on roads clogged with other wagons and military vehicles, many of the refugees were overtaken by Soviet soldiers who stole their watches, pillaged their possessions, raped many of the women, and in some cases murdered them. The escape attempt was chaotic, disorganized, and delayed because government and Nazi Party officials—in particular, the infamous Gauleiter of East Prussia, Erich Koch—gave permission to evacuate only when the Red Army stood a few kilometers distant from East Prussian towns and villages. As a result, there was needless loss of life and great hardship when civilians attempting to escape to the west were apprehended by Soviet soldiers.

Many of the East Prussian refugees aimed to reach the Baltic but first had to cross the frozen Frisches Haff (the freshwater lagoon separated from the Baltic by the narrow spit of land known as the Frische Nehrung) where they were attacked by low-flying Soviet fighter planes and faced the ever-present danger of breaking through the ice. If successful in running this gauntlet and reaching the Frische Nehrung on the Baltic, they faced the challenge of finding a vessel that would transport them to central Germany. Although most East Prussian refugees survived the hazardous voyage on the Baltic, thousands died when Soviet submarines and planes attacked their ships, including nine thousand when the *Wilhelm Gustloff* was torpedoed in late January 1945. Chapter III concludes with a description of the last days of Königsberg and Samland, and the world's largest rescue of over two million refugees and military personnel from Baltic ports, including Pillau, Gotenhaven, and Hela.

During the invasion and subsequent occupation of East Prussia by the Red Army, civilians were completely at the mercy of the Soviet soldiers. The bestial behavior of these Soviet troops was unprecedented in Western Europe and quite different from the brief and less damaging Soviet invasion of East Prussia in World War I. An attempt is made to explain this behavior in Chapter IV, which includes eyewitness reports of brutal attacks on German women as well as accounts by Soviet officers, including Alexander Solzhenitsyn, that candidly depict acts of violence committed by their own soldiers in East Prussia. These attacks were partly due to a desire for revenge for the murderous and deliberately destructive German military operations against the Soviet Union. In addition, up until almost the very end of the war, the Soviet government undertook a relentless propaganda campaign, led by the Russian journalist and author Ilya

Ehrenberg, that was designed to incite Soviet soldiers with hatred for Germans. A description of the violent conduct of Soviet military personnel in Hungary and Soviet-occupied Germany shows that this conduct was not driven solely by revenge and the Soviet-government inspired hatred of Germans. Yet amid the generally horrific behavior of the Red Army there were individual acts of kindness and compassion on the Soviet side.

While the vast majority of German refugees made a successful escape across the Baltic, thousands met a watery grave. Almost one-quarter of the forty thousand who lost their lives at sea were on the former cruise ship, the *Wilhelm Gustloff*, when it was torpedoed at 9:15 p.m. on January 30, 1945; this was the greatest ship disaster in maritime history. Chapter V provides a vivid account of this catastrophe, including the fate of Commander Marinesko, the captain of the *S-13*, which sank the *Gustloff*. Simultaneously, a tragedy was unfolding on the Baltic coast of East Prussia. On the cliffs and beaches outside the town of Palmnicken roughly three thousand concentration-camp inmates, mainly young Jewish women from Eastern Europe, were being murdered by the SS and their henchmen. The massacre at Palmnicken was a continuation of the German campaign of death and devastation in the Soviet Union, including the extermination of Jews and non-Jews alike, which unleashed the Soviet counterattack on Germany that ultimately resulted in the destruction of East Prussia.

Many East Prussians failed in their attempt to flee the Red Army and returned to their homes, and after Germany surrendered on the night of May 8–9, 1945, a significant number who had managed to escape also returned. Unaware that the wartime Allies had decided that East Prussia would no longer be a part of Germany, they believed they would be able to resume the way of life they had known before the war. They were bitterly disappointed when they gradually realized this would not be the case. Chapter VI describes their fate under Russian and Polish rule. Immediately following the capitulation of Königsberg in early April 1945, the city's inhabitants were rounded up and removed from the capital on forced marches lasting several days. During these marches they were interrogated by Soviet secret police to ascertain if they had been Nazi officials in the Third Reich, and these interrogations subsequently continued in Rothenstein, a suburb of Königsberg, and in other camps in East Prussia. On these marches many of the women were raped, often repeatedly, by Soviet guards, and children and old men died from exposure and lack of food. While the Königsbergers were on the march, Soviet troops systematically looted the dwellings in the city and then set many on fire. Thousands of East Prussians, mainly young women, were transported by train to forced labor camps in the Soviet Union where up to half died from disease, overwork, dangerous working conditions, and malnutrition.

In the ruins of East Prussia, Germans in the early postwar years faced an unrelenting struggle to survive. Food was scarce, and if they could work for the Russians the pay was typically some bread, hardly enough to sustain life. In the first months after the war many East Prussians were able to keep themselves alive only by scavenging for food in bombed-out buildings, searching for potatoes and other crops left in the fields, and foraging for edible wild plants. To survive in these desperate conditions, they had to be cunning and resourceful. Chapter VI includes accounts of those who won the struggle to survive and those who did not. Even in hospitals meals were so meager that patients needed the additional food relatives brought them to escape death from malnutrition. Conditions in the countryside were hardly better because the Russians had stripped the farms bare of all usable agricultural machinery and equipment, livestock, and household goods.

East Prussians felt increasingly hopeless about their future in the second half of 1945 and 1946. Outcasts in what had been their homeland, they were subject to expropriation of what little property they had as more and more Soviet citizens settled in the northern third of the province and Poles moved into the southern two-thirds. The new arrivals could take their pick of the farms, houses, and apartments belonging to East Prussians, who were kicked out and had to find new accommodations wherever they could. Moreover, jobs became scarce for the Germans as the Soviet and Polish settlers took over their positions.

Facing such bleak prospects in their native land, East Prussians were soon desperate to escape. In the fall of 1945 some were allowed to leave what had become the Polish part of East Prussia, and more organized expulsions took place from 1946 to 1948 because the Polish authorities wished to cleanse their new territory of East Prussians. By 1950, the vast majority of Germans in Polish East Prussia had been evacuated by train to the Soviet zone of what remained of Germany. In Russian East Prussia the new Russian government used the local inhabitants essentially as forced laborers to bring in the crops and help in the reconstruction of the province, and only in the spring of 1947 did they permit the first East Prussians to depart. Highly organized deportations by train to the Soviet-occupied zone of Germany began in late 1947 and continued through 1948, by which time nearly all East Prussians had been expelled from the northern one-third of the former German province.

During the war, the Soviet Union had made plans to establish a military base on the Baltic in East Prussia, and Poland had laid the groundwork to achieve what it regarded as its long-standing claims to this German territory. As described in Chapter VII, the fate of East Prussia was sealed during the three major Allied conferences in Teheran (November/December 1943), Yalta (February 1945), and Potsdam (July/August 1945). At these conferences the leaders of Great Britain and the United States approved the Soviet plans and all three (Stalin, Roosevelt and his successor Truman, and Churchill and his successor Attlee) endorsed the Polish desire to expand at Germany's expense. The three Allies regarded East Prussia as the locus of the worst characteristics of the Prussian military mindset they believed had helped bring about World War II. Indeed, they had already agreed in 1943 that the province should be excised from Germany to ward off a reemergence of Prussian militarism. The decision to allocate East Prussia to Russia and Poland was taken during a time of very heavy fighting and Allied plans for postwar Europe made at Potsdam were influenced by the millions of lives lost in the war that had just ended. Nevertheless, this decision was taken in callous disregard of the Atlantic Charter, which was signed in August 1941 by the United Kingdom and the United States and which proclaimed that "they desire to see no territorial changes that do not accord with the freely expressed wishes of the peoples concerned," and that "they respect the right of all peoples to choose the form of government under which they will live."[1]

After long negotiations, the Allies further agreed that Poland should receive not only the southern two-thirds of East Prussia, but also a large slice of Germany's eastern territories, including Silesia, eastern Brandenburg, and eastern Pomerania (see Map 3. Germany after World War II). This additional land was calculated to compensate Poland for the territory on its eastern border taken by the Soviet Union. At the final conference in Potsdam in July/ August 1945, the Allied leaders also decided that all Germans in the territory acquired by Poland, as well as ethnic Germans living in other parts of Eastern Europe, should be transferred to one of the four occupied zones of Germany. The vast ethnic cleansing involved in this expulsion brought untold hardship and death for millions of Germans who were forcibly evicted from their homes.

———

The fate of East Prussians in World War II and its aftermath was by no means unique. Not only southern East Prussia but also the much larger area of Germany east of the Oder and Neisse rivers, comprising West Prussia, Posen, Silesia, eastern Brandenburg, and eastern Pomerania, was allocated to Poland by the Allies at Potsdam in 1945. Millions of German nationals living in these German territories were expelled by the Poles in a manner similar to that of the Germans from Polish East Prussia. Poland's objective was to rid this newly acquired land of all Germans and have it settled exclusively by Poles in order to create an ethnically homogeneous nation. In addition, World War II—and particularly the brutal Nazi conquest and occupation of Eastern Europe—unleashed an outburst of anti-German sentiment against *Volksdeutsche*, the ethnic Germans who had lived for centuries in eastern and southeastern Europe. The largest group (some three million) consisted of Sudeten Germans in western Czechoslovakia; almost two million ethnic Germans also resided in Hungary, Romania, and Yugoslavia. As the Red Army advanced into southeastern Europe in late 1944 and early 1945, many fled to the west, and those who remained were expelled following the German defeat. An eruption of violence against these ethnic Germans resulted in many deaths at the hands of local civilians, officials, and militias. Thousands died in internment camps from malnutrition and disease, as well as on the trains taking the expellees to Germany. It is estimated that nearly twelve million Germans were displaced, of whom over two million died from hunger and disease.[2] This expulsion of German nationals (including East Prussians) from eastern Germany and ethnic Germans from southeastern Europe constituted the largest population transfer in recent European history.

While it may have been the largest transfer, the expulsion of Germans was but one of many episodes of ethnic cleansing—the removal of a national, ethnic, or religious group from a specific territory—in twentieth-century Europe.[3] One of the earliest was the deportation of Armenians from Turkey in 1915 to the deserts of Mesopotamia. While some Armenians were transported by rail, most were driven like cattle on forced marches across the Anatolian plain. Many were murdered by their guards and hundreds of thousands died from exposure, malnutrition, and disease. Another case of ethnic cleansing took place as a result of the Greco-Turkish War in 1921–1922 in which a Greek expeditionary force was driven out of Turkey. A settlement between Greece and Turkey was reached on July 24, 1923, with the signing of the Treaty of Lausanne, which required the compulsory removal of Greeks from Turkey and Turks from Greece. Despite the fact that tens of thousands of Greeks died in the process, the Treaty of Lausanne was viewed by Churchill and Roosevelt as a successful example of the organized exchange of ethnic groups and predisposed them to the expulsion of millions of Germans from Eastern Europe, later agreed to by Truman at the Potsdam Conference.

During World War II both Nazi Germany and the Soviet Union carried out their own ethnic cleansings. Before the Holocaust began in earnest and eclipsed all previous ethnic cleansings, the Nazis engineered substantial population shifts designed to achieve *Lebensraum,* the territory believed necessary for the full flowering of national German, i.e., Aryan existence. Following the defeat of Poland in 1939, Germany annexed a huge swath of western Poland (known as the "Warthegau") and up to a million Poles and Jews were forced to move to German-administered central Poland (known as the "General Gouvernment") in order to make room for ethnic Germans resettled from the

Baltics, Italy, and the Soviet Union. There were also plans for the Germanization of northern Slovenia, involving the removal of about a third of the local population, but this was only partially carried out. Following the German invasion of the Soviet Union in June 1941, the Nazis developed ambitious plans (called the General Plan East) for the extension of German settlements to as far east as the Ural Mountains in central Russia. However, this German blueprint for ethnic cleansing on a vast scale was stillborn, thanks to the counter-offensive by the Red Army in 1943.

On the Soviet side, following the takeover of eastern Poland by the Red Army in 1939, over three-hundred-thousand Polish citizens were deported to central Asia and Siberia to facilitate the planned Sovietization of this newly acquired territory. When Germany attacked the Soviet Union, ethnic Germans in Volhynia and the areas around the Black Sea and the Volga were immediately suspected by the Soviets of supporting the enemy and were sent east to labor camps and specially created settlements in Siberia and Central Asia. In addition, in 1944 the Soviets carried out the forced deportation of Chechens and Ingushes in the Caucasus and Tartars from the Crimea to central Asia to prevent collaboration with the Germans and ensure Soviet control of their territory.

These ethnic cleansings provided ample precedent for the forced removal of Germans from Eastern Europe following the end of World War II. It is indeed ironic that the Nazi racial beliefs that motivated Germany's ethnic cleansing in Eastern Europe boomeranged against the Germans when their turn came to be expelled from their homeland in the east. But however much suffering and death were caused by the Nazi expulsions, these pale in comparison with the well-organized campaign of mass murder of the Jews that began in earnest with the invasion of the Soviet Union in June 1941, and was planned in detail at a villa on the Wannsee outside of Berlin on January 20, 1942. It was here that the earlier attempt at ethnic cleansing of European Jews was unequivocally transformed into the "Final Solution," which resulted in the Holocaust. This was the crowning barbarity of the Nazi regime which, together with the pervasive death and destruction wrought by German armed forces in Eastern Europe, ultimately led to the ethnic cleansing of Eastern European Germans. This connection was drawn by the German writer, Ralph Giordano, who responded to the loss of East Prussia:

> The mourning for an irreplaceable loss and anger against all who were at the root of this: Hitler and his adherents. They, their policies, their war and their crimes are primarily responsible for the loss of the regions beyond the Oder-Neisse Line, therefore also East Prussia. They created the preconditions for the decisions their historic conquerors made at Yalta and Potsdam, however right or wrong their decisions may have been.[4]

If the suffering and deaths of the East Prussians and so many other Germans were a consequence of the brutal war waged by their leaders and the atrocities committed by fellow Germans, what claim do they have to our empathy and pity? As Germans, they were tainted by Nazism and one might conclude that they deserved their plight. Is there then any reason to be concerned about their fate and in particular, the fate of East Prussians at the end of the war and subsequently under Russian and Polish occupation? Old men, women, and innocent children had not participated in the brutal Nazi campaign in Eastern Europe and the murder of the Jews. While one can understand what led to the disastrous consequences for the East Prussians—the revenge sought by Soviet soldiers and more generally, Hitler's quest for *Lebensraum* and genocidal ambitions—one cannot condone what was done to these people.

Furthermore, the cruel treatment of civilian East Prussians by Soviet forces was in violation of international human rights. These rights are embodied in the Geneva Conventions, which lay out the international laws governing the humanitarian treatment of the victims of war.[5] The Fourth Geneva Convention, which was published on August 12, 1949, deals with the protection of civilians during wartime and under military occupation by a foreign power. Article 27 reads, in part:

> Protected persons are entitled, in all circumstances, to respect for their persons, their honor, their family rights, their religious

convictions and practices, and their manners and customs. They shall at all times be humanely treated, and shall be protected especially against all acts of violence or threats thereof and against insults and public curiosity. Women shall be especially protected against any attack on their honor, in particular against rape, enforced prostitution, or any form of indecent assault.

Moreover, Article 49 expressly prohibits the deportation of the inhabitants of occupied territory. The treatment of East Prussian civilians at the hands of the Red Army must in retrospect be regarded as a flagrant violation of international standards governing conflicts and occupations. Yet at the time, with Nazi Germany waging the war to the bitter end, England and the United States needed the Soviet Union to bring the conflict to a speedy and successful conclusion, and considerations of international human rights did not enter into their negotiations with the Soviet Union regarding the conduct of the war and postwar developments.

One must resist the temptation to weigh in the balance the suffering of the East Prussians with the countless numbers of Russians, Poles, and other nationalities who suffered and died in the war, to say nothing of the victims of the Holocaust. This thought was well expressed by the former German president, Roman Herzog, in an address on February 15, 1995, marking the fiftieth anniversary of the bombing of Dresden:

> In this same spirit we mourn the German victims of our history, the countless people who lost their lives or whose health was ruined in the war or in camps, during flight, through expulsion or deportation, in houses and on the streets, in ditches and cellars. One cannot come to terms with the past, one cannot find peace or reconciliation unless one faces up to history in its entirety.
>
> We object to our mourning being seen as an attempt to square the suffering of the victims of crimes committed by Germans against people of other nations, and against fellow countrymen. Anyone

who, like the Germans of today, wants to break the vicious circle of injustice and violence, of war and inhumanity, anyone who seeks peace, friendship and reconciliation among nations, cannot simply strike a balance between the dead, the injured and those who suffered distress in the various nations. One cannot offset life against life, pain against pain, fear of death against fear of death, expulsion against expulsion, horror against horror, degradation against degradation. Human suffering defies accounting. We can only overcome it together, through compassion, reflection and learning.[6]

Notes

1 Statement by the Prime Minister of The UK and the President of the United States ("Atlantic Charter"), U.S. Government Printing Office, August 21, 1941, page 2.

2 This estimate is taken from de Zayas, *A Terrible Revenge*, 156.

3 For recent surveys, see Lieberman, *Terrible Fate*, and Naimark, *Fires of Hatred*. A useful perspective on ethnic cleansing in World War II is provided in Ther and Siljak, eds., *Redrawing Nations*. For a trenchant study of genocide—the systematic killing of all or part of an ethnic, national, or religious group—see Power, *"A Problem from Hell."*

4 Giordano, *Ostpreußen ade*, 24. "Der Trauer über einen unwiederbringlichen Verlust und des Zorns gegen alle, die die Wurzel für ihn gesetzt haben: Hitler und seiner Anhänger. Sie, ihre Politik, ihr Krieg und ihre Verbrechen sind primär verantwortlich für den Verlust der Gebiete jenseits der Oder-Neisse-Linie, also auch Ostpreußen. Sie schufen die Voraussetzungen für die Entscheidungen ihrer historischen Überwinder in Jalta und Potsdam, wie richtig oder falsch deren Entschlüsse auch immer gewesen sein mögen."

5 See Weisbrod and de la Vega, *International Human Rights Law*, and Michael Haas, *International Human Rights*. It goes without saying that the actions by the Allies in World War II that might have been regarded as war crimes, e.g., the bombing of civilian targets or crimes against humanity by the Soviets, were not considered at the Nuremberg War Crime Trials. See James, *Universal Human Rights*, 95.

6 Herzog, *Remembrance and Perpetual Responsibility*, 6. The German text is in Herzog, *Wahrheit und Klarheit*, 121.

CHAPTER I

HISTORICAL BACKGROUND: FROM THE CONQUEST OF THE PRUSSEN BY THE TEUTONIC ORDER TO THE EVE OF WORLD WAR II

A. Conquest of the Prussen by the Order of the Teutonic Knights: 1230–1283

The term "Prussia" is derived from the name of the original inhabitants of East Prussia. The first recorded use of the term was by the Spaniard Ibrahim Ibn Jacub, who in 965 ventured as far as Magdeburg in what is now the eastern part of Germany. He referred to the people living much further east as the "Brus." Somewhat later—around 990—the first Polish king, Mieszko, sent a document to Pope John XV in which he referred to his neighbors to the northwest as "Prussen." They were an ethnic group of Baltic peoples distinct from the Germans and the Slavs who spoke their own language. They occupied an area east of the Vistula River and south of the Memel River, with a coastline along the Baltic extending from Danzig (now Gdańsk) in the south to Memel in the north, and bordered on the east by what was then Polish and Russian territory. This area is referred to here as "Prussenland." The Prussen were not organized as a state, but consisted of ten tribes in geographically distinct areas whose leaders formed a kind of local aristocracy.

By the year 1000 the Prussen had lived in the area for at least a millennium. In AD 180 the Greek geographer Ptolemy mentioned the two Prussen tribes in the southeast part of the region as the Galindians and the Sudovians. In the period from 600 to 900 the Vikings tried to subdue the coastal area of Prussenland, but King Alfred of England's informant Wulfstan reported that the inhabitants had a keen sense of their independence and were strongly organized, which made them difficult to conquer. Like other ethnic groups in the Baltics, the Prussen were pagan and did not take kindly to attempts to convert them to Christianity. An attempt at peaceful Christianization around the first millennium was unsuccessful and St. Adalbert of Prague was killed by the Prussen in 997, as was another Christian proselytizer, Bruno von Querfurt, in 1009. Further efforts by the Poles to conquer and convert the Prussen were repulsed. Such was their resistance and belligerence that around 1220 the Polish historian Vincent Kadlubek characterized such conversion campaigns as "tanto brevior, quanto coactior," i.e., "the harder [they] pressed, the shorter [they] lived."[1] Pope Honorius II had assembled a strong force of German and Polish knights at the Polish fort at Kulm (now Chelmno) on the Vistula with the aim of subduing the Prussen, which was soundly beaten by the pagans.

The Polish duke Konrad I of Masovia (an area bordering Prussenland to the south) found it very difficult to protect his lands from the Prussen's onslaughts. In 1226 he sought the assistance of the Order of Teutonic Knights, then located at St Mary's Hospital in Acre on the Mediterranean in the Holy Land (now northern Israel). This order of celibate monks was founded in 1190 with the help of German merchants and initially consisted of German knights who had participated in the Third Crusade.[2] In return for their services, Duke Konrad promised the Teutonic Knights the territory around Kulm along the Vistula in the southwest part of Prussenland, even though he had no legal claim to this land. The possibility of coming into possession of Kulmerland came at an opportune time for the Teutonic Order because in 1225 it was unable to retain its territory in the Transylvania part of Hungary and prospects for further expansion of the Order in the Holy Land were unlikely.

Known as the Grand Master ("Großmeister des Deutschen Ritterordens"), the head of the Order at that time was Hermann von Salza. He was quick to seize the opportunity for an expansion in Europe of the territory under the Order's control. As he was on good terms with Friedrich II, the then emperor of the Holy Roman Empire, Hermann von Salza persuaded the emperor in 1226 to grant him dominion over the Prussenland, which was granted in a document known as the Golden Bull of Rimini.[3] In 1234 the legal claims of the Order to the Prussenland were further bolstered by the Bull of Reiti in which Pope Gregory IX declared that all conquered territory in this area would become property of the papacy and all rights to this territory would be vested in the Order; the primary responsibility of the Teutonic Knights would be the conversion of the pagan Prussen to Christianity.[4] The claims of the Order to Prussenland were thus established by both the highest secular and spiritual authorities of the time and reflected the fact that emperors and popes competed with each other to extend their own spheres of influence in Europe.

The subjugation of the Prussen by the Teutonic Knights was organized systematically.[5] Previous attempts to conquer and convert these pagan tribes had involved forays into dense forests where the invaders were vulnerable to ambushes by the Prussen, who had the advantage of knowing the local terrain. Hermann Balk, the captain of the Teutonic Knights in the Polish fortress of Kulm (Chelmno), adopted a different strategy, one that involved the construction of a string of fortifications along the Vistula. These were used as a base from which to subdue the tribes along the river up to the Baltic coast: starting in 1230, forts were built at Thorn, Marienwerder, Reden, Elbing, and Christburg. This method of securing the surrounding countryside was so successful that by 1239 a fortress had been constructed at Balga on the Frisches Haff, a lagoon thirty-five miles northeast of Elbing bordering the Baltic, which was important for coastal trade.

At first, the Order was able to exercise control over Prussen lands fairly easily and losses were limited. However, the Teutonic Knights now had to deal with the fact that their settlements were upsetting existing trading relationships in the area. Up to this point Duke Swantopelk of Danzig (now Gdansk) had been an ally of the Order, but he soon realized that the traders at the newly established forts in Thorn, Marienwerder, and Elbing were in direct competition with his own merchants in Danzig, and that the new fort at Balga on the Frisches Haff undercut his control of the sand spit called the Frische Nehrung, which separated the Haff from the Baltic. To counter this threat to his commercial interests, Duke Swantopelk joined forces with the Prussen in 1242, and over a ten-year period they waged an effective campaign against the Order, capturing all but three of its forts and settlements.

However, the tide turned against Duke Swantopelk and his Prussen allies. First, Pope Innocent IV enjoined the duke to join forces with the Teutonic Knights in order to mount a more effective crusade to Christianize the Prussen. Second, the Poles were competing commercially with the duke and wished to eliminate his sphere of influence from the mouth of the Vistula on the Baltic. Faced with this new alliance against him, Duke Swantopelk agreed to stop his attacks and to share the mouth of the Vistula with the Order. But in return for this Papal and Polish support, the Teutonic Order had to agree to endow three bishoprics in Prussenland, to share their territory with Lübeck and the Polish princes, and to allow King Håkon IV of Norway to take over Samland, an unconquered area to the north of Prussenland.

Fortunately for the Order, three new developments enabled it to avoid keeping these promises. First, King Ottokar II of Bohemia joined forces with the Order in the crusade to conquer more of Prussenland, and in 1255 he subjugated Samland. In honor of King Ottokar, a "castrum de Coningsberg" (i.e., a castle of the king, or Königsberg in German) was built in a strategic part of southern Samland on the heights above the Pregel River. Using this fortress as a base, the Order was able to control economic activity in the area, especially the trade in amber, a highly prized and valuable commodity found in deposits on the coast of Samland. Second, the conversion to Christianity of King Mindaugas in neighboring Lithuania made it possible for the Teutonic Knights to build two forts in the north of Samland in 1259 and thereby gain control of all Samland, thus preempting the neighboring Poles and Norwegians who also had designs on this territory. Third, the Russian prince, Daniel of Galicia, together with two Polish dukes, undertook a campaign against the Prussen from the east, which persuaded King Mindaugas and his successors not to contest the Order's control of Samland.

Nonetheless, the independence-loving Prussen tribes resisted the yoke of the Teutonic Order and rose up in general revolt in the early 1260s. Many knights and settlers in the forts and settlements were killed, and the first reinforcements coming to their aid were defeated in a battle at Pokarwis, just east of Königsberg, which itself survived only because of the arrival of additional Teutonic Knights from the north. The Prussen were now much better organized and had adopted the warfare techniques of the Order, such as fighting on rivers and in the open, conducting sieges, and using the crossbow. Moreover, some Prussen had learned German through contact with members of the Order and settlers and had infiltrated the knights' garrisons to discover their weak points. As a result of this Prussen resurgence, by the mid-1260s the area controlled by the Order was reduced to just a few of its strongest forts.

Nearly wiped out as rulers of Prussenland, the Teutonic Knights were again rescued from oblivion, this time by a large infusion of German crusaders, including the Duke of Brunswick (1265), the Landgrave of Thuringia (1265), the Margrave of Brandenburg (1266), and the Margrave of Neissen (1272). Thanks to these reinforcements, the Order retook the lost forts and regained control of the rivers, and the Prussen either had to submit to the Order's authority or emigrate to the east or the north beyond its reach. With the exception of limited attempts at revolt in 1286 and 1295, the task of subjugation was essentially completed by 1283, roughly fifty years after the onset of the Christianization campaign in the early 1230s.

The crusades in the northeast territory of Europe were quite different from those in the Holy Land. Both shared the objective of Christianizing pagan peoples, but in the Holy Land this objective was coupled with short-term exploitation—seizing the available riches—and the knights typically returned home after a year or two.[6] By contrast, the crusade in northeast Europe aimed from the very beginning at permanent settlement and colonization, which reflected the strong commercial and trading orientation of the Teutonic Knights since the Order's founding in 1190.

The Order had started out at the beginning of its campaign to subjugate the Prussen with relatively few members—about six hundred in the 1230s compared with around two thousand in the late 1270s. Consequently, the conquest and settlement of Prussen land required recruiting crusaders from many parts of the Holy Roman Empire. In order to attract people from the West to settle in the East, the Order adopted an explicit policy of encouraging the growth of towns. The prospect of establishing a new and better life in the East was embodied in a popular Flemish song of the time:

> Naer Oostland wille wij rijden,
>
> Daer isser een betere stel.
>
> To the Eastland we want to go,
>
> There is a better life.[7]

The influx of farmers, traders, craftsmen, and burghers from the West led to the "Germanization" of the Prussen territory. Estimates of the area's population before the start of the northern crusade in 1230 are on the order of 140,000; by around 1400 the total population is estimated to have remained more or less unchanged. The large-scale immigration of about 100,000 from what is now Germany roughly offset the decline in the indigenous population, as many Prussen were either killed during the conquest and settlement, or had fled and resettled to the east in Poland, or to the north in Lithuania. By the beginning of the fifteenth century the German language was clearly dominant, and by the seventeenth century the Prussen language was largely extinct.

The considerable decline over the years in the number of native Prussen reflected a harsh policy of subjugation.[8] However, the Order wanted its newly conquered land to be settled, and as there was a vast expanse of thinly populated territory, the indigenous inhabitants were not driven off the land. Moreover, the Teutonic Knights had come to convert the pagans, not to eradicate or expel them.[9] In fact, the Order tried to gain support among the various factions of the local population by playing one off against the other. The Order also successfully attracted a number of better-off Prussen by allowing them to become knights and several rose to become high administrators (*Komtur*) in the Order. Lower positions, such as interpreters and officers who carried out economic and military functions, were also filled by Prussen, and many landowners survived and managed to extend their land holdings.

By contrast, when, seven centuries later, the Soviet Union invaded East Prussia and occupied the northern part of the province in World War II, its objective was to rid the conquered territory of the indigenous population and re-settle it with newcomers from the Soviet Union. The Poles also pursued a similar policy of expelling Germans and re-settling Poles in the southern part of East Prussia, which they acquired at the end of World War II. While in the first colonization of East Prussia the remaining Prussen were absorbed by the German conquerors and settlers and ultimately became extinct as an ethnic group, the second colonization in the twentieth century by Russia and Poland resulted in the explicit expulsion of Germans from what had become their native land, i.e., ethnic cleansing.

B. Rule of East Prussia by the Teutonic Order: 1283–1525

Having established its authority over the lands of the Prussen, the Order turned its attention to the territory west of the Vistula, an area named Pomerelia (later part of West Prussia), in order to establish secure communication and trade links with the Holy Roman Empire in the West. At that time, Pomerelia was contested by both the Poles and the Margraves of Brandenburg, who occupied Danzig at the mouth of the Vistula. King Vladislav of Poland asked the Teutonic Order to help him dislodge the Brandenburgers from this territory, and in 1308 the Order agreed to do so. But for its services the Order demanded excessive financial compensation, which Poland could not afford to pay, and thereby created hostility with Poland that had severe consequences for the Order a century later. At the same time, the Teutonic Knights compensated Brandenburg for its claims to Pomerelia and thereby extended the Order's control over Thorn, Kulm, Elbing, the city of Danzig, and the territory west of the Vistula. This expansion of the territory under the Order's control was in turn not well received in Lithuania and helped sow the seeds for a Polish-Lithuanian alliance against the Order.

With the Prussen subdued and the Order's activities now largely concentrated in the newly conquered territory in northeast Europe, in 1309 the Teutonic Knights decided to move their headquarters to Marienburg (now Malbork in Poland) from Venice, where it had been established after the Order left Acre in the Holy Land. Marienburg was located about halfway between Thorn in the south and Königsberg in the north. Siegfried von Feuchtwangen, the first Grand Master to reside in the new headquarters, put considerable emphasis on consolidating the Order's hold on its territory, a policy that was subsequently pursued in particular by Grand Master Winrich von Kniprode (1352–1382), who completed the Order's headquarters building, a magnificent Gothic brick fortress (see Illustration 1. Marienburg Castle around 1944).

The relatively peaceful fourteenth century in this area enabled the Order to devote its considerable administrative talents to the development of East Prussia. The high price of wheat provided an incentive to undertake large-scale cultivation of East Prussia's fertile fields, and trade was actively encouraged, in part through the introduction of uniform weights and measures. The exploitation of minerals—as well as the fossilized resin amber—was encouraged, and to facilitate trade the Order fostered the use of cash transactions. By 1410, fifty-five cities, fourteen hundred villages, forty-eight castles of the Order, and one hundred castles of other knights had been established in the territory ruled by the Teutonic Knights.[10] From the eastern bank of the Oder River in the south to beyond the Memel River in the north, the region was now largely settled by Germans.

Three developments—one external and two internal—led to the decline in the power and reach of the Order from its apogee in the fourteenth century. First, the marriage of Prince Jagiello of Lithuania in 1386 to Jadwiga, the heiress to the crown of Poland, created a strong alliance between Lithuania and Poland, and the prince subsequently became King Vladislav II of Poland. This Lithuanian-Polish alliance had a major impact on the Order in the fifteenth century. Second, as the Knights became more preoccupied with their own material well-being, the Order failed to look after the interests of the landed gentry, the peasants, and particularly the town dwellers, and these groups sought out the Lithuanian-Polish alliance to redress their grievances with the Order. Third, a significant decline in the price of wheat from the end of the fourteenth century into the fifteenth century reduced the Order's revenues. This depleted resource base made it difficult to hire the mercenaries needed to replace the volunteers whose ranks had dwindled because conversions in northern Europe had been completed and the crusading zeal to convert pagans was gone.

Emboldened by the growing weakness of the Teutonic Order, the combined Lithuanian-Polish forces marched into southern East Prussia in mid-July 1410. They were met a few miles inside the southern border near the village of Tannenberg (now Grunwald in northern Poland) by a large army raised by Grand Master Ulrich von Jungingen. The Order was outmatched by a force of roughly twice the size and in the ensuing battle the Teutonic Knights suffered grievous losses: their commanders—including the Grand Master—were killed and the soldiers were killed, captured, or routed from the field of battle.[11] The Order appeared once again to be faced with extinction, but their fortress headquarters in Marienburg withstood a fifty-seven-day siege by King Vladislav II. The siege was lifted because his artillery was unable to smash the castle walls and his troops were suffering from dysentery. In the First Peace of Thorn on February 1, 1411, the Teutonic Order retained all its territory except Samogitia to the north of East Prussia, but was required to pay Poland and Lithuania the considerable sum of £ 850,000, ten times the annual income of the King of England at that time.[12]

The need to raise taxes to make this payment resulted in the founding in 1412 of an assembly of the estates—representatives of the cities, towns, bishoprics and the landed gentry—by the Grand Master, Heinrich von Plauen. This assembly was intended as a reform measure that would enable the estates to have a voice in the determination of the taxation they were subject to, as well as in other matters affecting the territory administered by the Teutonic

Order. Nonetheless, conflict between the Order and its subjects continued and in 1440 the estates founded the Prussian League in direct opposition to the Order. To bolster its position, in 1454 the League offered its allegiance to the Polish crown. Expelled from Marienburg in 1457 by mercenaries from Bohemia, then Grand Master Ludwig von Erlichshausen moved to Königsberg, where he established the Order's new headquarters. Königsberg had joined the Hanseatic League in 1340 and by the mid-fifteenth century had developed into an important trading center and port in the southeastern Baltic area.

With the Order in a much weakened position, Grand Master von Erlichshausen was forced by the Poles to accept a far-reaching division of his territories in the Second Peace of Thorn, signed on October 19, 1466. In the west, he was compelled to cede to the Polish crown the lands on either side of the lower Vistula, including Danzig, which had been taken from Poland in 1309, as well as some of the territory conquered by the Teutonic Knights before 1250, namely Kulm, Elbing, and some bishoprics. These lands became an autonomous area of the Polish crown and became known as "Royal Prussia," a large part of which later constituted the German province of West Prussia. The territory in the east—later to become the province of East Prussia—remained an independent principality headquartered in Königsberg. Although the Grand Masters of the Teutonic Order were allowed to continue their rule, they were forced to recognize the formal authority of the Polish king.[13] A far-reaching consequence of the Second Peace of Thorn was that the easternmost part of the German lands became separated from German territory in the west by the autonomous area under Polish rule.[14] While sovereign authority rested with the Polish king in both the territories of East and West Prussia, the people remained ethnically German in language, customs, and law, albeit with a large Polish minority in the west and some surviving Prussen in the east.

During the fifteenth century the Teutonic Order was faced with a problem which ultimately proved to be its undoing. It had been founded and had enjoyed considerable success as a crusading order of celibate monks whose purpose and structure were eminently suited to the dual objectives of converting pagans by military means and then colonizing the conquered territory. Thus the Christianizing and fighting functions of the Order were mutually reinforcing to achieve a common purpose. However, once the pagan Prussen had been subdued and converted, and their lands had been settled largely by Germans and to some extent by Poles, a religious order of military knights was no longer suited to the administration of a stable and static society.

There were two opposing options to resolve this underlying dilemma.[15] On the one hand, the Teutonic Order could give up its control of East Prussia and return to its original function of fighting and subduing the pagans. By the fifteenth century, these were the Ottoman Turks, who posed a major menace to Catholic Europe. On the other hand, the ruling knights could maintain their control of East Prussia by severing their ties to the Order, renouncing their vows as monks, and becoming part of the secular ruling class. Given that they had made a substantial investment in their lands, and had what they regarded as a clear ownership claim to them—although constantly operating under threats from their Polish and Lithuanian neighbors—it is perhaps not surprising that the knights chose the latter option. However, this revolutionary development did not take place until the early part of the sixteenth century, when its catalyst was the Protestant Reformation initiated by Martin Luther.

In 1511 the Teutonic Knights in East Prussia elected Albrecht (the son of the Margrave of Brandenburg and a cousin of the Elector of Brandenburg) as their Grand Master in Königsberg, and thereby established a connection between East Prussia and Brandenburg. Grand Master Albrecht provoked an ill-fated confrontation with Poland that put him in a precarious position vis-à-vis the Poles. He also faced an internal threat as the new Lutheran doctrine was widely embraced by the Prussian laity and some of the clergy, including the bishop of Königsberg. To help resolve his political and religious difficulties, Albrecht traveled to Wittenberg in 1522 to meet Luther to seek his advice. Luther counseled that the Teutonic Knights under Albrecht's control should renounce their monastic vows and marry, thereby enabling Albrecht to avoid a confrontation with his anti-Catholic subjects. Albrecht followed this advice and summoned the East Prussian Teutonic Knights to Königsberg in May of 1525 to approve his decision to leave the Order. At this meeting seven knights initially refused, but fearing they would be hanged, ultimately gave their approval and cut the Teutonic cross out of their habits.[16] (The Order continues to exist largely as a charitable organization with headquarters in Vienna.)

Luther also urged Grand Master Albrecht to set himself up as a secular duke in order to solidify his control over East Prussia. Albrecht was able to persuade King Sigismund of Poland to recognize him as a hereditary duke of East Prussia and this elevation of his status was officially codified in the Peace of Cracow in April 1525.[17] This document formally established what then became known as the "Duchy of Prussia" and was later to become the German province of East Prussia. In return for the dukedom, Albrecht agreed to recognize the sovereignty of the Polish crown, as stipulated in 1466 in the Second Peace of Thorn.[18]

C. The Duchy of Prussia: 1525–1701

Administratively, the Duchy of Prussia was organized much as before under the Teutonic Order, although now the power resided in the hands of a duke instead of the grand master. One major difference was that while the grand master was elected by members of the Teutonic Order, the position of a duke was inherited. The tenure of the grand master had generally been quite short, often only two to three years, whereas a duke held power for life, and whether his rule and that of his heirs would be beneficent or destructive depended largely on the duke's temperament and character.

It was fortunate for the Duchy of Prussia that Albrecht, the first duke, was unusually farsighted. He pursued an external policy of peaceful coexistence with his neighbors and an internal policy of economic development. He revived the Teutonic Order's encouragement of the settlement of uninhabited territory, especially in border areas, and for this purpose he attracted settlers from Holland and Bohemia. He established schools and in 1544 founded the Albertina University, named after him in the capital, Königsberg, whose most illustrious professor would be Immanuel Kant two centuries later. The duke also encouraged printing and ordered that the catechism and hymn books be printed not only in German but also in the languages of the minority populations in the duchy (Prussen, Polish, and Lithuanian). He also endowed a library in the castle in Königsberg. Through his support of trade and economic development, the Duchy of Prussia prospered during his forty-three-year rule, and by 1550 Köngisberg was a thriving city of about fifteen thousand inhabitants.

Underlying this prosperity was the development of extensive landed estates, which were eminently suited for growing grain. Large-scale farming was aided by the fact that the Duchy of Prussia avoided the land-holding practice in some other parts of Germany whereby property was divided into smaller and smaller units when the father died and there were multiple heirs. Also, the landowning nobility in the duchy managed their own estates and were motivated to make the most productive use of their considerable resources. As a consequence, the vast stretches of arable land in the duchy were organized as large, highly efficient estates producing a surplus of grain for export to the German principalities in the west and to the rest of Europe. Eventually, the duchy (and later East Prussia) earned a well-deserved reputation as the *Kornkammer*, or granary, of Western Europe. The wealth generated by grain exports provided the foundation for the economic prosperity of Königsberg, with its flourishing urban culture.

Duke Albrecht died in 1568 at the then exceedingly old age of seventy-eight. His only son, Albrecht Frederick, inherited the dukedom, but it was soon evident that he was mentally unfit to rule. In 1577, Margrave George Frederick of Brandenburg was appointed regent and thus the connection to Brandenburg, which was ruled by the Hohenzollerns, was maintained. During his long regency George Frederick displayed considerable energy and adroitness in furthering the development of the Duchy of Prussia. He continued the policy of settling undeveloped areas, encouraged trade in wheat through the port of Königsberg, founded three schools to prepare students for entry into the Albertina University, and employed his own building master to construct the west wing of Königsberg Castle (see Illustration 2. Königsberg Castle around 1900; also Illustration 3. Damaged Königsberg Castle with

Soviet Tanks). When he died in 1603, George Frederick of Brandenburg left a well-ordered duchy to the two Electors of Brandenburg who succeeded him in turn as regents.[19]

The first elector, Joachim Frederick, served unremarkably as regent for five years, 1603–1608. His successor, Johann Sigismund, had already forged a link in 1594 between Brandenburg and Prussia by marrying Duke Albrecht Friederick's oldest daughter, Anne. He had also had the foresight in 1611 to undertake a formal arrangement with the Duchy of Prussia that put him in the line of succession. Thus, when Duke Albrecht Friederick (referred to by the people as "the retarded one") died in Königsberg in 1618 without leaving a son as heir, the right of succession to the Duchy of Prussia went to Johann Sigismund of the House of Hohenzollern in Brandenburg. He was now ruler of both Brandenburg and the Duchy of Prussia; these two territories became inextricably linked under the Hohenzollerns and formed the original core of the future state of Prussia. The size of the lands ruled by the Hohenzollerns doubled, extending from the east, with Poland and Russia as neighbors, to the west, bordering on Holland (see Map 4. Union of the Duchy of Prussia and Brandenburg). Brandenburg, with its capital in Berlin, covered 697 square miles—about the same size as the Duchy of Prussia's 672 square miles, whose capital, Königsberg, was then of much greater commercial importance than any town in Brandenburg, including Berlin.[20]

Soon after becoming ruler of the Duchy of Prussia in 1618, Johann Sigismund became ill and died in 1620. His son and successor, George William, placed primary importance on his formal investiture as Duke of Prussia by King Sigmund of Poland, as the Duchy of Prussia remained under the sovereignty of the Polish crown. Meanwhile, George William's mother had plans to marry her daughter to King Gustavus Aldophus of Sweden, then at war with Poland. This confrontation between Sweden and Poland marked the beginning of the Thirty Years' War, 1618–1648, which would engulf much of Europe. Not surprisingly, King Sigmund viewed such a marriage as forming an alliance between Brandenburg-Prussia and Sweden against Poland, and he therefore delayed the investiture. But when Swedish forces threatened Poland from the north, King Sigmund saw advantages in stabilizing the situation on Poland's western border by formally investing George William with the title of Duke of Prussia. The ceremony of investiture took place on September 23, 1621, and made George William a vassal of Poland owing allegiance to her king.

George William of Brandenburg-Prussia attempted to pursue a policy of neutrality between Sweden and Poland, but this proved impossible when Swedish troops reached the walls of Berlin and he was forced to take sides and become embroiled in the Thirty Years' War.[21] Brandenburg, in particular, was severely damaged by the fighting and lost over fifty percent of its population. It appeared to observers at the time that Brandenburg was on the verge of collapse when George William, Elector of Brandenburg and Duke of Prussia, died at forty-six on December 1, 1640.[22]

He was succeeded by his son, Frederick William, who at twenty inherited both of his father's titles. His father had kept him away from the affairs of state and he had little experience in governing, yet he was energetic and quickly learned how to negotiate with his counterparts in Europe. Such skills were essential to maintain the territorial integrity of Brandenburg-Prussia while the Thirty Years' War was raging and during the conflicts afterward. One of Frederick's key achievements during his long rule from 1640 to 1688 was the creation of a well-trained, professional army, which was sorely needed both to protect Brandenburg-Prussia from foreign invasions and to provide support to other rulers in the various alliances he pursued.[23] As historian H. W. Koch has noted, "From an instrument of a military entrepreneur, [the army] … was transformed into an instrument of state."[24] Frederick William introduced discipline into the ranks of the army: plundering by soldiers was punishable by hanging, an officer who attacked a civilian was stripped of his rank for a year, and officers were prohibited from beating their troops. He also founded cadet schools for the training of army officers. In peacetime, the army consisted on average of about seven thousand troops, while in wartime the ranks rose to around fifteen thousand, and at times reached a peak of thirty thousand.

To finance a large standing army, a uniform system of tax administration was developed. This included the introduction of a tax on consumption, which soon constituted one of the most important sources of revenue in

Brandenburg-Prussia. The close link between the army and financial policy can be seen in the fact that the most senior army general was placed in charge of the General War Commissary, which was responsible for the collection of taxes.

Another hallmark of Frederick William's reign was his ability to shift his alliances with other countries in order to further the interests of Brandenburg-Prussia. In particular, he managed to go back and forth in his support of Poland and Sweden, as both posed actual or potential threats to his lands. In 1653, he was put on the spot when war broke out again between Poland and Sweden; owing allegiance to the king of Poland, Frederick William was obliged to come to the his defense when he was attacked. But as Sweden had become the dominant power at this point, Frederick William allied himself with Sweden to avoid being on the losing side. In a three-day battle near Warsaw in mid-1656, the combined Swedish and Brandenburg-Prussian forces won a decisive victory over the Poles. Yet these forces did not establish control over Poland and revenge from the Polish side was soon forthcoming. The Polish king, John II Casimir, formed an alliance with Crimean-Tartar troops under the leadership of the Polish-Lithuanian general Gonsiewsky, and on October 8, 1656, their armies invaded East Prussia and largely destroyed the small force of Swedish and Prussian soldiers in a battle near Prostken, south of Lyck. Large stretches of East Prussia were laid waste: thirteen cities, 249 villages, and thirty-seven churches were ravaged and thousands of farmsteads reduced to ashes. Nearly eleven thousand inhabitants were killed and thirty-four thousand taken as slaves to the Crimea and Turkey, only a few of whom returned home many years later.[25]

During this difficult time, the election of a new emperor of the Holy Roman Empire turned out to be advantageous for Frederick William. When Emperor Ferdinand II died in April 1657, the House of Habsburg in Vienna needed Frederick William's support as an elector for their candidate.[26] As a condition for backing their candidate, he demanded nothing less than full independence of the Duchy of Prussia from Poland. The Habsburg court agreed to this demand and exerted considerable pressure on the Poles, who finally acquiesced. In the Treaty of Wehlau signed on September 1, 1657,

King Casimir of Poland renounced all claims to the Duchy of Prussia and made Frederick William the Duchy's fully independent ruler. Thus, the territory conquered and settled by the Teutonic Knights again became a sovereign German entity and no longer owed allegiance to Poland. This change in status was confirmed by Poland and Sweden in the Peace of Oliva, signed near Danzig in May of 1660, whereby Frederick William became the sovereign duke of the Duchy of Prussia in his own right and at the same time remained the Elector of Brandenburg.

However, the estates—representatives of the towns and landed gentry—of the Duchy of Prussia, wishing to preserve their authority and independence, insisted that the duke's new status required their approval. This conflict came to a head in 1661 when the first *Landtag*, or Diet, meeting in Königsberg after the Peace of Oliva, refused to accept Frederick William's sovereignty over the duchy. The duke did not back down and in 1662 traveled from Berlin, where he resided, to Königsberg with an army of two thousand men. Faced with this force, the estates decided not to resist and acceding to Frederick William's claim, swore an oath of fealty in the courtyard of Königsberg Castle in October 1663. However, in 1669 the estates refused to raise money to support the military activities of Brandenburg. Once more the elector would brook no opposition from the East Prussian estates and in 1772 ordered an opposition leader captured and beheaded in Memel. When Brandenburg again demanded that Königsberg pay taxes, the city complied, but the elector's troops remained stationed in Königsberg without the consent of the estates. The attempts by the estates in the Duchy of Prussia to maintain some degree of independence from the Elector of Brandenburg had come to an end.

In late 1674 conflict again arose with Sweden when Swedish troops invaded northern Brandenburg just as the elector's army was moving to its winter camp far away in Franconia. After a rapid march across Brandenburg with his troops, sixty-nine-year-old General Derfflinger inflicted a decisive defeat over the superior Swedish force at Fehrbellin on the Rhine in June 1675. This battle firmly established the fame of the elector's army, and from that time on Frederick William was referred to as the "Great Elector" ("Der große Kurfürst") even though it was General Derfflinger who had won the battle.

Notwithstanding this defeat and their loss of Pomerania at the end of 1677, the Swedes undertook a new campaign against Brandenburg-Prussia near the northern border of the duchy during the winter of 1678–1679. In a dramatic move to head off the Swedish forces, the Great Elector loaded his troops onto twelve hundred sleds and led them from Heiligenbeil in the south, crossed over the frozen Frisches Haff and Kurisches Haff to near Heydekrug in Memelland in the north. In a battle in the neighborhood of Tilsit the Swedes were defeated; of an invading force of twelve thousand, only three thousand returned to Sweden.[27] (Nearly three hundred years later during World War II in the frigid winter of 1944–1945, the frozen Frisches Haff again played a critical role when it became the only escape route for thousands of German civilians fleeing the advancing Soviet Army.)

Throughout his rule the Great Elector pursued a policy of religious tolerance and maintained an open-door policy for immigrants. In the last three years of his life, he took advantage of the revocation of the Edict of Nantes in 1685 and attracted to Brandenburg-Prussia around twenty thousand French and Walloon Huguenots by providing them with subsidies and tax benefits. Some five hundred of these settled in Königsberg.[28] The Huguenot immigrants were typically better educated than the local population, and as they had more advanced commercial and industrial skills, they contributed significantly to the economic and intellectual development of East Prussia.

D. Kingdom of Prussia: 1701–1815

When the Great Elector died in 1688, his son Frederick III demonstrated neither the political and administrative talents of his father nor the desire to assume for himself the reins of state. As Koch notes, "[p]referring the appearance and outward trappings of absolutist monarchy to its actual substance, he entrusted the conduct of the affairs of state to the hands of prime ministers."[29] His primary aim in life was to become a king and enjoy all the perquisites of that royal office, but he did not wish to subordinate himself to the emperor of the Holy Roman Empire. He based his claim to royalty on the fact that he was the sovereign and independent duke of the Duchy of Prussia and therefore needed only the acquiescence of Emperor Leopold to become King of Prussia. Negotiations to this end began in 1690, but it took until November 1700 for the emperor to grant his approval. In return, Frederick III agreed to supply him with troops in a war against France and to support the House of Habsburg in a future imperial election.

In case the winds shifted against him, Frederick III wasted no time and traveled from Berlin to Königsberg, where on January 18, 1701, he crowned himself King of Prussia in the castle.[30] To pay for the costly coronation a special tax was levied on the populace. Following a glittering ceremony, Fredrick III henceforth called himself King Frederick I.[31] His official title was "King *in* Prussia," not "King *of* Prussia," to alleviate Polish concerns that he might exert claims to the Polish part of Prussia known as Royal Prussia (later to become West Prussia). He also remained Elector of Brandenburg.

By becoming a king in his own right with independent authority derived neither from the Holy Roman Emperor nor from the King of Poland, King Frederick I conferred prestige not only on himself but also on the Prussian territory he ruled: "The new title also had a psychological integrating effect: the Baltic territory formerly known as Ducal Prussia was no longer a mere outlying possession of the Brandenburg heartland, but a constitutive element in the new royal-electoral amalgam that would first be known as Brandenburg-Prussia, later simply as Prussia."[32] Whereas the term "Prussia" was once restricted to the easternmost German territory, it now became the name of the much larger area that encompassed Brandenburg. The Kingdom of Prussia became the most dynamic and powerful German political entity at the time.

Not wishing external disturbances to interfere with his enjoyment of royal prerogatives, King Fredrick I pursued a peaceful foreign policy. As his Prussian territories were quite dispersed—extending from East Prussia to the Rhine—they were vulnerable to foreign incursions. But instead of building up his army, King Frederick I devoted himself to the arts and non-military activities, founding the University of Halle and the Prussian Academy of Arts. To support these endeavors and himself in the grand style he had become accustomed to, he had essentially bankrupted his country by the time he died in February 1713.

With empty coffers, his administration was unable to deal effectively with the Black Death that ravaged East Prussia from the very cold winter of 1709 to the beginning of 1711. Of a population that by then had reached 600,000, nearly 240,000—or forty percent—died of the plague, and in the capital of Königsberg, roughly one-third of the twenty-eight thousand inhabitants did not survive.

The King's son, Frederick William I, was by nature quite different from his father. A deeply religious man, Frederick William I was also motivated by a strong sense of duty to the state of Prussia to improve its army, administration, and economy. He changed course 180 degrees from that of his father immediately upon inheriting the crown in February 1713. First, he ordered severe spending cuts throughout the government, especially in the staff and support for the royal household. Two-thirds of the servants were dismissed, including the chocolate maker, a number of castrati singers, and musicians, composers, and organ makers. The royal stables were reduced from six hundred to 120 horses, and salaries were cut in many cases to twenty-five percent of the level during his father's reign. The new king then turned his attention to expanding and improving the army and doubled its size to around eighty thousand. Initially, recruiters used force in many cases to recruit soldiers, but this had the adverse effect of driving the peasants out of Prussia to escape compulsory military service. The depopulation of the countryside was particularly severe in East Prussia and a solution was found that balanced the needs of the military with the need for labor to sustain and increase agricultural production: beginning in 1730, peasants had to serve in the army only three months a year; the other nine could be spent working their masters' estates.

In addition, Frederick William I reformed the state administration. To reduce competition between the two main branches, the General Finance Directory (responsible for the royal properties) and the General War Commissary (responsible for the army and taxation) were combined into one central administrative unit. To upgrade the quality of the administrative staff, retired soldiers (most often noncommissioned officers) were hired to fill positions in the state bureaucracy. They introduced military discipline and professionalism into the Prussian civil service, setting the tone thereafter in the administration of Prussia and forming part of what later was referred to as the "Prussian Spirit" or "Prussianism."

Frederick William I's third major initiative was the revival of agricultural production, especially in East Prussia, which had been devastated by the Black Death. Thousands of farms were left vacant and the settlement of immigrants was a major part of the initiative to increase agricultural output. Attracted by government assistance in the form of agricultural tools, livestock, and seeds, about half of the thirty thousand Protestants expelled in 1732 from the Salzburg region of Austria moved to land lying fallow in East Prussia. Frederick William I took great pride in this re-colonization of East Prussia, which helped to bring the population at the time of his death in 1740 back to the level it had been before the Black Death.

His successor was Frederick II—later called Frederick the Great. In his younger years he displayed a temperament quite different from that of his pious and duty-driven father. He was consumed by literature and other intellectual pursuits: music—Frederick II was an accomplished flute player and wrote music for the instrument; philosophy—he had a lifelong, albeit often stormy relationship with Voltaire; and science. The two opposing personalities of father and son have been described as follows: "Given Frederick William's firm religious conviction that the prosperity of the state was a sign of divine approval, and his belief that the duty of the monarch was that his every action be an example to his subjects lest divine approval be withdrawn, his son's interests and his way of life were the very opposite of all that he believed in."[33]

Not surprisingly, conflict between father and son eventually came to a head. To escape the repressive atmosphere of his father's court, in 1730 at age eighteen, Frederick planned to flee to England where his grandfather on his mother's side was King George I. His father caught wind of the plan and outraged at what he regarded as the crown prince's desertion from the army, had him courtmartialed. While the court rejected the charge and Frederick was acquitted, his good friend, Lieutenant von Katte, who had assisted him in his plot to escape, was sentenced to death for treason and lèse-majesté. His father ordered that Frederick be forced to watch the beheading of his friend from the window in his prison cell in the fortress in Küstrin. Frederick remained confined to his cell for six weeks and was permitted to leave Küstrin only after he had made three promises to his father: to never take revenge for his imprisonment, always obey his father, and never marry without his father's consent. He kept all three, but the last only with considerable difficulty. In February 1732, his father wrote and told him in no uncertain terms that he was to marry Elisabeth Christine of Braunschweig-Beven. Frederick had no love for the match proposed by his father, nor for any other heterosexual relationship; in deep despair he nonetheless wrote back two weeks later that he would comply with his father's wishes.

Contrary to expectations, when his father died on January 31, 1740, and he became king, Frederick did not give himself over completely to the pursuit of his intellectual interests. Rather, he followed in his father's footsteps and immediately began building up the ranks of the military by adding seven regiments to the army, bringing it to a force of one hundred thousand soldiers in 1741. This military buildup was essential to realize his ambition of enlarging and unifying Prussia's territorial holdings and thereby forging it into a major European power that had to be reckoned with.

When Emperor Charles VI died unexpectedly in Vienna on October 20, 1740, Frederick lost no time in seizing the opportunity afforded by the temporary lack of leadership of the House of Habsburg in Austria to take over economically well-off Silesia, then part of the Habsburg Empire. He invaded on December 16, 1740, and rapidly occupied Silesia, thus precipitating what was later called the First Silesian War. After a number of battles, Empress Maria Theresa of Austria ceded most of Silesia to Prussia in the Peace of Breslau signed on July 28, 1742. But the peace did not last long. Concerned that Austria might mount a counterattack against Silesia, Frederick again took the initiative and started the Second Silesian War by invading Bohemia in August 1744. After several battles Frederick eventually emerged victorious over Maria Theresa's army, and she now ceded all of Silesia to Prussia in the Treaty of Dresden, signed on Christmas Day, 1745. These victories earned Frederick II the title "Frederick the Great." In only five years he had achieved his ambition of establishing Prussia as a major European power.[34]

In the ten years of peace before the outbreak of the Seven Years' War, Frederick the Great devoted himself to the economic development of the newly conquered province of Silesia, in particular, and Prussia, more generally. By reducing the number of days peasants had to work on royal lands from six to three, he allowed them more time to work their own plots, which increased agricultural production. He also continued his predecessors' policy of attracting and settling immigrant farmers, resulting ultimately in the establishment of 275 peasant villages. To encourage trade and manufacturing, he created a new department in the Prussian administration with specific responsibility for industrialization. He continued his father's mercantilist policy by imposing heavy duties on imported goods to protect domestic markets from foreign competition.

Following in his father's footsteps, Frederick the Great never ceased to utilize Prussia's strong economy to provide resources for the expansion of the army. Thus, when the Seven Years' War broke out in August 1756, he had 150,000 troops at his disposal and a war chest of thirteen million thalers. He invaded Saxony in August 1756 to preempt a move by Empress Maria Theresa, whom he believed to be sending troops into Bohemia and Moravia as a prelude to an attack on Prussia. Over the next few years battle followed battle, and, with only England as an ally, Prussia was hard pressed by the combined forces of Austria, France, Russia, and Sweden. In August 1759, Frederick the Great was decisively defeated at the Battle of Kunersdorf near Frankfurt on the Oder and in November he proposed peace negotiations, but as Austria now had the upper hand, it rejected his offer.

To retain Russia's continued participation in the war against Prussia, Empress Maria Theresa promised East Prussia as compensation in the event the anti-Prussian coalition emerged victorious and Silesia was returned to the Habsburgs.[35] In fact, the Russians had already invaded East Prussia and occupied Königsberg. In 1758, they forced the inhabitants to swear an oath of fealty to Tsarina Elizabeth, who had been on the Russian throne since 1741. While the Russian occupation lasted five years, there was no intention to make East Prussia a Russian province.[36] (As described in Chapter VII, some two hundred years later the situation was vastly different at the end of World War II.) Rather, Russia's aim was to exchange East Prussia for the Duchy of Kurland (now the southwest part of Latvia) and thereby provide a route for Russian trade from the Black Sea to the Baltic.[37] Frederick the Great was also prepared in his negotiations with Russia to offer East Prussia in exchange for a guarantee that Prussia would be able to keep Silesia.[38]

In the event, neither exchange took place. On January 5, 1762, Tsarina Elizabeth died and was replaced by her nephew, the Duke of Holstein-Gottorp, who became Tsar Peter III. The new tsar thought highly of Frederick the Great and peace was agreed to between Prussia and Russia on May 22, 1762. The Russian occupation of East Prussia ended soon afterward in August. Frederick had high hopes that Peter III would side with him against Austria, but these hopes were dashed when Peter III was overthrown six months after becoming tsar. He was reputedly murdered at the instigation of his German-born wife, who took over the throne and reigned as Catherine II.

Weakened by the war, Austria chose not to continue hostilities with Prussia to regain Silesia. The Seven Years' War came to an end with the signing of the Peace of Hubertusburg on February 15, 1763. Prussia retained Silesia but had to give up the part of Saxony that it had occupied. The status quo was thus re-established at great cost, with Frederick the Great able to retain only Silesia. Chastened, he returned to Berlin via side streets, not wishing to face his subjects on the main avenues.[39]

In the postwar period Frederick the Great devoted himself in his usual energetic fashion to the reconstruction and further economic development of his dominions. In agriculture, he encouraged the planting of potatoes and promoted large-scale dairy farming, especially in East Prussia where the royal lands were more advanced than in other parts of Prussia. As cattle raising succeeded sheep farming, the latter moved to the eastern parts of the province. Frederick also turned to re-settlement and re-colonization, and Prussia's population rose from 4.1 million in 1756 to 4.5 million in 1775.

The period following the end of the Seven Years' War was marked by an expansion of Prussian territory in the east. In the 1760s, Poland was wracked by inner turmoil caused in part by an unstable political system. This instability was exacerbated by both Russia and Prussia, who viewed it as an opportunity to expand their territories at Poland's expense. On August 5, 1772, Austria joined these two powers in signing a document that later became known as the First Partition of Poland. This partition, which involved about thirty percent of the country, enabled Frederick to regain land that had been ceded to Poland by the Teutonic Order over three hundred years earlier in 1466 in the Second Treaty of Thorn, and that separated East Prussia from Brandenburg. This area, which had been called Royal Prussia ("Königliches Preußen") because it was that part of Prussia ruled by the King of Poland, was now officially called West Prussia. For some time Frederick the Great had had his eye on this territory: in his Second Political Testament (1768) he had written how "useful" it would be to "round out" Prussia's borders and enhance the defensive capability of its easternmost province.[40] However, Danzig and Thorn remained in Polish hands. The territory of the original Duchy of Prussia was enlarged by the addition of the bishopric of Ermland and was henceforth officially called East Prussia. The state of Prussia was now fully contiguous with its easternmost province, and from that point on Frederick was "King *of* Prussia," as his kingdom encompassed both East and West Prussia.

When Frederick the Great died on August 16, 1786, after a reign of forty-six years, he left no heir to the throne. As his younger brother had died thirty years earlier, his nephew was next in line of succession and consequently became King Frederick William II. His uncle would have been a hard act for anyone to follow, but Frederick William made little attempt to do so. "'The much beloved' as Berliners used to call him because of his paramours, or 'fat William,' because of the width of his girth as well as his truly Herculean proportions"[41] assumed the throne at the age of forty-two and reigned eleven years. Worn out by an inconclusive war against France, his health deteriorated sharply in the early 1790s, and after a long illness, he died on November 16, 1797.

During his reign two further partitions of Poland took place. In the Second Partition, concluded between Prussia and Russia in January 1793, Prussia gained the entire territory lying south of East and West Prussia and north of Silesia in the south (known as South Prussia), and the towns of Danzig and Thorn were incorporated into West Prussia. In the Third Partition, signed

by Austria, Prussia, and Russia in October 1795, Prussia obtained most of
Masovia in east-central Poland, including Warsaw, as well as Bialystok and
the surrounding territory. Of the roughly eight million inhabitants within
the expanded borders of Prussia, around three million were now Polish speaking.[42] The remainder of what was left of Poland was divided between Russia
and Austria, with the result that Poland vanished from the map of nations.
However, one of the consequences of the Napoleonic Wars early in the nineteenth century was that this expansion of the territory on Prussia's eastern
borders lasted less than fifteen years until the Treaty of Tilsit in 1807.

Frederick William III, the firstborn son of Frederick, the "fat William,"
ascended to the throne in 1797 at the age of twenty-seven. By temperament
he was much closer to his "Great" uncle, who had taken responsibility for
his education and training. King Frederick William III tried to remain neutral in the conflict that had emerged between France and England and allied
himself with Russia. But Napoleon had his eyes on Prussia and war became
inevitable; on October 14, 1806, he decisively defeated Prussian forces at the
battles of Jena and Auerstädt. Later that month he entered Berlin and at the
Tomb of Frederick the Great in Potsdam was reported as saying: "Gentlemen,
if this man were still alive, I would not be here."[43] Pursued by the French
army, Frederick William III and his court fled to Königsberg, but by the
time French soldiers entered the city on June 16, 1807, he and his court had
already escaped to Memel on the Baltic at the northern tip of East Prussia.
Napoleon and his army quickly followed in pursuit and apprehended the king
in Memel. Peace negotiations then took place on June 25 between Napoleon
and Tsar Alexander I on a well-appointed barge in the middle of the Memel
River, which separated the French and Russian forces near the East Prussian
town of Tilsit.

Frederick had been excluded from the negotiations and sent his Queen Luise
to try to obtain more lenient terms for Prussia by having her appeal directly to
Napoleon at a meeting in Tilsit on July 6. Napoleon apparently was impressed
by the queen's firmness and graciousness, but he conceded nothing in response
to her entreaties. In the Treaty of Tilsit, signed on July 9, 1807, which ended
this phase of the Napoleonic Wars, Prussia lost most of the Polish land it had

acquired in the Second and Third Partitions, but retained much of West Prussia linking East Prussia with Brandenburg; Danzig became a free city under French rule; and the borders of East Prussia were not altered.

The second phase of the Napoleonic Wars began in June 1812, when Napoleon invaded Russia by crossing the Memel River with his large army. East Prussia, as the borderland with Russia, served as the staging ground for the Russian invasion and a force of some 300,000 soldiers (French, German, Italian, Dutch, Walloon, and other nationalities) was marshaled there. Before the invasion, Napoleon inspected his troops in Königsberg on June 12.

Because it was occupied by France and in a very weak military position, Prussia had entered earlier in 1812 into an alliance with France against its former ally, Russia. This alliance committed Prussia to furnish troops to France in the event of war between France and Russia. As a state of war now existed between these two countries, Prussia was forced to participate in the conflict on the French side and Prussian soldiers, commanded by General Johann von Yorck, joined the French invasion of Russia.

Napoleon's campaign was initially a success and Moscow was captured, but the bitter winter weather forced his army to beat a disastrous retreat. With the tide now turning against Napoleon, General von Yorck decided on his own initiative to abandon the French side and join forces with the Russians. On December 30, 1812, he met with the Russian general Hans Carl von Diebitsch and signed the Convention of Tauroggen (a Lithuanian town forty kilometers from the Prussian border), which formally dissolved Prussia's alliance with France. On the night of January 4/5, 1813, the last remaining French soldiers retreated from Königsberg and Russian troops again entered the city, but not as an occupying force as had been the case in the Seven Years' War.

On March 16, 1813, Prussia declared war on France and in a battle that raged in and around Leipzig between October 16 and 19, the combined armies of Austria, Prussia, and Russia decisively defeated Napoleon in what became known as the Battle of the Nations (Völkerschlacht bei Leipzig). On March 31, 1814, the allied forces against France entered Paris and Napoleon abdicated. He was exiled to the island of Elba a few days later, but in March of 1815 managed to escape to France and resumed fighting with those French forces still loyal to him. He was finally vanquished in June at Waterloo by the English Duke of Wellington and the Prussian general Gebhard Blücher.

Prussia's earlier defeat by the French in the battles of Jena and Auerstädt in October 1806 had a galvanizing effect on its leaders. Spearheaded by a group of enlightened noblemen, including Freiherr Karl von Stein, Prince Karl August von Hardenberg, Wilhelm von Humbolt, General Gerhard von Scharnhorst, and Carl von Clausewitz, the Prussian Reform Movement implemented a wide range of measures.[44] The October Edict of 1807 dealing with agrarian reform had three main elements: restrictions on who could purchase land owned by the nobility were eliminated; occupations of all kinds were opened to people of all classes, thereby creating a free labor market; and hereditary servitude of peasants on the land was eliminated. Wilhelm von Humbolt pioneered educational reform by introducing a single, standardized educational system that included new teacher training colleges. He also founded the Friedrich-Wilhelm University in 1810 (since 1949 Humbolt University) in Berlin, where students were encouraged to engage in critical and reasoned thinking rather than memorize facts. General Scharnhorst's ideas for reform of the Prussian army—largely implemented in July 1809—involved the abolition of corporal punishment, the opening up of the officer corps to the middle class, and making higher education a requirement for advancement to the top levels of the army. Finally, in March 1812, the Edict Concerning the Civil Condition of the Jews in the Prussian State considerably enhanced the position of Jews; it made them citizens of Prussia, eliminated restrictions on Jewish occupational and commercial activity, and lifted special taxes and levies on them.

All these farsighted, liberal reforms were aimed at making the state of Prussia more efficient and productive. Together with the high standards of honesty and efficiency in the Prussian civil service and military administration introduced by King Frederick William I and his son, Frederick the Great, they facilitated the economic, social, and political development of Prussia and later the German nation. These positive features of Prussia were lost sight of during World War II when, as described in Chapter VII, Churchill,

Roosevelt, and Stalin believed that East Prussia embodied the worst Prussian traits and should therefore be excised from the map of Europe.

E. From the Congress of Vienna in 1815 to World War I

Following the defeat of Napoleon, the principal objective of Austria, England, Prussia, and Poland was to re-establish the political order that existed before his rise to power and to forge a stable balance of power and establish boundaries that would preserve the peace for the foreseeable future. This restoration of the status quo ante was achieved at the Congress of Vienna in 1815. Nearly all European states participated, and Prussia was one of the principal beneficiaries. On its eastern borders Prussia regained southern West Prussia as well as Danzig, which became the capital of West Prussia; Ermland, which became part of East Prussia; and Thorn and Kulmerland.[45] Prussia also took possession of the Grand Duchy of Posen, an area to the south of West Prussia largely inhabited by Poles. While Prussia gained lands in the west along the Mosel, Saar, and the central region of the Rhine, it remained divided into separate territories in the east and the west, with Hanover and Hesse separating the two.

A feature of the new political order was the formation of the German Confederation (*Deutscher Bund*) consisting of Austria and Prussia as the major participants, thirty-four German principalities ruled by princes, and the city states of Lübeck, Frankfurt, Bremen, and Hamburg. This new grouping of various German political entities was intended to serve as a replacement of the Holy Roman Empire, which had been relegated to the dustbin of history in 1803 by Napoleonic decree (*Reichsdeputationshauptschluß*) and ended in 1806 when the ruling Emperor Franz II removed his crown and thereby abdicated the throne. As East and West Prussia had not been part of the Holy Roman Empire, they were not allowed to join the German Confederation. In 1824, at the direction of King Frederick William III, they were united to form the province of Prussia. The East Prussian Theodor von Schön was appointed *Oberpräsident* and had his office in the Königsberg Castle. Von Schön was an energetic administrator who did much to develop the province of Prussia, including constructing schools,

roads, and the Art Academy in Königsberg, and reconstructing the former headquarters of the Teutonic Order in Marienburg.[46] He resigned in 1842 because
of a difference of views with the new king, Frederick William IV. In 1878 East
and West Prussia were once again separated because Danzig wished to resume its
role as a provincial capital and because of the growing nationalism of the Polish
minority in West Prussia (see below).

The battles that had been fought to liberate German territory from the
yoke of France in the Napoleonic Wars had brought forth a strong feeling of
German national identity. Wishing to become part of the German nation and
concerned that East and West Prussia, being exposed at the farthest reaches
of German territory, might again be threatened by Russia, the Provincial
Assembly in Königsberg made an appeal on April 3, 1848, to King Frederick
William IV to join the German Confederation:

> The Province of Prussia, as the guardian of Germany's eastern fron-
> tier, can maintain this dangerous forward position with unlimited
> devotion only by knowing that it also belongs constitutionally
> to the great German fatherland to which the vast majority of its
> inhabitants are already united in their minds through language,
> education and disposition.[47]

The province of Prussia became a member of the Confederation a week
later, but membership lasted only three and a half years because conservative
forces took over the National Assembly in Frankfurt and ousted it from the
Confederation on October 3, 1851. Following Austria's defeat by Prussia in
1866, the German Confederation was dissolved and a year later the province was incorporated into a new German entity called the North German
Confederation (essentially the German Confederation minus Austria and
southern Germany). The Confederation's president was King William I, who
had crowned himself in the chapel of Königsberg Castle in October 18, 1861,
with great pomp and circumstance.

The German Empire (which excluded Austia) was established on January
18, 1871, when William I of Prussia became Emperor William I in the Hall

of Mirrors at the Palace of Versailles. The location of this ceremony was a deliberate insult to France, which had gone to war with Prussia in 1870 in a dispute over a Hohenzollern candidate to the Spanish throne, but was defeated. The chancellor of the new empire and the power behind the throne was Otto von Bismarck. Previously the minister-president of Prussia, he was the leading German statesman of the nineteenth century and instrumental in the formation of Germany as a nation-state. Up to this point Germany had existed as a loose collection of political entities of which Prussia was clearly the dominant force. With the establishment of the empire, Prussia was united with both the kingdoms of Bavaria and Württemberg and the grand duchies of Baden and Hesse (see Map 1. Germany before World War I). As a result, a unified Germany came into existence for the first time. (Note on terminology. The German word for "empire" is "Reich" and when East Prussians traveled west to the central part of Germany, they would often say they were going "ins Reich," i.e., to the Reich.)

With Bismarck's strong support, the northeastern French region of Alsace-Lorraine—taken from France following its defeat—was annexed to the empire. This acquisition of French territory poisoned relations between Germany and France, and one of Bismarck's biographers described the annexation as the worst mistake of his political career.[48] Some opposition had arisen in Germany to the annexation of Alsace-Lorraine on the grounds that it reflected the military power of the victor and did not represent the desires of the inhabitants. Johann Jacoby, a political liberal from Königsberg, expressed his strong reservations with words that were prophetic of what would happen later in World War II: "How would it strike us liberals if at some point a victorious Poland—on the basis of force of arms—wished to take over and annex the provinces of Posen and West Prussia? And indeed considered as valid the same reasons that are now used to justify the annexation of Alsace and Lorraine?"[49] Jacoby was imprisoned for protesting the annexation and proposing a plebiscite in Alsace-Lorraine.

In fact, during the nineteenth and early twentieth centuries there was growing tension between Germans and Poles in the eastern provinces.[50] It began in 1830 with a Polish uprising against the Russian rule of the Grand

Duchy of Warsaw and it spilled over to the Prussian-controlled Grand Duchy of Posen. In response, the Prussian governor of Posen introduced a policy of Germanization of the Poles, which included the prohibition of school instruction in Polish. This policy aroused considerable opposition not only in the Grand Duchy of Posen, but also in East and West Prussia, where there were significant Polish minorities. There also was Polish opposition when East and West Prussia successively became part of the German League, the North German League, and the German Empire. In 1871, the Reichstag held a debate led by a representative from Posen on the rights of Poles in this region. During this debate another Polish representative recalled that the wishes of the inhabitants of Alsace-Lorraine to be part of France had not been taken into account at the time of its annexation.

Concurrently with growing anti-Polish sentiment in Germany, economic factors provided incentives for Poles to work in both Germany's eastern and western provinces. The rapid industrialization in the western part of Germany, particularly in the Ruhr area of the Rhineland, attracted German and Polish workers from East and West Prussia and Pomerania. Their departure in turn provided opportunities for Poles to settle in these provinces and the large estates in the eastern provinces became very dependent on Poles for seasonal farm work.[51]

The German–Polish conflict was exacerbated in 1876 when a law was passed stipulating that German was the only language to be used for official purposes. The policy of Germanization went hand in hand with attempts to impose state control on the Catholic Church in all of Prussia (the so-called *Kulturkampf*). In 1887, a new law forbade religious instruction in Polish. Public opposition to school instruction in German broke out in 1901 in Posen where German was the mother tongue of only one-third of the population, and school boycotts spread to West Prussia in 1906 and 1907. A petition to the Pope protesting the policy of severely restricting the use of the Polish language bore 147,000 signatures from Posen and 26,900 from West Prussia.[52]

German–Polish tensions in eastern Germany reflected a strong feeling of national identity among Polish people living in the region. West Prussia had, in fact, been part of Poland for three hundred years and East Prussia had owed allegiance to the Polish crown for hundreds of years. These factors became important at the end of World War I, when historic Polish claims to this German territory were partially realized in the Versailles Peace Treaty. In the Potsdam Agreement following the end of World War II, they were crucial for the decision to excise East Prussia from Germany.

While East Prussia was much less affected by these tensions, in World War I it became a major battleground between Germany and Russia. In the early days of the war two Russian armies advanced quickly into East Prussia and defeated the German army in the Battle of Gumbinnen on August 19–20, 1914. Many villages and towns were destroyed, there were considerable civilian casualties, and many inhabitants fled west to avoid the advancing Russian forces. An official document in the Reich archive reported sixteen hundred civilian deaths, four hundred wounded, ten thousand taken prisoner, and thirty-four thousand buildings destroyed. Of the 2.5 million inhabitants east of the Vistula, some eight hundred thousand fled their homes, with half fleeing all the way to the west of the Vistula.[53] The considerable plundering, damage to property, and civilian loss of life were in sharp contrast to the benign occupation of the province by the Russians during the Seven Years' War and the brief incursion of the Russian Army at the time of the Napoleonic Wars. However, the civilian losses and property damage were but a foretaste of the widespread death and destruction wreaked during the Soviet invasion some thirty years later at the end of World War II.

In World War I the tide quickly turned against the Russians when the commander of the German Eighth Army, General Maximilian von Prittwitz, was relieved of his command. His replacement was sixty-six-year-old General Paul von Hindenburg, who was called out of retirement. Hindenburg immediately assigned General Erich Ludendorff as his chief of staff. Under this new leadership the Eighth Army defeated the Russian forces in southern East Prussia in the Battle of Tannenberg during the last week of August.[54] In the winter of 1914–15 southeast Prussia was once again briefly occupied by the Russian Army and considerable destruction took place. The province was finally freed of Russian occupation for the remainder of World War I in the battles fought in Masuria from February 17–21 and in Tilsit on March 21, 1915. In that same year the reconstruction of East Prussia began with aid from German cities in the west. To cite one example, Breslau provided considerable assistance to the East Prussian town of Pillkallen (renamed Schloßberg by the Nazis and then Dobrowolsk when this area became part of Russia), which had been almost totally destroyed by the Russians.[55]

F. From the Versailles Treaty of 1919 to the Eve of World War II in 1939

Germany's defeat in World War I resulted in significant changes to its eastern provinces, as stipulated in the Versailles Peace Treaty. The most far-reaching change was the separation of East Prussia from the rest of Germany. This isolation of East Prussia was foreshadowed in the Fourteen Points that US President Wilson presented to a joint session of Congress on January 8, 1918. Influenced by the famous Polish pianist and politician Ignace Paderewski, Wilson proposed in Point 13 the creation of an independent Polish state, consisting of regions with a Polish majority population, and that Poland should have a land connection to the sea. Poland's territorial demands at Versailles included not only Danzig and West Prussia but East Prussia as well. Roman Dmowski, president of the Polish National Committee and head of the Polish delegation to the Versailles peace conference, proposed the creation of a Republic of Königsberg with a close connection to Poland. When this demand was rejected by Great Britain and the United States, he then floated the idea of a Republic of Königsberg under the protection of the League of Nations and linked to Poland by a customs union. Again, he was unsuccessful.[56] When the peace treaty was signed on June 28, 1919, in the Hall of Mirrors at Versailles, East Prussia lost to Poland only the town and surrounding area of Soldau because it was on a railroad line that fitted into the Polish transportation network.[57] In addition, in northern East Prussia the Memelland was put under international control and later ceded to Lithuania.

The Versailles Treaty did provide Poland with a connection to the sea that became known as the Polish Corridor (see Map 2. Germany after World War I with Polish Corridor). This was accomplished by transferring to Poland most of West Prussia, an area of nearly sixteen thousand square kilometers and a population of 965,000. Danzig (part of West Prussia) was declared a free city under the protection of the League of Nations and became part of the Polish customs area. By far the largest area (twenty-six thousand square kilometers with a population of two million) that was transferred from Germany to Poland was the province of Posen located south of West Prussia.

As a consequence of the Versailles Treaty, East Prussia became isolated from the Reich by Poland. Always vulnerable at the outer eastern edge of Germany, East Prussia's geographic position was now even more precarious and the negative economic effects of separation soon became apparent. The far-reaching political and military implications of East Prussia's exposed location became evident twenty-five years later at the end of World War II.

Of the eastern territories taken from Germany under the Versailles Treaty, only Danzig had a clear German majority; ninety-five percent of the population of three hundred thousand were German speaking. By contrast, in Posen the German-speaking part of the population was thirty-four percent, in West Prussia forty-three percent, and in the Memel area fifty-one percent.[58] It became apparent, however, that a person's mother tongue did not necessarily indicate a preference for citizenship in the country where it was the language of the majority of the population. The plebiscites mandated by the Versailles Treaty in those parts of East Prussia with large Polish populations took place on July 11, 1920. The results indicated an overwhelming preference for Germany on the part of the Poles: in the southern part of East Prussia (the voting district of Allenstein), ninety-eight percent of the population voted to be part of Germany; in the area of East Prussia east of the Vistula (the voting district of Marienwerder), ninety-two percent voted to go with Germany.[59] In the East Prussian area of Ermland, only six thousand voted for Poland, although almost forty-two thousand reported Polish as their mother tongue, and in the plebiscite in East Prussia east of the Vistula, eight thousand voted for Poland although twenty-two thousand indicated that Polish was their mother tongue.[60]

It seems reasonable to conclude that West Prussia would have remained part of Germany if the citizenship preferences of its inhabitants had been allowed to determine the outcome.[61] And yet as described above, the history of West Prussia going back several centuries shows that Polish influence and connections were pronounced; indeed, more than forty percent of the population of West Prussia spoke Polish as their mother tongue. This strong Polish link makes Poland's claim to West Prussia understandable, while its claim to East Prussia, by contrast, has no such ethnic basis.

Being cut off from the rest of Germany by the Polish Corridor inevitably put East Prussia at a significant economic disadvantage. (This isolated position was similar to that of Berlin, isolated in the middle of the German Democratic Republic after World War II.) Although Poland was obligated under the Versailles Treaty to permit unhindered transit traffic between East Prussia and the Reich, it insisted that German merchandise and passengers be transported on Polish trains at full cost, albeit without passport controls and the imposition of tariffs.[62] Automobile traffic, on the other hand, was subject to the full extent of such controls and was allowed only on specially designated highways.[63] The cost of transportation therefore rose considerably between East Prussia and the rest of Germany. The economic squeeze on the province became particularly acute in January 1936, when Poland required that payment for transportation services across the corridor be made in foreign currency, such as the English pound, instead of Reichsmarks. Because of the severe shortage of foreign exchange in Germany at this time, this requirement led to sharply reduced transit traffic and to significant additional transportation costs as alternative, more expensive, transport routes via land and sea to the Reich had to be developed.

The economic difficulties posed by East Prussia's isolation became the subject of a number of studies to ameliorate the situation.[64] Eventually, the decision was made to provide East Prussian industry and agriculture with government subsidies, but systematic and long-term assistance for the province was hindered by the worldwide economic depression and the political instability in

Germany in the early 1930s. Although the government in Berlin had limited budgetary resources, efforts were nonetheless made to bring new settlers to East Prussia and measures were enacted in 1929, 1930, and 1931 in the Reichstag to provide these settlers with considerable support in the form of credits and subsidies. This program of incentives had some success: from 1919 to 1937 the total number of settlers had reached nearly twenty-eight thousand.[65]

Because the economy of East Prussia was largely based on agriculture, it was the least well-off province of Germany except for West Prussia: income per capita in East Prussia in 1913 was only sixty-four percent of the average for the Reich as a whole. However, by 1936 income per capita had risen to seventy-three percent of the average, the largest gain in income of all the German provinces. Moreover, the absolute level of income had risen by seventeen percent between 1913 and 1936, whereas in parts of Germany more dependent on manufacturing and therefore more susceptible to the worldwide Great Depression, a decline in absolute income per capita occurred over this period. For example, in Hamburg income per capita dropped by twelve percent during this time.[66]

Königsberg, the capital of East Prussia, had the good fortune from 1919 to 1933 to have Hans Lohmeyer as its mayor (*Oberbürgermeister*).[67] He was an exceptionally able civil servant who did much to enhance the city's position as a leading commercial center. His administration established the Eastern Trade Fair, which fostered trade links with Scandinavia and countries in Eastern Europe, particularly Poland and Russia. New docks were built in the harbor and modern storage facilities, including one for cold storage, were constructed. The sea canal to the Baltic through the Frisches Haff was deepened to eight meters to allow larger vessels to serve the port, and new railroad stations were built south and north of the city. Thus, East Prussia, and particularly its capital Köngisberg under Oberbürgermeister Lohmeyer, adjusted fairly well to the unfavorable economic situation resulting from the Versailles Treaty, which separated it from the rest of Germany and transformed it into an island bordered by Poland and Lithuania (see Map 5. East Prussia 1923–1939).

Throughout its history, East Prussia, situated at the far eastern edge of Germany, was open to attacks from its neighbors, particularly Russia, and was coveted by Poland, which regarded it as Polish territory. It nonetheless survived for seven hundred years through adroit acts of statecraft and fortuitous political developments. East Prussia remained intact as a German province following the wars waged by Frederick the Great and the last German emperor, William II. Yet the immediate legacy of World War I—especially the Treaty of Versailles—and the Great Depression fostered the conditions for Hitler's rise to power and ultimately led to World War II. Cut off from the rest of Germany by the Polish Corridor, at war's end East Prussia was ripe to be taken over by Poland and Russia, a fate that had nearly befallen it in the past. Such an outcome was by no means inevitable, but the history of East Prussia shows that it was clearly vulnerable to being excised from the body of Germany, a fate foreseen by Frederick the Great:

> Frederick assigned clear priority to the central provinces of the kingdom. In a revealing passage of the Political Testament of 1768, he even declared that only Brandenburg, Magdeburg, Halberstadt and Silesia "constituted the actual body of the state." This was in part a matter of military logic. What distinguished the central lands was the fact that they could "defend themselves, as long as the whole of Europe [did] not unite against the sovereign." East Prussia and the western possessions, by contrast, would have to be given up as soon as hostilities began.[68]

When the hostilities of World War II began on September 1, 1939, East Prussia became the staging ground for the invasion of Poland. It enjoyed a false sense of security as long as the war was being waged far in the east. Life on this island of relative calm before the storm is described in the next chapter. Only at the end of the war did Frederick the Great's prediction come true, when Germany was forced by the three wartime Allies to give up East Prussia to Russia and Poland.

Notes

1 Christiansen, *The Northern Crusades*, 104.
2 The Teutonic Order was officially recognized by Pope Celestine III in 1196 and was confirmed by Pope Innocent in 1199. While it was a distinctly German institution, it did accept foreigners, especially Poles and other Slavs, into its ranks. Its close association with German burghers since its founding had important implications for the later colonization of East Prussia. In the early thirteenth century the Order received considerable support from the Holy Roman Emperor at the time, Frederick II, who recruited prominent members and imbued it with an effective administrative structure similar to that of his court.
3 This valuable parchment document with a gold seal, hence the name "Golden Bull," is in the Königsberg Historical State Archives in Berlin. The text is reproduced in Gornig, *Das nördliche Ostpreußen*, 229–31.
4 The text of this document is reproduced in op. cit., 234–35.
5 For a full description of these crusades, see Christiansen, *The Northern Crusades*.
6 See Koch, *A History of Prussia*, 11.
7 Ibid.
8 Both Koch and Boockmann, *Ostpreußen und Westpreußen*, argue that the policy of the Order toward the Prussen was one of subjugation, not extermination.
9 There was, of course, tension between the Order's religious and political-economic objectives. According to Koch, *A History of Prussia*, 11, the conversion of Prussen in large numbers would have undermined the political dominance of the Teutonic Knights. He reports that the Papacy had to intervene in 1237 against the Order on behalf of the Prussen.
10 Gornig, *Das nördliche Ostpreußen*, 32.
11 As described below, in another Battle of Tannenberg some five hundred years later at the beginning of World War I, the German Army achieved a major victory over Russian forces. More recently, almost six hundred years later, the battle of 1410 is regularly re-enacted by participants from Germany, Poland, and other eastern European countries. Tannenberg (Polish Grunwald) has been transformed from a symbol of German-Polish antagonism into a place manifesting the integration of central Europe after World War II. *Amerika Woche* 33/34 (August 17/24): 2009, 20–21.
12 Christiansen, *The Northern Crusades*, 228.
13 There appears to be some controversy among scholars as to whether this was in fact a feudal "oath of allegiance," a *Lehnseid*. Gornig argues (*Das nördliche Ostpreußen*, 36) that this was not the case.

14 This separation of East Prussia from the rest of German territory lasted three hundred years until the First Partition of Poland in 1772. It can be seen as a precursor of the creation of the Polish Corridor in the Versailles Treaty in 1919, which once again separated East Prussia from what had then become the state of Germany.

15 Christiansen, *The Northern Crusades*, 245.

16 Ibid., 47.

17 Albrecht was in fact the nephew of King Sigismund, who was his mother's brother. Upon returning to Königsberg, Albrecht renounced his vows, converted to Lutheranism, and married Princess Dorothea of Denmark.

18 It is ironic that Catholic Poland undertook this initiative to maintain the integrity of its newly minted Protestant neighbor. This can be understood as a defensive measure vis-à-vis the Holy Roman Empire. See Koch, *A History of Prussia*, 34.

19 The main function of an elector was to elect the Holy Roman Emperor. Though not a title of nobility—such as king, duke, margrave, or count—the position of elector was extremely prestigious. In addition to the Margrave of Brandenburg, there were six other electors: the archbishops of Cologne, Mainz, and Trier; the Count Palatine of the Rhine; the Duke of Saxony; and the King of Bohemia.

20 For a concise account of the development of Brandenburg and how it became linked to the Duchy of Prussia, see Clark, *Iron Kingdom*, Chapter I, "The Hohenzollerns of Brandenburg."

21 The Thirty Years' War ravaged central Europe from 1618 to 1648. It was largely a conflict between the Habsburg Holy Roman Emperors Ferdinand I and II, together with their Spanish cousin Philip IV, mainly against France and Sweden, but also Denmark and Holland. It was partly a religious war, with the Catholic Habsburgs pitted against Protestant Sweden and Frederick V of the Palatinate in southwest Germany. It was also a German civil war, as the German principalities fought for or against the Habsburgs at different times during the war's thirty years.

22 Koch, *A History of Prussia*, 42.

23 Clark, *Iron Kingdom*, Chapter 3, "An Extraordinary Light in Germany," describes in detail Frederick William's rule and the energy and care he devoted to the administration of Brandenburg-Prussia.

24 Koch, *A History of Prussia*, 59.

25 Stamm, *Frag mich nach Ostpreußen*, 84.

26 Frederick William was one of seven electors of the Holy Roman Emperor. See footnote 19 for the list of the other six.

27 Stamm, *Frag mich nach Ostpreußen*, 85.

28 The Edict of Nantes was issued by Henry IV of France in 1598 and granted Huguenots (Calvinist Protestants) substantial rights in what was a predominantly Catholic country. Louis XIV, grandson of Henry IV, renounced the edict in October 1685, and declared Protestantism illegal. As a result, hundreds of thousands of Protestants left France in the following two decades.

29 Koch, *A History of Prussia*, 67.

30 Since the founding of Königsberg in honor of King Ottokar of Bohemia in 1255, it was by name and by tradition the city of kings. For this reason, Frederick III crowned himself in the castle in Königsberg, rather than in Berlin, the capital of Brandenburg.

31 Clark, *Iron Kingdom*, 68, provides a vivid description of the lavish celebrations and crowning ceremony. He cites an estimate on the order of six million thalers for the cost of the ceremony and associated festivities, roughly twice the annual revenues of the Hohenzollern administration.

32 Ibid., 77.

33 Koch, *A History of Prussia*, 99.

34 Frederick is referred to as "the Great" not only because of his military exploits, but also because of his enlightened rule of Prussia, which included the introduction of many far-reaching laws.

35 Koch, *A History of Prussia*, 129.

36 The Russian occupation of Königsberg was quite benign. See Manthey, *Königsberg*, 277–93. This same view is conveyed in a recent biography of Kant: "…on the whole not much changed [with the occupation]. Prussian officials continued to do the work they had done before, and everyone continued to draw the same salary. The Russians especially favored the university and its members. The army officers attended many lectures, and professors were invited to official receptions and balls.… All in all, the Russian occupation was good for Königsberg.… The Russians contributed to a change in the cultural climate of Königsberg. There was more money, and there was more consumption." Kuehn, *Kant: A Biography*, 113. Kant in particular benefited from the occupation, as many officers attended his lectures. He also gave them private instruction, for which he was paid handsomely.

37 Gornig, *Das nördliche Ostpreußen*, 48.

38 Ibid.

39 Koch, *A History of Prussia*, 158.

40 Clark, *Iron Kingdom*, 186.

41 Koch, *A History of Prussia*, 141.

42 Gornig, *Das nördliche Ostpreußen*, 51.

43 Koch, *A History of Prussia*, 160.

44 See Clark, *Iron Kingdom*, Chapter 10, "The World the Bureaucrats Made," 312–44, and Koch, *A History of Prussia*, Chapter 8, "The Prussian Reform Movement," 163–87.

45 Gornig, *Das nördliche Ostpreußen*, 54.

46 Boockmann, *Ostpreußen und Westpreußen*, 357.

47 Ibid., 364. "Die Provinz Preußen als Deutschlands Grenzwächter gegen Osten kann diese vorgeschobene gefährliche Stellung mit unbeschränkter Hingebung nur im Bewußtsein behaupten, daß sie auch stattsrechtlich dem großen deutschen Vaterlande angehöre, mit welchem sie durch Sprache, Bildung und Gesinnung in der weit überwiegenden Zahl ihre Bewohner geistig schon vereinigt ist."

48 Clark, *Iron Kingdom*, 553. Bismarck was undoubtedly the most outstanding Prussian statesman of the nineteenth century. He was guided by a pragmatic sense of what would work to balance the competing interests of various states and groups, rather than by a fixed ideology. He was therefore identified as a practitioner of realpolitik and was quoted as saying "having to go through life with principles is like walking down a forest path with a stick in one's mouth." His pragmatism was noteworthy in social legislation of the 1880s, which included health, accident, and old age and disability insurance. His chief concern was the mollification of Social Democrats rather than the welfare of workers.

49 Boockmann, *Ostpreußen und Westpreußen*, 364–66. Original in German, translated by the author.

50 See ibid., 376–91, for an extended discussion of this issue.

51 German agriculture depends on Polish workers to harvest seasonal crops to this day. As reported in *The Economist* (May 7, 2005, p. 58), the spring harvest of asparagus in Germany relies heavily on seasonal Polish workers because they are cheaper, more reliable, and more eager to work than unemployed German workers.

52 See Boockmann, *Ostpreußen und Westpreußen*, 385–91, for a description of these developments.

53 This report is cited in Gornig, *Das nördliche Ostpreußen*, 61. See also Fritz Gause, *Die Russen in Ostpreußen 1914/15*.

54 As pointed out by Boockmann, *Ostpreußen und Westpreußen*, 394, this battle was waged over a wide area and many localities could have been chosen as the name of the battle. However, as one of these was Tannenberg, it was chosen to designate the entire conflict in order to make clear that the victory in 1914 reversed the defeat of the Teutonic Knights there in 1410 by the Poles and the Lithuanians.

The German victory at this historic site also helped enhance the reputations of Hindenburg and Ludendorff to near-mythic status. For an account of the Battle of Tannenberg that combines historical reconstruction with imaginative flair, see Alexander Solzhenitsyn, *August 1914.*

55 For a description of the reconstruction of East Prussia after World War I, see Erich Göttgen, *Der Wiederaufbau Ostpreußens.*

56 Manthey, *Königsberg,* 653.

57 Gornig, *Das nördliche Ostpreußen,* 63.

58 These figures are taken from Boockmann, *Ostpreußen und Westpreußen,* 398. By way of comparison, in Alsace-Lorraine, which was transferred back to France, eighty-seven percent of the population was German-speaking.

59 At least one account of the history of Poland, written by two Polish authors, does not contest the results of this plebiscite: "While fighting for its very survival against the Bolsheviks in the summer of 1920, the fledgling Polish state was unable to press its territorial claims effectively in southern East Prussia, where the Polish-speaking Mazurians, whose national identity was still indeterminate, voted overwhelmingly to remain in Germany rather than risk inclusion in a Bolshevik Poland." Lukowski and Zawadzki, *A Concise History of Poland,* 203.

60 Gornig, *Das nördliche Ostpreußen,* 64. The figures for the language reported as the mother tongue were obtained in a survey undertaken in 1910. The fact that the language survey and the plebiscite took place at different dates, and involved somewhat different samples of the population, means that the comparison of the figures for mother tongue and citizenship preference can only be interpreted as indicative that the former do not necessarily determine the latter.

61 This is the conclusion of Boockman, *Ostpreußen und Westpreußen,* 401.

62 The many issues involved in transit traffic are described in Morrow, *The Peace Settlement in the German Polish Borderlands,* Chapter VI, "The 'Corridor' Problem: (1) Transit Traffic," 201–15.

63 Gornig, *Das nördliche Ostpreußen,* 66.

64 For an extensive discussion of these developments, see Friedrich Richter, "Wirtschaftsprobleme Ostpreußens 1919 bis 1945: Ausgangslage, Politik, und Entwicklung," in Jähnig and Spieler, eds., *Das Königsberger Gebiet,* 45–71.

65 Ibid., 55.

66 Boockmann, *Ostpreußen und Westpreußen,* 404.

67 For an extensive description of Königsberg between World War I and World War II, see Gause, *Die Geschichte der Stadt Königsberg,* Vol. III, Chapter III, "Königsberg in der Democratie," and Chapter IV, "Das Dritte Reich."

68 Clark, *Iron Kingdom,* 244.

CHAPTER II

PRELUDE TO THE END
OF EAST PRUSSIA

A. Germany's Invasion of Poland and Russia:
Sowing the Seeds for Revenge

World War II began when Germany invaded Poland at 4:45 a.m. on
September 1, 1939. Hitler's objective was to conquer Polish territory as quickly as possible in order to provide living space (*Lebensraum*) for
Germans.[1] Given the vastly superior resources of the German armed forces,
the military outcome was never in doubt and most Polish forces were defeated
by the end of September. In the brief military campaign and the occupation
that followed, Germany waged war not only against the Polish Army but
also against civilians. The unprecedented brutality of this campaign against
civilians reflected the official Nazi view that Poles were inferior human beings
who should be uprooted or annihilated in order to make room for German
settlers in Polish territory. The destruction of Poland's political and cultural
elites in particular was designed to ensure that the country had no future as
an independent nation.

Russia shared this objective. The successive partitions of Poland in the
eighteenth century by Prussia and Russia described in Chapter I were earlier manifestations of the intention of these two powers to suppress a sovereign Poland and to share its territory. To cement Russia's collusion with his

conquest of Poland, Hitler engineered a Non-Aggression Pact between Nazi Germany and the Soviet Union, which was signed in Moscow on August 23, 1939, by Germany's foreign minister, Joachim von Ribbentrop, and that of the Soviet Union, Vyacheslav M. Molotov. It contained secret provisions dividing Poland and other parts of Eastern Europe between Germany and the Soviet Union. The Soviet attack on eastern Poland on September 17 enabled the German forces to concentrate on crushing the remaining Polish resistance in the western part of the country.

When armed conflict ceased in early October, about one million Polish soldiers had been captured by the Germans and the Russians, and over one hundred thousand had perished in the brief, brutal conflict.[2] A large number of these casualties resulted from military conflict, but by one estimate the number of summary executions of Poles by Germans reached fifty thousand by the end of 1939.[3] This joint conquest constituted the Fourth Partition of Poland by Germany and Russia.

Some attempts had been made in the wake of World War I to determine the preference of members of various ethnic groups regarding the nation-states they wished to be part of. In the case of Poland at the start of World War II, the exact opposite was the case.[4] In those parts of western Poland directly annexed by Germany, including the major cities of Poznan (Posen) and Lodz (re-named Litzmannstadt by the Germans), Poles lost all their property rights and were subject to compulsory work or deportation; they were thereby reduced to an underclass. That part of Poland not incorporated into Germany was called the "General Gouvernement," and the governor-general was Hans Frank, one of Hitler's top lieutenants, who was eventually sentenced to death at the post-war war crimes trial at Nuremberg. Under his rule the Poles were subjected to extremely harsh treatment, including mass executions of the political, cultural, and religious elite; random killings of civilians; widespread forced labor and resettlements; and beginning in the winter of 1941–1942, the wholesale slaughter of Polish Jews. It is estimated that forty-five percent of all Polish doctors, fifty percent of all Polish engineers, and fifty-seven percent of all Polish lawyers died in mass executions or in concentration camps. The Poles in the General Gouvernement were treated as a workforce at the beck and call of the

Nazi regime, and from 1939 to 1944, out of a population of thirty-five million in 1939, 2.8 million were sent to Germany as forced laborers.[5]

The conquest and brutalization of Poland by the Nazis was a prelude to Hitler's "crusade" against Bolshevism. On June 22, 1941, Hitler abrogated the Non-Aggression Pact and launched an invasion of the Soviet Union: Operation Barbarossa.[6] It was named after Emperor Frederick I Barbarossa (Red Beard) of Germany and the Holy Roman Empire, who led the Third Crusade in 1189 against Saladin's Muslim armies, which had captured Jerusalem earlier that year.[7] He was the most powerful emperor of the Middle Ages, and with the flowering of German national identity in the nineteenth century, was glorified as a pinnacle of Germany's history.

Hitler directed his "crusade" from his eastern front headquarters known as the *Wolfschanze*, or wolf's lair, located near Rastenburg (Ketrzyn) in East Prussia. Construction of the barracks and bunkers in a mosquito-infested forest had already commenced in the fall of 1940, and these quarters were constantly expanded, improved, and reinforced to provide Hitler with state-of-the-art security measures. Nevertheless, Count Claus von Stauffenberg, head of the anti-Nazi conspiracy called Valkyrie, was able to penetrate the tight security at the Wolfschanze and attempted to assassinate Hitler on July 20, 1944. The attempt failed and Stauffenberg and many others involved in the conspiracy were executed. In January 1945, the Wolfschanze was abandoned and partly destroyed by the Germans in the face of the advancing Red Army. The ruins in Ketrzyn are now a tourist attraction in territory that is now Polish.[8]

During the first stage of the Blitzkrieg, or lightning war, German forces succeeded in destroying the Soviet forward defenses and crossed the Dvina and Dnieper Rivers by early July. The tank forces of Army Group North advanced rapidly through the Baltic countries of Estonia, Latvia, and Lithuania in the direction of Leningrad; Army Group Center—with Moscow as its goal— moved in the direction of Smolensk; and Army Group South drove toward Kiev, the capital of Ukraine. In the second stage of Operation Barbarossa, from late July through most of August, Army Group North captured the cities of Riga and Pskov and then advanced toward Luga and Novgorod, Army Group Center spent much of August in a fierce battle to wrest Smolensk from the Soviet armies, while Army Group South eliminated two Soviet armies southwest of Kiev. In late August, Hitler made the fateful decision to order a pause in the all-out thrusts to take Moscow and Leningrad, and instead directed German forces to eradicate the Soviet armies that were staunchly defending Kiev and central Ukraine.

In the third stage of the campaign from late August to the end of September, Army Groups Center and South joined together to defeat the Soviet forces in the Kiev bulge. This German victory opened the way for the final assault on Moscow, which began in early October. Reinforced with troops from Army Groups North and South, Army Group Center advanced toward Moscow on a broad front stretching from north of Smolensk to south of Briansk. Meanwhile, to the south, the Second Panzer Army, under the command of General Guderian, had advanced toward Tula, a major armaments manufacturing center nearly two hundred kilometers south of Moscow, which was of strategic importance for the Soviet defense of their capital.

After a delay caused by rains and mud in early November, the German forces launched a massive assault against the Soviet armies defending Moscow. However, in the face of bitter cold and heavy snow, lack of adequate supplies, especially fuel for the tanks needed for the assault, and die-hard resistance by the defending Soviet forces, the German attack stalled. On the night of December 4–5, a large-scale Soviet counterattack was mounted against Army Group Center, which fell apart after sustaining heavy causualties and lost its effectiveness as an offensive force. Thus, the Germans were stopped almost within sight of Moscow, and the Blitzkrieg, which had been so successful in the summer and autumn of 1941, was finished, having become frozen fast in the depths of the Russian winter.[9]

The harshness with which the Germans waged war on the Soviet Union was, if anything, even more extreme than the campaign against Poland. It reflected the core belief of Nazi ideology that the Germanic race, as the "Herrenvolk," was superior to others, and in particular to the Slavs in the Soviet Union. The Nazis regarded the Slavs as subhuman (*Untermenschen*) and hence believed that the conventional moral code embodied in the Geneva Convention regarding the humane treatment of prisoners of war and noncombatants was not applicable to them. The deliberate brutality of the campaign against the Slavs was stated succinctly by General Erich Hoepner in an order to the Fourth Panzer Group on May 2, 1941, seven weeks before the start of the Russian campaign:

> It is the ancient struggle of the German people ("Germanen") against the Slavs, the defense of European culture against the Russian-Asiatic flood, the repulsion of Jewish Bolshevism. [...] In concept and execution, each fighting engagement must be guided by an iron will to annihilate the enemy totally and without pity.[10]

The commander-in-chief of the Sixth Army, Field Marshal Walter von Reichenau, issued a similar order on October 10, 1941, which was praised by Hitler and distributed throughout the German armed forces:

> RE: Conduct of the troops in the East. In many instances, confusion still prevails regarding the conduct of the troops in their dealing with the Bolshevist system. The primary goal of the campaign against the Jewish-Bolshevist system is the absolute destruction of the means of power and the eradication of Asian influence in the European cultural sphere. As a result, tasks arise for the troops that transcend traditional one-dimensional soldiership.
>
> The soldier in the East is not only a fighter according to the rules of the art of waging war, but also the bearer of the inexorable *völkische* [national] concept and the avenger of all the bestialities that were visited on the Germans and related peoples.... Therefore the soldier must fully understand the necessity for severe but just atonement by the Jewish subhumanity.... This has the further goal of nipping in the bud uprisings to the rear of the Wehrmacht, which, as experience shows, are always instigated by the Jews....

The soldier has two tasks to fulfill, far removed from all political considerations about the future:

1. The utter destruction of Bolshevist heresy, of the Soviet state and its war machine.
2. The merciless extermination of foreign cunning and cruelty, thereby securing the life of the German Wehrmacht in Russia. This is the only way we can live up to our historic task of liberating the German people once and for all from the Asiatic-Jewish peril.[11]

For the conduct of the entire Operation Barabarossa, what are referred to as the "criminal orders" were issued, which governed the behavior of German military personnel vis-à-vis Soviet troops, Communist Party officials, and civilians.[12] These orders were embodied in four specific sets of instructions:

1. Regulations pertaining to the activities of the quick response units (*Einsatzgruppen*) of the SS (*Schutzstaffel*) and SD (*Sicherheitsdienst*) commanded by Reinhard Heydrich (until he died of wounds from an assassination attack on June 6, 1942). These regulations allowed these special units to operate relatively independently as roving murder squads in areas controlled by the German army.
2. The restriction of military jurisdiction (*Die Einschränkung der Kriegsgerichtsbarkeit*), directed that partisans as well as civilians suspected of being collaborators be executed by the army, and severe measures be implemented against civilians in areas of partisan activity where the culprits could not be found.
3. The "Commissar Order," probably the best known of the instructions, stipulated that political commissars in the Soviet armies captured by German troops were to be summarily executed.
4. The "Guidelines for the Conduct of the Troops in Russia," specifically ordered that extreme measures were to be taken against "Bolshevik agitators, guerrillas, saboteurs, and Jews," as well as the total suppression of any active or passive resistance.

Given the guiding principle of Nazi ideology that Russians and other Slavic ethnic groups did not deserve to be treated as ordinary human beings, these "criminal orders" meant that the enemy should be dealt with pitilessly and all segments of the Soviet population—soldiers, civilians, Communist Party officials, and partisans—were subjected to extremely harsh treatment during the German conquest and occupation of the western part of the Soviet Union.

More than half of the estimated 5.7 million soldiers captured by the Germans died in captivity.[13] This high mortality rate arose from an acute lack of food, medical care, and clothing allocated to prisoners of war (POWs), as taking appropriate care of millions of Soviet soldiers in prison camps would have imposed a substantial economic burden on the German economy and diverted supplies from the front-line troops. Moreover, as the winter clothing of the Soviet soldiers was much better than that issued to German troops, the latter stripped the Soviet POWs of their warm clothes and boots, leaving them with little protection against the subzero Russian winter in the outdoor fenced-in compounds that served as prisons. The German Army did not provide any medical care for the prisoners, but allowed Soviet medical personnel to use whatever equipment and medicine they had to treat their POWs. Not surprisingly, thousands died of epidemics that raged in the prison camps.

The inhumane treatment of POWs was so severe that it posed a problem for the German Army because once Soviet troops became aware of the dire fate that would confront them if captured, they put up much stiffer resistance in battle. A specific order that was given in a German army division reflected an awareness of this problem: "[The troops] must understand what the ultimate result of the maltreatment or the shooting of POWs after they have given themselves up in battle would be…a stiffening of the enemy's resistance, because every Red Army soldier fears German captivity."[14]

Not all German soldiers engaged in brutal acts against POWs, but the often indiscriminate shooting of captured Soviet troops by German soldiers raised concerns on the part of their officers that this could lead to a breakdown of discipline. At the same time, official German army policy encouraged such behavior. For example, on September 13, 1941, the German Army High Command (OKH or *Oberkommando des Heeres*) in charge of the

Eastern Front ordered that Soviet troops who had fallen behind the German lines and then re-organized into fighting units should be regarded as partisans and shot on the spot. But when it was decided that Soviet POWs could play a useful economic role in the German war effort, attempts were made to stop the indiscriminate shooting of prisoners and to improve the conditions in POW camps so that prisoners could not only provide services to the German troops at the front, such as building roads, collecting war booty, and burying corpses, but also work in factories and farms in Germany. Yet only a small proportion of POWs could provide useful labor in Germany. Johannes Gutschmidt, a commander of a POW camp near Smolensk, wrote in his diary in early March 1942:

> Now all the POWs capable of work are to be sent to Germany to free up armaments workers there for the front. Of the millions of prisoners only a few thousands are capable of working. So unbelievably many have starved to death, many are ill with typhus and the rest are so weak and pitiful that they can't work in this state. The German administration failed to provide them with enough provisions....[15]

While there was some protection of POWs from summary execution, this was not the case with partisans and with civilians if they were suspected of engaging in partisan activity or harboring and supporting guerrillas. The orders were clear that such individuals were to be immediately shot or hanged. The same treatment applied to civilians suspected of being Communist Party officials or Jews. For example, the archives of the German 12th Infantry Division reported that on January 30, 1942, "[when] a few of its sledges had driven on mines in the vicinity of the village of Nov. Ladomiry, the whole male population of the village was shot and the houses burned down as a 'collective measure.'"[16] The same archives reported, on July 4, 1941, "the execution of ten civilians in the village of Dukszty, accused of membership of the communist party or youth organization and of belonging to the Jewish race."[17] The archives of the 16th Army noted that between November 29 and December 5, 1941, "[their units] had killed 77 'partisans' in the combat zone and a further 265 in the rear."[18] In addition to what had become routine actions taken against actual or suspected partisans, large-scale operations were undertaken in partisan areas in an attempt to suppress guerrilla activity. For example, between November 19 and December 5, 1941, "units of the II Corps operating in the area of Polisto Lake killed 250 'partisans,' destroyed fifteen 'camps' and burned down sixteen villages, taking away cattle and horses and destroying food supplies."[19]

Soviet civilians were also slaughtered in wholesale fashion. For example, in the village of Polykowitschi some six kilometers from the city of Mogilew in eastern Belorussia, around ten thousand men, women, and children were executed between the end of 1941 and the fall of 1943, some by shooting and others by gassing in trucks.[20] The dead were buried in mass graves and an attempt was made to hide the atrocity by planting grain on top of the graves. After the war the graves were discovered and an investigative commission ordered that the bodies be exhumed. The harshness of the German occupation in the Soviet Union manifested itself in the smallest details. In the Ukraine, the commander of the occupation authority in Kiev promulgated an order on October 22, 1941, which stipulated the penalty for the possession of pigeons: "All pigeons in the area of the city of Kiev are to be gotten rid of immediately. Whoever is found still in possession of pigeons after October 26 will be shot on account of sabotage."[21]

The barbaric way in which Soviet civilians were put to death at times took its toll on those responsible for these atrocities. A young army officer who had recently arrived on the Eastern Front had:

> received an order to shoot three hundred and fifty civilians, allegedly partisans but including women and children, who had been herded together in a big barn. He hesitated at first, but then was warned that the penalty for disobedience is death. He begged for ten minutes' time to think it over, and finally carried out the order with machine-gun fire. He was so shaken by this episode that [after being wounded] he was determined never to go back to the [Eastern] front.[22]

The savage suppression of actual or suspected partisan activity in Operation Barbarossa proved to be counterproductive because it encouraged civilians to participate in the guerrilla war against the German Army. This in turn heightened the ferocity of German reprisals against civilians. The commander of the Army Group North, Field Marshal Ritter von Leeb, therefore issued the following order on January 31, 1942:

> The recent revival of partisan activities in the rear area...together with the battles at the front, demand that action be taken...with the greatest ruthlessness. Partisans are to be destroyed wherever they appear, as are their hiding places [i.e., their villages] if not needed by our troops for accommodation.[23]

The barbarous treatment of the Soviet people also included the German Army "living off the land" when it retreated from the Soviet Union. Due to the great difficulties the Gemans encountered in supplying their troops with adequate food at such a vast distance from the Reich, explicit orders were issued to exploit all available resources in the conquered territory. Army units therefore requisitioned from Soviet peasants huge quantities of food, such as potatoes, butter, eggs, and milk, as well as other supplies, including cattle, horses, pigs, calves, sheep, oats, and hay. This rapaciousness led not only to widespread starvation of the local peasants, but also to the reduction of future food supplies as the fields were not tilled and new crops were not planted.

In addition to requisitioning food and other supplies in the occupied territories, the Germans also exploited the human resources. They conscripted large numbers of civilians to work near the front lines building fortifications, digging trenches, constructing roads, burying the dead, and performing chores for the soldiers in their camps. As the majority of able-bodied German males were in the armed forces rather than engaged in civilian or armaments production, millions of Soviet citizens were also sent to Germany to work in the factories, farms, and mines to support the German war effort.

Finally, in its long retreat from the Soviet Union in 1943–1944, the German Army pursued a "scorched earth" policy aimed at depriving the Soviet forces of any assets—food, livestock, machinery, houses, and able-bodied inhabitants—in the territories that had been held by the Germans. As they were pushed inexorably westward by the advancing Red Army, German soldiers took prisoner men between the ages of fifteen and fifty-five and sometimes women as well; at other times they allowed women and children to go free and sent them east toward the advancing Soviet forces. Food supplies and livestock that could not be used by the troops or sent to the rear were destroyed; houses, other buildings, and machinery were burned, and wells poisoned. As a result of this scorched earth policy, vast stretches of the Soviet Union were left completely desolated.

The explicitly brutal policy pursued by the Germans in their campaign of annihilation in Poland and the Soviet Union inevitably sowed the seeds for revenge, with dire consequences for the East Prussians when the tables were turned. Enraged by the murder of their family members, friends, and countrymen, as well as by the wholesale destruction of what little property they had, and incited by a Soviet campaign of hatred against Germans, Red Army troops wreaked vengeance on the first German civilians they encountered in East Prussia in late 1944 and early 1945.

B. An Island of Comparative Calm before the Storm

While battles were raging on the Eastern Front, East Prussia remained relatively untouched by the war until the intense bombing of Königsberg in August 1944, and Soviet troops entered the easternmost part of the province later that year. Until then, the region was largely spared the destruction and death that had been visited upon the cities of Germany by frequent and massive American and British air raids. Of course, the war's activities and its effects made themselves felt. Shortages of food and heating coal were particularly pronounced in the cities. Most men between the ages of eighteen and forty-five had been drafted into military service, and their wives and other relatives personally experienced the direct consequences of the war when they were notified of the deaths of their husbands or other family members. As East Prussia was dotted with military training facilities and hospitals, members of the armed forces were not only constant reminders of the war being waged elsewhere, but also sometimes generated friction with the local residents when they purchased large quantities of scarce food to send to their families. Moreover, those with relatives in the western parts of Germany were kept apprised of the widespread destruction and death there due to air raids. During the course of the war, East Prussians also were ordered to provide accommodation in their houses and apartments as more and more bombed-out civilians in the West, principally from Berlin and Hamburg, were evacuated to the relative peace and safety of this far-eastern German province. Not surprisingly, relations were at times strained between the hosts and their wartime "guests."

Marianne Peyinghaus, in her book *Quiet Years in Gertlauken: Memories of East Prussia,* provides a particularly poignant description of the contrast between the calm and quiet of East Prussia and the rest of Germany during most of World War II.[24] She describes her experiences in East Prussia from the time she arrived in the fall of 1941 until January 1945, when she narrowly escaped from the invading Red Army. At age twenty, following her training to be a teacher, she was sent for her first assignment to a school located in the small village of Gertlauken, about halfway between Königsberg and Tilsit. Marianne was from Cologne and she noted the stark contrast between the sophistication of one of the biggest cities in Germany and the rural agricultural community of Gertlauken, where the main economic activities were farming and forestry. She was young, innocent, and open-minded, and any prejudices she may have had against her new home soon disappeared. The letters she wrote to her parents and brother in Cologne nearly every week provide a fresh, vivid, and sympathetic portrait of her fellow villagers, her school and pupils, and the rituals of village life. They also depict how she soon became an integral part of the village community that she loved and cherished the rest of her life.

An ever-present theme in her letters home is the contrast between her bucolic existence in Gertlauken and the terror of the incessant Allied bombings visited upon Cologne and other German cities she heard of from her parents, who described the destruction of neighborhoods familiar to her and the deaths of friends and acquaintances. She naturally became extremely concerned about the survival of her parents and other close relatives. Her sensitivity to the contrast between Gertlauken and Cologne was heightened by her appreciation of the natural beauty of East Prussia. She made many trips to the Courland Spit (*Kurische Nehrung*), a long, narrow, sandy strip of land that runs nearly sixty miles (one hundred kilometers) from Memel (Klaipeda) in the northeast to Cranz (Zelenogradsk) in the southwest and that separates the fresh water lagoon (*Kurisches Haff*) from the Baltic Sea. It is so narrow one can easily walk from the lagoon on one side to the sea on the other in twenty to thirty minutes. Like many others, Marianne was taken by the strong colors and dramatic vistas seen from the spit. In a letter of May 7, 1942, she wrote:

> and so for the first time I saw the sea, endless water that collides with the sky. I was overwhelmed, could hardly bear to leave. I like this land, I like the people, they are so friendly. [...] Life here appears to be so calm, as if we are living in a time of utter peace, that your reports come from out of a different, terrible world.[25]

In a letter sent a little over a week later she wrote in the same vein:

> My dear parents, it was a beautiful, infinitely peaceful day that one could forget the whole horrible war and all its miseries. That such opposites can exist in the same country, at the same time.[26]

In early June 1942, Marianne received two letters from her parents and broke out in tears while reading about more bombings, terrible fires, and the devastation in Cologne. She was particularly distraught to learn that her favorite church, in which she had been confirmed, had been destroyed in the most recent air raids. Overcome by the striking contrast between her idyllic surroundings and the suffering and danger endured by her parents, she described her feelings:

> I always have a bad feeling when I think of what danger you are in and what security I have here. I spend incredibly peaceful, quiet

days in Gertlauken. I am embarrassed to tell you how well I spent last Sunday. On Saturday Paula came to visit and on Sunday we got up at 5:00 a.m. and biked to Labiau. There we took a steamer across the Haff, past Rossitten and Pillkoppen, to Nidden, an extremely picturesque village, a favorite place of artists....Finally, we climbed the high dunes and had a grand view over the quiet blue Haff and the wide green Baltic. To run down the dunes with huge steps and sink deep into the sand is a wonderful pleasure.[27]

Marianne Peyinghaus regularly visited Königsberg, which was easily reached by train. As a young woman from the big city she was naturally attracted to the cultural, historical, and entertainment offerings of East Prussia's capital and she enjoyed going to the movies and visiting the cafes and restaurants, such as the Alhambra Café, Café Bauer, Café Gehlhaar, and the Berliner Hof where—much to the chagrin of her father—at the crowded tables she invariably met soldiers on leave before they returned to the front. The Parade Place (*Paradeplatz*) made an unforgettable impression on her. In earlier times, on the birthday of the Kaiser, the seven regiments of Königsberg would march there in formation before it became the center of the city. On one side of the Parade Place was the imposing façade of the Albertina University and on the other side was one the largest bookstores in Europe, Gräfe und Unzer, where she spent many hours exploring the vast collection this emporium had to offer.[28] She visited the massive Königsberg Cathedral on an island in the Pregel River and was impressed by the statues of Duke Albrecht I and his two wives, as well as the nearby monument marking the grave of Immanuel Kant, the most renowned philosopher and professor at the Albertina in the eighteenth century.

One of the historical sights she liked most of all was the Königsberg Castle (see Illustration 2. Königsberg Castle around 1900). In front of the castle were some of the city's imposing monuments, including statues of Bismarck and Kaiser Wilhelm I. Inside, she viewed with awe the famous Amber Room (*Bernsteinzimmer*).[29] The castle's cellar had been transformed into the *Blutgericht*, a well-known restaurant and wine cellar, and she tasted its many offerings. In September 1943, she took her seven oldest pupils on an excursion to Königsberg, where they spent half the morning touring the castle. In the Coronation Hall, they were all ears when the tour guide explained how Frederick, the first Prussian king, placed the crown on his head with his own hands, and then crowned his wife, Sophie Charlotte. Following these history lessons she took her pupils to the nearby Castle Pond (*Schloßteich*), where they rented and had fun rowing one of the flat-bottomed skiffs.

In her explorations of the region around Königsberg, Marianne Peyinghaus visited the small port of Pillau located at the opening of the Frische Nehrung. A canal dredged in the Frisches Haff allowed ships to steam between Pillau and Königsberg to load and unload cargo. Pillau was a major German naval base crowded with military personnel, and in the harbor were the steamships *Robert Ley* and the *Pretoria,* which would play a vital role in the evacuation of refugees and soldiers seeking escape from the advancing Soviet Army in the winter and spring of 1945.

Over time, the far-off war intruded ever more into Marianne's peaceful existence in East Prussia. In a letter to her parents in April 1943, she told them about a radio report she had just heard about developments on the Eastern Front:

> I lead such a good life here that it almost bothers my conscience. I am now listening to the radio report from the German military forces [Wehrmacht]. How technically cold and militarily concise it sounds: "The expected counterattack of the Soviet armies on the Kuban bridgehead [on the Taman Peninsula in the Black Sea] began yesterday. The battles are continuing...." And how much distress and death and misery and hardness and courage is hidden behind that, one cannot express in words.[30]

Toward the end of 1943 and the first part of 1944, more families were evacuated from Hamburg and Berlin, some of whom were assigned to houses in Gertlauken. In February 1944, Marianne reported that she had forty to fifty pupils who had been evacuated from areas in the western part of

Germany threatened with bombing, and in June children were also sent from Königsberg to the relative safety of Gertlauken. By July, the Eastern Front had moved so close to East Prussia that in Gertlauken on a quiet night she could hear the distant muffled sound of the heavy artillery. On July 17, 1944, a general prohibition of travel by civilians went into effect and made it impossible for her to visit her parents in Cologne. With Gertlauken now threatened by advancing Soviet forces, she wrote to her parents that the women and children who had been evacuated from Berlin and Hamburg were being moved back to the West, to the provinces of Thuringia and the Sudetenland.[31] By one estimate, some fifty-five thousand *Luftkriegsevakuierte* (those evacuated on account of air raids) from Berlin were sent back to the capital.[32] Some East Prussian women and children were also evacuated to the West at this time. In late July, 1944, Marianne reported observing Russian planes attacking Tilsit and Insterburg on the eastern edge of East Prussia, as well as hearing anti-aircraft fire defending these towns.

Marianne's glowing account of her stay in East Prussia is in no small part due to the fact that she spent most of her time in a small, isolated village that was largely self-sufficient. She never complained about the lack of heat or food; on the contrary, she described how well she was treated by her hosts and was often astonished at the abundance of food which the farmers' wives set out at mealtimes and on special occasions, such as birthdays, when the tables were loaded with a wide assortment of cakes, despite the supposed austerity of wartime. As an outsider, she might not have been fully cognizant of—or chose not to report—the stresses and strains experienced by the East Prussian population in the urban areas while the war raged on the Eastern and Western fronts.

The challenges of daily life faced by the East Prussians were described in considerable detail in bimonthly reports from President Max Dräger and Chief Prosecutor Fritz Szelinski at the Provincial Court of Appeals in Königsberg to the Ministry of Justice in Berlin.[33] These secret reports were initiated by the minister of justice in Berlin who wished to have his own source of information, independent of the security services of Himmler and the NSDAP (the Nazi Party), on the mood of the population and key developments in the judicial districts throughout Germany. The fifty-two reports stored in the Central German Archives (*Bundesarchiv*) cover the period from January 5, 1940, to January 18, 1945.[34]

These judicial reports reveal that for many East Prussians, especially for those in urban areas, the war increasingly impinged on their daily lives. Shortages of heating coal and food were common and sometimes very acute. The winter of 1939–40 was especially long and cold, and in some areas in the province schools and theaters as well as certain offices of the courts had to shut down. Some homes were completely without heat and it was so cold that the hands of children froze while they slept.[35] According to these reports, the situation became so severe that the population became embittered, and it was especially upsetting to people experiencing frigid temperatures in their homes when it became known that some parts of the province were well supplied with coal. The shortage of heating coal in the winter of 1940–41 was again severe and in parts of East Prussia retail stores were forced to close and cases of children with frostbite were reported.

Insufficient food supplies were a constant problem in urban areas. Food rations were cut in early April 1942, when for the first time since 1939 the amounts of meat and fat allotted to families were substantially reduced (by twenty-five percent), raising concerns about the nutrition of young children. Many residents complained about insufficient supplies of vegetables and that housewives had to stand for hours in long lines in front of shops to try to buy the meager stocks available. The lack of fresh vegetables caused outbreaks of boils and an increased incidence of gum disease. The scarcity of tobacco products and alcoholic beverages also led to long lines in front of stores selling whatever was available.

Given the widespread shortages of just about everything, people with access to goods took advantage of their privileged position and a flourishing black market developed. These activities were illegal under the laws governing the war economy (*Kriegswirtschaftsgesetze*) and were often mentioned in the reports of the judicial authorities. For example, in retail stores the availability of non-food products, such as clothing and furniture, declined significantly because storeowners withheld these items in order to either barter them for food for themselves or to sell them to their steady customers. Withholding of goods from the general populace also occurred at the wholesale level and the apprehended culprits received stiff prison sentences or fines. The scarcity of meat for sale in stores reflected widespread illegal slaughtering of animals (*Schwarzschlachtungen*). This illegal slaughtering was heavily penalized; prison sentences depended on the size of the animal slaughtered and whether the meat was used for family consumption or sold on the black market. In fact, a number of Polish farmers in eastern East Prussia received the death penalty for this crime. The judicial reports noted that the severe penalties imposed on Germans who broke these laws were not always well received by the population, and military officers and enlisted men complained that such stiff penalties were not good for morale.

Food in Lithuania was relatively abundant, but a major problem developed when military personnel smuggled this food into East Prussia on a massive scale. The judicial authorities permitted soldiers to bring in small amounts of food for their families but took exception to the military using their vehicles to import truckloads of goods with the intention of selling them at high prices on the black market. One case was cited in which a doctor on a hospital ship in Tilsit called the main customs office because he was outraged at the extent to which the crew was engaged in smuggling. By the time the customs authorities boarded the ship, they found only several hundred eggs, as the other contraband goods had already been removed. Because neither the customs authority nor the police had legal authority over the military, they decided to give the eggs to the army because the hospital ship was already fully supplied with eggs.[36]

The huge number of military personnel stationed in East Prussia had other economic consequences for the province. While food supplies were tight, they were nonetheless in greater abundance than in other parts of Germany; as a result, soldiers purchased goods in considerable quantities and shipped them back home. The local population was particularly annoyed with the proclivity of the troops stationed in East Prussia to buy up poultry for home consumption in the Reich, especially geese, which were purchased in large quantities and at almost any price. Even Marianne Peyinghaus mailed a goose to her parents in Cologne. (In Germany, it is a tradition in many families to serve roast goose on Christmas.) As the large purchases by military personnel contributed to the high food prices paid by the East Prussians, complaints arose that these high prices constituted an implicit form of taxation supporting the war effort.

With most husbands and young men away at the front, many women in East Prussia had considerable contact with both POWs, largely from France and Poland, and civilian workers imported from the conquered countries in the east who worked in cities and on farms. In most cases these "forced guest workers" had friendly relations with their hosts and in some cases they were considered part of the family.[37] There were even reports of Polish workers and prisoners of war having drinks with the locals.[38] However, such fraternization was not considered desirable by the authorities and could be punished.

More serious, and receiving much greater coverage in the judicial reports, were sexual relations between German women and foreign civilian workers and POWs. The judicial reports attributed this behavior to the declining morality of women who lacked normal peacetime constraints and who did not have to work because they received subsidies from the government while their husbands were away at the front. The reports also mentioned that these women neglected their children and that they had nothing better to do than to go to the hairdresser, enjoy themselves, and associate with foreign men. The laziness of some East Prussian women was noticed by a hard-working farmer in Passenheim (now Pasym in Poland, southeast of Allenstein, now Olsztyn) who wrote in his memoir:

> We were most irritated by the old resident families whose men were in the war or killed in action. These women and their adolescent children wouldn't lift one dammed finger, and so they often made our blood boil. The state threw so much support money at the women that they could live off it—and royally. Why, then, should they do more than what absolutely had to be done, such as the most necessary house cleaning? We watched as these previously hard-working and simple-living women, fortified by the help of the *L. Schein* [a food-stamp-like subsidy given to people during

the war]…were suddenly seen out buying themselves new clothes
and bicycles. And soon they could only be found on their way to
the hairdresser or the movie theater.[39]

The promiscuous behavior on the part of some East Prussian women was
cited as causing an increase in the number of divorces and a rise in out-of-
wedlock births. Intimate contact between Aryans and non-Aryans was strictly
illegal and both parties were subject to penalties. For the women, this often
entailed having their hair cut off and being paraded through the streets, and
some were given prison sentences. For the imported workers and POWs
found guilty of sexual relations with German women, the penalty was severe:
a public hanging.

The number of death penalties imposed by the courts in East Prussia for
sexual contact with foreigners and other offenses rose considerably as the
war continued. In the first half of June 1942, the State Court in Königsberg
reached 635 verdicts, of which fifty-six resulted in death sentences. In the
State Court in Zichenau (a Polish area incorporated into East Prussia for
the duration of the war), 309 verdicts were handed down, of which seventy-
two were death sentences.[40] The death penalty was imposed much more frequently in the Polish area (twenty-three percent) than in Königsberg (nine
percent) because of the ever-increasing resistance of the local Polish population. The Nazi authorities tried to suppress any resistance with harsh penalties, typically public hangings, with the local population assembled to witness
the executions in an attempt to deter further resistance activity. However, in
the judicial report of March 30, 1943, the author asked whether such public
hangings did not, in fact, make martyrs of the executed and generate solidar-
ity among the Poles. He noted that one of the condemned shouted "Long
live eternal Poland" and was enthusiastically echoed by the Polish witnesses.[41]

Of course, much harsher penalties were meted out to Jews for far lesser
crimes. For example, in the Mielau (formerly Mlawa) ghetto in the Polish area
incorporated into East Prussia, police discovered large quantities of fresh pike
and tench. As such fish were not among the rations supplied to the ghetto,
the police summarily hanged ten Jews for what was deemed illegal activity.

The roughly five thousand inhabitants of Mielau were forced to witness these executions and started to riot, whereupon the police shot twenty-seven dead; fifty more Jews were shot in the days following.[42] A similarly severe penalty was meted out in Allenstein (Olsztyn), where a Jewish textile mill owner by the name of Max Hirschfeld was convicted in April 1942 of the "economic crime" (*Wirtschaftsverbrechen*) of bartering a sewing machine for a goose. He was executed in March 1943 in Königsberg.[43]

Severe penalties were also handed down for Germans convicted of what during wartime were considered serious crimes. As already noted, this was the case for those found guilty of illegally slaughtering animals. In another example, in the district of Lyck (Elk) a special court condemned to death two nurses in a home for crippled children for sending their relatives the food ration cards intended for the children.[44] The judicial reports also noted that the German population did not always view sympathetically the heavy judgments of the special courts:

> There are many reasonably thinking members of society from all walks of life, including the armed forces, who do not understand the length of certain sentences against Germans reached by the special courts. Severe sentences for the illegal slaughter of animals, for example, may be necessary in the interests of the food production economy. On the other hand, these sentences do not support the morale of troops at the front if the convicted are relatives of soldiers. At the front such sentences are noted with bitterness and are not understood…. In any case it must not be overlooked that civilians criticize the severe penalties just as sharply. For the mood of the people in general is very nervous and tense, and accordingly, they express themselves with much greater candor than was the case heretofore.[45]

Freedom of speech was, of course, not allowed under the Nazi dictatorship and much was kept hidden from the public. Even President Dräger of the Provincial Court of Appeals was not always kept informed about certain activities undertaken by the Nazi regime that were considered too sensitive and likely to arouse the opposition of the population. For example, on January 4, 1941, he reported that inmates of the insane asylums in East Prussia had been transported in the previous year to other parts of Germany, and when inquiries were made to a lower court by the inmates' guardians regarding their new whereabouts, they did not receive any information. However, on a strictly confidential basis, an official in the office of Gauleiter (provincial Nazi Party leader) Erich Koch informed the court in Königsberg that the location of those under guardianship was unknown at that time. Further inquiries proved fruitless. In a later report on March 5, 1941, President Dräger noted that there had been no clarification of this matter and that the Chancery Courts (*Vormundschaftsgerichte*) under his jurisdiction were having great difficulties with the guardians and relatives because the judicial authorities could not provide a satisfactory response to their petitions for information about the fate of their charges. He reported that he had been in contact with Gauleiter Koch, who told him he was attempting to find out from the authorities in Berlin how the question should be answered.

President Dräger was finally informed of the fate of the inmates at a secret conference in Berlin at the Ministry of Justice on April 23–24, 1941.[46] At that meeting he learned that, in accordance with the directives of the euthanasia program, in May and June 1940, 1,558 mentally and physically handicapped inmates in institutions in the East Prussian towns of Allenburg (Druzhba), Carlshof (Karolewo), Kortau, and Tapiau (Gvardeysk) were transported to Soldau (Dzialdowo), a town in Polish territory southwest of East Prussia.[47] There a former army barracks had been turned into a concentration camp where Jews, members of the Polish intelligentsia, and the handicapped were executed. Between May 21 and June 8, 1941, the mentally and physically handicapped from East Prussia were packed forty at a time into a truck and during a three-hour journey were gassed to death. The truck then returned empty to the camp to pick up another load of victims. Their execution assignment completed, the special unit (*Sonderkommando Lange*), composed of security police (*Sicherheitspolizei*) and members of the security service (*Sicherheitsdienst*), celebrated in the camp dining room with a farewell dinner during which they received an amber box with a dedication from Gauleiter Koch. Members of the unit were given some time off, which they spent on vacation in German-occupied Holland. This special unit had been promised ten Reichsmarks by the head of the SS in Königsberg to cover the transport and other costs involved for each "evacuated" East Prussian asylum inmate. It appears that after considerable negotiations, this "fee" was in fact paid.[48]

Either Marianne Peyinghaus was unaware of most of the developments described in the judicial reports, or in her letters to her parents she chose not to describe fully what she experienced in East Prussia. However, she mentioned one aspect of what was happening there during the war that also appears in the reports, namely, tension between the evacuees and their hosts. In a letter sent in late September 1944, she reported that when they first arrived, the women who had been evacuated from Königsberg complained vehemently about the primitive conditions in Gertlauken, but later when they were evacuated with their children to Saxony, they were not happy having to leave behind the good food and quiet they had become accustomed to. These complaints were mild compared to those of the Berlin evacuees, who made themselves much disliked by the locals when they arrived by demanding better accommodations and food, complaining about the absence of theaters and movie houses, and purchasing large amounts of what limited commodities were available in the shops to send back home. Some Berliners were so put off by what they regarded as primitive conditions in East Prussia that they forthwith returned home. As time wore on, however, relations between the locals and the evacuees became less strained, perhaps because they discovered the generous East Prussian hospitality that Marianne Peyinghaus had also experienced and wrote about.

———

On only one occasion during her stay in East Prussia did Marianne remark on the situation of Jews in the province. In July 1942, she and two other young teachers from Labiau joined a group of over two hundred BDM girls (*Bund Deutscher Mädel*—a state-organized women's youth group) to help with the harvest in southeastern East Prussia.[49] On the way, they stopped to visit Tannenberg and she reported that the towers and the honor guard at the memorial made a powerful impression on her. They then traveled via Zichenau to Nasielsk, which had been Polish but in 1939 was incorporated into Germany. She described Nasielsk as a dirty, run-down town with small, decrepit houses. She also noticed a magnificent building, which she identified as a synagogue, and she remarked that of the town's seven thousand inhabitants, four or five thousand were said to have been Jews. Their group went on to Joniec, where they helped bring in the harvest. From Joniec she accompanied one of the group leaders to the nearby county seat of Plöhnen (Plonsk) to pick up a skirt at a tailor's shop in the town, and as it was not yet ready, they took a walk through the town, which she described as follows:

> Imagine you are walking through streets where all the windows and doors have been nailed shut with thick boards from the outside, and yet inside there is a never-ending sound of murmurings and movement. Then between the houses there is a long wooden fence, which does not quite touch the earth, and below it one sees feet, countless feet, some bare, others in slippers, in sandals, and in shoes. The babble of voices gets louder, it smells of many people, and if you stand on tippy-toe and look over the fence, you see bald heads. Then you suddenly realize that this is a ghetto and the packed-together people are Jews. We then very quickly returned to our tailor and he told us that he, too, is Jewish and is allowed to leave the ghetto during the day to work. He was in the midst of ironing a pair of pants with great dexterity.... We praised him and he smiled at us sadly. I was very glad when Plöhnen was finally behind me.[50]

Marianne Peyinghaus's sole reported brief encounter with Jews in East Prussia demonstrates that she knew about Jewish ghettos, but she did not reveal if she knew why they were incarcerated, although her short interaction with the tailor seems to show that she was aware of something unpleasant.[51]

———

The fate of the remaining Jewish population in Königsberg has been conveyed in gripping terms by one of the few survivors, Michael Wieck.[52] While his mother was Jewish, he survived in Nazi Germany largely because his father was Christian and therefore Michael was of mixed race (*Mischling*). However, because he and his older sister Miriam were raised as Jews, they were designated by the Nazi regime as "certified or deemed Jews," which meant as of September 1941, they had to wear the yellow Star of David. They were subject to increasingly oppressive laws that deprived them of all rights and made them outcasts.[53] While not as "privileged" as children born of mixed marriages who had been raised as Christians, the fact that Wieck's father was Christian conferred some protection on Wieck, his sister, and their mother. Nonetheless, they lived in constant dread that they would be forced to leave Königsberg by train to what they feared would be certain death. Victor Klemperer, the author of two volumes of memoirs, also survived the Nazi regime because his wife was Christian.[54]

Wieck described in vivid detail Kristallnacht, the night of broken glass on November 9–10, 1938, when throughout Germany members of the SS and the SA ransacked and burned synagogues and Jewish businesses. In Königsberg, well-organized SS units used a previously prepared list of Jewish stores to go from one to the next, breaking the storefront windows, plundering the goods inside, and destroying the interiors.[55] The synagogue that housed Wieck's school was set on fire and destroyed, the Torah scrolls were ripped apart and thrown into the street, and the cantor and assistant cantor were badly beaten. Wieck was stunned when his parents told him about this desecration and wanted desperately to contact his schoolmates, but his parents forced him to stay in the apartment because he could be killed if caught on the streets that night. As soon as he was allowed to leave, he went immediately to the synagogue and found its burnt-out hulk. This was the first time Wieck had seen a destroyed building and in his memoirs he reflected that this was exactly what Königsberg looked like a few years later when the war came home to the capital of East Prussia.

Wieck also recounted the many restrictions and indignities Jews were subject to as outcasts. Two examples are cited here:

> Food rations for Jews were continually being cut and, as an extra restriction, the ration cards were also stamped with a "J." We could buy food only in special shops at given times. We were not allowed to take part in air raid drills. A curfew prohibited Jews from being on the street after eight o'clock in the evening. At fourteen, all Jews were drafted to work, mostly in dangerous jobs, such as chemical factories, mines, or collecting garbage. My mother was already working ten hours a day in the chemical factory of Gamm & Son.[56]

> Another time...I was going to work as usual when a civilian came up to me. Bellowing as if giving an order, he demanded that I, a "Jewish pig," should have the decency to walk in the street and not use the sidewalk that was there for "decent" citizens. I had to walk in the gutter of the street along with the horse carts, automobiles, and bicyclists until I was out of sight of this gentleman. Refusal to do so—especially if this was someone who held a high office—meant resistance to the authority of the state and could have led immediately to deportation.[57]

Particularly poignant is Wieck's description of the assembly of Jews and their departure on the first train out of Königsberg, which he later learned took them east to their deaths.[58] Hundreds of people (but not the Wiecks) had received orders to gather on June 24, 1942, at the designated assembly point in the old riding school. They had been told to bring only thirty kilograms of baggage, but naturally took much more, and many had to stop to rest before proceeding with their heavy luggage. "Their faces were expressionless, tense, resigned. They looked like prey, creatures without hope." Among them were his German teacher Rosa Wolff, whom he greatly admired; Ruth Marwilski and her family; and many classmates and friends. All morning people arrived at the assembly point and he entered the open door of the riding school to say goodbye and perform small favors for those departing. He knew that his favorite Aunt Fanny, who had taken care of him when he was a child, had received the order to join the transport, but he had lost sight of her in the large hall. Suddenly the order was given to march to the North Train Station (*Nord Bahnhof*) to board the transport. Wieck found himself near his German teacher and as he wanted to stay with those leaving as long as possible, he immediately picked up some of her luggage. Soon after the column—surrounded by armed guards—had departed the riding stable, Wieck came upon Aunt Fanny sitting on a street curb, utterly exhausted, her eyes imploring him for help. Loaded down with his favorite teacher's luggage, he did not know what to do. He hesitated, but was carried along with the moving column of people. Quickly turning around, he saw his beloved Aunt Fanny for the last time looking at him with reproachful eyes. This traumatic parting was a deep wound which would stay with him forever.

Once the column reached the heavily guarded train station, his teacher had become very concerned that he might be forced to board the train and ordered him to leave the station immediately. The guards naturally assumed he was among those ordered to take the transport and would not allow him to leave. He was almost resigned to having to join the group when another guard gave him a sign to leave at once, so he ran as fast he could and was soon out of danger. This was one of many narrow escapes by which Michael Wieck survived not only Nazi Germany but also the Soviet occupation of Königsberg that followed the defeat of Germany.

In his memoirs Wieck wrote that the destination of that train transporting hundreds of Jews to the east never became known. Recent research, however, has revealed that its final destination was Minsk in Belorussia.[59] This particular train, which has been identified as "Da 40," departed at 10:34 p.m. the night of Wednesday, June 24, 1942, with 465 Jews from Königsberg seated in passenger cars. The first stop was at 1:49 a.m. on June 25 in Korschen (Korsze), where two or three passenger cars coming from Allenstein (Olsztyn) were attached to it, with an estimated eighty to one hundred Jews from southwestern East Prussia, including the son and daughter-in-law of Dr. Heinrich Wolffheim, the head of the Jewish community in Allenstein.[60] The train then traveled to Bialystok via Prostken (Prostki) and arrived at 4:30 the afternoon of June 25 in Wolkowysk (then Poland, formerly Belorussia, now Belarus), where the passenger cars were emptied and everyone loaded into twenty-six freight cars. Sometime in the morning of Friday, June 26, train "Da 40" arrived at the freight depot in Minsk with 770 Jews, according to documents revealed in the 1962 trial at the State Court in Koblenz, Germany, of one Georg Heuser, then active in the security police in Minsk. It thus appears that between Königsberg and Minsk, "Da 40" had picked up an additional two hundred Jews. With the exception of sixty-five to seventy relatively healthy Jews selected for forced labor, all on the train were loaded into trucks and driven to recently excavated pits (*Gruben*) near the village of Maly Trostinez, a few miles southeast of Minsk, where they were shot by members of an SS unit. This is corroborated by an "activity report" written by an SS officer on August 3, 1942:

> The work of the remaining men here in Minsk remains as before, pretty much the same. The transports with the Jews arrived regularly in Minsk and were taken care of [sic] by us. So we were busy already on June 18 and 19, 1942, with the digging of pits in the area of the housing development. On June 26 the train with Jews from the Reich arrived as expected.[61]

And so it was outside of Minsk that Wieck's Aunt Fanny, his teacher Rosa Wolff, his friend Ruth Marwilski, fellow students and friends, as well as hundreds of others from Königsberg exhaled their last breath as a result of the murderous policy of Nazi Germany to exterminate the Jews. They and nearly all of the Jewish residents of Königsberg did not live to see the firestorm that engulfed their city a little over two years later, when the war came home to East Prussia in earnest.[62]

C. The War Comes Home: The Bombing of Königsberg in August 1944

Until August 1944, the air raids over Königsberg had not been particularly destructive. At the beginning of the war in 1939, nine-year-old Wolfgang

Degner, who was living in the Juditten suburb, remembers waiting for an attack to come in the mild summer night of September 1–2. He was in bed when the bombers from Poland arrived around 5:00 that morning and recalls being frightened by the detonations of the bombs that fell on the city. Several houses were destroyed, including one in the Hufen district, where the mother of his sister's friend was killed. The friend was taken in by the Wagner family until her father could find a place where the survivors could live.[63]

The next raid took place a day after the start of Operation Barbarossa when, in the early morning of June 23, 1941, Russian planes dropped bombs mainly on residential areas in the city and most of the damage was inflicted near the zoo. The Russians caught the city almost completely by surprise by flying in from the Baltic at a high altitude; the air-raid alarm sounded just before the bombs hit; sixteen people were killed. The air raid the following night did little damage as most of the bombs fell where there were no buildings. The final attack came in the evening hours of June 24, when the same area was bombed and caused three casualties. In the following three years Soviet aircraft carried out a number of nighttime bombing raids on Königsberg (November 13, 1941, August 30, 1942, and April 13, 1943), but while there were some casualties and property damage, the city remained largely unscathed.[64] By contrast, a large Soviet air raid on Tilsit in mid-April 1943 caused considerable casualties and damage: 104 killed, 113 houses completely destroyed and 158 heavily damaged, and over forty-six hundred inhabitants made homeless. In a letter to her parents on April 16, 1943, Marianne Peyinghaus described hearing waves of Russian bombers, which she thought were on their way to Königsberg, and then hearing anti-aircraft guns firing at the planes.

The British air raids on Königsberg at the end of August 1944 were on such a massive scale that they destroyed the center of the city and caused thousands of casualties. Brief official British accounts of the two separate raids read as follows:

August 26–27 (Sunday)

174 Lancasters of 5 Group to this target, which was an important supply port for the German Eastern Front. The route to the target

was 950 miles from the 5 Group bases. Photographic reconnaissance showed that the bombing fell in the eastern part of the town but no report is available from the target [then Königsberg], now Kaliningrad in Russian Lithuania [sic]. 4 Lancasters lost.[65]

August 29–30 (Wednesday)

189 Lancasters of 5 Group carried out one of the most successful 5 Group attacks on this target at extreme range. Only 480 tons of bombs could be carried because of the range of the target but severe damage was caused around the 4 separate aiming points selected. The success was achieved despite a 20-minute delay in opening the attack because of the presence of low clouds; the bombing force waited patiently, using up precious fuel, until the marker aircraft found a break in the clouds and the Master Bomber, Wing Commander J. Woodroffe, probably 5 Group's most skilled Master Bomber, allowed the attacks to commence. Bomber Command estimates that 41 percent of all the housing and 20 percent of all the industry in Königsberg were destroyed. There was heavy fighter opposition over the targets and 15 Lancasters, 7.9 per cent of the force, were lost.[66]

Eyewitness reports from people on the ground confirm that the first air raid was not as destructive as the second.[67] The night of August 26–27 was clear when the sirens started blaring shortly after midnight, rousing the residents of Königsberg out of their beds and into the rehearsed routine of quickly getting dressed, grabbing a packed bag of essential possessions, and hurrying to their allotted air-raid shelters. These were typically rooms in the cellars of apartment buildings where the doors had been reinforced and the ceilings shored up with heavy wooden beams in case the building collapsed. While making their way to the shelters the residents could already hear in the distance the muffled droning of many bombers, which grew louder by the minute. The night was nearly turned to day by the illumination of the so-called "Christmas trees," high-intensity flares that quietly floated down on parachutes to enable the bomber pilots to identify their targets on the ground. The bright beams of searchlights coming up from the ground also lit up the night and swept the sky to catch a bomber in its grip and make it a better target for anti-aircraft guns to shoot at.

As the chattering fire of these guns became more persistent, people soon realized this air raid would be more intense than past attacks. The thunder of exploding bombs drew nearer and nearer, and then the floors began to shake and the walls to shudder from detonations in the immediate vicinity. The deafening noise continued for what seemed like forever to people huddled in their bunkers fearing a direct hit on their building. The terrifying roar appeared to let up from time to time, but then returned with renewed intensity. Gradually, the earsplitting racket died down and the sinister droning of the bombers receded into the distance. Eventually, at the all-clear signal, the survivors emerged from their shelters to see the sky red from the many fires burning in the city and clouds of smoke billowing in the distance. As it was a Sunday during summer vacation, many Königsbergers had left for the weekend for the nearby seaside resorts of Cranz, Nidden, and Rauschen, and thereby escaped injury or death in their apartments in the city.

While the first August raid caused much damage to Königsberg and a significant number of casualties, it was a mild harbinger of the death and destruction inflicted by the second raid. Shortly before 1:00 a.m. on Wednesday, August 30, the sirens screamed again and woke the residents from their slumber, driving them into their cellars. The sky was heavily blanketed with clouds, but this cloud cover ultimately provided no protection from the bombers because after a delay of some twenty minutes, the Lancasters finally found an opening in the clouds and proceeded to bomb their targets. This time the attack came more quickly and the hellish combination of the insistent growling of the bombers' motors, the sharp staccato of the flak, and the roar of exploding bombs sounded like the apocalypse had come to those huddled in their shelters. As the attack reached fever pitch, people in the shelters dreaded being hit any second. In the din one could hear glass panes breaking and walls collapsing, the red glow of the fires raging outside could be glimpsed from within, and the smell of smoke soon began to permeate many of the shelters. After about an hour of this ceaseless pounding and just when it seemed that a further stay in the cellars would be unendurable, the intensity of the raid diminished and then was over.

When they emerged from the shelters, people were nearly overwhelmed by the smoke and heat, as the center of the city from the North Train Station to the Central Train Station was in flames, having been systematically subjected to a combination of high explosives, napalm, and other incendiary bombs. A firestorm gripped the central city and many inhabitants were incinerated in their shelters or consumed by the flames on the streets when they tried to escape the burning buildings. Some tried to reach a safe haven on the banks of Castle Pond (*Schloßteich*), but were burned by the flames from nearby buildings; the water in the pond had become so hot from the inferno that it provided no protection from the searing heat. One witness reported that roughly two hundred women and girls sought refuge in an air-raid shelter on the banks of the Pregel River, which winds through the center of the city, and when this shelter was hit by phosphor bombs, many ran out of the shelter burning like torches and sprang into the Pregel, where they died. One resident intended to escape the flames by jumping into the Pregel but thought better of it when he found that the wooden pilings were burning in the river.

When Michael Wieck, then seventeen, looked out over Königsberg at dawn from his parents' apartment balcony—the building was located in the Hufen, an outlying district of the city that was only partially destroyed—he saw a massive cloud of smoke towering over the city, which he later described as looking like an atomic mushroom cloud. The updraft from the blazing conflagration sucked up half-burned bits of paper, cartons, wood, cloth, bedding, and curtains, which then floated down over the city and out to the countryside. Marianne Peyinghaus wrote to her parents that ashes and pieces of burned paper rained down on her village of Gertlauken nearly forty miles (sixty kilometers) from Königsberg the day after the big raid.

Wieck described what he found when he attempted to go into the city center a few hours later:

> The misery was beyond words. Hundreds of thousands of homeless people were moving their things by handcart, wheelbarrow, baby carriages, anything with wheels, into city parks. Everywhere suitcases, sacks and baggage, the remnants of saved possessions.

As could be expected, the sight reminded me of Jews gathered for transport. Still, this was completely different; these people had survived and could count on others helping them. Many were covered in soot, wearing burnt clothing, and were weeping for the missing. Full of compassion for mothers, children, and helpless old men and women, I covered my star of David and went back home. For almost three days no one could enter the city. Even after the flames had died down, the stones and ground were incandescent, cooling off only gradually.[68]

Königsberg had largely escaped the ravages of the conflict until then, and Wieck reported that the survivors were stunned by this new dimension of the war that had now reached them. Overcome by fear that another raid might be imminent, many Königsbergers fled the city in overcrowded trains to spend the night in Cranz (Zelenogradsk) or elsewhere, as well as in large camps, and returned to Königsberg the following day. Only a few cases of plundering in the ruins of the city came to the attention of the State Supreme Court in Königsberg, whereas in the Memel area plundering was much more widespread and death penalties were handed down in fifteen cases through September 9, 1944.[69]

As an officially declared Jew, Wieck feared for his life every day, but he nevertheless condemned the senseless loss:

> The Allies must have known that such air raids killed civilians, women, and children while scarcely influencing the outcome of the war. These acts of revenge were neither heroic nor reasonable; they were manifestations of a mentality equally corrupt. This was not the way to stop Hitler's war machine—on the contrary. It bred bitterness and desperate acts.[70]

Other eyewitnesses noted that the raid had clearly aimed at Königsberg's city center, with its closely spaced apartments and historic public buildings, and had left unscathed targets of obvious military importance, such as the main railroad station and the huge Schichau-Werft dockyards, which employed nineteen thousand workers for the war effort.[71] Their impressions are supported by the official British description of the raid undertaken by the British Bomber Command cited above, which reported that forty-one percent of the housing in the city was destroyed, but only twenty percent of the industry.[72] Thus it would appear that this was a terror raid specifically designed to kill civilians and to break their will to continue the war. Air Chief Marshall Arthur Harris stated as much in October 1943, when he urged the U.K. government to openly announce that "...the aim of the Combined Bomber Offensive should be unambiguously stated [as] the destruction of German cities, the killing of German workers, and the disruption of civilized life throughout Germany."[73] The raid succeeded in achieving the former objective, as estimated fatalities ranged from thirty-five hundred to ten thousand. Approximately fifty percent of all dwellings in Königsberg were severely damaged or completely destroyed and thousands of people became homeless. Using photographic reconnaissance, the British estimated that 134,000 residents lost their homes and that the homes of a further sixty-one thousand had been damaged.[74] The city center lay in ruins and many of its historic buildings, such as the castle, the cathedral, the two universities, the old grain storage buildings, and the opera house, were partly or fully destroyed. Königsberg, a city that had taken seven hundred years to create, no longer existed.[75]

In the wake of this devastation, many women and children were evacuated to Saxony and Thuringia. As Peyinghaus noted, even before these raids some civilians had been evacuated to other regions in Germany and others had been settled in the countryside outside of Königsberg, including in Gertlauken.[76] In her letter to her parents of September 29, 1944, Peyinghaus described how she had helped the earlier evacuees from Königsberg pack up their belongings for their journey to Saxony.

In her reminiscences of her childhood in East Prussia during the war, Erika Morgenstern wrote that she and her mother and sister were suddenly evacuated from Königsberg to the nearby village of Almenhausen, and from there they and other villagers sadly viewed the dark red glow on the horizon of burning Königsberg.[77] In this village they lived in one room of a small farmhouse, where a Polish prisoner of war who worked for the farmer treated her like his own daughter. This comfortable existence came to a sudden and early end when Erika and her mother were forced to return to bombed-out Königsberg and move into a dark, dingy room in a building surrounded by other structures that had been heavily damaged.

The bombing in August 1944 was a foretaste of the death and destruction Königsberg would experience when it was finally conquered by the Red Army in April of the following year. During 1944, the Germans were pushed back from the Soviet Union and Soviet forces made incursions into East Prussia in the fall of that year. The days of the easternmost province of Germany were numbered.

Notes

1 Hitler articulated his view of the necessity for Lebensraum for the German people (the Volk) in an address to five thousand officer cadets on December 18, 1940, at the Berlin Sport Palace. He first argued that there is a natural increase in the population of the Volk, but the available space for the Volk remains fixed unless some way is found to expand it. "Sooner or later, there will be a discrepancy between the increase in the Volk's numbers and the available Lebensraum. There are only two ways to overcome this discrepancy. Either the Volk's numbers are adjusted to the available Lebensraum…or the Lebensraum is adjusted to accommodate this discrepancy." Hitler obviously preferred the latter. "There is another way yet. It stands in opposition to this latter path leading to the adaptation of the Volk's numbers to the Lebensraum. It is the natural way and the one willed by Providence: namely, that man should adjust the Lebensraum to his numbers. In other words: that he should partake in the struggle for this earth. For it is nature which places man on this earth and leaves it to him. Truly, this earth is a trophy cup for the industrious man. And this rightly so, in the service of natural selection. He who does not possess the force to secure his Lebensraum in this world and, if necessary, to enlarge it, does not deserve to possess the necessities of life. He must step aside and allow stronger people to pass him by. This was so at all times." Hitler

then compared the population density of Germany to that of England, France, Russia, and the United States and concluded that Germany was the worst off: "By contrast, if we compare the percentage of Lebensraum occupied by the German Volk to that of the earth as such, then we must remark that the Volk is one the most disadvantaged peoples in the world." Germany's invasion of the Soviet Union was designed to correct this disadvantage. Domarus, *Hitler: Speeches and Proclamations*, vol. 3: *The Years 1939 to 1940*, 2160–162.

2 Weinberg, *A World at Arms*, 57.

3 Browning, *The Origins of the Final Solution*, 35. See also Snyder, *Bloodlands*, 120–22, for examples of the murder of Polish soldiers and civilians by the Wehrmacht.

4 In the territory taken over by Russia, the Soviet authorities staged plebiscites in an attempt to show that the inhabitants wished to be incorporated into the Soviet Union, but these were completely fraudulent. Davies, *Heart of Europe*, 65.

5 Lukowski and Zawadski, *A Concise History of Poland*, 229. The Poles suffered a similarly harsh treatment at the hands of the Russians. It is estimated that upward of two million Polish civilians were deported to Russia and Kazakhstan in 1939–1940, with at least half dying within a year of deportation. Most notorious was the execution estimated by Davies, (*Heart of Europe*, 67) of forty-five hundred Polish officers by the Russians in the Katyn Forest near Smolensk in April 1940. However, the total number of Poles executed by the NKVD was much larger. Based on the information included in the secret order for the execution of Polish, Ukrainian, and Belorussian prisoners of war signed by Beria on March 5, 1940, roughly 24,400 Poles were killed. These included not only Polish army officers, but also police officers, intelligence officers, border guards, prison guards, civil servants, landowners, factory owners, and those referred to in the order as "members of various counterrevolutionary and insurgent organizations and various counterrevolutionary elements." See Document 84 in Koenker and Bachman, eds., *Revelations from the Russian Archives*, 165–68.

6 See Megargee, *Barbarossa 1941*, for a concise description of Barbarossa and the atrocities committed by the Germans in the Soviet Union.

7 Glantz, *Barbarossa: Hitler's Invasion of Russia 1941*, 13.

8 The Wolfschanze is described in Roy, *The Vanished Kingdom*, Chapter 16, "Rastenburg: Madness, Assassination, Honor," 253–84. See also Dieckert and Grossman, *Der Kampf um Ostpreussen*, 36–41.

9 For a vivid description of the havoc caused by the ferocious Russian winter, see, in particular, Chapter 9, "The Battle of Moscow," in Clark, *Barbarossa: The Russian German Conflict 1941–1945*.

10 Klee and Dreßen, "*Gott mit uns,*" 1. "Es ist der alte Kampf der Germanen gegen das Slawentum, die Verteidigung europäischer Kultur gegen moskowitisch-asiatische Überschwemmung, die Abwehr des jüdischen Bolschewismus. [...] Jede Kampfhandlung muß in Anlage und Durchführung von dem eisernen Willen zur erbarmungslosen, völligen Vernichtung des Feindes geleitet sein." The author of this order, General Erich Hoepner, changed his views on Hitler and the Third Reich during the course of the war. When the Russians launched their counterattack in December 1941 to defend Moscow, Hoepner withdrew his tank forces in defiance of explicit orders from Hitler to stand fast. In 1942 he was expelled from the army, joined the resistance movement, and for his participation was condemned to death by the Peoples Court ("Volksgerichtshof") and hanged in Berlin-Plötzensee in August 1944. Klee and Dreßen, "*Gott mit uns,*" 255.

11 Hamburg Institute for Social Research, *The German Army and Genocide*, 94. This volume is the English translation of the catalog of an exhibition in Hamburg that took place in 1995.

12 The description given here of the "criminal orders" and how they were implemented follows closely that provided by Bartov in Chapter 4, "Barbarism and Criminality," *The Eastern Front*, 106–41.

13 This estimate is from Bartov, op. cit., 107, who cites a figure of 3.7 million deaths in prisoner-of-war camps. By one estimate, half a million Soviet POWs were shot by the Germans. Snyder, *Bloodlands*, 184.

14 Cited in Bartov, op. cit., 119.

15 Quoted in Mazower, *Hitler's Empire*, 166.

16 Bartov, *The Eastern Front*, 120.

17 Ibid., 121.

18 Ibid., 122.

19 Ibid., 123.

20 Klee and Dreßen, "*Gott mit uns,*" 186–89.

21 Ibid.,197. "Alle im Stadtgebiet von Kiev befindlichen Tauben sind sofort abzuschaffen. Wer nach dem 26. Oktober noch im Besitz von Tauben angetroffen wird, wird wegen Sabotage erschoßen."

22 Clark, *Barbarossa: The Russian-German Conflict, 1941–1945*, 193.

23 Bartov, *The Eastern Front*, 123.

24 The German title is *Stille Jahre in Gertlauken: Erinnerungen an Ostpreußen.*

25 Peyinghaus, *Stille Jahre in Gertlauken*, 36. "und so habe ich zum ersten Mal das Meer gesehen, endloses Wasser, das mit dem Himmel zusammen stößt. Ich war überwältigt, konnte mich kaum trennen. Mir gefällt das Land, mir gefallen die Menschen, sie sind so freundlich.[...] Das Leben hier wirkt so ruhig, so in tiefsten

Friedenzeiten—da kommen Eure Berichten aus einer anderer, schrechlichen Welt."

26 Ibid., 37. "Meine lieben Eltern, es war ein schöner, unendlich friedlicher Tag, daß man den ganzen schrecklichen Krieg mit all seinem Elend vergessen konnte. Daß solche Gegensätze bestehen können—im selben Land, zur gleichen Zeit."

27 Ibid., 44. "Ich habe immer ein schlechtes Gefühl, wenn ich daran denke, in welcher Gefahr Ihr schwebt und in welcher Sicherheit ich hier bin. Ich verlebe unglaublich friedliche, stille Tage in Gertlauken. Ich schäme mich, Euch zu erzählen, wie gut ich den vergangenen Sonntag verlebt habe. Samstags kam Paula zu mir, Sonntag standen wir um fünf auf und radelten nach Labiau. Dort bestiegen wir einen Dampfer und fuhren übers Haff, vorbei an Rossitten und Pillkoppen nach Nidden, ein Höchst malerisches Dorf, Lieblingsaufenthalt von Keunstlern…. Zum Schluß bestiegen wir die hohen Dünen und hatten einen erhebenden Blick auf das stille blaue Haff und die weite grüne Ostsee. Mit Riesenschritten die Dünen hinunter zu laufen und tief in den Sand zu sinken ist ein herrliches Vergnügen."

28 After World War II this bookstore relocated to Munich.

29 The Amber Room consisted of finely put together panels of amber that were sent in 1717 as a gift from Frederick I of Prussia to Peter the Great of Russia. It ended up in Catherine the Great's palace at Tsarskoe Selo outside St. Petersburg. Visitors were amazed at the rich yellow glow of the amber panels. It was hidden when the German Army invaded Russia in 1941, but was discovered and shipped off to Königsberg and assembled in the castle there. Following the surrender of the city in early April 1945, the Amber Room disappeared and its fate has been the subject of considerable speculation and investigation ever since. The most recent book on the topic (Scott-Clark and Levy, *Amber Room*, 356) comes to the conclusion that the Amber Room was destroyed by the Soviet Army in the pillage of Königsberg April 9–11, 1945, and to avoid embarrassment the Russian authorities have kept this unfortunate outcome a secret to this day. Ironically, in a gesture of reconciliation following the collapse of the Soviet Union, the German government financed a re-creation of the Amber Room in the Catherine Palace, which was unveiled on May 31, 2003, nearly three hundred years after the original had been sent from Prussia to Russia.

30 Peyinghaus, *Stille Jahre*, 95. "Hier führe ich so ein gutes Leben, daß es fast mein Gewissen belastet. Soeben höre ich den Wehrmachtsbericht. Wie sachlich kühl und militärisch knapp das klingt: 'Der erwartete Gegenangriff der Sowjetarmeen auf den Kubanbrückenkopf setzte gestern ein. Die Kämpfe dauern fort….' Und was steckt an Not und Tod und Leid und Härte und Mut dahinter. Das kann man in Worten nicht ausdrücken."

31 This evacuation of Berliners is also reported in Steinert, *Hitler's War and the Germans,* 263.

32 Meindl, *Ostpreußens Gauleiter,* 417.

33 These two high-ranking judicial officials from Königsberg met an untimely death toward the end of the war, as described below.

34 These reports have been published in Tilitzki, *Alltag in Ostpreußen.*

35 Ibid., 108.

36 Ibid., 163.

37 Chapter III below, which describes the flight of civilians from the advancing Soviet army, cites examples of the considerable help provided by foreign workers to their host families in their time of need.

38 See Tilitzki, *Alltag in Ostpreußen,* 103 and 113.

39 Thiel, *The Wolves of World War II,* 25.

40 Tilitzki, *Alltag in Ostpreußen,* 210.

41 Ibid., 233.

42 Ibid., 209.

43 Sommerfeld, *Juden im Ermland,* 60.

44 Tilitski, *Alltag in Ostpreußen,* 196.

45 Ibid., 205. "Es gibt viele und vernünftig denkende Volksgenossen aus allen Berufen, einschl. der Wehrmacht, welche gewisse Sondergerichtsurteile gegen Deutsche wegen ihre Höhe nicht verstehen. Harte Strafen wegen Schwarzschlachtungen, z. B. mögen zweckmäßig sein im Interesse unserer Ernährungswirtschaft. Andererseits dienen sie nicht dem guten Geist der Front, wenn es sich bei den Verurteilten um Angehörige von Soldaten handelt. Dort werden solche Urteile mit Erbitterung vermerkt und nicht verstanden.... Jedenfalls sollte auch nicht übersehen werden, daß das Volk an den scharfen Sondergerichtsurteilen eine ebenso scharfe Kritik übt. Denn die Stimmung ist im allgemeinen sehr nervös und gespannt und äußert sich demgemäß auch mit viel größerer Freimutigkeit, als bisher der Fall war."

46 Ibid., 131 and 138–39.

47 The cruel fate of the handicapped East Prussians is described in section 4, "Das Sonderkommando Lange vergast für ein Kopfgeld von 10 RM: Die 'Evakuierung' ostpreussischer Kranker," in Klee, *Euthanasie in NS Staat,* 190–93.

48 Burleigh, *Death and Deliverance,* 132.

49 Peyinghaus, *Stille Jahre,* 46–50.

50 Ibid., 50. "Stellt Euch vor, Ihr geht durch Straßen, wo alle Fenster und Türen von außen dick mit Brettern vernagelt sind, und doch herrscht dahinter ein unentwegtes Geräusch—Gemurmel und Bewegung. Dann kommt zwischen den Häusern ein

langer Bretterzaun, der nicht ganz bis zur Erde reicht, und darunter sieht man Füße, nackte, in Pantoffeln, in Sandalen, in Schuhen. Das Stimmengewirr schwillt an, es riecht nach vielen Menschen, und wenn du dich auf die Zehen stellst und über den Zaun blickst, siehst du kahle Köpfe. Dann geht es einem plötzlich auf, daß das ein Getto ist und die zusammengepferchten Menschen dahinter Juden sind. Wir sind ganz schnell zu unserem Schneider zurückgegangen, und er erzählte uns, daß er auch Jude ist and das Getto tagsüber zum Arbeiten verlassen darf. Er bügelte gerade mit unendlicher Behendigkeit eine Hose.... Wir lobten ihn, und er lächelte uns traurig an. Ich war sehr froh, als Plöhnen endlich hinter mir lag."

51 Marianne Peyinghaus may have been aware of the virulently anti-Jewish newspaper, *Der Stürmer,* published by Julius Streicher, but she never made any mention of it in her letters.

52 Wieck, *A Childhood under Hitler and Stalin.* According to Wieck, only four Jews from Königsberg who wore the Star of David survived persecution under the Nazis, World War II, and the Russian occupation that followed.

53 According to Paul H. Haagen, Duke University Law School, "The classification of a Mischling changed if he voluntarily associated himself with the Jewish community. Such a person was reclassified as a 'Geltungsjude,' or a 'deemed' Jew. A person deemed to be a Jew was treated as a Jew for the purposes of the discriminatory statutes and orders issued by the Nazis." See his article, "A Hamburg Childhood: The Early Years of Herbert Bernstein."

54 Klemperer, *I Will Bear Witness.*

55 Schüler-Springorum, *Die jüdische Minderheit in Königsberg,* 349.

56 Wieck, *A Childhood under Hitler and Stalin,* 51.

57 Ibid., 65.

58 Ibid., 18–21.

59 Gottwaldt, "Zur Deportation der Juden aus Ostpreußen in den Jahren 1942/43," in Alfred Gottwaldt, Norbert Kampe, and Peter Klein, eds., *NS-Gewaltherrschaft,* 152–71. For a detailed chronology of the deportation of Jews out of the German Reich during World War II, see Gottwaldt and Schule, *Die "Judendeportationen" aus dem Deutsches Reich.*

60 Dr. Wolffheim survived the war and in 1947 wrote a report in Palestine concerning the situation of Jews in Allenstein in the 1930s and their deportation in the early 1940s. See Christa Alheit, "Allenstein 1933–1943: Die Erinnerungen des Artztes Heinrich Wolffheim von 1947," in Alfred Gottwaldt, et al., eds., *NS-Gewaltherrschaft,* 172–86.

61 Reproduced in Gottwaldt, "Zur Deportation der Juden aus Ostpreußen," in Gottwaldt, et al., eds., NS- *Gewaltherrschaft,* 167. "Die Arbeit der restlichen

Männer hier in Minsk bleibt nach wie vor ziemlich dieselbe. Die Judentransporte trafen in regelmäßigen Abständen in Minsk ein und wurden von uns betreut [sic]. So beschäftigten wir uns bereits an 18. und 19.6.42 wieder mit dem Ausheben von Gruben im Siedlungsgelände.... Am 26.6 traf der erwartete Judentransport aus dem Reich ein."

62 Sixty-nine years later, on June 24, 2011, a plaque was dedicated in Kaliningrad, near the site of the former North Train Station, in memory of the 465 Jewish men, women, and children who were on the "Da 40" train. Michael Wieck participated in this ceremony. See *Königsberger Bürgerbrief,* Ausgabe 78 (Winter 2011): 81–83.

63 I am grateful to Wolfgang Degner, currently living in Cologne, Germany, for sharing this information with me in an email communication and for sending me a fourteen-page description of his life in Königsberg and subsequent flight from the Russians in 1945.

64 This account is taken from Werner Krömke, "Der Untergang von Königsberg," in *Königsberger Bürgerbrief* 62 (Summer 2004): 24, and Tilitzki, *Alltag in Ostpreußen,* 155 and 238.

65 Middlebrook and Everitt, *The Bomber Command War Diaries,* 573.

66 Ibid., 575.

67 The following description of the August air raids is based largely on Wieck, *A Childhood under Hitler and Stalin,* 98–102, and Königsberger *Bürgerbrief* 62 (Sommer 2004): 22 –27, and 63 (Winter 2004): 24 –29.

68 Wieck, *A Childhood under Hitler and Stalin,* 101.

69 Tilitzki, *Alltag in Ostpreußen,* 281.

70 Wieck, *A Childhood under Hitler and Stalin,* 101.

71 *Königsberger Bürgerbrief* 64, special issue, "750 Jahre Königsberg: Geschichte und Kultur einer europäischen Metropole," 78.

72 See Tilitski, *Alltag in Ostpreußen,* 279, for a description of the damage and the casualties caused by this raid.

73 Garret, *Ethics and Airpower in World War II,* 32–33.

74 Webster and Frankland, *The Strategic Air Offensive Against Germany,* 3: 180.

75 One can take issue with the deliberate bombing of civilian targets in German or any other country's cities from both moral and strategic standpoints. A critique of the bombing of Königsberg and other German cities from a moral perspective was delivered in February 1944, by the English bishop Bell of Chichester:

"I desire to challenge the Government on the policy which directs bombing of enemy towns on the present scale, especially with reference to civilians who are non-combatants.... It is of supreme importance that we, who are liberators of Europe, should use power that that it is always under the control of Law.

It is because our bombing of enemy towns—this 'area bombing'—raises the issue of bombing unlimited that such immense importance is bound to attach to the policy and action of His Majesty's Government." (This passage is cited in Hastings, *Armageddon*, 307.)

From the strategic perspective, evidence is lacking that these target terror raids on civilians hastened the end of the war by undermining the resistance of Germans and depriving the German war machine of military personnel and labor for armaments production. Hence it is untenable to argue that carpet bombing was a necessary evil to achieve the Allied war objectives. One estimate is that this bombing of Germany destroyed nearly two million homes and killed upward of 600,000 civilians, with many of the deaths taking place in the last months of the war. Hastings, *Armageddon*, 299. On the contrary, it seems clear that the strategic bombing of German cities—spearheaded by Sir Arthur Harris, commander-in-chief of the Royal Air Force (RAF) Bomber Command—in fact delayed the end of the war by diverting the destructive firepower of aerial ordnance away from industrial and transportation targets as well as oil production facilities, which were essential for the German war effort. By the end of 1944 Britain's chief of air staff, Sir Charles Portal, became convinced that RAF bombers should concentrate more on noncivilian targets and he communicated his views to his subordinate, but "Bomber" Harris would have none of it and continued his carpet bombings of German cities, behavior that was tantamount to insubordination. Hastings, *Armageddon*, 335.

76 At this time the author's future wife, together with her mother and brother, were evacuated from East Prussia.

77 Morgenstern, *Überleben war schwerer als Sterben*, 40 and 45.

CHAPTER III

THE BATTLE OF EAST PRUSSIA AND THE FLIGHT FROM THE RED ARMY

"No true German can possibly think that East Prussia will fall into the hands the Russians." Gauleiter Erich Koch[1]

A. The Center Does Not Hold

By early 1944 Soviet forces had defeated the German Army in Ukraine and had pushed it back to Galicia and the borders of Romania and Czechoslovakia. Following this major offensive, in May and June of 1944 a lull in the fighting took place on the Eastern Front. On the Soviet side, the Soviet Supreme Command (STAVKA) gave instructions for army units to organize troop training, to undertake reconnaissance of the German lines, and to clear a sixteen-mile (twenty-five-kilometer) strip behind their own lines to bolster their defensive positions. The STAVKA also ordered a major buildup of forces opposite the German Army Group Center in Belorussia (now called Belarus), which was commanded by Field Marshal Busch.[2] This German Army Group consisted of the Second, Fourth, and Ninth Armies, and the Third Panzer Army. The massing of Soviet troops and supplies was so skillfully concealed that it eluded the Eastern Intelligence Branch of the German High Command, the OKH (*Oberkommando des Heeres*), which was in charge of the entire Eastern Front. Busch, however, received reports from the intelligence services of his own armies that indicated a large-scale deployment of enemy forces, which would make his position vulnerable to an attack. When he conveyed his concerns to the OKH, they argued that these troop movements were a ploy by STAVKA to divert attention from where the OKH firmly believed the next Soviet assault would be concentrated, namely, in Ukraine.

OKH's unwillingness to change its view on Soviet military intentions in spite of mounting evidence to the contrary, as well as Busch's inability to argue his case forcefully, led to considerable concern on the part of General Hans Jordan, the commander of the Ninth Army. He wrote on June 22 in his Ninth Army war diary:

> Ninth Army stands on the eve of another great battle, unpredict- able in extent and duration. One thing is certain: in the last few weeks the enemy has completed an assembly on the very greatest scale opposite the army.... The army has felt bound to point out repeatedly that it considers the massing of strength on its front to constitute the preparation for this year's main Soviet offensive, which will have as its object the reconquest of Belorussia.... The army, therefore, looks ahead to the coming battle with bitterness, knowing that it is bound by orders to tactical measures which it cannot in good conscience accept as correct.... The Commanding General [Jordan] and Chief of Staff presented these thoughts to the army group [Army Group Center] in numerous conferences, but there, apparently, the courage was lacking to carry them high- er up, for no counterarguments other than references to OKH orders were given. And that is the fundamental source of the anxi- ety with which the army views the future.[3]

On May 31, STAVKA sent to Soviet commanders at the front the final operational plans for the attack against Army Group Center. Their objectives were to liberate Belorussia and to advance all the way to the Vistula River and the eastern border of East Prussia. Stalin named this operation "Bagration" after a Georgian general who was a hero of the 1812 Battle of Borodino against the armies of Napoleon. Operation Bagration was designed to envelop the salient (the outward projection of the front into Belorussia) held by Army Group Center in fifty days and to advance 160 miles.[4] One key part of the plan was a pincer movement that would surround the Fourth Army, with the pincers converging at Minsk. In June 1944, the Eastern Front was still some distance from East Prussia, stretching from Lake Peipius on the eastern border of Estonia with Russia, to Pinsk in eastern prewar Poland, with the salient that included Polazk, Witebsk, Orscha, Mogilew, and Rogatschew. While Army Group Center had thirty-eight divisions, three panzer or panzer grenadier divisions, and two infantry divisions in reserve (a total force of almost 900,000 men), it also had to defend the longest stretch of the Eastern Front, a total of 488 miles.[5]

On June 22, the third anniversary of the German attack on Russia in 1941, the Soviets launched a massive assault against Army Group Center with an advantage of four to one in troop strength and six to one in tanks.[6] In addition, the Soviet commanders demonstrated considerable skill in breaching the German lines with tightly concentrated troop forces and artillery fire. They also orchestrated rapid advances much like the Blitzkrieg tactics that had been used so effectively by the Wehrmacht in its invasion of Russia. Moreover, the Soviets had overwhelming air superiority and used it to great effect to wipe out German artillery located close to the front.

From the start, the battle went poorly for the Germans. The Third Panzer Army was taken completely by surprise near Vitebsk and was soon in dire straits. As Soviet forces swiftly advanced toward Orsha and Mogilev, the Fourth Army's front began to fall apart and the Ninth Army's left flank south of the Beresina River was near the breaking point. By the end of the fourth day of fighting, all the Army Group Center's reserves had been committed without having any discernable effect in slowing down the Russian assault. Five German divisions were encircled at Vitebsk and the Ninth Army was retreating toward Bobruysk. The Ninth was ordered to hold Bobruysk at all costs, but the Soviets quickly surrounded it and about seventy thousand German troops were trapped in and around the city. On the morning of June 28, Field Marshal Ernst Busch reported to his superior officer, General Kurt

Zeitzler, the chief of staff of the OKH, that the Ninth Army was severely damaged; the Third Panzer Army had been reduced to only one corps; and the Fourth Army was decimated. When informed of the rapidly deteriorating situation on the Belorussian Front, Hitler replaced Busch as commander of Army Group Center with Field Marshal Walter Model, at the time arguably one of the Wehrmacht's best tacticians.

Field Marshal Model also proved incapable of stemming the advancing tide of Soviet troops, who took Minsk, the capital of Belorussia, on July 3. In the twelve days since the onslaught had begun, Army Group Center lost twenty-five divisions (almost 450,000 men), casualties that would be considered unconscionable today. The Ninth Army had been so battered that it was taken out of the fighting on the front and sent to the rear to reorganize. The staff of Army Group Center assumed that when the Russians reached Minsk—their first major objective—they would pause for a few days to resupply their units. They were mistaken; the Soviets pressed their advantage and pushed the Germans farther west, toward Kaunas and the Neman River in Lithuania, and Bialystok in eastern Poland.

By the third week of July the German Third Panzer and Fourth Armies were finally able to establish a defensive line from Ukmerge east of Kaunas and along the Neman River to south of Grodno (Hrodna) in western Belorussia. The Second Army consolidated its position near Bialystok, and the Ninth Army staff organized the establishment of a protective line at the East Prussian border. The Soviet forces had advanced much more quickly than planned and paused to reestablish their supply lines by rebuilding bridges and rail lines that were essential for the support of further advances. In the meantime, fifty-seven thousand German prisoners were paraded on July 17 through Red Square in Moscow to celebrate the victory in Belorussia. This marked the end of the first stage of Operation Bagration, which was described by one American author as "not only the most effective Soviet offensive of the war but perhaps the most overwhelming and devastating single military assault in history."[7]

The next stage of the Soviet offensive involved a move against the flanks of German Army Group Center. On the southern flank, large-scale attacks were launched in mid-July against both the German Army Group North Ukraine and the Ninth and Second Armies of Army Group Center. By July 24, 1944, the front had moved to just outside Bialystok and Brest, and by the end of the month Soviet armies were rolling west through the broken German divisions. On the northern flank, a gap had been opened between Army Groups Center and North. Pressure was particularly intense on Center's Third Panzer Army and on July 30 its flank collapsed, allowing the Russians to advance to Mariampol in Lithuania, just twenty miles from the East Prussian border. On August 1, the German Third Panzer Army shifted the right half of its front to form a defensive line to shield East Prussia from the onslaught, but a Soviet attack force pierced this forward defense of German territory in three locations and took Vilkaviškis in Lithuania, only ten miles from East Prussia.

Having been pushed back far to the west and close to German territory, the staff of the Third Panzer Army set up its headquarters on the western side of the border between East Prussia and Poland, in Schloßberg (known as Pillkallen until re-named in the 1930s by the Nazis, now Drobrowolsk in the Kaliningrad Russian territory). This peaceful, well-functioning German town stood in stark contrast to the chaotic conditions Third Panzer soldiers had experienced on Soviet soil. The commander of the Third, General Georg-Hans Reinhardt, was aghast when he discovered that the Gauleiter (provincial Nazi Party leader) of East Prussia, Erich Koch, had done nothing in his capacity as civil defense commissioner to draft a plan to evacuate women and children from this German territory so close to the front.[8] In his daily communications with his superiors, the Ninth Army's chief of staff was also critical of this lack of an evacuation plan, but to no avail. Koch viewed any discussion about evacuating civilians as smacking of defeatism and refused to make any preparations for an orderly withdrawal of the mostly women, children, and old men in the border areas. Nearly all the able-bodied males were in the armed services.[9]

But with Soviet forces advancing rapidly westward, it became impossible to ignore the imminent threat that the enemy would, in fact, soon be on German soil. The heavy air raids on Tilsit (Sovetsk) in July and August may have persuaded Koch to modify his views. Given the near certainty of further aerial bombardments, he decided that in border areas that were particularly threatened, women with children, the elderly, and the infirm would be permitted to leave, but only if they could prove they had accommodations elsewhere.[10]

This evacuation order did not apply to the world-famous horse stud estate, Trakehnen, located only nine miles (fifteen kilometers) from the border. In early August 1944, Ernst Ehlert, the estate's manager, sought permission to evacuate his horses, but was abruptly turned down by the party authorities in Königsberg. He tried again on September 1 and reached Gauleiter Koch himself on the phone. Koch first told him that if the Russians should temporarily advance into Trakehnen, the horses would prove their exceptional performance in competition with the Soviet tanks, but he then relented and authorized the removal of one of the farm's best studs.

In mid-October the Soviet army advanced into East Prussia at the border town of Eydtkau (until 1938 known as Eydtkuhen, now Chernyshevskoye) twelve miles (twenty kilometers) from Trakehnen; on October 17, Ehlert received a telephone call at 5:00 a.m. from the authorities in Königsberg ordering him to evacuate all the inhabitants and horses within three hours. Amazingly, only one horse was lost in the confusion, delays, and Soviet aircraft attacks by that evening, when the personnel and horses reached a provincial stud farm in Georgenburg (Maewka) near Insterburg (Chernyakhovsk), some thirty-four miles (fifty-four kilometers) from Trakehnen.[11] However, the evacuation of four outlying stud farms west of Trakehnen in the neighboring administrative district ("Kreis") of Gumbinnen (Gusev) was forbidden under threat of punishment. Notwithstanding this prohibition, with Russian soldiers advancing ever closer, the people living on these horse farms fled some thirty hours later. While many were soon overtaken by Soviet tanks, most of the women and children escaped on foot, but a number of the drivers of the wagon teams were shot. The official order to evacuate these four farms was finally issued on October 20 at a time when Soviet troops had already reached them. This is one example of many evacuation orders that were issued too late and that thereby caused untold hardship and death for the East Prussians.

Eventually, the Wehrmacht was able to get approval to evacuate civilians living in the border-area administrative districts of Ebenrode (Stallupönen until 1938, now Nesterov) and Schloßberg (Pillkallen until 1938, now Dobrovolsk). Moreover, as a large-scale Soviet attack between Tilsit and Memel was expected in the beginning of August, the area north of the Memel River was also evacuated. Long lines of refugees, some in wagons and others on foot, crossed the Queen Luise Bridge in Tilsit and moved south from Memelland into the more secure area of East Prussia. Ultimately, this Soviet attack failed to take place and many returned home—tragically, as it turned out, because they were caught when the Red Army finally invaded later in the fall of 1944. The fact that this evacuation proved unnecessary may have persuaded Gauleiter Koch to deny many subsequent such requests, and in cases when he did give his approval, it was far too late for many of the civilians to escape.[12] While Koch allowed women and children to move out of Königsberg to the countryside in the summer of 1944, he was unwilling to consider a comprehensive and systematic plan for the evacuation of civilians from East Prussia.

Nonetheless, he was clearly aware of the threat posed to the province by the massed Russian forces and, in mid-July 1944, he proposed to Hitler that a defensive wall (*Ostwall*) be built in Poland twelve miles (twenty kilometers) east of the border; Hitler authorized Koch to proceed with the construction. On July 16, large numbers of workers, horses, and wagons crossed the border to the building sites in Poland. Thousands of men—young and old, laborers, government officials, office workers and managers—were summarily relieved of their positions and dispatched to the construction area. There they built a defensive line consisting of tank trenches, foxholes, and bunkers, which became popularly known as the "Erich Koch Wall." The location of these entrenchments was determined by the Wehrmacht's construction engineers in charge of defense, but the actual building was in the hands of local Nazi party officials or their appointees, who did not have the appropriate training for such an undertaking. As a result, many of the fortifications were of questionable value and were later re-built under Army supervision to form a proper defensive network, which did provide some protection for the retreating German soldiers. A major part of this defensive effort involved the construction of tank ditches, which required the most resources.[13]

By mid-August 1944, the German defenders had barely been able to keep the Soviet forces from invading German territory. In just two months, Operation Bagration had taken Soviet forces to the border of East Prussia and had reduced Army Group Center to a force of 445,000, about half its original size.[14] However, the rapid advance of the Red Army again led to the overextension of its supply lines, which precluded the immediate exploitation of the advantage it had achieved over the much-weakened Army Group Center. This overextension led to a pause in the fighting in this sector of the Eastern Front, albeit not for long.

B. Two Incursions into East Prussia in the Fall of 1944

During the Soviet offensive in the summer of 1944, the situation of German Army Group North became increasingly precarious. The front it defended stretched from roughly the Memel River in the south to Lake Peipus in Estonia in the north. This left East Prussia dangerously exposed to an attack from the north in the event of a collapse somewhere along this extended defensive line. As late as the morning of October 5, 1944, the staff of Army Group North estimated that the enemy forces facing them needed more time to redeploy their armies and hence did not expect a Soviet assault in southern Lithuania. The commander of Army Group North, General Ferdinand Schörner, was convinced that the next Soviet offensive would take place in the north in Estonia, near Riga, where the Russians would attempt to encircle the units of the German Army Group. Yet one of his subordinates, General Erhard Raus, commander of the Third Panzer Army, reported that intelligence sources in his army had detected a buildup of Soviet troop levels in the south in preparation for an attack, which he believed was aimed to cut off Army Group North from Army Group Center in East Prussia.[15] His report was ignored.

On the morning of October 5, the assault commenced precisely where General Raus had predicted. Following a heavy concentration of artillery fire, the Soviets mounted a major thrust west and southwest from Schaulen in Lithuania toward Tilsit and Memel on the Baltic coast. The full force of the attack fell on two inexperienced German divisions, which suffered heavy losses. The tanks dispatched to come to their rescue ran out of fuel and were in imminent danger of being surrounded and destroyed by advancing Soviet units. A counterattack by the besieged German troops held off the assault long enough for fuel to be siphoned off from trucks and other vehicles, making it possible for the tanks to roll again.[16] Nonetheless, the overpowering Soviet force quickly broke through the weakened German lines and in four days reached the Baltic coast north and south of Memel, separating Army Group North from Army Group Center exactly as General Raus had feared. By October 15, the Red Army had conquered much of Memelland.

On the first day of this assault General Raus had recommended to party officials in Königsberg that Memelland be evacuated and an orderly withdrawal of civilians be prepared. The order was given the following day (October 6), but ironically the local population was in no hurry to comply. As mentioned above, many had already left their homes in early August in response to the first evacuation order. To cite one example, the wife of a farmer in Memelland explained that she and her husband had fled in early August when Memelland was first threatened by the advancing Red Army, and when this evacuation proved to be a false alarm, they joyfully returned to their farm three weeks later to harvest the fully ripened rye and other grains.[17] Unfortunately for them, this time an attack on Memelland was in fact launched, but they delayed their escape even while the battle raged only a few miles away. Many living south of Memel were still able to take the train to Tilsit and points farther south in East Prussia, while civilians in Memel itself and to the north of the city made their way to the Kurische Nehrung or escaped by ship or ferry. However, those in the long lines ("Treks") of farmers' wagons on the road from Memel south to Heydekrug (Silute) were cut off by Russian tanks that smashed into their wagon trains. The wagons were plundered, some of the women were raped, and a few of those on the wagons were shot. In a panic to save themselves, large numbers of refugees abandoned their wagons and fled on foot to the Kurisches Haff, where small boats were still able to transport them over to the Kurische Nehrung.[18]

By now the Soviet incursion had also made itself felt inside East Prussia some distance from the border with Memelland. Dr. Hans Graf von Lehndorff worked as a surgeon in a hospital in Insterburg (Chernyakhovsk) some fifty miles (eighty kilometers) east of Königsberg. Insterburg was close enough to the front that at night Dr. Lehndorff could see the red glow in the east where frontier towns were burning after heavy Soviet air raids. He described how, in the largely agricultural East Prussia, farm animals also suffered in the war:

> Enormous herds of cattle came down along the stream beds and gathered in the flat valley through which the Pregel winds its way. They had been driven out of the eastern part of the province and now stood, an overwhelming sight, by the thousands in the wide meadows. For a short time there was enough food for them there; but if you went nearer and looked at the animals one by one, your heart was wrung with pity. With no relation between them, regarding human beings as enemies, they stumbled through the countryside, trampling down the hedges, forcing their way into paddocks and gardens, and stripping trees and bushes bare.[19]

The breakthrough of the Red Army into Memelland was a foretaste of the storming of East Prussia that was about to commence. Since the beginning of October, Luftwaffe reconnaissance flights in the area had detected a massive Soviet buildup in Lithuania to the south and southwest of Kaunas, directly opposite the Army Group Center's Fourth Army. With an attack expected in this sector at any moment, the Army again pressed for a timely evacuation of civilians from the threatened areas of East Prussia near the front, but party officials in Königsberg refused to issue the order. Moreover, Hitler refused to declare East Prussia a "theater of operations," which would have given Army Group Center the responsibility for the safety of civilians in their sector of the front. Consequently, Gauleiter Koch, in his capacity as *Reichsverteidigungskommisar* (Reich Defense Minister), remained in complete control of civil defense matters up to the front line and held firm against the wholesale evacuation of civilians, which in his mind would signify defeatist views.[20] In the administrative districts of Ebenrode and Schloßberg, civilians residing in the easternmost villages near the border were eventually permitted to evacuate. But in those areas further from the front, civilians were not allowed to leave, and the result was helter-skelter flight when the inevitable Soviet assault commenced.

This attack began at 4:00 a.m. on October 16, when artillery fire of every possible caliber as well as explosives dropped by bombers rained on the forward German Army positions. The two-hour firestorm was of such intensity that it could be heard far from the front.[21] It destroyed much of the German artillery and many anti-tank guns, and without their support, German troops were largely defenseless and suffered very high casualties. On the first day they were pushed back nearly seven miles in some places, and the border area of East Prussia was penetrated along a wide front. On the following day the town of Schirwindt (Kutusovo) fell after fierce house-to-house fighting, and other border towns were overrun despite strong resistance by vastly outnumbered German soldiers, who, as they were now defending their homeland, fought almost to the last man. On the third day a cloudless sky allowed the Soviet attackers to use their overwhelming air power to pulverize German gun emplacements and troop concentrations.

It now became obvious that Germany was in danger of being quickly defeated on the Eastern Front. On October 18, Hitler proclaimed the formation of the *Deutscher Volkssturm* (German Home Army), which involved drafting all able-bodied men between the ages of sixteen and sixty who could bear arms and who were not already in the armed services. This call to arms contained the following exhortation:

> While the enemy believes he can go in for the kill, we are determined to undertake the second supreme effort of our nation. We will and we must succeed, as in the years 1939–1940, in building solely on our strength not only to break the destructive intent of our enemies, but also to turn them back and keep them away from the Reich until the future of Germany, its allies, and thereby Europe's secure peace is guaranteed.[22]

The duties of the Volkssturm included assisting antiaircraft units and helping fire brigades deal with the destruction and casualties caused by air raids. Even Hitler admitted that because of a lack of training, equipment, and weapons, they were not effective fighting units.[23] While many of the youthful members showed considerable enthusiasm in carrying out their duties, the elderly displayed much less eagerness to risk their lives defending the homeland. The effectiveness of the Volkssturm units was also hampered by the fact that they were organized and at first largely trained by party officials, who typically had little military experience. Gauleiter Koch, in particular, wished to deploy the Volkssturm in East Prussia as his own private army, with the result that coordination with the Wehrmacht regarding the disposition of these units was often sporadic or nonexistent. Also, many of the men drawn into the Volkssturm came from farms and villages and had to leave their wives and daughters to face the marauding Soviet soldiers alone.

Faced with the rapid advance of enemy forces into German territory, the local authorities near the border in Ebenrode, Schloßberg, and Goldap at the last minute took the initiative to order the evacuation of civilians in their districts. In a village just south of Nemmersdorf (Mayakovskoye), residents were given permission to make preparations to flee as late as 5:00 in the afternoon of October 19; up to then such preparations would have risked arrest on the grounds they would cause a panic.[24] In the district of Gumbinnen, the evacuation order was given on October 20, when the Russians had already penetrated the surrounding area.[25] Soon long lines of wagons filled with refugees and their possessions jammed the roads from Goldap, Gumbinnen, and Schloßberg, all trying to escape to the west.

The deepest incursion of Soviet troops and tanks into East Prussia, and hence German territory, took place in Nemmersdorf, about seven miles (twelve kilometers) southwest of Gumbinnen. A column of Soviet tanks broke through the weak German defense line and crossed the Rominten River at Grosswaltersdorf on October 20. Not encountering any opposition, it kept advancing and crossed the Angerapp River into Nemmersdorf on October 21. This sudden thrust through the German defenses posed an immediate threat to Gumbinnen, to the north of Nemmersdorf. To avoid being overrun, General Friedrich Hossbach, commander of the Fourth Army, asked for and received reinforcements, which he used to mount a north-south pincer operation centered on Grosswaltersdorf designed to cut off the Russian units in Nemmersdorf. After very fierce fighting the pincers closed and the Germans were indeed able to ambush the advance Russian units and re-take Nemmersdorf.

When German soldiers and members of the Volkssturm returned to Nemmersdorf following the successful counterattack, they found evidence that Soviet troops had committed atrocities against German civilians. What exactly transpired on that fateful October 21, 1944, remains unclear and is the subject of debate to this day. Karl Potrek provided one version of what may have happened in a deposition in 1953 to a commission that assembled massive documentation of the expulsion of Germans from eastern Europe.[26] Potrek, a native of Königsberg who had been recruited into the Volkssturm, described thirteen years later what he had witnessed when he entered Nemmersdorf:

> At the edge of town, on the left side of the road, stands the large inn "Weisser Krug".... In the farmyard further down the road stood a cart, to which four naked women were nailed through their hands in a cruciform position. Behind the "Weisser Krug" towards Gumbinnen is a square with a monument to the Unknown Soldier. Beyond is another large inn, "Roter Krug." Near it, parallel to the road, stood a barn and to each of its two doors a naked woman was nailed through the hands, in a crucified posture. In the dwellings we found a total of 72 women, including children, and one old man, 74, all dead ... all murdered in a bestial manner, except only for a few who had bullet holes in their necks. Some babies had their heads bashed in. In one room we found a woman, 84 years old, sitting on a sofa ... half of whose head had been sheared off with an axe or a spade....

We carried the corpses to the village cemetery where they lay to await a foreign medical commission.... On the fourth day the bodies were buried in two graves. Only on the following day did the medical commission arrive. And the tombs had to be re-opened. Barn doors were set on blocks on which to lay the bodies so that the commission could examine them. This foreign commission unanimously established that all the women, as well as the girls from eight to twelve years and even a woman of 84 years had been raped. After the examination by the commission, the bodies were again buried.[27]

Two other reports of the atrocities in Nemmersdorf, made by German Army officers, could be cited to corroborate Potrek's description.[28]

More recent research, however, has called into question some of the details of the atrocities that Potrek described.[29] The number of civilians murdered in Nemmersdorf may have numbered only twenty-six, as reported in the Nazi Party newspaper *Völkischer Beobachter* on October 28. Moreover, the *Völkischer Beobachter* and other newspapers made no mention of naked women nailed to barn doors; some witnesses could not confirm that such murderous acts had, in fact, taken place; and the bodies of those murdered were found fully or at least partly clothed. Bernhard Fisch has written the most complete account of what happened at Nemmersdorf, and on the basis of extensive eyewitness reports and other information, he has concluded that only nineteen inhabitants were killed when Soviet forces overran the village, and that at least four, and possibly as many as ten, of those passing through Nemmersdorf in treks were also killed.[30]

The murder of innocent civilians was seized upon by Joseph Goebbels' ever resourceful Propaganda Ministry in an effort to rally the German population to resist the onslaught of the Red Army on German soil. Graphic photos of the bodies were printed in the newspapers, and newsreels of victims lying in the field where they had been assembled were shown in movie theaters for inspection by German newspaper reporters and foreign press from neutral countries (Sweden and Switzerland) (see Illustration 4. Nemmersdorf Dead on Field). One inflamatory German press report on October 27, 1944, described the scene as follows:

> The pale October sun shines wanly and accusatorily on the grey bloody terror on the Angerrapp [river flowing through Nemmersdorf]. Grey and calloused are the hands of the men and women who were murdered by the Soviets.... The German soldiers stand without tears in front of them.... Their eyes express the will to fight even harder and more relentlessly against the Soviets.... These are not the individual deeds of a sadistic horde—this is systematic mass murder, as known only by the Soviets.... The war has entered into its most merciless phase. Here ends everything that one could until now have conceived. The bestial bloody deed at Nemmersdorf will come to cost the Bolsheviks dearly.[31]

The free press in Germany had long been silenced and at no time was there any mention in the press or other news media of comparable atrocities against civilians committed by the Germans in a systematic manner on the Eastern Front.

The widespread distribution of the photos and newsreels in Germany of the Nemmersdorf massacre was intended to instill fear and horror in the population and to steel the armed forces for a fight to the finish against the advancing Soviet troops. The gruesome display of the victims on the field was designed by the Propaganda Ministry to achieve maximum shock effect, and it is possible that exposed to such graphic pictures of the terrible fate that could befall their women and children, Germany's soldiers did indeed become motivated to put up a more stubborn defense of the homeland. Among German civilians, however, this propaganda campaign generated panic on the home front. In the weeks following the atrocities in Nemmersdorf a renewed, spontaneous wave of East Prussian refugees moved westward in an attempt to escape from the now inevitable onslaught

of the Red Army. As described by the writer Arno Surminski, the East
Prussians now knew what to expect:

> Basically, Nemmersdorf triggered the flight of the refugees.
> Otherwise, many would have said: "Oh, what should we be
> doing on the street in winter, we will stay home no matter what
> happens." As a result of Nemmersdorf, even the last holdouts had
> become so scared that they wanted to leave because they had a
> forboding that it would not end well.[32]

While the precise details concerning the killing in Nemmersdorf will probably never be known, the fact remains that the Soviet invaders committed atrocities against innocent villagers, many women and children among them, when
they entered German territory. For East Prussians, Nemmersdorf conveyed a
dire picture of their vulnerability to the excesses of war and it proved to be a harbinger of the cruel fate that would befall all of East Prussia within a few months.

Meantime, at the end of October 1944, Nazi Party officials (*Gauleitung*) in
Königsberg finally acceded to the urgent pleas from both the military and the
civilian government and ordered civilians to evacuate a zone about nineteen
miles wide behind the front. People not engaged in agricultural pursuits were
evacuated to Pomerania, Saxony, and Thuringia, while farmers, their families, and farm workers moved in columns of wagons with what animals they
could take with them to the western areas of East Prussia. Either as a result
of spontaneous flight or organized evacuation, roughly half a million people,
or twenty percent of the population, had left East Prussia by the time of the
final Russian offensive in January 1945.[33] Another estimate puts the figure
higher, at 650,000.[34]

C. The Invasion of East Prussia and the Flight
from the Red Army in January 1945

From November 1944, to mid-January 1945, both sides used the lull in the
fighting to bolster their positions. Despite an overwhelming superiority in

men and weapons, Soviet forces were not yet prepared to push their advance farther into East Prussia in the face of the unyielding fighting spirit of the German troops. According to a STAVKA report: "The unsatisfactory results of October show that we needed to rest those divisions that have been on the front a long time, to regroup our troops, to bring forward the services behind the lines, and provide the necessary material supplies for a breakthrough as well as for the next stage of the operation."[35] Intelligence reports at the German OKH—the high command of the German Army—put the advantage for the Soviet side at eleven-to-one for the infantry, seven-to-one in the number of tanks, and twenty-to-one for artillery and air support; the Soviet attack was estimated to commence on January 12.[36]

Apprised of the overwhelmingly superior force facing him, the commander-in-chief of the OKH, General Heinz Guderian, made an attempt on December 24 to persuade Hitler to strengthen German defenses in the east. As the Wolfschanze in East Prussia had been evacuated on account of the impending Soviet attack, Guderian traveled to Hitler's new headquarters in Ziegenberg (a peaceful, hilly area near Bad Nauheim in the state of Hessen). There he argued forcefully for an immediate shift of forces from the Western and Northern Fronts (including the bridgehead in Memel and the divisions stranded in Kurland in Lithuania close to East Prussia) to bolster the Eastern Front. His entreaties for more resources were summarily rejected by Hitler, who asserted that the intelligence estimates of large enemy troop concentrations reflected a Soviet bluff and shouted, "It's the greatest imposture since Ghengis Khan." Guderian wrote in his memoirs that he "spent a grim and tragic Christmas Eve in those most unchristian surroundings...and was dismissed with instructions that the Eastern Front must take care of itself."[37]

To further buttress his case, Guderian visited his commanders on the Eastern Front in early January, and finding that their assessments of the military situation mirrored his, made one final attempt on January 9, 1945, to convince Hitler that reinforcements were absolutely essential for a viable defense in the east. He was again rebuffed, nor did he receive any support from General Jodl, chief of the general staff. When Hitler argued that the reserve forces at his disposal were sufficient to defend Germany in the east,

Guderian replied prophetically, "The Eastern Front is like a house of cards. If the front is broken through at one point all the rest will collapse...."[38]

He returned in a depressed state of mind to his headquarters at Zossen in Brandenburg, about fifty-six miles (thirty-five kilometers) south of Berlin. In his memoirs, Guderian—who was born in the town of Kulm in West Prussia—reflected on what might be the reason for Hitler's intransigence:

> I do not know how much their [Hitler and Jodl] incomprehension was due to the fact that they both came from parts of Germany far away from the threatened area.[Hitler was in fact born and raised in Austria.] At my last conference I came to the conclusion this fact played a not unimportant part in the decisions they were taking. For us Prussians it was our immediate homeland that was at stake, that homeland that had been won at such cost and which had remained attached to the ideals of Christian, Western culture through so many centuries of effort, land where lay the bones of our ancestors, land that we loved. We knew that if the assault from the East succeeded our homes were lost. After the examples of Goldap and Nemmersdorf we feared the worst for the inhabitants. But even these fears fell on deaf ears. A request from the generals at the front that civilians be evacuated from the most immediately threatened areas was turned down by Hitler; he said it was just another manifestation of the generals' alleged defeatism and he was afraid that such evacuation would have a bad effect on public opinion. In this attitude he was supported by the Gauleiters, and especially by Gauleiter Koch of East Prussia.[39]

Indeed, as late as January 11, 1945, Koch's deputy defense commissioner (*Reichsverteidigungskommissar*) Dargel rejected insistent requests from the military for a civilian evacuation with the claim, "East Prussia will be defended, an evacuation is out of the question" ("Ostpreußen wird gehalten, eine Räumung kommt nicht in Frage"). No arrangements had been made for an orderly and comphehensive evacuation of East Prussia if it were attacked, and any preparation for leaving the province that was not expressly authorized was subject to a stiff penalty.[40]

The defense of East Prussia from the expected attack was the responsibility of the Army Group Center, headed by General Georg-Hans Reinhardt, who was in overall command of three separate armies:[41]

1. The Third Panzer Army (General Erhard Raus) in the north, entrusted with the defense of the East Prussian capital of Königsberg;
2. The Fourth Army (General Friedrich Hossbach) in the center, which held a long front bulging into Polish territory east of the Masurian Lakes; and
3. The Second Army (General Walter-Otto Weiß) in the south, facing the Soviet bridgeheads across the Narew River, with its right flank extending to the boundary with Army Group A, north of Warsaw.

Facing Army Group Center and preparing for the attack were two Soviet so-called "fronts," which were the equivalent of a German army group and consisted of up to ten armies:

1. The Third Belorussian Front (Marshal I. D. Chernyakovsky) in the north, which aimed to drive toward Königsberg from the east; and
2. The Second Belorussian Front (Marshal Konstantin Rokossovsky) in the south, which was to attack west-northwest to West Prussia and Pomerania, with the objective of cutting off East Prussia from the rest of Germany.

The Soviet plan of attack, but not the precise date, was known on the German side. The mayor of Insterburg, Dr. Wander, reported that a German Army officer stationed there had informed him in November that the two massive Soviet forces described above were posed to invade East Prussia at any time.[42] The defense of East Prussia became more precarious when many divisions were transferred from the Eastern Front to the west to fight the Americans and their allies. Despite the imminent invasion of East Prussia,

Gauleiter Koch continued to forbid evacuation plans for the civilian population. Obviously exasperated by the Gauleiter's unwillingness to act, Dr. Wander developed, in early November 1944, his own detailed plan for the evacuation of Insterburg; this entailed delegating specific responsibilities to city officials and making arrangements with the German railroad (the Reichsbahn) for trains to transport the inhabitants when the time came. Although many people were involved with the evacuation preparations, party officials in Königsberg never got wind of it. If they had, Dr. Wander would have faced severe penalties and possibly execution.

The date for the Soviet attack on East Prussia had been set between January 15 and 20. Churchill did not know this and on January 6 he sent a secret message to Stalin asking whether a renewed offensive on the Vistula could commence during January, as the "battle in the West is very heavy." Stalin replied the following day that he was waiting for "clear flying weather and the absence of low mists that prevent aimed artillery fire."[43] He added that large-scale offensive operations would begin no later than the second half of January regardless of the weather, but did not mention that the weather had been wet and mild, which would make it difficult for tanks to attack in the muddy conditions on the battlefield. However, by January 9 a cold front was approaching and prisoners captured by the Germans revealed that the Soviet offensive was now scheduled to be launched between January 11 and 16.[44]

The attack in the north by the Third Belorussian Front against Raus's Third Panzer Army began on the foggy and frosty morning of January 13. This Army had just nine divisions (roughly 100,000 troops) to defend northern East Prussia against forty-four Soviet rifle divisions (about 270,000 soldiers).[45] (Note that German divisions were roughly twice the size of Soviet divisions.) Moreover, Raus's forces were completely outgunned from the start, with just fifty tanks, four hundred artillery pieces, and very few airplanes, compared to the eight hundred tanks, three thousand guns, and considerable air support on the Soviet side for their ground forces.[46]

The opening Russian artillery salvos between Gumbinnen and Schloßberg were so intense that Dr. Lehndorff in Insterburg reported being awakened at 7:00 a.m. that January 13 by a roaring and rumbling sound that rattled the windows; toward noon the roar had become so loud that it sounded like an avalanche. By January 17, Gumbinnen—just sixteen miles (twenty-five kilometers) to the east—was on fire and at night the entire east looked to Dr. Lehndorf like a sea of flames.[47] On January 19, the hospital in Insterburg was evacuated and the patients and most of the nurses were transported to the relative safety of Pomerania west of East Prussia. Dr. Lehndorff packed his personal belongings and took them to the railroad station for shipment to Königsberg. On the way he noticed a woman standing by the roadside and when he passed her, she asked if he knew of a furniture mover. It seems that two years earlier she had transported eight huge pieces of furniture from Wuppertal in the Rhineland to Gumbinnen to be safe from the bombs that were by then raining down on her hometown. Somehow, she had managed to save them from being consumed by the fire in Gumbinnen by moving them to a yard in Insterburg. Knowing full well that it would be impossible to move these massive furniture pieces, Dr. Lehndorff tried to persuade her to leave Insterburg without her furniture. The woman then confessed that they were the only possessions she had left in the world: she had no children, her husband had been killed in the war, and her house in Wuppertal had been bombed out. Dr. Lehndorff was unable to help her. Late in the evening the following day (January 20), with Insterburg under intense bombing attacks, Dr. Lehndorff departed by car for Königsberg together with a young female assistant doctor in the hospital whom he refers to only as "Doctora." When they passed the railroad station, they came upon the woman from Wuppertal waiting to leave on the next train, apparently having freed herself from the furniture she had held so dear. On the drive from Insterburg he reported that all roads on the way west to Königsberg were completely deserted and he could not detect any signs of measures being taken to defend East Prussia along the route.

The well-orchestrated evacuation plan for Insterburg conceived by Dr. Wander in late 1944 worked to perfection. As he put it, "[a]nd now happened what I had hardly dared to hope. The theoretical evacuation plan proved its worth in its smallest details. Everyone did as ordered or as intended with exemplary cooperation and fulfillment of assigned responsibilities."[48] The dedication of those involved in this effort was remarkable. For example, because the railroad station in Insterburg was under enemy fire, many inhabitants were directed instead to the train station in the nearby village of Waldhausen. By noon on January 21, some seventeen hundred people had gathered there and a middle school teacher named Noetzel (a member of the evacuation team) was dispatched to Waldhausen to engineer their flight to safety. As soon as he arrived at the village, he was on the phone to officials in Königsberg, who sent a rescue train to Waldhausen. It arrived at 2:00 that afternoon, but as there was room for only half of the women and children waiting at the station, Noetzel again phoned Königsberg with urgent pleas for another train. Hours passed and none appeared. Russian troops were by now on the outskirts of Waldhausen and German military officers had been given orders to demolish the railroad bridge and station. They desisted when Noetzel pleaded with them for just a little more time before proceeding to dynamite the structures. Finally, around midnight a long train pulled into the station, but it was immediately stormed by a group of prisoners of war who in the meantime had assembled at the station and packed the train with their baggage. The two guards accompanying them were incapable of imposing any semblance of order. Consequently, not enough room was left on the train for all the remaining women and children. At this point Noetzel hit upon a brilliant gambit. He let it be known that the train would only depart when the last woman had been taken on board. This had the desired effect; the prisoners discarded enough baggage to make room for the remaining civilians and the train left the station at 1:00 a.m. on January 22. Thanks to the planning of the mayor, Dr. Wander, and the heroic efforts of members of his evacuation team, such as the teacher Noetzel, most of Insterburg's inhabitants escaped and managed to survive.

General Raus, the commander of the Third Panzer Army, had fully anticipated the massive bombardment of the initial attack. He ordered his troops to evacuate the two forward lines at 10:00 p.m. on January 12, allowing them to escape the brunt of the initial Russian pounding.[49] However, the overpowering Soviet forces soon blasted through the German lines in northeastern East Prussia and fierce house-to-house fighting ensued in Schloßberg and Kattenau. On January 14, Soviet troops and tanks penetrated German defenses south of Schloßberg, and Kattenau fell to the Russians, was then retaken, and continued to change hands several times, with severe losses on both sides. Schloßberg remained heavily contested until the early morning of January 16, when the few remaining German defenders received the order to fight their way westward to join up with the rest of the Third Panzer Army. By now the German front was breached in many places and a strong Soviet tank force broke through and captured Breitenstein (Ulyanovo) on January 18. By January 20, the front in the north had collapsed. Soviet forces took Tilsit and Gilge, and almost reached the shore of the Kurisches Haff, which put the Red Army within striking distance of Königsberg.

The rapid advance of Russian soldiers in northern East Prussia, together with the lack of preparations for an orderly evacuation, caused chaos for the civilians. Hundreds of hastily packed wagons, jammed with fleeing women, children, and old men, together with many others on foot—some pushing baby strollers and prams and others pulling wagons—were now on the roads trying to escape to the west from the Soviet forces advancing from the east (see Illustration 6. Flight on a Wagon). So many refugees were on the move that travel conditions became chaotic and forward progress very difficult. Moreover, the roads were often reserved exclusively for German weapon and troop movements. As a result, the civilian population which was making every effort to escape was incessantly delayed and often forced to flee across the frozen fields through heavy snowdrifts. The road westward from Insterburg to Wehlau (Znamensk) was completely stopped up, with two and sometimes three lines of wagons next to each other.

Marianne Peyinghaus, whose idyllic years in East Prussia are described in Chapter II, was at this time on the road from Gertlauken to the north of Wehlau hoping to reach the railroad station in Labiau (Polessk). She described the incredible confusion on the roads, where abandoned wagons with baggage spilling out were pushed into the ditches, animals wandered loose, and desperate people searched for lost relatives.[50] Given such slow progress, the fleeing East Prussians were often overtaken by advance columns of Soviet tanks, and if the wagons did not move to the side of the road quickly enough, they were crushed or pushed into the ditch as the panzers rolled through. Red Army soldiers following the tanks almost always looted the wagon trains and many women were raped.

While the German front was collapsing in the north, in southern East Prussia the Russians were rapidly advancing in the area near Tannenberg, the site of the memorial to General Field Marshal von Hindenburg commemorating his victory over the Russians in World War I. The commander of the military district that encompassed East Prussia (*Befehlshaber des Wehrkreises I*), General Otto Lasch, called the OKH to seek approval for the removal of the caskets containing the remains of Hindenburg and his wife to the safety of the western part of Germany known as the Reich. Hitler responded, "East Prussia will be defended and therefore the Tannenberg Memorial does not have to be removed." ("Ostpreußen wird gehalten und somit braucht auch das Tannenbergdenkmal nicht geräumt zu werden.")[51] However, Hitler had second thoughts and an hour later the order came from his headquarters to carry out Lasch's plan. Lasch assigned the task of transporting the caskets to Hindenburg's son, Lieutenant General Oskar von Hindenburg, who took them to Pillau from whence they were sent west by ship. After the caskets had been removed, the Germans dynamited the memorial on January 22.

Meanwhile, the Soviet divisions of the Third Belorussian Front in the north were moving ever closer to Königsberg, taking Wehlau on January 22, and after heavy fighting, Allenburg, Tapiau, and Labiau on January 24 and 25. By January 25, Soviet units had reached Waldau (Nizovye), some nine miles (fourteen kilometers) north of Königsberg. Here a group of retreating German soldiers was shocked to find that the imminent Soviet takeover had not yet penetrated the pedantic mind of the army quartermaster in charge of a supply depot:

> There we found a mighty store of provisions in a gymnasium, which was stocked with things like coffee, chocolates and spirits—great

treasures which for a long time had existed for us only in rumors. We were infantrymen, and therefore the last troops to arrive before the Russians, and yet the resident quartermaster refused to yield up anything without the appropriate Forms A and E, which had to be signed by an officer.[52]

A more serious example of the failure of the different branches of the German armed forces to coordinate their military supplies was reported by the senior quartermaster of the Third Panzer Army. When the battle began in January, the Army had only a three-day supply of ammunition and fuel, but the fighting was so intense that in one day a single corps would use up three trainloads of ammunition. It was therefore with considerable amazement that by sheer chance units of the Third Panzer Army discovered in the woods in Samland north of Königsberg a huge underground supply depot of invaluable munitions and fuel that belonged to the Navy (*Kriegsmarine*) and the Air Force (Luftwaffe). With the Russians hot on their heels, they did not have time to take these supplies with them on their retreat and destroyed them on the spot in order to keep them out of enemy hands.[53]

Irene Eckert-Möbius provides a particularly vivid description of the civilian flight from Soviet troops advancing on Königsberg in her detailed account of the fate of the nearly one hundred inhabitants of her father Ernst Overkamp's estate, Trömpau, about nineteen miles (thirty kilometers) northeast of Königsberg.[54] Toward the end of January, the front was just a short distance away; in the east the sky was red from burning houses and shells were hitting Trömpau. Some rooms in the manor house had been turned into a field hospital where the wounded were brought in from the front; other rooms were jammed with refugees, many with small children who had fled to the estate for protection from the advancing Soviet forces. These were now so close that when the wife of the estate manager answered the telephone, a Russian was on the other end of the line. While ordinary German soldiers slept in the horse barn, their officers took over some rooms in the manor house. Sanitary conditions broke down because the plumbing was overwhelmed by all the military personnel and refugees who were crowded into every available space on the estate.

By the time it became clear, on January 26, that the Russians were about to enter Trömpau, Ernst Overkamp had made preparations for an orderly evacuation. This evacuation was greatly facilitated by an Army repair unit that had set up a base in Trömpau and was servicing heavy Tiger tanks. Arrangements had been made for many on the estate to leave with this military unit. On the afternoon of January 26, more or less at the last minute, trucks and other vehicles of the repair unit were ready to depart in the yard of the manor house and horse-drawn covered wagons had driven up outside the houses of those villagers who wished to leave by their own means. They waited until it became dark (between 3:00 and 5:00 p.m.), hoping to avoid attacks from Russian airplanes, and then left Trömpau in bitter cold (–4°F, –20°C) and deep snow. January was always very cold in East Prussia, but the winter of 1945 was particularly severe and caused untold hardship for all the refugees on their flight to the west. Altogether, fifty-nine departed from Trömpau in the repair unit's military vehicles, twenty-one in a military bus, and sixteen in horse-drawn wagons. Most were women and children, a few old men, and a number of essential craftsmen who were exempt from military service and had remained on the estate.

Five inhabitants chose to remain in Trömpau: an elderly married couple, Karl and Johanna Wittenberg (both seventy-two); the oldest woman living on the estate, Louisa Schmidtke (eighty-one); and Erna Schmidtke's grandparents (referred to as "Oma" and "Opa" below).[55] Johanna Wittenberg was a pious Seventh Day Adventist who believed that the Russians would not harm her. Unfortunately, this was not the case; she was treated brutally by the Russians when they occupied Trömpau, and died that year. Her husband survived and was expelled to Saxony in 1948. Louisa Schmidkte did not survive the harsh living conditions under the Russians and died in 1945.

As the column of vehicles and wagons was getting underway, some remembered things they thought needed to be done before they departed. Elise Stobbe (thirty-five) was about to board the military bus, but hurried back to the barn to give her cow "Julla" some hay as well as to untie her and make sure the barn door was left open. When a bullet slammed into her neighbor's house, she ran back to the bus as fast as she could. After the bus had reached the outskirts of Trömpau, one of the passengers—Harry Siebert (fourteen)—remembered that all his family's photos had been left behind. He jumped out of the bus and rushed back to his house past endless lines of refugees and soldiers fleeing from the Red Army so close behind them. In his house he made his way through rooms by now crowded with wounded soldiers and went to the closet, where he retrieved the much-cherished carton of family photos. By now it was getting dark, but the glow of burning houses in the distance allowed Harry to find his way back to his bus, which had not gone very far because of the congested roads. Once on board, he was roundly scolded by the soldiers for his dangerous escapade. In the gathering gloom, Harry looked back for the last time and saw wagons with broken axles that had tipped over and had been pushed to the side of the road by their distraught owners. He also saw horses so exhausted they collapsed on the snow-covered street unable to move.

One family—the Schmidkes (father Herman, mother Elisabeth, daughter Erna, her husband, and their six-month-old daughter)—delayed their departure from Trömpau for too long, with fatal consequences. By the evening of January 26, shells were beginning to rain down on the estate. One came so close to the Schmidke's house that it knocked the plaster off the wall and Erna (twenty-one) pleaded, "Let's finally get out of here!" ("*Laßt uns endlich wegfahren!*") Two horses were hitched to the covered wagon and by the time the Schmidkes got going, it was nearly midnight. They did not make much progress that night because, as they too discovered, the roads were jammed with countless military vehicles and refugee wagons all trying to outrun the Russians. Toward daybreak, being shot at from the air, they sought protection in a farmhouse near the road and tied up their horses in the adjacent barn. Later that morning they were about to resume their escape when they were taken by surprise by Russian soldiers who set the barn on fire, killing their two horses. The Russians forced the Schmidkes and other Germans who had delayed their escape to walk to a school building about one thousand feet distant; they came under fire almost immediately and, dropping to their hands and knees, crawled along the snow-covered road as the bullets whizzed by them. The next day (January 28), they returned to the farmhouse and retrieved from their wagon what they could carry with them. Having failed to outrun the Russians, they decided to walk the roughly two miles (four kilometers) back to their house in Trömpau where they found that Oma and Opa, Erna Schmidke's maternal grandparents, had survived the Russian assault on Trömpau.

It was then that the horror truly started. Erna's father and husband were picked up and taken away by the Russians, who provided no explanation of where they would be taken. As German forces had launched a counterattack, Trömpau had to be evacuated and the remaining family members were forced to leave their house with nothing but the clothes on their backs. By the time they came to the next village, Oma was so weak she was losing her eyesight and decided to stay behind. The following night Erna's six-month-old child died of starvation. They placed his tiny body in a carton and buried it in a hole in the ground. Somewhere on their journey, Opa simply disappeared. Erna's mother became very weak from malnutrition and died on March 23, 1945. An old man helped Erna bury her in a shallow grave. She found a few snowdrops and laid them on top of the fresh earth over the grave. Now Erna was all alone— her father, husband, and grandparents were never heard from again. How she survived until her deportation in 1948 is described in Chapter VI.

Those who had departed Trömpau in the military convoy in the late afternoon of January 26 were more fortunate. They had an earlier start and the military had the right of way. If the roads were impassable, the military vehicles could drive across the snow-covered fields. This made it possible for the convoy to keep just ahead of the advancing Russian Army. The military convoy took them all the way to Groß Blumenau (Kwiatuszki Wielke), not far from the Frisches Haff, where the civilians had to leave the vehicles because the soldiers had received orders to fight the Russians, who were hot on their heels.

From Groß Blumenau, the Trömpauers walked to Fischhausen (Primorsk) and reached the port of Pillau (Baltiysk) by the end of January or early February. Harry Siebert, then fourteen, reported bursts of gunfire and shelling from the Russians, who were all around him as he stamped his way through the high snow to Fischhausen. There all the houses were full to overflowing with refugees, but Harry met someone from Trömpau and together they "bribed" some soldiers with their remaining provisions—bacon—to take them in a military bus to Pillau. After much searching, they found a room crowded with refugees. They were allowed to stay and immediately fell asleep.

Pillau had become a place of hope—where refugees looked for a ship to take them on the final stage of their flight to the safety of the West—but in the bitter cold winter of 1945 it had also become a place of misery and death. In the streets parents abandoned baby carriages with babies frozen to death, horses roamed all over the port town unattended by their owners, and all manner of abandoned wagons and household goods littered the sides of the streets. Attacks from the air were an ever-present danger, and the refugees milling around the docks and wandering the streets were sitting ducks for low-flying Russian fighter planes that raked them with machine-gun fire. One of the Trömpauers described such an attack:

> At any rate, this afternoon we experienced a terrifying air attack in the harbor. In no time at all the planes were over us like a swarm of bees. They flew low and shot indiscrimately into the crowd of people. In this area we scattered in all different directions, and I ran into a railway station waiting room…. The station building collapsed over us—I lay at the bottom, all the others on top of me. So nothing happened to me—you might say that I lay under cover…. In the hall where I lay boards and glass splinters had fallen on us. Many were injured by the splinters. This "hell" lasted perhaps 10 minutes. Then it was all over. But my goodness, what damage the attack had inflicted in these few minutes![56]

Pillau was now bursting at the seams with thousands of refugees all clamoring to board the ships sent by the German Navy that were docked at the piers, making the process of embarkation extremely chaotic (see Illustration 7. Refugees Boarding Ship at Pillau). Whoever was on the pier when a ship docked had the best chance of getting on board, especially women, children, and wounded soldiers, who were given preferential treatment. In most cases, ships took the refugees from Pillau to nearby ports in the Bay of Danzig, such as Oxhöft (Oksywie), Gotenhafen (Gydnia), and Hela (Hel). There they boarded another vessel that transported them to western Germany or Denmark. These intermediate stops usually lasted less than a week, but sometimes stretched out much longer. Two families from Trömpau chose not to take a ship to the Danzig area: one went by wagon over the primitive road along the narrow spit—the Frische Nehrung—the other risked the "ice street" on the frozen Frisches Haff. Waltraud Abraham, who was not from Trömpau, described how the refugees were in such a panic to escape the Russians that huge sums were paid for ship tickets and evacuation certificates.[57]

All who escaped from Trömpau were fortunate that two men made special efforts to get them on board ships in Pillau. One was Herr Krause, whose wife and three children had been evacuated to Trömpau from Königsberg and had fled with the others from the Trömpau estate. The other was a local party official ("Ortsgruppenleiter"), Herr Friedrichs, from a town near Trömpau. Harry Siebert describes how Herr Friedrichs enabled him and his family to board a ship:

> Word spread that a ship was coming. It was a freighter named *Deike Rickmers.* At once chaos broke out!!! Pillau was of course filled beyond capacity with refugees. We were ordered to go on board, but armed naval soldiers then took over the embarkation at the gangway and we no longer had any hope of getting on board. Then our group leader, Friedrichs from Schmeidehenen, suddenly appeared and pushed us past the soldiers onto the ship. Lucky for Frau Pläp that she was with us because it was said that women without children could not go on board. Now what? We simply pretended that my brother was her son and she went on board with us.[58]

Sometimes it required sheer willpower to board a ship. Maria Stobbe (age thirty-five) from Trömpau described how she and her family had spent a week in early Febuary 1945 in Gotenhafen trying to find a ship that would take them.[59] Finally, they were successful and were about to board the large former cruise ship, the *Cap Arcona*, when an SA officer attempted to keep her two oldest children off the ship and ordered them to make their way along the frozen Frisches Haff to Danzig (see Illustration 15. *Cap Arcona*). Frau Stobbe pretended she had not heard the officer and commanded her children to board the ship: "Go ahead, go ahead onto the ship—we are all going together onto the ship!!!" ("*Geht vor, geht vor aufs Schiff—wir gehen alle zusammen auf das Schiff!!!*"). Her gambit worked; they also were able to bring on board what was left of their possessions from Trömpau: a baby carriage, their backpacks, and family papers.

A few from Trömpau were thus lucky to be evacuated by ship shortly after arrival in Pillau, while others had to wait three or four days for a ship and a hoped-for safe passage to the west. Elise Stobbe (age thirty-five) and her five children spent only one night in a home for naval officers and the next day—perhaps because of the naval officers' connections—were given passage on a coal freighter to Gotenhafen near Danzig. There she attempted to get on the large former cruise ship, the *Wilhelm Gustloff*, which had been pressed into service to ferry the hordes of refugees to safety, but was unsuccessful because the ship was already filled with refugees and preparing to depart (see Illustration 11. *Wilhelm Gustloff*). No doubt with a certain amount of envy, she watched as Berta Riemann (age forty-two), a friend from Trömpau, and her two daughters, Edith (age fifteen) and Adelheid (age nine), were allowed to board the *Gustloff* at the last minute. As fate would have it, Elise Stobbe was extremely lucky, as was another Trömpauer, Bertha Schwill (age thirty-one), who was at the dock that same day with her four children. She had also tried to board the *Gustloff*, but because she was pregnant and labor pains had just begun, a sailor at the gangway prevented her from boarding. The *Gustloff* with its teeming human cargo finally steamed out of Gotenhaven into the Baltic around midday on January 30, 1945, and was torpedoed shortly after 9:00 p.m. by a Russian submarine. Some nine thousand of the over ten thousand on board did not survive, including the Riemanns from Trömpau. (A detailed description of the last voyage of the *Wilhelm Gustloff* is given in Chapter V.)

Countess Marion Dönhoff, the longtime editor and publisher of the respected German weekly newspaper, *Die Zeit*, has written a vivid account of her escape from East Prussia.[60] Living on an estate in Quittainen seven miles (eleven kilometers) south of Preußisch Holland, she called the local administrative office on January 21 and found out that the district had to be evacuated by midnight that very evening. When she inquired where the Russians were, the man on the other end of the line said, "No idea." Dönhoff then asked how those living in Quittainen should escape, he replied, "That is all the same to us, by land, by sea, in the air...." She noted acidly that up until that point government officials had never tired of emphasizing that they were taking care of everything and there was no need to panic.

With only a few hours to get ready to leave, there was no time to implement the detailed plans that Dönhoff had worked out for the evacuation of the estate. A few days before, an official from the district office had warned her that if she persisted with her "defeatist preparations for the flight," she would suffer severe consequences. Now she barely had time to tell everyone what they needed of the barest essentials to take with them, and she herself quickly packed a few clothes, several photographs, and family papers in a backpack, and stuffed into a saddlebag some toiletries, bandaging material, and her old Spanish crucifix, which had already been wrapped up for the flight. She shared her last meal at the estate with the two secretaries who worked there. (One of them was an enthusiastic follower of Hitler who somehow was able to make her way ahead of the Russians to Gotenhaven where she boarded the *Gustloff* and was among the thousands who perished on January 30.) When they were finished eating, they left the remaining food and the silverware on the table and went out through the main door without locking it.

It was now midnight and those living on the estate had assembled their wagons for the flight west. After Dönhoff had saddled and mounted her horse, the trek departed in the light of a full moon for Preußisch Holland, normally a journey of about one hour. With the streets covered with sheer ice, the horses stumbled and slipped, and because countless other wagon trains jammed the road and every crossing, it took six hours to reach the outskirts of town, at which point all forward progess ceased. She rode ahead to find out the cause of the problem and discovered that all the roads leading into Preußisch Holland were completely jammed, making it impossible to move forward or backward. She went to the Nazi Party headquarters and found it deserted, with files strewn all over the floor and burned paper blown about by gusts of wind coming through the open door. "They naturally are the first to go, the pigs," exclaimed a farmer who had followed Dönhoff into the office. She returned to her trek, where everyone was by now freezing in the –4°F (–20°C) cold and in deep despair. They all agreed that it would be better to deal with the Russians in their own homes, and they had convinced themselves that the Russians would need them to milk the cows and clean out the barns. But if she were caught by the Russians, they were sure she would be shot, so they urged her to make her way west on horseback. She needed little convincing. After perfunctory goodbyes, she mounted her horse and rode westward, passing through Elbing and Marienburg, and arrived in Dirschau on the western side of the Vistula.

She became exasperated with the wretchedness of the masses of people struggling westward and regretted that she had not returned with her people back home. She thought that perhaps she could take a train to Königsberg and from there another eastward to Friedrichstein, where her family had a second estate. She made her way to the train station in Dirschau where thousands of people had gathered in the vain hope of finding a train to the west. But there was nobody behind the counters and no train information. Finally, Dönhoff found a railway official who was amazed that she wished to travel to Königsberg. He looked at her as if she wanted to go to the moon and shook his head: "No, nobody traveled to the east anymore."

After fourteen days of flight, Dönhoff happened upon Otto von Bismarck's magnificent estate in Varzin (Warcino) in the western part of Pomerania. There, the lady of the house was a very old, but still fine-boned woman, Bismarck's daughter-in-law. Despite all entreaties by her staff to leave, she intended to stay and enjoy the last moments of her life at home in the surroundings she enjoyed. Her old retainer served dinner in grand style and poured one bottle of red wine after the other from the best vintages. She entertained Dönhoff with lively stories of how it was in the old days of

Bismarck and the emperor's court, and at no point did she allow the horror of the war and the flight of the refugees going on outside to disturb the refined conversation. As much as she enjoyed the hospitality of the lady of the manor house, after two days Dönhoff decided that it was time to leave. It took her many more weeks to cross Mecklenburg and Lower Saxony until she finally reached the Mettternichs in Vinsebeck in Westphalia. When she arrived it was spring and the birds were singing.

The East Prussians who delayed their departure—such as the Schmidkes from Trömpau—were enveloped in the maelstrom when East Prussia was overrun by Soviet forces. This was also the fate of the Soine family living near the village of Borchersdorf, located about twenty-five miles (forty kilometers) south of Trömpau and roughly twelve miles (twenty kilometers) southeast of Königsberg. Their plight is representative of that of thousands of other East Prussians. The residents of Borchersdorf received the official order to evacuate only on January 26, but on the Soine family farm preparations had been made long in advance for the flight from the advancing Red Army.[61] While others in the village had already fled, Grandfather Soine (age eighty-two) spoke Russian and Grandmother Soine (age seventy-four) spoke Polish, and he assumed that if the Russians came, he would still be able to work the family farm. The family therefore hesitated until the last minute and departed only when the order to evacuate was finally given. At dusk that same evening, the family—the grandparents, mother Hertha, and two young daughters, Christel (age fifteen) and Elli (age eleven)—began their flight on a heavily loaded wagon in bitter cold and through deep snow. Again, the road was so jammed with soldiers, army vehicles, and other refugees in wagons or on foot that forward progress was very difficult. Exploding shells and the thunder of artillery fire made everyone very fearful and anxious, all the more so as several houses along the road had already been hit and were on fire.

Making their way at an agonizingly slow pace across the winter landscape, it was so cold (−4°F or −20°C) that the Soines often walked beside their wagon in order to keep their circulation going. After spending two nights at different farmhouses, they arrived at a large house on an estate teeming with refugees. Late that night, a hand grenade suddenly smashed through a window and exploded, wounding many in the room, including Grandfather Soine, who was hit in the head by a grenade fragment. In the ensuing panic everyone quickly ran into the cellar and closed the door. They had just enough time to bandage Grandfather's grenade wounds when a loud banging on the door announced the arrival of Russian soldiers, who rushed in and herded the terrified Germans upstairs at the point of machine guns, shouting all the time, "*Davai, Davai*" ("Hurry, Hurry").

What followed was a scene repeated countless times when East Prussian civilians were overwhelmed by Red Army soldiers. With cries of "*Uri, Uri*" and "*Frau komm*" ("Watch, watch" and "Woman come"), the conquering soldiers demanded everyone's watches and raped whichever women took their fancy, all accompanied by the insistent refrain of "Davai, davai." Women were raped repeatedly by one soldier after another, and only the very old or very young were unmolested. Husbands who attempted to protect their wives from assault were often shot to death and pregnant women were not spared. In the room next to the Soines were mothers with their children, one a baby. The Soines could hear the desperate screams of the mothers who were being raped and the terrified cries of their children, which did not in the least deter the soldiers from assaulting the women. The Soines' teenage daughter, Christel, would have quickly attracted the soldiers' attention, but she hid under a large table until the soldiers left the house.

In addition to physical assaults, the plundering and looting were so extensive that most refugees lost all their personal possessions. Crowds of soldiers stormed the wagons, threw everything onto the snow-covered ground, and took whatever suited their fancy. Once the looting spree was over, the Soines searched through what was left of their belongings and found some useful and personal items. They were particularly gratified to find a few priceless family photos.

By now Grandfather and Grandmother Soines had become despondent—especially Grandfather with his head wound—and they gave up any further attempt to survive under these terrible conditions. Grandfather informed Hertha of their decision, who told Christel and Elli: "Mother was completely distraught when she broke the sad news to us; we embraced each other tightly and shed bitter tears."[62] Later they searched the animal stalls, barns, and haylofts in vain for the elderly couple. It seems likely that the the elderly Soines had gone off and let themselves be overcome by the cold and certain death.

Hertha and her two daughters then decided to return to their farm near Borchersdorf on the same road they had taken a few days earlier in their failed attempt to flee the Russians. When they finally approached the familiar buildings, the sight confronting them was heart-wrenching: the barns and the stalls had burned to the ground, and the farmhouse, while still standing, had been blasted by artillery fire and was no longer habitable. In front of the house lay a dead soldier and next to the burned-down stalls some of their cows lay dead and bloated in the snow. There was no possibility of resuming their life on their farm, and with a heavy heart the three Soines joined a group of other refugees—mostly women and children—and over the next several weeks were marched under armed Soviet guard from one primitive accommodation to another: typically a barn or stalls, where sometimes fresh straw made a welcome clean bed; once a filthy henhouse; another time a church empty of pews; and once a school building, where they slept on bare classroom floors. Often the only food to eat was a watery soup, and to alleviate their thirst they melted snow or drank water from dirty puddles. In such unhygienic conditions, dysentery soon spread among the refugees. Whatever toilet facilities were available were continually in use; at one place a large milk can served this function. Nocturnal bouts of diarrhea were especially difficult because one had to step carefully but quickly over people sleeping on the floor to get to the privy.

At a large farm near Fuchsberg (Gora Lisa), the three Soines had the great fortune to come upon an old baby carriage. As they had become physically much weaker, it helped immensely that they could stow their few possessions in the carriage, which they pushed and pulled from place to place on their forced marches under the watchful eyes of their Soviet guards.

For fifteen-year-old Christel this march would have been disastrous had it not been for the timely intervention of her younger sister Elli. Their group of refugees was standing in formation in a large yard and those capable of performing physical labor—mainly younger women—were selected and stood apart from the others. A Russian soldier brutally seized Christel and dragged her to this group, which then started to march away. Seeing what was happening, Elli ran to Christel and clung tightly to her, all the while ranting and raving. The fear of losing her older sister had given Elli unsuspected strength, and by behaving like a wild animal, she saved her sister from being shipped to a forced labor camp in the Soviet Union. On numerous occasions Soviet soldiers took pity on their captives (especially where children were concerned), and luckily the Russian guard marched away with the selected group of women, leaving Christel with Elli. (Christel later learned that these women, like many others in East Prussia, were taken to work camps in Siberia where many died under the extremely harsh living and working conditions.)

From the end of March to early May, the three Soines continued to march eastward with other refugees under Soviet armed guard and had reached Schloßberg, in the easternmost part of East Prussia, when the war came to an end. Their major preoccupation all this time was finding food to assuage their ever-present hunger. They constantly scoured the fields and gardens for anything edible, such as turnips, potatoes, chives, parsley, or sorrel leaves. When they came across a cow, they immediately milked it, but typically other refugees on the road had already extracted what little milk was left in the udder. "When absolutely necessary, the devil devours flies" ("*In der Not frißt der Teufel Fliegen*") is a German saying; when Christel became very sick in late April, to provide desperately needed nourishment, her mother joined other women in cutting strips of meat from dead horses in the fields, which had frozen in the winter but by April had thawed out. These pieces of horsemeat were cooked for hours, but to Christel they still smelled awful and tasted worse, and though terribly hungry, she could not get herself to take a bite. Finally, with the greatest difficulty ("*mit Hängen und Würgen*") she was only just able to force herself to eat a piece of bread smeared with cold horse fat.

The all-consuming challenge was to avoid assaults by Russian soldiers and hiding from them was a constant preoccupation. Once, when they were spending the night in a barn and had barricaded the doors to prevent nocturnal intrusions, Red Army soldiers nevertheless found a way in through a hatch in the hayloft and raped many of the women, one of whom was assaulted more than twenty times. Christel's mother covered her with her body and saved her from being raped. On one occasion, Christel hid in a large wardrobe that had been turned over and covered with straw, and on another, at a farmstead, she concealed herself behind the branches of a large arborvitae tree in the yard. Ultimately, her luck ran out, as it did for so many German women (see Chapter VI).

Like Christel, other young women were able to steer clear of marauding Soviet soldiers for many months. In her diary, written from October 1944 through January 1946, Emma Kirstein describes how her daughter and two other young women were hidden whenever enemy soldiers were sighted.[63] By the time the Russians had overtaken them on January 30, 1945, on their flight from Goldap in eastern East Prussia, they had found refuge on a farm outside a small town near Rastenburg (Ketrzyn). They were visited at the farmhouse nearly every day by soldiers who demanded food, stole nearly everything they could lay their hands on, and always searched high and low in all the buildings for women. The three young women escaped detection because they hid in the cramped quarters under the roof over a porch, which could only be reached by a hatch in a room inside the house. From early morning to late evening someone stood watch at a window on each side of the house to look out for approaching soldiers. Whenever the alarm was given, the three girls would quickly and quietly rush to their hiding place over the porch, and in freezing temperatures often had to spend the whole day and sometimes the night in this confining space. Emma Kirstein described her extreme anxiety and nervousness when Russian soldiers spent the night at the farmhouse:

> It is Saturday, the 24th of February. Twelve horses were brought to be shod and then it was said that the Russians would spend the night here. My heart stopped with fright. What are the three doing. Hidden the whole day and then even at night. Oh God, it is terrible, every day something new and increasingly excruciating.[64]

Thanks to the effective warning system and their inconspicuous hiding place, the three young women were never discovered.

The Situation in Königsberg[65]

In late January 1945, Königsberg was under siege by the Red Army. It had become packed with thousands of refugees who were terrified at being caught by the Soviet onslaught and had streamed in from the northern and eastern parts of East Prussia. The hospitals were overflowing with wounded soldiers as well as sick or injured civilians.

When he arrived in Königsberg after escaping from Insterburg, Dr. Lehndorff went to work as a surgeon at the Südpark Restaurant Ponarth, which was used to house patients brought in from hospitals in the east. The woman physician, "Doctora," who had driven with him from the hospital in Insterberg, visited him there. One afternoon they went to the Königsberg suburb of Juditten to see how Doctora's parents were surviving the siege. They found them grappling with the question of whether they should try to escape from Königsberg or take their own lives. If they attempted to flee the city, they risked being separated from each other after thirty years of a happy life together, a prospect they could not bear. Others in Königsberg were facing this same question. Dr. Lehndorff reported hearing people talking matter-of-factly about the dose of cyanide needed to kill oneself. The poison apparently was readily available in the city. When Lehndorff and Doctora left later that afternoon, they had the feeling that they had been unsuccessful in convincing her parents not to take their own lives. Concerned about her parents, they returned to Juditten that same night and found the couple dead in their beds, where they had been carefully laid out by their elder daughter, who had already left the house. The window had been opened and the bedroom was frigid. After a moment of silence, they recited the Lord's Prayer and departed.[66] The couple was buried a few days later.

When ordered by the civilian or military authorities to leave the besieged city, some residents were only too glad to comply, whereas others chose to remain and face an uncertain future at the hands of the Russians.[67] Several professors on the medical faculty at the Albertina University were among those instructed to leave the city. Dr. Lehndorff described how upset he was with this order and the enthusiasm with which the professors obeyed, while thousands of wounded and dying in the city needed urgent medical attention. Some of these patients had been abandoned in a large hospital that no longer had a medical supervisor. When offered the position as doctor in charge of this hospital, Dr. Lehndorff accepted without hesitation and immediately took up his new duties. The following day, January 27, the chief of the Army Nurses Corps phoned the hospital with instructions that all female staff members were to be discharged immediately and were to leave the city that very night. The nurses conferred briefly and then asked Lehndorff for permission to disobey this order because they wished to stay with the wounded; he readily assented. Even though the other support staff (orderlies, cleaners, kitchen help, etc.) had been warned what their fate would be if they should fall into the hands of the Russians, they too chose to stay. At the same time, Dr. Hetzar, who had been the doctor in charge, returned because the seat in the car that was to have been his means of escape from Königsberg had been assigned to someone else. Completely depressed by this quirk of fate, he talked incessantly about his imminent demise. This indeed came just a few days later, when he was the only person killed in an air raid that severely damaged parts of the hospital.

Gauleiter Koch and his associates had done nothing to mitigate the desperate condition of the teeming masses of refugees jammed into Königsberg, and in this highly uncertain and precarious situation, wild rumors began to spread among the local population and the refugees about what would happen next. With Soviet forces fast closing in on the ring of twelve nineteenth-century forts just outside the city center, Königsberg's fate seemed sealed. Yet at this very moment, Nazi Party officials authorized an escape attempt and used loudspeakers to order all civilians to evacuate and move to Pillau. However, they failed to provide any plan or direction for such a large exodus and a wild flight immediatedly ensued in the direction of Pillau as countless cars, trucks, people on foot, all kinds of wagons, and mothers pushing baby carriages tried to make their way out of Königsberg. The inevitable result was an immense traffic jam, which stopped all movement along the escape route. Only the intervention of Landrat (head of county administration) Klaus von der Gröben brought a degree of order and enabled some of the escaping throng to reach Fischhausen (Primorsk) on the Frisches Haff and then make their way over the ice to Pillau. But because Soviet troops to the west of the city had already reached the Haff and cut off the overland escape route to Pillau, many others were forced to return to Königsberg. In this confusion, Gauleiter Koch appointed district leader (*Kreisleiter*) Wagner as the Nazi Party official in charge of Königsberg and promptly made his own getaway with his entourage on January 28 to Neutief, across the channel from Pillau.

Before leaving, Gauleiter Koch apparently recommended the death sentence for the chief justice of the Court of Appeals (*Oberlandesgerichtspresident*), Max Dräger, and Chief Prosecutor (*Oberstaatsanwalt*) Fritz Szelinski, who, as described in Chapter II, had prepared the judicial reports for Berlin and had attempted to ascertain the fate of the handicapped East Prussians early in the war. As Ralf Meindl reported in his biography of Koch, on January 25, 1945, Dräger and Szelinski traveled to Swinemünde in what they alledged was an effort to make preparations for the evacuation of judicial staff from Königsberg.[68] Koch had given the order that these officials were to remain in the city and hence regarded their behavior as desertion. He informed both Heinrich Himmler, Reichsführer of the SS, and Reichsjustizminister Otto Thierack of the escape attempt, which led to their being sentenced to death for demoralization of the troops (*Wehrkraftzersetzung*). Dräger was executed on April 20, 1945; Szelinski commited suicide in prison.[69]

With Königsberg facing imminent occupation by the Russians, the Nazi Party authorities ordered the evacuation of the nearby town of Metgethen (Lesnoye), located on the western side of the city, on January 29, 1945. That afternoon, the train waiting at the Metgethen station rapidly filled with people seeking to escape, but it did not depart until the early morning hours of January 30. The delay had dire consequences because the Russians had advanced so rapidly that the train was stopped not far from Metgethen by a Soviet tank, which had taken up a position on the tracks. The passengers were driven outside and robbed, several were killed, and many women were raped.

There was still hope that some of the thousands of wounded could be transported out of Königsberg by rail to Pillau. On the very cold and clear night of January 29–30, Dr. Lehndorff observed a long train on the last track of the freight station being loaded two to a berth with wounded soldiers from hospitals all over Königsberg, including some from his hospital. He was doubtful that the train would make it through the enemy lines, as the red sky surrounding the city seemed to indicate that it was completely encircled. On passing the station the following afternoon on his way to his room in Ponarth, he saw that the train was still there. It turned out that the train had departed before daybreak, but unable to get through the enemy lines encircling the city, it had returned. It would make another attempt that night. When he reached Ponarth, Dr. Lehndorf discovered that the house where he was staying had been hit by enemy shells. An elderly couple on the third floor had been killed, but his room had suffered no damage from the shelling. In the evening, he passed the station again on his way back to the hospital and was very relieved that the train with the wounded was gone. He learned later that despite repeated attempts, the hospital train had been unable to get through the Soviet forces surrounding the city and had had to return to the freight station. It was still there two weeks later and Dr. Lehndorff noted in his memoirs the horrors the wounded stranded on that train must have endured without proper medical attention. The survivors of this ordeal were ultimately transferred back to various hospitals in the city.

The German forces defending Königsberg were by now stretched so thin that a concerted effort by the Third Belorussian Front of the Red Army could easily have conquered the city within days. In the evening of January 28, Soviet tanks and infantry were advancing toward Königsberg along the road from Cranz (Zelenogradsk) and were not far from the nineteenth-century Fort Quednau, on the outskirts of the city. That morning, General Lasch had been named commander for the defense of Königsberg (*Befehlshaber der Befestigungen bei Königsberg und der Festung Königsberg*), and when he later wrote a book about the battle of Königsberg, he included a report by Major Schaper about that fateful day.[70] Major Schaper's Grenadier Regiment 974 was rushed by train from Rastenburg, in the south, to Rothenstein, a northern suburb of Königsberg. The road north from the city was so jammed with refugee wagon trains that Major Schaper abandoned his car and with his troops walked along the road to the outer defenses of the city. In the early evening of January 28, he found the situation there so precarious that he asked his division headquarters for a detachment of assault weapons and was told they would arrive sometime that night. When the expected Russian attack came late that evening, the enemy tanks and masses of soldiers were only 650 feet (nearly two hundred meters) away. Major Schaper wrote that the crisis both for his troops and for Königsberg had reached its peak and if no help came now, their position would be untenable:

> At this juncture, like a gift from heaven, the assault guns arrived on the scene and rolled forward on the road to Cranz. Russian tanks were driving to meet them, but in the light of the illuminating shells the Germans were able to recognize them in good time. With considerable skill our five or six assault guns took up position behind a swell in the ground, and they shot up between six and eight tanks in short order, including some Stalins. The whole landscape was as bright as day with the light from the exploding and burning tanks.[71]

Thanks to Major Schaper, his troops, and the timely arrival of the assault weapons, the Soviet attack on Königsberg was repulsed that evening. The city had received a reprieve. It would be a little over two months before Soviet forces would begin their final attack on the capital of East Prussia.

———————

Since late October 1944, Memel (Kleipeda) had been surrounded by the Red Army and had become an indefensible enclave. As the remaining German troops in the city were urgently needed to defend East Prussia from the onslaught unleashed in mid-January by Soviet forces, Hitler gave the evacuation order on January 22, 1945. Eight ferries operated continuously for three nights to transport these troops the short distance from Memel to Sandkrug, on the northern tip of the Kurische Nehrung. On January 28, at 4:00 a.m., the last German soldiers were evacuated from Memel and that same night the German ships and ferries used in the evacuation operation reached the safety of Pillau. These vessels were put to immediate use in evacuating the thousands of refugees who had fled to Pillau ahead of the advancing Soviet troops. The rail link from Königsberg to the west via Elbing (Elblag) and Marienburg (Malbork) had been cut on January 23, and the land connection between East Prussia and the rest of Germany had been severed when Soviet forces advancing rapidly to the south of Königsberg reached the Frisches Haff on January 24. Consequently, the sea route from Pillau had become the only means of escape for the East Prussians.

In the face of fierce resistance by the German Third Panzer Army, the Third Belorussian Front in northern East Prussia advanced fairly slowly westward between the Memel and Pregel rivers. By contrast, the advance of the Second Belorussian Front against the German Second Army across the southern part of the province below the Masurian Lakes proceeded much more rapidly since the Soviet invasion began in mid-January. This swift attack was part of a pincer movement designed to surround the Fourth German Army in central East Prussia and to cut off the province from the Reich. Despite the crumbling of German defenses in East Prussia, Hitler nevertheless gave the fateful order in the early hours of January 15 to transfer battle-ready reserve forces from East Prussia to Poland. In his memoirs, General Guderian wrote:

> On January 15th Hitler interfered for the first time in the defen-
> sive battle, by issuing an order, despite my protests, for the transfer
> of the Gross-Deutschland Corps from East Prussia to Kielce [in
> Poland] where it was to block the break-through that the Russians
> were threatening to make towards Posen. It was obvious that this
> move could not have been made in time to stop the Russians
> and would have involved a weakening of East Prussia at the very
> moment when the enemy's attack there was about to become
> highly dangerous. If the corps was taken away the same disastrous
> situation must develop in East Prussia that already existed along
> the Vistula. So this powerful striking force...led by the trusted

General von Saucken sat in railway sidings while its destination was the subject of argument. My refusal to carry out this order infuriated Hitler. He would not rescind it....[72]

As General Guderian had predicted, the whole front began to break down like a house of cards in the face of the overwhelming superiority of the Soviet forces. Quickly taking advantage of a wide gap in the German defenses, the Russians captured Neidenburg (Nidzika), near the border with Poland, on January 20, and Osterode (Ostróda) on the following day. The assault took place with such astonishing speed that civilian and military authorities were often taken completely by surprise. For example, at 3:00 a.m. on January 22, units of the Soviet III Guards Cavalry Corps entered Allenstein undetected and attacked the Germans, who were unloading tanks and artillery pieces from railroad cars. On January 23, Soviet tanks had raced as far as Elbing, while the Oberbürgermeister was still assuring the population that the front had stabilized. The Soviet tanks had inserted themselves into the huge stream of refugees and German troops coming in from Preußisch Holland (Pastęk), in the southeast, and because the Soviet tank crews had disguised themselves in German field-gray uniforms, they were mistaken for German defenders and entered Elbing undetected. For a time the Soviet tanks rolled along the main street together with street cars and shoppers, but when they commenced firing at buildings they revealed their true identity and quickly became the target of young German recruits in the local garrison, who used *Panzerfausts* (handheld antitank rocket launchers) to knock out four of the Soviet tanks. Despite the overwhelming Soviet advantage in troops, guns, and planes, Elbing was fiercely contested for three weeks and was not taken by the Soviets until February 10.

A medical student, Josefina Schleiter, on her escape from Osterode, was overtaken by Russians outside of Preußisch Holland.[73] A Russian tank crashed into the wagons of the group of refugees she had joined and pushed them into a ditch, where horses were soon dying and injured women and children screamed for help (see Illustration 8. Abandoned Wagons on Trek). A Russian officer on horseback ordered captured German soldiers to be brought forward and to stand at attention in front of him. He then took out his revolver and shot them in the head. Schleiter described how they lay dead on the ground with a look of horror on their faces. Shocked and frightened by the brutal murder they had just witnessed, the refugees did not dare go over and cover the dead. As it was getting dark, Schleiter and others in her group found a nearby farmhouse for shelter during the night. Later, when she was cooking potatoes, drunken young Russian officers came into the room but did not threaten the women. One of the officers spoke some German and warned the group, "Your lives are in danger. Run away at once." They knew immediately he was referring to rape and they quickly put on their coats and rushed to their wagons in the farmyard, only to find that they had been plundered— their clothes, food supplies, and trunks were gone; only pieces of torn linen lay scattered on the ground.

They were not assaulted that evening when they returned to the farm-house, but their good fortune did not last. As there was no longer any hope of escaping the Russians, Schleiter and others in her group decided to return to Osterode. On the way they spent a night in a large cow barn:

> Terrible hours followed, particularly for the women. From time to time soldiers came in, also officers, and fetched girls and young women. No shrieking, no begging, nothing helped. With revolvers in their hands they gripped the women round their wrists and dragged them away. A father who wanted to protect his daughter was brought out into the yard and shot. The girl was all the more prey of these wild creatures. Towards morning she came back, terror in her child-like eyes, she had become years older during the night. She sank down into the straw, because her body was no longer capable of giving expression to her feelings. We were all overcome with sadness and desperation. We waited. No more soldiers came, thank God.[74]

Josefina Schleiter had escaped rape that night, but ultimately her luck ran out (see Chapter IV).

The Encirclement of the Fourth German Army

As the German Third Panzer Army, in the north, and the Second Army, in the south, were being pushed back to the Baltic, the Fourth Army, in the middle, became dangerously exposed in a salient stretching far to the eastern border of East Prussia. General Georg-Hans Reinhardt, commander of Army Group Center (renamed Army Group North on January 25) soon realized that the entire Fourth Army risked being enveloped from the north by the Third Belorussian Front and by the Second Belorussian Front from the south. He therefore urged Hitler to allow him to withdraw the Fourth Army in order to establish a shorter and more defensible battle line. When Reinhardt was told by Guderian (the commander of the OKH) early in the morning of January 21, that Hitler continued to object to a pullback by the Fourth Army, General Reinhardt replied: "But that's quite impossible. It means that everything is going to collapse."[75] It was only after a long telephone conversation later that day between Reinhardt and Hitler that the latter finally agreed to a modest withdrawal of the Fourth Army. The commander of the Fourth Army, General Friedrich Hossbach, was then able to engineer a breakout of his troops from their exposed position and push west of the Masurian Lakes to establish a better defensive position.

It was during this withdrawal, on January 24, that the heavily built-up fortress of Lötzen (Gizycko), near the Masurian Lakes, was abandoned to the Soviets after only limited resistance. General Guderian described how this news hit like a bombshell in Hitler's headquarters, which had assumed that Lötzen would be defended because it was the best-armed and best-manned fortress in Germany. Hitler became enraged and his distrust of his generals increased.[76]

Realizing the ever-growing danger to Königsberg resulting from the collapse of the German Third Panzer Army in northern East Prussia, General Reinhardt proposed to the OKH on January 26 that the front line of the Fourth Army be withdrawn to the Alle River, south of Königsberg. He repeated his proposal in a phone call to Hitler. After a long debate with the general, Hitler said that his decision would be forthcoming by 5:00 p.m. that evening. No word had come by 7:00 p.m. and attempts to get in touch with Hitler were unsuccessful. General Reinhardt then informed the OKH that the withdrawal would be implemented as he had proposed. Two hours later a message came to the headquarters of Army Group North that Reinhardt was relieved of his command because of his decision to withdraw without Hitler's approval.[77]

The commander of the Fourth Army, General Hossbach, also stood up to Hitler and implemented his own breakout plan for the army, knowing full well that it could cost him his job and possibly his life. He aimed to break through the thinly stretched Soviet units to the west and link up with the Second Army at Elbing. While this attack westward caught the Russians by surprise, after three days of heavy fighting the German attempt to break out of the Soviet encirclement was thwarted and the gap between the Second and Fourth Armies could not be closed. Thus, the very outcome feared by generals Hossbach and Reinhardt—the entrapment of East Prussia—had come to pass. For his efforts to prevent this outcome, General Hossbach was dismissed. His case was not helped by a telegram sent to Hitler by Gauleiter Koch from his refuge in Neutief on the Frisches Haff: "The Fourth Army is fleeing in the direction of the Reich. In its cowardly way it seeks to break through to the west. I shall continue to defend East Prussia with the Volkssturm."[78] True to form, Koch was grandstanding and did nothing of the sort.

The Fourth Army was now isolated in the coastal region of central East Prussia, with its back to the Frisches Haff and connected to Königsberg by only a narrow strip of land along the Haff. This bridgehead was called the "*Heiligenbeil Kessel*" (the "Cauldron of Heiligenbeil") after a town near the Haff, and consisted of a roughly square-shaped area about thirty miles (fifty kilometers) on each side (see Map 6. The Heiligenbeil Cauldron). The army's objective was to maintain the connection to Königsberg and the bridgehead to enable as many refugees as possible to escape. Most went over the ice on the Haff to the narrow spit of land, the Frische Nehrung, and from there they could either make their way southwest along the spit to Danzig or be evacuated by ship from the naval harbor of Pillau at the spit's northern end. Because the overland escape route was overcrowded with refugees, and thus subject to long delays, and the sea route was prone to attack from Soviet aircraft and submarines, some refugees chose to flee along the frozen Haff itself to reach Danzig (see Map 7. Towns on the Bay of Danzig). To facilitate this escape route, members of the German youth group, the Pioneers, marked out a "Haffstraße" on the ice, which at some points was only a short distance from the shore and therefore subject to Russian artillery fire.

To assist the movement of thousands of refugees from the Heiligenbeil Cauldron to the Nehrung, the army marked out passages over the ice from Rosenberg and other villages on the shore of the Frisches Haff to points on the Nehrung. Ramps were built from the land to the ice and the route was indicated by poles and by lamps at night to guide the way. These "iceways" were constantly monitored and detours set up around holes in the ice caused by Soviet bombing attacks from the air and artillery fire from the coast. Toward the end of January, the flight over the Haff along the iceways was briefly interrupted when an icebreaker made a passage about one hundred feet (thirty meters) wide through the ice so that three nearly completed torpedo boats would not fall into the hands of the Russians, who were advancing toward the shipyard near Elbing where these ships had been constructed. As soon as these ships had passed through the narrow waterway, Pioneers built bridges over the gap using the tallest trees they could cut down in the nearby forests, and the stream of refugees continued to flow to the Nehrung.[79]

Thousands were thus able to escape over the iceways across the Haff, but when they reached the Nehrung they faced long delays in moving westward to Danzig (see Illustration 9. Trek Crossing the Frisches Haff). With this escape route temporarily blocked, soldiers in the Army Group North directed hundreds of wagons eastward to Pillau and used dozens of trucks to transport to Pillau the crowds that gathered in the open near the small village of Narmeln. To speed up the westward movement of refugees along the Nehrung, a corduroy road of logs laid side by side was built in a very short time by large numbers of Pioneers and personnel from the Organization Todt, a military construction group named after its founder, Fritz Todt. Due to the heavy traffic of countless wagons, this crude road had to be constantly repaired and damaged logs replaced. The few who managed to escape by automobile found it easier to drive along the firm sand of the beach on the Baltic side of the Nehrung.[80]

Hundreds died along this escape route westward along the Nehrung from wounds inflicted by strafing Soviet fighters, from exhaustion, and from starvation. One refugee (identified only as a high-school student from Lyck) described what she saw as follows:

> On the way we witnessed shocking scenes. Demented mothers threw their children into the sea, people hanged themselves; others fell upon dead horses, cut flesh out of them and fried pieces over open fires; women gave birth to children in carts. Everyone thought only of himself; no one was able to help the sick and the weak.[81]

Another refugee, Else-Marie Schlewski, had escaped from Allenstein in late January with her elderly mother and they were only able to pack a few belongings on a toboggan.[82] When they finally reached Leisunen, one of the designated crossing points across the Haff, long columns of wagons waited endlessly until allowed to proceed across the well-marked "ice street." The long delay was caused by the need to keep a distance of one hundred feet (thirty meters) between the wagons in order not to put too much weight on the ice at any one spot. Halfway across the Haff, Schlewski's group was fired on by enemy planes, and while they were unhurt, a woman right next to her was killed (see Illustration 10. Treks on the Ice—Photo by Soviet Plane). Once they reached the sheltering woods of the Nehrung, they encountered further delays when wagons broke down and had to be moved to the side of the primitive road. All the while, German troops moved in the opposite direction eastward toward the front, and one of them cursed the refugees as he went by: "We will lose the war yet because of you" ("*Wir werden wegen Euch noch den Krieg verlieren.*") Schlewski did not know whether to laugh or be amazed.[83]

The constant stress and privations on the flight from Allenstein took their toll on Schlewski's mother. She grew weaker every day until she confessed that she could go no further. Else-Marie went looking for a place to stay for the night and finally at a farm came upon an empty pigsty with fresh straw. She lay bedding on it for her mother to sleep on. The farmer and his wife generously gave Schlewski freshly boiled potatoes to share with her mother for supper. The next morning, she found a wagon jam-packed with refugees who were willing to take her sick mother on board, but there was not enough room to shelter her from the pouring rain. That night, they found a room in a house that was also crowded with refugees, and the only remaining place was a bench, where they slept sitting up. In the early morning, when Else-Marie was returning with her mother to the wagon, something caused her to turn around and she heard her mother say, "That's it" ("*Das ist das Letzte*"), whereupon she collapsed and died. Two nearby German Army officers found boards and nails to fashion an improvised casket, and some young people dug a grave near the road, which Else-Marie marked with a wooden cross. She eventually reached Danzig, and on March 18 boarded an empty coal ship that was jammed with two thousand other refugees and arrived safely in Copenhagen on March 22, 1945.

Many who fled from the Trakehner stud farm had sought refuge at a horse farm in Braunsberg (Braniewo) near the Frisches Haff. In late January 1945, they heard the depressing news that the Red Army had captured Elbing and cut off East Prussia from the rest of Germany. Most then decided to risk crossing the frozen Frisches Haff and make their way along the Frische Nehrung to the west. Martin Heling and his wife Annie left Braunsberg in an open wagon pulled by a team of two black Trakehner stallions.[84] At the crossing point to the Haff, at Alt-Passage, they drove onto the ice in a driving snowstorm with the temperature at –4°F (–20°C). Visibility was only a few meters, which had one advantage: they would not be attacked by Soviet planes. When they crossed the makeshift bridge, constructed of long spruce logs, over the channel in the ice, they had difficulty controlling the trembling stallions, who were unsure of their footing on the swaying bridge. The Helings were shocked at the sight of desperate refugees dragging themselves across the ice, many with small children. Although their wagon was filled with hay and water cans for the horses, they managed to make room for a young mother who was pulling her child on a toy sled.

When they reached the spit—the Frische Nehrung—the Helings found that their nightmare was by no means over. The narrow road over the dunes was clogged with hundreds of refugees on foot and in horse-drawn wagons, which were constantly pushed into the snowdrifts beside the road by army vehicles and endless columns of prisoners. After twelve hours of painfully slow progress, they finally arrived at the village of Stutthof at the western end of the spit, roughly twenty-five miles (forty kilometers) east of Danzig. Here their wagon became stuck in a snowdrift and the exhausted stallions, up to their bellies in snow, were unable to pull it farther. Luckily, a wagon train with refugees from the stud farm in Braunsberg emerged out of the snowstorm and with their help Martin Heling extricated the wagon and dragged it to a nearby guest house, where they spent the night. Heling stayed up all night in a frigid barn with his pistol drawn to guard his two Trakehner stallions from marauding German soldiers.

The following morning, Heling set out in the still-raging snowstorm to find other quarters for his Braunsberg group. By chance, he happened to meet an acquaintance, a company commander in the SS, who told Heling that he was under orders to evacuate the inmates of a nearby concentration camp located in Stutthof (Sztutowo) (see Map 7. Towns on the Bay of Danzig).[85] This surprised Heling, who like many East Prussians claimed to have no idea that a concentration camp had been set up in the region. Others making their escape on the Nehrung—grateful to find refuge in the camp buildings—never mentioned that they were aware that it was, in fact, a concentration camp.[86]

By contrast, in his memoir *Peeling the Onion*, the writer Günter Grass wrote that in the early 1940s he and his classmates in Danzig had heard about the camp at Stutthof.[87] When people disappeared from Danzig, it was assumed that they had been incarcerated there: "But when our Latin teacher … was suddenly no longer there to test us on our vocabulary, when he suddenly disappeared, I again asked no questions even though the moment he was gone the word 'Stutthof' was on everyone's lips by way of warning."[88] If school children in Danzig were aware, however dimly, of what was going on in Stutthof, one wonders whether most East Prussians could have been completely ignorant of the concentration camp there.

While in Stutthof, Martin Heling was able to trade his wagon for a sled, and when the snowstorm finally let up on February 1, he and his wife made their way over the Vistula to Danzig. After many narrow escapes—several times they managed to take the last train ahead of the fast-approaching Red Army—by early April they ended up in Celle, not far from Hanover, in what later became the British Occupation Zone.

While thousands of refugees made their way over the frozen Haff and escaped by ship from Danzig or Pillau, many others delayed their flight until it was too late. This is what happened to the Wermter family, which was living on a farm some forty-five miles (seventy kilometers) southwest of Königsberg in the village of Heinrikau (Henrykowo), roughly four miles (seven kilometers) north of the town of Wormditt (Orneta).[89] This family's lengthy unpublished documentation of their flight provides a vivid account of their failed attempt to escape and how they endured Russian rule. This eyewitness report is therefore drawn on extensively to illustrate another struggle to survive in East Prussia in the waning days of World War II.

On February 1, 1945, young Otto Wermter's uncle, who was in the army and stationed in East Prussia, visited the family and warned that they should flee at once to escape the Russians, who were fast closing in. They spent four days thoroughly preparing three wagons for the journey, loading them with warm clothing, bedding, food, and hay and oats for the horses. When they were finally ready to leave, it was bitter cold (–22°F, –30°C) and the snow was over three feet (one meter) deep. By then, Soviet forces had advanced almost to Wormditt and their artillery shells were exploding nearby, some hitting farmhouses, which then burned brightly and lit up the sky. On the first wagon were the father, Otto Wermter (age fifty-one), the mother Erna (age thirty-seven), Helene (age ten), Steffan (age eight), Brigitte (age six), and Joachim (age four); on the second, Erhard (age twelve) and *Haustochter* (live-in maid) Ursel (age twenty); and on the third, Otto (age fourteen) and Aunt Theresel Wasserzier (age twenty-four).

After an all-day and all-night journey of only fifteen miles (twenty-five kilometers) at an agonizingly slow pace along roads jammed with streams of refugees, wagons, and military vehicles, they passed burning Mehlsack (Pieniezno), then under Russian attack, and arrived in Lilienthal on the evening of February 6 at the farmhouse of their uncle, Clemens Bludau. It was already filled to capacity with family members and other refugees. That same evening Aunt Theresel continued her flight in the company of some soldiers from the farmhouse and eventually escaped by ship to the island of Rügen on the north coast of Germany. The rest of the family, however, procrastinated because the three oldest men in the family could not agree on when to continue their flight. The decision to leave was finally made for them on February 12 when the army gave the order to evacuate and a much-enlarged family group of twenty-six in eight wagons again joined endless columns of other refugees trying to make their escape over snow-covered roads. On February 14, they reached Leisunen on the Haff. (Along the way Grandfather Bludau, who was about seventy-five years old, somehow disappeared without a trace and nothing was ever heard of him again.)

At 8:00 the following morning the family started out on its journey over the frozen Haff to its western end, rather than directly across it to the Frische Nehrung, the route preferred by most other refugees who wanted to spend the least amount of time on the treacherous and exposed ice. (Although not mentioned in the Wermter family documentation, presumably they took this more direct route to Danzig to avoid the long delays along the Nehrung.) This "ice street" was marked along the sides by small Christmas trees and tree branches stuck into holes made in the ice. Their wagons had to maintain a minimum distance of over sixty-five feet (twenty meters) to avoid putting too much weight on the ice in any one spot. At the crude wooden bridge over the gap in the ice made by an icebreaker, soldiers ordered them to throw all superfluous heavy objects out of their wagons because the bridge could only support a maximum weight of 2,750 pounds (1,250 kilograms). Nearly all the wagons had excess baggage and a huge pile of discarded household items was building up on the ice nearby. Unfortunately for the Wermters and their relatives, it was a clear, sunny day, and soon Russian fighter planes strafed the column of wagons and killed two of the women in their group (see Illustration 10. Treks on the Ice—Photo by Soviet Plane). They were buried in a cemetery in Neukrug (Nowa Karczma) on the Frische Nehrung the following day when the Wermters temporarily left the frozen Haff.

The Wermter family group then resumed its journey and spent an excruciating night on the frozen Haff hearing anguished calls for help as wagons and horses broke through the ice when they stopped too long in one place or when they were bunched up together in the darkness and put too much weight on one spot. A depression would form in the ice where water collected and rose up the wagon wheels and the ankles of the horses, until finally the entire wagon and the horses in their traces crashed through. People had to jump quickly from the sinking wagon to escape a cold, watery grave, and it would have been too dangerous to respond to calls of distress from others. It had become a matter of sheer survival; if they did not look out for themselves and keep their wagons moving over the ice, the Wermters might have met the same horrible fate as so many who went under the ice.

The next day began with sunny weather and in the distance the Wermters could see the town of Frauenburg (Frombork) burning on the shore of the Haff. In the afternoon it began to snow again, which protected their column of wagons from air attack but not from the artillery fire of Soviet guns on the shore. They first heard a crack when a gun fired, then nothing, then a whistling sound as the shell came nearer, and finally the sound of the shell exploding under the ice. The shelling made relatively small holes of about six feet (two meters) in diameter, which the wagons had to circumvent, but only a direct hit caused casualties. The Wermter family escaped injury that day, but along the ice street they passed the bodies of less fortunate refugees as well as horses killed by enemy bombs or shells and wagons split apart by explosions, which scattered all kinds of personal effects across the ice. There was a great sigh of relief when toward 5:00 p.m. on February 17 they finally reached a wooden bridge that took them over the thin ice at the shore to the relative safety of Bodenwinkel (Kąty Rybackie) near Stutthof, at the western end of the Frisches Haff.

After leaving the frozen Haff, for the next three weeks the Wermters made their way toward Pomerania in the west, always hoping to stay ahead of the advancing Red Army. They spent one night in a warm house from which the owners had fled only hours earlier. On the way westward they passed through what had been the Polish Corridor, where there were still a large number of Polish farmers. In East Prussia it had been fairly easy to find feed for the horses in the barns of deserted farms, but this area was much poorer and the task of foraging (*organisieren*) fell to the two boys, Otto and Erhard. They stole feed from the silos of Polish farmers and ran as fast as they could if caught in the act. Shortly after reaching Pomerania, the Wermters became discouraged when they heard that the Red Army had already reached the Baltic, thereby cutting off their escape route. Their delay of six days in Lilienthal in East Prussia had cost them dearly.

A week later (March 9), three Russian riders galloped into the yard of the farm where the family was staying, shot into the air and yelled "*Uhr, Uhr, Uhr*" ("Watch, watch, watch"). Trembling with fear that they would be shot, everyone handed over their watches. One Russian took a liking to the pants and leather boots worn by Otto Wermter, who handed them over on the spot and returned to the farmhouse in his underwear. That evening sleep was impossible as a rampage of rape continued through the night; the Russian soldiers started with the youngest, who was around thirteen years old, and ended up with the oldest. They heard "*Mattka komm, Mattka komm*" in the darkness followed by cries and shrieks when the women tried to defend themselves. Suddenly, a drunken Russian soldier came into their room, turned on a light, and demanded watches, but they had all been handed over as part of the "surrender ceremony" earlier that day. The situation became extremely tense when the soldier aimed his rifle at Otto Wermter and threatened to shoot him. Instead, he shot into the ceiling and everyone in the room screamed in fear. In response to the shots and the screams, another Russian entered the room, disarmed the drunken soldier, and led him out of the room. All the while, in the very next room a woman was being raped by a group of soldiers.

Shortly thereafter, the Wermters were on the road again, this time retracing their steps and going east in the direction of Danzig. Their wagons were stopped by three Soviet soldiers, who also demanded watches, which of course had already been handed over in their first encounter with the Soviet troops.

The three soldiers then decided to take all the German males with them, at which point everyone began to weep, knowing full well that their survival would be jeopardized if they were split up. They thought it a miracle when a Russian officer appeared and handed them a piece of paper on which was written: "These wagons have been checked." This paper enabled the entire family to continue together on its way.

The villagers of Wussowke (Wussow) in Pomerania (now Poland) who had not fled greeted them in a friendly manner and took them to rooms in a relatively intact house where they could stay. They remained there for three months, receiving food in exchange for the use of their four horses by a village farmer for the spring plowing. Word got around that the Russians were conscripting all young men and women to herd the large number of surviving livestock along the roads all the way to Russia. To avoid what was likely to be a fatal conscription, a "security procedure" was developed at the house whereby a bell would be rung whenever Russians were spotted to warn those at risk to run quickly into the woods; a white cloth on a pole was raised when the coast was clear again. Once Otto and his two sons were not quick enough in making their escape and warning shots were fired at them by two approaching soldiers. Trembling with fear and expecting the worst, they walked up to the soldiers and were greatly relieved when one of them—an officer—quietly asked in good German: "*Wohin wollt ihr, warum seid ihr weggelaufen?*" ("Where are you going, why did you run away?") After Otto's identity papers were checked, they were allowed to go on their way.

Over time, food became scarce in the village and considerable resourcefulness was needed to stay alive. Stalks of rye grain were found in a nearby barn, and after the kernels had been separated from the stalks with handmade flails, they were ground into flour using coffee grinders. Crayfish, caught in a small stream, provided a welcome addition to their meager diet. Once a village youth was cunning enough to drive a cow that was being herded to Russia with other cattle into the woods; it was immediately slaughtered to provide precious meat for the inhabitants of the village. Eventually, so little food remained that the decision was made to return to East Prussia. This was all the more urgent as the family had a keen desire to locate Frau Wermter's parents, who had stayed behind when the Red Army was invading East Prussia. (The Wermters had no way of knowing that the part of East Prussia where their farms were located was already under Polish administration.) And so on June 11, 1945, about a month after the war had ended, they packed what little they had into their backpacks along with some food—a loaf of bread for each adult—and after a teary goodbye to the villagers, the Wermter family and their relatives started out walking in the direction of East Prussia. (Their journey back to their farm and what happened after they returned are described in Chapter VI.)

Toward the end of February and into March, the ice on the Frisches Haff was thinner and more dangerous to cross; big cracks appeared, which were bridged with wooden timbers. It became even more critical for the refugees to stick to the marked paths across the ice in light of the risk of falling into the growing number of holes from exploding bombs and shells. Along the ice routes there were increasing numbers of corpses of refugees who had succumbed on the way or were killed by the gunfire from low-flying Russian fighter planes (see Illustration 10. Treks on the Ice—Photo by Soviet Plane). Countless damaged wagons littered the ice, as well as all kinds of household goods that had been abandoned to lighten the wagons of those trying to make it safely across the thawing ice. The distance between wagons had to be increased and the treks could not halt, as otherwise the weight of the horses and the wagons would cause horse, man, and wagon to disappear through the softening ice into the frigid waters of the Haff. By mid-March the ice had become so thin from the warmer weather that the Army permitted only very light wagons to make the crossing.

The End of the Fourth Army in the Heiligenbeil Cauldron

Meanwhile, the bridgehead held by the Fourth Army in the Heiligenbeil Cauldron was gradually compressed as the overwhelmingly superior Soviet forces inexorably pushed back the German defenses, which were weakened by staggering casualties and lack of ammunition and fuel. Repeated requests to Hitler to withdraw the army to the Nehrung were rebuffed, with the inevitable results. On March 13, the Soviets launched their decisive assault on the vastly reduced area of the Heiligenbeil Cauldron (see Map 6. The Heiligenbeil Cauldron). In the northeast, Brandenburg on the Haff fell on March 17, thereby severing once and for all the land link to Königsberg, and in the southwest, Braunsberg was taken on March 20. Following a devastating artillery barrage on March 21, the German positions were continuously assaulted by Soviet tanks and infantry units. In the town of Heiligenbeil all usable spaces—including two churches, public buildings, and industrial workrooms—overflowed with wounded soldiers, who sat on steps and filled the hallways. Ambulances often took hours driving from one overcrowded hospital to another before they found one that would accept their wounded cargo. Yet through superhuman efforts by the army medical corps and the German Navy, nearly all the sick and wounded were evacuated before Heiligenbeil fell to the Soviets on March 24.

A German doctor in the Wehrmacht described how he and his medical team converted an abandoned airplane factory near Heiligenbeil into a military hospital. Every day they admitted from two to four hundred wounded.[90] One day they had a total of twelve hundred patients being cared for in their makeshift hospital. Soldiers who had sufficiently recovered from their wounds were transported by ships and barges from the nearby port of Rosenberg to Pillau through a channel cut by icebreakers in the ice of the Frisches Haff. When this channel froze over, horse-drawn carts commandeered from local farmers were driven over the ice, with the wounded kept warm during the six- to eight-hour journey to Pillau by heated bricks packed next to them. Soldiers with severe head wounds were evacuated by air as long as the airport remained open. When it came under artillery fire, Luftwaffe pilots had to be bribed with sugar discovered in a nearby processing plant to induce them to fly the wounded out. The pilots would then wait up to ten extra minutes on the runway and run the risk that their planes would be hit by incoming shells while an ambulance with three wounded soldiers on stretchers and one stretcher stacked with sacks of sugar raced to the plane. It was then hastily loaded with the wounded and the precious sweet cargo.

As the noose around the Fourth Army grew ever tighter, Rosenberg on the Haff was the only port still capable of loading ships with heavy equipment, and hundreds of trucks, personnel carriers, and all types of wagons were concentrated in a small area around the port. All were soon destroyed by a hail of bombs and shells. When Soviet ground forces approached, panic broke out among the masses of refugees who had gathered there and desperate attempts were made to escape over the Haff from Rosenberg or along the road to the two last remaining open ports of Balga and Kahlholz. Rosenberg was taken on March 27, and Balga—one of the original garrisons founded seven hundred years earlier by the Teutonic Knights in 1239—fell on March 28. All kinds of boats and ships were pressed into service by the German Navy to evacuate refugees and surviving soldiers. On March 29, a heavy fog prevented attacks by Soviet aircraft on the departing vessels and the last ship was able to leave Kahlholz at 6:30 that morning. The Fourth German Army had been crushed and all that remained of East Prussia in German hands were Königsberg, the western part of Samland, and the Frische Nehrung, where the port of Pillau provided the last chance for escape.

D. The End of Königsberg[91]

Königsberg had enjoyed a period of relative tranquillity from the end of January until early April 1945. It experienced only one heavy attack by bombers and artillery fire, on February 1, which caused considerable loss of life of both soldiers and civilians. The city was now completely surrounded by Soviet forces except for a very narrow corridor along the Haff, south of the city. This provided a vital connection to the Fourth Army through which essential food and other supplies could reach the beleaguered Königsberg garrison and population. While the populace remained weary, some sense of normalcy returned following the assault on the city in late January as newspapers again became available in the kiosks, films were again shown in movie theaters, and banks, shops, and restaurants reopened their doors for customers. Dr. Lehndorff wrote in his memoirs: "The reopening of banks… has spread a wave of reassurance; the possibility of paying money in again and drawing it out is evidently proof for the people that things cannot be so bad after all."[92] The water supply became critical when the reservoirs north of Königsberg fell into the hands of the Russians. However, old plans were discovered that showed the location of about eighty wells scattered around the city; these were opened up and pumps were installed, which soon made water available to the inhabitants and the fortress garrison.[93]

The commander of Königsberg, General Lasch, wrote that during this period of relative quiet he tried to boost the morale of civilians and soldiers in the encircled city by urging them to mail postcards to friends and relatives in the rest of Germany. These would be sent from the main Königsberg post office in the event that the siege was lifted. One such postcard was mailed by a lawyer (*Justizrat*), who wrote that things did not look good in Königsberg, that the party had completely failed to take care of the inhabitants, and that Gauleiter Koch had fled. In totalitarian Germany, Nazi Party officials examined every piece of mail looking for what they regarded as "defeatist" views, and in due course this postcard came to their attention. Although he had simply stated the facts known to everyone in Königsberg, the man was convicted for undermining the morale of the troops ("*Zersetzung der Wehrkraft*") and denigrating party and public officials ("*Verunglimpfung von Partei und Staatsbehörden*") and was condemmed to death in the spring of 1945. General Lasch regarded this judgment as "[a] shocking example of the extent to which the perception of right and wrong had been extinguished in many minds." In his capacity as fortress commander, Lasch had the authority to countermand death penalties and he prevented the implementation of what he called a ludicrous judicial decision.[94]

At the same time, General Lasch remained firmly convinced that his decisions regarding the defense of Königsberg were in the best interest of everyone living within the city's perimeter. As he wrote in his often self-serving memoirs, he also believed that he had the population's full support:

> The civilian population and the troops have worked together during these three weeks as a large family looking out for each

other, come what may. All lived and worked with the thought in mind to hold Königsberg so long until freedom came either because of the continually promised relief from outside, or through the end of the war by negotiations.[95]

He also believed that there might still be the possibility of a successful breakout:

Especially considering the population of Königsberg, which still believed in the Wehrmacht, the attempt had to be made to defend the fortress. Perhaps possibilities would still arise to help the civilian population, under the protection of its defenders, to escape first to the Samland and then via Pillau into the Reich or over to Denmark.[96]

It wasn't long before the German Army laid plans to break out of its encirclement. The western part of the Samland peninsula was still held by German forces, which included two army divisions that had been withdrawn from Memel in the last week of January. In the first half of February, these troops, under General Hans Gollnick, fought their way to within seven to seventeen miles (twelve to twenty-seven kilometers) of Königsberg. On February 17, Army Group North, under General Lothar Rendulic, who was in overall command in East Prussia, ordered the two German forces—one inside and the other outside Königsberg—to attack the Red Army simultaneously and to link up and re-establish the land connection to the port of Pillau. Rather than limit his forces to those units designated in the orders he had received from Army Group North, General Lasch took the considerable risk of committing to the attack the three entire divisions he had at his disposal because he firmly believed that only a very large concentration of troops would have any hope of achieving the aimed-for breakthrough. He also ordered that the resulting gap in the eastern defenses of Königsberg be filled by police and Volkssturm units.

General Lasch's incredible gamble paid off. The attack commenced in the early morning hours of February 19 and caught the Russians so much by surprise that soldiers jumped out of their beds in their underclothes when their positions were overrun by the Germans. Lasch's troops met stiff resistance in Metgethen (Lesnoye), where a girls' school had been heavily fortified by the Russians, but after a hard fight with considerable losses, the Germans were able to advance six miles (ten kilometers) by the end of the day. General Gollnick's divisions in Samland, which were supported from the nearby Baltic by the guns of the heavy cruiser *Admiral Scheer,* made slow progress against heavily fortified positions and advanced barely two miles (four kilometers) in two days. Nonetheless, the two German forces made contact on February 20 northwest of Groß Heydekrug and over the next several days were able to carve out a corridor through which refugees could once again escape from Königsberg to Pillau. Lasch's gamble also paid off in that the Soviet Supreme Command (STAVKA) did not take advantage of Königsberg's weakened defenses to attack while the breakout was in progress. STAVKA had decided that the German Army was too strong in Königsberg and in the Samland for it to mount an offensive at that time, and on February 26 it ordered the two Soviet armies in this region to take up defensive positions.[97] As a result, Königsberg was spared further attacks until early April.

After German troops had secured Metgethen and other towns, they were greeted by the grisly sight of bodies lying in the streets as well as charred corpses in smoke-blackened ruins. In one area, some thirty civilians had been held in a fenced-in tennis court and were killed by a mine that exploded in their midst (see Illustration 5, Massacre at Metgethen). The survivors reported that all the women and girls from the ages of fourteen to sixty-four had been raped, some many times over. The German troops also found all kinds of furniture and household goods that had been taken from the ransacked houses—radios, sewing machines, vacuum cleaners, bicycles, beds, upholstered furniture, and dishes—and had been carried to the railroad tracks to be loaded on trains, although most of this booty was damaged and no longer usable.[98] Metgethen joined Nemmersdorf as an example of the nightmare that befell East Prussians when the Red Army took over their towns and villages, and the population of Königsberg became even more fearful and felt the overpowering urge to flee.

When the connection to Pillau was reopened, thousands of Königsbergers and other East Prussians therefore descended on this small port in hopes of escape. In many cases their hopes were dashed because not enough ships had been requisitioned for their evacuation. With Pillau becoming increasingly overcrowded, temporary barracks were built at Peyse (Baltiyskiy Les) on the Frisches Haff to house the refugees until sea transport became available. Owing to poor preparation and organization, not enough food was provided for the hungry refugees and disease became ramport. Despite protestations by local party officials, General Lasch allowed those wishing to return to their apartments in Königsberg to do so, as they would be better off than in Peyse because at least they could buy their own food in the city.

During the lull in the battle for Königsberg, Gauleiter Koch again made his presence felt in ways that once more revealed that his sole concern was for his own welfare. From the relative safety of his headquarters in Neutief, just across from Pillau, he had already made preparations for his escape. Nonetheless, he ordered that his estate, "Friedrichsberg," in East Prussia be repaired and expanded; that a large building in the center of Königsberg on the corner of Tragheimer and Gartenstraße be remodeled with princely furnishings for his own use; and that an airplane runway be built on the Paradeplatz so that he could escape at a moment's notice. The construction of the runway required the demolition of whole building blocks and involved the diversion of a large number of civilian workers from the war effort. Entreaties by General Lasch to stop this insane project fell on deaf ears. He reported that Koch appeared briefly in Königsberg only once during this period of relative quiet under the cover of darkness; according to Lasch, the Gauleiter no doubt feared the wrath of the residents whom he had abandoned.[99]

In the meantime, following the expulsion of the German Fourth Army from the Heiligenbeil Cauldron at the end of March, the German Army High Command (OKH) in Berlin determined that the staff of the Army Group North was no longer needed to oversee the much reduced military presence in East Prussia and it was transferred back to Germany. Overall command of the remaining German forces in this sector was then placed in the hands of the former commander of the defeated Fourth Army, General Friedrich-Wilhelm Müller. On April 2, just after he had been given this new command, he made an appearance at General Lasch's command bunker beneath the Paradeplatz. General Lasch was amazed that notwithstanding the disastrous defeat in the Heiligenbeil Cauldron, General Müller was full of illusions about the prospects for the war and refused to hear his pessimistic assessment concerning the defense of Königsberg. General Müller, who was Lasch's superior officer, asked all division and unit commanders, and especially party leaders, to assemble in the basement of a building at the Albertina University. There he gave a stirring oration full of optimism about the outcome of the war and evinced complete conviction in Germany's final victory (*"Endsieg"*). When Lasch asked him where the minimum four or five battle-ready divisions would come from that would be needed to expel the Russians from East Prussia, General Müller replied that he had no idea where he would get these troops but that "everything would work out" (*"Er meinte aber, das würde schon alles werden"*[100]). Following his harangue before the assembled army officers and party officials, General Müller informed General Lasch that he would be relieved of his command of Fortress Königsberg. He added that his dismissal would not take place immediately because Lasch's previous commanding officers had such high regard for him, but that he, Müller, had connections and would request his dismissal directly from Hitler. This was the only discussion General Lasch had with General Müller, who survived the war but was turned over to Greece. There he was executed for his participation in the German operations in Crete.

By this time—early April 1945—survival for the people in Königsberg had become increasingly difficult. Walking on the streets on a clear day was a nightmare as Russian planes had complete command of the sky and would strafe or bomb anything that moved. Michael Wieck, then aged seventeen, described in vivid detail what happened one cloudless day when he and his mother returned home to the Hufen district from the chemical factory where they worked, which was near the Alhambra movie theater.[101] Because of the danger of aerial attacks, they took a circuitous route through parks and

past cemeteries, the Veilchenberg, and the Neue Bleiche toward Luisenwahl
to get home:

> Mother and I are going by foot. We can take cover more quickly
> and, most importantly, hear the planes sooner. This time we avoid
> the streets and are going along some earthworks from which we
> have an unobstructed view of the entire sky. To our left are the gas
> storage tanks for Königsberg, completely full and undestroyed.
> We have to go past them just as do a small troop of soldiers going
> in the same direction a hundred yards in front of us. Just as we're
> very close to the storage tanks—about three hundred yards sepa-
> rate us from them—we hear the drones of planes again. They
> are flying higher and there are lots of them. Before we can figure
> out what they are aiming at, we see the soldiers looking for cover
> and signaling us to do the same. They had seen the bombs being
> released. There is nothing nearby but a pile of railroad ties and
> we press ourselves flat on the ground against them. Then all hell
> breaks loose. Heavy bombs are dropped on the storage tanks, but
> miss. Our thoughts are fixed on the fact that if the storage tanks
> right next to us explode, we will be annihilated. We stay pressed
> against the ground. We hold our mouths wide open to relieve the
> pressure from the explosion. The dirt kicked up as the bombs hit
> the ground rains down on us; then it's all over. The storage tanks
> remain untouched. We can see what would've happened…. The
> soldiers are also relieved. They ask us where we are going and give
> us friendly advice.[102]

On Thursday, April 5, the trip home from the factory became more dangerous as Soviet artillery fire continued unabated. The front had moved
closer to the city and rifle and machine-gun fire sounded nearby. German
troops had by now established defensive positions near the Wieck's apartment building. To pass through these troop units, Wieck and his mother
had to show their worker's pass every few yards, and when they heard the

distinctive high-pitched whine of incoming shells, they threw themselves flat on the ground. It was with incredible effort and considerable luck that they were finally able to reach their home unhurt. But when they entered their air-raid shelter in the basement, they found that it had been damaged by the bombardment. It became very clear to Michael Wieck that the battle for Königsberg was now so intense, they would have to remain in the shelter and either be buried under the collapsed building, or leave it only after the arrival of the Russians, who seemed about to engulf the city at any moment. He expressed what he and others in the air-raid shelter felt that day about the continued defense of Königsberg:

> No one could comprehend why the civilian population was being subjected to this murderous bombardment. Lord knows everyone had suffered enough. We choked with impotent rage at the commanders who were squandering their troops. Everyone cursed openly and loudly.[103]

On the other side of the city, Dr. Lehndorff was working at the Charity Hospital, which faced the Castle Pond (Schloßteich). He described the horrendous attack from the air that day:

> From early morning until late in the afternoon on this lovely sunny day they [the airplanes] circled, first at fifteen hundred feet then much lower, over every quarter of the town. More than a hundred were always in the air at the same time, dropping heavy bombs and firing on the streets with all their guns.... A powerful spectacle met our eyes every time we passed the exits of our building facing the Castle Pond. In the steel blue sky a violent storm, blowing toward the center of town, sent the rising smoke clouds whirling about. Over the center of town lay a black cloud bank like a mountain range out of which flames were shooting, and above it circled the planes, pressing in from all sides, plunging into the witches' cauldron and climbing up again unharmed on the other

side. The stone stairs in front of our door were littered with shell splinters; but only when the planes were directly overhead, did we run back a few steps into the cellar. Otherwise we stood outdoors, staring spellbound at the infernal racket. We could not hear what the other said, but it was not necessary....[104]

The day before—April 4—had been Iris Rörup's twelfth birthday. It could not have been much of a celebration as she and her mother were huddled in a bunker. They had been transferred to this air-raid shelter from Fort Quednau, outside the city, where they had sought refuge from air attacks between January and March. Fort Quednau was located about 650 feet (two hundred meters) from their house at 195 Ringstraße in the surburb of Rothenstein.[105] Between air raids they would run back to their house, where her mother prepared warm food and they would wash up as best they could. When Iris's mother came upon a few of her possessions in a neighbor's house, she was shocked that some people would steal from other residents when the bombardments were underway.

Before the air raids, the dirt-covered top of the fort had been a favorite playground for Iris; the many old trees and berry bushes provided excellent hiding places for the neighborhood children when they played games there. Now, right next to the fort, an antiaircraft battery had been erected. It was soon destroyed by bombs. The cries of the wounded, who had manned the guns, unnerved everyone when their mangled bodies were taken into protected quarters under the fort. No one dared speak openly and it was through tight lips that someone muttered, "The war was lost long ago" ("*Der Krieg ist längst verloren*").

Iris's father and nearly all of the other men in the family were either at the front or had already been killed in the war. One three-year-old relative (Urte) had drowned when the *Wilhelm Gustloff* sank at the end of January 1945, and Iris's maternal grandmother had died in the bombardment of Königsberg in August 1944. A cousin and her two children were evacuated before this massive air raid, first to Saxony and then to Thuringia, and an aunt fled first to Fischhausen and then to Pillau, where she escaped by ship at the end of

January 1945.[106] One uncle, too old to be in the army, explained why he and his wife chose to remain in Königsberg: "I went through World War I. Where should we go? Our houses at the outskirts of the city are still standing. Just look at the misery of the refugees."[107] Other family members also chose to remain in Königsberg, with tragic consequences for many. Iris and her mother survived the final brutal Soviet assault described below, although Iris suffered a leg wound from a stray shell fragment. How they managed to stay alive until their expulsion from East Prussia in 1948 is described in Chapter VI.

Friday, April 6, 1945

The final assault on Königsberg began in earnest the morning of Friday, April 6. The attack was concentrated in two main thrusts: one from the north, centered on the suburb of Charlottenburg, and the other from the south, aimed at the surburbs of Kalgen and Ponarth. The Soviet objective was to carry out a pincer movement that would cut off the city once again from the Samland and the escape route to Pillau. Before the Soviet troops and tanks advanced, an ear-shattering barrage of artillery fire from thousands of guns prepared their way. Even with his extensive tours of duty on both the Eastern and Western Fronts, General Lasch confessed that he had never before experienced such a powerful weapons assault. The Luftwaffe was unable to mount any air defense and the city was pounded by bombs delivered by wave after wave of Soviet planes striking with impunity from a clear, cloudless sky. The German anti-aircraft batteries lacked adequate ammunition and many had already been put out of commission by enemy guns and air attacks. By evening, fires raged throughout a city now enveloped in clouds of smoke and dust, and the streets were littered with the bodies of animals and civilians, destroyed vehicles, and the ruins of collapsed buildings. Communication between German units became very difficult and messengers on foot had a very hard time finding their way through the rubble in the streets.

By the end of the first day's assault, Soviet forces had made major inroads into the city's defenses. There was a terrific roar outside the Wieck family's air-raid shelter when their building received direct hits from Russian artillery. By now the German defensive line had moved closer to their apartment building and soldiers fully equipped for battle moved through the relative safety of the cellars, which were linked by passageways. The civilians exhorted them to have pity and stop the fighting, but to no avail. The soldiers always responded that they were under orders to continue their resistance to the advancing Russians.

Saturday, April 7, 1945

The second day of the assault opened with further massive artillery salvos and heavy air bombardments of the entire city. To the north and west of Königsberg, the Red Army had penetrated into Amalienau and Juditten, and in the south, the suburb of Ponarth was taken and heavy fighting took place around Königsberg's main railroad station. By evening, Russian troops had reached the mouth of the Pregel in the west and the south bank of the river in the east; north of the city they had captured the railway line to Pillau. Faced with the rapid deterioration in Königsberg's defenses, General Lasch asked the OKH for permission to break out to the west and re-establish the link to Pillau. He recommended using all remaining troops, tanks, and artillery pieces in Königsberg because the application of such a concentrated force was the only hope that some of the remaining 100,000 civilians might yet be able to escape the Russian grip on the city. The OKH in Berlin brusquely denied his request.[108]

During this intense bombardment, the Charity Hospital near the Schloßteich where Dr. Lehndorff continued to operate was hit by several large bombs that blew out the remaining doors and partitions on the second floor. He was sleeping in the operating room on the ground floor and was awakened when four ceiling lights crashed to the floor and one landed on him. A bomb detonated right next to the operating room, but fortunately the outer wall held. Another huge bomb carved out a crater forty-five feet wide that blocked off one of the entrances to the hospital. In the course of the afternoon, Soviet soldiers advancing from the east of Königsberg drove the defending Germans to the west bank of the Schloßteich; it had been so ravaged by enemy fire that Dr. Lehndorff described it as looking like a cabbage patch destroyed by hail. The hospital was caught in the middle of the two opposing forces, and shelling from the new German defensive line across the Schloßteich knocked off parts of the hospital roof. For some, the deafening onslaught and imminent arrival of the Russians was too much to bear, and Lehndorff came across people who had killed themselves with an overdose of sleeping pills.[109]

In the western part of Königsberg the front had moved to the Hufen district, where the Wiecks sat cowering in their shelter with their hands over their ears to keep out the continuous roar of shells bursting in their block. When a German sergeant and four soldiers entered their shelter to take up a position by a corner window, there was consternation among the civilians that the cellar would attract enemy fire. They implored the sergeant not to shoot at the Red Army soldiers. He replied, "Don't worry, we'll disappear at the right moment."[110] They found it reassuring that at least the soldiers in their midst would not endanger them by putting up resistance. During the course of the afternoon the shelling became more intense and two large bombs exploded just outside the building, violently shaking it and gouging out holes in the wall. Dust began to fill the shelter and with the rise in air pressure it seemed their heads would explode. Things had reached a breaking point: the Wiecks' neighborhood was now the front line and fighting was going on outside their building. Any resistance would have been fatal, but somehow the sergeant and the four soldiers had disappeared from the shelter without anyone noticing. Toward evening the shelling diminished markedly as the front moved toward the city center. In the eerie quiet Michael Wieck looked out of the unprotected windows of the shelter and saw a white sheet hanging on the door across the street. The people in his shelter then decided to do the same thing and there was immense relief that they had survived the battle. Nothing was left to do but wait for the Russians to arrive. This did not happen until noon the following day.

Sunday, April 8, 1945

The third day of the massive attack on Königsberg began with a hail of artillery fire and bombs exploding in all sectors of the city. The noose of Soviet forces pushing inexorably forward from all sides to the city center tightened even further. By now even party officials could see that the situation was hopeless. General Lasch put it bluntly, "Even the deputy Gauleiter and his minions had become very frightened. It dawned on them that Königsberg is lost." Deputy Gauleiter Großherr and a few of his subordinates appeared in General Lasch's bunker to telephone Gauleiter Koch in Neutief to ask permission for a break-out even at this late date. Koch relayed this request to army headquarters in Berlin and General Lasch received the official order from headquarters at 8:00 that evening, which read, in part: "For the time being the fortress has to be held, and for the breakout of party members and the civilian population, only limited forces are to be used."[111] General Lasch knew that an attempt to break out with only limited forces against overpowering Soviet might was bound to fail. He made a final appeal to his commanding officer, General Müller, arguing that only by using all the forces of the fortress garrison would a breakout to the west have any chance of success. To no avail: General Müller told him that it was his duty to hold Königsberg to the last man.

Night of April 8–9, 1945

Even if army headquarters had approved General Lasch's request, it is doubtful whether committing all his troops would have succeeded in breaking through the Soviet noose. Because of the incessant bombing raids and artillery fire, the streets were filled with bomb craters, destroyed vehicles of all kinds, and the rubble of collapsed buildings. With the streets nearly impassable, the assembly of the troops, specified in the orders from headquarters, was delayed from 11:00 p.m. to 2:00 on the morning of April 9. Once the group of soldiers and civilians started moving along the escape route, the noise of the vehicles alerted the Russians to the attempted breakout and a hail of artillery fire rained down on the column and caused considerable casualties, among them

Deputy Gauleiter Großherr, the very man who had instigated the breakout to save his own skin. Most survivors fled back to Königsberg and only a smattering of troops succeeded in escaping the ring closing in on the center of the city. A vivid description of conditions in Königsberg that night is provided by Major Lewinski, leader of Grenadier Regiment 192:

> Over and over were heard the detonations of incoming bombs, shells, and fire from heavy Stalin organs [multiple rocket launchers]; in between, the still-standing house façades plunged onto the street and huge bomb craters were torn open. Into this hell from the south and the north pushed wagons, trucks, artillery, and weapons until they were so jammed together, they could go neither forward nor backward. It was a horrendous picture. Through this inferno the regiment had to make its way, always seeking a path to avoid tank obstacles or huge bomb craters. In no time at all our artillery and battle wagons sat inextricably stuck between vehicles of all kinds, cut off by new craters and destruction.[112]

Monday, April 9, 1945

With the German defensive lines crumbling, battles were now being fought only at individual strong points such as the Wrangel and Dohna towers, Königsberg Castle, and the area around the Paradeplatz where Lasch's headquarters were located. Conditions had become so chaotic that communications became impossible, and Lasch was unable to transmit commands to the remaining troops. Artillery pieces could not be shifted around because of impassable streets, and air-raid shelters were filled with wounded soldiers and civilians. Many soldiers gave up fighting and joined civilians cowering in cellars to escape the inferno. General Lasch reported that desperate women tried to tear the guns out of the hands of the German soldiers and hung white cloths from windows to bring an end to the carnage. He finally realized it was hopeless to continue the battle because doing so would needlessly sacrifice thousands of soldiers and civilians: "I could no longer answer to God and my conscience for such a decision [to continue the battle]."[113]

On the morning of April 9, Lasch informed his staff of his decision to capitulate. He sent a short note to a unit commander, Oberstleutnant Kerwien, at the nearby Trommelplatz, with instructions to contact the nearest Russian command post to seek a ceasefire and request that Russian Army officers be sent to Lasch's bunker. With the inner city of Königsberg in chaos, Kerwien found it difficult to get in touch with the Soviet command. Following hours of tense waiting, it was not until evening that he and officers of the Soviet Third Belorussian Front finally appeared in Lasch's bunker below the Paradeplatz. After protracted negotiations, General Lasch signed the capitulation document at 9:30 p.m., April 9, 1945. He and his remaining staff were taken into Soviet custody the following morning.

Gauleiter Koch in Neutief was one of the first to hear the news of the surrender. Always looking to present himself in a good light, Koch immediately radioed Hitler: "The commander of Königsberg, Lasch, used a moment of my absence to capitulate cowardly. I continue to fight in the Samland and on the Nehrung."[114] Koch omitted to add that he had already abandoned Königsberg on April 4 before the final assault had begun. Because General Lasch, a professional soldier, had failed to follow explicit orders to fight to the last man, he was immediately sentenced to death in absentia and his family was arrested on Hitler's orders. (He survived ten years as a prisoner of war in Russia and in the late fall of 1955 returned to Germany where he was reunited with his family.)

In his memoirs, Michael Wieck expressed outrage that Lasch had waited until the last minute to capitulate, as the lives of thousands of soldiers and civilians would have been spared if the surrender had taken place on April 6 when the final Russian assault on Königsberg was launched. Rather than sentence Lasch to death, Wieck commented acidly that Hitler should have rewarded him for being a faithful general who followed orders to the end, and he regarded as "poppycock" Lasch's later self-serving claim that he saved lives before God and his conscience. Wieck observed scathingly that the general had certainly saved his own life by surrendering only when the Russians were closing in on his bunker, and he was so outraged that he could not read the following passage from the general's memoirs without shuddering:

> From numerous accounts of the battle for the Festung Königsberg, it can been seen that every soul had done his duty in exemplary fashion to the last. The final battle for East Prussian soil shall remain forever a glorious chapter in the history of the German military tradition and in the history of the people of East Prussia.[115]

During the second breakout attempt, Major Lewinski and a few of his men were able to fight their way out of Königsberg, and looking back at the city, he described Königsberg's final hours:

> During the day we saw behind us the dying city enveloped in a coat of smoke and fire into which the streaks of fire of heavy artillery shells ate their way through. At 5 p.m. the fire gradually died down. In some places a few machine guns still sputtered until finally these last signs of battle also died down. In the darkness of evening the sinister red-tinged black clouds caused by the many continuing blazes vaulted over the dead city. The fortress of Königsberg had perished....[116]

E. The End of East Prussia

Königsberg fell on April 9, 1945, but German forces were still in the Samland, the last remaining corner of East Prussia which had not surrendered. Six ill-equipped divisions were all that survived of Army Group North (by now renamed *Armee Ostpreußen*). They were now commanded by General Dietrich von Saucken, as General Müller had been relieved of his command by Hitler because of the capitulation of his subordinate, General Lasch. General von Saucken was a native of Fischhausen on the Frisches Haff in East Prussia and had gone to school in Königsberg. Intimately familiar with the Samland terrain, he was determined to use the six divisions under his command to put up stiff resistance in order to enable as many East Prussian civilians and troops as possible to escape from Pillau. General von Sauken and his soldiers were up against the entire Third Belorussian Front with an overpowering advantage in troops, tanks, assault weapons, ammunition, and some Lend-Lease military supplies delivered to Russia by the United States. The outcome of the ensuing final battle was never in doubt.

The Soviet attack on the Samland came on the morning of April 13. Once again the Russians chose the thirteenth of the month to launch their attack—just as January 13 had marked the beginning of the final assault on East Prussia and March 13 the start of the offensive against the Heiligenbeil Cauldron. The Russians had the additional advantage that April 13 was a clear spring day; Soviet air force pilots were able to find their targets easily and attacked with impunity. The Germans did not have sufficient fuel to mount a concerted counterattack with their few remaining fighter planes. Consequently, their ground troops suffered grievous losses from the bombs and cannon fire that rained down on them whenever they moved out of their defensive positions. On the first day of the attack, the Soviets broke through the German defensive lines in many places and their tanks rolled into the northwest of the Samland. The local inhabitants and refugees fled along the roads to Pillau, where the long lines of wagons became sitting ducks for low-flying Soviet fighter planes.

In Rauschen (Svetlogorsk) on the Baltic, the order to evacuate was given at 5:00 a.m. on Saturday, April 14, and thousands of residents and refugees were told to make their way however they could to Palmnicken (Yartany).[117] Frau Anna Grohnert had been bombed out in Königsberg in the massive air assault on August 30, 1944, and in early 1945 had taken a train to Rauschen together with an elderly married couple, the Tiedtkes. Frau Grohnert's husband had been forced to join the Volkssturm and remained behind, as did her youngest daughter, a Red Cross nurse assigned to the hospital in the Tragheim district of Königsberg.[118] In Rauschen, Frau Grohnert and the Tiedtkes spent most of their time in cellars to avoid attacks by low-flying fighter planes. On April 14, the order was given to leave as soon as possible for Palmnicken. When they arrived, they found it so tightly packed with refugees, they decided to continue on to the nearby town of Sorgenau (Pokrovskoje), but it too was completely packed with refugees. The three joined a group of about forty other refugees without a place to stay. Their only hope was the last train out of Palmnicken, which was scheduled to arrive in Sorgenau at eight o'clock that evening and to continue on to Pillau. But when the train arrived, every conceivable space—the roofs, the steps, the platforms, wherever one could stand or hold on—was already taken by desperate refugees, and the train passed through the station without stopping. Fortunately, the stationmaster was able to arrange for their group to be picked up at midnight by a munitions train, which took them to Neuhäuser (Mechnikov) near Pillau. They arrived at 4:00 a.m. on Sunday, April 15, and the following day Frau Grohnert and the Tiedtkes walked to Pillau and learned that ships were not available to evacuate them via the Baltic to the Reich.

Now their only escape route was to make their way by foot along the Frische Nehrung to the west. To avoid Russian air attacks, they were transported around midnight by ferry to Neutief on the Nehrung, just across the channel from Pillau. By now completely exhausted, they were stunned when a soldier informed them that the western end of the Nehrung was nearly fifty miles (seventy-five kilometers) distant. The following day they were so weak they walked only six miles (nine kilometers) along the narrow Nehrung road, which was jammed with various types of vehicles, healthy and wounded soldiers, and other refugees. The roadsides were littered with all kinds of discarded personal belongings. They considered themselves lucky to find shelter for the night in a police barracks, while most refugees spent the night in holes dug in the earth with their legs sticking out into the open and their heads and parts of their bodies hidden inside the hole. The next day they walked to Stutthof, at the western end of the Nehrung, and from there to Nickelswalde (Mikoszewo), where they were able to take a ferry to Hela (see Map 7. Towns on the Bay of Danzig). They had the good luck to board a large freighter, which transported several thousand refugees and soldiers to Copenhagen on

April 22. When they learned that Copenhagen was their destination, they were deeply upset because they had hoped to land in Schleswig-Holstein in northern Germany. (Frau Grohnert was interned in Denmark for twenty months before she was sent back to Germany. Her husband and her daughter were captured by the Russians, but they survived three years of captivity.)

––––––––––

By April 16, 1945, Soviet troops had advanced so far south in the Samland that they separated the two remaining German defensive points on the Frisches Haff, Fischhausen, and Peyse. During the night of April 16–17 some German troops were evacuated by boat, while other soldiers used tree trunks and oil drums to fashion makeshift rafts to cross the six miles (ten kilometers) of the Frisches Haff from Peyse to Pillau. On April 17, both Fischhausen and Peyse were taken by the Soviets and now only a sliver of the Samland coast, from heavily fortified Tenkitten to Pillau, was still held by the Germans. They took down the cross in Tenkitten commemorating the attempt in 998 by Bishop Adalbert to convert the heathen Prussen as well as his defeat and martyrdom, because it would have served as an orientation point for Soviet artillery. The German soldiers continued to put up stiff resistance, making it possible to evacuate more wounded troops and refugees from Tenkitten by sea. As the harbor in Pillau was now blocked by a sunken freighter, gangways were erected on the shore between Pillau and the village of Neuhäuser; small boats picked up soldiers and refugees and brought them to the larger ships waiting at anchor further out in the Baltic. This shuttle service ran continuously at night to avoid attacks by low-flying Soviet fighter planes. Tenkitten held out for four days and Pillau another four days until it was taken on April 25, barely long enough for nearly all of the remaining refugees and troops to escape.

Throughout the battle for the Samland, Gauleiter Koch had remained holed up in his headquarters in Neutief, just across the channel from Pillau. With the Russians advancing inexorably and Neutief now subject to heavy bombing, he decided to make his escape on April 23, when the enemy was four miles (six kilometers) away, just outside Neuhäuser. He had arranged for two icebreakers, the *Ostpreußen* and the *Pregel*, to wait for him at the jetty in Pillau. He took with him his close staff and departed in the half-empty *Ostpreußen* without taking on board any refugees or wounded. The *Ostpreußen* made an intermediate stop in Hela, the small port at the end of the peninsula on the Bay of Danzig, where Koch again refused to take any refugees or wounded on board. Before leaving, Koch discovered that the first engineer had managed to bring his family from Königsberg on board and he ordered them to leave the ship immediately. Upon hearing this, the first engineer told Koch that if his family did not come along, the ship would never depart from Hela. After conferring with the commandant of Hela, Koch allowed the family to stay on board.[119]

After he arrived in Copenhagen, Koch switched into a German Army uniform and took on the identity of "Major Rolf Berger." He made his way back to Germany and lived under this assumed name as a farm worker in Hasenmoor near Hamburg in what was then the British-occupied zone. In 1949, his true identity was discovered and a British court had him transferred to Poland, where he was tried in the fall of 1958. In his closing statement at his trial, Koch maintained that he should be set free because he had only followed orders and was not responsible for any deaths. On March 9, 1959, he was sentenced to death for his role in the killing of hundreds of thousands of Poles, but his brutal regime as *Reichskommissar* (chief civil administrator) from 1941 to 1944 in Nazi-occupied Ukraine was not considered at his trial. His sentence was, however, commuted to life imprisonment. In prison, Koch had a special cell and other privileges. In his later years he developed cancer and was operated on by leading Polish doctors. He died on November 12, 1986, at the age of ninety in what had been East Prussia but was now Poland, never having expressed the slightest remorse for either the millions of East Prussians he did nothing to protect from the Soviet Army, or for the hundreds of thousands of Poles and Ukrainians whose deaths he had caused.[120]

Another party functionary who escaped in similar fashion, Gauleiter Albert Forster, had been in charge of the Danzig - West Prussia region. On March 27, two torpedo boats, the *T23* and the *T28*, were protecting the warship *Lützow* in the waters near Danzig when their crews noticed a

ferry overcrowded with refugees lying dead in the water, having been hit
by an attacking Soviet fighter plane. At the same time, a luxury steamer
was approaching at high speed and was clearly paying no heed to the ferry's desperate situation. Enraged, Captain Weilig of the *T23* contacted
the steamer by radio and ordered it to take the ferry in tow to the relative safety of Hela. From the steamer came an immediate and authoritarian
reply: "Here on board is Gauleiter Forster. You have no business giving us
orders!" In response, both torpedo boats rapidly approached the steamer
and trained their guns on it. In the meantime, the two commanders had
received authorization from Vice Admiral Thiele to use force if necessary to
compel the steamer to take the ferry in tow. Before Captain Weilig could
convey this message, Gauleiter Forster himself appeared on the steamer's
deck and shouted "Here speaks Gauleiter Forster of Danzig! I will call you
to account for this!" Captain Weilig retorted, "And here speaks Lieutenant
Captain Weilig. This is an order: Arrange promptly for your steamer to take
the ferry in tow. Otherwise you will be shot at!" The order was obeyed and
the steamer took the ferry in tow.[121]

After the war, Forster escaped detection for over a year near Oldenburg,
in northern Germany, until he was arrested by the British authorities in
Hamburg and handed over to the Polish authorities on August 12, 1946. He
was sentenced to death on April 29, 1948, and was executed in Warsaw on
February 28, 1952.

Other high officials also made their escape from the east during the last
days of the war. In late February, a refugee, Paul Bernecker, arrived after a
harrowing voyage from Danzig to Saßnitz on the island of Rügen, where
he observed with outrage the arrival of a luxury steamer from Danzig filled
with Nazi Party functionaries and their families.[122] All were well dressed and
had made the trip in the ship's luxurious staterooms, bringing a great deal
of baggage, including bicycles, while countless women and children waited
for days to get on board a rescue ship in Pillau. He also reported that when
the airport in the Heiligenbeil Cauldron was still open, civilians who were
airlifted out were not ordinary refugees but relatives and friends of high-level
Nazi officials.[123]

Following the fall of Pillau on April 25 and Neutief on April 27, Soviet troops pushed down the narrow Frische Nehrung and took Kohlberg (Kolobrzeg) on May 3, and Pröbbernau on May 5. Refugees were still trying to escape the advancing Red Army and those able to reach Schiewenhorst (in the middle of the last remaining German bridgehead on the Baltic on both sides of the Vistula) were taken by boats of all kinds across the Bay of Danzig to Hela. There, military personnel worked feverishly to house and feed thousands of refugees and troops awaiting evacuation to the west by ship. The scale of this desperate effort to escape the Russians can be seen in the fact that on April 15 alone, eighteen thousand wounded soldiers, thirty-three thousand refugees, and eight thousand members of the Volkssturm arrived at Hela.[124] By midnight on May 8, 1945, when Germany capitulated to the Allies, nearly all the remaining refugees had been evacuated. But thousands of German troops remained in Hela after the last German ships had departed and soon became Russian prisoners of war.

It has been estimated that roughly 2.5 million German civilians and soldiers were evacuated by ship from East Prussia, Danzig, and West Prussia between the second half of January and May 8, 1945.[125] Through this incredible effort, over a million East Prussians were able to flee from the Soviet invasion and occupation that was to follow. The fate of those who remained behind is described in Chapter VI.

Notes

1 Ziemke, *Stalingrad to Berlin*, 340. "Kein echter Deutscher darf nur daran denken, daß Ostpreußen in Russische Hände fällt." It appears that Koch was following a directive issued by Hitler.

2 Army Group Center was massed along the Belorussian Front, running from Pinsk in the southwest to Vitebsk in the northeast. It consisted of the Second Army, under General Weiß, covering the southern flank along the Pripet Marches near Pinsk; the Ninth Army, commanded by General Jordan, in the area of Bobruisk; the Fourth Army, under General Heinrici, south of Orsha; and the Third Panzer Army, commanded by General Reinhardt, near Vitebsk in in the north. The Center's southern flank was covered by Army Group North

Ukraine and its northern flank was protected by Army Group North. See
Seaton, *The Russo-German War*, 432–34.

3 Quoted in Ziemke, *Stalingrad to Berlin*, 316.

4 For a comprehensive account of Operation Bagration, see Zaloga, *Bagration 1944.*

5 This estimate of the number of men in Army Group Center is from Glantz and
House, *When Titans Clashed*, 215.

6 Clark, *The Russian-German Conflict*, 382.

7 Mazower, *Hitler's Empire*, 16.

8 Erich Koch was born in Elberfeld, Germany, on June 19, 1896. He served in
the German Army during World War I and worked for the German railways
(*Reichsbahn*) after the war. He became an early member of the NSDAP (Nazi
Party) in 1921 and in September 1927 was appointed Gauleiter in East Prussia.
There he was so effective in increasing membership in the party that it won an
absolute majority in the election of 1933. Through illegal means he took over
more than one hundred firms, including the Park Hotel in Königsberg, and
transferred their capital to the "Erich Koch Foundation." In 1945, it had assets
of 331 million marks. From 1941–1944 he was head of the civil administration
(*Reichskommisar*) in Ukraine, where in a speech in March 1943 he proclaimed
the Nazi Party's racial views: "We are a master race, which must remember
that the lowliest German worker is racially and biologically a thousand times
more valuable than the population here." (www.holocaustreseachproject.
org/nazioccupation/erichkoch, page 1) When the Soviet Army recaptured
Ukraine in 1944, he returned to East Prussia. At the end of the war he went
underground but was found in 1949 and extradited to Poland. There he was
condemned to death in 1959 for war crimes against Poles, but was never put
on trial for crimes committed in Ukraine. The sentence was never carried out,
however, and Koch, who was treated for cancer, died in prison on November 12,
1986, at the age of ninety in what was formerly Wartenburg, East Prussia, now
Barczewo, near Olsztyn in Poland. Why Koch was not put to death still remains
a mystery. The most recent and comprehensive account of Koch's life does not
provide an answer, but speculates that "[a]pparently, with growing temporal
distance from the deeds of the Nazi leadership, the Polish authorities had doubts
about whether the execution of the 'last war criminal' was still appropriate."
"Offenbar wuchsen in den polnischen Behörden mit wachsendem zeitlichen
Abstand zu den Taten des NS-Führers die Zweifel, ob die Hinrichtung des
'letzten Kriegsverbrechers' immer noch angebracht sei." Meindl, *Ostpreußens
Gauleiter*, 485.

9 Evacuation plans were, in fact, drawn up in East Prussia but were never implemented: "When a plan for evacuating the population of East Prussia was put before Koch by the *Oberpräsidium* [civil administration] of Königsberg, in the summer of 1944, the Gauleiter refused to pass it on even as a mere secret instruction to the administrative and party authorities in East Prussia." Schieder, *The Expulsion of the German Population,* 10. In addition, a letter dated June 24, 1952, from Walter Marquardt to Dr. Hoffmann in connection with the Schieder Dokumentation exercise (Ost-Dok 1, Nr. 1, pages 607–11, Bundesarchiv Bayreuth) describes a detailed evacuation plan that was worked out in October 1943 by the Oberpräsidium Königsberg, where Marquardt was employed. The letter also states that the plan was never implemented because at the beginning of 1944 the responsibility for evacuation was shifted from the Oberpräsidium to the party authorities. By contrast, in other areas in eastern Germany, such as Danzig - West Prussia, Pomerania, and Silesia, detailed plans for evacuation had been drafted in the summer of 1944 and secret instructions had been issued in the event of an attack.

10 Dieckert and Großmann, *Der Kampf um Ostpreussen,* 29.

11 For a gripping account of the escape from Trakehnen to Georgenburg, see Clough, *In langer Reihe über das Haff,* Chapter 6, "Endlich: Der Aufbruch," 84–91.

12 Dieckert and Großmann, *Der Kampf um Ostpreussen,* 33.

13 Ibid., 31.

14 Glantz and House, *When Titans Clashed,* 214.

15 This account of differences in views between German army commanders is contained in Raus, *Panzer Operations,* 297–98. As General Raus was directly involved in the fighting in this sector, it is not clear whether he in fact came to his views before or after the attack.

16 Ibid., 299.

17 Schieder, *The Expulsion of the German Population,* 3.

18 Dieckert and Großmann, *Der Kampf um Ostpreussen,* 48.

19 Lehndorff, *Token of a Covenant,* 4.

20 As the military situation in East Prussia became more desperate, Koch's authority first extended up to six miles (ten kilometers) and then finally to twelve and a half miles (twenty kilometers) from the front. Dieckert and Großmann, *Der Kampf um Ostpreussen,* 58.

21 For example, Wieck reported (*A Childhood under Hitler and Stalin,* 109) that from a rooftop in Königsberg he could hear the muffled sound of the battle in the far distance.

22 Dieckert und Großmann, *Der Kampf um Ostpreussen*, 63. "Während der Gegner glaubt zum letzten Schlag ausholen zu können, sind wir entschlossen, den zweiten Großeinsatz unseres Volkes zu vollziehen. Es wird und muß uns gelingen, wie in den Jahren 1939–1940, ausschliesslich auf unserer Kraft bauend, nicht nur den Vernichtungswillen der Feinde zu brechen, sondern sie wieder zurückzuwerfen und so lange vom Reich abzuhalten, bis die Zukunft Deutschlands, seiner Verbündeten und damit Europas sichernder Friede gewährleistet ist."

23 Hastings, *Armageddon*, 248–49.

24 Dieckert and Großmann, *Der Kampf um Ostpreussen*, 66.

25 The conflict between the civilian administration and party officials regarding the evacuation of East Prussians is illustrated in the letter from Marquardt to Dr. Hoffmann cited in footnote 9. Marquardt reported that *Regierungspräsident* (chief civilian administrator in East Prussia) Dr. Rhode—with the support of the commanders of the Third and Fourth Armies—made repeated and ever more insistent requests to the *Gauamtsleiter* (chief party administrator in East Prussia), Paul Dargel, that the Gumbinnen district be evacuated. Dargel categorically rejected these requests and the two had very heated disagreements over the phone. Finally, Dr. Rhode gave the evacuation order on his own responsibility, but it was too late to prevent what happened in Nemmersdorf. Dargeld attempted to put the blame on Rhode for the atrocities committed there and tried to remove him from office. This was thwarted, however, by the intervention of *Staatssekretär* (secretary of state) Dr. Stuckart of the Interior Ministry, who had written evidence of Rhode's conversations and was so outraged with Dargel's behavior that he thought that Rhode should be given the German Silver Cross for his brave conduct.

26 De Zayas, *Nemesis at Potsdam*, 61–65.

27 Schieder, *Dokumentation der Vertreibung*, vol. I, part 1, 7–8. Potrek provided his report to the commission on January 14, 1953, that was preparing documentation of the flight and expulsion of Germans from eastern Europe from the end of 1944 through 1948. The translation provided here is taken from de Zayas, *Nemesis at Potsdam*, 63–64.

28 De Zayas, *Nemesis at Potsdam*, 62–63.

29 See Fisch, *Nemmersdorf, Oktober 1944*; Knopp, *Die große Flucht*; and Lachauer, *Die Brücke von Tilsit*.

30 Fisch, *Nemmersdorf, Oktober 1944*, 124–26.

31 Lachauer, *Die Brücke von Tilsit*, 277–78. "Die fahle Oktobersonne leuchtet bleich und anklagend über den grauen Blutterror an der Angerapp. Grau und verarbeitet sind die Hände der von den Sowjets hingemordeten Männer und

Frauen…. Tränenlos stehen die deutschen Soldaten vor ihnen…. Aus ihrem Blick spricht der Wille, nun noch härter und schonungsloser gegen die Soviets zu kämpfen…. Das sind nicht einzelne Taten einer sadistichen Horde—das ist systematischer Massenmord, wie ihn nur die Sowjets kennen…. Der Krieg ist in sein gnadenlosestes Stadium getreten. Hier endet alles, was man bisher in Begriffe fassen konnte. Die bestialische Bluttat von Nemmersdorf wird den Bolschewisten teuer zu stehen kommen."

32 This quotation is taken from Knopp, *Die große Flucht*, 51. "Im Grunde genommen hat Nemmersdorf die Fluchtbewegung ausgelöst. Ansonsten hätten viele gesagt: 'Ach, was sollen wir im Winter auf die Straße gehen, wir bleiben zu Hause, egal, was passiert.' Durch Nemmersdorf aber waren auch die Letzten so verängstigt worden, daß sie wegwollten, weil sie ahnten, es würde kein gutes Ende nehmen."

33 Schieder, *Dokumentation der Vertreibung*, vol. I, part 1, 12–13.

34 Meindl, *Ostpreußens Gauleiter*, 434–35. Meindl cites sources indicating that the population of East Prussia was roughly 2.4 million in March 1944, and had declined to about 1.75 million by the end of that year.

35 Knopp, *Die große Flucht*, 53. "Die unbefriedigenden Ergebnisse des Oktobers zeigten, daß wir den schon länger im Einsatz befindlichen Divisionen eine Ruhepause gönnen, unsere Truppen umgruppieren, die rückwärtigen Dienste nachziehen, und für einen Durchbruch sowie für die anschließende Entwicklung der Operation erforderlichen materiellen Vorräte schaffen mußten."

36 This assessment of the relative strength of Russian and German forces is given by Guderian, *Panzer Leader*, 382.

37 Ibid., 384.

38 Ibid., 387.

39 Ibid., 388.

40 Dieckert and Großmann, *Der Kampf um Ostpreussen*, 77.

41 For a comprehensive descrption of the battle for East Prussia, see Buttar, *Battleground Prussia*.

42 Report no. 5, "Die lezten Monate und Tage vor der Einnahme Insterburgs durch die Russen," in Schieder, *Dokumentation der Vertreibung*, vol. I, part 1, "Dokumente," 9–19.

43 Richardson, ed., *The Secret History of World War II*, 238–39.

44 Seaton, *The Russo-German War*, 532–34.

45 See Duffy, *Red Storm on the Reich*, 320 and 357–58, for estimates of the strength of Russian and German divisions.

46 Raus, *Panzer Operations*, 311–12.

47 Lehndorff, *Token of a Covenant*, 5–6.

48 Schieder, *Dokumentation der Vertreibung*, vol. I, part 1, 15. "Und nun geschah, was ich kaum zu hoffen gewagt hatte. Der theoretische Räumungsplan bewährte sich bis in seine Einzelheiten. In vorbildlicher Pflichterfüllung und Zusammenarbeit tat jeder, was ihm aufgetragen oder für ihn vorgesehen war."

49 Raus, *Panzer Operations*, 314.

50 See Peyinghaus, *Stille Jahre*, 198.

51 Lasch, *So fiel Königsberg*, 34.

52 Duffy, *Red Storm on the Reich*, 157–58.

53 Dieckert and Grossman, *Der Kampf um Ostpreussen*, 96.

54 Eckert-Möbius, *Flucht der Trömpauer*. The author herself did not, in fact, witness the flight from Trömpau because she had already left the estate on August 1, 1944, in considerable haste in response to an urgent telephone call from her mother-in-law in Halle (near Leipzig in eastern Germany). Her mother-in-law urged her to come to Halle as soon as possible to escape from the advancing Red Army. In the 1980s she contacted nearly all of the Trömpauer who had survived the war and obtained vivid descriptions of their fate on their flight from Trömpau.

55 There appears to be some inconsistency in Eckert-Möbius's account of what happened to those living in Trömpau. At several points in her narrative she states that only three chose to remain at the estate, and these three are mentioned in the text below. However, Erna Schmidtke was quite clear in her report that when her family returned to their house in Trömpau, they found "Oma und Opa," her maternal grandparents, so that it appears that five of those living there had decided not to escape as the Russians were closing in.

56 Report by Herta Rudnick in Eckert-Möbius, *Flucht der Trömpauer*. "Jedenfalls erlebten wir an diesem Nachmittttag am Hafen einen furchtbaren Fliegerangriff. Im Nu waren die Flugzeuge über uns wie ein Bienenschwarm. Sie flogen niedrig und schoßen wahllos mit Bordwaffen in die Menschenmenge. Auf diesem Gelände. Wir rannten auseinander. Da war eine Bahnhofshalle, in die ich hineinlief.... Das Bahnhofsgebäude fiel über uns zusammen—ich lag unten, alle anderen auf mir drauf. So passierte mir nichts—ich lag sozusagen in Deckung.... In der Halle, in der ich dann lag, waren Bretter und Glassplitter auf uns heruntergefallen. Es waren viele durch die Splitter verletzt. Diese 'Hölle' dauerte vielleicht 10 Minuten. Dann war alles vorbei. Aber meine Güte, was hatte der Angriff in den paar Minuten angerichtet!"

57 Abraham, *Flucht aus Ostpreußen*, 25.

58 Eckert-Möbius, *Flucht der Trömpauer*. "Dann hieß es: ein Schiff kommt! Es war ein Frachter mit Namen 'Deike Rickmers.' Jetzt began ein Chaos!!! Pillau war ja übervoll mit Flüchtlingen. Wir wurden aufgefordert, uns einschiffen zu lassen. Bewaffnete Marinesoldaten haben dann die Einschiffung an der Gangway übernommen. Wir hatten schon keine Hoffnung mehr auf das Schiff zu kommen. Da tauchte plötzlich unser Ortsgruppenleiter Friedrichs aus Schmiedehnen auf und schob uns an den Soldaten vorbei auf das Schiff. Ein Glück für Frau Pläp, daß sie bei uns war, denn es hieß: Frauen ohne Kinder dürfen nicht an Bord! Was nun? Wir haben einfach meinen Bruder als ihren Sohn ausgegeben und so ging sie mit an Bord."

59 As described in Chapter IV, the *Cap Arcona* was one of several large ships used to rescue refugees that was sunk with large loss of life. The sinking of this ship was particularly tragic because on board were several thousand concentration camp inmates, only 350 of whom survived.

60 Dönhoff, "Nach Ostern fuhr keiner mehr," in *Namen die keiner mehr nennt*, 7–33. For an eloquent appreciation of Dönhoff, see Egremont, *Forgotten Land*, 126–137.

61 Soine, *Vertrieben—geschunden—mißbraucht*.

62 Ibid., 65. "Mutter war völlig verstört, als sie mit der traurigen Nachricht zu uns kam; wir hielten uns fest umklammert und weinten bittere Tränen."

63 Kirstein, *Mein Tagebuch*.

64 Ibid., 53. "Es ist Sonnabend der 24.2. Zwölf Pferde wurden zum beschlagen gebracht. Und dann hieß es, die Russen übernachten hier. Mir blieb das Herz vor Schreck stehen. Was machen die drei. Den ganzen Tag in der Verbannung und auch noch die Nacht. O Gott, es ist schrecklich, alle Tage etwas Neues und immer qualvoller."

65 See Gause, *Die Geschichte der Stadt Königsberg*, Chapter V, 1. "Königsberg im Zweiten Weltkriege," 156–70.

66 Lehndorff, *Token of a Covenant*, 23.

67 Many relatives of the author's wife, including her maternal grandfather and grandmother, chose to remain in Königsberg and several did not survive the Soviet occupation.

68 Meindl, *Ostpreußens Gauleiter*, 452.

69 For a somewhat different account of the fate of Dräger and Szelinski, see Tilitzki, *Alltag in Ostpreußen*, 310. These two accounts agree, however, that both were arrested for leaving Königsberg without authorization and that Dräger was executed and Szelinski committed suicide.

70 Lasch, *So fiel Königsberg*, 49–51.

71 Duffy, *Red Storm on the Reich*, 161.

72 Guderian, *Panzer Leader*, 392–93.

73 Document no. 8, "Experiences on the flight and among the advancing Russians in the area of Osterode," in Schieder, *The Expulsion of the German Population*, 129–33.

74 Ibid., 132.

75 Duffy, *Red Storm on the Reich*, 169.

76 Guderian, *Panzer Leader*, 400–401.

77 Dieckert and Großmann, *Der Kampf um Ostpreusser*, 114.

78 Duffy, *Red Storm on the Reich*, 173.

79 Dieckert and Großmann, *Der Kampf um Ostpreusser*, 125. What were called in the German Navy "torpedo boats" were in fact much larger than the torpedo boats in the U.S. Navy in World War II. They were roughly the size of a U.S. destroyer escort. I am grateful to Charles McCain for pointing out this difference to me.

80 Ibid., 136–37.

81 Document no. 20, "Flight over the Haff to the west of the Reich," in Schieder, *The Expulsion of the German Population*, 135.

82 Schlewski, "Letzte Tage in Allenstein und Flucht nach Dänemark," in Reinoss, ed., *Letzte Tage in Ostpreussen*.

83 Ibid., 65.

84 Clough, *In langer Reihe über das Haff*, 113–23.

85 Ibid., 116.

86 The camp at Stutthof was set up in 1939 to house Polish prisoners taken following the attack on Poland on September 1, 1939. It was originally designed as a labor camp, but it became a concentration camp in 1942 and was the center of dozens of satellite camps, which received Soviet POWs, Jews from eastern Europe, as well as Gypsies and others considered undesirable by the Nazis. In the summer of 1944, as the Soviet forces were approaching the Baltic countries, Jews and other inmates in the concentration camps there were transferred to Stutthof and its satellite camps. The march of thousands of mainly Jewish women from these camps in January 1945 via Königsberg to their deaths in Palmnicken on the Samland coast is described in Chapter V. The Stutthof camp is described in Roy, *The Vanished Kingdom*, 241–52.

87 Grass, *Peeling the Onion*, 88.

88 Ibid., 37.

89 Wermter, *Flucht und Vertreibung der Familie Wermter*.

90 Bamm, *Die unsichtbare Flagge*, 326–61.

91 For a compact description, see Gause, *Die Geschichte der Stadt Königsberg*, Chapter V, 1. "Königsberg im Zweiten Weltkriege," 156–70. See also Denny, *The Fall of Hitler's Fortress City*.

92 Lehndorff, *Token of a Covenant*, 52.

93 Lasch, *So fiel Königsberg*, 65.

94 Ibid., 66. "Ein erschütterndes Beispiel dafür, bis zu welchem Grade des Empfindens für Recht und Unrecht in manchen Köpfen damals ausgelöscht war."

95 Ibid., 64. "Zivilbevölkerung und Truppe haben in diesen Wochen als große, auf Gedeih und Verderb angewiesene Familie zusammengearbeitet. Alle leben und schafften in dem Gedanken Königsberg solange zu halten, bis entweder von außen her der immer wieder zugesagte Entsatz oder durch eine Beendigung des Krieges auf dem Verhandlungswege die Freiheit kommen würde."

96 Ibid., 82. "Aber schon mit Rücksicht auf die Königsberger Bevölkerung, die immer noch gläubig auf ihre Wehrmacht vertraute, mußte der Versuch, die Festung zu verteidigen, unternommen werden. Vielleicht ergaben sich noch Möglichkeiten, die Zivilbevölkerung unter dem Schutz ihrer Verteidiger zunäschst ins Samland und dann über Pillau ins Reich und nach Dänmark hinüber zu retten."

97 Duffy, *Red Storm on the Reich*, 166.

98 Ibid., 166, and Lasch, *So fiel Königsberg*, 74–75.

99 Lasch, *So fiel Königsberg*, 78.

100 Ibid., 84.

101 As described in Chapter II, the Alhambra was the movie theater frequented by Marianne Peyinghaus when she visited Königsberg from the village of Gertlaucken where she was an elementary school teacher.

102 Wieck, *A Childhood under Hitler and Stalin*, 121–22.

103 Ibid., 124.

104 Lehndorff, *Token of a Covenant*, 62–63.

105 Rörup, *Also sprach Vielliebchen*, an unpublished manuscript entitled, "Mutterland-Gedächtnisband: Blinde Flecken," and a personal interview with the author, November 21, 2004.

106 One of the two children, Heide-Hede Könitzer (a second cousin of Iris Rörup) became the wife of the author.

107 Rörup, *Also sprach Vielliebchen*, 16. "Ich habe den ersten Weltkrieg erlebt. Wo sollen wir denn hin? Unsere Häuser am Rande der Stadt stehen noch. Seht euch das Flüchtlingselend doch an."

108 Lasch, *So fiel Königsberg*, 94.

109 Lehndorff, *Token of a Covenant*, 65–66.

110 Wieck, *A Childhood under Hitler and Stalin*, 127.

111 Lasch, *So fiel Königsberg*, 95. "Jetzt ist auch dem Stellvertretenden Gauleiter und seinen Getreuen der Schreck in die Glieder gefahren. Es dämmert ihnen die Erkenntnis, daß Königsberg verloren ist." "Die Festung ist weiterhin zu halten. Für den Durchbruch der Parteileute und der Zivilbevölkerung sind nur schwache Kräfte zu verwenden."

112 Ibid., 98. "Immer wieder krachten die Einschläge der Bomben, Granaten, und schweren Stalinorgeln, dazwischen stürzten stehengebliebene Häuserfassaden auf die Straße und wurden riesige Bombentrichter aufgerißen. In diese Hölle drangte sich von Süden und von Norden Trosse, LKWs, Artillerie- und Sturmgeschütze, bis sie sich so ineinander verkeilt hatten, daß sie weder vor noch zurück konnten. Es war ein grauenhaftes Bild. Durch dieses Inferno mußte das Regiment sich hindurcharbeiten, immer wieder nach einem Weg suchend, immer wieder vor einer Panzersperre oder vor Riesenkratern ausweichen. Unsere Artillerie- und Gefechtstrosse sassen nach kurzer Zeit rettungslos fest eingekeilt zwischen Fahrzeugen aller Art, abgeschnitten durch neue Trichter und Zerstörungen."

113 Taken from Wieck, *A Childhood under Hitler and Stalin*, 132.

114 Dieckert and Großmann, *Der Kampf um Ostpreussen*, 182. "Der Befehlshaber von Königsberg, Lasch, hat einen Augenblick meiner Abwesenheit aus der Festung benutzt, um feige zu kapitulieren. Ich kämpfe im Samland und auf der Nehrung weiter."

115 Wieck, *A Childhood under Hitler and Stalin*, 133.

116 Lasch, *So fiel Königsberg*, 101. "Am Tage sahen wir hinter uns die sterbende Stadt. Eingehüllt in einem Mantel von Rauch und Feuer, in den sich immer wieder die Feuerbahnen der schweren Werfergeschoße hineinfraßen. Um 17.00 Uhr erstarb langsam das Feuer. Nur von einigen Stellen kleckerten noch einzelne MG, bis schließlich auch diese letzten Zeichen des Kampfes verstummten. Im Abenddunkel wölbten sich nur noch die von vielen Bränden unheimlich rot angeleuchteten, schwarzen Rauchwolken über der toten Stadt. Die Festung Königsberg war untergegangen...."

117 Palmnicken was the scene of the massacre of hundreds of Jewish women by the SS at the end of January and is described in Chapter V.

118 Dokument 1 (report of Frau Anna Grohnert from Königsberg) in *Vertreibung und Vertreibungsverbrechen 1945–1948*, 134–37.

119 This account of the first engineer on the *Ostpreußen* standing up to Koch is from Lass, *Die Flucht*, 316–17. An alternative account of Koch's escape is that he departed from Neutief by plane on April 24 and flew to Hela, where he boarded the icebreaker *Ostpreußen*. See Meindl, *Ostpreußens Gauleiter*, 455.

120 Dieckert and Großmann, *Der Kampf um Ostpreussen*, 196–97, and *Welt am Sonntag*, November 16, 1986, no. 46, 4.

121 Dieckert and Großmann, *Der Kampf um Ostpreussen*, 167–68, where they quote a passage from *Ostsee, Deutsches Schicksal 1944/1945*, by Cajus Bekker. "Hier an Bord Gauleiter Forster. Sie haben uns gar nichts zu befehlen!" "Hier spricht Gauleiter Forster von Danzig-Westpreußen! Ich werde Sie zur Rechenschaft ziehen!" "Und hier spricht Kapitänleutnant Weilig. Dieses ist ein Befehl. Veranlassen Sie sofort, daß Ihr Dampfer die Fähre abschleppt. Sonst werden Sie beschoßen!"

122 Paul Bernecker, "Flüchtlinge im Raum Heiligenbeil," in Reinoss, ed., *Letzte Tage in Ostpreussen*, 59.

123 As described above, this airport was also used to evacuate soldiers with severe head wounds. See Bamm, *Die unsichtbare Flagge*, 338–39.

124 Dieckert and Großmann, *Der Kampf um Ostpreussen*, 203.

125 Schmidtke, *Rettungsaktion Ostsee 1944/194*, 298.

CHAPTER IV

THE BRUTAL BEHAVIOR OF SOVIET TROOPS: WHY DID THIS HAPPEN?

A. German Eyewitness Reports of Rape

The raping of women, the brutal murders of innocent civilians, and the wanton destruction of property when Soviet forces invaded East Prussia and other eastern provinces in Germany were undertaken in wholesale fashion by soldiers and officers alike. When Soviet forces entered a town or village, women were hunted down to be raped—often repeatedly by a number of soldiers—and old women and young teenagers were not spared. In many cases these sexual attacks were carried out in public and in the presence of the victims' children. Husbands were often forced to witness bestial assaults on their wives, and if they tried to protect them, they were typically shot on the spot. At times, women put up stiff resistance and were left unmolested, but such resistance sometimes resulted in instant death. Giving in to soldiers' demands did not necessarily spare them from subsequent violence, as many victims were mutilated and killed after being raped. The extreme trauma of being violated in such brutal fashion scarred women for the rest of their lives and for many the experience was so devastating that they committed suicide.

Women were never safe from the marauding Russians. The previous chapter described how the young medical student, Josefine Schleiter from Osterode

(Ostróda) in East Prussia, had at first managed to avoid being assaulted when she was overtaken by the advancing Red Army.[1] However, her luck ran out when she was walking on a road to find refuge on a nearby farm:

> Suddenly a motor car stopped and three very tall fellows surround-
> ed and seized hold of me, and threw me into their car. My cries
> could not be heard in the snow storm. The car started off and I
> was standing in it, being gazed at by one of the Russians. I was ice-
> cold. Since mid-day I had been without food and had nothing but
> what was on my body. One of the fellows, who was covered up in
> rugs, grinned at me and asked cynically: "Cold?" The car slowed
> down and I sprang out, it stopped immediately and I was again
> thrown back. There then followed the most dishonoring moments
> in my life which I cannot describe. The car stopped again sudden-
> ly. I jumped out and driven by a terrible fear ran as quickly as I
> could into the winter darkness.... I ran without stopping until I
> came to a little bridge. Here I took refuge and would have liked
> best to lie down in the snow, in order not to wake up again.[2]

Christel Soine had also been able to elude Russian soldiers intent on attacking women, but in the fall of 1945 she fell victim to sexual assault. She and her mother had been working for the Russians on a collective farm in the village of Irglaken near Tapiau (Gvardeysk), which gave them a certain amount of protection from the attention of soldiers. When the fall harvest had been completed, the collective farm was disbanded and they were on their own:

> Since the "protective factor" of the collective farm no longer
> existed for our security, the fear of nightly attacks naturally rose.
> This fear was justified. Mother, Ellie, and I lived at this time in
> a tiny attic cubbyhole, and one night we were roughly awakened
> by a racket on the stairs. Shortly afterward a Russian stood in the
> doorway with a gun and a flashlight. He illuminated the room

and discovered me. Mother wanted to protect me and pleaded with the brute—I was still just a child—to let me go, but in vain. This "piece of shit" tore the blanket off us, pointed at me and said "you good." Then he chased mother and Ellie into the attic and attacked me brutally. I could not even yell as the sadist held my mouth closed. I do not want to describe details—in front of the door the next one was waiting!

This terrible experience caused me such a severe emotional shock that I was never quite able to overcame and it hindered me my entire life to develop a healthy attitude toward sexuality.[3]

Whether women escaped rape depended on the disposition of the Russians. A woman identified only as Frau E. H. described the different fate of two women and that of her own twenty-five-year-old sister on March 10, 1945, when Red Army soldiers took over the village of Groß Damerkow where she had fled after receiving orders to evacuate:

Suddenly a female neighbor came in screaming out that the Russians wanted to take her with them. There then came two Russians into our room: "Woman come," and seized two women by the hands. These women screamed and begged so much, that the Russians let them go and went away.

Thereupon, a big Russian came in. He did not utter a single word, but then went to the back where all the young girls and women were sitting. He beckoned once with his finger to my sister. As she did not stand up at once, he went close up to her and held his machine pistol against her chin. Everyone screamed aloud, but my sister sat there mutely and was incapable of moving. Then a shot resounded. Her head fell to the side and the blood streamed out. She was dead instantly, without uttering a single sound. The bullet had gone from her chin to her brain and her skull was completely shattered.

The Russian looked at us all, and went away again without uttering a single word. We laid my sister to her last rest in the cemetery of Gross Damerkow.[4]

A graphic description of rape is provided in a report by a Frau E. O. from Elbing (Elblag) in West Prussia:

> On January 29, 1945, at 6:30 in the morning, I was taken prisoner. Immediately on encountering Russian soldiers, my boots and coat were taken from me. In the pram I had my daughter Christa, 15 months old, and I held the hand of my son Horst, 7½ years old. The entire Richthofenstrasse was soon filled with men, women and children. A group of about 1500 people was driven into the railroad station waiting room.... Here already began the rapes of the young women. Visible to all in front of the station I saw a young girl H. N., 15 years old from Elbing-Trettinkenhof, being raped by Russian soldiers. The mother of H. N. defended her daughter because the Russian soldiers used her over and over again, and she paid for her courage and her fight two days later with her life....
>
> A short while later we were taken in the direction of the Tannenberger Allee and given temporary housing. The war rages on. Russian reserve troops marched into the Tannenberger Allee and were temporarily housed very close to our makeshift quarters. We were again looked over and sorted by age. I was then 39 years old. One room in these temporary quarters had been made ready for the rapes to follow. First came the younger women, my turn came towards morning and I was used immediately by three soldiers. These rapes were repeated twice daily, each time by several soldiers, until the seventh day. The seventh day was my worst day, as I was taken away in the evening and released in the morning. My vagina was completely torn and I had an arm-thick growth from the vagina down both thighs to the knee. Then followed three more

of those horrible days until the sixth. I could no longer walk or lie down…. Then the Russian soldiers were finished with us and we were chased naked out of this room of hell. Other women took our place. An older woman gave me a blanket. These horrors took place in the presence of ten women and also often in the presence of one's own children, but my two children were spared this. During these terrible days we did not get any food, only alcohol and cigarettes.[5]

The report from Frau E. S. in the East Prussian town of Rössel (Reszel) describes how German women were driven to suicide as a result of actual or threatened rape:

Around February 20, 1945, fixed formations arrived in Roessel which then became a garrison town. Plundering took place day and night and the rapes never ended. Many women, for example, Frau B., pleaded with Dr. N. from the hospital to give her some poison. He did not give it to her. Among those brutally mistreated by coarse men were children of 13 to 14, such as the fourteen-year-old daughter of W. F. and the thirteen-year-old daughter of businessman V. M. My girlfriend E. W. was taken by Russian soldiers to her mother, she was so weak she could not walk and was sick for a long time. A young girl from the housing development could no longer endure the rapes and took concentrated vinegar and died with terrible pain. Another young woman, also a refugee wife, hanged herself for the same reason. When a Russian appeared at the door, women and girls fled through the windows. Then the Russians surrounded the houses and fetched their victims.[6]

The raping of German women was by no means confined to East Prussia; it was prevalent in all parts of Germany invaded by the Red Army. The battle for Berlin—April 14 to May 2, 1945—has been particularly well documented, with extensive coverage of assaults on women.[7] Sometimes the women were successfully hidden; a husband was able to convince the marauding soldiers that his wife was dead, but he had dug a three-foot hole in the floor where he was able to hide her behind a sofa on which he stretched out while the soldiers looked around his living room. At other times women were raped, but the Russian, usually an officer, would stay with his victim to protect her from assaults from other soldiers. Pregnant women and those who had just given birth were not spared at House Dahlem, the orphanage, maternity hospital, and foundling home run by the Mission Sisters of the Sacred Heart in the Berlin suburb of Dahlem. The Mother Superior reported that the screaming went on day and night and that the victims included seventy-year-old women and girls of ten and twelve. Many who had suffered terribly at the hands of Red Army soldiers committed suicide. One mother of three small children had been taken away from her family and been raped the entire night. After being released in the morning, she raced back to her children only to find that her mother and brother had hanged all three and then themselves, whereupon she slit her wrists and also died. In the Pankow district of Berlin alone, 215 suicides were reported in a period of three weeks.[8]

The extent of the sexual assaults by Soviet troops was enormous and has been documented in countless eyewitness reports by German victims.[9] In addition, attempts have been made to estimate the number of women who were raped in Germany. One such statistical analysis, reported by Heike Sander and Barbara Johr, used hospital records and other sources and concluded that of 1.4 million women over the age of fourteen living in Berlin, at least one hundred and ten thousand (7.1 percent) were raped between the spring and fall of 1945, with the vast majority in the months of April, May, and June.[10] For the areas of Germany subject to expulsions—East Prussia, East Pomerania, East Brandenburg, and Silesia—Dr. Gerhard Reichling has estimated that 1.4 million German woman were raped, of whom one hundred and eighty thousand (12.9 percent) committed suicide.[11]

B. Soviet Accounts of Rape and Pillage by the Red Army[12]

The Soviet side has provided limited coverage of the atrocities committed by their troops, as Catherine Merridale has extensively documented in *Ivan's*

War: Life and Death in the Red Army, 1939–1945. When interviewed decades after World War II, dozens of surviving Red Army soldiers were uniformly reluctant to describe their experiences in the heat of battle, much less to recount assaults on German civilians by themselves or by their comrades. The internal records of the NKVD troops, who had the responsibility for maintaining discipline on the front line, were marked "absolutely secret" but hardly mention any incidents of gang rape and few incidents of individual crimes; instead, the great majority of cases in their reports dealt with drunkenness and absence without leave.[13]

While the official Soviet account of "The Great Patriotic War" fails to deal with the wanton behavior of their troops, a few individual Soviet accounts corroborate German eyewitness reports. Merridale cited one report that was written by a young officer named Leonid Rabichev who participated in the attacks on Insterburg (Chernyakhovsk) and Goldap (Goldap) in East Prussia:

> Women, mothers and their children, lie to the right and left along the route…and in front of each of them stands a raucous armada of men with their trousers down.… The women who are bleeding or losing consciousness get shoved to one side…and our men shoot the ones who try to save their children. Meanwhile, a group of "grinning" officers stood nearby, one of whom was "directing—no, he was regulating it all. This was to make sure that every soldier without exception took part.[14]

The soldiers under Rabichev's command were "less composed" when they discovered a building where the bodies of women who had been raped had also been mutilated and an empty bottle of wine had been shoved into each woman's vagina. Rabichev was encouraged by other officers to choose a German girl from among a group of cowering Germans and he complied, fearful that his fellow soldiers might regard him as a coward or, worse, as impotent if he refused.[15]

A Ukrainian artillery officer, Isaak Kobylyanskiy, reported in his war memoirs that he personally never witnessed a sexual assault. In fact, he protected a fifty-year-old woman in Königsberg from the unwanted attentions of a Russian soldier who was not in his regiment. However, he was aware that such assaults were widespread: "I think I ought not to pass over in silence the very troublesome topic concerning the sexual behavior and sexual crimes of our troops in East Prussia."[16] He related the horrific account conveyed to him (Kobylyanskiy was fluent in German) by an eighteen-year-old German woman named Annie whom he met in July 1945 in a hamlet outside of Pillau. When Soviet forces approached in late April 1945, she tried to escape to Pillau, but having badly sprained her leg, was overtaken by Russian soldiers just half a mile from the port and ordered to return to her hamlet. It took her a week: along the way she was incessantly raped day and night by passing soldiers, sometimes by three men one after another. Altogether she was assaulted by eighty soldiers by the time she had returned home and was sick for two weeks. She was still running a high fever when she told Kobylanskiy her awful tale. Her last words to him were, "I began growing stronger just recently, but the nightmares still stay with me."[17]

A vivid and moving account of the early days of the Soviet invasion of East Prussia was written by none other than Alexander Solzhenitsyn, but it was not published until 1974 and only in Paris. He had served as a captain in an artillery unit attached to the Second Belorussian Front. His unit advanced rapidly through the center of the province, reaching Neidenberg (Nidzica) on January 20, Allenstein (Olsztyn) on January 22, and the Baltic on January 26. His searing narrative poem, *Prussian Nights,* provides a graphic description of the horrific brutality, rape, and pillage inflicted on the province as his unit thrust into East Prussia. The following selected passages convey the endemic violence committed against civilians as the Red Army first set foot on German soil:

> Zweiundzwanzig, Höringstrasse.
> It's not been burned, just looted, rifled.
> A moaning, by the walls half-muffled:
> The mother's wounded, still alive.

The little daughter's on the mattress,
Dead. How many have been on it?
A platoon, a company, perhaps?
A girl's been turned into a woman,
A woman turned into a corpse.
It's all come down to simple phrases:
Do not forget! Do not forgive!
Blood for blood! A tooth for a tooth!
The mother begs, "Töte mich, Soldat!"
Her eyes are hazy and bloodshot.
The dark's upon her, she can't see.[18]

And … Cossacks go from carriage to carriage.
Sabres ring and rifles thud.
"O-u-t!" And down along the platform
In fur coats, hats, and boots they herd—
"Leave your things!" They drive the helpless
Terrified *civilians* now
On foot to the collection depot
Across the town, through rosy snow.
On the way, they start selecting
Those they feel they want to spend a
Hot five minutes with in a doorway
Or any corner that comes handy.
A limping general from Supply,
With orderly and ADC,
Just a shade distastefully,
Picks his way among the corpses,
Choosing stuff for sending home.
Probing with his stick, he shows
A scarf, a ring, some cloth, some shoes.
And at once they're seized and sunk
In the black depths of a trunk.[19]

Some soldiers have gathered around
A pram that's been abandoned,
                              Blue,

      Lace trimmings too:
      "Look, a little 'un.
        Still, he's a German!
He'll grow and put a helmet on.
Deal with him now, d'you think?
The order from the Supreme Command
Is *Blood for Blood!* Give no quarter!"
"To talk like that! What, are you drunk?
Are you Herod? Is your priest
Some abominable beast?"
"It's not me, grandpa!—Moscow's order!"[20]

The silver of the Prussian noons,
The crimson of the Prussian nights.
Two logs stand crossed upon the road
To signal detour. Iron fate's
Changed its route. Dreamlike there floats
Before us, somewhere to the side,
Silent, trackless, deep in snows,
Someone's solitary house,
With the virgin woods behind.
Someone's noisy column turned
Toward smoke rising from the hearth.
They've hardly cut the engines' noise
When they're out to find some warmth.
Slapping their shoulders, they reach the house.
Now they're in. She stands there, numb.
They laugh. "Get us some eggs then, mum!"
And the housewife does her best,
Brings them apples, ripe and brittle,
They grabbed them, walked around a little,

A crunch between their teeth like frost.
And then they shot the housewife first,
Spattering with blood the carpet's pile.
The husband was bedridden, ill:
They cured him with a carbine burst.[21]

Solzhenitsyn is aghast when he hears that one soldier intends to kill the German baby boy in the blue pram, and he is in anguish when a casual wave of his hand is interpreted by two soldiers under his command as a signal to murder a young German woman. Yet over time he becomes caught up in the spirit of uncontrolled license taken by the soldiers and officers around him to loot and rape. He tries to resist the temptation to join in, but ultimately succumbs and excuses his actions with, "Everyone behaves like that," "Carpe diem…seize the day," and "Life offers a drink, so bottoms up!"[22] At the end of *Prussian Nights* he confesses to some embarrassment when he moves among the women crowded in a room and picks one by the name of Anne whom he lures into an empty wing of the farmhouse where:

Questioning, and unsure,
She stepped back toward the threshold . . .
I strode to the still-open door,
And I shut it with a crash.
Condemned to action, without looking,
I gestured to her, "Komm!"
It wasn't passion, or the firm
Pleasure in the muscles ringing . . .
With my back to the mean bed I
Shortly heard that she—was ready . . .

And after, unnaturally close
To the pale blue of her eyes,
I said to her—too late—"How base!"
Anne, that moment, with her face
Sunk in the pillow, in an unsteady

> Voice that she could not control,
> Begged, "Doch erschiessen Sie mich nicht!"
>
> Have no fear. . . For—Oh!—already
> Another's soul is on my soul...[23]

Thus Solzhenitsyn is himself tainted with the stain of sexual assault, however much he may have felt remorse afterward. There is, moreover, other evidence suggesting he did not regard the rape of German women as a crime. After three weeks on the East Prussian front he was arrested for sending home letters deemed anti-Soviet. He was put in a cell with three tank soldiers who had been accused of attempting to rape two German peasant women. Solzhenitsyn considered this accusation to be a miscarriage of justice as they were being punished solely because one of the women was the "campaign wife" of the Soviet chief of counterintelligence.[24]

Solzhenitsyn is taken to task by Susan Brownmiller, author of *Against Our Will: Men, Women and Rape*, for his cavalier attitude toward rape. To make her point she quotes from his *Gulag Archipelago*: "Yes! For three weeks the war had been going on inside Germany and all of us know very well that if the girls were German they could be raped and then shot." She criticizes him because, "Never pausing to contemplate the problem or the meaning of rape in war, or a workable system of deterrence and punishment, Solzhenitsyn plainly considers the offense in question no offense at all, attributable to over-enthusiastic drunkenness."[25]

Lev Kopelev was another Soviet officer who witnessed what happened in East Prussia. Fluent in German, he rose to the rank of major in the Red Army's political department. His responsibilities included interviewing German civilians and identifying those German prisoners who could be persuaded to return to their units and sow confusion and dissension in their ranks. He participated with Solzhenitsyn in the same advance of the Second Belorussian Front into East Prussia in mid-January 1945. In his memoir, *To be Preserved Forever,* he described the same looting, rape, summary executions, arson, and wanton destruction witnessed by Solzhenitsyn. His book was not published until 1975, and not in

Russia but in the United States. An ardent member of the Communist Party, Kopelev strongly criticized the havoc wreaked by his fellow soldiers and officers as inconsistent with Communist ideology, and on numerous occasions he intervened to protect German civilians from attack by his compatriots.

Kopelev was also incensed by the senseless torching of buildings in East Prussia by Russian troops. Upon entering the very first villages on German soil, Groß Koslau and Klein Koslau, Kopelev's driver kept their Ford truck—the vehicle was part of the United States' Lend-Lease program to Russia—in the middle of the road because the houses on both sides of the street were in flames. It was like driving through a hot, fiery tunnel and the Ford could easily have caught fire from the clouds of sparks and burning pieces of wood generated by the conflagration. Kopelev's superior officer, Belyaev, kept shouting to the driver to drive faster to get them out of the inferno. After they made it safely to the town square, Kopelev asked other Russian drivers if there had been a battle with Germans in the village. One responded that all the German soldiers and civilians had left without firing a shot and that "our guys" had set fire to the buildings. Kopelev asked why they did it:

"Who the hell knows? Just did it, without thinking."

A mustached soldier said with a kind of indolent bitterness: "The word is: 'This is Germany. So smash, burn, have your revenge.' But where do we spend the night afterward? Where do we put the wounded?"

Another of the men stared at the flames. "All that stuff going to waste. Back home, where I come from, everyone's naked and barefoot these days. And here we are, burning without rhyme or reason."

Belyaev spoke up sententiously. "The Fritzes have plundered all over the world. That's why they've got so much. They burned down everything in our country, and Now we're doing the same in theirs. We don't have to feel sorry for them."

"No, not for them," I [Kopelev] said. "For ourselves. Senseless destruction does more damage to us than to them."[26]

That evening they reached the nearby town of Neidenburg and found that Red Army soldiers had finished plundering the houses and had set many on fire. After looking for loot in those not yet burned down, Belyaev ordered the men under his command to cart away a piano and other booty, and Kopelev persuaded him to load into their truck some books from an extensive library he had found in the house of a local judge. He rationalized his own participation in this pillage on the grounds that the houses had been abandoned and many had already been ransacked. Kopelev mentioned that shortly before the January 1945 winter offensive, Soviet troops had been given official permission to send parcels home, which he regarded as a direct and unequivocal "incitement to plunder." Indeed, in advance of the Russian New Year, on December 26, 1944, the Soviet Ministry of Defense had confirmed a regulation authorizing army soldiers and officers to ship parcels home from the front: soldiers were allowed to send eight kilograms (more than seventeen pound) per month, while officers were allotted twice as much.[27]

In reality, the amount of plunder shipped home exceeded these limits by a wide margin. Exposed to the much greater wealth in East Prussia, compared to the extreme scarcity faced by their own impoverished families in the Soviet Union, the Red Army troops took advantage of the opportunity to strip German houses of everything they could find. Senior officers commandeered automobiles to transport their booty, often fine china, bedding, and furs, and later in the war, requisitioned special trains to transport their plunder home. As food was in extremely short supply in the Soviet Union, many soldiers shipped canned goods, sugar, and chocolate to their families. Others sent useful items such as nails, panes of glass, tools, shoes, clothes, and cloth. Bicycles were another popular item even though most Russians did not know how to ride a bike. In Allenstein, Belyaev and Kopelev used axes to chop open a few of the crates that had been piled high on the platform at the train station and found them filled with blankets, mattresses, pillows, and overcoats. The shipment of parcels swamped the Soviet postal service and in the spring of 1945 the railhead at Kursk in Russia, as one example, took on the appearance of a huge warehouse.[28]

While in Allenstein, Kopelev and Belyaev came upon an old woman in a thin coat with a boa who was surrounded by several soldiers. Kopelev got out of the truck to help her, but Belyaev, sure she was a spy, yelled at Kopelev, "She's probably a plant! Shoot her and have done with it." He then jumped out of the truck, grabbed the old woman's handbag and emptied it, but only photos and spools of thread spilled out. Belyaev was nevertheless convinced she was a spy and he took out his pistol, whereupon:

> I [Kopelev] shout at him: "Are you out of your mind?" I grab his arm, argue, curse, cajole. There's a commotion behind us. One of the soldiers gives the old woman a push. She collapses on a bank of snow; there is a shot. She gives a rabbity whimper; the soldier fires his carbine a second time, and a third. The black bundle in the snow is still. The soldier, a mere boy, bends down looking for something—for her boa.
>
> I bellow, "What are you doing, you son of a bitch?"
>
> I turn on Belyaev. What to do now? Hit him between his stupid eyes? At this point I am not even indignant, just filled with a sense of helpless loathing.
>
> He [Belyaev] murmurs soothingly, "Come, now, don't take on so. Are you going to turn against your own people over a lousy German crone? To hell with her. She was bound to go, one way or another."[29]

Later that evening they drove to Neidenburg, where the streets were illuminated by the red glow of burning buildings. There they found a house where German civilians were hiding and discovered a woman covered with blankets and moaning in pain. Kopelev lifted the blankets and found the sheets covered with blood; the woman had been stabbed in the stomach and breast with a crude Plexiglas knife of the kind Russian soldiers fashioned from the windows of downed aircraft. Belyaev had no interest in the woman and looked around the house for booty. Not finding anything worth taking, he wanted to leave, but Kopelev objected:

"We can't just leave her here."

"What are we supposed to do? She'll croak anyway. She's probably a spy like the other one."

Again, a sense of humiliating helplessness. I can't leave her here in this state, in agony, with no one to come to her aid.

"Sidorych [Kopelev's orderly], finish her off." I give the order out of pity and helplessness, craven helplessness. Try to bandage her wounds? Run for the medics? Where will I find them? And will they come? And she has already lost so much blood.

I walk out of the house. Belyaev is saying, "There now, you did the right thing. You're a man after all."

There is a short burst behind us. We stand in the yard, smoking. Belyaev worries: "Where's that Sidorych?" He shouts for him. Sidorych comes out carrying a bundle.

"What took you so long?"

"Oh, I spotted these shoes for the old woman. They're worn, but they'll do."[30]

On these and other occasions during the East Prussian campaign, Kopelev was candid in making known to Soviet soldiers and officers alike his concern for the treatment of all civilians (Germans, Poles, and Soviet citizens doing forced labor in Germany), and he did not hesitate to try to protect German civilians from attacks by members of the Red Army. He argued that not all Germans were fascists and that seeking vengeance on innocent women, children, and old men was inconsistent with Communist ideology and the principles of Soviet internationalism. Above all, Kopelev gave vent to his feeling that the widespread pillage was corrupting and coarsening the Soviet Army. Eventually his outspokenness became known to his superior officers, and at his trial, Belyaev—whom at one time he considered to be his friend—gave damaging testimony against him. Despite his incessant attempts to clear his name, Kopelev was sentenced to ten years in prison for "having shown pity for the Germans" and for "bourgeois humanism." He was released in 1954.

Ultimately, the looting, rape, and drunkenness became so widespread that the troops' morale and fighting effectiveness were undermined. Kopelev reported that at his staff headquarters an order from the commander of the front, Marshal Rokossovsky, was read aloud; it decreed a court martial for looting, robbery, rape, and murder of civilians, and execution on the spot when necessary. He was also told of a division commander who shot a lieutenant who had assembled a group of soldiers in front of a German woman spread-eagled on the ground. Even Belyaev once tried to maintain order when he and Kopelev came across a truckload of Russian soldiers led by a sergeant stealing suitcases from Russian and Ukrainian women returning home from captivity in East Prussia. Belyaev took out his pistol and shouted, "'Orders of Marshall Rokossovsky—looters to be executed on the spot. Let's shoot this son of a bitch, to make an example for the others.' The sergeant pales and jumps back into the truck; the others hop onto the back, and the truck races off."[31]

These orders by Soviet generals and their occasional enforcement, as well as individual acts of kindness and protection by Soviet soldiers and officers, could not stem the tide of lawlessness and depredation that befell East Prussia, other eastern territories of Germany, and Berlin when they were invaded by the Red Army.[32] As Belyaev aptly put it after he had brandished his pistol at the sergeant: "'What can you do? It's war; people become brutalized.'"[33]

The excesses at the front were reported back up the chain of command. One such report is cited by Antony Beevor:

> "The number of extraordinary events is growing," the political department reported in its usual vocabulary of euphemisms, "as

well as immoral phenomena and military crimes. Among our troops there are disgraceful and politically harmful phenomena when, under the slogan of revenge, some officers and soldiers commit outrages and looting instead of honestly and selflessly fulfilling their duty to their Motherland."[34]

C. What Explains the Brutal Behavior of Soviet Troops?

1. Nazi Atrocities in the Soviet Union

One underlying motivating factor for the Soviet troops' brutality was vengeance for the atrocities committed in systematic fashion by the Germans in their invasion and occupation of the western part of the Soviet Union. The wholesale slaughter of civilians and wanton destruction of property that took place during Operation Barbarossa was summarized in Chapter II. The desire to settle accounts for the cruelty inflicted by the Germans appears again and again in the excerpts from Solzhenitsyn and Kopelev. Kopelev's superior officer Belyaev, in particular, constantly excused the barbaric behavior of Red Army troops as justified by the criminal behavior of German soldiers. The indelible memory of the savagery of German soldiers during their attack and occupation of the Soviet Union goes a long way in explaining the brutal behavior of the Red Army in East Prussia:

> "Our soldiers have not dealt with East Prussia any worse than the Germans did with Smolensk," a Russian combatant wrote home from a town inside the Prussian border. "We hate Germany and the Germans deeply. In one house, for example, our boys found a murdered woman and her two children. You can often see civilians lying dead in the street, too. But the Germans deserve the atrocities that they unleashed. You only have to think about Maidanek.... It's certainly cruel to have killed those children, but the cold-bloodedness of the Germans at Maidanek was a thousand times worse."[35]

Vasily Grossman has movingly described the suffering in the Soviet Union at the hands of the Germans. During the war he was a correspondent for *Red Star*, a Red Army newspaper, which was read more avidly by civilians than the official Communist Party newspaper *Izvestia*. He chronicled the Eastern Front and the notebooks he wrote to provide material for his newspaper articles formed the basis for his book *A Writer at War*.[36] Following the liberation of Ukraine in the fall of 1943 and winter of 1944, Grossman wrote that the destruction and murder by the Germans was so devastating that:

> Every soldier, every officer and every general of the Red Army who had seen the Ukraine in blood and fire, who had heard the true story of what had been happening in the Ukraine during the two years of German rule, understands to the bottom of their souls that there are only two sacred words left to us. One of them is "love" and the other one is "revenge".[37]

In his reporting on the wholesale slaughter of the Jews in Ukraine, Grossman—who was himself Jewish—brought home the horror of the extermination of innocent civilians. Rather than marshalling an array of statistics to make his point, he conveyed the immediacy of the crimes committed:

> There's no one left in Kazary [a village in Ukraine] to complain, no one to tell, no one to cry. Silence and calm hover over the dead bodies buried under the collapsed fireplaces now overgrown with weeds. This quiet is much more frightening than tears and curses.
>
> Old men and women are dead, as well as craftsmen and professional people: tailors, shoemakers, tinsmiths, jewelers, house painters, ironmongers, bookbinders, workers, freight handlers, carpenters, stove-makers, jokers, cabinetmakers, water carriers, millers, bakers, and cooks…dead are babushkas who could knit stockings and make tasty buns, cook bouillon and make strudel with apples and nuts…dead are eighty-year-old men and women

with cataracts on hazy eyes, with cold and transparent fingers and hair that rustled quietly like white paper, dead are newly-born babies who had sucked their mothers' breast greedily until their last minute.

This was different from the death of people in war, with weapons in their hands, the deaths of people who had left behind their houses, families, fields, songs, traditions and stories.... This was the murder of everyday traditions that grandfathers had passed to their grandchildren, this was the murder of memories, of a mournful song, folk poetry, of life, happy and bitter, this was the destruction of hearths and cemeteries....[38]

Grossman had grown up in Berdichev, a Ukrainian city of about sixty thousand some eighty miles (130 kilometers) southwest of Kiev. The Germans had captured it on July 7, 1941 as part of Operation Barbarossa. Shortly after it was re-taken by the Red Army two and one-half years later, on January 5, 1944, Grossman returned to look for his mother and other relatives. As his family was Jewish, he did not have much hope he would find them alive. In Berdichev, he visited the execution site close to the airstrip and interviewed the few Jewish survivors and local Ukrainians. He discovered that the Germans had used Soviet prisoners of war to dig five deep trenches in the field close to the airfield and that on September 14, 1941, units from an SS regiment had arrived in Berdichev to carry out the execution operation. It began the following morning, when the Jewish inhabitants were forced out of their homes and marched to the field. They were herded to the edge of the pits and then murdered by the SS troops using submachine guns. This slaughter went on all day until nearly all the thirty thousand Jews—half the population of Berdichev—had been killed. Grossman learned from a neighbor that his mother was among those murdered that day.

Grossman also relates the story of a Jewish boy of ten or eleven who miraculously survived the massacre. He was known as Mitya Ostapchuk but his real name was Chaim Roitman. He was with his family at one of the pits when his father, mother, and little brother were shot in front of him. He waited, thinking that he would be next, but then one of the SS soldiers came up to him and squinted. The boy saw a piece of glass glittering in the sun and said, "Look, there's a watch!" As the executioner went to reach for it, the boy ran away as fast as he could with the German running after him, firing his gun and hitting the boy's cap. He finally stumbled and fell, but was out of reach of his pursuer, who had given up the chase. Some time later, an old man, Gerasim Prokofievich Ostapchuk, picked him up and said, "Now you're Mitya, my son." Thus, Chaim became Mitya, the eighth son of the old man. Later some drunken German soldiers came to Gerasim Ostapchuk's house and asked who the boy was, as he had a dark complexion. They did not believe him when he said that he was the father, so he calmly elaborated, "He is my son by my first wife. She was a Gypsy."[39]

When the Red Army pushed into Poland during the summer of 1944, even greater atrocities were discovered in the extermination camps of Majdanek and Treblinka. Another reporter, Konstantin Simonov, wrote about the Nazi crimes at Majdanek for *Red Star*. Soviet soldiers were ordered to view the vast killing facilities where 1.5 million Jews and non-Jewish Europeans were killed. Grossman was assigned to describe what happened at Treblinka, about twenty-five miles (forty kilometers) northeast of Warsaw, where the Simon Wiesenthal Center has estimated that nearly 900,000 Jews were killed between the spring of 1941 and July 1944. Although the SS had tried to eliminate all signs of this extermination site, Grossman was able to piece together what had taken place from interviews with about forty survivors and local Polish peasants. His account was published in the November 1944 issue of *Znamya*, the monthly publication of the Soviet League of Writers, under the title, "The Hell Called Treblinka." It was considered sufficiently authoritative to be cited as evidence against Nazi war criminals at the Nuremberg International Military Tribunal. The extract below vividly conveys the horror of Treblinka and underscores Grossman's contention that Red Army soldiers had to be informed of what happened there in order to realize that they had to contend with a monstrous enemy:

Terrible torments awaited those who arrived from the Warsaw ghetto. Women and children were separated from the crowd and taken to the places where corpses were burned instead of to the gas chambers. Mothers who went mad with terror were forced to lead their children between the glowing furnace bars on which thousands of dead bodies were writhing in flames and smoke, where corpses were squirming and jerking in the heat as if they had become alive again, where stomachs of dead pregnant women cracked open from the heat, and unborn babies burned on the open wombs of the mothers. This sight could render even the strongest person insane.

It is infinitely hard even to read this. The reader must believe me, it is hard to write it. Someone might ask: "Why write about this, why remember all that?" It is the writer's duty to tell this terrible truth, and it is the civilian duty of the reader to learn it. Everyone who would turn away, who would shut his eyes and walk past would insult the memory of the dead. Everyone who does not know the truth about this would never be able to understand what sort of enemy, what sort of monster, our Red Army started on its own mortal combat.[40]

Letters from home to soldiers at the front vividly chronicled the suffering endured by Soviet citizens in areas occupied by Germans. In mid-1942, for example, twelve-year-old Mariya wrote to her father that there had been many deaths in the village near Smolensk where she lived. The family's home had been destroyed at the end of January and the livestock driven away. One son died of pneumonia in the damp dugout where they were hiding and another died and was buried in a nearby village. In her letter she wrote:

"...and the Germans took Yashka away. They burned the whole Liseyev family and the Gavrikovs too, and another fourteen girls who were on their way back from work in Yartsevo.... At the same time we also lost Uncle Petya, he was coming back from Ruchovo, and the Germans caught him and burned him too."[41]

"Many people have been killed in the villages around here," Mariya wrote her father. "And all they think about is the blood-thirsty monsters, you can't even call them human, they're just robbers and drinkers of blood. Papa, kill the enemy!"[42]

The depredations inflicted on the Soviet people naturally generated feelings of revenge in the Red Army soldiers when they first entered Germany in East Prussia. Drafted from throughout the Soviet Union—Azerbaijan, Belorussia, Mongolia, Siberia, Ukraine, and many other regions—they knew that millions of their comrades had been killed in battle. Many had lost their wives and children during Operation Barbarossa to execution, starvation, and disease. At the front they faced severe hardships as they were typically ill equipped, ill fed, and endured frigid winter conditions. When they crossed the border into East Prussia they were astonished at the wealth they found: the clean, well-ordered towns with paved streets and electricity; the large, well-constructed houses filled with furniture, bedding, and food; the indoor toilets and running water; and the barns full of fat cattle and strong, healthy horses. An artillery officer, Isaak Kobylyanskiy, described his impressions:

> East Prussia, which we entered in late December 1944, turned out to be totally different from our country as well as from neighboring Lithuania. Everywhere, in towns and in the countryside, you could see buildings with steep, red-tiled roofs. There were attributes of Western European family life in the houses that amazed even those of us who had been city dwellers before the war. We also encountered many small hamlets and independent farms with roomy barns, cowsheds, and stables, all built of red brick. There was amazing order and cleanliness everywhere. The German roads that reminded us of a careful mother's well-groomed children

especially impressed us all. Framed by straight rows of mature trees, the roads were all so clean, flat, and even![43]

Soviet soldiers could not understand why the Germans, who had so much, would want to invade their country and take and destroy what little they had. Vasily Grossman wrote:

> It was in Germany…that our soldiers really started to ask them-selves why did the Germans attack us so suddenly? Why did the Germans need this terrible and unfair war? Millions of our men have now seen the rich farms in East Prussia, the highly organized agriculture, the concrete sheds for livestock, spacious rooms, carpets, wardrobes full of clothes. Millions of our soldiers have seen the well-built roads running from one village to another and German autobahns…. Our soldiers have seen the two-storey suburban houses with electricity, gas, bathrooms, and beautifully tended gardens. Our people have seen the villas of the rich bour-geoisie in Berlin, the unbelievable luxury of castles, estates, and mansions. And thousands of soldiers repeat these angry questions when they look around them in Germany: "But why did they come to us? What did they want?"[44]

An answer to this question was provided at the Nuremberg Trials in 1945–1946. There, the Soviet prosecution made a strong case that German atroci-ties in the Soviet Union had been an integral element of the systematic Nazi campaign of terror aimed at the annihilation of what the Nazis regarded as *Untermenschen*, or inferior peoples. The so-called "Molotov Note," prepared by the Russian foreign minister V. M. Molotov in 1942, was entered at the trials as Exhibit no. 51, to document the murder, pillage, and destruction in the Soviet areas occupied by German forces. The note argued that

> …these atrocities do not constitute accidental excesses on the part of individual undisciplined army units, individual

German officers or soldiers. The Government has at its disposal documents …which prove that the bloody crimes and atrocities perpetrated by the Nazi army are carried out in accordance with plans of the German Government, carefully elaborated and worked out in detail, in accordance with orders of the German Command.[45]

As described in Chapter II, this brutal campaign of terror reflected the Nazi ideology that extolled the superiority of the German race. Indoctrinated to believe that Jews and eastern Europeans were inferior, many German soldiers felt little constraint in killing millions of Soviet citizens and destroying their meager possessions in wholesale fashion. By the time the Red Army entered East Prussia, there was a backlash and the Germans became victims in their turn. An argument has been advanced that:

The Russian soldier's desire for revenge was fed by his desire to restore his honor and manhood, to erase doubts about inferiority that were exacerbated by German well-being and self-satisfaction. Perhaps this is the reason there were so many cases in which a German woman was purposely raped in front of her husband, after which both husbands and wives were killed. This may also account for the unusually high number of complaints by Germans that the rapes were carried out in public.[46]

2. *The Soviet Campaign to Incite Hatred of the Germans*

The soldiers' desire for vengeance was stoked by a deliberate Soviet propaganda campaign designed to incite hatred against not only German soldiers but civilians as well. Leading this campaign was Ilya Ehrenburg, who, like Grossman, was a writer for *Red Star*. In one of his most widely cited passages, his message to Red Army soldiers was clear:

We are remembering everything. Now we understand the Germans are not human. Now the word "German" has become the most terrible curse. Let us not speak. Let us not be indignant. Let us kill…. If you do not kill a German, a German will kill you. He will carry away your family, and torture them in his dammed Germany…. If you have killed one German, kill another. There is nothing jollier for us than German corpses.[47]

Ehrenburg's writings were extremely popular among the Red Army troops. When *Red Star* arrived at front-line units the soldiers sought out his articles first, and if they could not read, implored their officers to read them aloud. They were read before battles and were found in the pockets of dead Soviet soldiers. Ehrenburg was held in such high esteem that knowing his fondness for things French, they would send him bottles of French wine they had looted from German homes.[48] In fact, his articles were treasured so much that in a large detachment of Soviet partisans fighting the Germans behind the lines, the order went out that all newspapers were to be used to make cigarettes after they had been read, except those with Ehrenburg's articles.[49] It was also reported that partisans were ready to exchange spare submachine guns for a collection of his newspaper articles.[50]

Ehrenburg often aped Nazi language, which referred to non-Aryans as rabid dogs, microbes, and bacteria. In *Red Star,* on August 13, 1942, he wrote:

> One can bear anything: the plague, hunger, and death. But one cannot bear the Germans. One cannot bear these fish-eyed oafs contemptuously snorting at everything Russian…. We cannot live as long as these green-eyed slugs are alive. Today there are no books; today there are no stars in the sky; today there is only one thought: Kill the Germans. Kill them all and dig them into the earth…. We shall kill them all. But we must do it quickly; or they will desecrate the whole of Russia and torture to death millions more people.[51]

Ehrenberg's theme of "kill the Germans" was a staple in leaflets distributed to Soviet troops during the invasion of East Prussia. His virulent anti-German writings were also featured in German newspapers, war diaries and histories, and contributed to the Germans' fear of the Russians.[52] By December 1944, with Soviet troops about to invade Germany, Ehrenburg was demonized by the Nazis. One German commander sought to inspire his troops to fight against the invaders by warning them that "Ilya Ehrenburg is urging the Asiatic peoples to drink the blood of German women." Even Hitler, in an order dated January 1, 1945, complained that "Stalin's court lackey, Ilya Ehrenburg, declares that the German people must be exterminated."[53]

The pervasiveness of Ehrenburg's reputation as a hate-monger among the Germans is illustrated by the following story he related in his memoirs. In January 1945, he was allowed to travel to East Prussia and was in Bartenstein just after it had been taken by Soviet forces. Ehenburg spoke German and the Soviet commander asked him to assure the staff of the local hospital that they and their patients did not have anything to fear from the Red Army. Ehrenburg conveyed this message to the doctor in charge, who then replied, "That's all very well, but what about Ilya Ehrenburg?" To which Ehrenburg responded, "Don't worry, Ehrenburg is not here. He's in Moscow." In his memoirs he says he found this episode "ridiculous and disgusting."[54] Even though Nazi propaganda exaggerated his vituperative language to motivate the defending German soldiers to defend their homeland against the Russian onslaught, it is undeniable that Ehrenburg's vast outpourings of hate-filled articles contributed to his fearsome reputation among Germans. Indeed, nearly twenty years after the end of the war a group of right-wing Germans protested the publication of his memoirs in the Federal Republic of Germany.[55]

In the Soviet Union, other writers were equally unequivocal in conveying the same message. Konstantin Simonov, a correspondent for *Red Star*, wrote the famous poem, "Kill Him!" which appeared in *Pravda* in the summer of 1942:

> If your home is dear to you where your mother nursed you;
>
> If your mother is dear to you, and you cannot bear the thought of the German slapping her wrinkled face;

If you do not want the German to tear down and trample on your father's picture, with the Crosses he earned in the last war;

If you do not want your old teacher to be hanged outside the old school-house;

If you do not want her, whom for so long you did not even dare kiss, to be stretched out naked on the floor, so that amid hatred, cries and tears, three German curs should take what belongs to your manly love;

If you don't want to give away all that which you call your Country, Then kill a German, kill a German every time you see one....[56]

Other examples can be cited of incitement to seek revenge on the Germans for what their soldiers had perpetrated in the Soviet Union. On the eve of the crossing into East Prussia, a directive from the Red Army's main political administration reminded the troops that: "On German soil there is only one master—the Soviet soldier, that he is both the judge and the punisher for the torments of his fathers and mothers, for the destroyed cities and villages … 'Remember your friends are not there, there is the next of kin of the killers and the oppressors.'"[57] A Soviet veteran of the East Prussian campaign described the propaganda to which they were subject when the Red Army approached the border: "As the front drew closer to the borders of Germany, the propaganda of hate not only of the German army, not only of the German people, but even of the German land itself took on a more and more monstrous character."[58] Lev Kopelev, too, seems to have been affected by this encouragement to defile the enemy. When he and his companions crossed the border into East Prussia, they jumped out of their truck and urinated on German soil.

Also contributing to the Soviet troops' violence against Germans and their property was the high propensity of soldiers to drink excessive amounts of alcohol. Analysts of Russian drinking habits have noted that Russians drink in binges and reach a high degree of intoxication for several days before sobering up until the next binge.[59] The soldiers—most of whom were uneducated—would lose all self control when drunk: "The drunken Russian is a wholly different person from the sober one. He loses all perspective, falls into a fully wild mood, is covetous, brutal, bloodthirsty."[60] Drunken Russian soldiers were above all prone to attack any German women in their vicinity.

The ready availability and high quality of liquor found in East Prussian homes contributed to drunken rampages, which resulted even in the deaths of Russian soldiers. Vasily Grossman recounts the following incident, which concerned "[t]he absurd death of Hero of the Soviet Union Colonel Gorelov, commander of a Guards tank brigade. At the beginning of February, he was sorting out a traffic standstill on the road a few kilometers from the German border, and was killed by drunken Red Army soldiers.... This wasn't the only example of bloody, drunken outrage."[61] The Red Army artillery officer, Isaak Kobylyanskiy, described in his war memoirs an incident when a thirty-year-old deputy sergeant major and his inseparable friend, a twenty-two-year-old artillery mechanic, became very drunk and began to quarrel furiously. Incensed, the sergeant shouted, "If you don't shut up, I'm gonna kill you!" whereupon the mechanic exploded, "Go ahead, shoot!" The sergeant shot and his good friend died immediately.[62] In Hungary, a Soviet soldier described the fatal effects of the local sweet Tokay wine: "'When I entered a huge wine cellar with rows of tall, black oak barrels I saw an incredible scene,' the old soldier recalled: 'The floor was knee-deep in wine, and floating in it lay three drowned soldiers. They had used their submachine guns to make holes in the barrels as "the easiest way" to fill up their mess tins and then, having tasted it, evidently could not stop drinking and became so intoxicated that they drowned in it.'"[63] Another explained that the use of alcohol made life on the front more bearable, "'It is nearly impossible not to be drinking,' a soldier wrote home in February. "What I am going through is indescribable; when I am drunk everything is easier.'"[64] Beevor reported that the ability of the Red Army to wage war was compromised by the excessive use of any kind of alcohol: "The situation became so bad that the NKVD reported back to Moscow that 'mass poisoning is taking place in occupied German territory.'"[65]

Ironically, even Ilya Ehrenburg became aghast at the violent behavior of Soviet troops against German civilians and property when he visited the East Prussian front in early 1945. On returning to Moscow in March he gave two lectures: one to the editorial board of *Red Star* and another to staff officers at the Frunze Military Academy. In both presentations he denounced the pillage, rape, and wholesale destruction of property by Soviet soldiers that he had personally witnessed in East Prussia. Such public criticism of the Red Army was unheard of and was brought to Stalin's attention. It was not long before Ehrenburg was castigated publicly in a prominent *Pravda* article, "Comrade Ehrenburg Oversimplifies," on April 14, 1945, by Georgy Alexandrov, the head of the Soviet government's political department. Using Ehrenburg's own incendiary wartime articles against him, Alexandrov argued that the Red Army "'never intended and would never have as its goal the extermination of the German people,' as Ehrenburg seemed to be advocating." The broadcast of Alexandrov's critical article on national radio and publication in *Red Star* further humiliated Ehrenburg and contributed to his sense of betrayal. Troops at the front wrote countless letters and telegrams to encourage him, but he felt stabbed in the back and betrayed by the government he had wholeheartedly supported during the war. He regarded Alexandrov's criticism as wholly without merit and wrote a letter to Stalin defending himself. He never received a response.[66] Notwithstanding this fall from grace, Ehrenburg managed to continue his career as a writer. He died in Moscow at the age of seventy-six on August 31, 1967, from the aftereffects of a heart attack.

During the war Stalin was aware of the attacks on civilians by his troops in Germany and elsewhere, but he did nothing to stop them. In fact, when Milovan Djilas (a Yugoslav partisan in World War II and later an author) criticized the behavior of Soviet troops in Yugoslavia, he was attacked by Stalin for insulting the Red Army. Djilas was present when Marshal Tito (leader of the wartime resistance in Yugoslavia and later prime minister and president of Yugoslavia) told General Korneev, the chief of the Soviet mission in Yugoslavia, that when the Red Army passed through the northeastern corner of Yugoslavia in the fall of 1944, many serious assaults on civilians and members of the Yugoslav Army had been committed. Later, 121 cases of rape were documented, 111 of which involved murder, as well as 1,204 cases of looting combined with assault. General Korneev completely rejected Tito's criticism of the Red Army. He became particularly incensed when Milovan Djilas pointed out that Germans were exploiting the assaults by Soviet soldiers in their propaganda and contrasted this behavior with that of English officers who did not engage in such excesses. When Djilas subsequently visited Moscow in the winter of 1944–1945 and attended a dinner with Stalin, he described how Stalin lashed out at him:

> He attacked only me personally. And in what a way! He spoke agitatedly about the suffering of the Red Army and about the horrors that it was forced to undergo fighting for thousands of kilometers through devastated country. He wept, crying out: "And such an army was insulted by no one else but Djilas! Djilas, of whom I could least have expected such a thing, a man whom I received so well! And an army which did not spare its blood for you! Does Djilas, who is himself a writer, not know what human suffering and human heart are? Can't he understand it if a soldier who has crossed thousands of kilometers through blood and fire and death has fun with a woman or takes some trifle?"[67]

D. How Soviet Troops Behaved in Budapest and Soviet-Occupied Germany

The brutal conduct of Soviet troops was not confined to Germany, as shown by the case of Yugoslavia above. The pillage and rape by Soviet soldiers in World War II was motivated not only by revenge for German aggression in the Soviet Union and the anti-German propaganda campaign by Ehrenburg and others, but also reflected a more general lack of discipline and a lust for booty when the Red Army moved into occupied territory. What occurred in Budapest when it was liberated by the Red Army is particularly well documented and shows that more than anti-German sentiment was at work. Moreover, rape by Soviet soldiers continued to be a major problem in the Soviet-occupied zone of Germany long after the end of the war. What happened in both situations is described below in order to provide a fuller picture of the behavior of Soviet forces in occupied territory at the end of World War II.

When the Red Army liberated Budapest in January 1945, the looting, pillage, rape, and destruction was almost of the same intensity and scale as that in East Prussia.[68] Some of the looting was organized and systematic. For example, Russian officers took the cash and other valuables stored in bank strongboxes and loaded trucks with the possessions of Jewish residents stored in the National Bank. But most of the looting was done by individual soldiers and officers. The looting was officially sanctioned for a limited period by Marshal Rodion Malinovsky, the commander of the 2nd Ukrainian Front, with responsibility for defeating Hungary, who granted the troops under his command three days of "free looting" to celebrate their victory. This license to celebrate included forcing women to serve as prostitutes and keeping them captive for a fortnight if they were found to be attractive. The Swiss Legation provided a graphic description of this mayhem in a report written in May 1945 after its members had left Budapest at the end of March and early April:

> During the siege of Budapest and also during the following fateful weeks, Russian troops looted the city freely. They entered practically every habitation, the very poorest as well as the richest. They took away everything they wanted, especially food, clothing, and valuables. Looting was general and profound, but not always systematic. It happened, for instance, that a man was deprived of his trousers, but his jackets were left to him.... Furniture and larger objects of art, etc., that could not be taken away were frequently simply destroyed. In many cases, after looting, the homes were also put on fire, causing a vast total loss.[69]

As in East Prussia, the rape of the local women was commonplace. The Swiss Legation report is emphatic on this point:

> Rape is causing the greatest suffering to the Hungarian population. Violations are so general—from the age of ten up to

seventy years—that few women in Hungary escape this fate. Acts of incredible brutality have been registered. Many women prefer to commit suicide in order to escape monstrosities. Even now, when order is more or less re-established, Russian soldiers will watch houses where women live and raid them at night, knocking down anyone who opposes them.... Misery is increased by the sad fact that many of the Russian soldiers are ill and medicines in Hungary are completely missing.[70]

Like so many women in East Prussia, one Hungarian woman described the ordeal she had suffered, "The Russians came in: they told me in Romanian to go with them. I knew exactly what they wanted. I don't know how, but I knew." She pleaded with the soldiers that her mother-in-law (Mami), who was with her in the room, would not let her go with them. But they simply pointed to the door of the tile stove and told her that they would bash Mami's head against it if she did not come with them. She then put on her boots and tied and untied her hair in a kerchief to delay leaving. While doing this she heard a thumping sound—it was the heels of her own boots, she was shaking so hard. Finally, she kissed Mami who started to cry. When they reached the corridor of the building, she attacked the three Russians, but they overpowered her and took her to the kitchen, where they threw her on the floor. Her head struck a hard object, causing her to lose consciousness, and when she came to, she was in a cold room lying on boards placed on a bed with a Russian on top of her:

> I do not know how many Russians worked over me or how many of them had before. When day began to dawn, they left me there. I got up, I could only move with great effort. My head, my entire body ached. I was bleeding profusely, did not feel that they had raped me but that they had attacked me physically. This had nothing to do with embraces or sex. It had nothing to do with anything. It was simply—I just now realize, as I am writing, that the word is accurate: aggression. That is what it was.[71]

The looting and destruction of private property in Hungary went on for some time, and the houses that were habitable remained occupied by Soviet soldiers for several months. The owners were lucky if they were allowed into their gardens to retrieve possessions that had been damaged and thrown out. One owner recalled what she discovered when she was finally able to return to her house:

> The Russians stayed in the villa for more than six months. All that time they had not even carried the rubbish out of the wrecked rooms.... They had taken away practically everything that had not burned as firewood or was thrown into the bomb craters. The piano, the paintings, the furniture, the carpets—at least those they had not cut up to make horse blankets or "curtain fringes" for their trucks—they had taken them all. And they had also taken 13 doors and a total of 72 window frames....
>
> In every room the remnants of my grandfather's library were stacked high: a pile of human excrement, an open book placed on top of it, another pile, another book, and so on.... The paper required for this "activity" had of course been torn out of the books in handfuls.... These towers stood in rows like proud skyscrapers, giving off an unbearable stench.[72]

This graphic description of Russian bathroom practice reflected the fact that Budapest was the first major metropolitan area where ordinary Soviet troops were exposed to "bourgeois" amenities. Flush toilets in particular were a mystery for most. Not knowing what they were used for, they referred to them as "stealing machines" because when they were flushed, they swallowed whatever was in them, such as items stored there that soldiers wished to clean or cool.

There was thus a definite culture clash at the end of World War II when the Hungarians were relieved of the German oppressor only to be burdened with Soviet occupiers. As Karisztian Ungvary observed, "[t]he Hungarians regarded the Germans as civilized but capable of great cruelty, and the Soviets as basically well-meaning but savage, with ideas very unlike their own about the meaning of private property, duty, and responsibility."[73] The Hungarians experienced the same sense of defenselessness as the East Prussians when the Red Army invaded their homeland, the same pervasive lawlessness and insecurity, which reflected the willful and unpredictable behavior of Soviet troops who had received minimal training and limited exposure to military discipline. There were often spontaneous acts of murder and mayhem, and at the same time acts of kindness and consideration. A group of looters might shoot all the members of a family, whereas another might play with the children and their toys and leave the family unharmed. As in East Prussia, individual Soviet soldiers and officers would protect women, children, and families from attacks by their Red Army comrades, sometimes posting guards outside apartments and houses. People were attacked, killed, raped, robbed, and sent off to labor camps irrespective of religion. To cite one example, when a rabbi revealed to a Russian soldier that he was a Jew, the soldier responded that he was also a Jew and kissed the rabbi on both cheeks, but then thoroughly searched his house and departed with all the valuable objects. The Israeli writer Ephraim Kishon, who lived through the siege and occupation of Budapest, characterized Soviet soldiers as follows: "They were simple and cruel like children. With millions of people destroyed by Lenin, Trotsky and Stalin, or in war, death, to them, had become an everyday affair. They killed without hatred and let themselves be killed without resisting."[74]

A Hungarian woman, a victim of the brutality of both the Germans and the Russians, compared them as follows:

> The Germans returned, then the Russians came again. I was always more afraid of the Germans. When they said there would be an execution, then you could be certain they would execute someone. The fear began with the Gestapo, and it was regressive. The persecution of the Jews intensified it.
>
> With the Russians, you could never know anything, never figure out anything. It was amazing that something actually developed from this lack of organization. When they left, they never said

good-bye; they simply vanished. When they returned, they greeted us with tremendous joy, took us into their laps, tossed us into the air, as if they were meeting their dearest relatives. They were warmhearted but unusually impulsive.[75]

Another time—I no longer know what happened—they injured me and then carried me to the Russian doctor in their arms. He bandaged me, petted me, and took me to the military dining hall for dinner.... That is what the Russians were like. They hit me with one hand, petted me with the other. Sometimes they came to grips over me: one wanted to spare me, the other to rape me, one to beat me, the other to heal me. One to take something from me, the other to give me something.[76]

Soviet soldiers did not stop raping women when World War II ended in May 1945. The endemic robbery, rape, and physical violence against civilians was then adversely affecting the reputation of the Red Army and the Soviet Union:

On August 3, three months after the surrender in Berlin, Zhukov had to issue even tougher regulations to control "robbery," "physical violence" and "scandalous events." All the Soviet propaganda about "liberation from the fascist clique" was starting to backfire, especially when the wives and daughters of German Communists were treated as badly as everyone else. "Such deeds and unsactioned behavior," the order stated, "are compromising us very badly in the eyes of German anti-facists, particularly now that the war is over, and greatly assist fascist campaigns against the Red Army and the Soviet government."[77]

In the Soviet zone of occupation in Germany, which later became the German Democratic Republic, German women continued to be attacked by the occupation troops on a large scale. Norman Naimark has extensively documented this postwar scourge.[78] In June 1946, for example, a report that described widespread violence in the Mecklenburg region was sent to the leadership of the German Communist Party. In some cases, people who resisted turning over goods to Soviet soldiers or resisted rape were shot and sometimes killed. The report also mentioned that farmhouses were entered and the women inside were raped, and that in the first three weeks of May 1946, twenty-four cases of breaking and entering had occurred in which rape also took place. In another example, the commander of the Soviet garrison in Potsdam listed criminal activity against Germans in July and the first half of August 1946 in which rapes and attempted rapes were as prevalent as robberies, unauthorized expropriations, and assaults. Similar lists were compiled in Brandenburg, Saxony, and Mecklenburg. In garrison towns, such as Frankfurt on the Oder, and those with Soviet naval personnel, such as Rostock and Warnemünde, rape was an endemic problem and women had to barricade themselves in their homes to protect themselves from assault.

Local leaders of the German Communist Party and the Socialist Party often raised this problem of rape and assault with their party bosses, but these party functionaries were generally reluctant to press the issue of rape with the Soviet authorities in Moscow. On one occasion, when it was brought up with Stalin, he is reported to have responded, "In every family there is a black sheep." When a member of the visiting German delegation pointed out the potentially grave consequences of such behavior for German socialism, he was cut off by Stalin, who said, "I will not allow anyone to drag the reputation of the Red Army in the mud."[79]

The unwillingness of the Soviet, and later the Russian authorities to confront the issue of rape by Soviet soldiers during World War II and afterward continues to this day. As noted by Beevor, reports of rape were made using euphemistic language:

> Rape itself, in a typically Stalinist euphemism, was referred to as an "immoral event." It is interesting that Russian historians today

still produce evasive circumlocutions. "Negative phenomena in the army of liberation," writes one on the subject of mass rape, "caused significant damage to the prestige of the Soviet Union and the armed forces and could have a negative influence in the future relations with the countries through which our troops were passing."[80]

The atrocities committed during the campaign against Germany have been omitted from official Soviet histories of the war. In her comprehensive history of Red Army soldiers in the war, Catherine Merridale has written, "The time for an honest assessment of the war is still far off...."[81] The suppression of public discussion of Soviet atrocities, rape in particular, began with demobilization, when the troops had to sign a statement that they were obliged to keep most of their wartime experiences, such as battlefield casualties and atrocities, to themselves.[82] When sixty years later Merridale interviewed veterans of the Great Patriotic War, they did not speak about the worst aspects of their wartime experience and instead used the official line, which emphasized the honor and pride of the Soviet soldier in defense of the Motherland.[83]

Notes

1 See Chapter III, page 131–132.
2 Eyewitness report no. 8 in Schieder, *The Expulsion of the German Population*, 1: 131.
3 Soine, *Vertrieben—geschunden—missbraucht*, 88–89. "Seit der 'Schutzfaktor' Sowchose für unsere Sicherheit nicht mehr existierte, wuchs zwangsläufig die Angst der nächtlichen Überfälle. Und sie war berechtigt. Eines Nachts, Mutter, Ellie und ich wohnten zu dieser Zeit in einer winzigen Dachkammer, wurden wir durch Gepolter auf der Treppe unsanft geweckt. Kurz darauf stand ein Russe im Türrahmen mit Gewehr und Taschenlampe. Er leuchtete den Raum ab und entdeckte auch mich. Mutter wollte mich schützen und flehte den Unmenschen an, mich zu verschonen, ich wäre doch noch ein Kind—doch vergeblich! Dieses 'Miststück' riß die Zudecke von unserem Lager, zeigte auf mich und sagte 'Ti charascho' (Du gut). Dann jagte er Mutter und Ellie auf den Dachboden hinaus und fiel in brutaler Weise über mich her. Nicht einmal schreien konnte ich, dieser

Sadist hielt mir den Mund zu. Einzelheiten möchte ich nicht beschreiben—Vor der Tür wartete der Nächste!

Dieses schreckliche Erlebnis hat mir einen schweren seelischen Schock versetzt, den ich nie ganz verwinden konnte und der mich mein Leben lang daran hinderte, eine gesunde Einstellung zur Sexualität zu entwickeln."

4 Eyewitness report no. 69 in Schieder, *The Expulsion of the German Population*, 1: 145–46.

5 Eyewitness report no. 15 in Schieder, *Die Vertreibung der Deutschen Bevölkerung*, part 1, 62–63. "Am 29. Januar 1945 morgens 6:30 kam ich in Gefangenschaft. Sofort bei Begegnung mit russischen Soldaten wurden mir meine Stiefel und Mantel ausgezogen. In meinem Kinderwagen hatte ich meine Tochter Christa, 15 Monate alt, und meinen Sohn Horst, 7½ Jahre alt an der Hand. Die ganze Richthofenstraße wurde mit Männern, Frauen und Kindern zusammengetrieben. Ein Zug von etwa 1500 Menschen wurde jetzt in die Bahnhofshalle gejagt.... Hier beginnt schon die Vergewaltigung der weiblichen Jugend. Auf offenem Bahnhofplatz sah ich, wie ein junges Mädchen H. N., 15 Jahre alt, aus Elbing-Trettinkenhof von Russischen Soldaten vergewaltigt wurde. Die Mutter dieser H. N. verteidigte ihre Tochter, weil die russischen Soldaten sie immer wieder gebrauchten, und besiegelte ihr Leben für den Mut und den Kampf nach zwei Tagen mit dem Tode....

Nach geraumer Zeit wurden wir in Richtung Tannenberger Allee abgeführt und in Behelfsheimen untergebracht. Der Krieg tobt weiter. Auf dieser Tannenberger Allee marschierten die russischen Nachschubtruppen und wurden in unmittelbarer Nähe der Behelfsheime vorübergehend untergebracht. Wir wurden jetzt noch einmal gemustert und nach Alter sortiert. Ich war damals 39 Jahre alt. Ein Zimmer von diesen Behelfsheimen war für die Vergewaltigungen hergerichtet die nun erfolgen sollten. Zuerst kamen die jüngeren Frauen dran, ich erst gegen Morgen und wurde gleich von drei russischen Soldaten gebraucht. Diese Vergewaltigungen wiederholten sich täglich zweimal, jedesmal mehrere Soldaten, bis zum 7. Tag. Der 7. Tag war mein schrecklichster Tag, ich wurde abends geholt und morgens entlassen. Ich wurde am Geschlecht ganz aufgerißen und hatte ein armstarkes Geschwulst vom Geschlechtsteil an beiden Oberschenkeln bis an die Knie. Ich konnte nicht mehr laufen und nicht liegen. Dann folgten noch 3 dieser schrecklichen Tage wie bis zum 6. Tag. Dann waren wir nach Ansicht der russischen Soldaten fertig und wurden nackt aus diesem Höllenraum herausgejagt. Andere Frauen traten an unsere Stelle. Eine ältere Frau gab mir eine Decke. Diese Scheußlichkeiten wurden im Beisein von 10 Frauen und oft im Beisein der eigenen Kinder durchgeführt. Meinen beiden Kindern blieb jedoch dieses erspart. In diesen schrecklichen Tagen erhielten wir kein Essen, sondern nur Alkohol und Zigaretten."

6 Eyewitness report no. 25 in Schieder, op. cit., 101. "Etwa am 20. Februar 1945 kamen feste Verbände nach Rössel. Damit wurden wir Garnisonstadt. Tag und Nacht wurde geplündert. Die Vergewaltingungen nahmen kein Ende. Viele Frauen, z. B., Frau B, baten Dr. N. vom Krankenhaus um Gift. Er gab es nicht. Unten den von wüsten Männern viehisch Mißhandelten befanden sich Kinder von 13–14 Jahren, so die 14-jährige Tochter von W. F. und die 13-jährige Tochter von Kaufmann V. M. Meine Freundin E. W. wurde von russischen Soldaten zu ihrer Mutter gebracht, sie konnte vor Schwäche nicht mehr gehen und war lange krank. Ein Mädel aus der Siedlung konnte die Vergewaltigungen nicht mehr ertragen, nahm Essigessenz und starb unter furchtbaren Schmerzen. Ein anderes Mädel hängte sich aus demselben Grunde auf, eine Flüchtlingsfrau ebenfalls. Wenn ein Russe an der Tür erschien, flohen Frauen und Mädchen durch die Fenster. Dann umstellten die Russen die Häuser und holten sich ihre Beute."

7 In addition to Ryan, *The Last Battle*, see Anonymous, *A Woman in Berlin;* Beevor, *Berlin: The Downfall 1945*; and Kuby, *The Russians and Berlin, 1945.*

8 Ryan, *The Last Battle*, 484–93.

9 For a recent description of the raping of German women by Soviet soldiers and officers and their horrific consequences, see Jacobs, *Freiwild: Das Schicksal deutscher Frauen 1945*. For a brief survey of the prevalence of rape in conflicts since World War II, see "Violence Against Women: War's Overlooked Victims," *The Economist*, January 15–21, 2011, 63–65.

10 Sander and Johr, eds., *BeFreier und Befreite*, 54.

11 Ibid., 59.

12 Oleg Budnitskii has written a comprehensive article describing the experiences of Soviet officers in Germany: "The Intelligentsia Meets the Enemy: Educated Soviet Officers in Defeated Germany, 1945," *Kritika: Explorations in Russian and Eurasian History* 10, no. 3 (Summer 2009): 629–82. This article cites many of the same sources and confirms the description of the behavior of Soviet soldiers and officers given here. The author is indebted to Steven Grant for bringing this article to his attention.

13 Merridale, *Ivan's War*, 319.

14 Ibid., 309.

15 Ibid., 310.

16 Kobylyanskiy, *From Stalingrad to Pillau*, 242.

17 Ibid., 243–44.

18 Solzhenitsyn, *Prussian Nights*, 37, 39.

19 Ibid., 63, 65.

20 Ibid., 65, 67.

21 Ibid., 67, 69.

22 Ibid., 89.

23 Ibid., 103, 105.

24 Brownmiller, *Against Our Will.* 72.

25 Ibid., 72.

26 Kopelev, *To Be Preserved Forever*, 37.

27 Ibid., 52.

28 Merridale, *Ivan's War*, 322–25, describes these and other details of the wholesale looting by Soviet troops.

29 Kopelev, *To Be Preserved Forever*, 41.

30 Ibid., 42.

31 Ibid., 56–57.

32 Kopelev (ibid., 57) contrasts the behavior of Russian soldiers in East Prussia in 1945 with that in 1914: "'I've got a book here in my bag published in Königsberg twenty years ago: *Russian Troops in East Prussia*. It's about August 1914. Written by a German historian—a civil servant, a nationalist. He did his best to dig up everything bad about the Russians. And what did he come up with? Two cases of rape. Several cases of robbery, beatings, one or two cases of murder. And in each case, Russian officers stepped in, tried to stop it, handed out punishment. The German author enumerates all the chickens killed, all the fruit trees smashed, all the faces slapped. Whenever he can, brings in the rudeness, the barbarousness. And do you know, to read that book today is frightening—frightening and humiliating. Those were Czarist armies. And to think how much worse we are! And the shame of it falls on us, the officers, the political instructors.'" The book Kopelev cites may have been *Die Russen in Ostpreußen,* written by Fritz Gause and published in Königsberg in 1931.

33 Ibid., 57.

34 Beevor, *The Fall of Berlin 1945*, 121.

35 Merridale, *Ivan's War*, 301. Majdanek was an extermination camp located two miles outside the Polish city of Lublin. It was liberated by the Red Army in July 1944 and was the first such camp discovered by Soviet forces. The scale of the killing there far exceeds that in Auschwitz: "It was a vast and tightly organized facility, a group of prisons, gas chambers, and chimneys that covered twenty-five square kilometers. One and a half million people had been murdered there. The smell of corpses and of burning flesh forced Lubliners to shut their windows.

They could not breathe, and even with the window shut they could not sleep. The scale of the atrocity shocked every witness at the time." Merridale, *Ivan's War*, 294.

36 Grossman, *A Writer at War*.
37 Ibid., 248.
38 Ibid., 252–53.
39 Ibid., 256.
40 Ibid., 301.
41 Merridale, *Ivan's War*, 234.
42 Ibid., 146.
43 Kobylyanskiy, *From Stalingrad to Pillau*, 134.
44 Grossman, *A Writer at War*, 341–42.
45 Molotov, *The Third Molotov Note*, 2.
46 Naimark, *The Russians in Germany*, 115.
47 Cited in Rubenstein, *Tangled Loyalties*, 192. The source of this quotation by Rubenstein is the article "Kill," in *Red Star*, July 24, 1942, p. 4.
48 Rubenstein, *Tangled Loyalties*, 193–95.
49 Ehrenburg and Simonov, *In One Newspaper*, 1–2.
50 Werth, *Russia at War*, 411–12.
51 Ibid., 414.
52 Ryan, *The Last Battle*, p. 27 n.
53 Rubenstein, *Tangled Loyalties*, 230.
54 Goldberg, *Ilya Ehrenburg*, 207.
55 Ibid., 208.
56 Werth, *Russia at War*, 417. Rubenstein, *Tangled Loyalties*, 420 n 8, gives the source of this poem as *Red Star*, July 18, 1942, p. 3.
57 Cited in Naimark, *The Russians in Germany*, 72.
58 Cited in ibid., 72.
59 Ibid., 113, and the references cited there.
60 Ibid., 112.
61 Grossman, *A Writer at War*, 324–25.
62 Kobylyanskiy, *From Stalingrad to Pillau*, 186.
63 Merridale, *Ivan's War*, 313.
64 Ibid., 313.
65 Beevor, *The Fall of Berlin 1945*, 31.
66 Rubenstein, *Tangled Loyalties*, 222–24.
67 Djilas, *Conversations with Stalin*, 87–89, 95.

68 This account of the behavior of the Soviet occupying forces in Budapest is based on Ungvary, *Battle for Budapest*, 279–95.

69 Taken from Appendix III, "Swiss Legation Report of the Russian Invasion of Hungary in the Spring of 1945," in Montgomery, *Hungary the Unwilling Satellite*, 239.

70 Ibid., 240.

71 Polcz, *One Woman in the War*, 88–89.

72 Ungvary, *Battle for Budapest*, 348

73 Ibid., 359.

74 Ibid., 360–61.

75 Polcz, *One Woman in the War*, 103

76 Ibid., 105.

77 Cited in Beevor, *The Fall of Berlin 1945*, 413.

78 Naimark, *The Russians in Germany*, Chapter 2, "Soviet Soldiers, German Women, and the Problem of Rape," 69–140.

79 Cited in Naimark, *The Russians in Germany*, 71.

80 Beevor, *The Fall of Berlin 1945*, 107.

81 Merridale, *Ivan's War*, 425 n 49.

82 Ibid., 356.

83 Ibid., 387.

Illustration 1. Marienburg Castle around 1944.

Illustration 2. Königsberg Castle around 1900.

Illustration 3. Damaged Königsberg Castle with Soviet Tanks. *Illustrations from the Front*, No. 8 (106) April 1945.

Illustration 4. Nemmersdorf Dead on Field.

Illustration 5. Massacre at Mergethen.

Illustration 6. Flight on a Wagon.

Bundesarchiv, Bild 146-1972-093-51
Foto: o.Ang. | 1945

Illustration 7. Refugees Boarding Ship at Pillau.

Illustration 8. Abandoned Wagons on Trek.

Illustration 9. Trek Crossing the Frisches Haff.

Illustration 10. Treks on the Ice – Photo by Soviet Plane.

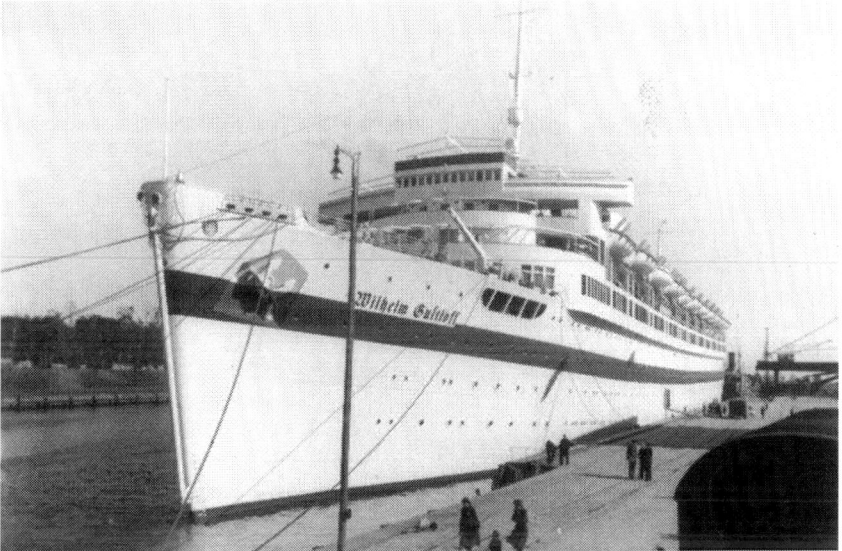

Illustration 11. *Wilhelm Gustloff.*

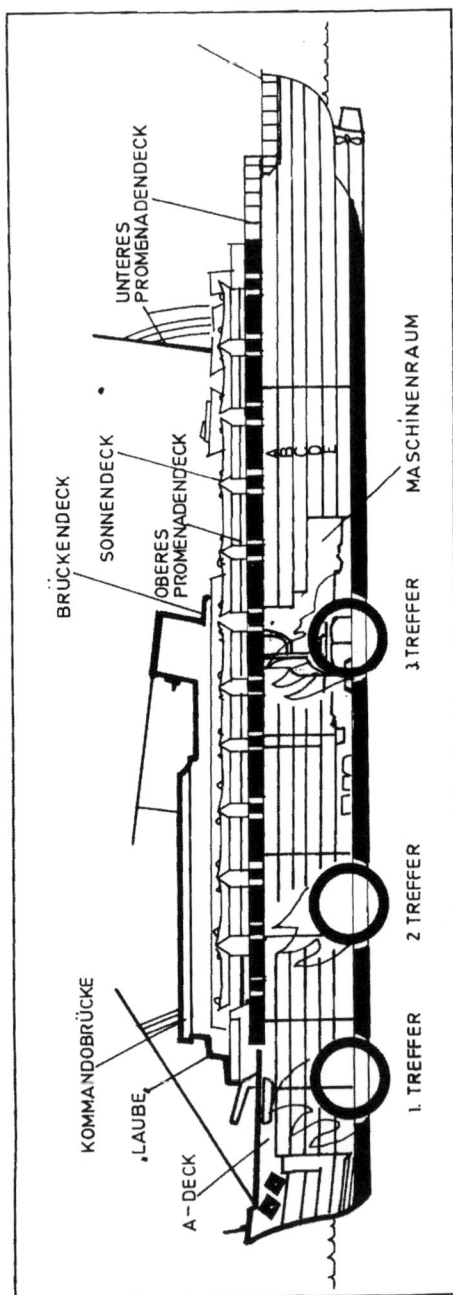

KOMMANDOBRÜCKE

LAUBE

A – DECK

BRÜCKENDECK

SONNENDECK

OBERES
PROMENADENDECK

UNTERES
PROMENADENDECK

MASCHINENRAUM

1. TREFFER

2 TREFFER

3 TREFFER

Illustration 12. Diagram of Where Torpedoes Hit the *Gustloff.*

Illustration 13. Torpedo Boat *Löwe*.

Illustration 14. Torpedo Boat *T 36*.

Illustration 15. *Cap Arcona.*

CHAPTER V

THE SINKING OF THE *WILHELM GUSTLOFF* AND THE MASSACRE OF JEWS AT PALMNICKEN

When the Red Army surged into the easternmost province of Germany in January 1945, thousands of East Prussians tried to escape from the advancing Soviet troops. The rigors, risks, and deprivations of the trek westward over land and the frozen lagoon, the Frisches Haff, weighed less on their minds than the apprehension of the brutal fate that would likely befall them if they were overtaken by Soviet soldiers. Beginning in the second half of January, the refugees crammed the German ports on the Baltic hoping that a ship would arrive soon to transport them to the relative safety of the coast of Schleswig-Holstein in north-central Germany. Most in fact made the trip successfully to western Germany or Denmark via this sea route, but thousands met a watery grave. Almost one-quarter of the forty thousand Germans who lost their lives in the Baltic were on the *Wilhelm Gustloff* when it was torpedoed at 9:15 p.m. on January 30, 1945, some fifty miles (80 kilometers) off the coast of Pomerania. It was by far the worst catastrophe involving a single ship in maritime history: 9,343 people died, more than eight thousand of them refugees, over half of whom were children. By contrast, the sinking of the *Titanic* in April 1912 resulted in the deaths of fifteen hundred passengers and crew. And the loss of the *Lusitania*, which was torpedoed by the Germans in May 1915, led to the deaths of 1,195 out of 1,959 on board.

Almost simultaneously an atrocity was unfolding some 170 miles (274 kilometers) to the east in Samland on the Baltic coast of East Prussia. Outside the town of Palmnicken thousands of Jews were dying on the cliffs and beaches of the Baltic, murdered by the SS and their foreign helpers in one of the last wholesale massacres of European Jews during World War II. The deaths of German civilians on the *Gustloff* and the Jews at Palmnicken are connected superficially by time and geography, but there is a more substantive connection as well. The German campaign of death and destruction in the Soviet Union, described in some detail in chapters II and IV, reflected the Nazi *Übermensch* ideology. A central tenet of this ideology was that all Jews should be eliminated; one manifestation of this murderous conviction was the massacre at Palmnicken in the waning days of the war. The sinking of the *Gustloff* and the massacre were a consequence of the same Nazi ideology that drove the Germans to try to annihilate the Soviet Union. The latter of course defended itself, with dire consequences for East Prussia. The Nazi *Weltanschauung* was the common factor between the massacre and the inevitable, and fully understandable, attack on East Prussia, which resulted in the sinking of the *Gustloff*. There is of course no causal link between the massacre of the Jews in Samland and the fate of the *Gustloff*. Rather, both can be seen as consequences of the Nazi regime's murderous actions.

A. The Sinking of the *Gustloff*

The *Wilhelm Gustloff* was a passenger ship launched on May 5, 1937, in Hamburg from the Blohm and Voss shipyard (see Illustration 11. *Wilhelm Gustloff*). It measured 680 feet (207 meters) long, 184 feet (56 meters) from its keel to the top of its mast, and a draft of 21 feet (6 meters), and had a top speed of 15.5 knots (18 miles per hour). With a crew of 417, it had accommodations for up to 1,463 passengers and all the features of a trans-Atlantic liner: a swimming pool, seven bars, a library, a music room, a movie theater, a smoking room, a sun deck, and two promenade decks from which to view the waves and take in the coastal sights. The lower promenade deck was completely enclosed in glass, which made it particularly popular in inclement weather. The ship was named for the leader of the Nazi Party in Switzerland. He was assassinated on February 4, 1936, by a young Jewish medical student, David Frankfurter, who was sentenced to eighteen years' imprisonment by a Swiss court.

The *Gustloff* was commissioned by the German Labor Front and its subsidiary, Strength Through Joy (*Kraft durch Freude* or KDF), which provided recreational and cultural activities for German workers. The flagship of the KDF, the *Gustloff*, took workers on comfortable and inexpensive cruises to Africa, the Mediterranean, and Scandinavia. Unlike other passenger liners of the day, it was deliberately designed with one class service to convey the unity of German people of all backgrounds and classes. At the christening ceremony, the head of the *KDF*, Robert Ley, gave a wildly enthusiastic speech in which he proclaimed to Hitler and a crowd of thousands:

> My Führer, you are leading our people to something beautiful. You give our people a new style of living and an inner and outer standard of living, which aims for the beautiful. You give our people beautiful highways, large and beautiful buildings in Nuremberg, in Munich, and soon also here in Hamburg. We want everyone to become strong and healthy, because then Germany will live and be forever![1]

The *Gustloff's* last peacetime cruise was in the early summer of 1939 to Norway and Sweden. Following the outbreak of World War II, she returned to Hamburg for conversion to a hospital ship and was used in this capacity for a little over a year for wounded German soldiers in Norway. In November 1940, the *Gustloff* was sent to the Baltic, where she was docked at a pier at Gotenhafen (now Gdynia in Poland) on the Bay of Danzig to serve as a floating barracks for the trainees in the Second Submarine Training Division of the German Navy. For over four years the *Gustloff* did not move from its berth and its crew was reduced far below its normal peacetime complement, as many had been assigned to other ships or drafted into naval infantry brigades to fill the gaps in the depleted ranks of the German Army. The projectionist was retained because he was needed to show movies in the ship's theater. When the *Gustloff* finally put to sea again at the end of January 1945, at least a third of the sailors on deck were from Croatia and other non-German countries.

The master of the *Gustloff* was a merchant marine officer, sixty-three-year-old Captain Friedrich Petersen. He had been in command of the ship for a short time in 1938, but had served mostly on other vessels. He was captured by the British and then repatriated because they did not believe that he would be useful for the German war effort. As part of the joint British-German repatriation arrangement, Petersen signed a document stating that he would not put to sea again as master of a ship. Without recent experience at sea, he was made a "sleeping captain" (*Liegerkapitän)* of the dock-bound *Gustloff* on February 20, 1944. His position was undercut, however, by the fact that the ship's military commander, Wilhelm Zahn, was a regular naval officer in charge of the operations of the *Gustloff* as commander of the Second Submarine Training Division, which was stationed on the ship.

On January 21, 1945, after the Red Army invaded East Prussia, the commander of the German Navy, Admiral Dönitz, ordered the two submarine training divisions in the Bay of Danzig to be evacuated as soon as possible, along with all ships and boats assigned to this operation. In addition to the *Gustloff*, these included the passenger liners *Hansa, Hamburg,* and *Deutschland,* all berthed in Gotenhafen. These ships were to use all their available space to transport those civilians in the Gotenhafen-Danzig area who were unfit for military service (*Nichtkampffähige*) as well as the refugees from East and West Prussia who had crowded into Gotenhafen seeking to escape. The *Hansa, Hamburg,* and *Deutschland* safely made the voyage to the west with thousands of refugees on board.

In addition to the Second Submarine Training Division, the *Gustloff* was ordered to take on board the Women's Naval Auxiliaries (similar to the Navy Waves in the United States) and a number of severely wounded soldiers. To get on board the ship, the refugees had to obtain a special pass, which was issued by the local Nazi officials. It was printed on the ship's own press with the heading "Identity Pass for the MS *Wilhelm Gustloff.*" The women of the Naval Auxiliary, who were between seventeen and twenty-five years old, were eager to get on board. Like everyone else, they had heard reports of rape and murder by the Soviet forces, and escape by ship, especially one as apparently impregnable as the *Gustloff*, appeared to be much safer and quicker than the long and hazardous journey west by train, trek, or truck in the frigid winter weather. A few of the submariners in the Second Training Division received permission to take their families on board. The wife of Franz Klammer remembered feeling very apprehensive when she saw the *Gustloff* and decided to try to get on one of the last trains to the west: "I packed my backpack and went straight to the train station…but then I saw the overcrowded trains, the dead children, and I hurried back as quickly as possible."[2]

The four ships—the *Gustloff, Hansa, Hamburg,* and *Deutschland*—received instructions to take on a total of twenty thousand passengers, of which the *Gustloff*'s share was six thousand, roughly four times the number it was designed to take on cruises. Yet twenty thousand refugees represented a small fraction of the roughly 100,000 who were jammed into the houses, sheds, shops, restaurants, movie theaters, warehouses, hospitals, and streets of Gotenhafen. When the *Gustloff* began boarding refugees on January 25, the pier at which it was docked was crowded with thousands waiting to get on the ship. At first only those with a proper pass were allowed on the ship, but it soon became difficult for the sailors supervising the boarding process to turn away refugees without a pass who were on their last legs and nearly frozen through on account of the bitter cold. Only women with children were permitted to board, but there was no clear cutoff age for children. Mothers argued that their fourteen- or fifteen-year-old sons were needed to look after their younger siblings, and sometimes women without children "borrowed" a child from another family to fulfill the boarding requirement. All passengers were registered when they boarded the ship and they were asked, "Who shall be informed if something happens to you?" (*Wer soll benachrichtigt werden—wenn Ihnen etwas zustößt?*[3]). It was a strange question to ask in wartime, when many of the refugees' relatives were fleeing for their lives elsewhere, had been killed, were missing on the front, or had been bombed out in central Germany, and in many cases that part of the registration form was left blank.

Once registered, passengers received a numbered boarding card that showed their assigned cabin or public room on one side, and on the other the number of pieces of luggage they had been allowed to take on board. Large pieces had to be given up and stored in locker rooms on the ship, and only hand luggage could be taken to one's assigned accommodations. The pier soon was filled with all kinds of left-behind personal possessions: baby carriages, bicycles, sleds, wagons, and animals, including hundreds of horses and dogs. These animals had been abandoned by their owners and now wandered the streets of Gotenhafen and the dock area looking for something to feed on.

Once the personnel of the *Gustloff* had received Dönitz's order to take on passengers, they immediately began feverish efforts to prepare their ship for departure. The ship's engines had not been used for over four years and the skeleton crew on board had been unable to maintain them properly. As a result, the few engineers and machinists aboard ship had their hands full to bring the engines into working order to undertake the voyage safely and reliably. Although the ship would be at sea a short time—less than two or three days—great quantities of food were taken on board to feed the growing number of passengers: tons of flour, sugar, potatoes, bread, and powered milk as well as thirty slaughtered hogs. The German Navy was able to requisition these large stocks of food despite their limited availability to civilians. Each passenger was given one hot meal a day, which was more than many had enjoyed during their escape to the coast and while waiting for a ship. As the *Gustloff*'s cabins could accommodate only one-fourth of the expected six thousand passengers, all public rooms and other areas were re-configured to handle the huge numbers streaming onto the ship. The only person on the crew soon made redundant by the evacuation order was the projectionist: all the seats in the movie theater were removed to provide space to squeeze in more passengers. Even the swimming pool on the lowest deck (E deck) of the ship below the waterline was drained and used to provide space for the members of the Women's Naval Auxiliaries; they were among the last to board the *Gustloff,* as the pool was one of the few remaining places where they could be squeezed in.

Most refugees were so relieved to be on board a vessel, which seemed the apex of safety and security, that they did not give much thought to the possibility that they might have to abandon ship. However, a few did worry about the dangers at sea, one of whom was thirteen-year-old Gunther von Maydell, one of Baroness Ebbi von Maydell's two sons. By birth a Lithuanian, the baroness was the widow of a German aristocrat and since 1939 had lived in Gotenhafen where she owned a perfume shop. She had the good fortune to be a friend of Professor Adolf Bock, who had assumed the position of the ship's artist specializing in marine drawings and paintings. He had his own cabin on the *Gustloff* and had used his influence to obtain passes for the baroness and her two sons to join him on the ship. But sixteen-year-old Bernard believed that the Baltic was infested with Russian submarines and refused to board the *Gustloff,* choosing instead the overland route to the west. Perhaps alerted by his older brother's concerns about the ship's safety, once on board the younger Gunther set about exploring the *Gustloff* and checking out the lifeboats. While the ship was supposed to have twenty-two in all, half on either side of the sun deck, Gunther counted only twelve lifeboats in their davits and these were filled with snow and the launching ropes and pulleys were iced up. It turned out that during the four years that the ship was docked, the other lifeboats had been requisitioned for special purposes in the harbor, such as providing smokescreens during air attacks. This loss was partially made up by the first officer of the *Gustloff,* the sixty-eight-year-old Louis Reese, who had searched in storehouses and on other ships and had been able to locate and requisition eighteen small boats. These were lifted onto the *Gustlof's* sun deck and tied down in such a manner that they could be quickly released in an emergency. In addition, a number of naval rafts were stacked in piles around the upper decks. As all passengers needed to have life jackets, truckloads were delivered to the ship, instructions were issued on how to put them on, and a number of evacuation drills were carried out.

Others on the *Gustloff* also had concerns about the ship's safety. Paul Uschdraweit, the county administrator (*Landrat*) of Angerapp in East Prussia, came on board on January 29. On deck he started a conversation with a midshipman (*Fähnrich*), who painted a grim picture of the dangers the ship would face from mines, torpedoes, and air attacks: "Given this immense overcrowding and the insufficient life-saving equipment, the panic on board will be indescribable should something happen to us."[4] Shocked by this revelation of the dangerous situation he might have to face, the Landrat panicked and made a quick inspection of the ship to find an escape route from his assigned quarters to the deck in case of an emergency. To his consternation he realized that in case of panic many exits would be blocked and that it would be next to impossible to break the safety glass in the windows that wrapped all around the lower promenade deck. After more searching, he found two iron bulkhead doors that could easily be opened and led to a ladder that would take one to the highest open deck. Once he had his escape route figured out, the Landrat calmed down.

When the *Gustloff* finally departed at noon on January 30, several hundred refugees still on the pier next to the ship were bitterly disappointed that they had been left behind. Many mothers and their children wept when four tugboats towed the large ship into the Gotenhafen channel. At that moment a small ship, the *Reval*, filled to overcapacity with between five and six hundred refugees making their way west from Pillau, entered the harbor and headed straight for the much larger *Gustloff*. As the *Reval* approached, people crammed on its deck shouted in unison "Take us with you" (*Nehmt uns mit!*[5]). Captain Petersen took pity on them and lowered the gangway to take them on board. As almost every conceivable space had already been taken, they were allowed to camp on the stairways and passageways, which until then had been kept open as escape routes in case of an emergency. The refugees were hardly dissatisfied with their "accommodations"; they were only too relieved to have reached the safety and warmth of the *Gustloff* and to have escaped the advancing Soviet front.

There then followed a series of decisions that sealed the fate of the *Gustloff*. Normally, there would have been a number of escort vessels to provide some protection from any Russian submarines lurking in the area. The Ninth Escort Division of the German Navy, which was responsible for providing these escorts for ships carrying refugees and wounded soldiers westward from the Gulf of Danzig, consisted largely of torpedo boats, minesweepers, converted trawlers, and small fishing vessels. On January 30, however, all the ships under its command were already at sea, but Commander Wilhelm Zahn was on the bridge of the *Gustloff* and was eager to get his men in the Second Submarine Training Division to the safety of the west as soon as possible. Earlier, at naval headquarters, he had checked reports of Russian submarine activity and found no evidence of enemy submarines in the waters through which the ship would sail. Thus encouraged, he used his connections at the submarine branch of the navy, stationed in Gotenhafen, to requisition two vessels to escort the *Gustloff*: the torpedo boat *Löwe* and the torpedo recovery boat *TF-19*, which was used to hunt and pick up practice torpedoes fired by submarine training crews.

As the *Gustloff* made its way out of Gotenhafen into the Gulf of Danzig, it was hit by strong winds and heavy seas. It was snowing and as the temperature dropped during the afternoon to considerably below freezing, the decks of the ship were soon coated with ice. Buffeted by high waves, the small *TF-19* escort vessel developed a crack along a welded seam and was forced to return to Gotenhafen, leaving the *Löwe* as the sole remaining escort vessel. More bad news arrived when the *Gustloff* reached Hela, where the Gulf of Danzig ends and the Baltic begins. There it was ordered to meet up with the large passenger liner *Hansa*, which was also jammed with refugees, and together the two ships were to form a convoy to the west. However, the *Hansa* had developed mechanical problems and was unable to make the trip. Captain Petersen now faced an excruciating decision: should the *Gustloff* wait outside the port of Hela for other ships to form a convoy to the west and for more escort vessels, thereby risking an enemy attack; should it return to Gotenhafen and possibly incur a rebellion of the thousands of refugees on board; or should it risk making a run for it alone with only one small escort vessel? After conferring with his officers on the bridge, Captain Petersen opted to proceed into the Baltic with the *Löwe* leading the way. Observing the small torpedo boat bouncing in the waves ahead of the huge passenger liner, he is reported to have commented sarcastically: "A dog leads a giant through the night." (*Ein Hund führt einen Riesen durch die Nacht*[6]).

The officers on the bridge made three more fateful decisions that day. First, Commander Zahn, who as a former submarine captain knew the tactics of enemy submarines, argued forcefully that the *Gustloff* should proceed full speed ahead—about fifteen knots per hour—in order to outrun any Russian submarines that might be in the area. He was overruled by Captain Petersen and First Officer Reese, both of whom insisted that the maximum speed at which the ship's engines could safely be run was twelve knots per hour because they had not been properly maintained during the years at dockside and had been repaired in only makeshift fashion from bomb damage in the fall of 1943.

Second, there were also strongly divergent opinions on the course the ship should take to the west. Captain Petersen maintained that they should stay clear of the coast in order to avoid hitting a mine—which he regarded as a greater risk than a submarine attack—and to stay out of the range of Russian artillery, which he believed posed a danger if they steered a course close to land. First Officer Reese, by contrast, argued vehemently for the coastal route because given the shallow depth of the water there, a submarine attack was quite unlikely, and should the ship hit a mine, the passengers could be brought safely to land. But Captain Petersen outranked him and gave the order to steer the ship into the deeper waters of the Baltic.

A third issue arose when, toward 6:00 p.m., a radio petty officer notified the bridge that the *Gustloff* was on a collision course with a group of German minesweepers headed in the opposite direction. Radar was not then in use, and after a heated debate among the officers, it was decided to turn on the ship's navigation lights in order to reduce the possibility of being rammed by the minesweepers. This decision was favored by Captain Petersen and Commander Zahn, who both doubted that Russian submarines were operating in the area, but it was vigorously contested by the other officers, who argued that turning on the navigation lights risked giving away the *Gustloff*'s position. Although the snowstorm that had raged in the afternoon had let up and visibility had increased to several hundred yards, the lights nevertheless remained turned on. All the while, the escort vessel *Löwe* could not detect Russian submarines because its position finder was totally iced up and not operational.

Early on January 11, the Russian submarine *S-13*, commanded by Captain Alexander Marinesko, slipped out of the Finnish port of Hangoe. Marinesko had received orders to search the Baltic for German ships, but after a two-week patrol none were found. The *S-13* was then instructed to join two other Russian submarines, patrol the coast off Memel, and sink any German ships that might try to evacuate the remnants of Hoßbach's Fourth German Army still holding out in that area. Before dawn on January 30, the *S-13* received a radio message that Memel had fallen to the Soviets and from this information Marinesko concluded it was unlikely that any quarry would be found in that area of the Baltic. Earlier, he had received a radio message that gave him a vital clue about where he was likely to find enemy ships: "From HQ Baltic Fleet to all submarines: Red Army offensive targeted on Danzig going well and likely to force enemy to evacuate Königsberg soon. Expect significant increase in movement of enemy transports in the region of the Danzig Bay."[7] After conferring with his officers the morning of January 30, Marinesko made the decision to leave the patrol route he had been ordered to follow and instead set the *S-13* on course to arrive that afternoon off the Hela Peninsula outside the Bay of Danzig.

Night had fallen and the *S-13* had spent several hours on the surface looking for enemy ships. It was shortly after 7:00 p.m. when the lookout on the submarine suddenly spotted the lights of a large vessel. Marinesko was sleeping in his bunk, but when informed, immediately shot up to the conning tower to take a look. From the size of the ship's superstructure he realized that it was a German transport of at least twenty thousand tons, but he had no way of knowing that it was the *Gustloff*. To minimize the risk of being detected, he put the *S-13* on a surface course between the *Gustloff* and the coast, hoping that against the dark background of the land the submarine would be nearly invisible and that the lookouts on the *Gustloff* and its escort would not be expecting an attack from this quarter because of the relatively shallow water along the coast. By the same token, it was a daring maneuver for the *S-13* because if discovered, it would not be able to submerge and escape would be extremely difficult.

For Marinesko, such a high-stakes gamble was necessary to achieve the success that he sorely needed to salvage his career. He had a reputation as a heavy drinker and a womanizer, which he had "polished" by going on a monumental three-day binge starting on New Year's Eve, 1944, at the submarine base in the Finnish port of Turku (the Germans having been expelled from Finland by Soviet forces by then), during which he enjoyed the favors of a number of local women. The *S-13* had been ordered to leave the port and go on patrol, but it could not do so without its commander, who had gone AWOL. Military police searched for him and could not find him until he returned to base on January 3, after sobering up in a sauna. He was now in serious trouble for his land-based exploits and the local NKVD (secret police) official recommended that he either be court-martialed or sent under armed escort to the main Soviet naval base at Kronstadt, in Russia. However, Marinesko's commanding officer, Captain Oryel, who was also a submariner, argued that he should only be given a reprimand. Marinesko was further supported by the officers and crew of the *S-13*; they sent a petition to Captain Oryel asking that their ship, with Marinesko as commander, be allowed to continue the battle against the Germans. Oryel temporarily resolved the dispute when he ordered the *S-13* to put to sea to remove Marinesko and his crew from the tense situation in Turku while he waited for a report from Kronstadt on whether the *S-13* commander would be court-martialed. When he set sail, Marinesko therefore had a clear idea of what might await him upon his return to base and that the successful sinking of a large German ship would certainly help his case.

———————

While the *S-13* was on high alert as it stalked the *Gustloff* on the surface of the Baltic to get into an advantageous firing position, all was quiet on the German ship. After the anxious moments and the delays surrounding the departure from Gotenhafen, many women and children were already asleep. Heinz Schön was a trainee purser on the ship. He subsequently devoted his life to research and writing books about the *Gustloff*. He reported what he saw when he made his way around the ship shortly before 9:00 that evening:

> On the lower promenade deck and on the A deck I see in the large halls hundreds of people lying on mattresses. Despite an explicit

order, many have undressed and are sleeping as if they were dead. The life preservers, which they really should have put on, serve as pillows for many.[8]

Those on watch on the bridge were now engaged in the normal routine of keeping track of the ship's position (see Map 8. Last Voyage of the *Wilhelm Gustloff*). With everything apparently in order, Captain Petersen and Commander Zahn retired to the cabin of First Officer Reese for their first meal since the voyage began. As the steward got ready to serve the first course—pea soup—the captain toasted his follow officers with cognac: "Gentlemen—here's to a good voyage." (*Auf eine gute Fahrt, meine Herren*).

At around 8:45 p.m., the *S-13* was running parallel between the coast and the *Gustloff*. It then turned toward its target and when the submarine was about twenty-two hundred yards from the ship, Marinesko ordered that four torpedoes be loaded into the forward firing tubes. By 9:05, the submarine had closed to within 765 yards of the former cruise liner and when the bow of the *Gustloff* came within the crosshairs of the periscope of the *S-13*, Marinesko gave the order to fire. At 9:15 a torpedo hit the bow on the port (left) side of the *Gustloff,* making a terrific explosion. This was quickly followed by a second, which blasted the ship at E-deck level, where the swimming pool was located. A third torpedo struck amidships, where the engines were located (see Illustration 12. Diagram of Where Torpedoes Hit the *Gustloff*). The fourth torpedo remained dangerously lodged in the forward firing tube of the *S-13*. The lights went out on the *Gustloff* and its siren started to wail. The three officers—Captain Petersen, Commander Zahn, and First Officer Reese—jumped up from their dinner and ran to the bridge to assess the damage. There they could see that the bow was already sinking into the sea and the ship was starting to list to port where it had been hit. An attempt to contact the engine room was unsuccessful and it soon became clear that the ship had lost all power. Orders were given to signal the *Löwe* that the ship was sinking, to shoot off red signal flares, and to send an SOS radio message. Unfortunately, the *Gustloff's* main radio was out of commission and its back-up transmitter was not operating properly; it had a range of only two thousand yards and therefore could not be picked up at the navy headquarters in Swinemünde (now Swinoujscie in Poland). But at least this faint signal was picked up on the *Löwe* and the SOS was then transmitted by its more powerful radio. However, the frequency of the *Löwe's* radio had been set for the original members of the convoy; hence the SOS was picked up by the *Hansa*, and not the Ninth Escort Division. Valuable time was therefore lost in alerting nearby ships on the coast of the disaster that had befallen the *Gustloff* and in setting in motion a rescue operation.

Once the officers on the bridge grasped the full extent of the damage to the ship, they had to make the traumatic decision to immediately close the bulkheads, sealing off the forward part of the ship, where the first torpedo had hit, in order to prevent the onrush of water through the huge hole from quickly swamping the rest of the ship. Closing these bulkheads sealed the fate of the seamen in the forecastle, who were on the wrong side of the steel watertight doors but had survived the initial blast. They were unable to escape to the ship's decks and they drowned as the water rose inexorably in their quarters. The death of these sailors would have dire consequences because they were the crew members who had been trained to help the passengers abandon ship and man the lifeboats.

As the naval auxiliary women had been quartered in the swimming pool on the lowest deck, the E deck, nearly all were instantly killed by the explosion of the second torpedo. Only the few in the cabins between the swimming pool and the engine room managed to escape. One of these, Gertrud Agnesons, lit a match in the pitch-black cabin following the explosion, but the tiny flame was extinguished by a sudden stream of water that entered the cabin from the ceiling.[9] She seized a flashlight and with others in the cabin managed to open the door, but in the passageway the water already reached up to her thighs and Agnes was horror-stricken when the body of a dead girl floated by. She headed for an emergency exit she had seen earlier while the others waded through the water to the main staircase, and she was alone when she climbed a ladder and emerged into an empty corridor. Completely disoriented, she shouted at a passing sailor to tell her where the stairway was and he pointed to a door. She opened it and immediately found herself swept up by a tightly packed throng of screaming, fighting passengers pushing against each other remorselessly as they fought their way up the stairway. Anyone who stumbled was mercilessly trodden under foot and when a small child fell from its mother's arms, it was immediately trampled to death by the panic-stricken crowd.

Those who reached the vestibule leading to the boat deck were hemmed in by the narrow doors opening out to this deck. Their escape was further delayed by some ship's officers who were trying to limit the number of passengers on deck in order to expedite the process of boarding the lifeboats. The traditional order, "Women and children first!" was given but in the melee was adhered to only sporadically. In exasperation, one of the officers fired his pistol into the air to control the surging crowd, but this had little impact. He became angrier when he discovered that some of the crew had taken a lifeboat for themselves, but he could only watch helplessly as they rowed away from the sinking ship with space for dozens of passengers in the nearly empty lifeboat. Sigrid Bergfeld, one of the few naval auxiliaries who had managed to make it to the boat deck, reached a lifeboat station where some semblance of order was maintained. A sailor told her to board the boat, but at that moment she was pushed back by a woman with a baby, who got in instead. The boat was lowered to the water but then capsized when it hit the waves, throwing all those aboard into the frigid sea. Sigrid moved through the crowd to board another lifeboat, but this was filled before she could get in. Again, she was lucky, because the boat was launched improperly and ended up hanging vertically by only one rope, spilling its screaming passengers into the sea. The rope then broke and the lifeboat smashed on top of those who were struggling in the water below. She finally was able to get on a small raft and she and others on the raft were picked up by a rescue vessel after spending hours on the water.

As the *Gustloff* listed more and more to port, many passengers slipped on the icy surface of the decks and fell into the sea. Others jumped from the ship, some taking off their clothes before doing so and therefore died of hypothermia in a matter of minutes. The ship's barber had collected a large number of silver coins and was determined to take them with him when he left the ship.[10] He loaded them into his rucksack, put it on his back, and fought his way through the desperate masses to the deck. He jumped from the ship with the intention of landing in one of the lifeboats, but he missed and was pulled under the sea by the weight of his hoarded coins.

While some of the crew looked out only for themselves, others were heroic in helping to save the passengers. The ship's purser, Gerhardt Luth, a powerful, strapping man, took off his life jacket and tied it on a woman who was standing helplessly on the deck. Later, he leapt overboard and was picked up by one of the boats that had been successfully launched from the ship. A sailor frantically worked his way down a corridor on a lower deck to force open cabin doors that had been jammed by the force of the torpedo explosions. Hearing a pistol shot in one of the cabins, he pushed open the door and found the bodies of a woman and a small child on the floor. A naval officer stood with smoking gun in his hand while his petrified young son clung to his leg. The officer yelled "Get out!" and the sailor surmised that he had just interrupted a suicide pact. Other passengers likewise lost the will to survive. A high Nazi Party official had managed to reach the open deck with his family when his wife shouted "Put a quick end to us all!"[11] The official pulled out a pistol and shot his wife and two children dead, but the weapon jammed when he pointed it at himself. He turned to a nearby sailor to borrow his pistol but slipped on the icy deck and fell into the sea instead.

Thousands of passengers remained trapped inside the *Gustloff*, including the mostly women and children who were crowded into the music room. When the ship suddenly tilted on its side, people not holding on to anything slid across the floor into a heap on the port side. A piano that had not been tied down rolled across the room and crushed everyone in its path before it smashed into the port bulkhead. Hundreds of others had gathered on the lower promenade deck; some had been herded there by armed sailors attempting to maintain order and others had been reassured by the announcements coming from the bridge that help was on the way and they would be rescued. This deck was surrounded on all sides by heavy shatterproof glass. As the *Gustloff* listed at an increasingly steeper angle, people tried desperately to break the glass to escape the water rapidly seeping into their sealed deck, but the glass did not give way. Rose and Ursula Petrus reached a window and futilely tried to break it until an officer shot holes in the glass with his pistol and the two sisters bloodied their hands frantically pushing on the glass and were able to get out through the opening where they were swept into the sea and survived. Maria Kupfer also managed to escape the lower promenade deck by climbing on a man's back and crawling through a broken window on the starboard (right) side of the ship that was now almost directly overhead. Except for these and a few others, all other passengers and crew on the lower promenade deck drowned (see Map 8. Last Voyage of the *Wilhelm Gustloff*).

Forty years before the movie *Titanic*, at the end of the 1950s a black-and-white film was made about the sinking of the *Gustloff* called *Night Fell Over Gotenhofen*. Directed by Frank Wisbar, it was a German-American production with German movie stars. The *Gustloff* was also the subject of a novel by Günter Grass, *Crabwalk* (*Im Krebsgang*), which was published in 2002. It includes historically accurate details of the sinking, but in one passage Grass chose to describe scenes from the movie to convey the full horror of the disaster:

> But what took place inside the ship cannot be captured in words…. So I won't even try to imagine those terrible sights and to force the gruesome scene into painstakingly depicted images…. Such an attempt was undertaken by that black-and-white film, with images shot in a studio. You see masses of people pushing, clogged corridors, the struggle for every step up the staircase; you see costumed extras imprisoned in the closed promenade deck, feel the ship listing, see the water rising, see people swimming inside the ship, see people drowning. And you see children in the film. Children separated from their mothers. Children holding dangling dolls. Children wandering lost along corridors that have already been vacated. Close-ups of the eyes of individual children. But the more than four thousand infants, children, and youths for whom

no survival was possible were not filmed, simply for reasons of expense; they remained, and will remain, an abstract number....[12]

———————

Those passengers familiar with the layout of the *Gustloff* had a much better chance of survival. Landrat Uschdraweit from Angerapp ran up to the boat deck to find a lifeboat and came upon one already filled with passengers being lowered into the water. He then witnessed when it turned end-to-end and the people fell into the sea and were swallowed by a large wave. The Landrat decided to make his way forward on the icy deck to the bow of the ship, only to find that it was already underwater. Holding on to the railing for dear life in order not to slip on the inclined deck, he turned to four other men nearby, who were also searching for an escape. One pointed to an empty raft in the water and in desperation the Landrat released his grasp on the railing and shot past the front of the bridge on the angled deck down into the sea. Luckily, waves propelled the raft in his direction and he managed to grasp a rope hanging from its side. The other four men also careened down the precipitous deck into the water and took hold of the rope. A large wave catapulted them against the window of the bridge and the shapes of men were visible in the still-illuminated room until another wave washed them free of the ship. They paddled with their arms until their raft was about one hundred yards from the stern of the *Gustloff*, which towered over them out of the water.

Another survivor was the ship's artist, Professor Bock. In Gotenhafen he had observed the preparations for the sea voyage and knew that several small boats had been loaded onto the sun deck behind the ship's funnel. He and his friends, the von Maydells, crawled on hands and knees across the slanted, slippery deck toward one of these boats. Just as they reached it, a wave came surging along the deck, but they managed to climb into the boat in time. And whom did they discover crouching at the bottom of the boat: none other than Captain Petersen. He and another officer had boarded it some time earlier. A large wave then swept their boat off the deck and carried it away from the *Gustloff*'s smokestack and out to the open sea.

Unlike Captain Petersen, who was intent only on saving his own life, Commander Zahn remained on the bridge to oversee the destruction of the *Gustloff*'s papers and codes. It was now 9:50 p.m. and the ship was listing at such a sharp angle that waves were crashing into the port side of the bridge. At one point Commander Zahn looked out the window and saw a big wave toss a raft against the bridge. It must have been the same raft containing Landrat Uschdraweit and the other four men. Max Bonner, the steward, had somehow managed to carry in a tray with filled glasses and offered the officers on the bridge a last cognac. After downing the welcome liquor, they smashed the glasses on the slanted floor. Zahn then left the bridge and crawled on the starboard deck toward a raft where two seamen shouted for help to free it, but at that moment a wave engulfed them and swept them away from the ship. Zahn was wearing a life preserver that propelled him to the surface, where he found an empty raft floating nearby and managed to climb in. He could see hundreds of heads moving up and down in the waves, while nearby there were twenty to thirty empty life rafts.

When the *Gustloff* started to plunge into the Baltic, Zahn and others who had escaped the doomed ship witnessed her final death throes: as she went under, her boilers exploded, somehow her generators came on and lights illuminated those parts of the ship still above water, and her siren wailed one last time. Many passengers still clung to the ship and screamed in desperation as the *Gustloff* slipped into the Baltic, extinguishing the lights and the siren and taking thousands with her. For one survivor, Ingeborg Dorn, the sound of the screams would stay with her for the rest of her life: "It was the scream, the muted scream of the people who were still on the ship. It is still ringing in my ear. That was the death scream of the *Gustloff*."[13] The Landrat on his raft also heard these same terrified cries coming from the stern of the ship: "From there resound the screams of hundreds of women and children, screaming in mortal fear, so horrible that nobody can ever describe it who has not heard it himself. The screaming intensified to shrill howling when it appeared that the ship would capsize."[14] This was at 10:15 p.m., about an hour after the three torpedoes had hit the ship.

While the *Gustloff* sank to the bottom of the Baltic, taking along several thousand passengers, the cries of hundreds in the frigid water became more distinct. Many soon succumbed to hypothermia, and if they did not wear a lifejacket, desperately tried to survive by swimming, but it did not take long before they, too, sank beneath the sea. Some with lifejackets—especially children—had put them on incorrectly and drowned with their heads in the water and their lower body sticking above the surface of the sea. Others used their last remaining ounce of energy to make their way to nearby lifeboats or rafts, but when they tried to get on board, a mortal struggle often ensued. In some cases armed men even opened fire on people trying to clamber on board.[15] While not a particularly strong woman, Ursula Birkle succeeded in hauling three pleading survivors—a young girl, a soldier with one leg, and another man—out of the water into her boat. But then those already on board warned her not to fish any more out of the sea or their boat would sink. The soldier Rudolf Geiss later confessed that he did not want to risk his own survival when three swimmers pleaded to be taken on board his raft and were pushed away. When the boat containing Captain Petersen filled up as more survivors were taken on board, he protested "If we take any more, we shall all die." A woman clung to the side of the boat and others hit her hands to try to dislodge her. But Professor Bock, in the same boat, insisted that she could not be left to drown and pulled her on board, whereupon Petersen shouted that he had no right to do that.[16]

The only ship in the area in a position to undertake rescue operations immediately was the *Gustloff*'s escort vessel, commanded by Lieutenant Captain Paul Prüfe (see Illustration 13. Torpedo Boat *Löwe*).[17] Nets and rope ladders were let down over the sides of the boat and people with enough strength climbed up to the deck, while others too weak from their exposure in the frigid Baltic were hoisted up by sailors. Within an hour the *Löwe* had taken on board two hundred people from the rafts and lifeboats. After four hours of extraordinary efforts, Captain Prüfe's crew was totally exhausted after packing every nook and cranny of the *Löwe* with 472 survivors of the *Gustloff*. These included Gertrud Agnesons, one of the few naval auxiliaries who had managed to fight her way up from below deck; Maria Kupfer, one of a handful of survivors of those trapped in the glass-enclosed lower promenade deck; the *Gustloff*'s first officer Louis Reese; and the officer of the watch, Heinz Kohler. With no more room to take additional survivors on board, Captain Prüfe left the scene of the disaster at 2:30 on the morning of January 31. He set the *Löwe* on course for Kolberg on the Baltic coast further to the west.

Among the nearby ships that had picked up the radio report of the disaster from the *Löwe* were the cruiser *Admiral Hipper* and its escort, the torpedo boat *T-36*. They had departed from Gotenhafen a few hours after the *Gustloff* but were traveling at much higher speed and as a result reached the scene of the catastrophe while the stricken *Gustloff* was still above water. The *Admiral Hipper* had taken on board 1,530 refugees in Gotenhafen but still had room for many of the survivors struggling for life in the ice-cold water. Hardly had it arrived at the scene when it received a message from the *T-36* that a Russian submarine was in the area. Captain Henigst was faced with the excruciating choice of either joining the rescue effort and running the risk that his ship would also suffer the *Gustloff*'s fate, or leaving the scene at once to ensure the safety of those on board. He chose the latter and the *Admiral Hipper* killed several survivors who were caught in its wake with its propellers as it sped off amid the anguished cries of those in the water nearby who had believed that their rescue was imminent.

By contrast, the twenty-seven-year-old commander of the *T-36*, Robert Herring, decided to face the risk of a submarine attack and proceeded to take on board as many of the survivors as possible (see Illustration 14. Torpedo Boat *T-36*). A wide climbing net (*Seefallreep*) was dropped over the side of the ship and the crew began the difficult task of heaving the survivors out of the water and up to the deck of the vessel. The shipwrecked were so exhausted they could hardly move by themselves and their waterlogged clothes made them even heavier to carry. Once on deck, they were immediately taken below and undressed, in some cases put in hot showers, and then dressed in warm clothes. To help revive them, they were given hot tea, coffee, or schnapps. The care of the survivors on board was in the capable hands of Commander Herring's mother, who had boarded the *T-36* as a refugee in Gotenhafen.

Among those picked up by the *T-36* were Captain Petersen and Commander Zahn, as well as a Dr. Ralph Wendt, who was quickly taken below deck to help a woman give birth. Although he was an army doctor who had never delivered a baby, he had no problems dealing with the birth of a healthy boy whose umbilical cord he cut with one of the ship's kitchen knives. That same night he delivered two more babies on board the *T-36*.

While the rescue operation was underway, the *T-36* was under continuous threat of a submarine attack, and indeed at one point sonar did pick up the position of a submarine fourteen hundred yards distant moving toward the *T-36*.[18] To present the smallest possible target, Herring maneuvered his torpedo boat so that its bow was pointed in the direction of the approaching submarine. When it was less than one thousand yards distant, Herring followed the advice of Commander Zahn to break off the rescue efforts and get underway. As the engines of the *T-36* roared loudly, the torpedo boat moved so quickly that three sailors assisting survivors to board were thrown off and the *T-36*'s bow wave was so high that it knocked some of the shipwrecked from their rafts. It was reported that two torpedoes were sighted, one to port and the other to starboard, and that sonar had also detected a submarine under the stern of the *T-36*. For twenty minutes Herring ordered his ship to circle the area and fire depth charges into the water to try to cripple the underwater enemy, but this effort was unsuccessful. At a quarter past midnight on January 31, sonar detected torpedoes coming straight toward the *T-36* and Herring abruptly turned his boat to starboard and thereby avoided them just in time. When his first officer entered the bridge and reported that there was no more room on board for additional survivors, Herring decided that there was no point in further delay and ordered his torpedo boat to proceed at high speed—seventeen knots—to the west. At 4:30 that morning the *T-36* had caught up with the *Admiral Hipper* and finally arrived at 2 p.m. in Saßnitz on the island of Rügen, where a hospital ship took on board the survivors from the *Gustloff*.

The most up-to-date estimates indicate that 1,252 of the 10,595 passengers and crew on the *Gustloff* were rescued after she was torpedoed: 564 by the *T-36*, 472 by the *Löwe*, and 216 by seven other ships that came to the scene of the catastrophe.[19] The last survivor to be rescued was an eighteen-month-old boy, who was found shortly after 5:00 a.m. by the crew of the old, rusty patrol boat *VP-1703*. He had been wrapped in a blanket and was the only one still alive in a lifeboat containing the frozen bodies of four passengers (a man, a woman, and two older children) who had succumbed to the effects of exposure to the bitter cold (0°F, −18°C). The little boy was adopted by his rescuer, Petty Officer Werner Fisch, whose wife was incapable of having children.

As more than eight thousand innocent women and children were among the victims, it is natural to ask whether the *Gustloff* was a legitimate target at a time of war. The Institute for Maritime Law (*Institut für Seerecht*), located in Kiel, Germany, considered this question soon after the war. In its opinion, the ship should be considered a military vessel because it was transporting hundreds of navy officers and men and was also armed with anti-aircraft guns. Moreover, even though it was carrying many wounded military personnel on board, it had no markings that would have identified it as a hospital ship.[20] The fact that the sinking of the *Gustloff* was not considered to be a war crime provided little solace for the relatives of the thousands who perished on that frigid January night.

———————

The *Gustloff* was one of many ships carrying German refugees that were sunk with considerable loss of life in the waning months of World War II. Some twenty-five other vessels met the same fate, with casualties totaling roughly forty thousand (refugees, soldiers, and sailors), in the huge evacuation operation in the Baltic from January to May 1945 called Operation Hannibal. The loss of those on board the *Gustloff* comprised almost one-quarter of the total.[21] The sinking of the freighter *Goya*, which was hit by torpedoes at 11:58 p.m. on April 16, 1945, shortly after taking on thousands of refugees at the port of Hela, resulted in the second-highest number of deaths. Two torpedoes hit the ship—one amidships and one astern—and caused such gaping holes in the ship's hull that it broke in half and sank within four minutes, with a loss of life of around seven thousand and only 147 survivors.[22]

The fate of the former luxury liner *Cap Arcona*, a somewhat larger ship than the *Gustloff*, was particularly poignant (see Illustration 15. *Cap Arcona*). In late April 1945, it had been ordered to take on board thousands of inmates from the concentration camp Neuengamme near Hamburg, as well as from others, including Stutthof and Mittelbau-Dora, and to transport them to Denmark. Captain Bertram delayed carrying out this order for as long as he could, because he did not want to be a party to the deaths of thousands of inmates. But finally he was given an ultimatum by two SS officers: "Tomorrow afternoon the *Cap Arcona* must begin the boarding of eight thousand KZ inmates. If you refuse, we have orders to shoot you."[23] He complied and early in the morning of May 3 the ship was just outside the harbor of Neustadt in the Bay of Lübeck when Captain Bertram learned that units of the English armed forces were expected to enter the town toward the middle of the day, raising the possibility of a peaceful takeover of his ship. But this was not to be the fate of the *Cap Arcona*. Around 2:30 p.m. the ship was attacked by Squadron 198 of Group 84 of the RAF led by "Jonny" J. Baldwin, a twenty-seven-year-old highly decorated pilot. To identify themselves, the camp inmates on deck waved white sheets and formed the letters "KZ" (the German abbreviation for "concentration camp") in an attempt to avert an attack, but to no avail. The *Cap Arcona* was hit by forty rockets, which turned it into a mass of flames. It capsized at 5:30 p.m. Only 450 survived while roughly seven thousand perished, most of whom were KZ inmates.[24] One of the few inmates to survive wrote movingly about the fate of those who did not:

> The *Cap Arcona* went under and in its hull swam human beings, our comrades, who had awaited all those long years the end of the war and the return home. Others lost their lives in the waters of the Baltic, which were cold at that time of year. We had imagined that the first day of freedom would be different.[25]

The third-largest loss of life in the Baltic rescue operation involved the steamer *Steuben*, a 17,500–ton former luxury liner, built in 1920, which ran between New York and Europe during the 1930s. Starting in July 1944, it was used in the Baltic area to transport wounded soldiers and refugees to the west. Its last voyage began on February 9, 1945, from Pillau, where it took on board close to three thousand wounded soldiers and almost a thousand refugees, which, together with doctors, nurses, and crew, brought the total on board to 4,267, more than any of its previous voyages. Helping to load the wounded on board the ship was Pastor Johannes Jänicke from Palmnicken, who was serving as a medical officer in the Wehrmacht. As he was leaving the *Steuben* to return to his quarters in Pillau, he was surprised to find several members from his church waiting to board the ship. They could only exchange a few parting words, and in his memoirs he recalled having a certain feeling of bitterness because his friends would shortly be sailing to safety, while he would be facing—admittedly of his own free will—either a Russian prisoner-of-war camp or death.[26]

Shortly after noon on February 9, the *Steuben* departed from Pillau and steered toward Hela to meet its escort vessels, the torpedo boat *T-36* (which had rescued hundreds of survivors from the *Gustloff*) and the torpedo recovery boat *TF-1*. Around midnight the one-time luxury liner and its escorts reached the vicinity of the sinking of the *Gustloff* ten days earlier. Undetected by the escort vessels, none other than Commander Marinesko in the *S-13* lay in waiting. At 12.52 a.m. on February 10 he gave the order to fire two torpedoes from the stern tubes of the *S-13*. The two torpedoes hit their target, one near the bow and the other amidships, and the *Steuben* immediately began to sink bow first. It took only thirty-three minutes for the ship to slip beneath the waves, with loss of life of 3,608 and 659 survivors. Pastor Jänicke's church friends all drowned, and when he later learned of their fate, he felt ashamed of feeling bitter when they parted company in Pillau as they headed for the presumed safety of the west.

Notwithstanding these losses, Operation Hannibal was a huge success. By one estimate some 2.5 million people were evacuated in the last months of the war, mostly German civilians who were escaping the advancing Red Army.[27] Historian Philip Karl Lundberg has described this evacuation effort as the most successful rescue by sea in modern history.[28] This rescue operation exceeded by far the better-known rescue of more than 300,000 British troops from the beaches of Dunkirk in May and June of 1940.

Three days after sinking the *Steuben* on February 10, Commander Marinesko received orders to return to his base. When the *S-13* arrived in port, his fellow officers congratulated him for having sunk two very large German vessels. He and his crew were treated to a celebratory dinner, which normally would have included a suckling pig in honor of a successful patrol, but none was forthcoming. On April 20, 1945, the headquarters of the Soviet Baltic Fleet awarded orders and medals for officers and crews of the fleet for exemplary action in the first three months of the year, but Marinesko and his crew received only standard orders (the Order of the Great Patriotic War and the Order of the Red Banner). He was deeply disappointed not to have received the much greater honor of Hero of the Soviet Union and that no mention was made of the sinking of the *Gustloff* and the *Steuben.* It seems likely that his escapades in early January when he went AWOL before resuming his patrol in the Baltic had put a major blemish on his record and that the Russian naval authorities were loath to credit him with the sinking of these two ships.

Marinesko then began a campaign among staff officers of the Soviet Navy to obtain what he regarded as proper recognition for his exploits in the Baltic, but these efforts on his own behalf did not endear him to his colleagues. In fact, they were counterproductive and he was relieved of his command of the *S-13* in September 1945, and a month later was dismissed from the navy for an "indifferent and casual attitude to the service."[29] Rebuffed in his attempt to join the Soviet Merchant Fleet in January 1946, he took a job in Leningrad (now St. Petersburg) at an enterprise dealing with building materials.

While working there, he was undone by doing a good deed for his fellow workers. He suggested to the director of the enterprise that large piles of damaged and discarded building materials be given to the employees as New Year's gifts. The director agreed and Marinesko was assigned to supervise the delivery of the broken blocks and bricks, refusing all offers of money from his co-workers for these valuable building materials. For this act of generosity, Marinesko was accused of stealing state property and was sentenced to three years in the infamous Kolyma slave-labor camp. He was kept there much longer and was only released two years after Stalin's death in 1953.

He then made his way back to Leningrad, where he found work in a factory. It turned out that during his years in the gulag he had not been forgotten. Thanks to the persistent efforts of two Soviet writers and two admirals, Marinesko was eventually rehabilitated in 1960, restoring his naval rank and increasing his pension. He was also given recognition in Hall No. 8 of the Central Naval Museum in Leningrad for the sinking of three enemy ships. Final vindication came in October 1963, when, at the annual reunion at Kronstadt of Baltic submariners, he was treated to the roast sucking pig that had been his due eighteen years earlier. Three weeks later he died of cancer.

B. The Massacre at Palmnicken

Almost concurrent with the *Gustloff* disaster, a tragedy was taking place on the Baltic coast of East Prussia outside the town of Palmnicken. Between January 31 and February 1 roughly three thousand Jews, mainly young women from eastern Europe, were brutally murdered by the SS and their hired executioners. They had been marched there from the nearby concentration camp of Stutthof and six of its satellite camps to prevent their liberation by the fast-approaching Soviet forces. These two horrific events are connected. First, the deliberate extermination of peoples deemed *Untermenschen* by Hitler—manifested in the massacre at Palmnicken—came full circle with the death, destruction, and elimination of East Prussia by the Soviet Union in response to German atrocities on its soil. The suffering of the East Prussians at the hands of the Soviet troops, including the loss of life on the *Gustloff,* was brought about by retaliation and revenge for the monstrous acts of the Nazi regime's "Thousand Year Reich." The second connection is eloquently conveyed by Andreas Kossert: "While German East Prussia burned in all corners and its inhabitants, fearing for their lives, fled from the Soviets, at the same time just before the Soviet Army reached the East Prussian Amber Coast, people died who yearned to be freed precisely by these Soviets."[30] Finally, there is the horrible irony that in early 1945 the Nazi regime was more intent on eliminating the last remaining Jews on East Prussian soil than doing everything possible to help the East Prussians escape from the advancing Red Army.

The Palmnicken tragedy began in the Stutthof concentration camp located twenty-two miles east of Danzig.[31] (The buildings of the Stutthof KZ were also where many refugees were housed temporarily when they made their escape along the Frische Nehrung to Danzig.) In addition to the main Stutthof camp itself, some thirty satellite camps had been constructed in the surrounding area, of which six were in East Prussia: Seerappen, Jesau, Königsberg, Schippenbeil, Gerdauen, and Heiligenbeil. In August and September 1944, thousands of relatively healthy young women from Auschwitz were sent to work at these camps, clearing forests for the building of an airport, digging defensive trenches, and working on nearby farms.[32] When the Red Army advanced rapidly into East Prussia in early 1945, the six camps were closed between January 15 and January 20 and the inmates were marched to Königsberg under armed guard.[33] In the bitter cold, with only tattered rags for clothes and little to eat, many women collapsed along the way and were shot by guards on the spot.[34] Hundreds of bodies lined the edges of the roads leading to Königsberg. There, the survivors of the forced march were housed for several days in three separate locations: the Steinfurt factory, which produced railway cars, located near the North Train Station; a thread factory at Reichstraße 1; and the barracks in the Kalthof district.

The question then arose what should be done with the thousands of inmates now in the city. Herr Gerhard Rasch, the head of the Königsberg office of the government-owned amber mining company in Palmnicken, apparently provided the answer.[35] He advised Herr Gromig, the chief of the Gestapo in Königsberg, that the prisoners should be marched to Palmnicken, where they could be herded into the tunnels of the abandoned "Anna Grube" mine, which could then be closed off. Gormig followed this advice and ordered the roughly five thousand mostly Jewish inmates to begin the forced march of thirty miles from Königsberg to Palmnicken early in the morning of Friday, January 26, 1945. In overall charge of the march was SS officer Fritz Weber; the guard unit consisted of twenty-two other members of the SS and 120 non-German guards from Ukraine, Lithuania, Belgium, and the Netherlands.

Given little to eat while in Königsberg and nothing on the road, and dressed in skimpy clothing with no protection from the cold, hundreds of prisoners collapsed from exhaustion and hypothermia and were shot where they fell by the guards. A native of Königsberg, who had started out that same Friday on foot to Pillau, reported that the snow was nearly two feet deep and the temperature was $-9°F$ ($-23°C$).[36] What had turned into a death march went largely by side roads to avoid as much as possible exposing local East Prussians to the horror that was passing through their midst. Nonetheless, many became witnesses to the atrocity perpetrated by the SS. Two young girls, Rosemarie Black (fifteen) and Elfride Möller (seventeen) reported seeing a column of women shot by the guards and their bodies thrown into a truck. Renate Loatsch, an employee of the amber mine, was in a car with her driver on the way to Palmnicken to pay the mine workers. She reported that for the car to pass, the driver had to get out of the car to remove the bodies of dead women from the middle of the road. Along the one-mile stretch between Palmnicken and the neighboring town of Sorgenau, between two and three hundred corpses were found on Saturday morning. The bodies were picked up the next day, but the snow was heavily stained with blood where they had lain, clearly indicating that they had been shot.

One of the SS men stayed behind the columns of Jews with orders to execute anyone who had managed to escape. Maria Blitz was one of the very few who did escape from the column. She was helped and hidden by a number of residents of the village of Kirpehnen; they were eager for her to stay with them because they believed her presence would provide some protection from the Russian troops who were then advancing rapidly westward.[37]

By the time the columns of mostly Jewish women reached Palmnicken in the early hours of Saturday, January 27, two thousand had fallen along the way and been shot, and three thousand had survived the death march.[38] Martin Bergau (sixteen) was an eyewitness to the arrival of the columns and in his memoir he reported that the sound of shots wakened him at about 3:00 Saturday morning. He hastily got dressed, grabbed his machine gun (which he had been issued as a member of the Hitler Youth organization), and went out into the front garden. In the dark he glimpsed a woman who was about to open the garden gate, but seeing the armed figure of Bergau, she turned around and went back into the street. Bergau then heard shots and saw the woman collapse in a heap. He then witnessed an endless column of poorly dressed figures pass by and now and then saw one of the women break out of the column only to be shot down. The following day young Bergau realized what had happened:

> Next morning when I went to the street, directly in front of the gate to the yard a frozen puddle of blood within which lay frozen rags covered with a blanket of fine snow immediately recalled to me the horrible reality of last night. Palmnicken, my hometown, so far spared all the horrors of the war, had quite suddenly become the scene of ghastly murders. Looking down the street made clear that the death march during the night had not been a terrible dream. Bloody snow and scattered belongings—signs of the nightly march. Only the dead had been removed.[39]

Early that morning when SS Commander Fritz Weber arrived at the amber mine, he informed the mine director, a Herr Landmann, of his intention to force the prisoners into the unused mine tunnels. But Herr Landmann immediately rebuffed Weber, arguing that the tunnels could in no way be used to incarcerate the prisoners because they now provided water for Palmnicken. Herr Landmann succeeded in housing the exhausted and freezing prisoners in a large building that served as a repair facility of the amber works. Later that morning, Hans Feyerabend, the director of the large estates owned by the amber mines, went to Herr Landmann's office; the latter informed him of what had transpired. Feyerabend then made it clear to SS Commander Weber that as long as he lived, the Jews would not be harmed. He immediately ordered that fresh straw be put on the floor of the repair facility housing the survivors of the march and that they be fed meat, pea soup, and bread prepared by the kitchen of the amber works. Thanks to Feyerabend's resoluteness, commanding authority, and sheer force of personality, Weber's plans for their extermination were stymied for a time.

Unfortunately, the protection he provided the women lasted only three days. On January 30, Feyerabend, who had served in the German Army in World War I and was the commander of the local Volkssturm, received an order from the SD (Security Service) in Königsberg to march with his unit to the nearby town of Kumehnen to bolster the defenses there against the Soviet Army. When he and his men arrived at Kumehnen, he discovered that he was not expected and then realized that his order was a fabrication designed to get him away from the amber works in Palmnicken. He had also received a sinister communication from the SD threatening him with severe consequences if he did not cooperate with the SS. As such cooperation would have been antithetical to his principles—and as he no doubt realized that he could not prevent the murder of those he had protected—he found himself in an impossible situation. The available evidence indicates that Feyerabend committed suicide by shooting himself with his hunting rifle just outside Kumehnen. He was buried on February 3 in the park of the Dorbnicken estate near Palmnicken, and as he was held in very high esteem by the community, the ceremony was attended by hundreds of local residents. (For his courageous attempt to prevent the death of three thousand Jews, Hans Feyerabend was subsequently recognized in Yad Vashem in Jerusalem.)

Once the Volkssturm unit had departed from Palmnicken on January 30, the fate of the survivors of the march was again in the hands of the SS and their collaborators. One was the mayor, Kurt Friedrichs, who ordered twelve armed members of the Hitler Youth (Martin Bergau among them) to his office in the town hall. There he gave them a considerable amount of brandy to drink and then introduced them to two low-level SS men with an ice-cold demeanor whom they were to assist. Friedrichs told them to maintain absolute secrecy when they had finished the task that the SS would explain. It was already dark when they left the town hall and made their way out of town to

the run-down buildings that were part of the long-abandoned Anna Grube
amber mine. Martin Bergau describes what happened next:

> I noticed a group of forty to fifty women and girls. They were Jews
> who had been apprehended. A diffuse light source barely illumi-
> nated the ghostly scene. The women had to stand in two rows,
> and we were ordered by the SS men to escort them.... When
> the formation was ready, two women were led by two SS men to
> the back of the building. Shortly after, the reports of two pistol
> shots were heard. This was the sign for two more SS executioners
> to lead the next two victims in the twilight around the building,
> and shortly thereafter pistol shots again blasted the air. I had to
> position myself near the end of the long row.... A woman turned
> to me and in good German begged me to let her advance two
> places in the line. She wanted to go the last walk together with
> her daughter. In a voice made nearly inaudible by tears, I granted
> the wish of this brave woman.... Then I led a mother whom I will
> never forget to her daughter.[40]

On the night of January 31, the remaining prisoners were led out of the
buildings of the amber works under the pretext that they would be transported by ship to Germany to prevent them from falling into the hands
of the advancing Russians. They had to form rows of five abreast and were
marched in the dark out of Palmnicken southward along the coast, where
the Baltic lay frozen in large clumps of ice along the shoreline. The SS guards
and their foreign helpers soon separated fifty or more prisoners from the column and using the butts of their rifles, forced the group into the water and
onto the ice, and then shot them with their machine guns. Many were killed
instantly, but because of the darkness and the haste in which the execution was carried out, some were only wounded or not hit at all. Yet in the
frigid conditions (around 7°F, −15°C), most of them soon froze to death or
drowned in the gaps between the ice clumps. Even then, some remained
alive for a time among the hundreds of corpses that lined the shore of the

Baltic south of Palmnicken, as witnessed by a German woman who chose to return to Palmnicken along that shore because the roads were completely jammed with refugees:

> Shortly before Palmnicken…we suddenly saw many bodies on the beach and also heard desperate cries coming from the water. From what I could tell, all those on the beach were dead, only now and then one heard despairing calls from the water…. The water was frozen near the shore and ice floes floated around, between which were the dead and those severely wounded. Many of these wore striped clothes. Many women were among them…. I was so devastated by this sight that I held my hands in front of my eyes…. We then walked on quickly because we could not bear to look.[41]

Nonetheless, nearly two hundred of the almost three thousand who had been incarcerated in the amber works managed to crawl out of the water after the SS guards left the scene of the massacre at daybreak. Most did not survive for long, as they were either soon apprehended by the SS and police, or if they managed to find refuge in the homes of German civilians, they were subsequently turned over to the authorities and executed. Only fourteen women and two men were protected by local civilians and survived.[42]

One of these was Zila (Celina) Manielewicz, born in 1921 in Ozorkow, Poland. She had survived the shooting along with two other young women and together they were able to crawl up the embankment and stagger through the snow to a group of small houses in the village of Sorgenau. One of them knocked on the door of the best-maintained house and when the husband and wife (Herr and Frau Voss) responded, she told them they were the survivors of a massacre on the coast and begged to be hidden in their house. The husband responded "That is out of the question," but then hesitated and said he had to confer with his wife. After some time Herr Voss returned and said that he would hide them in his attic. They stayed there for eight days and every evening were given warm soup and some bread to eat. The Red Army was at this time advancing toward Sorgenau and Herr Voss may have thought that hiding the Jewish women would provide protection from the Russian troops. However, when the Soviet advance was beaten back by the German Army, Voss feared he would be found out and ordered the three women to leave his house.

As luck would have it, they spied a storage shed for coal and firewood in the neighbor's yard and quickly hid themselves under the coal and pieces of wood. Unbeknownst to them, the neighbor—Frau Harder—knew that they had been taken in by Voss and had observed the women when they left the Voss house and hid in her woodshed. She was determined to protect them from the police. She came out of her house just as Voss returned with two SS men and a police dog, and when they asked her if she had seen some escaped Jewish women, she replied: "Yes, I have seen three ragged women here but I can't tell you where they went. I think they went in the direction of the woods," pointing in the opposite direction of the shed.[43] One of the SS men thanked her and said that they would take a look in the woods. At great risk to themselves, Frau Harder and her husband kept the three Jewish women in their home and explained to their neighbors and the police that they were young German women from Memel who had fled so quickly from the onrushing Soviet troops that they did not have proper identification papers. This ruse worked and they escaped detection. When the Russian troops took Sorgenau in mid-April 1945, they did not believe that the three were Jewish women from Poland, as they were convinced that any Jew who had not been killed by the Germans must have been a collaborator. Only the testimony of the other survivors of the massacre convinced the Russians that the three women were, in fact, telling the truth.[44]

There is ample evidence that the local population knew about the Palmnicken atrocity, as documented in the testimony of men who were ordered to collect the corpses and load them into their wagons, as well as in considerable detail in Martin Bergau's book. He reports that witnesses described seeing large patches of blood on the snow and frozen corpses on the route between Königsberg and Palmnicken.[45] There is also a brief report written by Klaus von der Gröben, who in January 1945 was a county administrative official

(Landrat) in the district of Samland (which encompassed Palmnicken). In September 1952, he described the death march and massacre:

> On the way from Königsberg to Sorgenau [near Palmnicken] many people in the column, which still numbered hundreds, died from exhaustion, hunger, and maltreatment and remained unburied in the high snow, while the rest were driven into the sea or shot in Sorgenau by guards from Nazi-occupied countries. Some of the unfortunates are thought to have escaped, even though wounded. In the general confusion it was impossible to prevent this insane deed, which the population had good reason to consider inhuman cruelty, especially in face of the threatening Russian attack, which they viewed as endangering themselves, and as their own police forces were not available and the guards had higher orders to obey. Although the Russian front-line troops must have come upon living witnesses or evidence of dead victims of this horrifying event, it could not immediately be established that retaliatory measures took place.[46]

This report is remarkable for a number of reasons. First, the killing is attributed to "some kind of foreign auxiliary forces" rather than to the German SS, who were of course in command. In addition, the author points out that the local population viewed this "act of madness" both as an inhuman atrocity and as putting them in danger of retribution by the Russians. For these two quite different reasons, Herr von der Gröben believed that the death march and the massacre should have been prevented, but perhaps because he was part of the government bureaucracy and therefore may have felt some responsibility, he thought it necessary to add that this was not possible because of the breakdown in political administration and because the guard unit was acting on higher orders. Without someone of the character and conviction of Herr Feyerabend, it seems highly unlikely that the local administration in Samland would have attempted to interfere with this SS operation.

Shortly after Soviet forces occupied Palmnicken on April 15, they under-took an investigation of the massacre. The local inhabitants who had not fled, as well as the German refugees who had not escaped from Palmnicken, feared that they would be subject to retribution. Johannes Jänicke, the pastor of the Confessional Church (*Bekennende Kirche*) in Palmnicken reported this expec-tation of revenge by the Russians in his memoirs.[47] The local inhabitants' fate was uncertain until May 23, when a memorial ceremony for the victims of the massacre was held by two hundred officers and soldiers of the 32nd Division of the Red Army. At this ceremony some two hundred German women and girls from the area were forced to exhume with their bare hands the bodies of 204 women and fifty-nine men, who had been buried in a mass grave near the Anna Grube mine. The bodies were laid out in two rows on the ground and the women who had dug them out had to assemble behind them. Russian soldiers set up two machine guns aimed directly at these women. The German witnesses of the massacre were then called upon to describe when and how the Jews had been killed. This was followed by speeches given by officers of the Red Army in which they described in detail the horrors of the death march and the massacre. Finally, a Russian major—who was also Jewish—gave a speech in German, which he concluded with the following words: "We could have done it exactly the same as your army was accustomed to in such cases.—But we won't sink to that level!—You are free!"[48] After the major finished his speech, the Germans were ordered to bury the bodies of the victims properly in a new mass grave.

The Soviet authorities made a major effort to apprehend those who had taken part in the massacre, but none of the executioners were found. Three members of the Hitler Youth, who had participated in the search around Palmnicken for Jews who had escaped the death march and massacre, were arrested. On May 15, 1948, a Soviet military tribunal sentenced them to twenty-five years of forced labor. Long after the massacre, Fritz Weber, the SS commander of the death march, was apprehended, and on January 11, 1965, was taken into custody at the municipal court in Kiel. But he escaped the reach of justice: on the night of January 20—some twenty years after the massacre—he hanged himself in his jail cell.

Of the roughly sixty thousand Jewish and other inmates in concentration camps in East Prussia at the beginning of 1945, only fifteen hundred survived, according to documents at the Yad Vashem Institute in Jerusalem: the handful of survivors at Palmnicken; the five hundred in Camp Praust near Danzig, who were freed by the Red Army on March 23; and about one thousand, whom Rudolf Strücker, a German naval officer, transported in late April to freedom in Neustadt on the north coast of Germany (see below). All the others died in attempts to flee, in the massacre in Palmnicken, on the *Cap Arcona* and other ships, and on the forced marches to the west.[49]

An act of incredible courage saved the lives of about one thousand concentration-camp inmates, many of whom were Jewish, in the very last days of the war. Rudolf Strücker had been drafted in 1940 into the German Navy. On the night of April 25, 1945, he was the commanding officer of a tugboat, the *Bussard,* in the harbor of Pillau, which was then besieged by Soviet forces.[50] The crew was waiting listlessly for the battle to end and passing around a bottle of schnapps, when Strücker thought he heard someone call out his name and he went on deck to see who it was. He found no one and thought at first he had imagined it, but then he interpreted the voice as an inner call to action. He immediately ordered the incredulous captain of the *Bussard* to get underway and leave Pillau. Making its way through a gauntlet of Russian artillery fire that made geysers in the water all around the tugboat, the *Bussard* miraculously made it unscathed out of the harbor into the Baltic, unlike other vessels that attempted to make a getaway at the same time and were hit and sunk by the Russian shells.

Strücker set the course for Hela, which was still in German hands and was the last transfer point for thousands of escaping refugees and soldiers. No doubt he believed that at Hela he would somehow be able to get these Germans out of the Red Army's reach. When he arrived, he confessed to being amazed at the sight of three huge ocean-going barges filled to overflowing with malnourished, poorly clad individuals guarded by SS, Volkssturm, and members of the local defense units. He learned that the "cargo" of each barge consisted of about a thousand inmates from a concentration camp near Stutthof: mostly Jewish women, political prisoners, and Norwegians who had been resistance fighters. The *Bussard* and two other tugboats were ordered to tow the barges westward to Saßnitz on the island of Rügen. When the *Bussard* reached Rügen, Strücker received an order to proceed to Warnemünde, but on arrival they were again told they could not land but had to continue on to Travemünde. By this time, Strücker decided that he had to do everything in his power to save the prisoners on the barge and he became very concerned about whether they would be able to survive much longer without food and water. He knew he needed to land somewhere as soon as possible, but he had to get the SS and other guards off the barge before he could free the concentration-camp inmates. When the *Bussard* reached Travemünde, the conditions in the port were so chaotic that Strücker continued on to Neustadt in Holstein.

Shortly before reaching Neustadt, the *Bussard's* crew heard screams coming from the barge and a sailor told Strücker that the guards were throwing prisoners into the water. He ordered the towline to be hauled in so that the barge came up along side the tugboat. He mentioned that what he saw next took his breath away: the SS and other guards were pummeling the women prisoners with their rifle butts and pushing them over the side of the barge into the water. Seeing an SS major, who was obviously supervising the drowning operation, Strücker ordered him to step onto the deck of the tugboat. The following confrontation then took place:

> The SS officer, evidently caught off guard by Strücker, in fact stepped over. "What do you want?" he snapped at Strücker, but his voice did not sound very confident.
>
> "We are entering the Neustadt harbor. I must ask you to go with me to the town commander so that it will finally be decided what will happen to the prisoners.
>
> These people need food as soon as possible."

The hand of the SS officer went to his pistol holster. "You dare to give me orders? I should shoot you on the spot."

Strücker: "Shoot!"

For a long moment they faced each other, their eyes boring into each other. Then the SS officer relented. "Okay," he grunted. "After all, I will be glad when I am rid of this baggage."[51]

The two men then went together to the commander in charge of Neustadt and Strücker once again received the same order as before: do not disembark, but continue on to Lübeck. Hardly had the *Bussard,* with the barge in tow, left the harbor of Neustadt when Strücker heard on the ship's radio that English forces had already taken Lübeck and were advancing on Neustadt. Without delay, he ordered the *Bussard* to turn around and return immediately to Neustadt. He did not want to land at Lübeck for fear that the English would treat the old men in the Volkssturm and local defense units (*Landesschützen*), who had been pressed into service as guards by the SS but had not harmed the prisoners, as harshly as they would the SS. Strücker thought the SS would receive their appropriate punishment sooner or later. It was dark by the time the tug and the barge reached Neustadt. There Strücker found a complete breakdown of order; most of the German soldiers were drunk. Before going ashore he told the tugboat captain that he wanted to obtain new orders. This was a ruse; when he returned to the tugboat he informed the captain that he had been instructed to disembark the guards from the barge. Strücker grabbed his megaphone and shouted to the guards: "All military personnel immediately board the tugboat with weapons and ammunition!" Relief was written on the guards' faces when they stepped onto the deck of the *Bussard,* which then took them to a dock in Neustadt where they disembarked and vanished in the darkness. The advancing English troops were not far from Neustadt; the horizon was illuminated by fires and artillery explosions could be heard in the distance.

Before depositing the guards on land, Strücker had detached the cable connected to the barge and set it adrift in the harbor. The prisoners were now on their own. The Norwegian inmates took charge of the barge and, with the aid of makeshift sails made from sacks, were able to bring the barge to land. In the early dawn of May 3, 1945, Strücker observed from a dock in the harbor the prisoners leaving the barge and making their way into Neustadt. A few hours later, a unit of the Second British Army under General Dempsey entered the town and Strücker was taken prisoner, but the surviving concentration-camp inmates he had protected from the SS were finally safe.[52]

Notes

1 Knopp, *Der Untergang der "Gustloff,"* 36–37. "Mein Führer, Sie führen unser Volk zum Schönen, Sie geben ihm einen neuen Lebenstil und eine innerliche und äusserliche Lebenshaltung, die auf das Schöne hinzielt. Sie geben unserem Volke schöne Autobahnen, große und schöne Bauten in Nürnberg, in München, und bald auch hier in Hamburg. Wir wollen, daß jeder stark und gesund wird, denn dann wird Deutschland leben und ewig sein!"

2 Ibid., 49. "Ich habe meinen Rucksack gepackt und bin schnurstracks zum Bahnhof ... aber dann habe ich die überfüllten Züge gesehen, die toten Kinder und bin schleunigst wieder zurück."

3 Schön, *Die "Gustloff" Katastrophe*, 198.

4 Schön, *Die "Gustloff" Katastrophe*, 216. "Bei der ungeheuren Überbelegung und den nicht ausreichenden Rettungsmitteln wird die Panik an Board unbeschreiblich sein, wenn uns etwas zustieße, sagte der Fähnrich."

5 Ibid., 237–38.

6 Knopp, *Der Untergang der "Gustloff,"* 69.

7 Dobson, Miller, and Payne, *The Cruelest Night*, 47.

8 Schön, *Die "Gustloff" Katastrophe*, 270. "Im Unteren Promenadendeck und im A-Deck sehe ich in die großen Säle, in denen die Menschen zu Hunderten auf Matratzen liegen. Trotz ausdrücklichen Verbotes haben viele sich ausgezogen, schlafen fest wie Tote. Die Schwimmwesten, die sie eigentlich umgebunden haben sollten, dienen vielen als Kopfkissen."

9 Dobson et al., *The Cruelest Night*, 107.

10 Ibid., 114.

11 Ibid., 111.

12 Grass, *Crabwalk*, 144–45.

13 "Es war der Schrei, dieses dumpfe Schreien der Menschen, die noch immer im Schiff waren. Das habe ich noch immer im Ohr. Das war der Todesschrei der Gustloff."

14 Schön, *Die "Gustloff" Katastrophe*, 320. "Und von dort tönt nun das Schreien von Hunderten von Frauen und Kindern, ein Schreien in Todesangst, so furchtbar, daß es niemand jemals beschreiben kann, der es nicht selbst gehört hat. Das Schreien steigert sich zum schrillen Heulen, als es aussieht, als ob das Schiff kentern würde."

15 Dobson et al., *The Cruelest Night*, 124.

16 Captain Petersen survived the sinking of the *Gustloff* and never went to sea again. He died not long after the end of the war. <www.wilhelmgustloff.com/facts_keyplayers_ind>.

17 What was called a "torpedo boat" in the German Navy in World War II was much closer in size and function to a "destroyer escort" in the U.S. Navy at the time. I am grateful to Charles McCain for this point. See his blog in which he describes the nomenclature of torpedo and other boats: <http://blog.charlesmccain.com/2010/10/alphabet-soup-of-confusion-torpedo.html>.

18 Dobson et al., *The Cruelest Night*, 129.

19 Schön, *Die Tragödie der Flüchtlingsschiffe*, 59.

20 Dobson et al., *The Cruelest Night*, 141.

21 Schön, *Die "Gustloff" Katastrophe*, 248–49. Many more ships were attacked, damaged, or sunk in the Baltic in the last six months of the war, but these experienced little or no casualties. For a complete list of these ships and associated casualties, see Schmidtke, *Rettungsaktion Ostsee 1944/1945*, 299–303. Schmidtke's estimate of the deaths during the evacuation operation is somewhat lower—36,640—than that provided by Schön, which is more than accounted for by his lower estimates of the number of fatalities in the sinking of the *Gustloff* and the *Cap Arcona*.

22 See Dobson et al., *The Cruelest Night*, 165–68, for a vivid description of this sinking.

23 Schön, *Die Tragödie der Flüchtlingsschiffe*, 201–2.

24 For an account of the British attack on the German ships in the Bay of Neustadt on the afternoon of May 3, 1945, see Müller and Kramer, *Gesunken und Verschollen*, "Die britischen Fliegerangriffe auf die im Seegebiet der westlichen Ostsee befindlichen Schiffe und Boote am 03. Mai 1945," 182–90. The authors estimate that of the roughly eleven thousand onboard the four German ships in the Bay of Neustadt that afternoon—the *Cap Arcona, Deutschland, Athen, and Thielbek*—about eight thousand died as a result of the British attack, and that 350 KZ inmates on the *Cap Arcona* were saved. Particularly tragic was the fate of Dr. Sumner Jackson, an American doctor who had remained in Paris during the German occupation and hid British and American servicemen in the

American hospital there. He and his son were imprisoned in the Neuengamme camp and were aboard the freighter *Thielbek* when it was attacked on May 3. The son survived but his father did not. See Vaughan, *Doctor to the Resistance,* and Glass, *Americans in Paris.*

25 Stanislaw Osika, "Bericht," in "Der zweite Auschwitztransport und die größte Schiffskatastrophe," "Und veilleicht überlebte ich nur deshalb, weil ich sehr jung war," in Erdelbrock, *Verschleppt ins KZ Neuengamme,* 68. "Die *Cap Arcona* ging unter und in ihrem Innern schwammen Menschen, unsere Kameraden, die die ganzen Jahre auf die Beendigung des Krieges und die Rückkehr nach Hause gewartet haben. Andere verloren das Leben im zu dieser Zeit kalten Wasser der Ostsee. Anders hatten wir uns den ersten Tag der Freiheit vorgestellt."

26 Jänicke, *Ich konnte dabeisein,* 114–15.

27 Schmidtke, *Rettungsaktion Ostsee,* 298. However, considerably lower figures have been given by Heinrich Schwendemann, who estimates that 900,000 refugees and 350 wounded were evacuated in the operation. Schwendemann does not credit Dönitz with the success of the evacuation, but rather low- and mid-level naval personnel who, largely on their own initiative, organized the rescue operation. See his "'Deutsche Menschen vor der Vernichtung durch den Bolschewismus zu retten': Das Program der Regierung Dönitz und der Beginn einer Legendenbildung," in Hillman and Zimmermann, *Kriegsende 1945 in Deutschland,* 13 fn. 13.

28 *American Historical Review,* April 1960.

29 Dobson et al., *The Cruelest Night,* 176.

30 Andreas Kossert, "Nachwort," in Bergau, *Todesmarsch zur Bernsteinküste,* 223. "Während das deutsche Ostpreußen an allen Ecken brannte und seine Bewohner vor den Sowjets davonliefen, weil sie um ihr Leben fürchteten, starben zeitgleich kurz vor dem Einrücken der sowjetischen Armee am ostpreußischen Bernsteinstrand Menschen, die von eben diesen Sowjets ihre Befreiung herbeisehnten."

31 The most complete description of the origins and operation of the Stutthof camp is in Benz and Distel, *Der Ort des Terrors.* See also Graf and Mattogno, *Concentration Camp Stutthof,* and Weber, "Stutthof: An Important but Little-Known Wartime Camp," *Journal of Historical Review,* 2–6. For a description of the hellish conditions in Stutthof by an inmate who was incarcerated there from the fall of 1944 through early January 1945, see Katz, *One Who Came Back,* 172–80.

32 Bergau, *Todesmarsch zur Bernsteinküste,* 9–10, and Graf and Mattogno, *Concentration Camp Stutthof,* 2. For a concise description of the Palmnicken massacre, see Blotman, *The Death Marches,* 117–125.

33 From mid to late January 1945, many thousands of Jews and other inmates were being marched from their camps to the west as the Red Army advanced from the east. Elie Wiesel has vividly described the horror of the march with his father from Auschwitz to Buchenwald in *Night*, 85–97. Himmler had ordered the evacuation of the camps in the east and that no prisoners should fall into the hands of the Soviets, but there was no overall plan on how this should be done. See Kershaw, *The End*, 229–35, 331–36.

34 It seems clear that these forced marches were undertaken with the intent that many of the inmates would die or be killed along the way. However, there is also evidence that those guarding the columns of prisoners made sure that that they were not killed all at once, as otherwise there would be the distinct possibility that the guards would be sent to the front lines. See Joachim Neander, "Vernichtung durch Evakuierung? Die Praxis der Auflösung der Lager: Fakten, Legenden und Mythen," in Garbe and Lange, *Häftlinge zwischen Vernichtung und Befreiung*, 52. But the massacre at Palmnicken was clearly carried out with the aim of killing all those in the group of inmates who had been in the satellite camps of Stutthof.

35 Bergau, *Todesmarsch zur Bernsteinküste*, 20.

36 Report by Therese Erdtmann in Kempowski, *Das Echolot*, 2: 627. Another resident of Königsberg traveled by car the next day (Saturday) and reported that it was so frigid ("Die Kälte ist fast unerträglich….") that her limbs were stiff at the end of the trip. Report by Erika Reich in Kempowski, *Das Echolot*, 666.

37 For an account of how Maria Blitz escaped the death march and managed to elude the SS, see Bergau, *Todesmarsch zur Bernsteinküste*, 35–41, and Blitz, *Endzeit in Ostpreußen*.

38 This forty percent death rate calls into question Mark Weber's claim that "most Stutthof victims apparently lost their lives in the grim and hastily organized evacuations by foot or sea. As harsh as they were, these evacuations were not part of any extermination program." Weber, "Stutthof: An Important but Little-Known Wartime Camp," 5. See also footnote 97.

39 Bergau, *Todesmarsch zur Bernsteinküste*, 44. "Am nächsten Morgen, als ich auf die Straße trat, holten mich die unmittelbar vor der Eingangspforte unter einer feinen Schneedecke liegende, gefrorene Blutlache und der darin festgefrorene Lumpen in die fürchterliche Wirklichkeit der letzten Nacht zurück. Palmnicken, mein Heimatort, bislang von allen Schrecken des Krieges verschont, war urplötzlich zum Schauplatz eines grauenvollen Mordgeschehens geworden. Der Anblick der Straße machte deutlich, daß der nächtliche Todesmarsch kein schrecklicher Traum gewesen war. Blutiger Schnee und verstreute Habseligkeiten—Spuren des nächtlichen Marsches. Nur die Toten waren entfernt worden."

40 Bergau, *Der Junge von der Bernsteinküste*, 111–13. "Ich bemerkte eine Gruppe von etwa vierzig bis fünfzig Frauen und Mädchen. Es waren aufgegriffene Juden. Eine diffuse Lichtquelle beleuchtete spärlich eine gespenstisch anmutende Szenerie. Die Frauen mußten sich in Zweierreihen aufstellen, und wir wurden von den SS-Männern angewiesen, sie zu eskortieren…. Als die Aufstellung beendet war, wurden jeweils zwei Frauen von zwei SS-Männern um das Gebäude geführt. Kurz darauf peitschten zwei Pistolenschüße auf. Das war für zwei weitere SS-Henker das Zeichen die beiden nächsten Opfer um das im Dämmerlicht liegende Gebäude zu geleiten, wo dann kurz darauf die Pistolen erneut knallten. Ich hatte mich ziemlich am Ende der langen Reihe positieren müssen…. Eine Frau wandte sich nun in gutem Deutsch an mich mit der Bitte, um zwei Plätze weiter nach vorn zu dürfen. Sie wollte zusammen mit ihre Tochter den letzten Weg gehen. Mit fast tränenerstickter Stimme erfüllte ich den Wunsch dieser tapferen Frau…. Dann geleitete ich eine Mutter, die ich nie vergessen werde, zu ihrer Tochter."

41 Kossert, *Ostpreussen: Geschichte und Mythos*, 314. "Kurz vor Palmnicken … sahen wir am Strand plötzlich zahlreiche Leichen liegen und hörten auch noch vom Wasser her verzweifelte Schreie. Die am Strand Liegenden waren nach meinen Beobachtungen alle tot, nur ab und zu hörte man aus dem Wasser heraus verzweifelte Rufe…. Das Wasser war am Ufer ein kurzes Stück gefroren, und Eisschollen trieben umher, dazwischen die Schwerverletzten bzw. Toten. Viele derselben waren mit gestreiften Bekleidungsstücken gekleidet. Viele Frauen waren auch darunter…. Ich war über den Anblick dermaßen erschüttert, daß ich meine Hände vor die Augen hielt…. Wir sind dann schnell weitergegangen, weil wir den Anblick nicht ertragen konnten."

42 Bergau, *Todesmarsch zur Bernsteinküste*, 120.

43 Ibid., 125. "'Ja, ich habe drei zerlumpte Frauenzimmer hier gesehen,' sagte sie, 'doch, wohin sie gegangen sind, kann ich Ihnen nicht sagen. Mir scheint, sie sind in Richtung Wald.'"

44 Ibid., 120–29, and Horbach, *So überlebten sie den Holocaust*, 7–31.

45 Bergau, *Todesmarsch zur Bernsteinküste*.

46 Individual Report no. 30 by von der Gröbben, in Schieder, *Dokumentation der Vertreibung*, Vol. I, Part 1, 136. "Auf dem Wege von Königsberg bis Sorgenau [near Palmnicken] sind dann zahlreicher Mitglieder des noch immer noch Hundertern zählenden Zuges durch Entkräftigung, Hunger und Mißhandlung umgekommen und unbeerdigt im hohen Schnee liegen geblieben, wärend der Rest von den—irgendwelchen ausländischen Hilfsvölkern angehörenden—Wachtmänner in Sorgenau in die See getrieben bzw. erschoßen wurde. Ein

Teil der Unglücklichen soll verwundet entkommen sein. In dem allgemeinen Durcheinander war es nicht möglich, diese Wahnsinnstat, die die Bevölkerung mit Recht als unmenschliche Grausamkeit und angesichts des drohenden russischen Einfalls als Gefährdung ihrer selbst ansah, zu verhindern, zumal eigene polizeiliche Kräfte nicht mehr greifbar waren und das Wachkommando höhere Befehle hatte. Obwohl die russischen Vorhuten auf lebendige oder tote Zeugnisse dieses grauenhaften Geschehens gestoßen sein müssen, waren Vergeltungsmaßnahmen nicht unmittelbar festzustellen."

47 Jänicke, *Ich konnte dabeisein*, 118. Jänicke writes that while there were no acts of revenge against the Germans in Palmnicken, there was punishment in that many died from disease and starvation under the Soviet occupation. In fact, he is quite explicit on this point. When the German men in Palmnicken were interrogated by the Russians about what he, Pastor Jänicke, now preached to his congregation, they all answered that "our minister says that we now suffer what the German people deserve. We now experience God's judgment." "Unser Pfarrer sagt, wir erleiden jetzt, was das deutsche Volk verdient hat. Wir erleben jetzt Gottes Gericht." Jänicke, *Ich konnte dabeisein*, 120.

48 Bergau, *Todesmarsch zur Bernsteinküste*, 146. "Wir könnten es genau so machen, wie Ihre Wehrmacht es in solchen Fällen zu tun pflegte—Aber dazu lassen wir uns nicht herab!—Sie sind frei!"

49 Horbach, *So überlebten sie den Holocaust*, 30–31. Joseph Katz cites figures of the same order of magnitude: "By the end of World War II, a total of 52,000 prisoners had passed through Stutthof. Of these, about 3,000 survived." Katz, *One Who Came Back*, 228 n. 1. One account describes how SS troops, marines and cadets from the U-boat school in Neustadt fired on the inmates when the barges got to shore, killing hundreds. Hence it appears that not all in the barge pulled by the *Bussard* survived. See Jacobs and Pook, *The 100-Year Secret*, 81.

50 Horbach, *So überlebten sie den Holocaust*, Chapter 13, 296–310.

51 Ibid., 306. "Der SS-Officier, offenbar überrumpelt von Strücker, stieg tatsächlich über. 'Was wollen Sie?' fuhr er Strücker an, aber seine Stimme klang nicht sehr sicher. 'Wir laufen in den Hafen von Neustadt ein, Ich muß Sie bitten, mit mir zum Stadtkommandanten zu gehen, damit endlich entschieden wird, was mit den Häftlingen geschehen soll. Die Leute müssen schnellstens Verpflegung erhalten.' Der Hand des Officiers fuhr zur Pistolentasche. 'Sie wagen es, mir Befehle zu geben? Ich sollte Sie über den Haufen schießen.' Strücker: 'Schießen Sie!' Einen Augenblick lang standen sie sich gegenüber, und ihre Blicke bohrten sich ineinander. Dann gab der SS-Officier nach. 'Also gut,' knurrte er. 'Schließlich bin ich froh, wenn ich das Pack los werde."

It is estimated that from 1939 to 1945, between sixty-three and sixty-five thousand inmates died in Stutthof and its satellite camps. Of these, 21,500 died on the death marches and the evacuations by ship. Some forty-three percent of the victims were Jews, the vast majority of whom were killed between July 1944 and May 1945. Benz and Distel, *Der Ort des Terrors,* 520.

52 Benz and Distel, *Der Ort des Terrors,* 519, estimate that roughly twelve hundred of those who had been on the barges survived in Neustadt.

CHAPTER VI

THE FATE OF EAST PRUSSIANS UNDER RUSSIAN AND POLISH RULE

While over a million East Prussians had escaped by war's end in May 1945, those who did not faced an epic struggle for survival in devastated East Prussia. Hundreds of thousands died from starvation, disease, and violence in the grim postwar conditions. The new rulers of East Prussia—Russians in the north and Poles in the south—tolerated their presence as long as they were needed for postwar reconstruction, and then they expelled to Germany those who had somehow survived this precarious existence. This chapter describes how the East Prussians sought to stay alive in conditions of extreme scarcity and deprivation, and how many succumbed in their struggle to survive. Chapter VII describes the political process that eliminated East Prussia from the state of Germany.

A. The Immediate Aftermath of the Soviet Victory in Königsberg[1]

Following General Lasch's capitulation on April 9, 1945, the survivors of the battle for Königsberg experienced the same brutal treatment by victorious Soviet soldiers as East Prussians had endured during the invasion. Cowering in their air-raid shelters, the Königsbergers did not know what to expect, but many feared rape and worse. Their anxiety was sharply intensified when they were joined by retreating German troops seeking refuge from the ongoing battle. They knew that if the Russians came upon these soldiers in their midst, they themselves risked being killed in the ensuing exchange of fire. Hildegard Rosin described her fears as she waited anxiously for the end to come: "In the small bunker silence reigned, a trembling, listening silence…. I was sick with fear…. What will they do with us, I brooded, as in my mind I saw photos of dead children and raped women."[2]

When the Russian front-line assault troops entered the air-raid shelters in early April, they first searched for German soldiers who might be hiding there, and if they found any often shot them on the spot, before moving on to the next shelter. Other troops then stormed into the cellars shouting "*Uri, Uri*" ("Watches, watches") and relieved those in the shelters of their watches. Hildegard Rosin described what happened in her bunker:

> Shortly afterward Russian soldiers tore open the basement door and yelled as they stormed in. With their pistols they shot into the ceiling and floor. Their flashlights shone into our faces…. They then demanded our watches. The beam of one flashlight fell on my face. "Watches, watches," the soldier roared. With a heavy heart I gave him my small gold watch, a present from my husband. When the soldier pulled the watch over his hand and lifted his sleeve, I could see that his forearm was full of watches.[3]

Once the shelters had been cleared of German soldiers, the Soviet troops turned their attention to the women. Women often attempted to make themselves look old and ugly by putting on ragged, dirty clothes and smearing their face with dirt, and in some cases this ruse worked. Another ruse was to tell their assailants that they were sick ("*bol'naia*"), and the fear of being infected with a sexually transmitted disease kept many attackers at bay. Other women were not so lucky and were brutally raped, sometimes by a gang of soldiers. The attacks were particularly violent when the Russians found alcohol, and after they were drunk they raped any woman they could lay their hands on, young or old.

Michael Wieck vividly conveyed the wholesale pillaging and rampaging by drunken Russian soldiers that took place in the Hufen district located outside the center of Königsberg:

> Everyone could see the Russian soldiers now on the streets were no longer troops from the front. The frontline troops had moved on about half a mile toward the city center. The soldiers were hungry for booty, taking watches and hand baggage, wandering through abandoned apartments and cellars as they looked for things to send home. The rich supplies of wine and schnapps thoughtlessly left behind obliterated any remaining inhibitions…. Incited to a frenzy, wild in their joy of victory, astonished at a civilization full of luxurious items, and drunk, they were beyond control. They knew no bounds. They indulged every instinct, be it sex, power, greed for possessions, gluttony, or murder. What blinding hatred! But, whosoever attacks and defends as ruthlessly as the Germans did, will be fought and vanquished with an equal absence of mercy.[4]

Mayhem and carnage were the order of day in the City Hospital (*Städtisches Krankenhaus*), located between Hinterrossgarten Straße and the Schloßteich, where Dr. Lehndorff was head of the surgery department.[5] When the Russian soldiers descended on the hospital early in the morning on April 9, the Russian woman who was his assistant tried to stop them but was thrown to the floor with such force that her jaw and some teeth were broken. She lay there soundlessly with blood streaming from her head while the soldiers burst into the wards, threw the patients out of their beds, and took off their bandages in search of valuables, such as watches and boots. Some nurses tried to avoid the attention of Russian soldiers wandering around the hospital by seeking refuge in the operating room where they pretended to be helping out with the surgeries. A dead woman was deliberately left on the operating table, and the nurses rushed to her side to give the impression they were treating her whenever Soviet soldiers appeared. Other nurses did not find a hiding place and were pounced upon and dragged off to be raped. From all parts of the hospital Dr. Lehndorff reported hearing the anguished screams of women being assaulted who cried out to be shot. When some lost their will to resist and became hysterical, it further incited the Russian soldiers.

Dr. Lehndorff confessed later he felt guilty that he was still alive and had not intervened to try to save the nurses from their tormentors. And yet on several occasions he was able to enlist Russian officers to help keep their riotous troops at bay. Once he removed a small wart from the face of a Russian major who was so pleased with the results of this minor surgery that for some time afterward he protected the hospital personnel from intruders. On another occasion, a Soviet officer called Dr. Lehndorff to the isolation ward where soldiers were attacking the patients. Upon learning from Dr. Lehndorff that they were sick with scarlet fever, typhus, and diphtheria, the outraged officer threw himself into the midst of the rampaging soldiers to restore some semblance of order, although by then it was too late for four women who had already died.

To facilitate their search for loot in the basement of the hospital, Russian soldiers burned mounds of paper to provide light in the dark rooms, forcing the hospital personnel to make frantic efforts to put out the fires. A wild mob stormed the main storeroom and pulled masses of provisions off the shelves, while fighting each other for the most prized goods. A heap of broken glass containers and opened cans soon littered the floor, over which sacks of sugar, flour, and coffee had been emptied. No one paid any attention to the lifeless body of a half-clothed man lying in the midst of this chaos. Dr. Lehndorff was extremely upset that these supplies, which could have supported the hospital for months, were pillaged in a matter of hours. The situation became even more desperate when the soldiers discovered the Menthal liqueur factory next door and its thousands of gallons of carefully hidden alcohol. Crowds of intoxicated officers, soldiers, and riflewomen soon stormed into the hospital in a drunken rampage and made it all but impossible to protect anyone from this out-of-control horde. Many sought to obtain sulfa drugs from Dr. Lehndorff to treat their venereal disease, but he could only point to the piles of crushed vials that littered the corridors.

In the maternity wards of the hospitals in Königsberg, women were raped irrespective of whether they were about to deliver or had just given birth.

A particularly tragic case took place at the Charity Hospital (*Krankenhaus der Barmherzigheit*) when Soviet troops rushed into the operating room just as Professor Unterberger was involved in a difficult forceps delivery.[6] They ruthlessly took the instrument out of his hands and it was only with great difficulty that he was able to complete the delivery. They then grabbed the woman out of the stirrups and abused her terribly. Professor Unterberger was so shocked and sickened by this barbaric treatment of his patient that he went to his office and took his own life. His staff buried him in the yard of the hospital.

Accompanying the invading troops were Soviet vagabonds who were equally intent on grabbing as much as they could of the hospital patients' remaining possessions. Dr. Lehndorff reported that in the evening the court-yard of the City Hospital took on the appearance of a ragged Gypsy camp as dozens of small wagons harnessed to Russian ponies drove up and shadowy figures started to cook food over small fires between two bricks. They were busily engaged in sorting out the loot they had collected from the trunks and suitcases of defenseless patients and their relatives. Dr. Lehndorff expressed shock that civilized Königsberg had been taken over by an uncontrolled mob and the scene in the courtyard seemed to him like one out of deepest Asia. He agonized about what might happen at the hospital that night, but to his relief the bandits suddenly broke camp and made their way down a major thor-oughfare, the Rossgarten, toward the center of the city. The next day he was amazed at Königsberg's transformation when he walked down the Rossgarten and was caught up in a maelstrom of Russian soldiers, riflewomen, vehicles, and animals all jammed together in a riotous crowd that made its way between the still-flaming buildings toward the castle in a kind of victory parade. He described it as akin to a scene out of Goethe's "Walpurgis Night."[7]

B. The Forced Marches out of Königsberg in April 1945

Shortly after the Soviet forces had secured Königsberg, the residents—young, old, infirm, and sick—were assembled into groups ranging from fifty to upward of five hundred people and marched outside the city. These were commonly referred to by the German survivors as propaganda marches (*Propagandamärsche*).[8] This evacuation of civilians served the principal purpose of allowing the Soviet soldiers to loot, undisturbed and unseen, all buildings that had not yet been destroyed in the battle. As mentioned in Chapter III, they had been given free reign by their commanding officers to take what they wanted as spoils of war for three days (April 10–12).[9] After the soldiers had removed everything they regarded as valuable, they set fire to many houses and other buildings in the city.

There is some direct evidence that the destruction of Königsberg reflected a deliberate decision to destroy much of the city. On April 10 the mayor (*Oberbürgermeister*) of Königsberg, Dr. Hellmuth Will, handed over the Municipal Hall to Russian officers, one of whom spoke excellent German. This officer remarked pointedly that all buildings in the city that were not needed by the occupying forces would be burned. Later, Dr. Will reported that during his ten-day march through the neighboring districts of Labiau and Wehlau, he saw the city burning like a torch in the distance.[10] Gerhild Luschnat also makes the case that the burning of Königsberg reflected the Soviet leadership's explicit objective to destroy the city that was regarded as the cradle of the hated Prussian order (*Preußentum*).[11]

While on the forced marches, Soviet soldiers robbed the Germans of the little they had managed to take with them, typically a knapsack packed with food, spare clothes, and a few valuables. During the first days of the marches they were given little or nothing to eat or drink. Many women were raped, and those who resisted parting with their belongings or did not submit to the soldiers' lust were sometimes shot. The worst time for women on the marches was at night when Russian soldiers entered the quarters where they were trying to sleep and shined their flashlights into the faces of those lying on the floor. Hugo Linck recalled that his column was put up in a barn with straw on the floor and that he tried to hide his wife from out-of-control soldiers by covering her with a mound of hay. The night was filled with the anguished shouts and cries for help from women being assaulted. When his wife was discovered, in desperation he used a few Russian words he had learned and which suddenly came to him, "*Moi matka balnoi.*" He meant to say that his wife was sick and he learned only later that "balnoi" had taken on a special meaning, namely, venereal disease. Her attacker recoiled in horror and let her go.[12] Lucy Falk found herself in a similar situation during her march. When a soldier was about to assault her, she put a pained expression on her face and he asked, "*Boljnaja?*" She guessed that he had asked if she were sick, so she groaned pitifully and the Russian left her alone.[13]

Some groups stopped in a suburb of Königsberg while others were marched for many days far away from the city. Once they had reached their destination, the marchers were typically housed in a farm building, shed, or barn of some kind. There Soviet security agents interrogated the adults to find out if they had been Nazi Party members or had been in the SS, the armed forces, the Volkssturm, or some other governmental unit. Once the interrogations were completed, some groups were told by their guards simply to "go home" and were left to their own devices; other groups were marched back to Königsberg, while many men were escorted under guard to camps and subjected to further interrogation.

One survivor of the march, Iris Rörup, described in her memoir what she saw as a young girl with her mother on the road away from Königsberg:

> On the main road to the Baltic they were overcome by thirst and bloody dysentery. Indescribable things happen. Next to the streets, in the lanes. In the ditches, the bodies of all kinds of life. In turned-over baby carriages, still whimpering babies. Next to them their dying or already dead mothers. Scattered all around ransacked luggage, suitcases, backpacks, handbags. Bodies crushed by tanks. Wounded horses stretch their hooves like threatening fists towards the sky.[14]

She imagined that she, too, could be lying dead along the road, and overcome by sheer horror, decided then and there that she would fight to avoid such a fate (*"Sie will nicht krepieren!"*). Even though she was only twelve at the time, she was interrogated by a Russian officer who asked her age. She lied and told him she was ten, and it was probably for this reason that he let her go. When she and her mother returned from their march to their house in the Königsberg suburb of Rothenstein, they found it damaged but still standing. On the second floor, where her grandmother had lived, a Russian was keeping careful guard over two cows he had somehow gotten up the stairs into her room. She also reported that when the Nazi block warden on their street was interrogated, he professed that he had always been a Communist. He did not convince the Russians and was shot.[15]

On April 12, Dr. Lehndorff went in search of the Russian "Kommandant" responsible for his district to request that he take steps to restore order in the City Hospital. But while on his search he was accosted by Russian soldiers and summarily marched off in a group of about fifty others; by evening Königsberg was fifteen miles behind them, and they were put in a barn on a small farm. When it was dark, the guards came with their flashlights and dragged the whimpering women outside to rape them. The next day the group was marched farther away from Königsberg, and when at nightfall they were nowhere near any buildings where they could sleep, a guard gave them a hatchet and showed them how to build a shelter out of tree branches. They got wet when it started to rain, but Dr. Lehndorff described how their makeshift shelter nonetheless provided them with some feeling of protection.

That night Dr. Lehndorff was interrogated in a nearby dugout and, as was often the case, Poles served as interpreters because they knew both Russian and German. Dr. Lehndorff responded candidly to the Russian questioner that his family had considerable property and buildings in East Prussia and he even enumerated the number of animals his family had possessed on their estate. The Polish interpreter told him he was stupid to reveal all this information because it would incriminate him as a staunch capitalist. Indeed it did: as a result of his "confession," he and about a dozen other German men also deemed to be dangerous were separated from their group and spent the rest of the night in another nearby dugout.

At dawn the dozen men were taken out of their hole in the ground and marched away at the head of a column with forty or so other Germans, with women in the rear. They were just behind the front in the Samland to the north of Königsberg where fighting was still raging. When passing through a burning village, which had been seized that day by Soviet forces, they walked as slowly as possible to warm themselves from the fires. Even though it was mid-April, it was still cold and wet snow was falling. It was dark by the time the column reached an empty farmhouse where Dr. Lehndoff and the twelve other men were crammed into a potato cellar just six feet square. Again they were helpless when they heard the raucous sounds of soldiers in the house assaulting the women above them. In the morning they were allowed outside to relieve themselves in a ditch behind the farmyard, and in the evening the Polish interpreter brought them some boiled potatoes to eat. The next morning at 4:00 they were taken out of the cellar and marched westward in bitter cold under a star-filled sky. Dr. Lehndorff tried to hold up a lawyer in his group who was so sick and exhausted that he kept falling down; he was finally allowed to ride on the wagon that followed the column. The sick lawyer's desperate condition convinced Dr. Lehndorff that he had to escape from what he feared would become a death march. That evening the guards were distracted by illumination rockets bursting in the sky and, assuming that the war had ended, shouted with joy "*Gitlair Kaput!*" (Hitler dead!) He took advantage of the general commotion and ran as fast as he could into the nearby forest; the guards fired a few shots in his direction but did not pursue him.

Dr. Lehndorff managed to elude Russian soldiers in the woods, but he was so weak that the following night he collapsed on the doorstep of a house. The door opened and the amazed Russian soldiers carried him inside, gave him soup to eat and took him to a barn next door where he lay down on the straw and instantly went to sleep. When he woke up late the next day, he found himself in the midst of women with small children, old men, and a few teenage boys from another march group. They had been given little food and several children had already died. All they had to eat were potatoes they had found in the fields, which they boiled over a fire between two bricks. When Dr. Lehndorff and this new column were on the road again, he passed a woman in what appeared to be a nurse's uniform who was pushing a wheelbarrow containing a blind and paralyzed man. She informed him that they were making their way to Königsberg from Rauschen on the Baltic where the man had become frightened of all the Russians who had encamped in his house. Dr. Lehndorff did not have the heart to tell her that the Russians occupied the city.

In the evening the only shelter the guards found for the group was the railroad station in the village of Watsum. The next day, when the guards were not looking, Lehndorff and a fifteen-year-old boy, identified as Helmut Z. from Palmnicken, climbed up the railroad embankment to search for food. They found a bag of oats in a dugout and hauled it back to the station where they cooked it over a fire on the station platform. The oats—normally used only to feed pigs—tasted like a delicacy. While they were eating, some Russians came onto the platform with a cow, tied it up, and immediately disappeared into the station building. Instantly, Lehndorff took a can and milked the cow while Helmut Z. kept an eye out for the Russians. Unfortunately, the container must have contained something that made the milk undrinkable, as the women discovered when they tasted the milk: it brought tears to their eyes.

The group spent another night in the railroad station and then the men were taken to Rauschen, where Soviet security officers again questioned them. These interrogations appeared to proceed in a rather arbitrary fashion: some men were soon set free, others were subjected to endless questioning, still others were sent to camps, and a few were executed. Dr. Lehndorff was dismissed by the interrogating officer after a comparatively brief hearing, whereas an old man who had worked for the German police did not return from his interrogation.

The next morning, the remaining group members were amazed when they were put out on the street and told "Go home!" Dr. Lehndorff decided to leave with Helmut Z. and go to Palmnicken, but on the road they met a seventy-year-old man pushing a wheelbarrow containing all his remaining possessions who warned them to avoid the Russians there. While this disturbing information did not deter Helmut from continuing on to his hometown, it caused Lehndorff to join the old man and together they walked to the village of Watsum, where Lehndorff had just spent the night. There they hid in an empty house that had been ransacked by Soviet troops in the usual manner: doors and windows were torn out; upholstery ripped up; furniture broken into pieces; and goose feathers, smashed dishes, bottles, and pictures made a knee-deep mess on the floor. At one point two Russians came into the house without taking notice of them; they tossed everything around looking for loot and then left. For the night they joined women and children in the house across the street who were lined up in one room according to the by-now standard protective arrangement: old women in front, children behind them, and young women and girls in back made up to look like old women.

The next day Dr. Lehndorff and the old man were walking along the road to Cranz (Zelenogradsk), when they were stopped by soldiers. Again, without any apparent rhyme or reason, the Russians allowed the old man to proceed on his way but interrogated Dr. Lehndorff and took him prisoner. They marched him in the direction of Königsberg and then threw him into a pig-pen that already held ten other men. Later, after marching under guard to the outskirts of Königsberg, they came upon the vehicle of a Russian officer that was stuck in the mud and that Lehndorff described as "one of those innumerable and hideous little American Jeeps that look like public lavatories."[16] The men were ordered to pull the Jeep out of the mud but were unsuccessful. They then walked further along the road until they came to the former Wrangel army barracks in the Königsberg suburb of Rothenstein and were marched through its gates. It was April 24. Dr. Lehndorff had survived—but just barely—his march, which had begun on April 12 and taken him nearly to the Baltic coast and back. Now he was incarcerated in the Wrangel barracks.

Sometimes generous acts of kindness on the march saved people who no longer had the strength to continue. In his memoir, *Ich sah Königsberg sterben* (*I saw Königsberg Dying*), Hans Deichelmann described how a fifty-year-old acquaintance with a broken leg was forced to walk nineteen miles (thirty kilometers) cross country with his leg in a plaster cast. Eventually, he became so exhausted that he could no longer keep up with his column. Miraculously, a Russian soldier—who emphasized that he was Jewish—befriended him and gave him a decent meal, strong tea, and a cigarette. Thus fortified, he was able to make his way back to Königsberg—sometimes crawling on all fours and after many detours—where he finally reached a hospital.[17]

Another report of a forced march comes from Michael Wieck. On the day General Lasch surrendered (April 9, 1945), he and his parents gathered up what belongings they could carry with them—backpacks, suitcases, and because they were musicians, their violins—and made their way to the corner of Luisenallee and Hermannallee, where the residents of the Hufen district in Königsberg had been ordered to assemble.[18] They no longer wore the Star of David because they had quickly come to realize that the Russians regarded them simply as any other Germans and they would receive no favors for being Jewish. In fact, the young Wieck felt a sense of relief that he was no longer an outcast among Germans and did not have to be afraid in their midst. After waiting for hours at the assembly point, his small group marched first to the suburb of Charlottenburg and then out of the city. They had had no water the entire day, and so when they came to a stream, Wieck ran down to fill containers with water and brought the precious liquid back up to his parents and others, who quickly gulped it down.

Farther along the way, Wieck's group came across the bodies of many German and Soviet soldiers as well as German civilians. Wieck found most depressing the sight of women beside the road or in the fields who had been so brutalized by so many rapes they could hardly move. The Wiecks had a close call when a Russian soldier demanded that Wieck's father hand over his violin. When he refused, the soldier held his pistol to his father's cheek. The younger Wieck made a gesture not to shoot and the soldier let his father go. Later his father lost his violin when a different soldier presented him with the choice of being shot or parting with his instrument in exchange for two rolls of bread. He handed over his violin but did not receive the promised rolls in return.

They spent their first night in the open on a grassy clearing. But they could hardly sleep because they were enveloped by the sights and sounds of war: Königsberg burning brightly in the distance, gunfire all around them, and the anguished screams and cries for help of women being assaulted by Soviet soldiers.

After another day and a half of marching, their group arrived at the village of Quanditten, where they were quartered in the undamaged buildings of an abandoned farm. Here a semblance of order prevailed; the women were not raped but brought to the kitchen to prepare potato soup. The Wiecks' hopes rose when they met a Jewish Russian lieutenant, but when they showed him their Jewish identity cards, he responded with a classic Catch-22, "We know that Hitler killed all the Jews. If you are still alive, you must have worked for the Nazis."[19] That evening they heard the Russian soldiers sing folk songs and Michael found it hard to square such beautiful singing with the heartless brutality he had witnessed since the fall of Königsberg. Later, the same lieutenant ordered Michael to play his violin. The lieutenant was curious about the instrument—how old it was and where it came from—which made Michael suspicious. Over the next two days their group was interrogated about the positions they had held under the Nazi regime and the whereabouts of German troops and weapons. The men were then divided into smaller groups, and, now without his parents, Michael and some others were marched off in the direction of Königsberg. They had to leave their baggage behind and Michael was outraged when the lieutenant, in fact, took his violin.

In Königsberg, young Wieck found that his neighborhood had burned to the ground. In other areas some partially destroyed buildings were still standing, but only a few houses remained with their interiors largely intact. He and about twenty others found shelter in a house that still had a roof. Inside it was very cold despite the fact that the broken windows had been sealed with whatever material was available, such as cardboard and the canvas of oil paintings. To survive, all had to scavenge for food. Wieck soon developed an uncanny ability to find food in the most unlikely places, for example, crevices in the corners of burned-out buildings. To assuage his ever-present hunger, he would take calculated risks, such as using a ladder to reach otherwise inaccessible places in hollowed-out houses that were about to collapse.

The Russians assigned Wieck to a work detail that buried the bodies of dead civilians in bomb craters. For this grisly task they were given gloves by the Russians because the bodies had begun to decompose after lying around for a week or more in the ruins. The dead were old men, women, and children, most of whom had been shot, some stabbed, while others had committed suicide. At first Wieck's work unit carried the corpses by the arms and feet to the bomb craters, but the Russians found this "method of transport" too time-consuming. They gave those in the unit lengths of rope to pull the corpses by the feet or hands to the nearest bomb crater, which significantly speeded up the burial process.

After a few weeks *Wieck's* fate changed dramatically. It was routine for Soviet soldiers to storm into his building at night in search of women. During one such incursion he was unceremoniously kicked awake by a Russian soldier and ordered to come with him at once, giving Wieck barely enough time to pack his few clothes and his invaluable woolen coat. Outside, he joined a number of male civilians. It turned out that someone in this group had escaped and the soldier had picked *Wieck* completely by chance to fill the quota of men who had been ordered to the Rothenstein camp.

C. The Internment Camp at Rothenstein

The Wrangel barracks, located in the Königsberg suburb of Rothenstein, were largely undamaged in the battle to conquer the city and served as the largest Soviet internment camp in the city.[20] The buildings consisted of the barracks themselves, which previously had housed German troops and other military personnel; the cellars beneath the barracks; administrative buildings; and nine large sheds for the tanks, trucks, and other equipment used by the German military units that had been assigned there.[21] The buildings were surrounded by a high fence, watchtowers, and barbed wire. The Russians used them as an internment camp for thousands of Germans from Königsberg and the surrounding area who were being held for further interrogation. Some men were released relatively quickly, while others spent weeks incarcerated in the most primitive conditions. Many died from disease and malnutrition.

Some were lucky to leave this camp after only a few days. Otto Thiel had been an automobile mechanic in the municipal car fleet (*Städtischer Fuhrpark*). After the capitulation he was marched, along with other men and a few women, to Tannenwalde, a suburb of Königsberg. They were then packed together so tightly into one room of a housing development (*Siedlungshäuser*) that there was no space to sit or lie down and everyone had to stand through

the night. Although the men tried to hide the women from the Soviet soldiers, some were discovered and taken out of the room; when they returned
they were weeping. One man was shot when he tried to save his wife from
being raped. Later, Thiel was taken from Tannenwalde to the Rothenstein
camp, where he was shoved into a room in the cellar, which he described as
crammed so full with men they were like sardines in a tin. On April 30, he
and the other men were let out of the cellar and those whose names were
called out from a list—which included Thiel's—were assembled in a long
column and marched into Königsberg. They were incarcerated in the cells
of the courthouse and were again interrogated, mostly at night. Around
mid-May, they were transported to an internment camp in Preußisch Eylau
(Bagrationovsk), where conditions improved for Thiel. Being a skilled auto
mechanic, he was assigned to repair the vehicles at the Russian barracks. Such
"specialists" were highly regarded by the Russians who by and large treated
them quite well.[22]

The printer Fritz Bartsch also was interned for a short time at Rothenstein.
On April 8, he and others were marched first to the suburb of Charlottenburg
to be interrogated; then moved to the Schliermacherstraße, where the last
three houses on the street were used to house civilian prisoners; and finally
they were taken to Camp Rothenstein, where Bartsch was incarcerated in a
cellar. At his interrogation he was told to confess that he had been a Nazi.
When he replied that this was not true, he received such heavy blows from
a broomstick handle that it broke and he fell off the stool he was sitting on.
Fearing further blows, Bartsch confessed that he had been a Nazi, whereupon
the Russian NKVD officer picked him up, sat him on the stool and after
giving him a cigarette, asked why he had not confessed immediately. Bartsch
replied, "I said that only because of the intense pain. I am really not a Nazi!"
("*Ich habe das nur vor lauter Schmerz gesagt. Ich bin wirklich kein Nazi!*") The
officer sent him back to the cellar and he was released shortly thereafter with
some other men and subsequently found work, first in a largely undamaged
paper factory, and then in a bakery.[23]

After only a two-day march around the outskirts of Königsberg, Pastor Hugo
Linck's group also arrived at the Rothenstein camp. The women were sent
to one of the barracks and the men were assigned to one of the nine huge
sheds where some thirteen hundred lay squeezed together on the cement
floor. The quarters were so cramped, there was no room for pathways for the
men to get to the buckets they used as toilets. Many of the prisoners suffered
from diarrhea and naturally it caused much shouting and cursing when they
inevitably stepped on the arms and legs of fellow inmates when they went
to relieve themselves at night. The buckets often overflowed and the stench
was overpowering. When the doors to the shed were unlocked at 6:00 a.m.,
the men rushed outside to relieve themselves in the open area surrounding
the camp. It soon became a field of excrement. In an attempt to deal with the
growing health hazard, the Russians ordered the prisoners to dig latrines in
the narrow yard between the sheds, one close by for the men and one at the
rear for the women. Often the urge to relieve themselves was so great that
women suffering from severe diarrhea could not run to their own latrine in
time, and overcoming any embarrassment, joined the men in squatting over
their pit.[24]

The daily food ration given the inmates in the Rothenstein internment
camp was barely sufficient to keep them alive: two slices of dried bread (about
two hundred grams), one-half liter of thin soup, and a tablespoon of sugar.
A detachment of men hauled water from a pump near the railroad station in
Rothenstein in whatever containers they could find, but this meager water
supply was hardly enough for the huge number of people interned in the
camp.[25] Because of this starvation diet and lack of water, many inmates
became so weak they did not have the strength to fetch their food at the midday distribution, and one of Pastor Linck's duties was to pick up the food for
the sick and weak.

Another of Linck's responsibilities was to supervise the transfer of the very
sick to the camp's makeshift hospital. The room set aside for dysentery cases
was so jammed with men lying on the floor and on top of and under the
tables that Pastor Linck could barely open the door when he visited his friend
Dr. Fett. Pointing to four empty places near where he was lying, Dr. Fett

whispered, "They died last night." It wasn't long before Dr. Fett also breathed his last in that room. Pastor Linck also officiated at the Protestant burial rites—a reading from the Bible, some prayers, and a blessing—for those who died in his shed. Inmates in other sheds arranged to have their dead taken out at the same time so that Pastor Linck could also perform the last rites for them. Crosses made out of fence boards with the names of the deceased were placed on the mounds of fresh earth, but a day or two later Pastor Linck always found that they had been pulled out. When a baby was born in the wretched conditions of the camp, Pastor Link was called upon to baptize the new arrival. He also instituted a morning prayer service and Bible reading for the inmates near his place in his shed. The circle of participants grew larger and larger until it finally included all thirteen hundred men in the building. According to Linck it was the largest congregation he ever had.

The German doctors in the camp valued highly the services Pastor Linck performed for the sick and dying. To enhance his living conditions in the camp, they asked if he would like to join them as a medical orderly in their hospital quarters. The offer was tempting because he would not only receive more food, but would also have his own "bed," namely, a straw-covered wooden platform instead of a narrow space on the concrete floor of the shed. After a few hours of reflection, however, it became clear to him that his place was in the shed with the hundreds of his new flock.[26]

Pastor Linck was kept in Rothenstein until May 1. He was then transferred to the internment quarters on the Schleiermacherstraße in the center of Königsberg, and on May 3 to the barracks in the Kalthof neighborhood. Shortly thereafter he was released and joined his wife, who had already returned to a house next to his church in the suburb of Liep. His first meal far exceeded what he had dreamed about in Rothenstein:

> I thought I was transferred to a fairyland. A long table, with a white tablecloth, with flowers on the table! The white tablecloth proved to be the back of wallpaper rolls, but the flowers were real, tulips, narcissus, crocuses, spring flowers, and whatever else bloomed in the many housing development gardens. Steaming

potatoes in big bowls and—unthinkable delight!—a roast! It was horsemeat, but nevertheless a roast.[27]

———————

One of those who almost did not survive in Rothenstein was sixteen-year-old Michael Wieck. When he first arrived he was temporarily sent to one of the sheds. When the thin soup was ladled out in the middle of the day, he had to go hungry because he did not have a pot or bowl. Later that day a guard led his group to a cellar that was already so crowded with inmates, it did not appear to have room for another person. The guard pushed Wieck and two other men into a pitch-black area under the stairs to the cellar. It turned out that German soldiers had once used this very spot as a pigpen. They found some wooden poles covered with pig feces and laid these on the damp floor to sit on, but they soon tired of this uncomfortable position and for the night stretched out on the filthy floor. Around noon the next day, they were taken out for their "meal" of dried bread; lacking any kind of container, they were unable to get their ladle-full of soup. Wieck realized that if he did not procure a bowl, he would soon starve to death. Upon emerging from the blackness of the cellar, he had noticed that some light bulbs were protected by transparent globes. When the guards were not looking, he quickly unscrewed one of the globes and hid it. At the next meal call, the Russian behind the soup pot smiled at him in apparent recognition of his resourcefulness and scooped up some potatoes and a little meat from the bottom of the pot, which he poured into Wieck's makeshift bowl.

With new-found strength from the soup, Wieck complained to the guards about the miserable situation in the pigpen. This complaint produced results: Wieck and the other two men were placed with a group of about eighty in a part of the cellar that appeared to have considerable space when everyone was standing. However, there was actually so little room that when some in the group sat down, they took up so much space that the men cursed and shoved as they tried to find a place on the floor. In fact, it was so cramped that some men had to lie on top of others. Anyone who fell asleep inevitably ended up at the bottom of a heap with arms, legs, and entire bodies on top of him, and on waking up would have to wriggle free from the bottom. As Wieck noted, "Our pigpen is dirty but it's a cabin between decks compared to this."[28]

He was lucky to be befriended by a sick man who suffered from a bad cough and struggled for breath. The man admonished Wieck not to get too close to him, but nonetheless let him lie on top of him for extended periods of time. The two windows in the cellar had been boarded up for protection against bomb fragments, and the two open slits did not provide nearly enough air for everyone in the room. As it was very dark, some of the men occasionally struck a match for illumination, but because of the lack of oxygen only the head of the match would burn. When Wieck noticed that fresh air seeped in from under the cellar door, he and his tubercular friend edged nearer to the door, and when lying on the floor, he kept his nose close to the ground where he had discovered the air was better.

The men were called for interrogation day and night. Some left the cellar hopeful to be released, only to re-appear hours later bruised, battered, and hardly able to speak. Others appeared more fearful and they, in fact, did not return, while some came back to the cellar without a scratch. As more and more names were called, Wieck became increasingly dispirited; he feared his name was not on any list, considering how he had been shanghaied in Königsberg, and that he would die in this dungeon. He grasped at any opportunity to escape. Once, a guard asked if there were a painter among the inmates and he volunteered immediately. He was escorted to a Russian officer who gave him colored pencils and paper to draw his profile. His effort was not sufficient to convince the officer of his painting talents, but he nonetheless gave Wieck a piece of bread before having him taken back to the cellar.

Disease, malnutrition, and lack of adequate medical care took their toll and every morning the dead were taken out and thrown on a pile in the yard. While this gave the survivors more space, it further discouraged Wieck, who could imagine only too well that this would also be his fate. One morning, when the cellar inmates were taken outside to the toilet pit, he returned late to the cellar and a guard gave him such a terrific whack on the back with his rifle butt that his ribs were injured. To add to his misery, on returning to his place on the cellar floor he discovered that someone had "exchanged" his woolen coat for a far too heavy coat that had once been worn by German soldiers on guard duty.

At this point Wieck lost his will to live and no longer went outside to pick up his food ration, knowing full well that this would lead to his death. At this nadir, his tubercular friend—dying and gasping for breath—incessantly encouraged him not to give up. The next day Wieck forced himself to get up and bring back his food on the very day when an additional teaspoon of sugar was allotted to the inmates. This unexpected addition to his meager diet changed his outlook from utter despair to newfound hope and the courage to persevere. Shortly thereafter, in the cellar hallway, he met by chance the Russian officer whose portrait he had attempted to draw and explained to him his dire situation. He had a feeling that the officer would help him, which further bolstered his outlook on life. But his spirits sank quickly the next morning when he found his sick friend was dead; like all the others, his body was taken outside and thrown on the mound of corpses.

Wieck was, indeed, saved by the Russian officer. A few days later he was taken out of the cellar with several other men and brought to a shed that had a plentiful supply of water from rain barrels. The men in this shed had boiled the water and shared it with the thirsty "cellar lice," who could not get enough of it. They were amazed that Wieck and the others had been able to survive in the cellar for so many weeks. The next day his group was marched to Königsberg; there, Wieck was assigned to a unit that had been ordered to fill up a huge bomb crater in the middle of an intersection. At this point Wieck was on the brink of collapse from his ordeal in the Rothenstein cellar and did not have the strength to lift a shovel. Taking pity on him, a Russian guard escorted him to the ruins of a nearby house and with a wave of his arm indicated that he should lie down on what remained of a bed. The following day, when Wieck went to work, he returned to the bed to rest and the same Russian guard gave him some of his own barley soup to eat. In Wieck's words: "I ate this delicacy in tiny portions, happy and touched. Indeed, there were more and more signs that some Russians began to see us as humans, which in turn allowed us to discover the heart and soul of the Russians. Still, the abuse inflicted on the women during the night was terrible. But in the bright light of day, we no longer needed to fear them so much."[29]

In Wieck's road-repair unit someone knew his parents and informed him that they had returned to Königsberg and were living only six blocks away on the Schrötterstraße. He set out to walk the quarter mile, but as he was still very weak, he only managed two blocks before he had to give up, utterly exhausted by the effort. The next day he was able to cover the entire distance only by resting after taking a few steps. When he finally reached the half-burned-out building and his parents, tears of joy flowed during the longed-for reunion.[30] To obtain food, his mother had bartered with the Russians some of the family's few possessions—a tablecloth, silver forks, a broken clock— and under her careful ministrations the sixteen-year-old Wieck gradually recovered some of his strength.

As his services as a medical doctor were needed in Camp Rothenstein, Dr. Lehndorff was treated much better than Michael Wieck. He arrived at the end of his "propaganda" march on April 24 and was placed in shed no. 8. It, too, was so tightly packed with upward of two thousand men that only a few could lie down to sleep on the cement floor while most squatted or had to stand. After climbing over bodies as best he could, Dr. Lehndorff was befriended by an old man who made room for him and apologized that he had no real food to offer, but gave him two of the four coffee beans he had managed to save in his pants pocket. It was not long before Dr. Lehndorff was able to leave these cramped quarters. Toward evening, a nurse entered the hall and escorted him to shed no. 2. There, he joined a Dr. Schreiner and two medical orderlies in a room that had been partitioned off from the rest of the shed and served as a dispensary. From then on, Dr. Lehndorff enjoyed the privileges accorded by the Russians to the medical profession in the camp: a place to call one's own, better food, some heat, and immunity from harassment by the guards.

At the end of April, dysentery started to ravage the camp inmates.[31] The most gravely ill were taken out of the sheds and soon nearly a hundred were lying in front of the dispensary on planks, on doors taken off their hinges, or on the bare cement floor, some half naked and without blankets. Most of the patients were too weak to get up and use the pail that served as a toilet, and they relieved themselves wherever they were lying. Consequently, the floor became a horrific sea of excrement and urine and forced Dr. Lehndorff and the other medical staff to jump from one uncontaminated island to another in order to reach their patients. Soon the death toll rose so precipitously that the Russians—fearing their own health would be compromised by the spread of infection—ordered Dr. Schreiner to supervise the removal of the sick from the sheds to the second floor of a huge barracks. By evening, about four hundred very ill inmates had been taken to the second floor, where their situation hardly improved; most had to lie on the bare cement floor, and because some of the windows had been smashed or removed and were not covered up, it was more drafty than in the sheds. In the morning, thirty-six dead men were found and collected in a pile several feet high. Several had died in the corridor, one of whom was found sitting on the toilet pail. During the day, so many more patients were brought into the barracks that roughly one hundred had to be housed in the loft above the second floor. Here, conditions were even worse because wind and rain came in through holes in the roof and the open windows. When Dr. Lehndorff checked on these patients, he found that some were already dead and he took off their coats and jackets to cover those still living. In face of the rising death toll, he spoke of his frustration that there was so little he could do to help the sick:

> There is no longer any question of doing anything properly; we merely help one another and now and then save a person from the worst. For however much we try to do something, we are in no position to judge if we have done any good or harm to our fellow beings. Although the sick have been separated from the crowds, they are even more uncomfortable than down in the halls. Fortunately the majority of them are so weak that they hardly know what is happening to them. We doctors have already

become co-workers in the death-mill of the camp, whether actively or passively makes no difference.[32]

Dr. Lehndorff also wrote that his most difficult assignment at the Rothenstein camp was making his rounds in the cellars. These visits were permitted every three or four days, and he estimated that some four thousand men and women were packed tightly into these loathsome dark and airless spaces under the barracks. All he could do was distribute bandages and some medications as well as identify the most seriously ill for transfer to the make-shift camp hospital. The sick were very eager to be put on the list in order to escape the hellhole that was the cellar, but Lehndorff knew they would not be much better off in the camp hospital. The inmates with dysentery were already so weak they could not get up, and he faced the difficult decision of whether it made any sense to put them on the transfer list, knowing that in either case they would likely be dead in a few hours. Frequently, all he could do was separate the living from the dead. Once, he and a chaplain were taken to the end of a corridor in a cellar, where an open door revealed a pitch-black cell with fifteen men whom the Russians probably had forgotten. Two of the men, blinded by the light from their flashlighs, crawled on the floor toward them. Dr. Lehndorff and the chaplain quickly examined the fifteen and found that seven were dead and the remaining eight were on their last legs. In this case, he decided to have them taken to the hospital. Dr. Lehndorff did not report what happened to these survivors, but in all probability they also died because, as he noted, inmates often expired soon after being taken to the hospital: "Tension has kept them alive until then; as soon as they relax, they pass away peacefully."[33]

In making his rounds in the cellars, Dr. Lehndorff observed that female inmates were much better at organizing their cells than the males. In one such cell, women were sitting back to back making a neat pattern on the floor, quite unlike the sprawl of bodies in the men's cells. The women's spokesper-son—a nurse Dr. Lehndorff knew—immediately rose when he entered and succinctly gave him the relevant information regarding the health situation of the women. This was in sharp contrast to the babble of voices that greeted him when he entered the cells occupied by men. Before he left, the women serenaded him with a cheerful song. Impressed by the practicality and organizational ability of the women, Dr. Lehndorff also noted that they had a higher survival rate in the camp than the men because they did not give up as quickly.

As the only surgeon in the camp, Dr. Lehndorff was in charge of the operating room. Given the lack of surgical instruments, he and his two assistants were not very busy and performed only the most necessary minor surgery. When the amputation of a leg was absolutely called for, he had to make do with a garden saw. The feet of one woman had turned black and fell off before they could be amputated. The lice were so thick, they sometimes covered the inmates to such an extent that they appeared to be gray when looked at from a distance. And yet these men refused delousing because they had to undress for this treatment and they knew that there was a good chance their clothes would be stolen. An old man was brought up from the cellar so infested with lice that he looked like an ant hill, and his fur coat had to be carried away on a pole to prevent the lice on it from spreading to others. The old man told Lehndorff in a low whisper that he had been the director of the local Cranz and Samland Railroad and implored him not to tell anyone because he lived in fear of being interrogated. He did not have to worry—he died an hour later.

Spring finally arrived in the second half of May and Dr. Lehndorff's spirits rose when dandelions sprouted and their leaves could be used for small salads. The inmates' rations still consisted largely of soup, but it had become somewhat thicker. Whitsunday, May 20, was a brilliant sunny day and the camp commandant had given permission for a church service. It was held in the operating room, which for the occasion had been decorated with spring flowers and greenery. By early June, the camp was gradually being broken up; some inmates were put out on the street while others were taken to Insterburg, where, rumor had it, there was a camp for Nazi Party members.

Dr. Lehndorff then had a pleasant surprise: a visit from his close friend, the "Doctora." Before the capitulation of Königsberg she had been a hospital colleague of his and now worked at the former provincial finance building (*Oberfinanzpräsidium*). It had been turned into what was called the "German

Central Hospital," where all the sick and wounded civilians in Königsberg had been taken from other hospitals in the area; those with infectious diseases were brought to the former University Clinic for Nervous Disorders. A few patients and doctors at Rothenstein had already been transferred to the German Central Hospital, and Dr. Lehndorff was among the last of the medical staff to join them there in mid-June. Just as he and others were departing from the camp, the commandant appeared and cordially wished them well, and as the camp gates were closing behind them, Dr. Lehndorff recalled that he almost felt like waving to the commandant, who was looking after them.

D. The Return of Refugees to East Prussia[34]

While the majority of East Prussians successfully escaped the Red Army in the winter and early spring of 1945, thousands fleeing to the west were overtaken by Soviet forces. These refugees could not conceive that their homes and land would be expropriated by the Soviet Union and Poland, and that their survival would be precarious at best in postwar East Prussia. Consequently, they expected that once the fighting had come to an end, they would be able to return home and resume their prewar activities. Little did they know that the trek home would involve worse dangers and difficulties than those they had already endured while trying to escape the advancing Soviet troops. The depredations these refugees suffered were on a par with those experienced by the survivors in Königsberg and its suburbs during the "propaganda marches." Along the way back to East Prussia, they were continually at risk of being forced to join work brigades to till the fields and clean up ruins, to dismantle machinery and railways for shipment to Russia, to perform services for Soviet troops, and to be deported to the Soviet Union as forced laborers. And if they did reach their home village or town in East Prussia, they found their houses heavily damaged and the contents carted away, the same depressing sight that had greeted the Königsbergers when they returned from their marches. In the southern part of the province the returning refugees often were shocked when they found that their homes were now occupied by Poles.

The returning refugees were of course unaware that during the war the three Allies—the United States, Great Britain, and the Soviet Union—had reached an understanding to eradicate East Prussia from German territory. As will be described in Chapter VII, once victory was achieved, the Allies had agreed in principle to partition the province into Soviet (the northern third) and Polish territory (the southern two-thirds) (see Map 3. Germany after World War II). This agreement was codified at the Yalta Conference (February 4–11, 1945) and at the Potsdam Conference (July 17–August 2, 1945). In their diaries and reminiscences, East Prussian returnees mentioned that they had been kept in the dark about these decisions regarding their homeland. Had they known what was in store for them, they would never have returned and the exodus to the west between late 1944 and early 1945 would have completely denuded East Prussia of all Germans. Soviet officers, on the other hand, knew that this easternmost province of Germany would be ceded to the Soviet Union and Poland at the war's end. When the Russian officer Lev Kopelev was engaged in the battle for East Prussia in early 1945, he wrote "We already knew then that we and Poland would keep the land." ("*Wir wußten damals schon, daß Polen und wir das Land behalten würden*").[35]

Soviet military commanders dealt in different ways with the refugees who had been overtaken by their forces. In many cases they ordered them to return to their homes or gave them official papers authorizing them to proceed to their home destination. In other instances the refugees were simply told they were free and could do as they pleased.

The overall objective of the Soviet authorities with regard to Germans in East Prussia was to use their skills and manpower in the Russian part of the province to reconstruct and develop this newly conquered territory until a sufficient number of Soviet citizens had been resettled there. As more and more Soviet settlers arrived in 1947 and 1948, the Germans were no longer needed for economic development purposes and were systematically expelled to the Soviet-occupied zone of Germany. The Polish authorities took a quite different approach in the portion of East Prussia allotted to them. As described in Chapter VII, they wished to create "facts on the ground" and quickly establish a Polish presence. Therefore, soon after the fighting ceased in the spring of

1945 in their newly acquired territory, Polish civilians were allowed to move onto the farms and into the houses of the East Prussians, some of whom were evacuated to Germany in the fall of 1945. As a consequence, the resettlement of the Polish part of East Prussia and the expulsion of the Germans proceeded much earlier than in the Russian section of the province.

Rough estimates indicate that two million East Prussians had fled the Soviet offensive, of whom about 200,000 returned to the province. In the summer of 1945, the German population of East Prussia was approximately 800,000, as opposed to 2.6 million before the war.[36] Postwar, the easternmost part of the province, in the district of Gumbinnen (Gusev), had the lowest population density, barely fifteen percent of its prewar level. The bulk of the remaining Germans—about half a million—were concentrated in the central and southern sections allocated to Poland, whereas some 300,000 were in the northern part ceded to Russia, of whom 110,000 lived in Königsberg.

A few examples will have to suffice to exemplify what happened to East Prussians who were caught by the Soviet Army on their flight and then returned home. The wife of a craftsman (*Handwerkersfrau*) described how she and her two daughters escaped on January 23, 1945, from Heilsberg (Lidzbark) in central East Prussia to Danzig, where they were put on a train they hoped would take them to the west.[37] But it was too late, and on January 31, 1945, they were overtaken by Russian troops near Küstrin on the Oder River. When a little girl looked out the train compartment window and exclaimed, "The Russians are here!" the craftsman's wife wrote that a bolt of lightning could not have cut through the passengers more deeply than this anguished cry. The Russian soldiers quickly entered the train and took their watches and other valuables. The mother became completely distraught when her fourteen-year-old daughter was taken away by a Russian soldier. She herself escaped being raped, but her thirteen-year-old daughter was not so fortunate. Later, their group of refugees was driven east by guards with whips and loaded pistols toward a deportation camp near Landsberg on the Weser River. They survived mainly on raw potatoes and turnips. Not knowing what would happen to them if they entered the deportation camp, she and her daughters escaped from the march and hid from the Russians in a wooden bunker in the forest that had a cache of food that lasted for a month. When in early May 1945 they left the bunker, they learned that Germany had surrendered.

After making their way west back across the Oder, the mother and her two daughters returned to Küstrin, where the mother's papers were examined by a guard. Noting that she was from East Prussia, he told her that she had to return home. By chance, she met two other families from Heilsberg and they decided to return the only way they could under the circumstances: on foot. Walking through the former Polish Corridor, they found little evidence of destruction and the local Polish people were not unfriendly and gave them food, drink, and a place to stay. By contrast, the towns and villages in East Prussia were heavily damaged and some villages had been completely leveled in the fighting. It took them twenty days to reach their hometown of Heilsberg on June 6, 1945, some four and a half months after their flight began. The mother knew many of the survivors, but did not find any of her relatives. Heilsberg was located in what had become the Polish zone of East Prussia, and she and her daughters were lucky to be among those who were deported to the Soviet-occupied zone in Germany in November 1945.

———

A farmer's wife, Frau L. Taschen, described similar experiences on the way back to her home in Schönwiese, in the district of Preußisch Eylau.[38] Her husband had been transferred in 1940 to a farm in the district of Dirschau in West Prussia to advise "*Volksdeutsche*" from Bessarabia on farming methods. It was from this farm that Frau Taschen set out on January 24, 1945, in flight with her three small children: eight-year-old Gerhard, seven-year-old Heini, and almost four-year-old Gretchen. (Her husband's official duties required him to remain on the farm.) They slogged through heavy snow for days on end and made very slow progress westward since the roads were clogged with wagons full of refugees also fleeing the advancing Red Army. The delay proved costly; by March 7, Soviet forces had reached Pomerania and cut off their escape route to the west. Soon they were being shelled and fired upon, and in the ensuing chaos ("Tohuwabohu" Frau Taschen called it) she and her children left their wagon and German soldiers helped them climb into an army truck. As the attack intensified, the truck was disabled when its radiator was hit by a shell splinter. Everyone jumped out of the truck and ran for their lives into the nearby forest. Russian troops took them prisoner shortly afterward.

The Taschens' first night as prisoners was spent in a half-destroyed house already filled with other refugees. Here, Frau Taschen was ordered to cook for the Russian soldiers and officers. At night, as soon as the oil lamps were extinguished, shouts and screams and cries for help pierced the night when the Russian soldiers began raping the women: "A half-crazed cry of horrific fear: 'Help, Help, refugees!' (*"Ein halb irrsinniger Schrei in grauenhafter Angst: 'Hilfe, Hilfe, Flüchtlinge!'"*). Frau Taschen escaped what she called a "symphony of horror" (*"Symphonie des Grauens"*) and was not raped. The following day she had a close call when she was questioned through a Polish interpreter. Her interrogator pointed the barrel of his gun at her when he asked about her husband. Thanks to a mis-translation by the Pole, her interrogator understood her answer to mean that her husband worked with farmers, and when she responded affirmatively, he told her that she would live (*"Dann bleibst leben"*).

During the next few days, Frau Taschen and her three children walked through half-destroyed villages, where she begged for food with little success. They were soon joined by many other refugees, all trudging east toward their homes in East Prussia. Frau Taschen discovered that it was dangerous to join up with a large group of refugees because the Russian guards would select women who appeared to be healthy and take them away to work, showing no concern for the abandoned children who had to fend for themselves. (As described below, these women were either forced to join work brigades in East and West Prussia or were transported by train to work in the Soviet Union as forced laborers.) Frau Taschen went on alone with her three children, always trying to avoid Russian soldiers. If they came up to her and asked for her documents, she would show them her German identity card, and because they did not know German, they would invariably hold it upside down and she would pass muster.

When she and her children reached the Vistula River, they could see East
Prussia on the other side but found that the bridges had been destroyed during the war. However, a number of enterprising local Poles had developed a
booming business ferrying East Prussians across the river, charging passengers
at least ten pounds of bacon ("Speck"). As Frau Taschen did not have the
"fare," all seemed lost. Fortunately, a Pole took pity on her and her three children and they were taken on board a fully loaded boat. As a thank-you gift,
Frau Taschen gave him the lice-ridden angora sweater she was wearing. Once
safely on the other bank of the river, she nevertheless gave vent to the then
not entirely uncommon prejudice of Germans toward Polish people, "Saved
from the Poles, I thought. We are in East Prussia!" using the derogatory term
"Pollacken" for "Poles." ("*Gerettet von den Pollacken,' denke ich. 'Wir sind in
Ostpreußen!'*")

By March 1945, Soviet forces occupied the Polish Corridor and most of
East Prussia. It is not surprising, then, that after climbing up the bank of the
river, she and her three children were almost immediately apprehended by a
Russian soldier on horseback, who escorted them to the nearest village shouting, "*Davai, davai*" ("Hurry, hurry"). Thanks to the protection from rampaging soldiers provided by the local Soviet army commander, they spent quiet
nights in an abandoned house along with other refugees. The children were
so exhausted they slept nearly twenty-four hours.

A few days later, with everyone's strength somewhat regained, they continued eastward in the direction of Marienburg (Malbork). Along the road
they found a still-usable handcart and some feather bedding. Little Gretchen
and the ailing Heini were placed on the bedding in the cart, and Gerhard
pulled on the drawbar in front while Frau Taschen pushed from behind.
Using this enhanced mode of transport for the two younger children, they
made their way through shot-up Elbing (Elblag) and devastated Braunsberg
(Braniewo) to Heiligenbeil (Manonovo), where they stayed for two weeks.
Frau Taschen found work with the Russians (not reporting what she did
for them) and was paid in bread and old horsemeat. When they continued
on from Heiligenbeil toward their hometown, Schönwiese, they found that
East Prussia had been turned into a wasteland. They passed one desolate,

abandoned, shelled village after another without livestock of any kind, and for long stretches not a human being in sight. Once, a stray, wild-eyed cat prowled across the road.

The family finally reached Schönwiese in the district of Bartenstein (Bartoszyce) on May 8, completely ragged, run down, and in frail health after a three-and-a-half-month odyssey. Frau Taschen searched everywhere for her-in-laws, but they were nowhere to be found. Because their farmhouse had been taken over by a dozen refugees, she and her children had to live in the empty attic of a nearby house, the rooms downstairs being occupied by three women and their children. Despite the cramped living conditions, Frau Taschen's children were happy to be back in Schönwiese: "Finally back home, the children exhult." (*"Endlich zu Hause jubeln die Kinder"*).

At first, the surrounding farms provided enough food and everyone stayed reasonably healthy. But during the course of 1946 conditions worsened and food became so scarce in the fall that Frau Taschen went begging in the nearby town of Landsberg. As Schönwiese was located in what had become the Polish part of East Prussia, she and other East Prussians were forced to work for the Poles after the Russians left at the end of 1945, work for which they received neither food nor cash. She did not have a kind word for the new proprietors of her homeland and she wrote that the Germans were now slaves of the Poles (*"Wir sind Sklaven der Polen"*). Facing starvation and with no prospects of supporting herself and her family, Frau Taschen feared they could not survive. When, in late 1946, survival seemed impossible, a ray of hope appeared and she quoted the German proverb, "When things are darkest, God's help is closest" (*"Wenn die Not am größten ist, ist Gottes Hilfe am nächsten"*). She had heard that a train would be taking the Germans in Schönwiese to the Soviet-occupied zone of Germany. Providentially, she had just sold her husband's coat for 2,000 zloty, which she used to bribe the mayor to allow her and her children to take this train. They left Schönweise on December 15, 1946, and arrived in Torgau on the Elbe River on December 24.

Chapter III described how the Wermter family had reached Lupow in Pomerania, some 193 miles (310 kilometers) from their village of Heinrikau, before the Red Army caught up with them.[39] In June 1945, food had become so scarce they decided to return to East Prussia. After a long march they arrived in the small town of Karthaus in what had been the Polish Corridor. They were completely exhausted and the father decided that in their weakened condition they would be incapable of walking the ninety-three miles (150 kilometers) from Karthaus back to Heinrikau. When they learned that Germans were allowed to take Russian freight trains back to East Prussia, the family—joined by about twenty others—climbed into an empty cattle car hooked to a freight train, which took them to Bromberg (Bydgoszcz).

The following day, the family and a group of some eighty East Prussians boarded a train to Graudenz (Grudzianz). At around noon, the train stopped at a small town and everyone was ordered to get off and march under armed guard to the courtyard of a factory. At the entrance, young Otto Wermter was taken aside by an older German-speaking man, who insisted that he go with him around to the back of the factory. Young Otto wanted to return to his family, but the man explained that in the courtyard the Russians were selecting healthy men, boys of his age, and women, and then separating them from their families (no doubt to be conscripted into work brigades). After half an hour Otto and the old man returned to the entrance of the courtyard where Otto's family had become very alarmed about his disappearance, completely unaware that this unknown man had saved Otto from the selection. The Russians also spared Otto's father because he had been encircled by his five children and was allowed to stay with his family. The Wermters had once again avoided conscription into labor brigades. They returned to the railroad station to complete the trip to Graudenz, where they spent the night in the railroad station.

Early the next morning, the Wermters made their way, together with other returnees, to the railroad tracks. They found two freight trains loaded with coal and a locomotive coupled to only one of them. The Polish train authorities ordered them to board the train with the locomotive, which would take them to Allenstein, also in Polish-occupied East Prussia. With much effort they clambered up the sides of the cars, and while they perched on top of the coal, the locomotive was uncoupled from this train and attached to the other string of coal cars. They clambered down and then up to the top of the other train, whereupon the locomotive was switched once more and they again laboriously changed trains. While the Wermters were pre-occupied with switching trains, their belongings were plundered by Polish thieves who made off with their bags and clothes. During this well-orchestrated robbery operation the Wermters lost their family book and identity papers. The train eventually did get underway and they arrived—dirty and hungry—in Allenstein. It was now mid-June, 1945.

Having lived in this area before and being familiar with the paths through the fields on the outskirts of Allenstein, the father led the family in the direction of the farm that belonged to his wife's parents, the Wasserziers. Frau Wermter's father had not joined them on their flight west because the Russians had not harmed him in any way when they invaded East Prussia in 1914, and as he was an old man, he did not believe that he would be in danger now. Along the way to the farmhouse the Wermters met a German from the neighborhood who knew the Wasserziers and gave Mrs. Wermter the sad news that her parents had been shot on January 30 when the Russian soldiers arrived at their farmhouse.[40] Later, the Wermters learned that her parents had been buried by one of the few remaining villagers in a hole dug laboriously in the frozen earth when the temperature was −22°F (−30°C).

The Wermter family never reached the village where the Wasserziers had lived and died because they were apprehended by the Russians and forced to work on a collective farm producing milk and butterfat to be shipped to Russia. By mid-July it became apparent that this farm would soon be closed down, and to avoid their likely fate of being transported as forced laborers to the Soviet Union, Herr Wermter led his family away from the farm late in the evening on July 17 toward Heinrikau some twenty-five miles (forty kilometers) distant. They again traversed a devastated countryside—shot-up houses, smashed furniture scattered about, dead animals, here and there a few bodies of German soldiers—and did not meet a single living creature. Around noon on July 19, 1945, they came to a stone marker indicating the boundary of Heinrikau, where they knelt down and recited the Lord's Prayer together. A short time later they arrived at the home they had fled five and a half months earlier.

They were relieved to find that all the buildings on their farm were intact. Not knowing what to expect, they held their collective breath and walked slowly and silently into the farmhouse. It was unoccupied, but all the windows had been smashed. Except for one chest, all the furniture had vanished. Every piece of farming equipment had disappeared and mice were the only animals extant. In the living room and bedrooms, the Russians had put down straw to sleep on that had not been threshed, and grain was now growing out of the rooms through the broken windows to the outside. To their great relief, Soviet soldiers had not discovered the large chest that Herr Wermter had buried just before their flight in the turnip storage room in the cow shed (*Rübenkammer im Kuhstall*). This chest contained hunting rifles and a large cache of preserved meat and sausages, which assured their near-term survival.

When Herr Wermter registered the family at the Russian command post in the village, he learned that only four childless families remained in Heinrikau out of a prewar population of eight hundred. The Wermters then began to put their house in order. The three boys found an ammunition wagon and used it to cart home the furniture and bedsteads they picked up in empty neighborhood houses. To provide meat for the household, they shot wild game in the nearby forest. At a neighboring farm they discovered a veritable gold mine (*eine echte Goldgrube*) in the form of a compartment full of unthreshed rye. Taking advantage of what they had learned in Pomerania, they threshed the stalks and with considerable time and effort used a coffee grinder to mill the grains. One of the boys found a small stone grinder that could be turned with a belt, which speeded up the milling process considerably and ensured a good supply of flour for baking bread. The surrounding gardens provided a plentiful supply of berries and apples. Without matches, making a fire was a challenge. Yet ever resourceful, when the sun was shining they used the glass lens from a flashlight to generate a flame. At night, they covered a piece of coal with hot ashes in the kitchen stove and the following morning they could generally start a fire from the still smoldering coal. With kerosene found in the tank of a piece of electrical equipment and kerosene lamps salvaged from some of the unoccupied houses, the boys also provided the family with illumination at night.

That summer, Herr Wermter and his two sons were forced to work for the Russians harvesting the grain that had been planted the previous fall by East Prussian farmers. They labored without a day off from sunrise to sunset until the entire crop had been brought in and were paid each day with a small bag of sugar and some bread (about four slices). Beginning in September 1945, the Russians began to leave Heinrikau because it was in the section of East Prussia allocated to Poland, and Poles from central Poland, especially from Warsaw, took their place. The arrival of the Polish settlers marked the start of another ordeal for the Wermter family, which did not end until November 1946, when they were transported by cattle car to the Soviet-occupied zone of Germany. From there they made their way to Braunschweig.

E. Deportations to the Soviet Union

The Wermters were lucky to have escaped conscription to work in the Soviet Union, but many thousands of other East Prussians were not so fortunate.[41] While the rapes, murders, and destruction of property largely reflected individual acts of violence by Soviet troops when they invaded East Prussia, the deportations of German civilians to work camps in the Soviet Union were systematically organized, carefully planned, and carried out by special units of the Soviet secret service, the NKVD (precursor of the KGB).[42] The deportations were implemented in accordance with the December 26, 1944, NKVD Directive 00-1538, entitled "Concerning the work of those held back in East Prussia and the utilization of their work capability" ("*Über die Arbeit mit den Zurückgehaltenen in Ostpreußen und die Nutzung ihrer Arbeitskraft*").[43] The deportations had begun at the end of January 1945, following the thrust of the Red Army into East Prussia, and were largely completed by the end of April. Germans living in what became the Russian zone of East Prussia—the northern third of the former German province—were needed as forced labor to re-develop this newly acquired territory and were thus less subject to deportation. By contrast, in what became the Polish zone of East Prussia, all able-bodied men and women were fair game to be rounded up by Soviet security forces and shipped off to work in the Soviet Union.

As described in more detail in Chapter VII, the Yalta Conference considered the issue of reparations for losses suffered by the Soviet Union during the war. The conference participants agreed to "reparations in kind" on the last day of the conference and Stalin interpreted this agreement as giving him carte blanche to deport as many surviving Germans as he wished to forced labor camps in the Soviet Union. As noted above, Stalin did not wait for a final go-ahead from the United Kingdom and the United States at the Potsdam Conference to start the deportations. Estimates vary as to the number of German slave workers sent to the Soviet Union. At least forty-four thousand were deported from East Prussia alone between January and April 1945, while estimates of the total number of German civilians transported to Soviet work camps from all the German territories east of the Oder-Neisse range from 200,000 to 400,000.[44]

The Germans were not told that they were being deported to Russia or other parts of the Soviet Union. Rather, they were ordered to report to the "*Kommandantur*" (local Soviet army headquarters), were rounded up from their homes, or were taken off the streets with no information as to what lay in store for them. Often they were told an outright lie, for example, that after working in labor brigades for a day or more, they would return to their homes. Instead, they were incarcerated, often for a few days but sometimes over a week or more, in cell blocks, cellars, or whatever buildings were readily available, and were interrogated as to whether they had belonged to a Nazi organization. Following these cross-examinations, many were transported to the labor camps.

Because most men in East Prussia were still on active military duty, had died in the war, or had been taken prisoner, the bulk of the deportees were women. The sudden round-ups and peremptory abductions were particularly traumatic for women with small children, who normally were not allowed to accompany their mothers, as often there was not enough time to make arrangements with relatives or neighbors to take care of the children. As a result, many such children ended up as orphans. Sometimes a woman's cries of anguish led to her being reunited with her child. In one instance, Russians in a truck were driving from village to village rounding up civilians when they came upon three women walking along a street. The truck stopped and two of the three women were ordered to get in. One woman had her child with her and was forced to give it to the woman left behind on the street. Once the truck got underway, the mother screamed and cried, and after a mile or two the truck halted beside two other women on the road. The Russians allowed the bereft mother to get off the truck and return to her child, but summarily took one of the women on the road in her stead.[45]

While small children as a rule could not accompany their mothers, occasional exceptions were made. When the Russians were about to take her mother away from their house, seven-year-old Christel Schack clung to her so tightly that they relented and allowed Christel to stay with her. One of the officers told her mother to dress Christel warmly but did not mention where they would be taken. When they left their house, they joined a large group of young, healthy women all without children.[46] In the selection process for deportation, the women chosen were those deemed most likely to endure both the hardship of the long journey to the labor camps as well as the brutal conditions in the Soviet Union. But as a rule they were told neither to dress for harsh weather conditions nor to bring food with them, as the Russians did not wish to reveal where the women were being sent. They did not appear to appreciate the fact that if the women had been properly clothed and fed, their chances of survival and of being ready to work upon arrival at the camps would have been significantly improved.

After the Germans were taken into custody and interrogated, they were either transported in trucks or forced to march for several days in long columns under heavy guard to an intermediate collection point. On these marches they were provided with little food or water; when they spent nights in barns or the cellars of empty houses, they searched for the odd potato, cabbage, or turnip to still their hunger. Some were so weak—especially older men—they had difficulty keeping up with the column and the guards beat them with the their rifle butts to force them to continue. This did not always have the intended effect and people who fell by the wayside were sometimes shot to death.[47]

Many of the Germans on these marches were sent from East Prussia to the Soviet Union as forced laborers producing goods for the reconstruction of the Soviet Union. While the Soviet intent was to utilize the East Prussians as a presumably valuable factor of production, they showed little concern whether the Germans perished or survived on the marches. This may have reflected a rough and ready calculation by Soviet government officials that because hundreds of thousands of German civilians were available for forced labor, to say nothing of the huge number of German POWs who could be put to work in Soviet camps, it made little economic sense to use the scant resources available in the Soviet Union to provide them with adequate food, clothing, and shelter. If many thousands died on the way to the camps, or perished while working there, the officials knew that thousands of others were available to take their place. As the German deportees were a free resource for the Soviet economy, earning barely subsistence wages, it is not surprising that only about one-third to one-half survived.[48]

The majority of East Prussians abducted for work in the Soviet Union were taken to the assembly camp (*Sammellager*) in Insterburg. There, they were again interrogated before being transported by train to Soviet work camps. Insterburg was the largest collection point in East Prussia set up by the Russians. Nearly fifty thousand civilians were imprisoned, registered, and interrogated there before it was shut down. In the town's prison, up to fifteen men were jammed into a single cell, and as already familiar from previous accounts, so many women were forced into a single small cell, there was no room to sit or lie down. Other prisoners were crowded into the grain mill and once a day were given dry bread to eat and black tea to drink. Already weakened by the exhausting march to Insterburg, many died from starvation, disease, and beatings during interrogations. Some prisoners were, in fact, released; they were typically old people who were so sick it was obvious they would not survive the trip to the Soviet camps.

However badly off the East Prussians were at the assembly camp at Insterburg, they endured much worse conditions during the journey by rail to the Soviet Union. They were marched to the railway station and then squeezed so tightly into cattle or freight cars, there was no room to lie down. The long, tortuous journey of three to six weeks into the depths of the Soviet Union began only after an average of two thousand deportees had been loaded onto the train. The best place in the dark, cramped, stinking compartment was near the door where more air came in, and the worst was near the groove cut into the wooden floor of the freight car sloping to the outside, which served as the latrine. Woefully inadequate food rations consisted of one or two slices of hard bread each day, sometimes supplemented by salty cheese or dried fish, which intensified the ever-present thirst. Every time the train halted, the incarcerated inside the car would pound on the door and yell for water. In February and March 1945, it was bitter cold and the prisoners were not dressed to cope with these conditions. While some of the cars had iron stoves that provided a little warmth, there was never enough wood to keep a proper fire going. Under such extreme conditions the death rate was high and on many trains reached ten percent of the deportees. When someone died, prisoners would bang on the side of the car until the door was opened and the guards either loaded the body into a special car on the train or simply dumped it on the side of the tracks. Sometimes children were born on the train and most soon died. In a few cases a newborn was bundled up with a name tag tied on and handed to a guard when the train halted in hopes the baby would survive in the hands of a kind-hearted Russian.

By the time the deportees arrived at the forced labor camps, they were so exhausted and weakened that they were given a few weeks to recuperate. They were then assigned jobs that consisted of the most backbreaking and dangerous work: in coal mines; in forests cutting down trees covered by heavy snow; in peat bogs; in factories, quarries, and brick kilns; and building roads, canals, and railway lines. In winter, the prisoners often cleared snow from roads and railroad tracks, and in the summer and fall generally worked on collective farms. (The working conditions they encountered will be familiar to readers of Solzhenitsyn's *Gulag Archipelago* and *One Day in the Life of Ivan Denisovich*.) They toiled twelve hours or more a day to meet onerous production quotas calibrated to each worker's state of health and strength. Yet the rations they received were hardly sufficient to undertake this heavy physical labor, and many died due to malnutrition and diseases rampant in the unhygienic conditions in the camps. Conditions were the worst in 1945 when up to half of the German deportees died in the camps. Gradually, the rations were increased and as the health of the prisoners improved, the mortality rate fell, but still remained quite high.

The camp inmates whose health did not deteriorate and who could continue to work were kept in the camps the longest. When inmates became sick and were incapable of performing productive tasks, they were sent to hospitals to get them sufficiently fit to resume work. If, after several months, it became clear that an incapacitated prisoner would not recover, he became a useless liability for the Soviet economy—in fact a drain on scarce resources requiring food and lodging—and he was certified by Soviet doctors as incapable of performing any useful work and sent back to Germany. It hardly needs mentioning that the deportees were overjoyed to leave. Such return trips began in the summer and fall of 1945, and although conditions on the trains were typically better than on the journey into the Soviet Union, many nonetheless died on the way back to Germany.

In his eyewitness account, an inmate who wished to be identified only as Herr J. H. reported that in camp no. 325, where he was incarcerated some 110 miles (175 kilometers) southeast of Moscow, the Russian doctors examined the prisoners every four weeks and divided them into four categories according to how much work they could perform.[49] Herr J. H. reported that the doctors did what they could for the sick inmates but were severely constrained by the lack of medicine and equipment. In the summer of 1945 he became very ill from malnutrition and suffered from extremely swollen legs; after spending three months in the hospital, he was sent back to Germany at the end of August. As fate would have it, his sister had been assigned to the same camp, but because she survived the heavy workload better than he did and did not become sick, she was not released from the camp. His sister's "good luck" eventually ran out and she died in Russia in the summer of 1946.

Frau H. B., who also chose not to give her full name, barely survived as a slave laborer in the Soviet Union.[50] She had fled from the advancing Red

Army but was overtaken in Heilsberg, which was in that part of East Prussia allocated to Poland. Here, the East Prussians were sometimes guarded by Russian soldiers, at other times by Polish troops. A Russian patrol rounded up Frau H. B. and others on February 9, 1945, and took them to the collection point in Heilsberg, where trucks were waiting to transport them to an unknown destination. Somehow, their relatives had gotten wind that they would be forcibly taken away for what could be a long time. They tried to hand them small bundles of food and clothes for the journey, but these were grabbed out of their hands by Polish civilians who had already arrived before the end of the war to settle in that part of East Prussia allocated to Poland. Frau H. B. also described how married couples and relatives who wished to say goodbye to each other were forcefully pushed aside by Russian guards with the butts of their guns.

When the trucks were fully loaded with their human cargo, they took the prisoners first to Rastenburg, where they were given warm soup that was so salty many could not eat it. The following evening they were transported by truck to Insterburg and incarcerated in a building that once had been used to grind and store the milled grain. The prisoners who had consumed the salty soup the day before were by now so thirsty that they begged for water. The Polish guards first beat them with rifles and sticks, but then appeared with a washtub full of water. Alas, it was a cruel trick: the tub was placed in front of the Germans but the guards kept them far enough away that they could not get a drink.

A few days later toward evening the men and women were given soup that was even saltier than the first. They were then herded to the railroad tracks and while being pushed into the waiting freight cars, were subject to heavy blows from the guards. Some begged to be allowed to scoop up a little snow to assuage their thirst, but the guards refused and told them that snow and water were only for Russians, not for Germans. On the journey to Moscow their daily rations consisted of two pieces of dried bread and a piece of salted herring less than an inch long. The death rate was so high that in some freight cars over half of the prisoners died. Every morning the bodies were stripped of their clothes and then loaded into two cars at the end of the train. By the time the train arrived in Moscow three weeks after leaving East Prussia, the cars were fully packed with corpses. Several Russian officers examined the survivors, and finding them all unfit to work, they criticized the train crew for their brutal treatment of the Germans. The crew, which according to Frau H. B. was drunk all the time and incessantly beat those in the cars and raped the women, explained to the officers that in Insterburg they had been instructed to allow as many as possible to die on the journey. If true, such deliberately inhumane treatment designed to maximize the number of deaths appears to have been the exception, because as pointed out above, the Germans were worth more alive than dead to the Russians and were being transported all the way to the Soviet Union to be exploited as slave labor.

When Frau H. B. reached her final destination on March 6, 1945, at a camp near the town of Kuibischew in eastern Russia not far from Novosibirsk, the deportees took a bath for the first time since their incarceration in East Prussia and were given three weeks to recuperate from the rigors of the train trip. The women judged to be capable of working were assigned to a brick factory, where they were grateful to receive a bowl of warm cabbage soup once a day. Nevertheless, the train journey and conditions in the camp took their toll: of the twenty-eight hundred who had started out in East Prussia, Frau H. B. reported that only seven hundred were still alive on September 15, 1945. Of these seven hundred, 130 (including Frau H. B.) were transported to another camp; after three weeks' rest to recover from the train journey, the women again had to work at a brick factory. During the icy winter of 1945–46, many became sick. In March 1946, Frau H. B. was sent to a hospital because of heart problems and stayed there until the end of August. She gave the Russian doctors and nurses credit for taking very good care of her. In September 1946, she was declared permanently incapacitated and was allowed to return to Germany.

Frau Käthe Hildebrand from Gerdauen in East Prussia also did not escape the advance of the Soviet forces.[51] After spending two weeks in a work brigade in the nearby town of Friedland (Pravdinsk), she and others from Gerdauen were ordered to return to their homes. Because the town had been reduced to rubble and ashes, she found refuge with women she knew on a farm where they had plenty to eat. But two days later, on March 11, 1945, Russian officers picked them up and took them by truck to the neighboring town of Nordenburg under the pretext that they would return home after working there for two days. Frau Hildebrand soon learned that this had been a ruse to keep them quiet, as shortly thereafter they were shipped by truck to a prison in Bartenstein (Bartoszyce). As in other similar situations, some thirty to thirty-five women were squeezed into a single cell designed for one person, making it impossible to sit or lie down. After a week's imprisonment, this group and many other women were transported by truck to Insterburg via Gerdauen. Frau Hildebrand described how heart-wrenching it was to pass through their hometown—the source of so many happy memories—perhaps for the last time. They wept bitterly and would have jumped off the trucks but for the heavily armed guards.

After a few days in the prison at Insterburg, on March 23 they were herded into the freight cars of a long train carrying about two thousand women and young girls ranging in age from fifteen to fifty-five, but only one hundred or so males who had not served in the German military. Their daily rations consisted of two slices of dry bread, one hundred grams of cheese, and one teaspoon of sugar. When the train stopped at larger stations, each car was provided with a milk can filled with water, but often they were not given enough and their thirst became unbearable. Every day a Russian doctor knocked on the door and asked if there were any dead in the car; if so, the door was opened and the corpse(s) removed. But when people inside yelled that someone was very sick, the door was never opened.

It took sixteen days for the train to reach Baku on the Caspian Sea and from there they were taken by ship to Krasnovodsk in Turkmenistan. This camp was located in a desert without a tree, shrub, or blade of grass. Every day except Sunday—when they had to clean their barracks—armed guards took the prisoners outside the camp to work in a quarry, build houses, and lay railroad tracks. The heat was overpowering and as they were not given water while working, they became completely parched. Frau Hildebrand reported that the number of deaths rose steadily, reaching forty-five to fifty prisoners a day. The bodies were stripped naked and every evening were deposited without ceremony in a mass grave and covered with sand. To replenish the stock of workers, a contingent of two thousand male prisoners from Upper Silesia was transported to the camp. By August 1945, roughly twenty percent of the inmates in the camp had survived and those who were too sick to work were repatriated to Germany. Those still healthy—Frau Hildebrandt among them—were loaded onto a small freighter on August 30 and, after crossing the Caspian Sea and traveling up the Volga River, arrived in the ruins of Stalingrad on September 4, 1945.

There had been enough to eat in the camp at Krasnovodsk, but in Stalingrad food was scarce. Fortunately, security was not overly tight and inmates were able to forage for potatoes and squash in nearby fields to supplement their meager rations. In the winter, when the fields were barren, they begged for food from the inhabitants of Stalingrad. At first, the locals took pity on the prisoners and were generous, but as the food available for the local population also dwindled, there was nothing more they would, or could, give to the prisoners. In these dire straits, an indomitable will to survive and return home led Frau Hildebrand and other young women to snatch dogs and cats off the streets whenever they could find them to cook and eat at the camp. After one and one-half years, almost all the women were incapable of working due to malnutrition and the camp in Stalingrad was closed. On January 21, 1947, Frau Hildebrandt and the other surviving deportees were loaded onto a train to Germany and arrived in Frankfurt an der Oder on February 4, 1947.

Maria Banner, from Voigtsdorf in the district of Allenstein, has also provided a detailed account of her experiences in Soviet forced labor camps. She was twenty-three at the end of March 1945 when she was deported to the Soviet Union together with her sister Hildegard (who left behind a young child) and her cousin Hedwig.[52] Of the some two thousand on her train, the great majority were women and girls, the remainder old men and boys under the age of sixteen. They were transported to various Soviet work camps where they did heavy labor. In Karelia, Maria and the other women dragged logs out of the forest and loaded large pieces of lumber onto ships. She, too, reported that food rations were meager: in one camp, for weeks on end they were given only dry bread and water, and only now and then a thin soup; in another camp their rations consisted of cabbage soup made from what remained after the preparation of sauerkraut. That summer, Maria was separated from her sister and cousin, and in November 1945, she and other women were selected to work in a Russian prison, where they cut out and sewed fur gloves and knotted fishing nets using thin twine. It was here that Maria learned that her cousin Hedwig had died of typhus in another camp. In the spring of 1946 she was transferred to a camp in the city of Medveschigorsk, where she was reunited with her sister. Both worked in the municipal sauna hauling water from the nearby river, sawing wood for the fire to keep the water hot, and keeping the sauna clean.

In the fall of 1946, Maria and Hildegard were taken by train to Borowsk in the Urals; there they spent a year working the frigid night shift in a wood products factory. It was there that for the first time the sisters were allowed to write home on a Red Cross postcard, using a maximum of twenty-five words. As they did not receive an answer to the card they had sent to their mother in East Prussia, they assumed that she was no longer there. They mailed a second card to relatives in the Rhineland in Germany. In May 1947, they received an answer from their uncle and soon afterward mail from their mother, along with a photo of Hildegard's daughter, who by now was three and a half years old. Tragically, Hildegard never saw her daughter again; in October 1947 she was scalded so severely on her arms, legs, and back in a plywood factory where she and Maria worked that she died from the burns. Maria was shipped to various factories during her last two years in the Soviet Union. It was shortly before Christmas 1948 that she first received mail from her husband. In October 1949, Maria was released and sent back to Germany, the only survivor of the three women who had been deported together in March 1945. Of the more than two thousand Germans who were transported in the same train that month to the forced labor camps in the Soviet Union, about five hundred returned.

As noted in Chapter IV, the topic of Soviet atrocities in East Prussia in late 1944 and the first half of 1945 received little public attention in Russia.

The same applies to the fate of the thousands of civilian Germans transported to the Soviet Union to forced labor camps. However, toward the end of the twentieth century, a gradual change in the political climate took place in Russia ("glasnost"), which permitted more open discussion and analysis of what had heretofore been a taboo topic.[53] A memorial was dedicated in 1995 on the grounds of the former forced labor camp no. 517 (Padozero) in the Russian Republic of Karelia, which borders Finland and lies north of St. Petersburg.[54] This memorial consists of plain crosses marking a small cemetery in the forest where those who died in the camp were buried. Instrumental in its construction was Ivan Chuchin, at the time a representative in the Duma and member of the human rights organization, Memorial. Chuchin has published a brief history of the Padozero camp.[55]

Another memorial took place on June 5, 1994, when a bus with twenty-two former women inmates of camp no. 1003 reached Konstantinovka, in far eastern Russia after a four-day journey from Munich.[56] The former inmates erected a twelve-foot (3.6 meter) high cross in the camp cemetery with a bronze tablet on which was inscribed, "In memory of those who died from 1945 to 1949 in Camp 1003," ("*1945–1949 Zum Andenken an die Verstorbenen Lager 1003*"). One of the participants described the dedication ceremony:

> Many inhabitants of the village had come, also German settlers who lived in Russia. The organizer of the trip, Georg Gehann, greeted the participants at the ceremony in an address and emphasized that "we have come as friends, with the good intention to build up the friendship between the two peoples so that we will never again have war." We shook hands with the Russians, sang the first verse of the Siebenbürgenlied [home song of a German minority that had settled in Romania] and prayed together the "Our Father." Not one eye stayed dry. After this, a Russian woman sang an evocative song, and the locals also addressed us briefly and underscored their willingness to take care of the cross with the memorial tablet in honor of the dead.[57]

F. Survival—or Extinction—in East Prussia under Russian Rule

For the East Prussians who escaped deportation, conditions were not a great deal better than in the forced labor camps in the Soviet Union. In fact, after the war's end, East Prussia had itself become a prison for the remaining German inhabitants. They were incarcerated in what had been their own country and were subject to depredations and humiliations first by the Soviet and Polish military occupying forces and then later by the settlers from the Soviet Union and Poland. The East Prussians did not know that their land had been given to Russia and Poland by the Allies and they expected that they would be able to resume some semblance of their prewar existence. They lost all hope for this benign outcome when they were forced to work for starvation wages, lost all their property, were at the mercy of the occupying authorities, and were gradually displaced by Soviet and Polish settlers. When they no longer served any useful purpose for the Russian and Polish administrations, they were expelled from their homeland to the Soviet-occupied zone of Germany.

In describing the conditions faced by the surviving Germans, it is important to distinguish between the northern third of East Prussia administered by Russia and the southern two-thirds taken over by Poland. The policies and attitudes of the Russian and Polish authorities toward the indigenous German population differed, in particular relating to the timing and organization of the expulsions of the East Prussians. Hence it is necessary to treat each region separately: the Russian-administered part of East Prussia is considered first, followed by the Polish section of the former province.

The Russian authorities forced many East Prussians to work on reconstruction projects and collective farms until they were displaced by civilian Soviet settlers in 1947 and 1948. They were paid paltry rations, often only about half a pound (five hundred grams) of bread a day. But if one remained unemployed, one was completely dependent on friends and relatives for food. Therefore, able-bodied East Prussians sought to work for the Russians despite the meager wages in order to survive. With little to eat, harsh living and working conditions, and poor hygiene and medical facilities, many thousands succumbed to starvation and epidemics of typhoid, dysentery, scabies, and malaria.

East Prussians had to be resourceful in finding ways to supplement their low wages and obtain nourishment essential for their own survival and that of those family members unable to work. For several months after the end of the fighting, people could still find stocks of food in abandoned and partially destroyed houses in the cities and towns, especially in Königsberg. Another alternative—not without significant risks—was to steal food and anything that could be sold or bartered. In the countryside, people scavenged for food in empty farmhouses and foraged in fields for grain and vegetables left over from the previous harvest.

In Königsberg and some other towns, black markets developed in which the residents obtained food in exchange for whatever personal belongings they had been able to keep in their possession as well as any useful articles they had scavenged from ruined buildings or had stolen from the Russians. In addition, Lithuania and Latvia became particularly important destinations because food could be obtained from the local farmers. While travel to these neighboring countries was prohibited, many risked being caught on these begging expeditions in order to bring back food for themselves and their relatives. Others chose to stay, particularly in Lithuania, where the farmers were sympathetic to the plight of Germans and hired a significant number to work on their farms.

The eyewitness reports cited here are representative of the immense difficulties East Prussians faced trying to survive under Russian rule in the northern part of the province from the end of the war until their expulsion in 1947 and 1948. Michael Wieck's striking memoir describes in vivid detail the relentless struggle to stay alive in the postwar period and it is again drawn on extensively to convey the desperate conditions in Königsberg at that time. Once the sixteen-year-old Wieck had recovered from near death in the Rothenstein internment camp, he devoted his energies to providing food for himself and his parents. He described how his father was incapable of adapting to the desperate situation the family faced; instead of scrounging for food or making himself useful in other ways, he set about learning Chinese. His father's passivity upset young Michael, who realized that survival depended on being cunning, creative, and resourceful:

> Father was completely helpless in the face of the new living conditions, which turned us all into predators crowded into a hunting preserve that was way too small. Now was the time to call on every instinct and to act swiftly. The skills needed to save our lives were a combination of keeping a sharp eye out and being creative—to make yourself indispensable to the Russians, to win their sympathy, to repair something, a clock for example or an oil lamp. For that you got bread or oatmeal, barley, or soup.[58]

Over time, Michael Wieck developed exceptional survival tactics and took advantage of every possible opportunity whenever and wherever it arose to provide enough food for himself and his parents. Once, when a Jeep careened along a street and hit a dog, he raced to the dying animal ahead of other starving Königsbergers and took it home. Before the Russians occupied Königsberg and food was already scarce, he had watched a neighbor skin and gut his pet rabbit to supplement the family's meager diet. He now applied what he had observed to the carcass of the dog, whose meat was then cooked and eaten as a tasty treat and a source of greatly needed protein. Another time he discovered that the Russians had fenced off a house that was only partly destroyed, no doubt to repair it for use by the military authorities. Wieck knew that it had been looted by the invading troops, but he surmised—correctly as it turned out—that it had not yet been scavenged by local residents. The house was situated near the ruins an adjacent one, which was not fenced off. Wieck hoped that he could enter it through the cellar of the neighboring house undetected by the guards. He was successful and was very pleased to find a large collection of pots and pans, dishes, cutlery, bed linens, and other useful items, all of which he managed to bring home and his mother then bartered for food. Eventually, the Russians discovered the break-in and blocked the passage into the house. Wieck felt lucky to have gotten away with so much; had suspicious guards caught him in the act, they would have shot him on the spot.

On another occasion, Wieck saw an advertisement for a carpenter to work in a bakery. Following the adage "nothing ventured, nothing gained," he thought he would have the opportunity to filch flour and perhaps even bread, and with considerable bravado he passed himself off as a carpenter by hammering a door together to the satisfaction of the officer in charge. He joined three other German carpenters who were already working in the bakery, and for a twelve-hour day they were paid at noon with a piece of bread and gruel (husked grain). By now the Russians had learned that their foodstuffs had to be closely guarded to safeguard them from the grasping hands of the starving Germans. As luck would have it, a window had to be repaired in the room where the flour was stored, and when the coast was clear, Wieck and the other carpenters stole flour from time to time. To smuggle the flour out of the bakery, he filled his pail half full with the flour and poured his gruel on top, thereby evading the tight inspection when he left the bakery. Eventually the Russians caught on that flour was somehow disappearing under their very noses and closed off this access to the storage area. The bread, which was baked on the premises, was so well protected that Wieck and the other carpenters were never allowed to get close to it.

While working at the bakery, Wieck noticed that the soldiers and workers parked their bicycles against the wall in back of the building. One day when no one was looking, he grabbed a bike and quickly hurled it over the wall where it landed amid the ruins on the other side. After he finished his shift that day, he intended to ride the bicycle home and barter it for food. He had not biked very far when he was confronted by one of the banes of existence in Königsberg at that time, namely, bands of orphaned Russian and Polish children who had followed in the footsteps of the advancing Soviet troops. They lived under the most primitive conditions in ruined buildings and survived largely by threatening civilians with the weapons they had found and robbing them of whatever they were carrying. Wieck's mother had been seriously injured when she was knifed in the hand in which she held the cigarettes she was selling. Now a gang of these brigands threatened Michael with knives and a cocked pistol, forcing him to hand over his valuable, just-acquired booty. With the memory still fresh of what had happened to his mother, he was thankful to have escaped with just the loss of the bike.

Wieck's career as a thief reached new heights of audacity and daring when he began to break into the apartments of Russians in search of something to steal. Knowing that the Russians had great respect for "specialists"—craftsmen with particular skills, such as mechanics, electricians, carpenters, and plumbers—Wieck put on the work overalls he had used in a cabinet maker's shop under the Nazi regime and tied the pouch with repair tools around his waist when he surreptitiously entered a Russian apartment he hoped would be empty. Thus attired, he could pass himself off as a repairman if he were caught in the act of a burglary, but he took enormous risks because he never knew if someone would be in the apartment when he broke in and how they would react. As the Russians were constantly being robbed by Germans, if they suspected someone was a thief, they were apt to shoot first and ask questions later. Young Wieck felt compelled to take such carefully calculated risks, because the alternative for himself and his parents was a slow death by starvation. Knowing full well the terrible danger he put himself in, he made careful preparations before every break-in: he figured out his escape route, identified possible hiding places, and prepared the particular story he would tell if he were apprehended in the apartment he was about to enter. In the course of his "career" as a thief he developed an uncanny ability to sense impending danger and such premonitions saved his life many times.

On one occasion, after he had knocked on an apartment door and nobody answered, he quietly entered using a skeleton key and found a bag of potatoes on the kitchen table, just the kind of booty he was looking for. A premonition of danger held him back from immediately grabbing it and he waited motionless for several minutes. All of a sudden a Russian—followed by his frightened wife—rushed into the kitchen swinging an axe aimed at Wieck's head. Their eyes met and somehow a look and a gesture from Wieck stopped the Russian in mid-swing, which gave Wieck a chance to explain that he was an electrician who had come to inspect the wiring and to point out that he had not stolen anything. Wieck's powers of persuasion calmed the man down and he thus escaped after what had truly been a "close shave."

In another audacious exploit he entered a four-story apartment building dressed in his electrician's "uniform" and made his way up the stairs to an attic that to his amazement was still intact. He searched for electrical devices, such as lamps and chandeliers, but found nothing useful other than two sockets. As he descended the stairs, a door flew open and Wieck was assaulted by a young lieutenant who knocked him to the floor, seized him by the hair, and dragged him down the stairs to the street. Consumed by rage, the lieutenant marched him to the nearest military police station, much to the bemusement of passing Russians who were glad to see that a German thief had been caught. At the station, the lieutenant explained the crime at the top of his lungs to the officer in charge and then started to beat Wieck so viciously that he collapsed on the floor. The policeman was not amused by this spectacle, but he turned to his typewriter and wrote up the report as dictated by the lieutenant, who then signed it and disappeared. Infinitely relieved that he had not been shot on sight, Wieck imagined that he would receive the usual sentence for theft, namely, to serve time in a Soviet work camp. He spent the afternoon at the police station, and now and then tried to explain his side of the story to the policeman, who said not a word. Finally, he came up to Wieck with the typed report in his hand and said: "I'll let you go this time, but make sure you never cross the path of this officer again or I'm in trouble too."[59] He then tore up the report, opened the door, and let Wieck go.

Michael and his parents lived off the food he stole, and his mother took the other filched items to the black market where she bartered them for food or sold them for rubles. The black market was located first on the Luisenmarkt near Hagen Straße and later on the square between Schrötter and Schleiermacher Straßen. This market made the difference between life and death for many residents of Königsberg, as the wages paid by the Russians were not high enough to survive on. All kinds of household goods—clothes, shoes, boots, dishes, cutlery, bedding, furniture—were offered for sale or were bartered. One could barter a towel for more or less a half pound of bread.[60] Farmers came from Lithuania to sell their vegetables, but charged very high prices. Average wages were between two hundred and four hundred rubles per month, but a loaf of bread cost forty to eighty rubles; half a kilogram of butter, eighty rubles; a kilogram of rye or wheat, twenty to forty rubles; a kilogram of bacon, 240 rubles; a kilogram of potatoes, thirteen to eighteen rubles; and an egg, five to ten rubles.[61] The grain had to be ground with great effort using a coffee grinder, but at least in this way the Germans could obtain flour to bake bread or rolls. The buyers were mostly Russians, whereas the Germans sold whatever they could lay their hands on to get enough food to survive for the next day or two. One had to be diligent and watch one's goods like a hawk, lest they disappear into the hands of prowling thieves, who were also adept at slicing open a backpack and removing the contents before the person carrying it noticed.

If Germans stole from the Russians, the latter also stole from the former. The Germans were never safe from being assaulted or robbed on the streets. In the Königsberg suburb of Morgenrot in February 1946 alone, 237 cases of assault and robbery were reported, and Germans were not safe even in their own homes. Pastor Linck reported such an incident; at ten o'clock at night he and his wife heard shots outside their house. Shortly thereafter, three Russian soldiers banged on the door and demanded to search the house for thieves who allegedly had broken into houses in the neighborhood. Pastor Linck showed them all over his house and the soldiers looked into every closet and under every bed before they left. The next morning, Linck found that his coat, gloves, and scarf, as well as a bag with medicines were missing, and he immediately realized that the soldiers had robbed him when they searched his house. In this case there was a rare happy ending. Pastor Linck was on good terms with the local Russian commander to whom he reported the theft, and the next day a Russian officer appeared with a soldier and asked Linck if the soldier had been in his house. Linck recognized the soldier and the officer commanded the soldier to open his backpack, and lo and behold, it still contained Linck's coat and medicine bag.[62]

In the depth of winter at the end of 1945, food was in such short supply that cases of cannibalism did occur. Doctors identified human flesh and hamburger meat made from human flesh for sale on the black market. In one case a Dr. Piontek appeared at a hospital carrying a heavy pail and was accompanied by a secret police officer. Apparently a buyer of meat on the black market had become suspicious of what exactly he was being sold and had notified the officer, who then contacted Dr. Piontek to confirm the buyer's suspicions.

Not wishing to deal with this grisly matter all by himself, the doctor asked the hospital's surgeon, a Dr. Riwold, to provide his expert opinion of what was in the pail. He carefully examined the contents and came to the conclusion that it was without doubt a human knee. Two days later, the culprit was arrested: an older man who lived with his niece in a tiny house on the former Hermann-Göring Straße and who was a permanent fixture on the black market where he sold hamburgers for five to six rubles apiece.[63] The two may well have obtained human flesh from bodies they had found in the ruins. But there is also the possibility, which Wieck mentions in his memoir, that people were lured into ruined buildings, where they were attacked and killed for their flesh and organs, which were then sold on the black market.[64] In the same vein, Pastor Linck reported that three women living on the Hufen in Königsberg lured women and children into traps, murdered them, and sold their flesh.[65] Several incidents of cannibalism in the Königsberg area were reported in a memorandum dated April 2, 1947, by the head of the Interior Ministry in Königsberg, Major General Trofimov, to the interior minister in Moscow, General Sergei Kruglov.[66] This graphic report attributed the cannibalism to hunger on the part of the Germans, but it did not address the issue of how to deal with the all-pervasive lack of food that drove a few Germans to such desperate measures.

As a result of severe malnutrition, Germans were susceptible to all kinds of diseases. Moreover, the lack of clean drinking water exacerbated their precarious health situation as people obtained water from wells or from bomb craters that in most cases were contaminated. The sewage system had completely broken down and ruined buildings were used as toilets, further contributing to extremely poor hygienic conditions. As soap and other cleaning agents were not available until mid-1946, skin diseases such as scabies also became a major problem. In addition, most people lived in damaged buildings that had been repaired in the most rudimentary fashion; when it rained, they were soaked by water coming in through holes in the roofs and broken windows. With so many houses in ruins, one or more families were squeezed into one room. In the winter, the rooms were freezing as there was no central heating, and little stoves improvised with exhaust pipes stuck through windows provided minimal warmth. In such wretched quarters, many Germans became sick and died.

1. A Death in Königsberg

One of the thousands of Königsbergers to die in such circumstances was Lotte Schwokowski. The story of how she survived for two years after the fall of Königsberg only to succumb to the effects of starvation was told in gripping and graphic detail fifty years later by her daughter, Hannelore Müller.[67] In the summer of 1946, Hannelore's mother was working at her last regular job in a rock quarry where, with other German women, she shoveled gravel and stones onto trucks. With so little to eat, she was soon worn out by this back-breaking job and suffered a grievous accident: she fell down a pile of sand and broke her knee. She was taken to the Charity Hospital, where she stayed several months because the break did not heal properly. When she was finally released in the fall of 1946, she limped noticeably and had to use a cane. From that point on, Lotte could no longer hold a job and was reduced to hobbling painfully from one garbage heap to another hoping to find something edible, such as potato peelings, uneaten cabbage leaves, or bread crusts. She also resorted to begging, which in the miserable conditions in Königsberg was not unusual. This greatly embarrassed her daughter, who also became upset when a passerby brusquely rejected her mother's entreaties for a handout.

In the fall of 1946 and the severe winter of 1946–1947 their situation worsened considerably. Hannelore's once-flourishing "business" of selling cigarettes to Russian soldiers dwindled and the gloves she knit from the wool of unraveled long stockings did not bring in much food when bartered on the black market. Mother and daughter were reduced to eating a thin soup of oats (*Schrottgetreide*) once a day, which they spooned out of a small enamel bowl, the only eating utensils they possessed. Eggs, fat, and sugar were completely unavailable; some days there was simply nothing to eat. In these dire straits their outlook was bleak: "We had absolutely no connection to the outside world. It appeared to us that we were forgotten."[68]

Around this time, on one of her foraging expeditions, Hannelore's mother met a young girl she knew who lived in an orphanage. After she found out that the Russians cared for orphans, she became fixated on the idea that Hannelore would be much better off in an orphanage, and in particularly desperate moments she painted a picture to Hannelore of how well she would be taken care of in such an institution. Hannelore thought this belief had fatal consequences for her mother, as she lost the will to live. She already had some of the symptoms of starvation: a puffy face and swollen feet and lower legs. But even in her much weakened state, Lotte Schwokowski continued to make her usual rounds in search of something edible.

In early 1947, conditions remained bleak. It was completely hit or miss whether they found anything to eat and often they would go to sleep on an empty stomach. The swelling rose up Lotte's legs and into her body. Still, when all appeared lost, she tried to encourage her daughter: "Hanneli, my dear, just when the thistles start to grow again, then it will get better for us again." ("*Hanneli, mein Liebling, wenn erst die Brennesseln wachsen werden, dann wird es uns wieder besser gehen*"). But her strength gave out before they could collect the edible thistles in the spring. On April 24, 1947, Lotte wrote a farewell letter to her daughter and other relatives, and again mentioned her hope that Hannelore would find refuge in an orphanage: "May God remain with my child, my dear Hanneli, and make a good person find her who will take her until perhaps she finds a home in an orphanage."[69] Hannelore reproduced this letter in its entirety in her memoirs because she wanted it to represent other Königsbergers who had died as her mother had, but had no witnesses of their fate.

Hannelore's mother died the morning of May 13, 1947, when Hannelore was twelve and a half and her mother was forty-seven. She was buried in a mass grave in the New Luisen cemetery. As for Hannelore, in the end her mother's prayer was answered. An aunt in Rinderort in the district of Labiau took her in for several months, but when food became very scarce in the fall of 1947, Hannelore made two trips to Lithuania, where she worked on farms. At the very end of 1947 Hannelore was placed in the orphanage Königsberg-Kalthof, and at the beginning of February 1948, she was transferred with roughly thirty other children to the orphanage in Preußisch Eylau. In mid-April 1948, these and other orphans, together with many orphans from Königsberg and environs, were loaded onto freight cars. Their train departed Königsberg in the early afternoon on April 14. Five days later, they arrived in Pasewalk in the Soviet-occupied zone of Germany, and were taken to the Eggesin quarantine camp. On August 26, 1948, Hannelore was reunited with her father, who had survived three years in a Soviet prisoner-of-war camp. The last words in her memoirs were: "Oh mom, if only you were also here!" ("*Ach Mutti, wärst du doch auch hier!*")

2. Conditions in the Hospitals in Königsberg

Other city residents were able to obtain medical assistance, often at one of the outpatient clinics established by the Russians in May 1945 specifically to treat German patients.[70] These clinics, staffed by German doctors, nurses, and other personnel, were set up to identify patients who were suffering from an infectious disease. The infected stayed in the clinic and were then transferred to one of the two hospitals, Yorck and St. Elizabeth, which dealt exclusively with infectious diseases ("*Seuchenkrankenhaus*").[71] People judged to be sufficiently sick with other illnesses to warrant admission to a hospital were sent to the German Central Hospital (*Deutsches Zentralkrankenhaus*). It was housed in the former provincial treasury (*Oberfinanzpräsidium*) until the end of June 1945, when all staff and patients were summarily ordered to move within twenty-four hours to the then-empty Charity Hospital (*Krankenhaus der Barmherzigkeit*) located on the Hinterrossgarten.

Germans regarded a hospital as a refuge and oasis of calm in the living hell of the city, where sheer survival was a daily challenge. Here one had a bed (although sometimes shared with another patient), protection from the elements and from assaults (if not always from thieves), some heat in the wintertime, medical assistance, and access to regular—albeit hardly nourishing—food rations provided by the Soviet military government. Confronted with a never-ending line of sickly, malnourished, ill-clad residents begging to enter the hospital, the admitting doctor faced the unenviable choice between allowing some to enter and sending others away to continue their incessant struggle to survive on the outside. One such physician was quoted as saying, "For us, the duty of the admitting doctor is to deny admission." ("*Der Dienst des Aufnahmearztes besteht bei uns darin, die Aufnahme zu verweigern*"). As everything in the hospital—beds, linen, medicine, food, doctors, nurses, and other staff, as well as space—was in short supply, only those on their last legs would be admitted. On one day, the admitting doctor had refused on three separate occasions to admit a destitute old woman who pleaded with him to let her enter the hospital. After her third attempt to persuade him, he had to put her out on the street again; the next morning she was found directly across from the hospital entrance sitting on the curb—dead.[72]

A similar dilemma arose when the decision had to be made to release patients. The still weak, barely recovered patients tried at all costs to remain in the sanctuary of the hospital. Doctors were loath to see their efforts to restore patients to some degree of health come to naught when those still sick were discharged, only to die soon after leaving the hospital. On the other hand, so many sick and dying needed to be admitted that room had to be made for them. This dilemma was particularly wrenching in the case of sufficiently recovered children who were not picked up by their mother or some other relative when they were released. The doctors knew full well the likely fate of children who had to fend for themselves on the city streets.

When Dr. Lehndorff was released from the Rothenstein camp in mid-June, he joined the medical staff at the German Central Hospital, where he was put in charge of the men's surgical ward. As noted above, at the end of June, the Russians ordered the hospital to be evacuated within twenty-four hours and all patients and staff moved to the Charity Hospital. This hospital had been emptied of patients on April 17 and was in a state of considerable disrepair: holes in the roof, all windows broken, doors torn off their hinges and lying in the corridors, drains clogged, and electric wires and water pipes ripped out of the walls. The new quarters for the former patients of the German Central Hospital were still being put in order when crowds of sick people appeared for treatment. Dr. Lehndorff described treating people for the symptoms of starvation:

> Nearly all the people brought to us are in the same physical condition: skeletons above, heavy watersacs [sic] below. Some can still walk to our place, on shapeless swollen legs, and sit down in front of the door, where many others like them are lying on improvised stretchers or on the floor. When their turn comes, they often give some trivial reason for their coming, for instance, a sore finger, for they can no longer feel their legs. This becomes evident when we put them on the operating table and slit the greasy, glassy skin from top to bottom with a knife, without their reacting at all. Each time we wonder whether there is any sense in amputating their legs, or whether we should not rather let these people die as they are. Usually we decided on the latter course.[73]

In addition to treating swollen legs, Dr. Lehndorff and his colleagues also dealt with malignant phlegmons, especially carbuncles on the neck, which in some cases extended from ear to ear. If they were teeming with maggots, there was some hope they would heal because the wounds tended to be cleaner. The surgeons also operated on hernias, intestinal obstructions—e.g., a woman's bowel was blocked by a huge quantity of seeds from unripe red currants—and sometimes cases of appendicitis. Occasionally, the doctors dealt with conditions they had never seen before, such as gangrenous stomatitis (noma), in which the diseased area of the face, including the cheeks, lips, and teeth, drop off and leave a massive hole. Many patients showed no improvement during their hospital stay because of the weak condition in which they were admitted and the limited supply of medications. According to Dr. Lehndorff, some thirty to forty patients died every day and their bodies were wrapped in the black paper used during the war to cover windows during blackouts. The corpses were piled up beside the back gate of the hospital and from there transported on a two-wheeled cart to the common grave next to the ruins of the Altrossgärter church.

When Dr. Lehndorff was not on surgery duty, he—like everyone else—was engaged in combing the city and the suburbs in a never-ending search for food and medical supplies. He would get up early to avoid Russians on the streets and would often be joined by a nurse, Erika, and his friend Doctora on foraging expeditions to Karolinenhof and Maraunenhof in the summer and fall of 1945. In the overgrown gardens in these suburbs they picked their fill of red currants and gathered large amounts of orach, which grew like a weed everywhere and had become a staple at the hospital because its spinach-like leaves were edible. On their way back, they would typically search through deserted houses on the Cranzer Allee. Although these dwellings had been worked over many times before by others, they sometimes found the odd potato or something else edible, which had been overlooked by earlier scavengers. On one expedition Lehndorff and five others left the hospital at 5:00 a.m. to search the ruined castle for medical supplies. As they had hoped, the guard normally posted at the entrance had not yet arrived for duty, and they quickly broke in and discovered a large quantity of bandaging material and other useful supplies. They also took one of the paintings that had been stored in the castle in a container marked "Brueghel." Back at the hospital they opened the box and were disappointed to find that the painting had been cut up into hundreds of pieces. Yet someone had painstakingly gathered up the pieces, no doubt with the intention of putting them together again—a seemingly impossible task.

While the staff and patients at the Charity Hospital were safe from assault by marauding Russian soldiers, they ran the risk of being interrogated at any time by the Soviet secret police and hauled off to a prison or camp on suspicion of having held an important position under the Nazi regime. A number of Germans in the hospital made their living working as spies for the secret police by informing about suspected anti-Soviet utterances by staff and patients, which included making plans to escape from Königsberg.[74] During the summer and early fall of 1945, Dr. Lehndorff had managed to avoid a confrontation with the secret police, but toward evening on October 18 his good friend Paula came by and whispered that he should try to escape because the police were coming to arrest him the following morning. He immediately packed some clothes and food in a rucksack and said goodbye to a few friends. His aim was to make his way south as quickly as possible to that part of East Prussia now under Polish administration. He was briefly joined in his escape the following morning by the nurse, Erika, who was then recovering from typhus at St. Elizabeth's Hospital. However, it soon became apparent that she was very weak and she collapsed when they reached the suburb of Schönfließ. She urged Dr. Lehndorff to continue without her, "Now you must go on, Doctor, I only wanted to see you out of the town. Remember me to the people and tell them they should search their hearts, so that what happened to us will not happen to them too."[75] He walked away slowly and reluctantly, but then picked up his pace. He looked back once and she was waving to him. They never met again and Dr. Lehndorff learned much later (January 1947) that Erika had died in Königsberg on December 22, 1945.

Pastor Linck entered the Charity Hospital on December 9, 1945, with a serious bladder infection. He learned firsthand about the high death rate in the hospital when another patient in the same room informed him that the two previous occupants of his bed had died quickly one after the other. He reported receiving a daily food ration of 250 to 400 grams of bread, a half liter of thin soup, and a tablespoon of sugar, and every week or so a small piece— perhaps twenty grams—of sausage. On New Years Day, 1946, all the patients received a special treat: an egg. As this diet was so lacking in nourishment, upon admittance patients were told that unless they received additional food from relatives, they would not be able to survive in the hospital, let alone recover. Following this advice, Pastor Linck's wife sold some furniture on the black market and used the rubles she had earned to purchase canned goods, preserved meat, butter, flour, sugar, and rice. She brought this food to the hospital every other day, and being a generous person, Pastor Linck occasionally shared it with his fellow patients. Thanks to this extra nourishment, he survived and was released on January 20, 1946, but he had to return to the hospital twice a week for follow-up treatment.[76]

One morning in December 1945, Michael Wieck could not move and spoke incoherently when he woke up. Suffering from a high fever (105.8°F), his condition worsened over the next few days and he could hardly breathe. His mother was able to find a Russian doctor, who examined him and then ordered that he be sent immediately by ambulance to the Charity Hospital. When Wieck was admitted, the doctor recognized that he would not survive delousing—a standard practice for new patients—and sent him straight to a sick ward. After X-rays were taken, Wieck was diagnosed with infection in both lungs, dry pleurisy, and malnutrition. As no medicines were available to treat these conditions, the attending physician, Dr. Schaum, could only aspirate his pleura and pericardium. The limited treatment in the hospital did not save the thirteen-year-old boy in the bed next to Wieck's whose lungs were also infected. He had no visitors to bring him the extra food, which might have made the difference between life and death. Wieck was deeply upset when the boy died and was buried in the mass grave along with countless other patients. Wieck was fortunate that his mother was able to bring him food nearly every day—bread, horse fat, and canned goods—bought on the black market in exchange for the hot coffee she sold there. He immediately ate almost everything she managed to bring him and shared only with the boy in the bed next to him. According to Wieck, if he had tried to save the food, it would have been stolen as soon as he went to sleep: "You can't share the slender reed to which you yourself are clinging. It was a terrible dilemma. Anyone who wasn't completely apathetic talked about food, about nothing else but food."[77]

Another story also makes clear the crucial importance of food for the survival of East Prussians. When the author and his wife visited Königsberg (Kaliningrad) in the summer of 1993 with a tour group that included former residents of the city and East Prussia, one older man recalled that as a young boy he had lived with his family in Königsberg while under Russian rule. His younger sister was sick, and after she was admitted to the Charity Hospital, he visited her nearly every day and brought her something to eat. One day he had a piece of bread that his parents had entrusted him to give to her, but he was so overcome by hunger he could not resist eating the bread. The next day he went to the hospital and discovered that his sister had died that night. Nearly fifty years later he was still anguished that he had deprived his sister of that slice of bread.[78]

After five months in the hospital, Wieck was on the mend when suddenly he again came down with a high fever. This time it was malaria, a disease heretofore unknown in Königsberg but now raging through the city. It was spread by mosquitoes that bred in the ponds polluted by decaying cadavers and garbage. He recovered gradually without any medicine, but he nearly starved to death because of a change in the city's administration. The Presidium of the Supreme Soviet of the U.S.S.R. passed decrees on April 7 and June 4, 1946, which incorporated the Soviet part of East Prussia, including Königsberg, into the Russian Republic. This change in status resulted in the replacement of the existing military government by a new civilian administration, effective June 1. Before the switch took place, the military authorities lost all interest in carrying out their responsibility for providing food to the Charity Hospital and for two weeks in May all food deliveries to the hospital ceased entirely. Existing stocks provided half rations for a few days, but then these small portions had to be cut back further. In the face of their patients' imminent starvation, the doctors in charge of the hospital ordered all nurses and ambulatory patients to search the fields, woods, and ruins in the outskirts of the city for anything edible, such as mushrooms, dandelions, stinging nettles, goutweed, and wild spinach. This stopgap measure no doubt helped some patients survive, but the death rate nonetheless rose precipitously to forty a day. Wieck survived this desperate period largely through the sustenance provided by his mother, but he needed to help her in the never-ending search for food and asked to be released from the Charity Hospital before he was fully cured.

The same conditions prevailed in the hospitals for patients with typhus, a severe disease often transmitted by body lice and marked by high fever, intense headache, and a dark red rash. Iris Rörup described how her mother developed a high fever in the fall of 1945 and was taken away in a truck with other sick women.[79] The twelve-year-old Iris searched all over the city for her and finally wangled her way into one of the typhus hospitals where she found her mother in such a feverish stupor that she did not recognize her own daughter. As Iris had also come down with typhus, the doctor in the ward admitted her as well. Fortunately, hers was not a severe case and she was able to take care of her mother in simple ways, pressing wet cloths to her feverish lips to provide some cooling comfort. As the hospital rations were limited, Iris confessed that she rustled up extra food by stealing from the dying or the meager remains left behind by the deceased that had not yet been picked up by the burial squad.[80] At night she slept next to her mother in the same bed and listened to the noisy gasps for breath of the women in the ward that all too often turned into a death rattle.

In February 1946, when their fevers had subsided, mother and daughter were released from the hospital. The doctor on the ward was obviously impressed with the efforts Iris had made to keep her mother alive and complimented her mother on her remarkable daughter. Since her mother was in no condition to walk, Iris once again proved resourceful. She found a sled and in the bitter cold pulled her mother several miles past mounds of bodies piled up on the sides of the streets. When they arrived at a relative's house, they discovered that several family members had died of starvation. Iris at once resumed begging for food and scrounging in the garbage for something edible, as well as bartering in the black market. Her mother recovered and found a job washing clothes for a Russian officer, for which she received half a loaf of bread and a piece of moldy bacon. Many German women worked in the homes of Russian officers and were paid with food.

Professor Wilhelm Starlinger, the director of the two hospitals that cared for typhus patients, reported that at the peak of the epidemic in the fall of 1945, some two thousand patients had stayed there, and that through March 1947, roughly thirteen thousand residents of Königsberg (more than one in ten) had passed through them.[81] He estimated the mortality rate at about twenty-five percent, which in his view compared favorably with the death rates from typhus in both civilian and military hospitals, especially in light of the absence of inoculation, the lack of appropriate medicines, and the unhealthy environment in Königsberg. For the city as a whole, he estimated that out of a population of about 100,000 in April 1945, some 25,000 had survived by the time large-scale evacuations began in 1947. This represents a staggering mortality rate of seventy-five percent and is significantly higher than that of East Prussians in the forced labor camps in the Soviet Union cited above.[82]

Unlike Dr. Lehndorff, Professor Starlinger was unable to escape arrest by the Soviet secret police. In 1947 he was taken into custody and tried twice for the crime of indoctrinating the hospital with fascism (*"faschistische Durchsetzung des Krankenhauses"*), but the case against him was thrown out for lack of evidence. Nevertheless, he was held in detention for a year and then sentenced to ten years in a forced labor camp for counterrevolutionary thinking and behavior (*"konterrevolutionäre Gesinnung und Haltung"*). He was released from the camp in December 1953, and arrived in West Germany on January 22, 1954.

When the Russians annexed the Soviet-occupied region of East Prussia into the Russian Republic, they changed Königsberg's name to Kaliningrad, after Mikhail Kalinin, a Bolshevik revolutionary and titular head of state (chairman of the Presidium of the Supreme Soviet of the U.S.S.R.) from 1919 to 1946. (For the sake of clarity, the city will be referred to by its original German name throughout this chapter.) This renaming of the German city irrevocably made it a part of Russia and dashed any slender hopes the residents might have held that their homeland would revert to Germany. When the Russians issued new identity papers that July, the Germans discovered to their consternation that their birthplace was given as Kaliningrad, irrespective of whether they had been born in Königsberg or some other place in Germany. Some Germans complained to the Russian officer responsible for issuing the identity cards, but he shrugged and explained that this was a completely insignificant clerical error and of no consequence.[83] Nonetheless, the issuance of these new identity cards increased the Germans' apprehension about what might happen to them. Would they become stranded in what was now a part of Russia for the rest of their lives, or would they be able to leave what most had come to regard as a god-forsaken place and start over again in Germany?

Their situation became more precarious in the summer of 1946 when increasing numbers of Soviet citizens began arriving. The Soviet settlers peremptorily took over many of the Germans' jobs and much of their housing. The loss of jobs meant that the Germans would have to find new sources of income to put food on the table. The loss of housing was very disruptive as entire households had to find and furnish new accommodations in the least desirable quarters because the new Soviet residents naturally chose the least damaged and best-refurbished housing for themselves.[84] The Germans were entirely at the mercy of the newcomers and had no legal recourse to the Russian civilian administration. In one case, in the Königsberg suburb of Ponarth, some Russians visited the local German pharmacist one morning and took an inventory of what was on his shelves. At noon he went out for lunch, hanging up his white coat before departing. When he returned, the door was locked, and when he knocked on the hinged window through which he dispensed his medicines, the window opened and one of the Russians handed him his white coat. He knew he had lost his job.[85]

One bright spot in this dismal situation was the resumption of mail in the summer of 1946 between the Russian and Polish parts of East Prussia and the four Allied-occupied zones of Germany. It took on average between ten and fifteen weeks for this mail to be delivered. For over a year the East Prussians had had no contact with the outside world, contributing to their feeling of isolation and hopelessness. The letters were a welcome sign that people in the west had not forgotten family and friends in the east, and they also provided information about their families in the west and what living conditions were like there. While the recipients of letters were overjoyed to re-establish contact with their relatives, many found it depressing that Germans writing from the occupied zones had very little conception of the degree of destitution in East Prussia; some had become so poor they could not afford the postage to send letters. The total lack of comprehension that all German authority and governmental administration in the former East Prussia had been eliminated is conveyed in a report from an eyewitness living in Gumbinnen:

> There came very many peculiar enquiries to the German authorities in Gumbinnen, such as the municipality, the police, and the district court, which no longer existed. Not only private individuals but even authorities in West Germany wrote asking for documents and certificates. Enquiries were made of the police, as to whether furniture was in this or that house, and had been well looked after, the church administration was asked, whether the graves were being looked after, and the real estate recording office was expected to give information about certain premises and lands.[86]

As Hans Deichelmann (pseudonym for Dr. Hans Schubert) recorded in his depiction of the demise of Königsberg, people sometimes just laughed when they read what they found to be incredible requests mailed from Germany. The writer of one letter included a legal authorization for the recipient to enter the sender's apartment and open the windows to air out the carpets and furs. In another letter the sender asked that twenty ping-pong balls be taken out of his apartment for safekeeping and when it was convenient, that they be shipped to Germany. But in the laughter Deichelmann also sensed desperation: "In the midst of laughter one feels the secret pain of disappointment. When those 'over there' have so little idea of what is really going on with us, when it is in fact possible to suppress so completely all this horror we have gone through and are going through for fifteen months, then—there is no hope for us."[87]

With no information forthcoming from the Soviet military authorities and later from the Russian civilian administration about what would happen to them, the East Prussians seized on every rumor circulating through the population. When the German Central Hospital vacated the Treasury (*Oberfinanzpräsidium*) at the end of June 1945, the story made the rounds that the building would now be used by the Allied Control Commission, which would govern Königsberg as a free city beginning July 6, and that members of the commission had been seen in the city. Around the same time, rumor had it that American troops were near Elbing; that American ships were seen anchored near Pillau; and that in six weeks it would possible to travel to the four occupied German zones. In September, the rumor mill generated three dates for departure to Germany—September 20, 25, and 29—which came and went, to everyone's great disappointment. The departures were then believed to take place in October, but again hopes were dashed. Toward the end of December, Germans working at Soviet military headquarters reported that lists were feverishly being drawn up. The Königsbergers interpreted this as a sure sign that they would be able to leave soon. As no concrete information was forthcoming from the Russian authorities, there was no limit to the rumormongers' flights of fancy. One particularly far-fetched report had it that Hitler was still alive and had given a radio broadcast in Australia in which he was supposed to have said that the East Prussians had to hold out only a little longer before they would be rescued.[88] These rumors were symptomatic of the despair those in the former East Prussia who yearned to escape from what had been their homeland and had now become a death trap.

3. Escape to Lithuania

One slender lifeline for people living in the Russian section of East Prussia was to the north, in Lithuania, where food was much more abundant and the local population was favorably inclined to the Germans. Lithuania had been annexed in 1940 by the Soviet Union, which treated the local inhabitants harshly, but was occupied by the Germans from 1941 to 1944, who were viewed as liberators from the hated Soviets. After the Red Army routed the German occupation forces in 1944, Lithuania was again annexed by the Soviet Union early in 1945. Driven by omnipresent hunger, many Germans made trips to Lithuania despite the risk of being caught by the Soviet police and the other dangers that lurked along the journey. Nearly all the trips were made by rail. As most East Prussians did not did not have money to buy a ticket, if they went by passenger train, they clung to the roofs of the cars or stood on the steps. If they took a freight train, they tried to hide among the goods being transported. In freezing cold or driving rain, there was the considerable risk of falling off the train. When they were apprehended by the police, in many cases they would be thrown off the moving cars. The Germans took the risks willingly because the alternative was starvation. One resident of Gumbinnen, not far from the Lithuanian border, reported on the rigors of the journey, which he had made many times:

> We traveled in summer and in winter, when the temperature was 20–25 degrees below zero Centigrade. The water ran out of our eyes, and our hands and feet were frozen. It was not so simple to hold out for hours in such cold, in order that the train personnel or the militia should not see us at the different stations. When our station came we sprang off, mostly in the darkness of the night. But we had to travel. Either one held out, or one perished, as there was nothing to eat at home, and many were waiting for something to be brought.[89]

Once the Germans had reached Lithuania, they headed for small towns and villages where the food supplies from the nearby farms were more abundant. They would go begging from house to house, hoping that whoever opened the door would give them some bread, an egg or two, butter, flour, or some grits. They soon learned that if a single person knocked and was seen at the door to be alone, he or she was likely to elicit a more generous response. The Lithuanians also tended to show more pity for the ragged, dirty, and emaciated German children. In one case, an old Lithuanian woman taught a small boy the proper local greeting and how to make the sign of the cross in order to make a more sympathetic impression on the locals.[90] These begging expeditions lasted a couple of days, sometimes a week or more, whatever time it took to fill a backpack, bag, or container to carry back to East Prussia with provisions for themselves and for close relatives whose survival for another week or two depended on this imported food. Even if the journey to Lithuania was successful in filling a knapsack, there was a considerable risk on the return trip that all or part of the precious contents would be confiscated by the Russian police or stolen.

A twenty-seven-year old farmer's wife described how the Lithuanians saved her. In January 1948, she was a forced laborer on a collective farm in Friedland, some twenty-five miles (forty kilometers) southeast of Königsberg.[91] The conditions were so atrocious that of the original work force of one thousand Germans, only three hundred remained alive, and her five-year-old son suffered such a severe case of malnutrition that he could no longer walk. Faced with starvation, she and nine other women decided their only hope was to make the trip to Lithuania. They walked to Gerdauen and from there rode on the footboards of railway passenger cars in icy weather first to Tilsit and then across the Memel River to Kelmen in Lithuania. There they split up into groups of two and went begging from house to house. She reported that even though the Lithuanians were extremely poor themselves, they never turned away anyone in her group without giving them some food, usually flour or grits. Paying tribute to their incredible generosity, she said, "They always took us in, although they did not know us. They saw, however, how poor and hungry we were and had mercy on us." The Lithuanians she encountered also gave them a place to sleep for the night, which was often just straw spread over a dirt floor in a room shared with chickens, goats, and sheep. They encountered other women, often with children, from many places in East Prussia, including Königsberg, Preußisch Eylau, Insterburg, and Gerdauen, who were also on begging expeditions. It took her group two weeks to fill their backpacks, but misfortune marred their return journey: only four of the ten women managed to bring their food home; the others had their backpacks plundered and arrived in Friedland empty-handed.

While many East Prussians went back and forth on these perilous but lifesaving trips, others chose to remain in Lithuania to work on farms, helping with the harvesting, planting, tending to farm animals, and doing household chores. Some stayed for a year or two and then returned to East Prussia when word spread that the Russians were allowing the surviving Germans to resettle in the occupied zones in Germany. These included Iris Rörup and her mother. As described above, they had survived the typhus epidemic in Königsberg during the winter of 1945–1946, but after the very hard winter of 1946–1947, they had come to the conclusion that their only hope for survival was to risk the journey to Lithuania. They made their way to the neighborhood of Kasloroda, where they dared to emerge from the woods and ask for food at an isolated farmhouse. The Lithuanians took them to the family table and gave them something to eat. Completely disheveled and dirty, Iris and her mother were then allowed to wash themselves and sleep for a long time. Before leaving the farmhouse, they were given a small linen sack with bread and cheese—for them long-forgotten delicacies. Iris and her mother continued making their rounds from house to house and were seldom turned away without receiving any food. The generosity of these often very poor Lithuanians left a lasting impression on the then thirteen-year-old Iris.

A few weeks later, her mother found work on a Lithuanian farm; the farmer's wife was quite ill and she helped take care of her six children and did household chores. Another family at a nearby farm took Iris in; she was put in charge of herding cows and kept busy from morning to night milking cows, cleaning out the stalls, feeding pigs, making soap, harvesting grain, and on bitter cold days cutting and hauling wood in deep snow to keep the big stove in the kitchen going. She recalled that in the kitchen she sometimes feasted on just-cooked new red potatoes topped with freshly made buttermilk containing clumps of butter, for her a delicious treat. Eventually, this new diet helped her regain her full strength.[92]

At one point Iris was almost caught in a police raid on the farm, but she had learned enough Lithuanian to pass herself off as a native. In the winter of 1948, during Lent, a Catholic priest came to the farm and after praying with the family, informed Iris that all Germans in the Russian part of East Prussia were being extradited and that she should return there as soon as possible. He warned her that she posed an increasing risk to the family that had rescued her because the Soviet police were deporting Lithuanians who harbored Germans to Siberia.

Iris informed her mother of this news and that very night they packed a small satchel with some bread and fat for the train journey back to East Prussia. They jumped into a crowded cattle car and were taken under the wing of an old Russian woman who was on her way to Königsberg in search of her son. The "babushka" told them that the Soviet police had already raided the train and had taken the women and girls away with them. As a precaution, she smeared their faces with dirt from the floor of the car. Hoping to be protected, they nestled up against the old woman, who crouched under a large cloth. When the train was again stopped by the Soviet police, they entered the cattle car and kicked everyone lying on the floor with their heavy boots, whereupon the feisty babushka threw her cloth over Iris and her mother. Swearing and screaming, she spat at the feet of the police and delivered a curse, "If you touch my children, the black devil will get you!" The police left them alone, but not before one of them kicked Iris and snatched the food satchel away from her.

At the Königsberg railroad station police officers apprehended Iris and her mother and forced them to spend the night in the cellar of a bombed-out building. They were released the following morning and were relieved when by chance they met a friend of Iris's mother, who took them to the basement of a building where she lived with two other mothers and their children. These two attractive young women—like many others in the city—had long-term relationships with Soviet officers, which enabled them to keep their children from starving. Iris regarded these women as true heroes because of the way they were able to take care of their children. Iris herself was befriended by Vasya, a Russian boy about her age, who managed to find a job for her and her mother in the kitchen of an officers' mess where his mother was the cook. They had their pick of the leftover food, which would otherwise have been thrown out and this provided more than enough to feed everyone in their basement abode.

A few weeks later they were taken by truck to the railroad station to be transported to Germany. Some Russians stood along the edge of the street and waved at the departing Germans, and a few even cried, including Iris's friend Vasya. At the railroad station, during the long wait for the train, other Russians robbed the departees of the little they had taken with them. It took ten days before they finally reached Leipzig in the Soviet-administered zone of Germany. They were the lucky ones: twenty-one of Iris's close relatives did not survive the war.

Other East Prussians stayed in Lithuania and began new lives there. Most were orphans. Without parents, relatives, or friends to look after them, their chances of survival in the hard postwar conditions in East Prussia were slim, and many orphans made the trip north, most choosing to go to Lithuania. They remained there working on farms, taking care of other children, doing household chores, and sometimes had the good fortune to be adopted by a childless couple. These children were later called "wolf children" ("*Wolfskinder*") because like wolves, they had to fend for themselves on the margins of existence.[93]

One such "Wolfskind," Gerhard H., was born in 1935 in Gerdauen in East Prussia, roughly thirty-seven miles (sixty kilometers) southeast of Königsberg.[94] In the fall of 1944, he and his mother and sister were evacuated to Berlin, where they lived with his grandmother and aunt. Not knowing the conditions in East Prussia and that it had been taken over by Russia and Poland, at war's end they and many other East Prussians journeyed eastward in hopes of re-establishing their prewar lives back home. In Gerdauen they found that Poles already occupied their house and farm, and that Soviet soldiers had plundered their possessions. They continued on to Insterburg, but conditions there were even worse, and in quick succession Gerhard's grandmother, his aunt, and finally his mother died of starvation. Gerhard and his sister had heard that in the Lithuanian countryside the people were extremely generous to German children, so they climbed on a freight train headed for Lithuania and got out at Kybartai. Here, they went begging from house to house and then moved on to Vilkaviškis. Just outside of town a Lithuanian woman with a small child gave them a ride in her horse-drawn cart and took them to her house in a neighboring village. Gerhard's sister stayed on and was given the responsibility of looking after the woman's children; Gerhard was taken in by an older couple in the same village whose children were already grown up. Both Gerhard and his sister established new lives in Lithuania.

Another Wolfskind, Lothar-Manfred W., was born in the Königsberg suburb of Ponarth in 1935.[95] He and his sister barely survived the extremely cold winter of 1946–1947 by scavenging in the garbage of Russian soldiers who occasionally took pity on them and gave them a slice or two of bread and some potatoes. Their mother had become quite sick and was growing progressively weaker, spending more and more time in bed. In the early spring of

1947, hoping to assure their survival, she prevailed upon two young women neighbors to take her children—twelve-year-old Lothar-Manfred and his not-yet-ten-year-old sister—along on one of their scavenging trips to Lithuania. After spending ten days in the district of Vilkaviškis, they had collected enough food and returned to Königsberg, where the children found that their mother's condition had deteriorated further. Not long afterward, she died on May 1, 1947. On the advice of their neighbors, the children made another journey to Lithuania—this time on their own—and on their return were enthusiastically taken in by the young women. A few days later they were told that there was nothing left to eat and they should make another trip to Lithuania. This request made Lothar-Manfred suspicious because he could not believe that the household had already consumed the food he and his sister had just collected on their trip.

Nevertheless, he and his sister did make another journey on their own to Lithuania. They traveled to the northern part of the country and ended up in the area around Biržai. There they found plenty of work because East Prussians begging for food and looking for work tended to congregate in southern Lithuania. In the fall of 1947, the two children helped a farmer with the potato harvest, and when it was finished he took them to his relatives, Feliksas and Brigita P. This kindly couple had no children of their own and gladly took them in. They worked hard on the couple's farm, but they were well-fed and clothed and Lother-Manfred was eternally grateful that this couple gave him and his sister a new home. They went to school in Lithuania and he pursued a career in forestry, got married and had two sons who also married Lithuanian women. In the spring of 1993 his sons emigrated with their families to Germany and eventually became German citizens, but Lothar-Manfred—who all this time had retained his German citizenship—remained in Lithuania because, as he wrote in 1994:

> Lithuania became my second home. I grew up here, experienced a great deal and spent the largest part of my life. I have good friends here. I love and honor the hardworking Lithuanian people. Nevertheless, in my thoughts I return over and over again

to the city of my birth, Königsberg, which in my memory was a most beautiful city filled with many historical sites. Never will I forget the beautiful environs…. It is very painful to watch how today, almost fifty years after the end of the war, the one-time northern East Prussia, has been ruinously mismanaged and gone to seed…. That hurts, but with the years, sometimes more often, sometimes less so, indefinable forces pull me there. And I go, how could I not go.[96]

G. Conditions Facing Germans in Polish East Prussia from 1945 to 1950

This chapter has so far focused on the Russian-administered part of East Prussia after the end of World War II. This largely reflects that fact that the literature—largely German—on what happened in this section of the former German province is much more extensive than that describing the fate of East Prussians in the southern section taken over by Poland.[97] Nevertheless, some consideration should be given to what happened to Germans in this part of the province after the war had ended.

The Provisional Government of the Republic of Poland did not wait for the Allies to reach an agreement at the Potsdam meeting where the division of East Prussia was decided; it had set in motion the Polish takeover of the southern two-thirds of East Prussia well before the end of the war. Poland had already received the green light to take over this territory in an agreement reached on July 26, 1944, between the Polish Committee of National Liberation and the Soviet Union, which laid out the different spheres of Soviet military and Polish civilian authority on Polish territory. Article 6 of this agreement stipulated that as soon as any territory of Poland was liberated from the Germans and no longer in the zone of direct military operations, the Polish Committee of National Liberation was to assume full responsibility for all aspects of the civilian administration. What was understood as "Polish territory" was defined in a secret border treaty signed the following day (July 27, 1944) as the area between the Oder-Neisse

Line in the west and the Curzon Line in the east. As described in detail in
Chapter VII, this extension of the western border of Poland with Germany
was agreed to by Great Britain, Russia, and the United States a year later at
Potsdam.[98]

The takeover of southern East Prussia, involving the uprooting and expulsion of the Germans living there and their replacement by Poles, was proposed by two members of the Masurian Research Institute, Jerzy Burski and
Hieronim Skurpski, in a memorandum delivered on November 22, 1944,
to Bolesław Bierut, the president of the National Assembly (*Krajowa Rada
Narodowa*). This memorandum recommended the following: the removal of
the name "East Prussia" and the establishment of a Polish Masurian province;
the introduction of Polish laws and jurisdiction; the expulsion of the German
population and the confiscation of all German property; the establishment of
Polish as the sole official language; and the elimination of German education
and its replacement by Polish education.[99] To accomplish these objectives,
Polish officials went to Allenstein (which became the administrative capital of
the new Polish province and was renamed Olsztyn) as soon as the Red Army
occupied this part of East Prussia in the winter of 1945. A representative of
the Provisional Government, Lt. Col. Jakub Prawin, went to the headquarters
of the Second Belorussian Front to coordinate Soviet and Polish occupation
and takeover policies. Prawin's deputy was none other than Jerzy Burski. The
rapid Polish takeover was designed to create a fait accompli. This objective
was made explicit on February 19, 1945, when the Polish Western Union
(an anti-German nationalist organization centered in western Poland) wrote
to the Council of Ministers of the Provisional Government: "The agreement
reached with the Soviet Union to secure Polish territorial holdings in East
Prussia not only ensures the demographic makeup of the territories, but it
is the only way to make clear to the world that we are ready to resolve the
complicated political problems that exist there."[100] Administrative authority
was transferred from the Red Army to the Polish civilian administration on
May 23, 1945, more than a year before the official transfer of authority took
place in northern East Prussia from the Red Army to the Russian civilian
administration.

To "ensure the demographic makeup of the territories" (i.e., an overwhelming Polish majority) was a daunting challenge because nearly three times as many Germans as Poles lived in the former German territory. A census report made in June 1945, showed that 145,573 Germans, 56,214 Poles, and 9,257 Masurians (the local indigenous population) lived in Polish East Prussia.[101] Yet before the planned drastic demographic transformation took place, the Germans were used to bring in the summer and fall harvests that would provide food not only for the existing population but also for the Polish settlers coming in from other parts of Poland. Moreover, in the under-populated districts of Polish East Prussia, German farmers were expelled only when Polish settlers had arrived and could protect the property from vandalism.[102] German skilled workers were also kept on to maintain essential public services (water, electricity, etc.) and to keep operating whatever manufacturing plants had not been dismantled and shipped to Russia. An effort was made to retain German workers for postwar reconstruction and some Germans were given special rations and housing privileges.[103] German physicians were well treated (two examples are cited below) and given positions of responsibility in hospitals until Polish medical personnel took their place. Also, during the transition period, when qualified Poles were unavailable, the Soviet military district administrators appointed experienced local Germans as mayors. As one Polish writer described the situation: "The German worker was exploited to the maximum as long as he was needed, i.e., until a Pole had been found for his position. Then the German had to be transferred as soon as possible."[104]

The atrocities committed against Germans by Soviet forces when they invaded East Prussia are described in detail in Chapter III. Less well-known is that the invading Red Army was not particularly discriminating in its choice of victims. Not only Germans, but also Masurians and Poles were recruited for forced labor and women were raped irrespective of nationality. A report by the Land Office, the first Polish civilian authority established in southern East Prussia in March 1945, complained about the treatment of Poles by Soviet soldiers: "The situation of the local population in East Prussia must be improved. If necessary, diplomatic efforts should be undertaken. What is happening to the people here is morally indefensible. Poles are being treated as slaves, in other words no better than Germans."[105] In addition, as in northern East Prussia, Soviet military occupation units expropriated farm animals (cattle, horses, pigs, cows, goats, sheep, and poultry) for their own immediate use or transported them back home. They also systematically looted machinery and equipment, dismantled factories, and took possession of transport and other vehicles for shipment to the Soviet Union. Because the Polish settlers brought very little with them when they arrived from central and eastern Poland, they were outraged that the Soviets had taken almost everything useful for themselves, making it very difficult for them to restart their lives in "their new land." The wholesale Russian expropriation of German goods and equipment thus led to considerable tension between Poles and the Soviet military occupation forces during the period they overlapped in southern East Prussia.

The situation was so intolerable for many settlers from central and eastern Poland that they left shortly after they arrived because they were terrorized by Soviet soldiers and members of the Soviet secret police. Moreover, robberies and other acts of violence were also inflicted on local Germans and Poles by other Poles as well. Some of these criminal elements came from Warsaw and Bialystok and had no intention of settling in Polish East Prussia; they came to loot whatever would help them rebuild their own war-devastated farms. Looting was also engaged in by officials at lower administrative levels, by the civil police, and by members of the Office of Public Security.[106]

In this "wild west" climate of lawlessness, Germans had no protection against Soviet and Polish expropriation of their property, theft, and acts of violence. As described in Chapter III, during the invasion of Poland and the terrible yoke of German occupation, Poles had suffered as much, if not more, than the population in the Soviet Union. The murder of millions of Poles, both Jews and non-Jews, and the widespread destruction of property had generated an understandable hatred of Germans and a desire for revenge once the tables had turned. The East Prussians were now at the mercy of Poles, who confiscated their property at will; when the Germans resisted, they were often beaten. For a period of time Germans were required to wear a black "N" (for "*Niemiec*," the Polish word for German) on their clothing, but this was forbidden in November 1945, when the Ministry of Public Administration ordered the local authorities to "resettle the German population as quickly as possible and not to employ methods redolent of Nazism."[107]

Even the Soviet military authorities were amazed at the Poles' ferocious behavior. On August 30, 1945, the Red Army's political section informed its headquarters in Moscow that:

> The German population is starving in many places, in other areas they are under the immediate threat of starvation in the near future. Not only does the plundering of the Germans not stop, but it gets stronger all the time. There are more and more frequent cases of unprovoked murders of German inhabitants, unfounded arrests, long prison confinements with purposeful humiliation.[108]

One eyewitness, a German farm official in Eichmedien in the district of Sensburg identified only by the initials "A. B.," described the looting first by the Russians and then by the Poles, as well confrontations between the two.[109] In February 1945, Russian soldiers carried off all his animals, plundered his farmhouse, and took away his two sisters. They set fire to many of the houses and barns in his village and in their rage burned piles of straw, wheat, rye, and rapeseed lying in the fields. On March 1, 1945, A. B. was arrested, cross-examined, and transported by truck with many others to the transit camp in Insterburg, where he feared that he was doomed to be sent to a forced-labor camp in the Soviet Union. However, his fears proved groundless when a Russian officer took stock of the new arrivals. He looked the fifty-nine-year-old A. B. up and down, crossed his name off the list of prisoners designated to take the next train to the camps, and told him to go home. A. B. surmised that his unkempt and emaciated appearance had led the officer to judge him as being too old and weak to survive the train journey, much less the harsh conditions in the camps. He later learned that the train had transported its human cargo far into Russia beyond the Urals and that those who had become too sick to work were sent back to the Soviet-occupied zone of

Germany, while many others in the camps died of overwork, starvation, and disease, including his acquaintances on the truck to Insterburg.

Meanwhile, A. B. watched as more and more Poles settled in Eichmedien. Rumors flew that the town would be placed under Polish control and, indeed, in late April 1945, a Polish official from the county government in Sensburg announced to a gathering of villagers that Poland would now administer the area and that they would henceforth be subject to Polish laws. At this meeting, A. B. was chosen to be mayor, in part because of his facility with the Polish language. On May 2, he went to the county seat in Sensburg, where he received a document in Polish confirming him in office. He hoped that a period of relative calm would prevail, but that proved not to be the case. He was immediately put in a terrible bind because Soviet military forces remained in the area and demanded weekly deliveries of food, while Polish authorities in Sensburg made similar requests and sent him lists of provisions, which as mayor of Eichmedien he was obligated to provide. As the farms in the area surrounding the village had already been stripped bare by Soviet military forces, it was very difficult for A. B. to persuade the farmers to part with some of the little food they still had. On one occasion, the Soviets stole a stock of victuals he had collected that was intended for the Poles. On another occasion, he was on his way to Sensburg with a cartload of food and Russian soldiers stopped him and confiscated everything on the cart. He tried to explain that the provisions were for the Polish county headquarters, but this argument carried no weight with the Russians. One responded, "The Poles have not conquered this country, therefore, they have no right to take anything from it. If they want anything, they must work for it themselves."[110] Given this attitude and the wholesale looting of the countryside by the Soviets, it is not difficult to understand why the Poles were loath to cooperate with them. When the latter ordered the Poles to use their carts and horses to bring in the summer corn harvest, their refusal led to a violent confrontation between the two sides.

In his capacity as mayor, A. B. had a number of official duties. One was to deliver to Poles who had worked for a German farmer during the war a certificate conferring the right to choose any farm as their property. The German owner and his family were then evicted and had to fend for themselves, while the new Polish owners equipped their farms by scavenging or stealing whatever had not already been carted off by the Russians. Another duty was to settle disputes. In one such case, a German farmer asked him to seek the return of a horse that some Russians alleged had been stolen by a Pole. He went with the farmer to Lötzen, where the relevant Polish authorities were located. There A. B. found that "drunken brawling Poles were everywhere. One Polish authority sent me to the other. Everywhere there was only cynical smiling, and shrugging of shoulders. Finally a drunken Pole held a pistol before my face and said, 'I always shoot Germans in the eyes.'"[111] Faced with this hostile reception, the two men breathed a sigh of relief that they were able to leave Lötzen unharmed and alive.

On this occasion, the Polish authorities did nothing, but sometimes Polish courts did consider judicial complaints by Germans and ruled in their favor. In one such case, Frau Taschen, the farmer's wife whose return to Schönwiese in the district of Bartenstein was described earlier, had a run-in with the town bully, whom she described as follows: "The terror of Schönwiese is Lubich Witkowski, the policeman, referred to by us in Schönwiese as 'Lulatsch,' a nineteen-year-old, bigmouthed lout, a scoundrel. Because of his reign of terror Schönwiese has become the most infamous village in the entire area."[112] On the evening of September 17, 1946, the much-feared Lubich stole nearly all the featherbeds Frau Taschen and another woman, Frau Pohl, had been keeping for the women of the village.[113] A plucky neighbor brought this theft to the attention of the Polish militia in Landsberg, where the district court was located, and a few days later Frau Pohl and Frau Taschen were summoned to the court to make their case against Lubich Witkowski. Much to Frau Taschen's surprise, the court convicted the man and ordered him to return the featherbeds and provide the two women with a basket of potatoes. They never saw the featherbeds again and the potatoes they received were rotten, but the two women had the satisfaction of having intimidated the hated Lubich.[114]

After returning to southern East Prussia to find their farms occupied by Poles, some Germans made a legal claim for the return of their property. In some cases, the Polish courts granted their claims. In the late fall of 1946,

Frau Anna Gehrmann made a legal claim for the farm that her father had owned and that was now occupied by a Pole named Rakowski. The Polish court in Allenstein ruled in her favor, granting her the right to live on her father's property and ordering Rakowski to vacate the farm's premises by May 1, 1947.[115]

On September 2, 1945, the German residents of Eichmedien received their first notification that they were no longer welcome and should move to Germany. It came as a shock to A. B., the mayor, who reported that he and his fellow Germans had given no thought to leaving their homes and consequently had planted potatoes on whatever patch of land they could find, which they intended to harvest to see them through the coming winter. They had hoped that their situation would improve over time and they could not imagine that the Russians and the Poles would take over their lands for good. A. B. became more concerned when, on September 25, he heard that all remaining Germans in a nearby village had been given fifteen minutes to vacate their homes. Because only one cart had been allocated to transport the belongings of the sixteen families in that village, they could take very little with them. And yet, at the same time the Poles were becoming more insistent that the Germans depart, they were also offering Polish citizenship to Germans to encourage them to stay and help populate this part of Polish East Prussia. Not one German took them up on the offer. A. B. was promised a farm if he would sign a form that would make him a Polish citizen, but he refused, and on October 1, 1945, he was relieved of his position as mayor. He reported that only when all his official documents and papers had been taken away, did he finally realize that he had no future in Poland. The new Polish mayor of Eichmedien reinforced A. B.'s decision to leave when he urged him to depart quickly "because the first to go would be treated better. The last ones who did not want to leave their homes at all, would be chased out by being whipped."[116] A. B. lost no time obtaining the necessary exit papers and settling his affairs in Eichmedien. Before leaving for Germany, he took one last look at the farm where he had worked for many years. It was a desolate, forlorn sight where only hungry cats and rats scampered about the yards and the paths were choked with nettles and thorns.

Another survivor in Polish East Prussia, Frau Anna Bodschwinn, had been evacuated in the summer of 1944 from the border town of Prostken to the village of Goldbach in the district of Mohrungen in western East Prussia.[117] On the afternoon of January 24, 1945, she heard on the German radio that enemy forces had penetrated deep into East Prussia and were just south of Mohrungen, but that "women and children were safe." She reported that this radio announcement—the last she listened to—was deeply ingrained in her memory because it was patently false: Soviet soldiers arrived in her village that same evening. In the first few days after the takeover, all the men were rounded up and taken away, never to be seen again. Many of the women and young girls, some as young as thirteen and fourteen, were also taken away and sent to the Soviet Union, a fate that Frau Bodschwinn avoided by dressing up as an old woman.

In early February, the first Poles arrived in Goldbach, and on February 14, Frau Bodschwinn, together with her mother and children, had to vacate the small room where they lived to make way for Poles to move in. Her seventy-year-old mother spent the rest of the winter packed together with other refugees in a cow barn where every night Soviet soldiers assaulted the women (her old mother just barely escaped being raped). Frau Bodschwinn found shelter for herself and her children in the village poorhouse. In May, an increasing number of Polish families arrived in the village and took over the houses of Germans. She reported that these Poles, too, arrived with few possessions and resorted to plundering to furnish their new dwellings. In one daring looting incident, she woke up to find that their featherbeds had been stolen while they slept. The Poles also used long, pointed poles to probe for what Germans had buried in the earth and had no qualms depriving them of what little they had managed to preserve until then. Frau Bodschwinn also described how she and her mother were beaten almost to death by a young Polish hoodlum who was notorious in the area for his vicious attacks on Germans, some with deadly consequences.

Gradually, the Poles took over all the farms, including the one where Frau Bodschwinn and her family were staying. A Polish family moved in with nothing more than two canaries and two chickens. For Frau Bodschwinn it

was particularly upsetting that she and the German owner of the farm had
to work for the Polish family doing all the heavy work, such as harvesting
and threshing the grain from the fields and digging up the potatoes, and
that all the food they harvested—down to last kernel of corn and the very
last potato—had to be handed over to the Poles, making them completely
dependent on the good will of the Polish family for any food they received.
Dispossessed of nearly everything she had owned, and with no prospect of
feeding her family during the coming winter, Frau Bodschwinn's only desire
was to escape her miserable existence in Poland. On December 1, 1945, her
wish was granted when she and her family were allowed to take a train from
Mohrungen to the Soviet-occupied zone in Germany.

Hildegard Diehl, then twelve years old, recalled the flicker of hope she felt
in May of 1945 when she returned with her mother, siblings, and cousins to
their farm near the village of Heilsberg.[118] The Russian military forces had
moved on and the family breathed a sigh of relief. More and more Polish
families moved into the village, and soon enough a Polish couple with two
small children appeared at their doorstep to inspect the premises. Hildegard's
mother showed them the parlor (*die gute Stube*), but as this was not what the
Poles had in mind, they summoned the village police and within half an hour
the family was forced to vacate the entire house except for the parlor, where
the nine Germans were allowed to stay. The Polish couple took whatever they
wanted, including the smoked pork ribs that the Russians had failed to find
in the dark smokehouse; their entire stock of potatoes, which Hildegard's
father intended to distill into brandy; and now and then some of the family's clothes from the wash line. For Christmas 1946, Hildegard had found
some ragged dolls, which she repaired and intended to give as presents to her
younger sister and cousin, but these were taken from her by the Polish children. The family learned to put up with these indignities: "We were without
rights and learned then to overlook such trifles." ("*Wegschauen lernten wir
Rechtlosen damals bei solchen Bagatellen*").

To find enough food to survive became the focus of the family's activity. The
children picked berries and walked nearly nine miles (fourteen kilometers) to
Heilsberg to sell them at the market. They scavenged for whatever they could

sell there and were happy when they got a loaf of bread in exchange. The boys went fishing in the ponds and sometimes caught enough fish to make soup. Hildegard went for walks in the woods with Dr. Ötker's mushroom guide under her arm to help her pick the non-poisonous varieties. The family was allowed to take the grain in the fields that had not already been harvested. They cut the stalks with scissors, then threshed them by hand and took the grain to the mill in Heilsberg; this laborious process yielded enough flour to last through the winter. Everyone tried to find some kind of work to earn a little food, and people who were unsuccessful went begging. Eventually, the family gave up hope that they could survive in Poland, and not wishing to become Polish citizens, they were able to take a train from Heilsberg to the Soviet-occupied zone in Germany in August 1947.

The fate of Germans in Polish East Prussia was not always as dire as that of Frau Bodschwinn and the others described above. As in the Russian part of East Prussia, German doctors, in particular, survived in relative comfort because Russians and Poles alike highly valued their skills. This was the case of Dr. Lehndorff, who had escaped from Königsberg in October 1945. He went on foot to Polish East Prussia, where he visited what remained of his family's estate in Januschau in southwestern East Prussia some thirty miles (fifty kilometers) west of Allenstein. In August 1946, he ended up in the nearby town of Rosenberg, where he worked in a small hospital until he was able to join other refugees on a train to Germany in May 1947. He described the town as follows:

> Rosenberg, which the Poles call Susz, used to be a peaceful small town of about six thousand inhabitants, the center of a district in which the large landed estates predominated. Now the town is lying in ruins, the country all around is desolate, and most of the beautiful manor houses have been reduced to rubble and ashes. Around the ruined inner town the Poles have moved into

the houses left standing, but only very few seem to be definitely settled. The majority are in a state of constant unrest, and the train, which is running once or twice over this section of the line, is packed with adventurers who come and go, because they have not yet found any place to stay, or look for more favorable opportunities. They come from every part of Poland.... The only thing they have in common is that they have lost their roots, otherwise they would probably not come here of their own free will, to a country which is laying waste, and with which they have no connection, except for the few who worked here on the land during the war and are now trying to build up a new existence for themselves on the deserted farms....

Only very few Germans are still living in the town; they can be counted on the fingers of both hands: two old men and a couple of women and children who sweep the streets, remove the rubble, and do domestic work in Polish families. Any other Germans left in this district live on the estates, chiefly under Russian supervision and in closed groups. Left to their own resources, they would hardly find the means to live and would be at everybody's mercy.[119]

Dr. Lehndorff also reported that he was treated with "great courtesy" at the hospital, which he ascribed to the fact that he had successfully performed minor surgeries during his first few days there. There were plentiful stocks of food and medicine, which had been sent from the United States, and he described the fare at the hospital as excellent. Occasionally, patients in the hospital gave him food for his services, fifteen or twenty eggs for pulling a tooth, whereas others paid him in zlotys, the Polish currency. As he was already well provided for, he passed on these additional supplies and his extra cash to the starving Germans in the area. He was often called upon to visit sick people in the town of Rosenberg and in the surrounding countryside, and he sometimes delivered babies on his rounds. At first he was treated with considerable reserve by the locals, but gradually he became a well-known and respected figure in the community. Once he passed by the barber shop and the barber came out and insisted on cutting his hair free of charge. The postmaster and others in the town sought him out to translate letters they had received from the United States and France and to draft their responses.

From his many contacts with the Poles, most of whom were very poor, he developed considerable sympathy for them, and when he visited their houses to deliver a baby, he would often stay for many hours and sometimes the whole night:

> Sleeping at intervals on some chair or other or on the floor, and offered now and then a schnaps, I get to hear many things which these people would normally not relate. The war had knocked them about in a pitiful way, and it was hard to tell from which side, west [German] or east [Russian] they had suffered more harm and injustice. I often feel deeply ashamed when they respond to a kind word with a readiness to restrain their justifiable feelings of revenge, looking upon all that was done to them in Hitler's name as an aberration alien to the German character. And it is just those who have lost and suffered most with whom one can talk most easily about these matters.[120]

Dr. Lehndorff also described the two encounters he had with the Polish authorities. Early on at the hospital, two older men in uniform visited him, whereupon his two nurses quickly retreated to another room. For some time the two men stood wordlessly in front of him, taking his measure from head to foot. When he asked if they were sick, they did not respond. Finally one pointed to his teeth, which appeared to be faultless, while the other slowly paced back and forth behind Dr. Lehndorff's back. Apparently finding nothing suspicious, the two men left without saying a word. The two nurses then reappeared, greatly relieved that their doctor had emerged unscathed from the encounter. They explained that these were the most dangerous men in the district: one, the commandant of the UB (the Polish political police) and the other, the head of the militia. On the second occasion, the UB summoned Dr. Lehndorff on April 10, 1947 (a month before he departed for Germany), to the nearby town of Deutsch Eylau. He went with considerable trepidation, knowing full well that there was a significant possibility that he might never return. His suspicions were not allayed even when he was spoken to in German in a non-threatening manner, as he speculated that the meeting could be a trap of some kind. But eventually it transpired that the UB was only interested in the conditions at the hospital, and specifically, the stock of alcohol supplied by America. They were greatly amused when Dr. Lehndorff told them that he and his staff had tasted it from time to time. As he was leaving, he was amazed to hear a kind of "thank you" for his services at the hospital.

Dr. Fritz Schilling also provided a detailed account of his experiences as chief of the district hospital in Rastenburg (Ketrzyn) from February 1945 until he was transported by train to Soviet-occupied Germany in August 1946.[121] On one occasion he visited the Russian military commander in Rastenburg whose adjutant confirmed the high esteem accorded to physicians by the Russians: "The doctor must live better, must have better housing, and eat better" (*"Der Arzt muß besser leben, er muß besser wohnen, und besser essen"*). This, in fact, turned out to be true. His situation was helped immeasurably in June 1945, when the responsibility for his hospital shifted from the Russian to the Polish authorities, and a doctor indentified only as "Dr. Pr." became the Polish chief physician. Dr. Schilling's new boss was a member of the Polish intelligentsia, fluent in both German and Russian, and before the war he had been sympathetic to Germans and welcomed the arrival of German troops on Polish soil. Nevertheless, the Gestapo incarcerated him several times and he came close to losing his life, but he still harbored no hated against Germans. The two doctors shared many of the same views and worked well together, and Dr. Pr. often invited Dr. Schilling for dinner in his apartment in the hospital.

Dr. Schilling described two occasions when his Polish superior intervened to provide crucial assistance to the hospital. The first was when the Russian Army major in charge of the hospital was getting ready to depart and planned to take the hospital's entire inventory of medical equipment with him. Dr. Pr. got wind of this and immediately ordered the Polish militia to surround the hospital. He then visited the Russian general stationed in Rastenburg to try to prevent what would have been a catastrophic loss for the hospital. He pointed out to the general that the Soviet Union and Poland had agreed that the property of German civilian authorities—which included the Rastenburg hospital and its contents—would revert to the Poles. Dr. Pr.'s argument convinced the general, who ordered the major not to touch the hospital equipment. The second occasion occurred in August 1945, when deliveries of food and coal to the hospital were cut back so much that the daily rations consisted of only a few slices of dry bread and a thin soup, which the Polish head doctor accurately referred to as "hardly-fit-to-eat soup" ("*Kaumzuessensuppe*"). Dr. Pr. solved this new problem in what Dr. Schilling described as a typically eastern European manner. With some of the money that the Polish government had allocated to the hospital, he purchased brandy to bribe the Russian troops in a nearby barracks where there was a plentiful supply of coal and food. Thanks to this resourceful deal-making, he managed to replenish the hospital's stocks of coal, potatoes, and grain.

In March 1946, the Polish government asked Dr. Schilling whether he would like to stay on in Poland, as there was no other doctor in the entire province of Masuria with his specialty (ophthalmology). He found this offer tempting because his personal situation was extremely good and he did not know what would be in store for him if he returned to Germany. To entice him to stay on, Dr. Pr. told him that a German physician, Dr. Mollenhauer, living in Allenstein, intended to take Polish citizenship. This aroused Dr. Schilling's curiosity, and in mid-March he accompanied Dr. Pr. on a trip to meet this doctor and seek his advice. Dr. Mollenhauer explained that he was doing very well in Allenstein: he had a very large practice, lived with his wife in his own comfortable house with all their own furniture, and he earned enough to enjoy the finer things of life. Nonetheless, he was considering leaving and was toying with the idea of emigrating to Australia, where he had relatives. After Dr. Schilling returned to Rastenburg, he corresponded several times with Dr. Mollenhauer until suddenly Dr. Pr. informed him that Dr. Mollenhauer had been arrested—for what reason he did not know—and was now in prison. Completely shocked by this news, Dr. Schilling at once decided that under no circumstances would he remain in Poland but would seek to leave as soon as possible. This happened in August 1946. While waiting for the train to take them west, German professionals and their families had gathered in a barracks.[122] There, Dr. Schilling again met Dr. Mollenhauer, who had just been released from prison and was allowed to join the other professionals. Although they had mistreated him in prison for several months, the Polish secret police had nevertheless asked him if he would like to remain in Poland and promised that his furniture would be returned. He had immediately declined the offer.

———————

While Russia never claimed that the northern third of East Prussia had historically been a part of its territory, Poland argued that the southern two-thirds of East Prussia had always been Polish. Linguistically, this area and other parts of Germany acquired at the end of World War II were referred to in Poland as "reclaimed territories" ("*wiedergewonnene Gebiete*" in German, "*Ziemie Odzyskane*" in Polish) and the resettlement of Poles there was called a "re-polonization program."[123] While it is true that many Poles lived in this area, they were not in the majority, and as described in Chapter I, historically East Prussia had remained largely German over the centuries, in contrast to West Prussia, which had been part of Poland for at least two centuries. In fact, in the plebiscite held in 1920, the vast majority (ninety-eight percent) of the residents voted to remain in East Prussia; only in Allenstein, in the heavily Catholic area of Ermland, did the vote in favor of Poland reach 13.5 percent. Nonetheless, when Poland "reclaimed" this territory in 1945, it insisted that the majority of the residents were Polish.

To ensure that the remaining Germans would be loyal Polish subjects, a registration of the population began in May 1945, in which residents were encouraged to declare their Polish ethnicity by signing a form. This procedure—known as "verification" to denote that the individuals verified that they were Polish—conferred legal rights and allowed those people signing to remain in what was now Poland. People who did not sign the form had no rights and were subject to plundering by bands of Poles. By October 15, 1946, two-thirds of the Germans remaining in the southern part of East Prussia had signed the document.[124] In the heavily Catholic district of Allenstein the vast majority opted for Poland, but in the strongly Protestant Sensburg district only thirty percent of the residents chose the Polish option.

Altogether, some thirty-four thousand Germans chose not to become Polish, but they were so attached to their homes and farms, language, and customs that they did not wish to give up their roots. These East Prussians who insisted on remaining German in Polish territory were viewed with suspicion by the Polish authorities, who did not want a German minority in their midst. At the end of 1948, the one-time chief of the secret police in Lodz, Mieczyslaw Moczar, became governor of the now Polish province headquartered in Allenstein (Olsztyn). He instituted what became known as the "Great Verification," which used material incentives as well as intimidation and force to "convert" these holdouts to Polish citizenship. Numerous eyewitness reports document the coercion that was used. In the district of Sensburg, where German opposition to conversion was particularly strong, one woman described how she was incarcerated, interrogated, and beaten until she finally signed the paper on which was printed: "I ask for Polish citizenship and promise to faithfully and loyally obey the Polish state" ("*Ich bitte um die polnische Staatsangehörigkeit und verspreche, dem polnischen Staat Treue und Gehorsam zu leisten*"). She said she felt as though she were signing her own death sentence.[125] Another eyewitness reported that he shared a prison cell with many men, including young boys and the very old. One man in the cell was beaten until he lost consciousness and then was revived after being doused with water. He held out for fourteen days until he finally signed the paper and was reported as saying, "Force breaks iron" ("*Gewalt bricht Eisen!*").[126] One woman from a village near Sensburg described how she and others were beaten and mistreated by the UB to get them to sign up for Polish citizenship. There were lengthy interrogations in which the UB used all kinds of threats and intimidations to force people to give up their German nationality. They were told that they were Polish, not German:

> We were asked over and over again why we did not sign. Our answers were convincing and well-founded, and yet nobody left the

building who was not forced to sign. We were told over and over again this land was Polish 700 years ago and the people who live here must be re-integrated back into Poland because their ancestors were Poles. Germans live on the other side of the Oder River.[127]

By April 1949, a majority of the Germans in Sensburg had opted for Poland.

H. Deportation of the East Prussians from Their Homeland

In both the northern (Russian) and the southern (Polish) parts of East Prussia, the Germans were kept virtual prisoners in their former homeland until their labor was no longer needed. In Polish East Prussia this lasted until the summer and fall harvests of 1945 had been completed, after which expulsions began, except for skilled workers. By contrast, in Russian East Prussia, Germans were exploited as workers until a significant number of Soviet settlers had arrived to take their place. The Russians took stringent measures to prevent the flight of East Prussians until late in 1947 when large-scale expulsions began in earnest. The different expulsion policies also reflected the fact that whereas the Russians had no historical attachment to their newly acquired territory, the Poles regarded southern East Prussia as a "regained" part of their country and deemed many of those living there—the Masurians and the Ermlanders—to be Polish. While the Potsdam Agreement codified the decision to expel Germans from the formerly German lands and provided some guidelines on how this expulsion was to be carried out (see Chapter VII below), it was silent on the fate of Germans in the Russian-administered zone.

1. Expulsions from Russian East Prussia

It was almost two years to the day of Königsberg's surrender to the Red Army that the first organized transportation of East Prussians out of the city took place. On April 2, 1947, a freight train with two cars filled with Germans departed in the direction of the border with Poland on its way to the Soviet-occupied zone in Germany.[128] The news of this unexpected development spread rapidly through the city and generated hope among the Germans that their misery might soon be over. Little did they realize that this train marked the beginning of a wholesale evacuation that would empty the region of nearly all Germans. This first officially sanctioned exodus had been authorized by General Trofimov, the head of the Interior Ministry in the Kaliningrad region. In a remarkable communication marked top secret, in April 1947, General Trofimov wrote to the director of the Interior Ministry in Moscow, General Sergei Kruglov, that in accordance with the directive dated February 14, 1947, from the Ministry's deputy director Ivan Serov, he had inaugurated the transfer of Germans and had approved 265 requests to leave the city.[129] He also noted that this first train had unleashed a deluge of applications to depart for Germany. General Trofimov provided a lengthy rationale for an organized deportation of East Prussians to the Soviet-occupied zone in Germany, namely: that many Germans were undernourished and could not work; that there was alleged to be widespread criminality among Germans, including cannibalism; that Germans had a bad influence on Soviet civilians and military personnel; and that there was a threat of sabotage by Germans. He summarized the case for resettlement as follows: "Because the German population…negatively influences the development of the new Soviet territory, I consider it appropriate to open up the question of an organized repatriation of Germans to the Soviet Occupation Zone of Germany."[130]

This memorandum led to others, which set in motion the resettlement of the East Prussians. On June 17, 1947, General Kruglov sent a memorandum to Alexei Kosygin, then the deputy chairman of the Council of Ministers of the Soviet Union. As Kosygin had requested, he attached the council's draft decision for the transfer to the Soviet zone of all non-working Germans, including the sick, invalids, children, and the very old. This was followed by a memo dated July 19, 1947, from Kosygin to Vyacheslav Molotov, also a deputy chairman of the council, requesting approval of the draft decision for resettlement. The council gave its approval in Directive No. 3547-1169s ("Concerning the resettlement of Germans out of the Kaliningrad region of the Soviet Union into the Soviet-occupied zone of Germany"), dated October 11, 1947, and which was signed by Stalin, the chairman of the council.[131] This directive assigned specific administrative responsibilities to various ministries for achieving the exodus of the Germans.

Much more substantive was Order No. 001067, dated October 14, 1947, from General Kruglov to General Djomin, the new head of the Interior Ministry in Kaliningrad, who was assigned responsibility for carrying out the resettlement operations.[132] Some of the key points in this fifteen-item directive included:

1. Thirty thousand Germans are to be resettled in 1947: ten thousand in October and twenty thousand in November. These are principally to come from Pillau (Baltiisk) and the coastal areas of the Samland, and those in other districts who are not capable of performing "socially useful work," as well as German children in orphanages and old people in homes for the elderly.

2. Each German family is permitted to take up to three hundred kilograms (660 pounds) of personal items, except for those objects and valuables which cannot be exported as determined by the customs authorities.

3. Medical assistance for the Germans is to be provided by one doctor and two nurses assigned to each train.

4. Each German is to be provided for the train journey with dried goods (*Trockenverpflegung*) for fifteen days in accordance with the norms for industrial and communication workers.

The initial focus on deporting Germans from Pillau and the Samland coast reflected Russia's primary objective in taking control of the northern part of East Prussia, namely, to set up a major naval base in Pillau—formerly an important German naval base—and to establish military bases in the Samland as well. All Germans therefore had to be evacuated from this area so that construction could proceed expeditiously under tight security. For many years thereafter, Kaliningrad (formerly Königsberg), and in particular Baltiisk (formerly Pillau), were closed to visitors and it was only after the dissolution of the Soviet Union that foreigners were allowed to travel to these areas.[133] The directive also clearly stated that the objective of expelling the unemployable as well as orphans and the elderly arose because feeding and housing them used up scarce resources. By contrast, skilled workers who performed essential services and had not yet been replaced by immigrants from the Soviet Union were not authorized to leave until the last stages of the deportation.

In the spring of 1947 German residents of Königsberg wishing to leave had to apply for exit permits. The application form had to be filled out in both Russian and German, and the applicants had to indicate their desired destination, a somewhat odd request as all the trains went to Pasewalk in the Soviet-occupied zone in Germany. In addition, they were required to fill out a questionnaire in German with thirty-one questions. Pastor Hugo Linck recalled that he had difficulties answering some of the questions.[134] For example, one asked if the applicant had ever been abroad. What did this mean in the current situation? If East Prussia had become Russian territory, did that mean that Germany was a foreign country? He also described the difficulties involved in submitting the application to the Russian militia, as it accepted only fifty a day. Because of the huge demand for exit permits, large crowds gathered outside the militia building, and people even came the evening before to stand in line to be among the fifty chosen the following day. After the application had been handed in, it took a minimum of fourteen days before a decision was forthcoming. The names of those whose applications had been approved were called out on a street corner in Königsberg by a Russian official, a major inconvenience for the applicants who had to appear at this location.

Pastor Linck turned in the applications for himself and his wife on April 8, 1947, but then was asked to fill out a new questionnaire, which he submitted on May 14. He and his wife sometimes went to the place where the approved names were called out, at other times he asked a neighbor to listen for his name. When their names were finally called, he went to pick up his travel papers on the Beethovenstraße, but he was told to come back in a week. A week later he was informed that there was a freeze on issuing exit papers. In late November he received an order from the Russian official responsible for church affairs in Königsberg (whom he referred to as the "*hoher Chef*" or "big boss") to be ready to leave the next day with eight others employed by his church.[135] The following morning, however, the "hoher Chef" informed him that not enough exit permits were available for his group. Completely depressed, he and his wife made their way back from the train station to their house in Liep with all the possessions they had hoped to take on their journey to Germany.

Nothing further happened during the next four months until at 10:30, on the evening of March 17, 1948, a militia official knocked loudly on the door and completely unexpectedly, handed over the exit papers for the Lincks. They spent the next day feverishly packing clothes, food, sheets, and eight books, which filled a wash basket that Linck and his wife carried between them. They also took with them knapsacks and a large suitcase. Russians appeared at the door to purchase furniture and household items that had to be left behind. The Lincks used the rubles thus obtained to buy food at the Königsberg freight station, where eighteen hundred expellees had gathered for their departure on the morning of March 19. Large stands had been set up with an abundance of food for sale—bread, butter, cheese, sausage, and tobacco—as well as other goods that were not normally available, such as shoes and socks. The Lincks bought tea, bread, margarine, and sausage for the seven-day journey, and used their last forty rubles—it was strictly forbidden to take Russian currency out of the country—to buy one pair of socks.

The official exit procedures began with an examination by customs officers (*Kontrolle*) of the goods that the Germans wished to take with them on the train. The Lincks had no difficulties—only two of their many bundles were searched—and the same was true at the next stage, when their travel documents were checked and found to be in order. They then had to declare all the currency in their possession. The Lincks had six hundred RM (Reichsmarks, the currency used in Germany before the Soviet takeover), of which 420 RM in large bills were confiscated. They received a receipt for this amount, but it was not clear what good this would do them. Pastor Linck reported that one woman in the line started to wail tearfully when all her money—180 RM—was confiscated. Whereupon the Russian officer not only returned the currency but also reached into his pocket and pulled out a wad of bills from which he gave her an additional three hundred RM.

At the last barrier in the station names were called out and people were told which train car to enter. The Lincks heard their names called, but just as they were making their way to the train they were suddenly told to return to their home. (Later they learned that one other man had been pulled off the train and told to repair a central heating unit somewhere in the city, after which he could take the next train out of Königsberg.) Completely dumbfounded, the Lincks made their way with their belongings to the room housing the Russian militia at the freight station where Pastor Linck asked the officer for an explanation. "On higher orders" (*"Auf höheren Befehl"*) was the response, which he interpreted as coming from the Soviet secret police, the NKVD. On leaving the militia room, Linck caught sight of a high-level Russian officer whom he had recently met and asked if at least his wife could take this train. After conferring with the militia, the officer returned and shrugged his shoulders, meaning there was nothing he could do. In desperation, Linck approached another Russian officer, showed him his valid travel document, and pleaded with him to intervene on their behalf. After an agonizing one and a half hours, the officer returned from the militia officer's room and whispered to them that they could both board the train.

By now it was evening. The train was still in the station when suddenly two hundred additional expellees climbed into the few remaining empty freight cars. It turned out that the train was supposed to depart with a human cargo of two thousand, but only eighteen hundred could be accounted for. The challenge for the Russian authorities was how to round up an additional two hundred Germans at short notice. Trucks were dispatched to the Charity Hospital where it was announced that anyone who wished to depart for Germany had to be ready in half an hour. Such was the overwhelming desire to escape from Königsberg that in no time at all two hundred nurses, children, and patients able to travel left the hospital for the train station.

At the very last stage of the departure process everyone was made to get off the train and ordered to leave all their belongings behind. Each car was boarded by an officer accompanied by two other men who used flashlights to search for blind passengers and Germans who did not have proper documentation. The expellees were counted for the last time and only then were they allowed to return to their assigned freight cars. The doors were closed, locked, and sealed; these measures were designed to prevent Russians from boarding the train and escaping to the west.

Pastor Linck and his wife survived the seven-day trip to Pasewalk without incident. They settled in Hamburg and only much later learned that it may well have been the "big boss" himself—the Russian official in charge of church matters in Königsberg—who had put up so many obstacles to their escape from the city.

Tens of thousands of Germans from the Russian part of East Prussia passed through the freight train station from the spring of 1947 until late in 1948 and underwent more or less the same control procedures. Hans Deichelmann had been yearning for months to leave the city and since the fall of 1947 had seen many of his medical colleagues receive the coveted *"propusk"* (emigration visa). Finally, on March 12, 1948, the Germans in the suburb of Ponarth where he lived began to receive orders to depart. Unlike 1947, when residents had to apply for exit permits, the Russian authorities now wished to get rid of all Germans except for a very few whose skills were still deemed essential. Deichelmann wrote that everyone had to leave whether they wished to or not.[136] A few women providing sexual services for Russian officers desired to remain in Königsberg, but they, too, had to join the exodus. Even the former "Schichau-Werft," a large shipbuilding enterprise the Russians had brought back into operation, was not exempt. The management of the Schichau-Werft was keen to retain the skilled German specialists, but it was unsuccessful in obtaining an exemption for these workers.

On March 15 at 8:00 a.m., Deichelmann and others were picked up in Ponarth by what he called a "good American truck." On the way to the station he took in the destroyed city for the last time and reflected on what leaving Königsberg meant to him:

> The hat that I wear is the inheritance of someone who starved
> to death. My walking stick is the legacy of someone who starved
> to death, everything I wear on my body is from people who fell

victim to the torment of Kaliningrad. We who are leaving the city are only alive because the passing of others made it possible for life to continue, because we were just a little stronger than the others who had to leave us their food, their clothing, their place of work. Whoever of us may see Germany again, was lucky, the luck of one of four, one of six. A last look in driving by the ruins of the old university, the cathedral, the grave of the great Königsberg philosopher. Each of us is absorbed with himself and his thoughts. The damp, cold March air blows without mercy through the racing, open truck. Thick clouds in the sky promise snow.[137]

When Deichelmann's group arrived at the freight station, Russian guards with fixed bayonets carefully watched the entrance to the station and allowed only Germans with proper documentation to enter. They had to stand in line for hours in the freezing cold, some smoking one Russian cigarette (*papirosa*) after another, until they were let into the train station, where they could buy food for the journey. More hours of waiting followed and the departure procedures commenced at nightfall. Deichelmann's account essentially corroborates that of Pastor Linck, while adding a few more details. First, Russian doctors examined Deichelmann's group of forty-five—men and women of all ages—for lice and gave them an injection against typhus. Then their *propusk* (exit visa) was given a small stamp, after which the bundles they had brought with them were laid out on long tables and searched by Russian officers who looked for currency and took any rubles and most of the Reichsmarks they found. Rummaging carelessly through their possessions, the officers took no interest in food, tobacco, or clothes, but confiscated their featherbeds or slit them open. In the final stage of the departure procedures, Russian secret police examined their documents and then assigned the group to the empty cattle car, no. 34. Lighting a few matches, they found places on the floor and bunched all together, they immediately fell asleep on what was left of their possessions.

After midnight the door of the cattle car was suddenly flung open and Russian workmen threw boards, stove pipes, and nails onto the sleeping

Germans. They were followed by another group of Russians who set up a stove in each car. Around 3:00 a.m. the oldest person in each car was ordered to go to the official in charge of the train to pick up a lantern, candle, and the set of rules that had to be adhered to during the journey. They were also told that they needed to have enough food with them to last for five days. One poor soul in Deichelmann's car had brought nothing with him to eat; after a long talk with the train official, he was given fifty rubles to buy himself bread and sugar. Around mid-morning the following day a squad of Russian secret police went from one cattle car to another and everyone had to get out while the car was searched for blind people and those without proper documentation. The expellees' names were checked off by the secret police against a list, and then they were shoved back into the car. In the car next to Deichelmann's a loud cry erupted from the children of a mother who was forced off the train because she was found to have been born in Russia. The father and children had to depart without her. To everyone's great relief, all in Deichelmann's car were properly accounted for on the list and the heavy door was banged shut and bolted after the last person had climbed back in. At ten minutes past noon on March 16, 1948, the train finally lurched forward and the voices of those leaving their homeland forever rose in unison in a hymn of thanks to the Lord: "Great God, we praise Thee" (*"Großer Gott, wir loben Dich!"*).[138]

Lucy Falk received her exit papers from Königsberg on March 20, shortly after Deichelmann's departure. She was waiting to leave late at night in a freight car after her name and others had been called from the list and the final exit procedures had been completed. She heard someone gently sobbing in the car and out of the darkness came a trembling plea in the broad East Prussian dialect, "Dear God, help us" (*"Lewet Gottke, help ons doch"*). Around midnight the train started to move with a jolt and Lucy stood up to catch a last glimpse of Königsberg through an opening in the door. The rubble of the city stood out clearly against the night sky, at first easily recognizable, then farther in the distance, farther still, until nothing more could be seen. Her parting words were "Farewell, Königsberg!" (*"Lebwohl, Königsberg!"*).[139]

2. Expulsions of Germans from the Polish Part of East Prussia

The deportation of Germans from the northern part of East Prussia proceeded more or less in an orderly and systematic fashion, and the confiscation and robbery of the few goods that the Germans were allowed to take with them on the train appear to have been the exception rather than the rule. Russian officials in Königsberg made major efforts to provide sufficient transport facilities and to ensure that the expellees had enough food to see them through to the end of their journey. By contrast, the expulsion of Germans from the southern Polish part of East Prussia was not as well organized. Little effort was made to provide them with the barest of necessities on their train journey to the west. Their belongings were plundered at all stages of the exit process: on the way to the train station, in the station while Polish authorities examined their papers and belongings, and when the train stopped along the way to the Soviet zone of Germany.

Confronted with the confiscation of their farms, houses, and other possessions, the harsh living conditions, and the government's discriminatory policy against them, many Germans decided that they had no place in what had become Poland and were eager to leave. Once the harvests in the summer and fall of 1945 had been brought in and it had become clear that the food supplies during the coming winter would be tight, the Polish authorities now desired the departure of many Germans who did not possess essential skills. Up until November 1, 1948, Germans intent on leaving were supposed to register for what was called "voluntary departure" ("*freiwillige Ausreise*"), and people who missed this deadline were to be interned in camps. This internment, in fact, never took place.[140] But Germans were no longer welcome, as clearly revealed in a statement by the state administration in Allenstein: "Through the enactment of retaliatory measures and norms, as they were applied during the occupation by the Germans against the Poles, thereby conditions will be created by means of which the departure out of the district will be a blessing for them."[141] The "voluntary" nature of the departure of East Prussians in the fall of 1945 is perhaps accurate only to the extent that the application for exit documents depended on the initiative of the Germans, and in that regard was similar to the situation in northern East Prussia in the spring and summer of 1947.

On October 1, 1945, the regional authority in Allenstein distributed to local officials the procedures and regulations governing the deportation of Germans from the region of Masuria ("*Wojewodschaft Allenstein*").[142] This directive stipulated that the "freely departing Germans" could take only the bare minimum with them: one change of clothes, one blanket, one small cushion, one small pot, food for the journey, and currency limited to the cost of a railway ticket. They were strictly forbidden to take jewelry, items made of gold and silver, watches, clothes, furniture, and household equipment. Moreover, the directive contained no guidance regarding measures to provide food and medical support for Germans on their journey. While the weak and infirm—the old, the sick, and children—were supposed to be transported from their homes to the collection points at railway stations, this was often not done due to a lack of wagons, carts, and other vehicles. In terms of security, the directive specified "that the units of the citizens' militia had to look after the departees at the collection points and watch and guard them until the departure of the trains."[143] Despite this directive, eyewitnesses as well as the Polish authorities themselves reported that the civilian militias generally made no effort to protect the Germans from thieves. On the contrary, in many cases they participated in the wholesale robbery of the goods the evacuees had taken with them.

Rather than dealing with the security of the people about to be expelled, the directive focused much more on protecting the property they left behind. To achieve this objective, the local administrators were ordered to undertake a complete inventory of the possessions of the Germans, who were told that severe penalties would be imposed if their goods were found to be damaged. No doubt to avoid encouraging the Germans to sell their household items to the local Polish population, the mayors and county officials were instructed not to reveal the purpose of the inventory. The officials were also told that once the Germans had left their homes, their properties and contents were to be constantly guarded by the civilian militia to protect them from vandals and thieves.

This same document also stipulated that all Germans in the region were to be expelled by the end of October 1945: "Citizen administrators, so that you know how to assess the importance and significance of the question of the deportation of Germans, you should use all the means put at your disposal to carry out this action so that by the end of October 1945, not one single German is left in the district of Masuria."[144] This goal was completely unrealistic and could in no way be achieved with the extremely limited means available to the authorities in the region. An official document dated August 25, 1945, estimated that the number of Germans living in the region at the time was 142,312, while another document dated January 15, 1946, estimated that 99,593 remained, from which it can be inferred that some 43,000 Germans had left or had been evacuated by then.[145] Because many Germans had made their way to Germany on their own initiative and without official exit passes, the figure of forty-three thousand is no doubt an underestimate of the actual number who had left. Indeed, others have estimated that from sixty to ninety thousand Germans left the region in 1945.[146]

When the deportations began in October 1945, in some cases it was necessary to bribe the Polish officials to obtain the necessary exit papers. Karl Kensy, a farmer from the town of Jägersdorf in the district of Neidenburg, described how he and his fellow Germans used all their remaining possessions, including clothes, furniture, beds, and machines, to bribe the relevant officials—including the mayor of Jägersdorf and his deputy—to secure a form indicating approval for departure.[147] This form then had to be taken to the county official in Neidenburg, who also needed to be bribed before he would release the necessary exit documents. On October 25, Kensy believed that all the required formalities for departure had finally been completed, but it turned out that the deputy mayor would not allow him and his family to leave until he had cut firewood for the local militia. Kensy and his family were fortunate that the Poles who had taken over their farm intervened with the militia on their behalf and they were allowed to depart that very day for the train station in Neidenburg. Before they left, however, the militia members insisted that they had to inspect the possessions in Kensy's group and they took their pick of whatever they pleased.

During the night in the train station in Neidenburg, a number of heavily armed Poles, including uniformed train personnel, helped themselves to what remained of the group's food and belongings. Later that night, two police officers came into the station and asked if they had been robbed. Not knowing how the officers would react, they hesitated to reply. Finally, Kensy responded with the lie that nothing had been stolen, which turned out to be the appropriate reply, as one of the officers said, "If nothing was stolen, you may continue with your travel." ("*Wenn euch nichts gestohlen wurde, so könnt ihr weiter fahren*").

The train for Allenstein left at 5:00 a.m., and when they arrived at the train station, they were ordered to clean up the waiting room, which the Poles had used as a toilet. The stench was so overpowering that their one thought was to escape as quickly as possible, and they managed to exit through a side door that opened to the tracks next to the station. There they came upon an empty Russian freight train and the Russian lieutenant in charge agreed to take them on board this train, which was headed to the Russian zone in Germany. At an intermediate stop along the way, Polish civilians climbed on and tried to throw them off the train, but the Russian lieutenant intervened. They were greatly relieved to have escaped the Poles when they finally crossed the border into Germany and arrived at Wittenberg in the Soviet-occupied zone.

A number of eyewitnesses described marching in long columns to the main collection point in Osterode, as well as their train journey. It began late in the evening on October 31, 1945, and ended twelve days later in Rostock.[148] One of these eyewitnesses, Hildegard Aminde, reported that she and others were allowed to take up to thirty pounds (fifteen kilograms) of food for the march to the train station and for the journey to the Soviet-occupied zone in Germany. They spent one night in a large house in the nearby village of Barwiese, where they were told that they would be registered; in fact, the purpose was to steal their valuables. As the Polish militia had already robbed Hildegard when they had ordered her to leave and had subjected her to a full body search ("*Leibesvisitation*"), little remained of her possessions for others to take. She also recalled the fall landscape the following morning when the East Prussians marched from Barwiese to the train station in Osterode:

> The march to Osterode began the next morning. It was a beautiful morning. Never in my life will I forget this scene! The fog lifted over the large Drewen lake, while above the sun was shining in the blue sky. The birch trees shone gold-speckled and the woods radiated the wonderful fall colors as only an East Prussian autumn can bring forth. It was as though God wanted to burn this unique beauty deep into our souls so that when we are gone, we do not forget our beloved East Prussia.
>
> Add to that, on the country road this kilometer-long, never-ending pitiful column driven away from the homeland.[149]

When her group reached Osterode, they were registered and checked several times, and were again robbed of food, clothes, and valuables. Some people were even ordered to take their clothes off and the pile of confiscated garments grew higher and higher until it almost reached the ceiling of the room where they were being registered. According to one account, the chief Polish official in the district of Osterode ("Landrat") was among the most energetic of the plunderers.[150] Another eyewitness of this same scene, Lilly Sternberg, the wife of an estate owner, described the horrific situation as follows:

> We went from one registration and checking to another, which consisted chiefly in our having to strip ourselves, and many of us being plundered down to our shirts.... We passed a shocking night in the warehouse of Korn and Spudlich in Osterode. We heard nothing but shrieking, crying, and groaning. Next morning at 7 o'clock we went through our "last" control, and came through it "enlightened" [relieved of their possessions]. We rushed like hunted game to the goods station, and suffered unspeakable fear, until the train actually moved off at 7 o'clock in the evening.[151]

In the early morning hours the following day the train arrived at Deutsch Eylau, where it stopped long enough for another round of plundering of what the Germans had still managed to retain. Bands of Poles roamed through the entire train and threw sacks of booty out of the windows or through the doors to their waiting accomplices outside. Many of the refugees also had to hand over the last of their bread, which was to have provided sustenance to the end of their journey. This happened to Lilly Sternberg and soon her children were crying from hunger. She had had the foresight to sew her grandfather's gold signet ring into of one her daughters' coats, and with a heavy heart she took it to the railroad car housing the Russian commandant and his soldiers who were supposedly guarding the train. After drawn-out bargaining, she managed to exchange the ring for two kilos of bread, enabling her family to have something to eat the rest of the journey.[152]

Another eyewitness of the same train journey described the wild conditions at Deutsch Eylau:

> At night the train stood on a station siding at Deutsch Eylau. At the station embankment were Poles with their horse-drawn wagons. Polish men went noisily through the cars shooting, beating, and robbing. My husband, meantime, had had a stroke and cramps and had lost consciousness. Despite my entreaties, they tore out the last pillow from under the sick man and pulled off his boots. They took away the last of my belongings. Later, a Pole returned to me what was most precious, bread, and a tin plate and an empty German soldier's kit. This was all I now possessed. On November 11, 1945, we arrived in Rostock at lunchtime and received from the German Red Cross the first warm meal and were brought to a camp. My husband was dead. God had released him from all suffering.[153]

This man was one of twenty who were reported to have died on this particular train.

Following these extremely disorganized efforts in late 1945 to expel Germans, there was a delay of many months before the expulsions resumed in 1946. The delay was due to conflicting objectives at different levels of the Polish government. On the one hand, there was a strong desire to quickly rid the country of all remaining Germans, particularly on the part of officials at the regional and district levels who faced a significant drain on their very limited budgets by providing social services, including food, for poor Germans. On the other hand, the central authorities in Warsaw wanted to ensure that the East Prussians who had, or were deemed to have, some Polish roots—the so-called "autochthons"—would remain in Poland.[154] The process of verifying who of the Germans were "Polish" proceeded slowly in the first half of 1946, as lists had to be prepared at the local level of people who were identified as fully German, and would therefore be allowed to leave, and those deemed to have sufficient Polish background, who would not receive permission to depart. As a result, no Germans were allowed to leave until the summer of 1946, when the deportations resumed.

The first train carrying Germans to the Soviet-occupied zone departed on August 14. Detailed instructions for this evacuation were contained in a document dated August 6, 1946, which was sent to all district officials and to the mayor of Allenstein.[155] Nearly sixteen hundred members of the German intelligentsia (doctors, teachers, ministers, etc.) were singled out and brought from all over the region to Allenstein. There, a sixty-car train had been assembled to take them to Stettin on the border of the Soviet-occupied zone, the destination of all the trains coming from the Allenstein region. The Polish authorities viewed these professionals as undermining the verification process and therefore wished to have them removed from Poland expeditiously. The directive made reference to the guidelines that the Polish Ministry for Reclaimed Territories had formulated for the deportation of Germans and it included instructions relating to food supplies, sanitary conditions, and medical care for this train.[156] Moreover, it specifically instructed the official in charge of the assembly location in Allenstein to ensure that the train had sufficient supplies of food on board before it departed. Hence, the evacuees on the Polish trains in 1946 were much better provided for than those in 1945.

Dr. Fritz Schilling, whose survival under Polish rule in southern East Prussia was described above, was on this train. He reported that when documents were checked and possessions examined during the exit procedures, many Germans were robbed of their money, valuables, and some of their clothes. Once on the train, the deportees continued to be plundered until it finally departed from the Allenstein station in the evening of August 14. During the train journey to Stettin the robbery ceased, and when the train halted for longer intervals, the Germans were provided with warm food. At one of the stops a Russian train had also halted on another track and when the Russian crew attempted to storm the cars to attack the German women, the Polish militia on the train protected them from assault. Dr. Schilling's description confirms the official directive cited above that the Germans were to be treated in a humane manner on their journey: "In general I must honestly say that this transport train of intellectuals was run humanely, notwithstanding the plundering in Allenstein. The food, even if I had not brought along more, would have been sufficient. The trip in this beautiful summer weather in the freight cars with open doors was a pleasure."[157] Nevertheless, those on the train were sad to be leaving their beloved East Prussian homeland, perhaps forever. Dr. Schilling described his feelings and those of others in his freight car:

> But how sad it was for every East Prussian to look at the once so fertile land. The fields had become nothing but acres of thistles. But the direction the train took was good, we went toward the West, not to Russia!
>
> When the sun was sinking, we crossed beyond Deutsch-Eylau, the old East Prussian border. Then we all became very sad that we had to leave this beautiful homeland, which, with its Oberlander Lakes, once more showed itself in all its magnificence in the evening light. For me this wonderful land had become home for nineteen years. Here were the graves of so many loved ones, in Goldap that of my mother, in Lyck that of my first wife, in Metgethen that of

my sister, and far, far in the northeast, in Estonia, that of my dear boy! We all had tears in our eyes, and out of the rolling cars came the wistful sounds of the old East Prussian folk songs. Yes, "Land of the Dark Forests and the Crystal Clear Lakes!" Many expressed the hope of being able to return home soon. But Ruth and I knew that it was goodbye forever.[158]

During the remainder of 1946, nine more trains transported East Prussians to the west. Official statistics indicate that 15,564 Germans left Poland that year, the majority from the northern districts of the region, where food supplies were extremely tight.[159] This was a very slow pace of resettlement; by way of comparison, in 1946 more than a million Germans were deported from the city of Breslau (Wroclaw) alone. The winter of 1946–1947 was bitterly cold, and in December this caused an increase in deaths on the transport trains. Two more trains departing in January 1947 experienced even higher death rates, and the central government halted all further trains to the west until April that year. From May through October 1947, four or five trains departed each month and transported Germans to the border town of Kohlfurt in the Soviet-occupied zone. Official data indicate that in 1947, a total of 45,475 Germans left what had been the southern part of East Prussia. In 1948, only 5,301 Germans were deported. For the combined years 1949 and 1950, 4,591 were resettled. In official Polish statistics the total number of East Prussians sent to the west since August 1946, is estimated to be 71,931.[160]

Notwithstanding the official guidelines stipulating the procedures the authorities were to follow in the resettlement of Germans, inspectors from the Ministry for Reclaimed Territories often found that these were honored in the breach. They reported numerous instances of poor hygienic conditions at assembly points, attacks on Germans, and the withholding of wages owed them by state-owned enterprises. The inspectors voiced particularly strong criticism of Polish civilian militia officers who robbed Germans and treated them badly, were corrupt, and were drunk while on duty.[161] A directive issued on September 15, 1947, by the regional government in Allenstein to the local authorities was very critical of the manner in which the resettlement procedures had been implemented and once again spelled out in detail the guidelines that had to be followed.[162] Nonetheless, the militia and other functionaries continued to treat the expellees poorly.

As noted above, when Mieczyslaw Moczar became governor of the region, the situation of the remaining Germans took a distinct turn for the worse. In September 1948, he was dismissed from his position in the Ministry for Public Security, but became governor in December of that year. According to the scholar Claudia Kraft, he pursued a more rigorous version of "verification" to demonstrate to the Communist Party leaders that he was a reliable member.[163] This so-called "Great Verification" began in early 1949, especially in the districts of Johannisburg, Ortelsburg, and Sensburg, when extreme measures were taken to force the remaining Germans to opt for Polish citizenship. These measures have often been described as a form of torture and have been documented in Polish as well as German sources.[164] Particularly graphic are letters written from the district of Sensburg, but similar letters were written from the districts of Allenstein, Lyck, Ortelsburg, Osterode, Rössel, and Treuburg.

One man identified only as R. G., from the village of C. in the district of Sensburg, sent a letter on March 11, 1949, to his friend Fritz in Germany. He reported the methods used to coerce him to sign a document that would make him a Polish citizen. He noted that in a meeting on February 8, 1949, "The Polish Landrat [district official] then said 'I demand that by tomorrow evening, at 6 o'clock, there is not a single German in C. By becoming Poles you obtain the same rights, indeed even better ones than any other Pole. You can choose landed property, receive a horse, a cow, and people to work for you, you could even perhaps receive your farms back. Anyone who needs support, will receive it, also pensions.'"[165] R. G. noted that no one was taken in by these offers, but the Polish authorities would not give up. At another meeting the following day, R. G. was asked why he would not sign the document. He replied that he and his wife had four grown children in Germany, and considering they were old, wanted to go live with them. His wife was allowed to go home, but R. G. was driven in a small truck with three other Germans to the cellar of the Secret Police building in Sensburg. After a night in the cellar, he was taken upstairs and interrogated by three men. He was again asked why he would not sign. He replied:

> "My father was German. I can't speak a word of Polish, and am going to remain a loyal German. My father would not rest in his grave, if I became a Pole; I want to go in my old years to my children in the Reich, in order that I do not have to work so hard any more." My face was then slapped, and I was ordered to clench the fingers of both my hands, and then one of these men struck my knuckles with a ruler and also my bald head. "Are you going to sign?" "After this, certainly not." I was again locked up.[166]

As he showed no inclination to become a Polish citizen, he was subjected to more severe beatings: he was hit with rubber tubes on the soles of his feet until they were black and blue, punched in the neck, and finally the back of his head was struck against the wall ten to twelve times in succession. As there seemed to be no end in sight to these assaults, R. G. feared that he would be crippled or tortured to death by the secret police. After five days and nights of beatings, he signed the document and became a Polish citizen. His final words in his letter to his friend Fritz were:

> We have only one desire, and that is to publish all this, in order that we may get out, for the signatures cannot be regarded as valid. About 13,000 Germans in the District of Sensburg were treated in the same way. Many had their arms and legs broken. See that the signatures of February are declared to be not valid....
>
> We now send you most hearty greetings from us enslaved Germans in C. I suppose we shall never meet again.[167]

Following the political thaw at the 7th meeting of the Polish United Workers Party (*"Polska Zjednoczona Partia Robotnicza"* or PZPR) on October 20,

1956, when Wladyslaw Gomulka became head of the party, there was considerable soul-searching by some Masurians in Allenstein who had been German and were now Polish. They drafted a memorandum to the party leaders in December 1956, stating that the Germans in the southern part of East Prussia had suffered injustice, depravation, and pain, that their history was full of tragedy and suffering, and that these Germans wished to have the freedom to maintain their traditions. The drafters of the memorandum expressed their conviction that the new party leaders would have the motivation and ability to redress this injustice and suffering.[168] After 1945, the Poles referred to the Masurians as either "*Szwab*" (Swabian = German) or "*Hitlerwoiece*" ("Hilterite") and treated them accordingly.[169] But it was too late to integrate many of the remaining Germans into Poland because of the intimidation and torture inflicted on them. Following the thaw, a wave of East Prussians left Poland and settled in West Germany. After an agreement was reached between German chancellor Helmut Schmidt and party chief Edward Gierek in 1975, more evacuees followed; it is estimated that between 1971 and 1988 some fifty-five thousand East Prussians emigrated from Poland to West Germany.[170] In 1990, a Polish historian delivered a devastating critique of Polish policy toward the southern part of East Prussia: "What the Prussians in over 400 years were unable to accomplish, we Poles accomplished in a generation, namely, to make out of the Masurians conscious Germans."[171]

Notes

1 For a compact description of Königsberg after the capitulation, see Gause, *Die Geschichte der Stadt Königsberg*, vol. 2, Chapter V, "Nach der Kapitulation," 170–77.

2 Rosin, *Führt noch ein Weg zurück?*, 18. "In dem kleinen Bunker herschte eine Stille, eine zitternde, lauschende Stille.... Mir war schlecht vor Angst.... Was werden sie mit uns machen, grübelte ich, sah die Bilder erschlagener Kinder und vergewaltigter Frauen vor mir."

3 Ibid., 22. "Kurz danach rißen russische Soldaten die Kellertür auf und stürmten mit Geschrei herein! Sie schoßen mit ihren Pistolen in die Decke und in den

Fussboden. Ihre Taschenlampen leuchteten in unsere Gesichter.... Danach verlangten sie Uhren. Der Strahl einer Taschenlampe traf mein Gesicht. 'Uri, Uri,' grölte der Soldat. Ich gab ihm schweren Herzens meine kleine goldene Armbanduhr, es war ein Geschenk meines Mannes. Als der Soldat die Uhr über die Hand streifte und den Ämellaufschlag hob, sah ich, daß er den Unterarm voller Uhren hatte."

4 Wieck, *A Childhood under Stalin and Hitler*, 137.

5 Lehndorff, *Token of a Covenant*, 68–87.

6 Deichelmann, *Ich sah Königsberg sterben*, 25.

7 Lehndorff, *Token of a Covenant*, 74–77. Walpurgisnacht is celebrated on the eve before May Day and was traditionally considered the night when witches gathered.

8 Linck, *Im Feuer Geprüft*, 15. Pastor Linck had served a congregation in Königsberg since 1930 and chose to remain with his church members under Soviet rule until he was allowed to leave in 1948. He elaborated on this term as follows: "'Propaganda-march' was a popular saying regarding the first order imposed upon the Königsberg population from the Russian side. This ironic word means the incomprehensible measures that, through efforts and deprivations, led to the great extermination." ("'Propagandamarsch'—so nannte der Volksmund die erste Anordnung, die russischerseits über die Könisberger Bevölkerung verhängt wurde. Dieses ironische Wort meint die für niemanden verständliche Maßnahme, die durch Anstrengungen und Entbehrungen den Auftakt zum großen Sterben bildete"). In another book he explained the term more vividly: "These marches were known ironically as 'propaganda marches.' This meant that all those who had had any illusions left about the workers' paradise in Russia thoroughly lost their idealism and their friendly feelings toward Russia." ("Diese Märsche nannte der Volksmund ironisch 'Propagandamärsche.' Es wurde nämlich allen, die irgendwelche Illusionen über das Arbeiterparadies in Rußland gehabt hatten, ihr Idealismus und ihre Russenfreundlichkeit gründlichst ausgetrieben."); Linck, *Königsberg 1945–1948*, 20.

9 Lasch, *So fiel Königsberg*, 126.

10 Lass, *Die Flucht: Ostpreußen 1944/45*, 292.

11 Luschnat, *Die Lage der Deutschen*, 49. Her argument, however, is based on circumstantial evidence, namely, quotations from un-named Russian authors describing the hatred in Russia of the Prussian conquerors, and the fact that the castle ruins were obliterated in 1969 to make room for a new city hall on the same spot. Considering that the Russian government knew at the time that Königsberg would become part of Russia, it is puzzling that so many buildings

were destroyed that could have been put to good use after the war. At some point a full opening and search of the Soviet archives may reveal the underlying rationale for the deliberate destruction of much of Königsberg after the battle for the city had been won by the Red Army.

12   Linck, *Königsberg 1945–1948*, 16–17.

13   Falk, *Ich blieb in Königsberg*, 9.

14   Rörup, *Also sprach Vielliebchen*, 18. "Auf der Landstraße zur Ostsee werden sie von Durst und blutiger Ruhr eingeholt. Es geschehen unbeschreibliche Dinge. Neben den Straßen, auf den Wegen. In den Graben Leichen von allen möglichen Lebenswesen. In umbekippten Kinderwagen noch wimmernde Säuglinge. Daneben ihre sterbenden oder schon erlösten Mütter. Dazwischen durchwühltes Gepäck, Koffer, Rucksäcke, Taschen. Von Panzern zermalmte Körper. Verwundete Pferde stricken ihre Hufe wie drohende Fäuste gegen den Himmel."

15   Ibid., 19.

16   Lehndorff, *Token of a Covenant*, 115.

17   Deichelmann, *Ich sah Königsberg sterben*, 28.

18   Wieck, *A Childhood under Hitler and Stalin*, 135–36.

19   Ibid., 142. The fact that one was a Communist Party member provided little or no protection. An eyewitness reported that when a convinced Communist raised his fist in the party salute to the Russian soldiers surrounding him and greeted them with "Heil Stalin, Kameraden, ich bin ein Kommunist," one responded "Wir nix Kamerad, nix Heil Stalin," and they took him away. When weeks later the eyewitness saw him again, he was in bad shape and depressed because the Russians had beaten him so long that he confessed (falsely) that he had been a Nazi, as otherwise they would have killed him. Lass, *Die Flucht: Ostpreußen 1944/45*, 296.

20   For a description of Camp Rothenstein and other internment camps in East Prussia, see Luschnat, *Die Lage der Deutschen*, 50–54.

21   Linck (*Königsberg 1945–1948*, 16) described this camp as the barracks of a tank reconnaissance detachment ("Kaserne einer Panzer-Aufklärungsabteilung").

22   Matull, *Vor 30 Jahren in Königsberg*, 52.

23   Ibid., 54–56.

24   Linck, *Königsberg 1945–1948*, 20–22.

25   Dr. Lehndorff credits Dr. Schreiner, whom the Russians had appointed medical director of the camp, with allowing water to be brought into the camp: "Dr. Schreiner finally succeeded in persuading a Russian officer, who had come to

him from time to time as a patient, to permit water to be brought to the camp. Consequently, twenty wretched men pushed a sewage cart out of the camp gates to the nearest pump which was about seven hundred yards away. It took them several hours to return with their load, but in this way the camp got at least a few hundred gallons of water." Lehndorff, *Token of a Covenant*, 122.

26 Linck, *Königsberg 1945–1948*, 27.

27 Ibid., 34. "Ich glaubte mich in ein Märchenland versetzt. Ein langer Tisch, weiß gedeckt, mit Blumen darauf! Die weiße Decke erwies sich als die Rückseite von Tapetenrollen, aber die Blumen waren echt, Tulpen, Narzissen und Märzbecher und Perlblümchen und was sonst in den zahlreichen Siedlergärten blühte. Dampfende Kartoffeln in großen Schüsseln und—unausdenkbarer Genuss!—Braten! Es war zwar Pferdefleisch, aber eben doch Braten."

28 Wieck, *A Childhood Under Hitler and Stalin*, 151.

29 Ibid., 157.

30 Ibid., 148–59.

31 Dysentery is caused by bacteria that usually enter the body through contaminated food or water, or by contact with a person who is already infected. The primary symptom is severe diarrhea, and other common symptoms are abdominal cramps, fever, and rectal pain. It can be fatal because of the loss of body water and salt, which are vital for the function of organs such as the kidney, brain, and heart. The mortality rate is particularly high among older, malnourished individuals. Dysentery is highly contagious and prevalent in areas with poor sanitation and an inadequate supply of clean water; source: BBC News Health Medical Notes website.

32 Lehndorff, *Token of a Covenant*, 125.

33 Ibid., 143.

34 A useful summary is provided in Schieder, Section II, "The return of parts of the refugee population at the end of the fighting," *The Expulsion of the German Population*, 54–62.

35 Kopelev, *Aufbewahren für alle Zeit*, 90.

36 These estimates are taken from Schieder, *The Expulsion of the German Population*, 61–62.

37 Schieder, *Dokumentation der Vertreibung*, vol. I, part 1, report no. 86, 330–33.

38 Ibid., report no. 88, 335–42.

39 Wermter, "Flucht und Vertreibung der Familie Wermter," 13–19.

40 There is no way of knowing, but it is possible that the elderly Wasserziers were the two victims in the farmhouse described in Solzhenitsyn's *Prussian Nights*, quoted in Chapter IV.

41 The chapter entitled "The Lost Children" ("*Die Verlorenen Kinder*") in Knopp, *Die große Flucht,* 216–93, provides a particularly vivid description of the deportation of largely East Prussian women and children to Soviet work camps.

42 This was not the first time that Germans were deported to the Soviet Union. Already in December 1944, thousands of ethnic Germans in Hungary, Romania, and Yugoslavia had been rounded up and transported as forced laborers to industrial areas in the Donez, to the Caucasus, and to the Urals. These deportations were carried out as a consequence of Stalin's Order No. 7161 of December 16, 1944, which directed the NKVD to mobilize in the Balkans all men from fourteen to forty-five, and all women from eighteen to thirty, for work in the Soviet Union. This directive was extended to all German territory in the east in Stalin's Order No. 7467 of February 3, 1945. Knopp, *Die große Flucht,* 220.

43 Kibelka, *Ostpreußens Schicksalsjahre 1944–1948,* 43–44, 48.

44 The estimate of a minimum of forty-four thousand deportees from East Prussia is given in Schieder, *Dokumentation der Vertreibung,* vol. I, part 1, 83 E. The lower figure for total deportations is from Schieder, *The Expulsion of the German Population,* 65, and the higher figure is cited in Knopp, *Die große Flucht,* 221. Somewhat larger numbers are given in Klier, *Verschleppt ans Ende der Welt.* The map on the inside back cover of Klier's book shows deportations to the U.S.S.R. and indicates that somewhat more than fifty thousand were deported from East Prussia, the vast majority in twenty-two trains from the assembly camp in Insterburg. On page 187 she gives a figure of 530,000 for the total number of German civilians deported to the U.S.S.R (an estimate that she attributes to the search service of the German Red Cross ("*Suchdienst des DRK*"), of whom 229,000 died in the Russian forced labor camps.

45 Knopp, *Die große Flucht,* 225.

46 Ibid., 223–24.

47 Ibid., 228, 248, and 250 for reported incidents of such shootings.

48 The estimate of the survival rate of one-half of the German civilians who were sent to work camps in the Soviet Union is given in Schieder, *The Expulsion of the German Population,* 67–68, and de Zayas, *A Terrible Revenge,* 118. The estimate of a survival rate of roughly one-third is found in Reichling, *Die deutschen Vertriebenen in Zahlen,* 1: 33, table 5. In this connection it is worth noting that slaves from Africa were not a free resource to the owners of plantations in the American South. They were a valuable capital good with a market price and for

this reason they were probably better taken care of than the German civilians forced to work in Soviet labor camps.

49 Report no. 137 in Schieder, *Dokumentation der Vertreibung,* vol. I, part 2, 3–5.

50 Report no. 141 in ibid., 13–16.

51 Report no. 146 in ibid., 29–33.

52 This report is contained in "Deportiert—Interniert—Verwaist: Das Elend der Frauen, Kinder und Greise in den Arbeitslagern der Sowjetunion von 1945 bis 1958," a special exibition of the Bund der Stalinistisch Verfolgten e. V., Landesverband Berlin. The author is indebted to Lorenz Grimoni for providing him with this material.

53 For an analysis of the deportation and internment of German civilians, which makes extensive use of Soviet archives, see Polian, *Against Their Will,* "International Forced Migrations," 239–303.

54 This description of the dedication is taken from a newspaper account, "Autorin weihte in Karelien Denkmal ein," in the reference cited in footnote 52. The author referred to, Ursula Seiring, was deported from East Prussia to the Padozero camp and took part in the dedication ceremony. She wrote a book, *Du sollst nicht sterben,* about her experiences there.

55 The English title of the book is: *Interned Youth—A History of the USSR NKVD Camp 517 for Interned German Women* (Moscow-Petrozavodsk: Memorial, 1995).

56 Olga Katharina Farca, *Allein die Hoffnung hielt uns am Leben,* part II (Villingen-Schwenningen: Farca Verlag, 1999), 330–32.

57 Ibid., 330. "Viele Einwohner des Dorfes waren gekommen, auch Rußland Deutsche. Der Organisator der Reise, Georg Gehann, begrüßte in einer Ansprache die Teilnehmer der Feier und unterstrich, 'daß wir als Freunde gekommen sind, mit der guten Absicht, die Freundschaft zwischen den beiden Völkern aufzubauen, damit es nie wieder Krieg gäbe.' Wir reichten uns mit den Russen die Hände, sangen dann die erste Strophe des Siebenbürgenliedes und beteten gemeinsam ein Vaterunser. Kein Auge blieb dabei trocken. Im Anschluß sang eine russische Sängerin ein stimmungsvolles Lied, und es wurden auch von seiten der Einheimischen kurze Ansprachen gehalten, in denen sie die Bereitwilligkeit unterstrichen, das Kreuz mit der Gedenktafel zu Ehren der Verstorbenen zu betreuen."

58 Wieck, *A Childhood under Hitler and Stalin,* 160.

59 Ibid., 193.

60 Deichelmann, *Ich sah Königsberg sterben,* 94.

61 Eyewitness report no. 171 by Hermann Balzer of Königsberg in Schieder, *The Expulsion of the German Population*, 193.

62 Linck, *Königsberg 1945–1948*, 58–59.

63 Deichelmann, *Ich sah Königsberg sterben*, 112–13. Linck (*Königsberg 1945–1948*, 95–96) describes this same incident but attributes the sale of human flesh on the black market to two Germans who were arrested and sentenced to death. Rörup (*Also sprach Vielliebchen*, 102) also reported that human flesh was sold on the market.

64 Wieck, *A Childhood under Hitler and Stalin*, 187.

65 Linck, *Königsberg 1945–1948*, 96–97.

66 Beckhern and Dubatow, *Die Königsberg Papiere*, 132–33.

67 Hannelore Müller, "Königsberg 1945–1948: Das war unsere Befreiung, Erinnerung 1995," in Ewert, Pollmann, and Müller, *Frauen in Königsberg 1945–1948*, 65–181.

68 Ibid., 147. "Wir hatten überhaupt keine Verbindung zur Außenwelt. Uns schien, wir waren vergessen."

69 Ibid., 152. "Möge Gott mein Kind, meine liebe Hanneli, nicht verlassen und einen guten Menschen in den Weg geben, der sich sie annimmt, bis sie vielleicht im Waisenhaus untergebracht ist."

70 For a description of these clinics, see Luschnat, *Die Lage der Deutschen*, 123–25.

71 These two hospitals were under the overall direction of Dr. Wilhelm Starlinger until he was replaced on August 30, 1946, by a Soviet doctor. Dr. Starlinger was retained in a consulting position until he was relieved of all responsibilities in March 1947. He has described his experiences and the death rates from infectious diseases in these two hospitals in *Grenzen der Sowjetmacht*.

72 Deichelmann, *I sah Königsberg sterben*, 58.

73 Lehndorff, *Token of a Covenant*, 163.

74 Deichelmann, *Ich sah Königsberg sterben*, 72.

75 Lehndorff, *Token of a Covenant*, 188.

76 Linck, *Königsberg 1945–1948*, 55–56.

77 Wieck, *A Childhood under Hitler and Stalin*, 186. Günter Grass, in his memoir *Peeling the Onion*, 175–90, wrote that he first experienced real hunger during the time he spent in a large prisoner-of-war camp in the Upper Palatinate in 1945. While there, he enrolled in a cooking course (one of many offered by inmates for inmates in the camp) to assuage his ever-present hunger. Although the instruction was completely theoretical, i.e., there were no ingredients and nothing was in fact cooked, a professional chef, now POW, made his lectures so

vivid that Grass used his imagination to savor the delicacies "prepared" by the chef, which eased his hunger pangs and made him into a lifelong amateur chef.

78 The story was told to the author and his wife when they were on the same tour group in the summer of 1993.

79 Rörup, *Also sprach Vielliebchen,* 20–22.

80 Starlinger, *Grenzen der Sowjetmacht,* 29, reported that the daily rations at the two epidemic hospitals under his direction consisted on average for each patient of four hundred grams of water-soaked bread, a little fish, a few grams of sugar and fat, and now and then some canned goods. Altogether, this daily fare amounted to roughly one thousand calories, i.e., half of the current recommended daily caloric intake in the United States. When deliveries of food from the military administration ceased completely in the first half of May, the patients received only green soup made from nettles, orach, and the leaves of young linden trees, ("Brennesel, Melde, und junges Lindenlaub") and other edible plants.

81 Ibid., 18.

82 Ibid., 40.

83 Deichelmann, *Ich sah Königsberg sterben,* 147. This change in the status of Königsberg to Kaliningrad and East Prussia to Kaliningrad Oblast is now politically correct and has been recognized by the U.S. Passport Agency in the passport issued to the author's wife, who was born in Königsberg before World War II. In her U.S. passports issued before 2006, her place of birth was given as Germany, but in the passport re-issued that year, her place of birth was changed to Russia. She was upset because this change erroneously implies that she is Russian rather than German. Indeed, on two occasions when she showed her passport to an immigration officer at an airport in Europe, she was addressed in Russian by the officer.

84 Weick, *A Childhood under Hitler and Stalin,* 173, reported that he and his family were forced to move six times during the Russian rule in Königsberg. Another eyewitness described the situation as follows: "The Germans, who had succeeded in finding adequate quarters, and in putting furniture into them out of apartments which had been left, had repeatedly to quit their quarters, mostly at very short notice, in order to accommodate Russian civilians who were moving in; the Russians determined what things were to be left in the quarters, which had to be evacuated. Thus I had to evacuate my apartment at 4–8 Arno-Holz Street in May 1946 within 2 hours…." Eyewitness report no. 171, Schieder, *The Expulsion of the German Population,* 194.

85 Deichelmann, *Ich sah Königsberg sterben,* 150.

86 Eyewitness report no. 179 in Schieder, *The Expulsion of the German Population*, 206.

87 Deichelmann, *Ich sah Königsberg sterben*, 142. "Aber mitten im Lachen spürt man den heimlichen Schmerz der Enttäuschung. Wenn man drüben so wenig ahnt, was bei uns wirklich los ist, wenn es tatsächlich gelungen ist, all dieses Entsetzliche, was seit 15 Monaten an uns geschah und geschieht, so restlos vertuschen, dann—gibt es keine Hilfe für uns."

88 Ibid., 133. Rumors are also described on pages 51, 55, 61, 63, and 95 in Deichelmann's book.

89 Eyewitness report no. 179, in Schieder, *The Expulsion of the German Population*, 207.

90 Kibelka, *Wolfskinder*, 85.

91 "The Lithuanians Had Mercy On Us," in Kurth, *Documents of Humanity*, 105–6. The author of this report did not wish to have her name published.

92 Rörup, *Also sprach Vielliebchen*, 96. Another young East Prussian girl, Hannelore Müller, also went to Lithuania and worked on a farm, where she ate the same tasty treat as Iris Rörup: "Ich bekam zu essen, was in jener Zeit am meisten zählte. Auf dem Bauernhof lernte ich Salzkartoffeln mit dicker Milch und Schmand kennen. Dieses Gericht gab es häufig, und es schmeckte jedesmal köstlich." Ewert, Pollmann, and Müller, *Frauen in Königsberg 1945–1948*, 162–63.

93 Ruth Kibelka provides a comprehensive description of the fate of these children in her book, *Wolfskinder*.

94 Ibid., 207–8.

95 Ibid., 209–18.

96 Ibid., 217–18. "Litauen wurde meine zweite Heimat, hier bin ich groß geworden, habe viel erlebt und den größten Teil meines Lebens verbracht. Hier habe ich gute Freunde, ich liebe und ehre das arbeitsame litauische Volk. Im Gedanken kehre ich jedoch immer wieder in meine Geburtsstadt, nach Königsberg, zurück, die in meiner Erinnerung eine wunderschöne Stadt voller historischer Sehenswürdigkeiten war. Niemals werde ich die hübsche Umgebung vergessen.... Es ist sehr schmerzhaft, mitansehen zu müßen, wie heute, fast fünfzig Jahre nach Kriegsende, das ganze ehemalige Nordostenpreußen total heruntergewirtschaftet und verwahrlost ist.... Das tut weh, aber mit den Jahren, manchmal mehr, manchmal weniger, ziehen mich unbestimmte Kräfte dorthin. Und ich fahre, wie konnte ich nicht fahren."

97 There is an extensive literature in Polish on the subject of the takeover and settlement of that territory of prewar Germany that was acquired by Poland

at the end of World War II. However, linguistic limitations have prevented the author from making use of these sources. One Polish publication dealing specifically with the takeover of southern East Prussia is Gieszczynski, *The Role of the State Office for Repatriation*. The author is indebted to Mrs. Regina Frackowiak, Reference Librarian, European Division, Library of Congress, for bringing this book to his attention and for translating a selected passage.

98 Zeidler, *Kreigsende in Osten*, 168–69.

99 Gieszczynski, *The Role of the State Office for Repatriation*, 13. The Masurian Research Institute was founded on March 18, 1943, in Radość, near Warsaw, by a group of pro-Polish Masurians from the district of Soldau. It developed a program for the takeover of Masuria (the southern part of what became Polish East Prussia) by Poland. See Kossert, *Masuren: Ostpreußens vergessener Süden*, 360.

100 Quoted in Claudia Kraft, "Who is a Pole, and Who a German? The Province of Olsztyn in 1945," in Ther and Siljak, eds., *Redrawing Nations*, 110.

101 Ibid., 111.

102 Ibid., 113.

103 Naimark, *Fires of Hatred*, 153.

104 Nitschke, *Wysiedlenie ludnosci niemieckiej z Polski w latach 1945–1949*, (*The Expulsion of the German Population from Poland 1945–1949*), 306. "Der deutsche Arbeiter wurde maximal ausgenutzt, solange er nötig war d.h. bis man für seine Stelle einen Polen gefunden hatte. Dann mußte der Deutsche so schnell wie möglich zum Aussiedlertransport."

105 Kraft, "Who is a Pole," in Ther and Siljak, eds., *Redrawing Nations*, 110.

106 Ibid., 114.

107 Ibid., 112.

108 Quoted in Naimark, *Fires of Hatred*, 127

109 Eyewitness report no. 187 in Schieder, *The Expulsion of the German Population*, 207– 18.

110 Ibid., 213.

111 Ibid., 215.

112 Eyewitness report no. 189, in Schieder, *Dokumentation der Vertreibung der Deutschen*, vol. I, part 2, 198. "Der Schrecken von Schönwiese ist Lubich Witkowski, der Polizist, von uns Schönwiesern ganannt 'Lulatsch,' ein 19-jähriger, großmauliger Lümmel, ein Schweinhund. Durch sein Schreckensregiment wird Schönwiese das berüchtigste Dorf im ganzen Umkreis...."

113 German featherbeds were particularly sought after by Polish vagabonds looking for booty: "In the late summer of 1945 the Russian occupiers moved on and

our region became Polish.... Settlers came from White Russia and from the region of Vilnius, but, unfortunately, there were as well groups of vagabonds who were also rootless and they robbed anything that wasn't nailed down fast, above all the featherbeds. These were just basic things, how would we survive the East Prussian winter without warm featherbeds?" ("Im späten Sommer 1945 zogen die russischen Besätzer weiter, unsere Region wurde polnisch.... Siedler aus Weißrußland, aus dem Wilnaer Gebiet, kamen, aber leider noch dazu vagabundierende Gruppen, die auch entwurzelt waren, und diese haben noch geraubt, was nicht niet- und nagelfest war, vor allen Dingen auch die Betten. Das waren ja nun elementare Dinge, wie würden wir die ostpreußichen Winter überstehen ohne warme Federbetten?"). Eyewitness report by Traudel Heyn-Schrade, "Lichtenau-Braniewo," in Karp and Traba, *Nachkriegsalltag in Ostpreußen*, 52.

114 Eyewitness report no. 189, in Schieder, *Documentation der Vertreibung der Deutschen*, vol. I, part 2, 199.

115 Eyewitness report by Johannes Gehrmann, "Zusammenleben mit Polen," in Karp and Traba, *Nachkriegsalltag in Ostpreußen*, 308–9.

116 Eyewitness report no. 187, in Schieder, *The Expulsion of the German Population*, 218.

117 Eyewitness report no. 184, in Schieder, *Documentation der Vertreibung der Deutschen*, vol. I, part 2, 165–69.

118 Hildegard Diehl, "Auf 'eigenem' Hof," in Karp and Traba, *Nachkriegsalltag in Ostpreußen*, 403–7.

119 Lehndorff, *Token of a Covenant*, 297–98.

120 Ibid., 301.

121 Dr. Fritz Schilling, "Orkan in Ostpreußen," in Joachim Hensel, ed., *Medizin in und aus Ostpreußen*, 75–103.

122 The governor ("*Wojewode*") of the Allenstein (Olsztyn) region issued a detailed directive on August 6, 1946, which described the plan for the compulsory transfer of German intelligentsia on August 14. Paragraph 2 of this directive states the plan's purpose: "The action has to take place. Its goal is the deportation of above all the German intelligentsia such as teachers, ministers, doctors, and other undesirable persons, who, especially in regard to the verification, are opponents and an unwanted factor. "Die Aktion hat sofort zu erfolgen, ihr Ziel ist die Aussiedlung vor allem der deutschen Intelligenz wie Lehrer, Priester, Ärzte und anderer lästiger Personen, die besonders im Bereich der Verifizierung ein Widerstand leistender und unerwünschter Faktor sind." This directive is

reproduced as Document 286 in Borodziej and Lemberg, "*Unsere Heimat ist uns ein fremdes Land geworden...*," 556–59.

123 Kossert, *Ostpreußen—Geschichte und Mythos*, 349.

124 Ibid., 354.

125 Glass and Bredenberg, *Der Kreis Sensburg*, 126–27.

126 Ibid., 128.

127 Eyewitness report no. 372 in Schieder, *Dokumentation der Vertreibung der Deutschen*, vol. I, part 3, 878. "Wir wurden immer wieder gefragt, warum wir nicht unterschreiben wollen. Unsere Antworten waren überzeugend und begründet genug, und doch hat niemand das Gebäude verlassen, der nicht zur Unterschrift gezwungen wurde. Immer wieder wurde uns gesagt, dieses Land ist vor 700 Jahre polnisch gewesen und die Leute die hier wohnen, müssen zurückgegliedert werden zu Polen, weil das ihre Stammeseltern waren. Deutsche seien hinter der Oder." This and ten similar reports from the district of Sensburg in the same author's volume paint a grim picture of the brutal measures undertaken by the Polish authorities in the period from 1949 to 1952 to force the remaining Germans there to declare themselves Polish.

128 Beckherrn and Dubatow, *Die Königsberg Papiere*, 155.

129 This memorandum is reproduced in ibid., 157–58.

130 Ibid., 158, "Da die deutsche Bevölkerung ... die Erschließung des neuen sowjetischen Gebietes negative beinflußt, sehe ich es als zweckmäßig, die Frage einer organisierten Aussiedlung der Deutschen in die Sowjetische Besatzungszone Deutschlands aufzuwerfen."

131 These three documents are reproduced in Eisfeld and Herdt, *Deportation, Sondersiedlung, Arbeitsarmee*, 469–73. "Über die Umsiedlung der Deutschen aus dem Gebiet Kaliningrad der RSFSR in die Sowjetische Besatsungszone Deutschlands."

132 This order is reproduced in Beckherrn and Dubatow, *Die Königsberg Papiere*, 201–4.

133 In the summer of 1993, the author and his wife visited Kaliningrad with a German tour group, and the Russian guide was able to obtain permission for the group to visit Pillau, now called Baltiisk.

134 Linck, *Königsberg 1945–1948*, 141.

135 Ibid., 186–91.

136 Deichelmann, *Ich sah Königsberg sterben*, 285.

137 Ibid., 286, "Der Hut, den ich trage, ist das Erbe eines Verhungerten. Mein Stock is Nachlaß einer Verhungerten, alles was ich am Körper trage, stammt

von Menschen, die den Qualen Kaliningrads zum Opfer fielen. Wir, die wir die Stadt verlassen, leben nur, weil andere durch ihr Weichen das Weiterleben ermöglichten, weil wir gerade noch kräftiger waren als die anderen, die uns ihre Nahrung, ihre Kleidung, ihren Arbeitsplatz lassen mußten. Wer von uns Deutschland wiedersehen darf, hat Glück gehabt, das Glück eines von vieren, eines von sechsen. Ein letzter Blick im Vorbeifahren zu den Trümmern der alten Universität, zum Dom, zum Grab des großen Königsberger Philosophen. Jeder is mit sich und seinen Gedanken beschäftigt. Die feuchtkalte Märzluft auf dem rasch fahrenden, offenen Wagen bläst unbarmherzig durch. Dicke Wolken am Himmel versprechen Schnee."

138 Ibid., 288.

139 Falk, *Ich blieb in Königsberg,* 141.

140 Claudia Kraft, "Flucht, Vertreibung und Zwangsaussiedlung der Deutschen aus der Wojewodschaft Allenstein (Wojewodztwo Olsztynskie) in den Jahren 1945 bis 1950," in Borodziej and Lemberg, *"Unsere Heimat ist uns ein fremdes Land geworden…,"* 456.

141 Cited in ibid., 457. "Durch die Inkraftsetzung von Vergeltungsrechten und Normen, wie sie während der Okkupation von den Deutschen gegenüber den Polen angewendet wurden, und in den Bedingungen geschaffen werden aufgrund deren Ausreise aus den Gebieten des Bezirks für sie zu einem Segen wird." The full text of the document from which this quote is taken is reproduced as Document 258, dated September 11, 1945, in Borodziej and Lemberg, *"Unsere Heimat ist uns ein fremdes Land geworden…,"* 514–16.

142 Document 260, in ibid., 517–21.

143 Ibid., 520, "daß die Einheiten der Bürgermiliz die Ausreisenden an den Sammelpunkten in Empfang nehmen und sie bis zum Augenblick der Abfahrt des Zuges eskortieren und bewachen."

144 Ibid., 521, "Sie, Bürger Starosten, sollten, indem Sie das Gewicht und die Bedeutung der Frage der Abschiebung der Deutschen richtig einzuschätzen wissen, alle Ihnen zu Gebote stehenden Mittel nutzen, diese Aktion so durchzuführen, daß es Ende Oktober 1945 keinen einzigen Deutschen mehr im Bezirk Masuren gibt."

145 The first estimate is contained in Document 255, ibid., 510–11, and the second in Document 270, ibid., 534.

146 Claudia Kraft, "Flucht, Vertreibung, und Zwangssiedlung," in ibid., 458.

147 Eyewitness report no. 313, in Schieder, *Dokumentation der Vertreibung der Deutschen,* vol. I, part 3, 719–21.

148 Eyewitness reports no. 314, 315, and 316 in ibid., 721–25.

149 Eyewitness report no. 314, in ibid., 722, "Am nächsten Morgen began der Marsch nach Osterode. Es war ein herrlicher Morgen! Nie in meinem Leben werde ich dieses Bild vergessen. Der Nebel hob sich über dem großen Drewenzee. Oben strahlende Sonne und blauer Himmel. Die Birken strahlten goldüberrieselt und die Wälder leuchteten in diesen herrlichen Herbstfarben, wie sie nur einmal der ostpreußische Herbst hervorbringt! Es war, als wollte uns der Herrgott diese einmalige Schönheit recht tief in die Seele brennen, daß wir unser geliebtes Ostpreußen in der Fremde nicht vergessen! Dazu auf der Chausse dieser kilometerlange, nicht abreissende Elendszug, aus der Heimat getrieben!"

150 Eyewitness report no. 316, in ibid., 725.

151 Eyewitness report no. 317, in Schieder, *The Expulsion of the German Population*, 305.

152 Ibid., 305–6.

153 Eyewitness report no. 316 in Schieder, *Dokumentation der Vertreibung der Deutschen*, vol. I, part 3, 725. "In der Nacht stand unser Zug auf einem Abstellgleis in Dt.-Eylau. An der Bahnböschung standen Polen mit ihren Fuhrwerken. Polnische Männer gingen lärmend, schießend, schlagend und raubend durch die Waggons. Mein Mann hatte inzwischen einen Schlaganfall und Krämpfe bekommen und war bewußtlos. Trotz meiner Bitten riß man unter dem Kranken das letzte Kissen vor und zog ihm die Stiefel aus. Mir nahm man das letzte Gepäck fort. Späterhin brachte mir ein Pole als das Wertvollste Brot zurück, einen Blechteller und einen deutschen leeren Soldatentornister. Das war alles, was ich noch besaß. Am 11. November 1945 kamen wir in der Mittagszeit in Rostock an, bekamen wir vom DRK [Deutsches Rotes Kreuz], das erste warme Essen und kamen in ein Lager. Mein Mann war tot. Gott hatte ihn von allem Leid erlöst."

154 For a discussion of this dilemma facing the Polish authorities, see Kraft, "Einleitung," in "Flucht, Vertreibung und Zwangsaussiedlung," 460–64.

155 Document 286 in Borodziej and Lemberg, "*Unsere Heimat ist uns ein fremdes Land geworden...*," 556–59.

156 Document 109, ibid., 245, stated that the departing Germans should be provided with food for four days, which would consist of eight hundred grams of bread, eighty grams of fat, and forty grams of sugar, as well as eighty grams of powdered milk for children up to seven years old and those who were sick.

157 Schilling, "Orkan in Ostpreußen," in Hensel, *Medizin in und aus Ostpreußen*, 102. "Überhaupt muß ich ehrlich sagen, dieser Intelligenz-Transport wurde durchaus human durchgeführt, wenn man von den Plünderungen in Allenstein

absieht. Die Verpflegung wäre, wenn ich nicht dazu gekauft hätte, ausreichend gewesen. Die Fahrt bei dem herrlichen Sommerwetter in den Güterwagen mit offenstehenden Türen war ein Genuß."

158 Ibid., 102. "Aber wie traurig war für jeden Ostpreußen wieder der Anblick des einst so fruchtbaren Landes. Die Felder waren ein einziger großer Distelacker. Die Richtung der Fahrt aber war gut, es ging nach Westen, nicht nach Russland!

Bei sinkender Sonne kamen wir hinter Deutsch-Eylau über die alte ostpreußsische Grenze. Da wurde uns allen sehr trauig zu Mute, daß wir diese schöne Heimat, die sich mit ihren Oberländer Seen in Abendschein noch einmal in ihre ganzen Pracht zeigte, verlassen mußten. Auch mir war dieses herrliche Land in 19 Jahren zur Heimat geworden. Hier lagen die Gräber so vieler Lieben, in Goldap das meiner Mutter, in Lyck das meiner erste Frau, in Metgethen das meiner Schwester und weit, weit in Nordosten, in Estland, das meines lieben Jungen! Alle hatten wir Tränen in den Augen, und wehmütig erklangen aus den rollenden Wagen die alten ostpreußischen Heimatlieder. Ja. 'Land der dunklen Wälder und kristallen Seen!' Manche sprachen die Hoffnung aus, bald in die Heimat zurückkehren zu können. Aber Ruth und ich wußten, es war ein Abschied für immer."

159 Kraft, "Flucht, Vertreibung und Zwangsaussiedlung," 466.
160 Kraft, "Flucht, Vertreibung und Zwangsaussiedlung," 477 n. 149.
161 Ibid., 469.
162 Directive no. 314, September 15, 1947, in Borodziej and Lemberg, "*Unsere Heimat ist uns ein fremdes Land geworden...,*" 601–5.
163 Kraft, "Flucht, Vertreibung und Zwangsaussiedlung," 475.
164 For Polish sources, see Kraft, "Flucht, Vertreibung und Zwangsaussiedlung," 476 n. 144.
165 Eyewitness report no. 374, in Schieder, *Expulsion of the German Population,* 340–41.
166 Ibid., 341.
167 Ibid., 341.
168 Kossert, *Masuren—Ostpreußens vergessener Süden,* 371–72.
169 Kossert, *Preußen, Deutsche, oder Polen,* 331.
170 Ibid., 332.
171 Quoted in ibid., 333, "Was die Preußen in mehr als 400 Jahren nicht geschafft haben, das haben wir Polen in einer Generation geschafft, nämlich, aus den Masuren bewußte Deutsche zu machen."

CHAPTER VII

DECIDING THE FATE OF
EAST PRUSSIA

On the night of May 8–9, 1945, World War II came to an end when
Germany surrendered unconditionally to the Allies. Even before the
surrender took place, both Poland and Russia were already operating as the
new rulers of East Prussia, though the final decision on the disposition of this
German province was only reached by Churchill (and later, Attlee), Stalin,
and Truman at the Potsdam Conference in early August 1945. How did this
decision come about? What led to the extinction of East Prussia as a part of
Germany?

The Soviet Union, the United Kingdom, and the United States were in
agreement long before the Potsdam Conference that East Prussia should be
excised from Germany. They shared a hatred of Prussia, which was seen as
the locus of German militarism and territorial expansionist ambitions, and
the province of East Prussia was associated with the worst Prussian traits. The
Allies viewed the elimination of this easternmost German province as a necessary step to reduce the risk of another war. This step was particularly important for the Soviet Union because it would thus be able to establish a major
military base in central Europe. It also enabled Poland to achieve its long-
standing objectives to reclaim what it regarded as historically Polish territory
and to improve its defensive position vis-à-vis Germany. The Allies were also
unanimous that Germans should be evicted from the land awarded to Russia

and Poland once the boundaries of post–World War II Europe had been redrawn. This expulsion was seen as the only long-term solution to avoiding conflict with German minorities. The Americans and British had some concerns about the hardship that would be imposed on Germans by their forced transfer to what remained of Germany in the west, but they had no compunction about the necessity of uprooting millions of Germans from their homes.

A. Polish Views on East Prussia before the First Conference of World War II Allies at Teheran

As described in Chapter I, the fate of East Prussia had been linked to that of her eastern neighbor, Poland, for centuries. In light of later history, it is ironic that the settlement of East Prussia began in 1226, when the Polish duke, Conrad of Masovia, called on the German Teutonic Order for assistance in subduing the heathen Prussen tribes. The Teutonic Order obliged and successfully governed this territory, but in 1410 suffered an almost fatal blow when its forces were decisively defeated at a village near Tannenberg by a joint Lithuanian-Polish army. In this weakened position, the Teutonic Order had to accept the terms of the Second Peace of Thorn, signed on October 19, 1466, whereby its eastern territory—later East Prussia—continued to be ruled by a grand master, but was now separated from German territory in the west by lands governed by the Polish crown. Thus, already in the fifteenth century the easternmost German territory was vulnerable to encroachment by Poland. The growing Prussian might in the seventeenth century, the partitions of Poland in the eighteenth century, and the extended reach of the German empire in the nineteenth century provided protection for East Prussia during this period. However, Germany's defeat in the two world wars led to the re-emergence of an independent Polish state, which finally realized its claim to part of East Prussia as historically Polish territory.

At the Versailles Peace Conference in 1919, Polish representatives had already made the case that the southern part of East Prussia was Polish and that the rest of the province should be detached from Germany. Roman Dmowski—head of the Polish National Democratic movement—presented Polish demands at a meeting of the Council of Ten on January 29, 1919, for a return to the Polish western boundaries as of 1772, i.e., before the First Partition, together with all of Upper Silesia and the ethnically Polish districts of East Prussia.[1] Similarly, a report by Polish academics for the Paris Peace Conference insisted that the part of East Prussia heavily populated by Poles should be incorporated into Poland: "All the POLISH DISTRICTS OF EAST PRUSSIA, namely the whole regency of Allenstein, together with the district of Olecko, MUST BELONG TO POLAND…." It went on to argue that: "The German part of East Prussia must NOT BE ALLOWED TO FORM ONE STATE WITH BRANDENBURG AS IN 1618. This led to the worse consequences. East Prussia, as the German Republic of Königsberg, can only be a perfectly neutral state under the protection and close control of the League of Nations or of a mandatory. This mandatory ought to be the Polish Republic, which has a historical right to East Prussia and had never done any wrong to its inhabitants." (The capitalized words are in the original text.)[2]

On March 18, 1919, the Commission on Polish Affairs of the Versailles Conference came out in favor of the Polish demands. However, the prime minister of Great Britain, David Lloyd George—who, according to some authors, had little confidence in Poland's capacity to govern itself—intervened and was successful in having the commission's proposals modified in Germany's favor.[3] Instead of the southern part of East Prussia being handed over without conditions to Poland, those living in this area were given the opportunity to vote in a plebiscite. This took place on July 11, 1920, and as described in Chapter I, the overwhelming majority voted to be part of Germany.[4] East Prussia thus remained German after World War I, but it was cut off from the rest of Germany by the Polish Corridor because the Versailles Peace Treaty allocated a considerable part of West Prussia to Poland to enable it to have access to the Baltic.

In the interwar period, 1919–1939, many publications appeared in Polish arguing that East Prussia was Polish territory and was a threat to Poland. Four of these have been conveniently summarized in English.[5] Stanislav Bukoviecki, who served as attorney general in the 1920s in Poland, published a pamphlet in 1922 with the English title, "The Policy of Independent Poland: Sketch of a Programme." He was a moderate who rejected the extremist views of the nationalist party, the National Democrats, and in the following passage he conveys a benign view of German colonization and development of its eastern territories:

> The Germans as a race had settled on these lands in very ancient times, long before the partition of Poland. Subsequently, they developed their colonization of the territories in a natural manner, as well as by means of coercion, and they became indigenous to such an extent that whole districts within these territories, especially the larger and smaller towns, became distinctly German in character. The German owners of Polish territories…introduced a rational administration which was advantageous to the occupied territory, since they succeeded in raising the cultural level of the country in all directions.[6]

While Bukoviecki praised the Germans for the economic development of their eastern lands, he nonetheless insisted that they lived there as "owners of Polish territories" and that "even the most intensive German labour could not legitimatize its ownership, because it was the labour of an unlawful owner" (p. 27). He singled out East Prussia as a particularly important thorn in Poland's side:

> And East Prussia, which occupies such a central position in the northern part of the Polish territory—does it not for us represent perpetual threat? Is a real connection with the sea and the necessary development of our navigations and commerce to be reconciled with Germany's possession of this territory?
>
> One may criticize the configuration of the boundaries of the Poland of today…but these boundaries in general are in accordance with our interests and do not constitute a danger to Poland.

It is otherwise in the case of East Prussia. Here lies for the Polish organism a particularly painful and, at the same time, particularly important spot. East Prussia penetrates the territory of the Polish Republic to a considerable depth; its frontier from Dirschau, through Soldau, to Suvalki, is of great length…it prevents our access to the sea in a central and easterly direction, more particularly affecting the north-eastern portion of our State, and compels these portions of our national territories to seek a connection with the sea by a long and circuitous route.[7]

Bukoviecki's moderate approach to the "problem" of East Prussia can be seen in the fact that he eschewed the use of any type of military action but instead hoped that a "rapprochement" between East Prussia and Poland could evolve naturally:

Finally, if we succeed in improving our country, from an economic and cultural point of view, and particularly in the districts neighboring on East Prussia, so that the tales of bad Polish management are refuted by the plain facts, this will undoubtedly have a favorable effect on the "rapprochement" of the East Prussian province to this country, to which East Prussia is united by the most permanent of all bonds, namely, by the bond of actual territorial continuity. Precisely this factor of the national geographical position, which outlasts all the ephemeral political conjunctures, however important they may be, and which speaks in favor of Poland, gives us reason to believe that all the difficulties will recede before the laws of natural development.[8]

Another publication that Ernst Hansen summarizes was written by Stanislav Grabski, a leader of the National Democrats who was minister of education and vice-premier in the 1920s. His pamphlet, "Observations concerning the present historical epoch in the development of Poland," appeared in 1923. As a strident nationalist, Grabski asserted Poland's right to those lands with significant Polish minorities, even if—as in the case of East Prussia—they had voted overwhelmingly in 1920 to remain German:

> the Polish people can never recognize the result of the plebiscite in Masuria [in East Prussia] as the final verdict of history. Were Poland to drop the Masurian question, she would deny herself. For one of two things is true: either our State is a Polish State, in which case its highest task is to reunite the national Polish territories; or else our State recognizes its rights only, but not its duties, toward the Polish territories...but in that case our State is not a national Polish State.[9]

Not surprisingly, Grabski was of the view that war over East Prussia was inevitable, but that Poland would be able to win only if it were well prepared militarily and if it first undertook the required political preparation "by the arousing of a Polish national consciousness in the Polish population of East Prussia." Poland fulfilled neither of the two conditions Grabski envisioned for a Polish victory, but he was prophetic insofar as he predicted that Poland would be engulfed "in the inevitable war with Germany, a war into which the latter will hurl herself as soon as she has recuperated from the defeat that she sustained in the Great War."[10]

In the summer of 1939, before the German invasion of Poland on September 1, a leading spokesman for the National Democratic Movement, Jędrzej Giertych, echoed Grabski's territorial objectives for Poland in an unequivocal manner. In an article that appeared in a series entitled, "Polish Districts under German Domination," he wrote:

> after the coming war, should it end with the defeat of Germany, Poland should annex Gdansk [Danzig], East Prussia, Upper and Central Silesia including Wroclaw [Breslau], and Central Pomerania including Kolobrzeg [Kolberg]; [Poland] should also create a chain of small buffer states under her protectorship and occupation in the territory along the lower Oder and even beyond the Lusatian Neisse (i.e., in Lusatia).[11]

The German invasion of Poland in 1939 clearly demonstrated the vulnerability of Poland's western borders, which had been agreed to at the Paris Peace Conference, and confirmed the apprehension expressed by the Polish delegation at the conference regarding the strategic danger posed by German control of East Prussia. The rapid victory of German forces generated discussion among Poles of how Poland's future borders with Germany could be rectified to enhance her future military security. Consideration of Poland's western boundaries appeared in a scholarly publication, called the "West-Slavonic Bulletin," which was printed in Edinburgh between September 1940 and June 1942. A passage from the "Bulletin" describes Polish territorial claims to German territory, which mirror those of Giertych:

> the "Bulletin" defined the frontiers "to which we must raise legitimate claims" as follows: "the Baltic coast from the mouth of the Nieman [Memel] to the island of Rugia [Rügen], the entire Oder basin as well as the basin of the upper Spree." In other words, East Prussia with Danzig, all of Pomerania, Upper and Lower Silesia, and east and southeast Brandenburg "including both banks of the Oder along its middle course," as well as Upper and Lower Lusatia.[12]

Another Polish publication in the early 1940s laying claim to Germany's eastern territory on both ethnic and historical considerations as well as those of Poland's security situation, was a book by Wladyslaw Palucki (under the pseudonym Antoni Blonski), with the English title *Return to the Oder*. Palucki criticized the borders agreed to at Versailles on the grounds that they exposed Poland to attack from the north and the west:

> Historical experience shows all too clearly that the greatness and security of Poland will depend above all on what boundaries we have in the north and west. The war of 1914–1918 did, to be sure, restore us to independence, but our independence...was neither complete nor secure.... [A]t the time of the conclusion of

the Versailles Peace, the western world, despite previous experiences, did not understand that Poland must either be large, with permanent and natural boundaries and broad access to the sea, or she will not be at all; and without her there will neither be peace nor equilibrium in Europe.[13]

In the north, Palucki proposed the inclusion of East Prussia and Danzig within the borders of postwar Poland, thereby eliminating what he called an "unprecedented historical-geographic monstrosity," and in the west Poland should seek the shortest possible border with Germany, which would "satisfy in every respect [her] strategic requirements."[14]

It should be emphasized that the publications cited here did not in any way link the issue of Poland's eastern frontier with the Soviet Union to the shift they proposed in Poland's borders with Germany. This shift in Poland's western and northern frontier to the vicinity of the Oder and Neisse rivers meant swallowing the whole of East Prussia. The western and northern extensions of Poland's boundaries were justified as the rightful return of territory that belonged to Poland on the basis of historical and ethnic considerations. These extensions of Poland's borders were also seen as necessary both to correct the errors of the Paris Peace Conference, which had made Poland vulnerable to German attack, and to make Poland a fully viable and functioning economic entity. It is ironic that Poland, in fact, achieved more or less these border adjustments in the west and north, but not primarily for these reasons. Rather, as explained below, the Soviet Union, the United Kingdom, and the United States awarded this territory to Poland at the meeting in Potsdam as compensation for a large swath of land taken by Russia on Poland's eastern frontier.

These views were largely shared by General Władysław Sikorski, prime minister of the Polish government-in-exile from its inception in Paris in September 1939 through its transfer to London in June 1940 until his death in an airplane accident in July 1943. Early in World War II before Germany invaded the Soviet Union, Sikorski laid out in a comprehensive memorandum his concept on what would be required for a viable Polish state in the postwar world. This document was delivered to the British Labor Party leader, Ernest Bevin, on November 19, 1940, because Sikorski believed that he was likely to be more sympathetic to the Polish cause than the then British foreign minister, Lord Halifax, who received it the following day. The document began with an historical overview of the growth of Germany's industrial and military might over the last one hundred years and advocated territorial changes that would weaken Germany both strategically and economically to prevent future aggression. One section dealt with the issue of East Prussia and is quoted here at length because it clearly delineates long-standing Polish concerns with the German province related to the requirements of a viable Polish state:

> The definite and final settlement of the secular conflict between Poland and Germany over the free access of Poland to the sea. This question, which, as far as Poland is concerned, was always of fundamental importance, has increased in importance to-day.... The Germans attempted twice—in the 18th century and contemporaneously—to resolve this conflict by the annexation to Germany of the Polish maritime province of Pomorze [Pomerania]. From the Polish point of view, the only solution which would prevent the interminable recurrence of this conflict would be the union of East Prussia and Danzig with Poland, which, *inter alia*, would put an end to the incessant German claims to a territorial connexion between Germany proper and East Prussia. The union of East Prussia with Poland would deprive Germany of the principal German outpost in the East, the only importance of which, as far as the Reich is concerned, rests on the fact that it constitutes a convenient bridge-head for Germany's expansion in the East of Europe. It would be one of the most effective blows aimed against German imperialism. Moreover, Poland would cease, as she was in 1939, to be threatened by Germany on two fronts, the western and the northern, of which the latter (East Prussia) dominated the central province of Poland and is removed only about 70 miles from the capital [Warsaw]...if East Prussia and Danzig were to

remain with Germany, it would have to be admitted that the Polish-German dispute which gave rise to the present war, would be perpetuated and continue to threaten with the same dangers.[15]

The Polish ambassador to Great Britain, Count Edward Raczynski, conveyed these same concerns about East Prussia in more graphic terms on January 2, 1941, to Anthony Eden, who had just become the British foreign minister under the new Conservative government. In his account of their conversation, Eden wrote that the ambassador described conditions in Poland under the German occupation as "harsh and cruel" and went on to say:

> In such conditions it was inevitable the Poles, whether in Poland or elsewhere, had one idea for the future: How was the problem of East Prussia to be dealt with? In their view, the future existence of Poland would continue to be indefensible unless the problem of East Prussia were got rid of. This was a matter of life and death for Poland. With the long arms of East Prussia and Silesia embracing the northern and southern confines of Poland, there was always a ready German pretext available for seizing and holding in subjection the 10 million Poles who lived in the territories between these two arms. Hitler had given them an example of how to deal with these population problems. Great movements of peoples which had been thought impossible twenty years ago were now being carried out in Eastern Europe with German thoroughness. It would be necessary one day to solve the problem of East Prussia. The Ambassador gave me the very clear impression that he thought that the problem could only be solved by a mass movement of the German population from that territory back to Germany.[16]

The Polish view was unequivocal: East Prussia had to be absorbed once and for all by Poland in order to reduce the threat Germany posed to its existence, and the solution of the "problem of East Prussia" required the expulsion of Germans from this territory. Thus the issue of the future territorial configuration of Poland was inextricably linked to the question of the fate of Germans living in Poland's newly acquired lands. It is highly ironic that Count Raczynski used the Nazi Germanization plans in their occupied territories in central and eastern Europe (the "*Generalplan Ost*" described in Chapter II) as a precedent for the transfer of Germans living in East Prussia. Moreover, the extreme brutality of the German occupying forces and the harsh manner in which they had forcibly resettled Poles and other eastern Europeans precluded any basis for the peaceful coexistence of German minorities living in Eastern Europe and contributed to their forced removal to Germany after the end of the war.[17]

Another irony is that the Poles recognized that their claims for postwar territorial acquisitions were inconsistent with the Atlantic Charter.[18] This charter was the result of the Atlantic Conference between Churchill and Roosevelt that took place August 9–12, 1941, on two warships off the coast of Newfoundland. The Atlantic Charter, issued on August 14, established common principles to guide nations in the postwar world. The second of these supported the right of self-determination: "Second, they [Churchill and Roosevelt] desired to see no territorial changes that do not accord with the freely expressed wished of the peoples concerned." When the Polish ambassador, Raczynski, visited Foreign Secretary Eden on August 18, 1941, according to Eden, he broached his concerns regarding the application of this principle to Polish designs on East Prussia:

> the Anglo-American 8-point declaration [Atlantic Charter], which, by its insistence on the principle of self-determination, would disappoint Polish hopes as regards their western frontier.... Danzig was undoubtedly a German town, but it was for economic reasons essential to Poland, and so long as Germans were in East Prussia, Poland's Western frontier was, from a military point of view, almost indefensible.... The Ambassador therefore suggested that...His Majesty's government might make some public

statement, or at any rate some communication to the Polish Government, to the effect that it was not their intention to insist on a rigid application of the principle of self-determination, to the exclusion of other considerations such as economics and defence. In all honesty, however, he felt bound to say that the 8-point declaration had caused misgivings in Polish opinion.[19]

In response, Eden pointed out that in all probability neither Churchill nor Roosevelt was thinking of the Polish frontiers when they drafted the eight-point declaration, and he emphasized that it would be difficult— except perhaps in the most general terms—for his government to provide an interpretation of that declaration along the lines desired by the Polish government. But the Poles persisted and in a letter to Eden a week later on August 25, the Polish ambassador made the suggestion "…that the British government make a gloss on Article 2 of the Atlantic Charter accepting the Polish right to territorial expansion at German expense."[20] Eden again declined to respond affirmatively to the ambassador's request, adding that it would in any case necessitate American acquiescence. The Poles believed that the Atlantic Charter would be applied uniformly and would protect East Prussia from a Polish takeover, but the Allies had no intention of preserving the easternmost province of Germany. As described in detail below, the Atlantic Charter posed no hindrance whatsoever to Polish territorial gains at Germany's expense because the Allies deemed such gains necessary to compensate Poland for extensive loss of lands on its eastern border with Russia.[21]

General Sikorski made three trips to Washington to consult with President Roosevelt on the progress of the war and postwar planning, and to enlist his assistance in furthering Polish objectives during and after the war. In his discussions with Roosevelt in April 1941, and March 1942, Sikorski likely raised the issue of East Prussia, but documentation is sketchy on this score.[22] No such ambiguity surrounds his third and last visit to Washington in December 1942. General Sikorski's own report of his conversation with Roosevelt on December 2, 1942, was matter-of-fact on the manner in which the fate of East Prussia and its German population was dealt with:

Roosevelt: And now, General, what do you think of the western frontier of Poland?

Sikorski: The frontier must be rectified and include East Prussia and Gdansk (Danzig).

Roosevelt: And what will become of the German population of this province?

Sikorski: They will escape to Germany. As a matter of fact, I think that we will apply the same methods of transfer of the population which the Germans applied to the conquered nations.

Roosevelt: How large is the population of [East] Prussia?

Sikorski: About 2,200,000.

Roosevelt: But this figure includes Poles, too.

Sikorski: A few years ago there were about 700,000 Masurians who will return to their nationality after Germany's defeat.

Roosevelt: That's right. East Prussia must be yours but this is a very difficult problem. We do not intend to finish this war by an armistice or a treaty. Germany must surrender unconditionally. We must dismember her and she must go in quarantine for a long period, perhaps thirty years. We have radically to uproot Hitlerism and build peace on its ruins.[23]

Thus Roosevelt fully supported Sikorski's aim of including East Prussia within Poland's postwar boundaries. While he referred to this as a "very difficult problem," Roosevelt, Churchill, and Stalin in fact never had any qualms about Poland receiving the lion's share of East Prussia. What is also striking in the passage quoted above is that Sikorski cited the methods employed by the Germans to resettle minorities in Eastern Europe as a precedent for how the Poles would transfer Germans from the newly acquired Polish territory, the same argument used by the Polish ambassador. It is clear, therefore, that long before the conclusion of the war and the defeat of Germany, the Polish government-in-exile was already entertaining plans to transfer Germans out of East Prussia.[24] It is also noteworthy that Roosevelt raised no objection to the fate Sikorski envisioned for the East Prussians.

The Polish government-in-exile in London remained tireless in promoting its claim to East Prussia through formal and informal contacts with the British and U.S. governments and through publications available to the general public. One of these summarized the arguments supporting this claim:

The incorporation of East Prussia and Danzig into Poland is justified on the following grounds:

1. The territory concerned forms geographically, historically and economically a unit with Poland.
2. East Prussia, as a German military base dominating Poland, constitutes a permanent danger to her security as well as to that of whole Eastern Europe.
3. East Prussia became the political symbol of the German *Drang nach Osten,* the main excuse of the German territorial claims against Poland and the stronghold of the reactionary *Junker* class. Its incorporation into Poland, together with Danzig, will help clear the atmosphere of Polish-German relations.
4. The incorporation of East Prussia into Poland will make Germany more dependent on food imported from abroad, and will deprive the German Army of a considerable reserve of man power.
5. The loss of East Prussia will weaken Germany politically and strategically, correspondingly strengthening Poland. From an

economic point of view, the gain for Poland will be far greater than the loss for Germany.

6. The final settlement of the problem of East Prussia and Danzig will remove one of the principal causes of friction and unrest in European policy, thus consolidating peace.[25]

B. Views of the Allies Regarding East Prussia before Teheran

The Allies' views on East Prussia were influenced by how they intended to conduct their campaign against their enemy and their plans for Germany after it had been defeated. When it became apparent that the Nazis were waging a war of incredible barbarity, any sympathy which the Allies might have had for the Germans evaporated and they issued many declarations and resolutions condemning German war crimes.[26] The desire to punish Germany for its conduct of the war led to the Allied demand for an unconditional surrender. Roosevelt made this clear at a press conference at the conclusion of his meeting with Churchill at Casablanca in January 1943. Among Roosevelt's notes for this press conference was the following:

> The President and the Prime Minister, after a complete survey of the world war situation, are more than ever determined that peace can come to the world only by the total elimination of German and Japanese war power. This involves the simple formula of placing the objective of this war in terms of an unconditional surrender by Germany, Italy and Japan. Unconditional surrender by them means a reasonable assurance of world peace, for generations. Unconditional surrender means not the destruction of the German populace, nor of the Italian or Japanese populace, but does mean the destruction of a philosophy in Germany, Italy and Japan which is based on the conquest and subjugation of other peoples.[27]

Consistent with the aim of eliminating once and for all Germany's ability to wage war, the Allies discussed at some length the possibility of dismembering

Germany into a few states. They ultimately rejected this idea as impractical and because they feared that splitting up the country might lead to a resurgence of German nationalism.[28] However, Cordell Hull, U.S. secretary of state from 1933 to 1945, reported that Roosevelt was strongly in favor of dismemberment. In a meeting with the president before departing for the foreign ministers' conference in Moscow in October 1943, Hull noted that Roosevelt was adamant that Germany should be partitioned into three or more sovereign states, which should be connected via postal, communication, and transportation networks. The president also insisted that "East Prussia should be detached from Germany, and all dangerous elements of the population should be forcibly removed."[29] In Moscow, the foreign ministers discussed the issue of dismemberment only briefly on October 25 and it did not elicit a great deal of support among them. In his report of this discussion, Hull concluded by saying, "We all agreed that Germany should be made to give up all her conquests and return to her pre-1938 borders, and that East Prussia should be separated from Germany."[30]

The groundwork for this agreement on the fate of East Prussia had been laid much earlier. The first discussion between the Soviets and the British on the issue of allocating part of East Prussia to Poland took place during British Foreign Secretary Anthony Eden's visit to Moscow from December 16–22, 1941, just days after Soviet defenders had stopped the Germans a few miles from Moscow. Eden's mandate was to undertake negotiations aimed at enhancing the cooperation of the two countries in waging war against Nazi Germany. To facilitate the achievement of their own objectives, the Soviets had drafted two treaties: one on mutual military assistance between the Soviet Union and Great Britain during the war, and the other on maintaining peace and security in the postwar world. The first meeting took place at 7:00 p.m. on December 16, attended on the Soviet side by Joseph Stalin, Vyacheslav Molotov (Soviet foreign minister), and Ivan Maisky (Soviet ambassador to Great Britain), and on the British side by Anthony Eden and Richard Cripps (British ambassador to the Soviet Union). Maisky acted as interpreter. Stalin distributed copies of the two draft treaties. After briefly examining them, Eden stated that he did not have any objections in principle, but would need to study them more carefully.

Stalin then mentioned that it would be desirable to attach to the treaty on postwar issues a secret protocol dealing with how European frontiers should be reorganized after the war. Paragraphs 10 and 17 of this protocol dealing with Poland and East Prussia are reproduced in part below:

10. To restore Poland to her 1939 frontiers, leaving the territories of Western Ukraine and Western Belorussia to the USSR except for regions with a predominately Polish population…as well as to increase the territory of Poland at the expense of the western part of East Prussia.

17. In respect to Germany…the following has been found expedient:

    (c)   the division of Germany into a number of independent States with Prussia made into an independent State, the territory of East Prussia being detached from her;

    (d)   part of East Prussia bordering on Lithuania (including Königsberg) shall pass to the USSR for a term of 20 years as a guarantee of compensation for losses sustained in the war with Germany. The other part shall pass to Poland (as stipulated in Paragraph 10).[31]

This is the first definitive written proposal by the Allies for the excision of East Prussia from Germany. As stated above, Stalin specifically claimed the northern third of the German province—including Königsberg—for the Soviet Union, with the remainder to be allocated to Poland. (Already in World War I, it appears that the annexation of East Prussia had been a war objective of Tsarist Russia.[32]) In elaborating on the secret protocol at the meeting, Stalin said, "The western frontier of Poland should encompass East Prussia and the Corridor, and the German population of these regions should be evacuated to Germany."[33] He thus added an issue not mentioned in the official protocol itself, namely, that all Germans in East Prussia should be expelled to Germany. In the subsequent discussion Eden had no difficulties with excising East Prussia from Germany:

"On the question of the future of Poland, he, personally, fully agreed that East Prussia should be within the Polish Republic. He had no grounds to assume that Churchill would be against this. Nonetheless, he could not speak for the Premier at the moment simply because he had never discussed this subject with him."[34]

Thus already in 1941 the Soviet Union and Great Britain had in essence agreed upon the fate of East Prussia and its population, although formal agreement among the three Allies was not reached until the Potsdam Conference in August 1945. The issue was apparently so minor that Eden and Churchill had not discussed it between themselves before Eden's departure to Moscow that December. One can conjecture that after being exposed to the Poles' incessant arguments that East Prussia was rightfully theirs, the British were prepared to support the Soviet proposal. In subsequent discussions among the Allies neither Roosevelt nor Truman raised any objections to the excision of East Prussia and the expulsion of the Germans living there. The end of East Prussia was a foregone conclusion long before final victory over Germany in May 1945.

East Prussia clearly was not the focus of these meetings. In his memoirs, Eden mentioned this easternmost German province only once when he noted that he and Churchill had not yet discussed this issue.[35] The real bone of contention between Eden and Stalin in Moscow was that Stalin wanted Eden to sign the secret protocol. This included a detailed scheme for postwar European borders and, in particular, that the Soviet border with Poland should reflect the Soviet takeover of a large slice of Poland's eastern territory achieved as a result of the Nazi-Soviet Non-Aggression Pact of August 23, 1939 (the Molotov-Ribbentrop Line). In his memoirs, Eden expressed his disappointment with the content of the secret protocol:

> Stalin's suggestions for this protocol showed me that the hope we had held in London, of being able to confine the discussion of frontiers to the general terms of the Atlantic Charter, had been in vain. Russian ideas were already starkly definite. They changed little during the next three years, for their purpose was to secure the most tangible physical guarantees for Russia's future security.[36]

Eden explained at length to Stalin that he could not sign the protocol because he had to consult with Churchill, the British cabinet, and the dominions (Canada, India, and other members of the British Commonwealth), as the latter were also involved in the war effort and he could not bind them to any agreement regarding postwar frontiers without their consent. He also informed Stalin that President Roosevelt had sent a message explicitly requesting that they not engage in any secret arrangement relating to the postwar reorganization of Europe without first consulting him, as Roosevelt did not want to participate in peace treaty discussions only to be confronted with matters that had already been settled without his knowledge. Stalin then asked if the British would at least recognize the Soviet Union's frontiers as they were in 1941 (thereby indicating the particular importance he attached to this extension of Soviet territory). Eden demurred, noting that Churchill had stated publicly that Britain could not recognize alterations in European frontiers that had resulted during the war. Over the course of the meetings in Moscow, Eden and Stalin went back and forth on this issue without reaching any agreement. In Eden's words:

> Stalin...soon made other difficulties and I had to repeat many
> times that we could not now recognize the Russian frontiers of
> 1941, because they affected other countries, one of which, Poland,
> was our ally. I told Stalin that I could not agree to definite frontiers
> without breaking pledges I had already made to other people, and I
> was not going to do that. Stalin merely said: "It is a pity." Molotov
> was completely unhelpful, and the close of our discussion frigid.[37]

Stalin invited the British delegation to a lavish banquet, which took place following the fourth meeting on the evening of December 20. With food very scarce in Moscow at that time, this was a major treat for the Russians present. During the course of the feast, which Eden described as "almost embarrassingly sumptuous," many toasts were made, including one at the stroke of midnight by Eden in honor of Stalin on his sixty-second birthday. The banquet lasted until 5:00 a.m., when Stalin retired. The Moscow meetings concluded officially with a joint communiqué that was completely innocuous, as epitomized by the last sentence: "Both parties are convinced that the Moscow conversations constitute a new important forward step towards closer collaboration between the USSR and Great Britain."[38]

The two sides aimed at such closer collaboration when they met in May 1942. Stalin again sought to obtain recognition from Great Britain of the 1941 Soviet borders and sent Molotov to London to negotiate a treaty that would achieve this Soviet objective. In the first meeting on May 21, Churchill informed Molotov that he was unable to accept the Soviet drafts of a treaty covering a military alliance and postwar collaboration because they were inconsistent with the Atlantic Charter and because they were objectionable to Roosevelt, who was strongly of the view that decisions on national boundaries should await the conclusion of hostilities.

Although the two sides were unable to agree on the Soviet-Polish border, they could see eye to eye on compensating Poland with East Prussia. This topic was discussed at the second meeting on May 21: "Speaking about the substance of the question of the Soviet-Polish frontier, Molotov said that the Soviet Government finds it expedient to satisfy the Poles, as Eden knows from the last December talks in Moscow, at the expense of East Prussia. It was quite legitimate for Germany to make sacrifices for the war against the USSR, Britain, Poland, and other countries."[39] While Britain and the Soviet Union shared the view that East Prussia should be transferred from Germany to Poland, they did not wish this to be mentioned in the treaty they were about to sign in London. The British Foreign Office was sensitive to the effect the detachment of East Prussia could have on German propaganda. To make explicit that Poland would be compensated with German territory was considered ill-advised, as a Foreign Office official noted:

> The question whether we can give any guarantee to Poland about East Prussia has already been considered and turned down. It may be that in our own minds we have already allocated East Prussia to Poland, but to allow this to become known, either directly or indirectly, at the present time, would be a great mistake. It would not only oblige us to give other territorial assurances in Europe, but it would completely wreck our propaganda policy to Germany.[40]

The Soviets had a different reason for not making public the planned transfer of East Prussia to Poland. In the meeting at 3:30 on May 21, Molotov was quoted as stating: "The Soviet point of view was that Poland should be compensated at the expense of Germany by receiving East Prussia. That would be entirely justifiable but it was not suitable that that should be included in the present Treaty. The effect of the British draft would be that the British Government were supporting one side of the Soviet-Polish frontier discussion."[41]

Even though East Prussia would not be mentioned in the treaty, there was already a realization that its transfer to Poland would require the removal of the Germans living there. This issue arose in consideration of Article 4 of the British draft of the treaty:

> In the case of European territories which now are or in consequence of the peace settlement may be placed under a sovereignty other than that under which they were on the 1st January, 1938, the High Contracting Parties recognize the desirability of making appropriate provision in the peace settlement to ensure to inhabitants of such territories who may wish to do so the right to leave such territories without hindrance and to carry their movable property with them.[42]

In the 4:00 p.m. meeting on May 22, 1942, Eden explained to Molotov that Article 4 had been added to take account of American concerns and he noted that the British were also supportive of the principle embodied in this article that the inhabitants of territories under new political authority had the right to leave. Eden then went on to apply this principle to East Prussia: "for instance, if it were agreed to transfer E. Prussia to Poland, it would certainly be desirable that arrangements be made enabling the German population to be removed."[43] Molotov replied that "he quite agreed that this principle should be applied in the case of E. Prussia," but he could not agree to its inclusion in the treaty because it would "encourage all kinds of propaganda on the part of dissatisfied elements" and "incite the inhabitants of the territories in question to make claims against the Soviet Government."[44] Molotov was thinking ahead to the end of the war, when he firmly expected that the Baltic countries would revert to the Soviet sphere of influence, and he was concerned about an exodus of the populations there if the principle of the right to leave were made public.

In the face of deadlocked negotiations over the treaty, Eden drafted an entirely new version that stressed both a wartime and a postwar alliance of the two powers but avoided the contentious issues of postwar frontiers and the mobility of populations. The British were puzzled why the Russians agreed to this new draft so quickly. When Eden and his personal assistant, Oliver Harvey, celebrated the successful outcome of the negotiations at the Ritz Hotel the day after the treaty was signed, Harvey asked, "But why the sudden agreement to the new treaty when they had got us to swallow the principles of the old?"[45] In his memoirs, Eden mentioned his own bafflement at the quick assent on the Russian side:

> The Russian motive in accepting the new text, which contained no mention of frontiers…is obscure. The chief purpose in the Soviet Government's negotiations was to secure a second front in Europe as soon as possible. At some stage in our talks Molotov probably became convinced he could not get his way over frontiers and decided more was to be gained in the military field by accepting our new terms…than by failure to agree.[46]

Now, thanks to access to Stalin's archives, we know why the Soviet side acquiesced so quickly to Eden's unexpected initiative. Molotov had, of course, sent a telegram with the draft of the new treaty to Stalin and asked for instructions as to how he should proceed with the negotiations in London. Stalin replied the same day with an unequivocal directive, part of which is reproduced below:

1. We have received the draft treaty Eden handed you. We do not consider it an empty declaration but regard it as an important document. It lacks the question of the security of frontiers, but this is not bad perhaps, for it gives us a free hand. The question of frontiers, or to be more exact, of

guarantees for the security of our frontiers at one or another section of our country, will be decided by force.

2. We propose amendments to the old draft treaties be discarded and that Eden's Draft uniting the two treaties be accepted as the basis.[47]

What is striking in this passage is the confidence Stalin displays in the Soviet Union's ability to achieve its territorial objectives on its own. In May 1942, the outcome of the war was by no means assured and the key victory of the Red Army against German forces at Stalingrad in January 1943, was still months away. Nevertheless, Stalin had the strong conviction that he would prevail in extending Russia's border to the west at Poland's expense and would compensate Poland with East Prussia and other parts of Germany. His confidence was not unfounded; at the Teheran Conference at the end of 1943 he obtained Churchill's and Roosevelt's acquiescence, in principle, to his territorial objectives.

The Soviet preoccupation with security was not limited to territorial borders but extended to precautions regarding personal safety as well. Churchill described what he termed the "inveterate suspicion by which Russians regarded foreigners," which was manifested during Molotov's stay at Chequers (the British prime minister's country house) when he was negotiating with the British. When the Russians arrived, they asked for keys to all the bedrooms. These were found with some difficulty and thereafter the guests always kept their doors locked. Only the staff at Chequers were allowed to enter the guests' rooms to make up their beds, and when they did so, they found pistols under the pillows. Churchill described the extraordinary precautions by the Soviets to assure Molotov's safety:

His room had been thoroughly searched by his police officers, every cupboard and piece of furniture and the walls and floors being meticulously examined by practiced eyes. The bed was the object of particular attention; the mattresses were all prodded in case of infernal machines, and the sheets and blankets were rearranged by the Russians so as to leave an opening in the middle of the bed out of which the occupant could spring at a moment's notice, instead of being tucked in. At night a revolver was laid out beside his dressing-gown and his dispatch case.[48]

The "infernal machine" Churchill referred to was presumably a device to record Molotov's conversations. No doubt the Soviets must have assumed that the British employed surveillance and bugging measures similar to those that they used on their foreign visitors in Moscow.

C. Preparations for the Teheran Conference

In the run-up to the Teheran Conference (held November 28–December 1, 1943), the American, British, and Soviet foreign ministers held a conference in Moscow from October 18–30 to carry out preparatory work. This was the first time the foreign ministers met to discuss cooperative efforts to wage war against Germany. The British ambassador in Moscow, Sir Archibald Clark Kerr, described the opening session in a telegram sent to Eden after the meeting had concluded:

> The conference opened in an atmosphere of appropriate but unforced politeness and jocularity, perhaps not wholly spontaneous on the part of the Russians. The chairmanship was imposed upon a modest and protesting Molotov. But once he assumed it, it soon became clear that it was the set determination of the Russians to make it a success. Molotov conducted the proceedings with sustained tact and skill and growing good humor, deferring any matter that seemed to threaten prickliness and only referring to it when its thorns had been withdrawn by talks over food and wine. The way he handled the debates impelled our respect and in the end our affection also. He has traveled a long way in the past year and a half.[49]

At this preparatory conference, the U.S. secretary of state, Cordell Hull, presented his counterparts, Eden and Molotov, with a detailed memorandum on the postwar treatment of Germany. Roosevelt had initiated this document in March 1943 and it had been worked on over several months in consultation with the British. The memorandum laid out the principles guiding Germany's unconditional surrender, its treatment during the armistice period, and its permanent status.[50] The question of frontiers was explicitly excluded from the document on the grounds that "[t]his is a matter which should come within the purview of the general settlement," i.e., that it should be a matter for consideration only after the war with Germany had been concluded. Nonetheless, the issue of East Prussia did come up in discussion and there was no disagreement regarding the outcome. Hull reported that at the session held on May 25, "We all agreed that Germany should be made to give up all her conquests and return to her pre-1938 borders, and that East Prussia should be separated from Germany."[51] At the same session there was some consideration of dismembering Germany. Eden said that his government would like to see Germany divided into separate states, and in particular, would favor a separate Prussia. Hull told his counterparts that although the United States was still in favor of dismemberment, convincing arguments could be made on both sides of the issue and there was an increasing tendency to keep an open mind. In his memoirs, Eden reported that he personally had always been opposed to dismemberment.[52] In his report to Roosevelt on the preparatory conference, the U.S. ambassador to the Soviet Union, Averell Harriman, observed that the Russians "did not exclude the possibility of a forced dismemberment of Germany."[53] Regarding reparations from Germany, he stated that the Soviets would be much tougher than the Americans: "Their measure of Germany's capacity to pay reparations in goods and services appears to be based on the concept that the Germans are not entitled to a postwar standard of living higher than the Russians."

As already noted, the American view at the meeting in Moscow was that territorial questions and those relating to borders should be deferred until after the war. However, this did not mean that the U.S. government had not been paying attention to these vital topics. In fact, the State Department set up planning units during the war to deal with postwar issues—especially those related to Poland's frontiers—and to provide recommendations to President Roosevelt.[54] In particular, the Advisory Committee on Postwar Foreign Policy was established on February 12, 1942. Chaired by Hull, it included not only State Department officials but also individuals from the private sector, such as businessmen, journalists, and scientists.[55] The scope of the committee's work expanded with the establishment of a number of specialized subcommittees, including the Subcommittee on Political Problems (chaired first by Undersecretary of State Sumner Wells and then by Secretary of State Hull), the Security Subcommittee (chaired by Norman Davis, at the time chairman of the American Red Cross and president of the Council of Foreign Relations), and the Territorial Subcommittee (chaired by the well-known geographer, Isaiah Bowman, then president of Johns Hopkins University).

At first, some members of the Committee were reluctant to modify the borders of Poland extant at the onset of World War II. Bowman, for example, expressed strong reservations about altering the prewar frontiers in Europe, and, in particular, allowing the borders of Russia and Poland to be shifted to the west, on the grounds that this would endanger western civilization:

> So far as blood and western forms of civilization are concerned it would not have been thought wise to give that great, growing, uncertain, unpredictable mass of Slav populations a chance to move farther west in Europe. Unfortunately national policies have become mixed up with that question of blood, and we are now allies of the greatest Slav power which has this great unpredictability.... It would be too short a view to assume that the Germans were all bad and the Russians were all good....[56]

Bowman was in the minority. The idea of excising East Prussia from Germany and allocating it to Poland was opposed by only one other member of the committee. The economist and diplomat Adolf A. Berle argued that this would involve a difficult and costly transfer of the Germans living in East Prussia and would incite strong anti-Polish feelings on the part of those repatriated. Hamilton Fish Armstrong—the editor of *Foreign Affairs*—proposed in the Territorial Subcommittee that Danzig should be combined with East Prussia and that this territorial unit should become an independent member of an East European federation. Benjamin V. Cohen—a prominent member of the Roosevelt administration—made essentially the same suggestion to the Subcommittee on Political Problems. It is clear from the early discussions in the various committees that the majority had no reservations about excising East Prussia from Germany; rather, the question was whether this easternmost province of Germany should be ceded to Poland and, if so, whether Germany should be compensated for this loss in territory.

Two influential committee members, while agreeing with the others that East Prussia needed to be eliminated from Germany, were unequivocal in their support of the view that Danzig and East Prussia should be incorporated into Poland. One was Leo Pasvolsky, a diplomat and an economist who was a special assistant to Secretary of State Hull. He emphasized that "Poland had already paid for East Prussia by the losses she had suffered as a result of German aggression and moreover was expected to lose territories in the east."[57] He argued that as the victim of aggression, Poland was not bound to provide any compensation to Germany and would in any case refuse to do so. Undersecretary of State Sumner Wells also felt strongly that East Prussia should be ceded to Poland and the entire German population expelled from this new Polish territory.

In March 1943, the three subcommittees reached different preliminary conclusions regarding Poland's western and northern frontiers in the postwar world. The Security Subcommittee was adamantly against the incorporation of East Prussia into Poland on the grounds that this would not improve Poland's security situation vis-à-vis Germany because it would incite Germans to agitate for the return of this territory. The Territorial Subcommittee remained undecided on the issue of ceding East Prussia to Poland, but was opposed to any compensation to Germany if it lost this province. Nonetheless, this committee expected that this territorial change would take place: "It expects that Russian conquest of East Prussia would be followed by the incorporation of East Prussia in Poland unless diplomatic efforts are at once undertaken to reach an agreement upon a different policy. If East Prussia is to be assigned to Poland by prior agreement, the subcommittee hopes that Russia will make counter-concessions in other areas and that an international body will facilitate the migration of Germans from East Prussia."[58] The Subcommittee on Political Problems supported the incorporation of East Prussia into Poland and agreed with the Territorial Subcommittee that Germans who wished to emigrate, or who were considered undesirable by the Polish government, should be helped to move to Germany.

While the members of the Advisory Committee differed on how to dispose of East Prussia, President Roosevelt was an early and consistent proponent of ceding this part of Germany to Poland. As described above, when General Sikorski visited Washington in December 1942, Roosevelt supported Polish claims to East Prussia. In a meeting with some members of the Advisory Committee on February 22, 1943, Roosevelt is quoted as saying: "East Prussia should go to Poland."[59] And when British Foreign Secretary Eden visited Roosevelt in March 1943, the president reaffirmed this view and added that the Germans living in East Prussia would need to be removed.[60]

The Advisory Committee synthesized the work of the specialized subcommittees in a memorandum entitled "Boundary Problems of Germany," which was transmitted to Cordell Hull on August 18, 1943.[61] This document had been drafted in anticipation of the First Quebec Conference held from August 14–24, but, as it turned out, a detailed discussion of Germany's borders did not take place then. However, the State Department was keenly aware that the issue of German boundary problems needed to be addressed because the Soviet Union insisted on the need to compensate Poland in the west for the territory it would lose to Russia on its eastern frontiers. The second paragraph of the document stated that: "The problem [of the boundary between Poland and Germany] has been rendered more acute by intimations from the Soviet Union that, in return for acquiescence in the loss of all or most of the Polish territories annexed by Russia in 1939, Poland should receive compensation along its western frontier at the expense of Germany."[62] The memorandum also pointed out that the matter was of some urgency because Russia wished to achieve a territorial settlement with Poland before the end of the war.

After lengthy consideration of alternative solutions to the problem of resolving Poland's western border with Germany, the document reached the conclusion that the transfer of Danzig and East Prussia to Poland without any compensation to Germany would be the "least bad" of seven possible solutions identified by State Department staff.[63] Such a transfer would confer on Poland economic and political advantages (echoing Polish arguments for this territorial change): it would significantly expand Poland's access to the Baltic, and by linking central Poland to the Baltic, it would increase agricultural production; it would also enhance Poland's security by considerably shortening its border with Germany and eliminate the risk of a future flanking attack from East Prussia.

But the memorandum also highlighted concerns raised earlier by some members of the committee that the expulsion of East Prussians could engender resentment among Germans and involve considerable costs in ensuring the economic well-being of those who had been resettled in Germany:

> In losing East Prussia [and Danzig], Germany would lose 7.9 percent of its pre-1939 territory, an area that is associated with great historical traditions not only for Prussians, but for other Germans. Such a transfer would undoubtedly be protested by the Germans as an alleged violation of the Atlantic Charter. The question of the future of the East Prussians and the Danzigers would be an extremely difficult one. Their mass expulsion to Germany would raise difficult problems of economic adjustment within Germany; on the other hand, for almost 3,000,000 Germans settled compactly and for centuries on this land to be placed under a traditionally despised Polish rule would multiply the problems of internal reconstruction with Poland itself.[64]

In early 1945, when the State Department again considered the potential economic implications of the incorporation into Poland of not only East Prussia but all German territories east of the Oder and Neisse rivers, it cautioned that a large-scale transfer of Germans would be difficult to absorb and would likely pose significant economic, social, and political difficulties in Germany:

> This enforced migration might well cause a tremendous psychological impact, although its manifestations might not appear immediately. The transferred Germans and the remaining German population might feel so embittered and sympathetic to violent nationalistic programs than an early revival of democracy in Germany would be practically excluded. An extreme German irredentism would in all probability be created constituting a barrier to attempts at permanent pacification of Central Europe.[65]

Moreover, as the loss of its eastern territories would deprive Germany of surplus agricultural production, the State Department also warned that the Western Allies would most likely have to fill the gap in food supplies, imposing on them a considerable financial burden. That this potential cost would have to be borne by the United Kingdom and the United States became important in the final negotiations at Potsdam in July 1945.

D. The Teheran Conference: November 28–December 1, 1943

The Teheran Conference took place from Saturday, November 27, through Wednesday, December 1, 1943, mostly at the Soviet Embassy. English and Russian were the working languages of the three conferences attended by the World War II allies. As the representatives of the Soviet Union spoke in Russian and the British and American delegates in English, translators were needed at every stage of the discussions.

The primary task of the Teheran Conference was to work out an agreement on a strategy for the conduct of the war, particularly the commitment of troops from the Western Allies in Europe, code-named Operation OVERLORD. The Soviet Union was bearing the full burden of fighting the combined German forces, and even though it had won decisive victories in Stalingrad in January 1943, and at the battle at the Kursk salient in the summer of 1943, the tide had not been turned decisively against Nazi Germany. Stalin was exasperated by the American and British delay in opening a second front in Europe, which would relieve pressure on the Soviet fighting forces. For their part, Churchill and Roosevelt wanted the Soviet military to continue to fight vigorously against the Germans because this would make their task easier when they finally launched an attack in Western Europe. Churchill and Roosevelt were also concerned about reports that Stalin might be tempted to conclude a separate peace treaty with Hitler and again divide Europe into Soviet and German spheres of influence, as had happened in 1939 with the Molotov-Ribbentrop Pact.[66]

While not the main focus of attention at Teheran, the question of Poland's borders with Russia and Germany, as well as the closely related issue of East Prussia, did arise. Roosevelt was averse to reaching any agreement on postwar borders, but Stalin was determined to bring this topic to the fore and did so at the penultimate meeting, which began at 6:00 p.m. on December 1. The subject was first broached, however, at a dinner meeting on November 28 at 8:30, in the context of a discussion of Germany's treatment after the war and how to prevent a return of German militarism.[67] Stalin took the lead in this discussion and argued that measures to control Germany and its disarmament would be insufficient to preclude a resurgence of German militarism. He did not specify exactly what he had in mind, but Charles Bohlen, the U.S. ambassador to the Soviet Union and the U.S. translator, reported that "Marshall Stalin particularly mentioned that Poland should extend to the Oder and stated definitely that the Russians would help the Poles to obtain a frontier on the Oder."[68]

Churchill and Roosevelt did not follow up on Stalin's remark during the remainder of the dinner. Following its conclusion, Roosevelt retired to his sleeping quarters while Churchill and Stalin continued to discuss the postwar treatment of Germany. Churchill also brought up the question of Poland and noted that Great Britain had gone to war because of Germany's invasion of that country and that his government was committed to a strong and independent Poland. Churchill saw Great Britain as playing the role of intermediary between the Soviet Union and Poland, and he wished to have a clear conception of Stalin's territorial designs vis-à-vis Poland, which he could then convey to the Polish government-in-exile in London. Churchill told Stalin that he did not have preconceived ideas of what Poland's frontiers should be—in particular, the border between Poland and the Soviet Union—but he appreciated that Soviet security on their western frontier was a key consideration for Stalin. Then Anthony Eden, the British foreign secretary, spoke up and asked if he had correctly understood Stalin to say during dinner that the Soviet Union favored the Oder River as Poland's western frontier with Germany, whereupon "Marshall Stalin replied emphatically that he did favor such a frontier for Poland and repeated that the Russians were prepared to help the Poles achieve it."[69] There followed a revealing exchange between Stalin and Eden:

> Stalin asked whether we thought he was going to swallow Poland up. Eden said he did not know how much the Russians were going to eat. How much would they leave undigested? Stalin said the Russians did not want anything belonging to other people, although they might have a bite at Germany. Eden said that what Poland lost in the East she might gain in the West. Stalin replied that possibly she might, but he did not know.[70]

Here, Stalin clearly revealed his intention to take a portion of German territory for Russia, and on the last day of the conference he made a specific claim for the northern part of East Prussia. This was not news to Eden because, as described above, Stalin had already informed him in Moscow in December 1941 that the Soviet Union wished to acquire part of East Prussia.

Noteworthy in the exchange with Eden is that Stalin was disingenuous regarding his views on Poland's borders. He had every intention of shifting them westward, but he played his cards close to his chest and allowed the British to take the lead in suggesting this approach for dealing with the "Polish problem." This ploy worked. Churchill remarked that it would be very useful if an "agreed understanding" on Poland's frontiers could be worked out in

Teheran that then could be taken up with the Polish government-in-exile in London. With regard to these frontiers, "[h]e [Churchill] said that, as far as he was concerned, he would like to see Poland moved westward in the same manner as soldiers at drill execute the drill 'close left' and Churchill illustrated his point with three matches representing the Soviet Union, Poland and Germany."[71] His demonstration presumably went as follows. With three matches on the table a little apart, the left one represented the German-Polish border of 1939, the right one the prewar Soviet-Polish border, and the middle one the new Soviet-Polish frontier established in 1939. By taking up the match on the right, the Soviet-Polish frontier of 1939—the middle match—became the new eastern border of Poland, and by placing this same match on the left, it became the new Polish-German border on the Oder.[72] Churchill reported that Stalin was pleased with his demonstration of how Poland's borders could be shifted westward, saying that reaching an understanding on this issue would be useful but would require further study. The meeting then broke up. In this informal after-dinner setting, Churchill and Stalin essentially laid the basis for the transfer of a huge swath of German territory to Poland. It was this "agreed understanding" that paved the way for the takeover of southern East Prussia by Poland and the expulsion of the German population described in Chapter VI.

Another reason why Great Britain took the lead in developing an "agreed understanding" on Polish frontiers at Teheran is that U.S. domestic politics precluded a major role for the United States. President Roosevelt described this political situation to Stalin in a one-on-one meeting that began at 3:20 on the afternoon of December 1.[73] Roosevelt first noted that there was an upcoming presidential election in 1944 and he did not wish to lose the votes of some six to seven million Americans of Polish descent. He went on to say that he personally shared Stalin's view on the restoration of a Polish state, but one with an eastern border moved farther to the west and a western border shifted as far as to the Oder River. He then explained to Stalin that in light of U.S. political considerations he would not be able to participate in any decision, or publicly take part in any arrangement, on the topic of Poland's borders not only at Teheran but the next year as well. Roosevelt's remarks indicate

that while he assented to Stalin's territorial ambitions, they were such a sensitive issue for Polish voters that he could not be a party to decisions regarding
Poland at Teheran. Roosevelt therefore left it to Churchill and Stalin to work
out the "agreed understanding" regarding "the Polish problem."

Such an understanding was reached at the meeting of the Big Three that
took place at 6:00 p.m. that same day.[74] Churchill again asked for the Soviet
view on the question of Poland's frontiers, and if some "reasonable formula"
could be worked out, he was willing to convey it to the Polish government-
in-exile in London. He also referred to his use of three matches in the after-
dinner discussion with Stalin to illustrate one possible solution to the border
issue. Stalin replied that he considered the 1939 border between Poland and
Russia as "just and right." Stalin, Churchill, and Roosevelt knew that this
was not acceptable to Poland. After some discussion of the precise location
of this border, Roosevelt asked Stalin whether Poland would be compensated by some of Germany's western land for the territory she would lose
to Russia in the east: "The President inquired whether in the opinion of
Marshall Stalin, East Prussia and the area between the old Polish frontier and
the Oder was approximately equal to the former Polish territory acquired
by the Soviet Union."[75] Stalin responded that he did not know. Roosevelt
followed up by asking whether a voluntary transfer of people living in the
affected areas would be possible, to which Stalin answered, "such a transfer
was entirely possible." It seems reasonable to conjecture that even though
Roosevelt did not wish to be a party to settling the border issue involving the
Soviet Union and Poland, he nonetheless wanted to understand what would
be involved and the likely implications for the transfer of populations in the
affected areas.

The Big Three also discussed Germany at this meeting. Stalin said that the
Soviet Union favored dismemberment, while Churchill emphasized that in
Germany "the root of the evil lay in Prussia, in the Prussian Army and the
General Staff" and that "he was primarily more interested in seeing Prussia,
the evil core of German militarism, separated from the rest of Germany."[76]
Roosevelt then described a U.S. plan that had been developed some months
earlier, which would split Germany into five independent, self-governing

parts, one being Prussia, which would be made as small and as weak as possible. Under this plan, the Kiel Canal and Hamburg, as well as the Ruhr and the Saar, would be placed under the United Nations or some other form of international control. Churchill again emphasized that the key was the isolation of Prussia, which he "would treat sternly," and in addition stressed the desirability of detaching most of southern Germany and making it a part of what he called a "Confederation of the Danube." Stalin expressed a preference for Roosevelt's proposal over Churchill's because it would make it more difficult for the separate German entities to coalesce back into a united Germany. After some further discussion, no conclusions were reached and it was agreed that they had undertaken only a very preliminary survey of what Churchill referred to as a "vast historical problem."

Particularly noteworthy in this discussion is the antipathy displayed by Churchill, Roosevelt, and Stalin toward Prussia as the source of German militarism and German aggression in Europe.[77] This anti-Prussian predisposition was a key factor underlying the conviction shared by the Big Three throughout the war that East Prussia should be detached from Germany and ceded to Russia and Poland. The three Allies saw the elimination of East Prussia as a means to achieve a reduced and diminished state of Prussia, of which the province of East Prussia was a part.

In the United States a virulent strain of anti-German sentiment was manifested in Robert Machray's book, *East Prussia—Menace to Poland and Peace*, published in 1943 by the American Polish Council in Chicago:

> No one who thinks realistically can to-day deny that certain features and instincts of the German nation, its traditions, institutions and ideas, defined for many decades by its leading thinkers and writers, have created a German organism which is morally degenerate, and mortally dangerous for other members of the international community. The aggregation of these qualities, defined as the "Prussian Spirit," because it reached its fullest development and manifestation in Prussia, must be thoroughly rooted out and destroyed for the good of humanity and of the Germans themselves.[78]

Machray further argued that because East Prussia had become the purest embodiment of this "Prussian Spirit," it was imperative that it be excised from Germany:

> So long as East Prussia remains a part of Germany there can be no possibility of a complete revolution in German policy and its emancipation from the dominant ideology. Contrariwise, separate East Prussia from Germany and the entire edifice built up by the Prussian Spirit will collapse and tumble down. And so the separation of East Prussia from Germany will be the most effective and expedient means of restoring the German nation to moral and political sanity.[79]

There is, moreover, evidence that some of the senior staff of the U.S. State Department and the British Foreign Office also shared the view that the province of East Prussia represented the purest form of the Prussian characteristics of obedience and military discipline, which were associated with the social class of the Junkers, the landlords of large-scale estates.[80]

This antipathy toward Prussia was manifested after the war in a largely symbolic act that extinguished Prussia as a political entity. On February 25, 1947, representatives of the Allied occupation forces signed Law No. 46 of the Allied Control Council. This law formally abolished the state of Prussia:

> The Prussian State, which from the early days has been a bearer of militarism and reaction in Germany, has de facto ceased to exist.
>
> Guided by the interests of preservation of peace and security of peoples, and with the desire to assure further reconstruction of

the political life of Germany on a democratic basis, the Control Council enacts as follows:

ARTICLE I

The Prussian State together with its central government and all its agencies is abolished.[81]

Churchill then turned the discussion back to the issue of Poland and emphasized that he was not asking for an agreed proposal, but that he would like to present to the Poles a "formula" about which he would say, "I do not know if the Russians would approve, but I think that I might get it for you. You see, you are being well looked after."[82] The "formula" he then conveyed to Stalin and Roosevelt ran along quite familiar lines: "It is thought in principle that the home of the Polish state and nation should be between the so-called Curzon line and the Line of the Oder, including for Poland East Prussia (as defined) and Oppeln [Upper Silesia]; but the actual tracing of the frontier line requires careful study, and possibly disentanglement of population at some points."[83]

Stalin was fully prepared to name the price he would demand for his agreement to this proposal:

> Marshel Stalin said that if Russia would be given the northern part of East Prussia, running along the left bank of the Niemen and include Tilsit and the City of Königsberg, he would be prepared to accept the Curzon Line as the frontier between the Soviet Union and Poland.
>
> He said that the acquisition of that part of Eastern Prussia would not only afford the Soviet Union an ice-free port but would also give Russia a small piece of German territory which he felt was deserved.[84]

These last words on Poland's borders and East Prussia at Teheran came at the very end of the final working meeting of the conference. Neither Churchill nor Roosevelt had any reaction or comment in response to Stalin's claim for "a small piece of German territory," namely northern East Prussia, including Königsberg. Stalin interpreted their silence as implying assent. Indeed, at the final Allied conference at Potsdam in July 1945, Stalin specifically referred to this discussion at Teheran and asserted that Churchill and Roosevelt had agreed then to the acquisition of this German territory by the Soviet Union. By raising this territorial issue at the very last minute of the Teheran Conference, Stalin no doubt hoped that it would not provoke any opposition from Churchill or Roosevelt. He was presumably aware that his demand for a piece of East Prussia was inconsistent with the Atlantic Charter and the oft-repeated pronouncements at Teheran that the Big Three eschewed all territorial ambitions after the end of the war, and it seems likely that he did not want to draw attention to this territorial claim on the part of Russia.

At the conclusion of this meeting there was also no desire to spell out in greater detail the nature of the "mutual understanding" on Poland's frontiers because of the domestic political sensitivity it posed for Roosevelt and because Churchill did not want to give the Poles the impression that this was a "done deal," which he had worked out in with the Russians behind their backs. This deliberate ambiguity is apparent in the last sentence of the minutes of this meeting: "Although nothing definitely was stated, it was apparent that the British were going to take this suggestion back to London to the Poles."[85]

Anthony Eden, in fact, conveyed this "suggestion" to the Poles three weeks later because illness had forced Churchill to spend time recovering in Marrakesh before his return to London. Eden invited senior officials of the Polish government-in-exile in London—the Polish prime minister, foreign secretary, and ambassador—to dinner on December 23, 1943, and he acquainted them with the formula worked out in Teheran. In a telegram to Churchill sent the following day he reported that the Poles were "very unhappy" with the proposed loss of their eastern territory to Russia.[86] Eden also wrote that he did not mention to the Poles that Russia claimed Königsberg, as this new demand would have confirmed the Poles' suspicions that Russia intended to encircle them and "would have closed their minds to all reason."[87] Eden proposed to Churchill that if the Poles were willing to consider the Curzon Line as their eastern frontier with Russia, then Stalin should be pressed strongly to drop his demand for Königsberg. Eden believed that Stalin's claim that Russia needed a warm-water port on the Baltic was bogus and that Stalin may have added this demand as an afterthought at the conclusion of the meeting in Teheran. He closed his telegram with the thought that, "at any rate when the time comes I think we should try hard to save Königsberg for the Poles, but this is all in the future."[88]

One writer on this period of Polish history, Antony Polonsky, described the British Foreign Office as surprised that Stalin demanded Königsberg at the Teheran Conference. He also cited a Foreign Office research department paper, which showed that Russia's need for an ice-free port on the Baltic was spurious, as there were other ports—Memel, Libau, and Windau were specifically mentioned—that were also ice-free.[89] Apparently, the deputy undersecretary of the Foreign Office, Sir Orme Sargent, was sufficiently convinced of the weakness of Stalin's argument that he is quoted as saying: "As regards Stalin's claim to Königsberg, this looks like a piece of bluff which I trust we shall call." Having taken Stalin's measure over the years, Eden was not so sure: "I should like to see Sir O. Sargent do it."[90]

As described in detail above, Stalin had already laid claim to the northern part of East Prussia, including Königsberg, when Eden visited Moscow in December 1941, but Stalin's remarks on this important territorial issue were apparently not taken seriously at that time. While the Foreign Office was correct that Stalin used the ice-free port argument as a pretext, it failed to probe beneath the surface of this weak justification to try to ascertain the real reason for Stalin's territorial ambition regarding East Prussia. In hindsight, it is clear that Russia wanted a military base close to Western Europe, but one wonders why this objective was not obvious to the Western Allies at the time.

It is also noteworthy that a luncheon meeting in Teheran on November 30 focused on the Soviet Union's need for warm-water ports.[91] The topic was introduced by a discussion of Russia's large landmass, which prompted Churchill to say that a country as large as Russia, with a population of nearly

200 million, should not be denied access to warm-water ports. Roosevelt agreed and said that all nations should have free access to the Baltic for merchant shipping. Stalin concurred and then inquired what could be done for Russia in the Far East regarding warm-water ports. Churchill mentioned Vladivostok, but Stalin noted that it was only partly ice-free in the winter and then pointed out that Murmansk was Russia's only ice-free port. This remark elicited a curious response from Churchill:

> I answered that I wished to meet the Russian grievance, because the government of the world must be entrusted to satisfied nations, who wished nothing more for themselves than what they had. If the world-government were in the hands of hungry nations, there would always be danger. But none of us had any reason to seek anything more.[92]

With this remark Churchill signaled to Stalin that he would look favorably on Russia's need for additional ice-free ports, but at the same time he seemed to be saying that this should satisfy Russia's territorial ambitions. It would have been an opportune moment for Stalin to mention that Königsberg was ideally suited for Russia's need for an ice-free port, but he refrained from doing so. Instead, he waited until the following day (December 1), at the very end of the last working meeting of the Teheran Conference, which dealt with Poland's borders and not East Prussia. Stalin, the master strategist and tactician, got his way with East Prussia without any objection whatsoever from Churchill or Roosevelt.

The communiqué released shortly after the end of the conference was full of noble sentiments and high-minded phrases: "We express our determination that our nations will work together in war and in the peace that will follow," and "We came here in hope and determination. We leave here, friends in fact, in spirit, and determination."[93] Perhaps the most concrete statement was a veiled reference to Operation OVERLORD, which had been the primary focus of the conference: "We have reached complete agreement as to the scope and timing of the operations which will be undertaken from the East, West, and South." Completely absent from the document was any mention of the proposed alterations in Poland's eastern and western frontiers and Russia's desire for a slice of East Prussian territory.

Nevertheless, one member of Congress was suspicious that behind this innocuous document, secret commitments had been made in Teheran regarding Poland. Roosevelt had to write to Congressman Mruk on March 6, 1944, to reassure him on this point. The full text of his letter reads as follows: "I am afraid that I cannot make any further comments except what I have written to you before—there were no secret commitments made by me at Teheran and I am quite sure that other members of my party made none either. This, of course, does not include military plans which, however, had nothing to do with Poland."[94] This statement may be technically correct, but of course Roosevelt did not refer to the "mutual understanding" and the "formula" dealing with Poland's frontiers proposed by Churchill to which neither he nor Stalin objected.

The conference participants consulted maps from time to time to ascertain the location of the relevant boundaries under discussion. One map was particularly relevant in connection with East Prussia because Stalin drew a line in red pencil on it to indicate the northern part of the province, which he wished to acquire for Russia. This map had been prepared earlier in the Office of the Geographer at the U.S. State Department in conjunction with the Advisory Committee on Postwar Foreign Policy. It was taken to Teheran and when the question arose at the December 1 meeting about the location of the Curzon Line, Charles Bohlen (first secretary of the American Embassy in Moscow and official U.S. translator) put it on the table. Later, Bohlen attached a note to the map, which reads in part:

> The marks in red pencil on the attached map were made by Stalin himself to illustrate the fact that if part of eastern Prussia, including the ports of Königsberg and Tilsit, were given to the Soviet Union he would be prepared to accept the Curzon line (the blue line "E" in the map) as the frontier between the Soviet Union and Poland.[95]

The fact that Stalin took the trouble to mark in red that part of East Prussia that he wished to reserve for Russia demonstrated that the acquisition of this territory was a major objective he had formulated in advance (see Map 10. Poland: Eastern Frontier with Stalin's Red Line).

E. The Aftermath of the Teheran Conference

While Stalin drew on the map roughly a straight line from Königsberg to Insterburg to the East Prussian border with Lithuania and Poland, bilateral negotiations determined the actual boundary between the northern and southern parts of East Prussia, which follows a line roughly twenty-five miles south of that put on the map by Stalin. This boundary was formalized without consulting the two Western Allies in an agreement signed in Moscow on July 27, 1944, between the Soviet Union and the newly formed Polish Committee of National Liberation (the "Lublin Committee"). The latter constituted a group of Polish Socialists and Communists set up by the Soviet Union to represent Poland, which was in direct competition with, and opposition to, the Polish government-in-exile in London.[96] This demarcation line was considered to be such a sensitive matter that it was regarded as top secret and was only published in Polish in 1967. Article 2 of this agreement divided East Prussia between the Soviet Union and Poland: the Soviet Union was allocated the northern part—including the city and port of Königsberg—while the entire remaining part—including the city and harbor of Danzig—was given to Poland. Article 3b specified that the border began in the east at the intersection of the borders of Lithuania, Poland, and East Prussia, and ran westward north of Goldap-Braunsberg to the coast of the Bay of Danzig.

What is also remarkable about this secret agreement is that in Article 4 the Soviet Union specified the western border between Poland and Germany:

> The Government of the U.S.S.R. has also recognized that the border between Poland and Germany shall be laid down along a line west of Swinemünde to the River Oder, whereby the city of Stettin remains on the Polish side, and that the border runs further

upwards along the River Oder to the Neisse River, and from here along the Neisse River up to the Czechoslovakian border. [97]

According to one author, R. C. Raack, the Lublin Committee had expected that all of East Prussia would be transferred to Poland and was very upset when it learned that Stalin claimed Königsberg and the northern third of East Prussia for the Soviet Union.[98] It was "only after strenuous negotiations, during which Stalin's notorious temper rose to a frightening level," that a deal was reached whereby Stalin agreed to compensate the Lublin Poles for their "loss" of Königsberg with the German city of Stettin.[99] In addition, Stalin agreed to support the Polish demand to move the Polish-German border to the west not only along the Oder River in the north, but also along the western (Lausitzer) Neisse River to the south from the point where it joined the Oder. Poland would thereby gain almost the entire territory of Silesia, some of the most productive agricultural and industrial land in eastern Germany, and not just what was referred to as Oppeln or Upper Silesia to the east of the Oder and the eastern (Glatzer) Neisse River which—as described in detail below—Great Britain and the United States intended to allocate to Poland. It was only at the Potsdam Conference in July 1945, that Stalin revealed to his American and British counterparts the true nature of the Polish demands for a large section of Germany's eastern territory. He did not disclose that he had already promised this land to the Lublin Poles in July of 1944.

The precise location of Poland's western border with Germany was sufficiently sensitive that the text of the agreement did not specify whether the river in question was the western or the eastern Neisse. Moreover, in a press conference on July 28, 1944, the day after the agreement was reached, the chairman of the Polish Committee of National Liberation (the Lublin Poles), Edward Osobka-Morawski, did not clear up the ambiguity when he described the Polish western boundary with Germany simply as the "Oder-Neisse boundary." Stalin also did not clarify the situation when he met a week later with Stanisław Mikołajczyk, the prime minister of the Polish government-in-exile. Mikołajczyk asked Stalin directly: "How do you see the future frontiers of Poland, Marshal?" To which Stalin replied: "How do

I see them?...well...in the East the Curzon Line, in the West along the rivers Oder and Nyssa (Neisse), Krolewiec (Königsberg)...(after a moment of reflection)...and the Krolewiec area will be assigned to Russia.... Yes, to Russia."[100]

Stalin's insistence on acquiring part of East Prussia for Russia had been made more forcefully earlier that year in a letter to Churchill dated February 4, 1944:

> As regards your statement to the Poles that Poland could considerably extend her frontiers in the West and North, we are in agreement with that with, as you are aware, one amendment. I mentioned this amendment to you and the President in Teheran. We claim the transfer of the north-eastern part of East Prussia, including the port of Könisgberg as an ice-free one, to the Soviet Union. It is the only German territory claimed by us. Unless this minimum claim of the Soviet Union is met, the Soviet Union's concession in recognizing the Curzon Line becomes entirely pointless, as I told you in Teheran.[101]

Two days later (February 6), Churchill finally informed the Polish government-in-exile in London that the Soviets wished to have the northern third of East Prussia, including Königsberg. This news came as a shock to the Poles, who emphasized that this would substantially reduce in size and economic importance the territory Poland would receive in compensation for its territorial losses to the Soviet Union in the east. Churchill was not moved by their arguments and stated that "this was a rightful claim on the part of Russia...."[102]

Roosevelt, by contrast, continued to hold out hope to the London Poles that they might still receive Königsberg. When Mikołajczyk visited Washington for nine days in June 1944, he had a meeting on June 12 with Roosevelt and officials from the U.S. State Department. In his summary of this discussion, Mikołajczyk wrote: "The President said that at the Tehran Conference he had made it clear that he held the view that the Polish-Soviet conflict should not be settled on the basis of the so-called Curzon Line and he assured the Prime Minister that at the appropriate time he would help Poland…to obtain East Prussia, including Königsberg, and Silesia."[103] His summary also included the following:

> III. In Premier Mikolajczyk's conversations with the President as well as in those with the Acting Secretary of State [Stettinus] the incorporation into Poland of former German territory and particularly East Prussia and Silesia, were discussed.
>
> The President favoured the incorporation of these erstwhile Polish territories into the future Polish State and a compulsory transfer of the German population.[104]

The U.S. account of this same conversation provides a little more detail:

> The President said that he was not worried about territorial matters, that they [the Poles] would get East Prussia and Silesia, and if they had to give up a little something somewhere else, he thought it was a pretty good exchange.
>
> The President said that he did not agree on the formula based upon the old Curzon Line. He did not feel the Russians would insist upon this. Further, the President stated he did not feel that Stalin would insist on Königsberg and that he felt Stalin would be willing to have Königsberg as a "shrine for the world," inasmuch as the city controlled Danzig and was an important locality. The President recalled Stalin having referred to it as the "Home of the Teutonic Knights."[105]

Roosevelt is also quoted as saying that he was convinced that the Russians were sincere in desiring a strong and independent Poland and that he believed that the Russians could be trusted to treat the Poles fairly. Mikołajczyk did not share this view, saying that "he could trust America to give them fair treatment politically and economically, but did not trust Russia."[106] Regarding the Russians, he was proved to be considerably more foresighted than Roosevelt.

Moreover, the U.S. president was disingenuous, to put it mildly, in conveying to the Poles that he would do what he could to intervene with the Russians to encourage them to give up their claims to Königsberg and northern East Prussia. Assurances along these lines were not to be taken seriously, Eden wrote bluntly on June 23, 1944: "The President will do nothing for the Poles, any more than Mr. Hull did at Moscow or the President did at Teheran. The Poles are sadly deluding themselves if they place any faith in these vague and generous promises."[107]

––––––––––––

The disingenuous manner in which both Churchill and Roosevelt dealt with the Poles in their negotiations with the Soviets became apparent in October 1944 when Churchill and Eden were in Moscow to discuss military and political matters with Stalin. Churchill wished to resolve the issue of Poland's borders with Russia in the east and with Germany in the west, and to this end he persuaded Mikołajczyk to join them in hopes of working out an agreement between Poland and the Soviet Union. At 5:00 on the evening of October 13, Churchill, Eden, Stalin, Molotov, Mikołajczyk, and his Minister of Foreign Affairs, Tadeusz Romer, as well as the American ambassador Averell Harriman as observer, held a meeting to discuss the Polish issue. Mikołajczyk has described in dramatic terms what took place.[108]

Molotov asked the Polish prime minister to describe his plan for postwar Poland. After he had heard the plan, Stalin said that it had two big defects: it left out the Lublin Poles (i.e., those supported by the Soviet Union), and it failed to recognize the Curzon Line "as an actuality" (see Map 9. Westward Shift of Poland's Borders). Stalin added that the rest of the plan was acceptable, but he was adamant that these two flaws had to be corrected. At this point Mikołajczyk described Churchill's reaction:

Churchill now expressed a great and sudden happiness.

"I now see a new hope for agreement," he said with enthusiasm. "Regarding the new frontier along the Curzon line, I must announce in the name of the British government that, taking into account the huge losses suffered by the USSR in this war and how the Red Army helped liberate Poland, the Curzon line must be your eastern frontier."

"Don't worry," he added, looking at me. "We will see to it that the land you lose in the east there will be compensations in Germany, in East Prussia, and Silesia. You'll get a nice outlet to the sea, a good port at Danzig, and the priceless minerals of Silesia."[109]

After a brief but tense interchange with Stalin about the role of the Lublin Poles, Mikołajczyk refused to back down and stated unequivocally that he had no authority to accept the Curzon Line as Poland's eastern border with the Soviet Union. Stalin then argued that the territory east of the Curzon Line was, in fact, part of White Russia (Belorussia) and the Ukraine. Mikołajczyk responded that even if Poland gave up this vast area, there would still be no guarantee of independence for what remained of Poland. Stalin retorted, "Who is threatening the independence of Poland? Soviet Russia?" Mikołajczyk wrote that he considered that then might be the time to say "Yes," but thought better of it and told Stalin that all Poland wanted was full independence and freedom. Mikołajezyk then continued to argue against the Curzon Line when he was brought up short by Molotov:

> "But all this was settled at Teheran!" [Molotov] barked. He looked from Churchill to Harriman, who was silent. I asked for details of Teheran. And then he added, still with his eyes on Churchill and the American Ambassador:
>
> "If your memories fail you, let me recall the facts to you. We all agreed at Teheran that the Curzon line must divide Poland. You will recall that President Roosevelt agreed to this solution and strongly endorsed the line. And then we agreed that it would be best not to issue any public declaration about our agreement."

Shocked, and remembering the earnest assurances I had personally had from Roosevelt at the White House, I looked at Churchill and Harriman, silently begging them to call this damnable deal a lie. Harriman looked down at the rug. Churchill looked straight back at me.

"I confirm this," he said quietly.

The admission made him angry, and he demanded that I agree then and there to the Russian demands. He reminded me of Britain's aid to Poland and of my duty now to accede to the demands that Britain had come to support. I could only answer that while there were no words to express Poland's gratitude for Britain's war aid, I personally had no authority to agree to give up half of Poland.

"I didn't expect to be brought here to participate in a new partition of my country," I shouted.

"You don't have to make a public announcement of your decision," Churchill urged. "I don't want to put you in a difficult position with the Polish people."

I could make no private deal either, I told him. So he went on:

"But you could at least agree that the Curzon line is the temporary frontier, and remember, you may appeal for adjustment at the peace conference."

Before he could continue, Stalin rose indignantly:

"I want this made very clear," he said gruffly. "Mr. Churchill's thought of any future change in the frontier is not acceptable to the Soviet government. We will not change our frontiers from time to time. That's all!"

Churchill held out his hands, looked up to the ceiling in despair, and wheezed. We filed out silently.[110]

Shortly after the meeting, Harriman received a letter from Mikołajczyk asking for clarification regarding Roosevelt's views on the Curzon Line at the Teheran Conference. Harriman provided this clarification orally in a meeting in London with Tadeusz Romer, the Polish Minister of Foreign Affairs, at which Harriman informed Romer that Roosevelt had not agreed to the Curzon Line and had made it plain that he did not wish to take a position on the boundary question either publicly or privately. Harriman added that he had not taken issue with Molotov's statement on this matter because he was at the meeting merely in the capacity of an observer.[111] Harriman's account of what Roosevelt said at Teheran was indeed correct and Molotov blatantly lied when he claimed that Roosevelt had strongly endorsed the Curzon Line. Nonetheless, Roosevelt had given Mikołajczyk to understand that he had argued against the Curzon Line at Teheran, which was incorrect; Roosevelt had merely remained mute on the topic and had thus not taken a position one way or the other.

F. The Yalta Conference: February 4–11, 1945

During the course of 1944 it became increasingly evident that the Allies would defeat Germany. The D-Day landing on June 6 in northern France had opened up a second front in Europe and the Soviets were rapidly retaking the territory they had lost to Germany earlier in the war. With military victory in sight, the Allies needed to resolve urgent matters, in particular: what would be done with a defeated Germany; how would reparations by Germany be handled; and how would the problem of Poland's borders in the east and the west, including the disposition of East Prussia, be resolved. Churchill, Roosevelt, and Stalin agreed that they needed to meet again in a further attempt to resolve these and other issues. After innumerable discussions and negotiations, Yalta in the Crimea was chosen as the meeting site largely because Stalin insisted that he needed to be near Moscow to continue to direct the Soviet offensive against Germany. The gathering of the Big Three had to wait, however, until the U.S. presidential election in November had taken place, the year-end holidays were over, and the U.S. Congress was back in session. A preparatory meeting of American and British officials was held in Malta from January 30–February 2, 1945. Churchill was present throughout, but Roosevelt arrived only on February 2 in time for luncheon and dinner meetings with Churchill.

The Yalta Conference itself was held from February 4–11, 1945, in the Livadia Palace, the former summer palace of the tsars.[112] During their occupation of the Crimea from July 1942 to May 1944, the Germans used this palace as their high command center, and when the Soviet offensive forced them to retreat, the building and grounds were heavily damaged and extensive German looting took place. Nonetheless, Soviet renovations and repairs in the three-week period immediately before the conference transformed the building into a comfortable and habitable site for the living quarters of the American delegation and for conference meeting rooms. The large former ballroom–banquet hall served as the main meeting room.

It was over a year since the first meeting of the Big Three in Teheran. The costs of the war in terms of lives lost and property destroyed by the Germans, borne particularly by the Soviet Union, were staggering. Inevitably, the suffering the Soviet people had endured affected Allied thinking about how they would deal with the defeated Germans. In a private meeting with Stalin on February 4 before the first plenary session devoted to military matters, Roosevelt remarked that he had been struck by the extent of the destruction in the Crimea and that as a result he was much more "bloodthirsty" regarding the Germans than he had been at Teheran. He added that he hoped Stalin would repeat the toast he had made in Teheran proposing the execution of fifty thousand officers of the German Army. Stalin did not respond to this suggestion but agreed that everyone was now more bloodthirsty than they had been a year earlier and pointed out that the destruction in Ukraine was far worse than in the Crimea, as the Germans had had time to carry out a calculated and methodical devastation of the country. The Germans were "savages and seemed to hate with a sadistic hatred the creative work of human beings."[113] Roosevelt shared this sentiment.

The question of Germany's immediate postwar future was the main item of discussion in the second plenary session at 4:00 p.m. on Monday, February 5.

Stalin quickly raised the question of Germany's dismemberment, and, noting that they had viewed this proposal favorably in Teheran, he asked whether Churchill and Roosevelt still supported this approach. They responded affirmatively, but Churchill would only commit to the establishment of the appropriate administrative machinery to put dismemberment into effect. He was adamant that Germany would have no say whatsoever in the decisions determining its fate. When Stalin asked whether the three Allies should mention dismemberment when the terms of the unconditional surrender were presented to the Germans, Churchill replied that:

> he did not feel there was any need to discuss with any German any question about their future—that unconditional surrender gave us the right to determine the future of Germany which could perhaps best be done after unconditional surrender. He said that we reserve under these terms all rights over the lives, property and activities of the Germans.[114]

The discussion then turned to the question of whether France—in addition to the American, British, and Soviet zones already agreed to—should have its own occupation zone. Stalin had no objection to France being given a zone carved out of the British and American zones, but thought it should not participate in the control of Germany. In this connection, he said that "the Soviet Government might desire to ask other states to help in the occupation of the Soviet zone without any right to participate in the decisions of the control commission."[115] This rather obscure remark probably related to Poland's occupation and administration of Germany's eastern territories (except for northern East Prussia, including Königsberg, reserved for Russia), which was announced that same day by Bolesław Bierut, the president of the Lublin Polish Government (formerly the Polish Committee of National Liberation). The *New York Times* on February 6, 1945, quoted Bierut as saying, "It is our feeling that on Polish soil there should be a Polish administration, regardless of the opinions that may be expressed at the international [Yalta] conference."[116] Neither Great Britain nor the United States took note at Yalta of the unilateral usurpation of authority by the Soviet-supported Poles concerning a matter that clearly was the responsibility of the Big Three. At that time—February 1945—both Poland and the Soviet Union were establishing "facts on the ground" in Germany's eastern territories, which the Western Allies did not contest.

When Stalin raised the question of German reparations, Deputy Soviet Foreign Affairs Commissar Ivan Maisky outlined the Soviet proposal whereby Germany would transfer eighty percent of its heavy industry within two years and pay reparations from its current production for ten years. Maisky argued that because the Soviet Union had contributed the most to winning the war and had suffered the greatest losses, it should receive the bulk of the reparations, which he estimated at ten billion dollars. Both Churchill and Roosevelt then recalled the unsatisfactory experience their countries had had with reparation payments after the First World War; the United States ultimately had to loan money to Germany to enable it to fulfill its obligations. Churchill added that he was "haunted by the specter of a starving Germany" and Roosevelt remarked that "he did not wish to contemplate the necessity of helping the Germans to keep from starving." Churchill asked if the Allies chose to provide assistance, who would provide the help: "if you wished a horse to pull a wagon that you would at least have to give it fodder." This prompted Stalin to observe that Churchill was correct, "but care should be taken to see that the horse did not turn around and kick you."[117] Given the strong differences in views, the reparations issue remained unresolved at Yalta.

The first extensive discussion of the Polish problem took place at the fourth plenary session on February 7 at 4:00 p.m. Molotov presented the Soviet proposals regarding Poland's borders. These included the familiar one that the eastern frontier should follow the Curzon Line (with some digressions of five to eight kilometers in favor of Poland), and a more specific proposal for Poland's western frontier with Germany: "It was decided that the Western frontier of Poland should be traced from the town of Stettin (Polish) and farther to the South along the River Oder and still farther along the River Neisse (Western)."[118] What is important here is the specific reference to the western Neisse River, which would involve considerably more German territory being allocated to Poland than if the eastern Neisse River became Poland's new western border with Germany (see Map 11. The Oder-Neisse Line). Stalin had already mentioned the western Neisse River in the third plenary session, but at that meeting his remark had not elicited comments or reactions from the American or British delegations. Now, however, when the issue was made explicit, Roosevelt asked for more time to study Molotov's proposals. Churchill voiced concerns raised in previous discussions in which he had qualified his support for moving Poland's frontier westward into German territory, saying that such a shift in frontiers should be no more than what the Poles wished or could properly manage. "It would be a great pity to stuff the Polish goose so full of German food that it died of indigestion."[119] He added that many in Great Britain would be shocked at the prospect of moving millions of Germans by force, although he himself had no problems in principle with the forced transfer of millions of Germans. He cited the example of the resettlement of some two million Greeks and Turks after World War I and called it "a great success."[120] If Poland took East Prussia and Silesia, that by itself, he surmised, would involve moving six million Germans back to Germany and could probably be managed, but shifting the frontier further to the west could create quite a problem because of the increased number of refugees involved.

Stalin observed that most of the Germans in these areas had already run away from the Red Army, to which Churchill responded, "this, of course, simplified the problem." But according to James Byrnes (a member of the U.S. delegation and later secretary of state), "Churchill reminded him [Stalin] that consideration must be given 'to where those Germans are that run away,' and asked, 'will there be room for them in what is left of Germany?'"[121] Churchill then elaborated on his concern about whether there would be room in what was left of Germany for millions of refugees from the eastern territories about to be taken over by Poland:

> Six or seven million Germans had been killed and another million (Stalin suggested two million) would probably be killed before the end of the war. There should therefore be room for these migrant

people up to a certain point. They would be needed to fill the vacancies. I was not afraid of the problem of transferring populations, so long as it was proportionate to what the Poles could manage and to what could be put into Germany. But it was a matter which required study, not as a matter of principle, but of the numbers which would have to be handled.[122]

Privately, Churchill confided to Byrnes that Molotov's proposal would entail the transfer of nine million Germans, who could never be absorbed by what remained of Germany.[123] Churchill was worried that Great Britain would have to pay for the support of many of the refugees who ended up in the British-occupied zone, a drain on its budget that it could ill afford.

The morning of February 8, Roosevelt sent the British and Soviet delegations a letter containing a counterproposal to Molotov's. The relevant part pertaining to Poland's western border with Germany reflected Churchill's concerns: "In regard to point Two, while agreeing that compensation should be given to Poland at the expense of Germany, including that portion of East Prussia south of the Königsberg line, Upper Silesia, and up to the line of the Oder, there would appear little justification to the extension of the western boundary of Poland up to the Western Neisse River."[124]

The last discussion of Poland's frontiers at Yalta took place at the penultimate plenary meeting at 4:00 p.m. on February 10.[125] A subcommittee of the three ambassadors had drafted a new proposal on Poland, which made no mention of Poland's frontiers. Churchill expressed concern that the world would wonder why Poland's borders were not dealt with. He pointed out that they had agreed on the eastern frontier of Poland, that the Poles should have part of East Prussia, and that be compensated with additional German territory in the west. Churchill had just received a telegram from the U.K. War Cabinet, which strongly objected to any reference to Poland's border as far west as the western Neisse because it would entail moving such a large German population that the operation would become unmanageable. Stalin and Molotov argued that there should at least be some statement about the eastern frontier, given that they were all agreed on this point, and Churchill concurred. Both Roosevelt and Churchill then proposed that the Poles be consulted regarding Poland's border in the west. Molotov suggested that it might not be necessary to be as specific about the western frontier of Poland as they had been about Poland's eastern frontier with the Soviet Union.

The meeting moved on to other matters but returned to the question of how to handle the issue of Poland's frontiers in the communiqué. Roosevelt proposed drafting amendments that would overcome the U.S. constitutional issue preventing him from committing the United States to boundary changes between countries because this was the prerogative of the U.S. Senate. These amendments were accepted and the following text for the communiqué was approved:

> The three Heads of Government consider that the Eastern frontier of Poland should follow the Curzon Line with digressions from it in some regions of five to eight kilometres in favour of Poland. It is recognized that Poland must receive substantial accessions of territory in the North and West. They feel that the opinion of the New Polish Provisional Government of National Unity should be sought in due course on the extent of these accessions and that the final delimitation of the Western frontier of Poland should thereafter await the Peace Conference.[126]

Molotov had one further suggestion to make, namely, to add to the second sentence "with the return to Poland of her ancient frontiers in East Prussia and on the Oder." Roosevelt asked how long ago this territory had been Polish and Molotov responded "very long ago, but they had in fact been Polish." Roosevelt's rejoinder was that "this might lead the British to ask for the return of the United States to Great Britain." Churchill shared Roosevelt's concerns and preferred not to have any mention in the communiqué of Poland's western frontier. After further discussion, Stalin withdrew Molotov's proposal. The agreed-upon paragraph on Poland's frontiers thus made no mention of East Prussia, although the Big Three were in complete accord that it would be extinguished as a part of Germany and divided between Russia and Poland.

Indeed, Churchill touched on this on February 27, 1945, when he explained to the House of Commons the decisions made at Yalta. Roosevelt did the same when he addressed the U.S. Congress on March 1, 1945.[127] The fate of East Prussia became official five months later at the last conference of the war at Potsdam when the question of Poland's western borders was finally resolved.

G. The Potsdam Conference (July 17–August 2, 1945) and the Expulsion of Germans from the Territory Ceded to Poland

While the Yalta Conference was underway in February 1945, thousands of German civilians, and in particular East Prussians, were attempting to flee the advancing Red Army. The plight of these refugees—described in Chapters III and VI—was far from the minds of the negotiators at Yalta, who decided that Germans still living in the territory ceded to Poland would have to be expelled to what remained of Germany. The outstanding issue for Churchill and Roosevelt was the size of the expelled group: the larger the number to be transferred into a shrunken Germany, the greater the economic burden imposed on the British and American zones of occupation to feed, clothe, and house the German population. Moreover, this issue was closely linked to that of German reparations: the larger the transfer of resources to the Soviet Union, the lower the level of resources available for the Germans in their zones of occupation. Mindful of the difficulties with reparations after World War I, neither Great Britain nor the United States wished to see a drain on their budgets to maintain living standards in postwar Germany. The linkage between Poland's western boundary with Germany and German reparations to Russia would be crucial for the final decisions reached at Potsdam.

In mid-July, when the Potsdam Conference commenced, war was still raging in the Pacific, but in Europe the conflict had been over for two months. Eastern Europe was firmly under Soviet control and millions of Germans were moving westward from eastern Europe, where they were no longer welcome. Some conference participants had firsthand exposure to the plight of these refugees. The chief U.S. representative was now Harry Truman, who, as vice president, had become president when Roosevelt died on April 12, 1945. Shortly after arriving in Potsdam, President Truman, U.S. Secretary of State James Byrnes, and Truman's military advisor William Leahy drove into Berlin on the afternoon of July 16. Truman reported that "[a] more depressing sight than that of the ruined buildings was the long, never-ending procession of old men, women, and children wandering aimlessly along the autobahn and the country roads carrying, pushing, or pulling what was left of their belongings."[128] Leahy was also moved by the endless line of refugees: "These helpless people seemed to be prodded by some urge to get to someplace where they could find food or shelter—anything, apparently, to get out of the Soviet-occupied zone."[129]

Leahy also reported that at dinner Truman's personal party discussed what they had seen that day. It must have made such a sobering impression that no one expressed any feelings of vindictiveness or revenge. It is difficult to say, however, how much impact this exposure to the pitiful sight of German refugees and the devastation of Germany's capital had on Truman's decisions at Potsdam. The British and American delegations had some concerns about what was happening to these refugees, but these did not significantly affect the outcome of the conference. By contrast, the Soviets showed complete disregard for the plight of the refugees. The only reference to this issue was a declaration in Article XIII of the Potsdam Protocol that any such transfers of people "should be effected in an orderly and humane manner." As described in Chapter VI, the expulsion of Germans from that part of East Prussia acquired by Poland was neither orderly nor humane, and the same was true for the millions of Germans expelled from other parts of Poland, Czechoslovakia, and Eastern Europe.

1. Sealing the Fate of East Prussia

The Potsdam Conference dealt with a wide range of issues, including how to deal with defeated Germany, reparations, refugees, and the future shape of postwar Europe. One of the least controversial topics was the final disposition of East Prussia. This issue was sufficiently unimportant for the

United States that it was not included as an agenda item for the conference in the State Department document submitted to President Truman on June 30, 1945.[130] However, Annex 13 of this document contained a large number of briefing papers on what were referred to as "lesser territorial issues," which would be available if needed for the negotiations. One of these was a briefing paper dealing with Germany's eastern frontier and Attachment 1 to this paper made the following recommendation: "East Prussia (except for the Königsberg district, which presumably will go to the Soviet Union) should be ceded to Poland."[131] It also noted that the Polish government would insist on deporting to Germany the remaining Germans from the part of East Prussia acquired by Poland. In addition, the attachment made explicit that the Soviet Union intended to annex the northeastern sector of this German province, including the port of Königsberg.

While East Prussia was not on the agendas of the American and British delegations, it definitely was on the minds of the Soviet delegates, who wished to gain definitive approval for the transfer of East Prussia to Russia. They therefore took the lead on this issue and Molotov raised it parenthetically at the end of a discussion of Turkey when he announced he would send a written proposal regarding Königsberg to the other delegations.[132] This proposal was circulated that same day, July 22. The following morning, Molotov chaired a meeting of foreign ministers at which he stated that Königsberg should be one of four agenda items at the gathering of the Big Three that afternoon. This proposal elicited no reaction from the American and British foreign ministers and the agenda was approved.

The Soviet proposal on Königsberg read as follows:

> On shaping the decision of the three Heads of Governments regarding the transfer to the Soviet Union of the Königsberg area. The Conference approved the proposal of the Soviet Union that pending the final settlement of territorial questions at the Peace Congress, the part of the western border of the U.S.S.R. adjoining the Baltic Sea should follow the line from the point on the western shore of the Danzig Bay indicated on the map annexed

hereto, eastward—north of Braunsberg-Goldap to the junction of the frontiers of the Lithuanian S.S.R., the Polish Republic, and former East Prussia.[133]

At the Seventh Plenary Meeting, which was held at 5:00 p.m. on the afternoon of July 23, Stalin again introduced the subject of the transfer of Königsberg to the Soviet Union by noting that this question had been discussed at Teheran in late 1943.[134] He repeated the arguments he had made there, namely, that it was necessary for Russia to have at least one ice-free port on the Baltic and that "the Russians had suffered and had lost so much blood that they were anxious to have some piece of German territory so as to give some small satisfaction to the tens of millions of their [Russia's] inhabitants who had suffered in this war."[135] Stalin reminded his listeners that all were agreed on this issue at Teheran and that he was anxious to have this agreement approved at Potsdam. Truman said he was ready to agree in principle, but that ethnographic and other questions needed to be studied. Churchill stated that he also agreed in principle and that His Majesty's Government would support "the Soviet wish to have this part of Germany incorporated into the Soviet Union," as he had pointed out in a speech to Parliament on December 15, 1944. However, he still had several concerns: there was a question of the legal basis for the transfer, the Soviet draft proposal presupposed that East Prussia did not exist and that the Königsberg area was not under the authority of the Allied Control Council in Germany, and the draft implied a recognition of the incorporation of Lithuania into the Soviet Union. Churchill said that all of these matters needed to be dealt with at the final peace conference. Stalin replied, "Of course, the matter would be settled at the peace conference." And to clinch the agreement he was seeking, he stated that the Soviets "were satisfied that the British and American Governments approved."[136] Churchill then closed the discussion of the transfer of the northern one-third of East Prussia to Russia by noting that the agreement of the Three Powers on this transfer would be recorded in the minutes of the meeting, but that the Russian proposal that they had just discussed needed to be redrafted in certain respects in order for it to be included in the conference communiqué.

The foreign ministers met in Potsdam for the last time on Wednesday, August 1. They discussed British and Soviet drafts of the proposal for the transfer of the northern part of East Prussia to the Soviet Union.[137] British Foreign Secretary Ernest Bevin prevailed upon Molotov to use the British draft as the basis for consideration because it took into account Churchill's concerns regarding the original Soviet draft.[138] After a brief discussion, there was agreement that the title of this section of the communiqué should be "City of Königsberg and the Adjacent Area."

Molotov then proposed a number of amendments to the British draft, arguing first that the word "provisionally" should be deleted from the sentence "the section of the western frontier of the Union of Soviet Socialist Republics should provisionally pass from a point on the eastern shore of the Bay of Danzig" on the grounds that the same paragraph already said "pending final decision." U.S. Secretary of State Byrnes asked Molotov if he agreed that there was no question that the transfer would be "pending final determination," whereby all parties understood that this wording referred to "the final determination of territorial questions at the peace settlement." Molotov replied, "Of course," whereupon Byrnes and Bevin agreed to delete "provisionally."

Molotov then objected to the statement that the new frontier would be "subject to expert examination," but Bevin argued that this wording was vital to the British, and Molotov backed down. The last amendment Molotov proposed was to delete "in principle" from the last paragraph in the British draft, which read as follows: "The President of the United States and the British Prime Minister have declared that they will support in principle this proposal at the forthcoming peace settlement." Molotov argued that these two words already appeared in the preceding paragraph, and Bevin and Byrnes agreed to this deletion.

Molotov's suggested changes were designed to remove any ambiguity that northern East Prussia was to be ceded to the Soviet Union. If the final communiqué had included "in principle" in the last paragraph, it would have been possible for Truman and Attlee—or their successors—to argue later that while they agreed in principle to support the Soviet proposal, in practice there were certain considerations that in their view militated against it. By removing these two words, U.S. and British support for the proposal became unequivocal. In addition, given the fact that by August 1945 the Soviets were already in full control and administering their part of East Prussia as if they were rightful owners, they had no reservations about the qualification that the transfer of this German territory to them depended on "the final determination of territorial questions at the peace settlement." The Western Allies believed this caveat meant that the territorial changes were not final and could be modified, whereas for the Soviets "facts on the ground" were what counted. They already behaved as permanent owners of their newly acquired property and neither the United States nor Great Britain objected to this assertion of property rights.

The final version of the agreement on the transfer of the northern third of East Prussia, which appeared in both the protocol of the conference proceedings and the communiqué, is as follows:

VI. City of Königsberg and the Adjacent Area

The Conference examined a proposal by the Soviet Government that pending the final determination of territorial questions at the peace settlement, the section of the western frontier of the Union of Soviet Social Republics which is adjacent to the Baltic Sea should pass from a point on the eastern shore of the Bay of Danzig to the east, north of Braunsberg-Goldap, to the meeting point of the frontiers of Lithuania, the Polish Republic and East Prussia.

The Conference has agreed in principle to the proposal of the Soviet Government concerning the ultimate transfer to the Soviet Union of the City of Königsberg and the area adjacent to it as described above subject to expert examination of the actual frontier.

The President of the United States and the British Prime Minister have declared that they will support the proposal of the Conference at the forthcoming peace settlement.[139]

Thus, in three short paragraphs, Königsberg, which had been founded in 1255 by the King of Bohemia and had over hundreds of years become a truly German city in which two German kings were crowned, ceased to be a part of Germany in 1945. The Soviet takeover of Königsberg and the northern third of East Prussia was entirely inconsistent with the Atlantic Charter, but the American and British delegations at Potsdam never mentioned this. Moreover, no consideration was given to what would happen to the Germans still living in Königsberg and northern East Prussia at war's end. Would the Russians expel them as the Poles intended to in their territory newly acquired from Germany? Would they be added to the mouths to feed in the American and British zones of occupation, which was one of the key issues for the American and British negotiators at Potsdam? If these questions arose, they never were expressed at the Potsdam Conference.

2. The Decision on Poland's Western Borders

In Potsdam, the Big Three were in full agreement on the disposition of the northern third of East Prussia. They were also in accord that the southern two-thirds should be allocated to Poland. However, the fate of this part of East Prussia hinged on reaching a decision on Poland's western borders and hence on the extent to which Germany's eastern territory (southern East Prussia, West Prussia, Pomerania, part of Brandenburg, and Silesia) would be lopped off and awarded to Poland. It eventually came down to the question of whether Poland's frontier with Germany would run along the eastern Neisse River, as proposed by the Western Allies, or along the western Neisse River, as demanded by Russia and desired by Poland (see Map 11. The Oder-Neisse Line). This border question proved to be one of the most contentious at Potsdam because it was inextricably linked to the number of German refugees who would be expelled from this region and to the size of the reparations the Soviet Union would receive from postwar Germany.

Poland's western frontiers were first considered at the Second Plenary Meeting in Potsdam on Wednesday, July 18, 1945.[140] Churchill began the discussion by posing the question: "What is Germany?" Stalin wanted a deal with postwar Germany, i.e., minus the territory it had lost in the war. He argued that it was not possible to ignore the results of the war and he was also emphatic with regard to the territory claimed by Russia: "If [a] German administration appears in Königsberg, we would expel it."[141] Stalin wanted to nail down the borders of Germany that he had in mind, but Truman felt that this was putting the cart before the horse and insisted forcefully that the starting point should be Germany as it existed geographically in 1937. Churchill concurred and Stalin eventually assented.

The Big Three continued their discussion of this topic during the Third Plenary Session on July 21.[142] Truman made a statement regarding Poland's frontiers in which he expressed concern that it appeared Poland had been given a zone of occupation without prior consultation and he did not see how reparations could be discussed if Germany were already carved up. Stalin claimed it was not accurate that Russia had given Poland a zone of occupation. He noted that his country had received communications from the Americans and the British protesting the establishment of Polish administration in certain areas before Poland's western boundary had been established.[143] He could not accept what he termed "suggestions" because, in the face of the advancing Red Army, the Germans had left these areas in need of a local administration, and "[h]e was unable to see what harm was done by the establishment of a Polish administration where only Poles live." This response generated a testy exchange between Truman and Stalin. The U.S. president "wanted it distinctly understood that the zones of occupation will be as established," as any other course would make decisions on reparations very difficult if parts of Germany were already excluded. Stalin retorted—in his *Memoirs* Truman reported that Stalin "boasted"[144]—that he was not afraid of the reparations question and would renounce them if necessary. He then challenged Truman by characterizing everything Truman had said as "interpretative since no frontiers had been ceded at the Crimea [Yalta] Conference except for the provision that Poland would receive territory. The western frontier question is open and the Soviet Union is not bound." Truman was obviously incredulous and turning to Stalin asked, "You are not?" Stalin replied, "No." Sensing that further progress on the border issue was impossible, Truman stated that this question could not be settled by heads of government and would have to be a matter for the peace conference.[145]

Stalin was determined to have this issue resolved at Potsdam. He had no intention of waiting for a peace conference to be convened at some unknown date in the future. He therefore continued the discussion and sought to persuade Truman that a Polish administration was needed because there were no German people left in this area. There then ensued a long discussion of how many Germans in fact remained in the eastern German territories at issue (southern East Prussia, West Prussia, Pomerania, part of Brandenburg, and Silesia). Stalin maintained that all the Germans had fled: "No single German remained in the territory to be given Poland." He even asserted that some Germans "had gone to the Königsberg area since they had learned that the Russians would be in Königsberg and they preferred to deal with the Russians than with the Poles."[146] (As noted in Chapter VI, in some cases East Prussians did implore the Russians to intervene on their behalf against depredations by the Poles, but Stalin's statement is demonstrably false, as Chapter III makes clear.) By contrast, Truman put the number of Germans remaining in the contested area at nine million, a figure that was about the same as the estimate of a prewar population of eight and a half million provided by Churchill. Repeating the argument he had put forth at Yalta, Churchill asserted that if what Stalin said were true, the question nonetheless remained of how the millions of people who had fled were to be fed in the rest of Germany, given that the land that they had left would not be available to help support the population of Germany—what remained of it. When Churchill emphasized that the Western Allies "did not wish to be confronted by a mass of starving people," Stalin responded, "there will be none." In his *Memoirs,* Truman reported that this remark prompted Admiral William Leahy to whisper to him, "Of course not…the Bolshies have killed all of them!"[147]

By this time Truman had become exasperated with what he considered to be endless debates on a matter that could not be settled at the conference, and given the need to deal with more urgent questions, he wished to avoid "any sharpening of the verbal clashes" and admitted, "I was becoming very impatient, and on a number of occasions I felt like blowing the roof off the place."[148] He did not "blow his top" but intervened to make his views unmistakably clear:

> At last I intervened to say that it seemed to be an accomplished fact that a large piece of Germany had been given to the Poles. The Silesian coal mines, I pointed out, were a part of Germany for reparations and feeding purposes, and these were now in Polish hands. We could talk about boundary and feeding problems, but the Poles, I emphasized, had no right to take this territory and remove it from the German economy.[149]

Truman then made what he called a frank statement of his views: "He could not agree to the separation of the eastern part of Germany under the circumstances. This must be considered in connection with reparations and the supply problems of the whole German people."[150] Stalin asked abruptly, "Are we through?" and Truman announced that the conference had apparently reached an impasse on this matter and adjourned the meeting.

The discussion of Poland's western frontier was resumed at the Sixth Plenary Session on July 22.[151] Truman said that he had nothing to add to what he had already stated on the matter, but Churchill said that he could not agree to the western Neisse River as part of Poland's western frontier because the British "would have a grave moral responsibility for the transfer of enormous populations." Truman observed that he did not see the urgency of deciding the frontier issue then and there, as a final settlement would have to wait for the peace conference. Churchill then explained why in his view this question was of considerable urgency: "If the settlement of the question were delayed the present local situation [in Germany's eastern territory] would be consolidated. Poles would be digging themselves in and taking effective steps to make themselves the sole masters of this territory. The longer the problem waited the more difficult it would be to settle it."[152] Stalin agreed with Churchill that a decision was needed that would definitively fix the western border of Poland: "The question to be settled was that of the frontier and not that of a temporary line. They could settle the matter or put it off, but they could not ignore it."[153]

During this discussion Stalin proposed several times that the Lublin Poles should be invited to Potsdam to present their views on the border issue to the foreign ministers, and Churchill and Truman finally agreed. As a result, President Bolesław Bierut, Prime Minister Edward Osobka-Morawski, Deputy Prime Minister Stanislaw Mikolajczyk, Deputy Prime Minister Wladysaw Gomulka, and four other officials attended the Seventh Meeting of Foreign Ministers on July 24.[154] They made a lengthy case for the western Neisse River as their western border with Germany. Soviet Foreign Minister Molotov urged his counterparts to be sympathetic to the Polish preferences, but U.S. Secretary of State Byrnes and British Foreign Minister Eden committed themselves only to conveying the Polish views to the Big Three. How much influence the Polish representations had on the Western Allies is difficult to say. Two American participants at Potsdam seemed resigned to Polish control of all the German territory they currently occupied. U.S. advisor William Leahy wrote: "It was my opinion that Russia would not take corrective action and that there was nothing we or Britain could do about it. We would have had to be prepared to take military action to overturn the Soviet *fait accompli*."[155] U.S. Secretary of State Byrnes expressed a similar view:

> We had recognized from the outset, however, that we would have to accept for the time being the Polish administration of this part of the Soviet zone. It was an accomplished fact and we could not force the Russians to resume the responsibilities they had voluntarily resigned. However, no agreement even on the temporary administration was reached until we came to grips with the issue of reparations.[156]

The issue of reparations turned out to be the key to the agreement reached on Poland's western frontiers. The Americans at Potsdam had come to the conclusion that the Soviets could not be budged from their insistence on the western Neisse River as Poland's border in the west. But they were loath to make a concession on this point, and the British even more so, because this would result in more German refugees coming into the American and

British occupation zones who would have to be fed and housed, and the additional land taken by Poland would further reduce the agricultural production available to support the German population. Moreover, if Germany were forced to pay large reparations to the victors, there was a high probability the Americans and the British would have to use their own resources to prevent the Germans from starving. There was thus a clear link between the western border issue and the magnitude of the reparations. Byrnes was well aware that the Soviets were very keen on obtaining the maximum possible reparations, but he feared that the more they received, the more likely the Americans and the British would have to foot the bill for feeding Germans. With a potential linkage between these two key issues, he saw the makings of a deal: if the Western Allies acquiesced to Stalin's border demands, the Soviets would have to make concessions on reparations.[157]

Before the deal could be brokered and sealed, a change occurred in the British leadership at Potsdam. On Wednesday, July 25, 1945, Churchill, Eden, and Clement Attlee (the leader of the Labor opposition, who had been in Potsdam as an observer from the beginning of the conference) flew back to London to await the results of the British national election held that day. In the morning they attended the Ninth Plenary Meeting of the conference, and after he had made his last statement, Churchill declared, "I am finished." Stalin commented, "What a pity." Striking an optimistic note, Churchill responded, "I hope to be back." Stalin then observed, "Judging from the expression on Mr. Attlee's face, I do not think he looks forward avidly to taking over your authority."[158] The following day the election returns were in: the Conservatives were voted out of office in a landslide victory for Labor and Attlee took over as prime minister and formed a new government. He returned to Potsdam late on Saturday, July 28, with his foreign secretary, Ernest Bevin, and as head of the British delegation attended the Tenth Plenary Meeting held at 10:30 the same evening, when the border issue was not discussed.

On Sunday, Truman and Byrnes met privately with Molotov—Stalin was indisposed with a cold—and attempted to get the Soviets to agree to the eastern Neisse as Poland's western border.[159] Molotov rejected this proposal because Stalin would insist that Poland receive all the German territory up to the western Neisse. Byrnes moved on to the question of German reparations and offered the Soviet Union twenty-five percent of the industrial capital equipment (i.e., factories, machinery, and equipment) as reparations from the Ruhr industrial area of Germany. To Molotov, "25 percent of an unde-termined figure meant very little and that they wished to have a fixed sum or quantity agreed upon." Byrnes refused to budge and argued that it was impossible at this stage to put a value on equipment that had the potential for reparations. He then suggested an alternative formula: instead of twenty-five percent exclusively from the Ruhr, the Soviets could receive twelve and a half percent of such equipment available for reparations from the combined American, British, and French zones. Molotov did not react to this new offer and instead returned to the issue of a fixed sum for reparations. This was again rejected by Byrnes and the meeting ended in a stalemate.

The following day, Monday, July 30, the U.S. secretary of state met pri-vately with Molotov at 4:30 p.m. and informed him that the United States was prepared to make concessions to meet Soviet desires and would agree to Polish administration of German territory all the way to the western, rather than just to the eastern Neisse.[160] This proposal included the condition that "[t]he three Heads of Government reaffirm their opinion that the final delimitation of the western frontier of Poland should await the peace settlement." It also made explicit that the "former German territories" to be put under the administra-tion of the Polish state included "that portion of East Prussia not placed under the administration of the Union of Soviet Socialist Republics in accordance with the understanding reached at this conference."[161] East Prussia was thereby completely and definitively extinguished as part of Germany at Potsdam.

Byrnes then moved to a second issue: the conditions for membership in the United Nations for Italy, Bulgaria, Finland, Hungary, and Romania.[162] This topic was not particularly contentious, but Molotov could not say at that point whether the U.S. proposal would be acceptable to the Soviet delega-tion. Moving to the third and most difficult issue, that of reparations, Byrnes handed Molotov a note with a revised U.S. proposal for Soviet reparations from the Ruhr: (a) the Soviet Union would receive twenty-five percent of industrial capital equipment deemed not necessary for a peacetime economy, and in exchange the equivalent value in food, coal, potash, zinc, timber, clay, and oil products would be delivered by the Soviets to the United States, France, and Great Britain; and (b) an additional fifteen percent of such industrial capital equipment would be transferred to the Soviet Union without payment or exchange of any kind.[163] Molotov proposed raising the amount listed under (b) from fifteen to twenty-five percent, but Byrnes doubted that the British would agree to such a high figure. It is not clear whether the Americans would have agreed either. Indeed, W. Averell Harriman, the U.S. ambassador to the Soviet Union, had come to the view that: "When I saw how completely the Russians had stripped every factory they could get their hands on [in the Russian zone] I realized that their conception of surplus tools and machinery which could be taken from Germany was far tougher than we could ever agree to."[164] The Russians took everything of possible economic value from their zone and shipped it back to the Soviet Union: "One thousand two hundred enterprises were hastily dismantled in a fortnight, possibly out of fear that the Allies would call a halt in favor of a systemic policy. Electricity cables and toilets were ripped out of private homes on 'orders' from Moscow."[165] Neither the British nor the Americans wanted this to happen in their occupation zones.[166]

The matter of reparations resurfaced at the Tenth Meeting of Foreign Ministers, which followed at 5:00 p.m. that same Monday. Byrnes reiterated the three proposals he had just discussed with Molotov. After a lengthy discussion, Molotov declared that Byrnes's proposal was largely acceptable, although he still would prefer some indication of the minimum amount of reparations that would be involved. Bevin then spoke up and said the proposal was not acceptable because all the equipment for reparations would come out of the British zone. Molotov seized on Bevin's concern and proposed that both British and American zones should constitute the basis for reparations to Russia. Byrnes countered that he was amenable to this suggestion if the percentages were cut in half, i.e., twenty-five reduced to twelve and a half percent and fifteen to seven and a half percent. Bevin regarded these figures as acceptable, but Molotov wanted higher percentages. Byrnes then argued that because a) the proposal on the Polish frontier involved a concession by the British and the Americans, and b) the proposal on membership in the United Nations also involved a concession on their part, the Soviets should also make a concession and agree to the percentages he had proposed. When it became evident that Molotov was still holding out for a definite figure for the amount of reparations, Byrnes presented a take-it-or-leave-it ultimatum: all three issues—the Polish frontier, conditions for U.N. membership, and reparations—had to be considered together as a package. If there were no agreement on reparations, he could not agree on the other two issues. Faced with an impasse, the foreign secretaries placed the three-point proposal on the agenda for the plenary session the following day.

At the Eleventh Plenary Meeting on Tuesday, July 31, Stalin no longer insisted on a fixed amount of industrial capital equipment; he agreed to the principle that reparations should be expressed as percentages but held out for more favorable figures for Russia. After further haggling over the numbers, Stalin proposed slightly higher figures: raising twelve and a half to fifteen percent, and seven and a half to ten percent. Truman and Churchill consented and the issue of reparations was finally resolved.

The meeting then turned again to the question of Poland's western frontier. Bevin's instructions were to hold out for the eastern Neisse River and he noted that the U.S. proposal stated that the territory up to the western Neisse River would be under the Polish state and would not be part of the Soviet occupation zone. While the territory would be under Polish administration, he presumed nonetheless that it would technically remain under Allied military control, as otherwise there would have been a transfer of territory before the peace conference. He also pointed out that the Control Commission's authority was to extend over what had been included in all of Germany's 1937 borders. Bevin thus put his finger on a delicate question of apparent inconsistency: how there could be no transfer of territory if, in fact, the Poles were already administering it. Byrnes was keen to get the deal done and provided a legalistic way to square the circle:

> Mr. Byrnes said that they all understood that the cession of territory was left to the peace conference. They had found a situation where Poland was administering with Soviet consent a good part

of this territory. By this action the three powers agreed to the administration in the interim by Poland in order that there would be no further dispute between them in regard to the administration of the area by the Polish Provisional Government.[167]

The "administration of the area" was thus regarded as an interim arrangement, whereas the actual transfer of territory would only take place at the peace conference. This language gave the appearance that a final decision had not been reached on the western frontier of Poland and—in principle—there was scope for reversion from the western to the eastern Neisse River. Moreover, by saying there would be "no further dispute" over the administration of the area, Byrnes clearly wanted to lay the matter to rest. His explanation apparently satisfied Bevin, who said he would not press the matter, but he then asked what would happen to the area and to the Soviet troops stationed there. Stalin claimed that four-fifths of Soviet troops had been removed from Poland, and "[a]s to the transfer of the territory to the Poles he pointed out that the territory was now actually already administered by Poles. There was no Russian administration." For Stalin, there was no doubt that a "transfer of territory" had in fact taken place.

Byrnes, on the other hand, was of the view that Poland's western frontier had not been fixed at the conference. He contrasted the promise made to the Soviet Union regarding Königsberg with the absence of such a promise on Poland's border with Germany:

> Our deliberate avoidance of a promise on the Polish border is emphasized by the promise we did make in the protocol about the transfer of the city of Königsberg to the Soviet Union, when we said: "the President of the United States and the British Prime Minister have declared that they will support the proposal of this conference at the forthcoming peace settlement."

To remove any excuse for Poland or the Soviet Union to claim that a line had been established or that there was any promise to support a particular line, the Berlin Protocol declared: "The three heads of government reaffirm their opinion that the final delimitation of the western frontier of Poland should await the peace settlement."[168]

Even though Byrnes stressed in this passage that in his view no promises had been made, he nonetheless recognized "that we would have to accept for the time being the Polish administration of this part of the Soviet zone. It was an accomplished fact...." Herbert Feis, in his book on the Potsdam Conference, was more straightforward when he observed that the fact that German territory east of the Oder and the Neisse would be under Polish administration and not part of the Soviet-occupied zone of Germany "meant the permanent detachment of this part of Germany," notwithstanding the qualification regarding the peace settlement.[169] The Soviet view was, of course, that the border between Germany and Poland had been fixed at Potsdam: "True, the resolutions of the Conference said that the final delimitation of Poland's Western frontier had to be deferred until the 'peace settlement.' But the mere fact that the Berlin Conference provided for the Germans to be evicted from the territories handed over to Poland meant that these decisions were irrevocable, i.e., final."[170] Indeed, the logic of this Soviet argument is unassailable. As the British and the Americans had agreed to the removal of all Germans in the territory of eastern Germany placed under Polish administration, once this land was emptied of Germans any claim that it was nevertheless German could not carry much force. The three Allies were therefore on board regarding Poland's western border with Germany and agreement was quickly reached on the issue of the admission of several countries to the United Nations. Byrnes was thus successful in obtaining Stalin's and Attlee's endorsement of his three-part package. At this final meeting of the Big Three to settle the outstanding issues of World War II, Stalin was able to get Great Britain and the United States to concur with the territorial objectives he had already achieved unilaterally with regard to East Prussia.

The decisions at Potsdam had far-reaching consequences not only for East Prussians but for all Germans and those living in Eastern Europe.

These decisions allowed the Soviet Union to dominate Eastern Europe and impose Communism on millions of people until the dissolution of the Soviet Union in 1991. They also led to the division of Germany into the Federal Republic of Germany (West Germany) and the German Democratic Republic (East Germany), which were not reunited until after the fall of the Berlin Wall on November 9, 1989.

The border between Poland and Germany was subsequently ratified by a treaty concluded between the Polish Republic and the German Democratic Republic on July 6, 1950.[171] This frontier lay between the German Democratic Republic and Poland, but the Polish government wished to have this boundary recognized by the Federal Republic of Germany as well. Such recognition was forthcoming in the first paragraph of Article I of the treaty between the two countries, signed on December 7, 1970, which stated that they were in mutual agreement that the existing boundary line, described in Chapter IX of the Potsdam Conference, "shall constitute the western State frontier of the People's Republic of Poland."[172] In the second paragraph, the two countries "reaffirm the inviolability of their existing frontiers," and in the third, they declared that "they have no territorial claims whatsoever against each other and that they will not assert such claims in the future." Thus twenty-five years after the Potsdam Conference, the issue of Poland's western boundary with Germany was settled once and for all.

East and West Germany were reunited in 1990, and following the so-called "two plus four" negotiations, a treaty was signed on September 12, 1990, in which they agreed that the borders of the united Germany were definitive.[173] Shortly afterward, on November 9, 1990, the Treaty of Good Neighbors, Partnership, and Cooperation between the Federal Republic of Germany and the Soviet Union was signed and the two parties committed themselves to observe unconditionally the territorial integrity of all European states in their current borders and that they viewed now and in the future the borders of all European states as inviolable. In addition, they declared that they had no territorial claims on others.[174] By signing these treaties, Germany agreed never to assert any rights to East Prussia and this easternmost province was irrevocably severed from the country of its origin.[175]

3. The Expulsion of German Minorities in Eastern Europe to Germany

At the Potsdam Conference the Allies were cognizant of the close relationship between the location of Poland's western border with Germany and the number of Germans likely to be expelled from Poland's newly acquired territory. Indeed, from early on Churchill's main argument against the western Neisse River as Poland's new frontier had been that the resulting huge stream of refugees would overwhelm the capacity of the British and the Americans to deal with them in their respective occupation zones. Great Britain had been economically devastated by the war and was keen to limit recourse to its own limited resources for the support of Germans from Eastern Europe. The Western Allies' primary consideration regarding the plight of the refugees themselves was economic rather than humanitarian. In his book on the expulsions, Alfred de Zayas characterized the Western view of the German transfers "as declaredly limited in scope—not out of pity for the Germans but out of practical considerations with respect to concrete problems of post-war reorganization."[176] Nevertheless, such "practical considerations" also extended to the manner in which the expulsions would take place, and the communiqué of the Potsdam Conference expressed the hope that these transfers would be handled in an "orderly and humane manner."

Long before the meeting at Potsdam, considerable time had been spent in discussion and analysis at the British Foreign Office on how to proceed with the removal of millions of Germans in postwar Poland and Czechoslovakia. By November 1943, the Foreign Office had already established a Committee on the Transfer of German Populations to explore this problem and to make recommendations for dealing with it.[177] At its very first meeting on December 7, 1943, the committee decided to proceed on the basis of the following two assumptions:

> (1) that if possible transfers of population should be carried out in such a way as to avoid inflicting very severe economic dislocation on Germany, and (2) that it was impossible to ignore the possible suffering by and cruelty to refugees involved in the transfers

contemplated, if only because of the reaction such suffering might have on public opinion in Allied countries.[178]

The committee's chair, John Troutbeck (head of the Foreign Office's German department), asked it to consider a number of aspects: Germany's capacity over the long term to absorb the refugees; the short-term measures needed to feed, house, and transport the expellees; the appropriate time frame for the transfer; and the possibility that some of the refugees could be accommodated outside of Germany, for example, in Siberia. In March 1944, Troutbeck modified the the committee's initial draft report in light of the additional difficulties that would arise if Poland received greatly expanded German territory and if expulsions of Germans from Hungary, Romania, and Yugoslavia also took place:

> 1. Problem of immense magnitude. Large-scale transfers will inevitably cause great suffering and much criticism, and be an obstacle to European reconstruction. They can be justified solely on grounds of (a) security, (b) saving transferees from maltreatment if they remain, (c) possibility that in the long run a Europe of homogenous States would work more harmoniously.[179]

The committee's final report highlighted the difficulties that would be associated with large-scale expulsions of Germans from the territory acquired by Poland and from other countries in central and eastern Europe. Orme Sargent, the deputy under-secretary in the Foreign Office, concluded on the basis of the report that the wholesale population transfers being considered would only be feasible if (1) they were carried out by the Russians, who would be prepared to act in a ruthless manner; and (2) the Germans were sent to Siberia, where they would be forgotten, rather than to Germany, where they would agitate for their return to their native lands. Richard Laws, the state minister in the Foreign Office, also emphasized the problems of wholesale transfers that were stressed in the report: "The Report brings out clearly the possible dimensions of the problem, and the very grave difficulties which would attend efforts to solve it on lines often approved in general public discussion of post-war questions."[180] In light of the challenges foreseen in the removal of millions of Germans from central and eastern Europe, the British Foreign Office did not see fit to send the report to the U.S. government because, according to Detlef Brandes (a German expert on this subject), if the British Cabinet nevertheless came out in favor of these transfers, the Foreign Office did not wish to be in a position of having to provide the U.S. authorities with counterarguments to the report's conclusions.

Prior to Potsdam there was also concern in the U.S. State Department about how the transfers would be carried out. A briefing paper prepared for the Yalta Conference, dated January 12, 1945, estimated that roughly 5.5 million Germans might be expelled from the German territory acquired by Poland (up to the eastern Neisse River) and from the Sudetenland in Czechoslovakia. It stated that "an indiscriminate expulsion of so many people would add enormously to the confusion likely to exist in that area, threatening the public health of much of Europe and jeopardizing the peace and good order of the continent."[181] Notwithstanding these reservations, the document argued that it would not be "expedient" for the United States to oppose such large-scale transfers if Poland and Czechoslovakia insisted they take place and if they had the support of the British and the Soviets. It recommended that the United States therefore pursue "a policy whereby these transfers would be kept to a minimum, would take place gradually in an orderly manner under international auspices agreed upon by the Principal Allies on the one hand and Poland and Czechoslovakia on the other."[182] Similar concerns were raised in a briefing paper, dated June 29, 1945, for the Potsdam Conference dealing with U.S. policy toward Poland: "We should facilitate insofar as our aid is requested the transfer of minority groups but we should not permit the forced repatriation of Poles now in the West or the uncontrolled deportation by unilateral Polish action of the 8–10 million Germans formerly domiciled in the areas claimed by the Soviet-sponsored Polish Government."[183] Such statements of concern did not help the Germans being expelled from the southern part of East Prussia controlled by Poland; in the summer of 1945 thousands of East Prussians were already being evicted from their homes.

The same issue arose with respect to arrangements for the transfer of Sudeten Germans from Czechoslovakia. In fact, the Czechoslovak government sent a note on July 3, 1945, to the U.S. Embassy in Prague (similar notes were sent to Great Britain and the U.S.S.R), which emphasized that it was essential for the "lasting peace and stability of Central Europe" that 2–2.5 million Germans be expelled from Czechoslovakia without delay. Given the magnitude of the task involved, the note indicated that the Czechoslovak government was preparing a plan for the organization of this transfer and suggested that the Allies consult with them regarding the timing and the number of Germans to be transferred to the different occupation zones in Germany. The note also requested that this topic be discussed at the forthcoming Potsdam Conference.[184] The State Department responded by first noting that it had already conveyed its views to the Czechoslovak government on the transfer of Germans in January, namely that these transfers should be carried out in an organized manner, with international agreement, and should be gradual so that facilities could be provided for the orderly settlement of those transferred. It then added that pending international arrangements, there should be no unilateral transfers of large groups.[185]

At Potsdam, the first discussion of transfers of populations took place at the Ninth Plenary Meeting at 11:00 a.m. on July 25.[186] Churchill pointed out that there were 2.5 million Germans who needed to be moved out of the Sudetenland and said that the British did not want them in their zone, as they "brought their mouths with them." Stalin observed that whereas the Czechs had given the Germans two hours' notice and then evicted them, Poland wished to keep 1.5 million Germans to help with the harvest and would then expel them. Churchill objected to this action by the Poles, but Stalin replied that "the Poles did not ask but did as they liked." Churchill pointed out that the Poles were expelling Germans from the Soviet occupation zone and this should not be done without consideration of food supplies and reparations, matters that had not yet been decided. When Stalin retorted that one had to understand that the Poles were seeking revenge on the Germans for all the harm they had caused them over the centuries, "Churchill pointed out that their revenge took the form of throwing the Germans into the American and German zones to be fed."[187]

Churchill and Stalin then turned to reparation and border issues, but Eden tried to steer the discussion back to the question of the transfer of populations by noting that Dr. Edvard Beneš, the president of Czechoslovakia, had asked that this subject be addressed at the conference. Stalin asked whether the Czechs should come to the conference. Churchill responded that he would be very glad to see his "old friend Dr. Beneš." This prompted Stalin to ask whether "this would not mean serving the mustard after supper"; since the transfers had already taken place, no purpose would be served by consulting Dr. Beneš. Churchill countered that he had heard that the Czechs and the Soviets had agreed not to transport more than one thousand Germans at any one time, and as 2.5 million were involved, the entire transfer would necessarily take place over an extended period. Stalin stated flatly that there was no such agreement. Stalin and Truman then accepted Churchill's proposal that the foreign ministers explore this question.

The question of the transfers of Germans was almost immediately taken up at the Eighth Meeting of the foreign ministers at 12:30 that day.[188] British Foreign Secretary Eden had by this time departed to await the election results in Great Britain, and in his absence, Alexander Cadogan, the British permanent under-secretary of state for foreign affairs, opened the discussion by noting that the problem included not only Sudeten Germans from Czechoslovakia but also Germans from western Poland (including southern East Prussia) as well as from Hungary. He stated that the British did not have a detailed plan, but that "in view of the difficulty that would be caused by this movement, the matter should be under the Allied Control Council, acting with the cooperation of the governments concerned." While Cadogan spoke of the difficulty the transfers would involve, he did not convey the dire message in the Foreign Office report cited above, which emphasized the suffering likely to be endured by the Germans in a mass exodus. U.S. Secretary of State Byrnes was more specific: he stressed the hardships that would be caused by unilateral action on the part of individual countries that forced the precipitate removal of Germans, and endorsed a gradual and orderly transfer so as not to exacerbate the problem of feeding the refugees. Favoring a more organized approach to this chaotic situation, he proposed that the Allied Control Council be authorized to regulate the transfers and to consult with the governments of Czechoslovakia, Hungary, and Poland to try to avoid what he characterized as "a very bad situation." In response, Molotov suggested that concrete proposals be drawn up and the Allies agreed to set up a subcommittee to prepare a draft on the topic.

The Allies considered this draft at the Eleventh Plenary Meeting on July 31.[189] At this meeting Byrnes reported that the draft—which became Article XIII of the Potsdam communiqué—was acceptable to all parties except for the last paragraph, which he urged his counterparts to agree to because it was needed to make the document effective:

> *Orderly Transfers of German Populations.* The Conference reached the following agreement on the removal of Germans from Poland [including southern East Prussia], Czechoslovakia, and Hungary:
>
> > The Three Governments, having considered the question in all its aspects, recognize that the transfer to Germany of German populations, or elements thereof, remaining in Poland, Czechoslovakia, and Hungary, will have to be undertaken. They agree that any transfers that take place should be effected in an orderly and humane manner.
> >
> > Since the influx of a large number of Germans into Germany would increase the burden already resting on the occupying authorities, they consider that the Allied Control Council in Germany should in the first instance examine the problem with special regard to the question of the equitable distribution of these Germans among the several zones of occupation. They are accordingly instructing their respective representatives on the Control Council to report to their Governments as soon as possible the extent to which such persons have already entered Germany from Poland, Czechoslovakia and Hungary, and to submit an estimate

of the time and rate at which further transfers could be carried out, having regard to the present situation in Germany.

The Czechoslovak Government, the Polish Provisional Government and the Control Council in Hungary are at the same time being informed of the above, and are being requested meanwhile to suspend further expulsions pending the examination by the Governments concerned of the report from their representatives on the Control Council.[190]

Molotov noted that while the document aimed at making the transfers orderly, it would likely be misunderstood by the three governments mentioned and a decision should not be made without consulting them. Stalin had even stronger reservations and contended that even if the document were approved, it could not be carried out because the Polish, Czechoslovak, and Hungarian governments had created conditions "which made the Germans want to leave" and were such that "it is impossible for the Germans to remain." He characterized the document as a "shot in the void."[191] Byrnes defended the document and argued that the last paragraph simply asked the three governments to suspend all action on the transfers until the Council could consider these problems. If the Poles, Czechs, and Hungarians were expelling Germans, then the three governments should be required to cooperate and to regulate the transfers in an orderly fashion. According to the information available to him, Germans were being forced to leave in some cases and "[t]heir departure for other countries increased burdens intolerably." Stalin countered that the Poles and the Czechs would inform the conference that their governments had not given any expulsion orders and that the Germans had fled. Nonetheless, if Attlee and Truman insisted on including the last paragraph, he would agree to it. This prompted Truman to interject that he appreciated very much Stalin's agreement on this matter, saying that "[p]erhaps the document would not change the situation very much, but it would help." Attlee concurred and the draft document reproduced above, entitled "Orderly Transfers of German Minorities," was approved and became part of the Potsdam communiqué.

The second and third paragraphs of Section XIII of the communiqué cited above are clearly aimed at mitigating this burden in the British and American zones. This is the judgment of Leahy, who in his account of the conference wrote that "Eviction of Germans from Czechoslovakia, Poland, and Hungary threatened to impose a severe burden on the occupation zones of Germany, particularly since most of the refugees were entering the British and American zones."[192] But he made no mention of the plight of the refugees themselves, and neither did Truman in his memoirs. While the first sentence of the document states unequivocally that the Germans will have to be removed from Poland, Czechoslovakia, and Hungary, the plight of the expelled Germans is recognized only indirectly in the second sentence, which states that the three governments at Potsdam "agree that any transfers that take place should be effected in an orderly and humane manner." Nothing was said of enjoining the governments of Czechoslovakia, Hungary, and Poland to carry out the expulsions in an orderly and humane fashion.

Thus, Herbert Feis is not very persuasive when, in his account of the Potsdam Conference, he describes the American and British governments as being "distressed…at the suffering that abrupt expulsion was causing old and young, poor and rich, healthy and sick. They thought it the duty of any humane people to subdue their impulse to punish and to show compassion to those who were losing their homes."[193] A more accurate picture is conveyed by Charles Bohlen, a special assistant to Byrnes and the official U.S. translator, who observed that three months after the end of the war, memories of Nazi atrocities, particularly against the Jews, were still fresh: "The spirit of mercy was not throbbing in the breast of any Allied official at Potsdam; there was no disposition to be lenient with the Germans."[194] The result for the expelled Germans was catastrophic. The expulsion of the East Prussians, in particular, from the territory Poland had acquired from Germany was hardly orderly or humane.

H. Concluding Observations

The end of East Prussia reflected long-standing territorial objectives of both the Soviet Union and Poland. Stalin persuaded his Allies that his country needed a warm-water port on the Baltic, and they apparently did not anticipate that the northern third of East Prussia would be used by the Soviet Union as a major military base in the heart of central Europe. Churchill and Roosevelt, and later Attlee and Truman at Potsdam, showed no hesitation in allowing this take-over of German land. They agreed with Stalin that the expansion of the Soviet Union was appropriate compensation for the sacrifices their ally had made in the war, and they never viewed the dismemberment of East Prussia as being at odds with the Atlantic Charter they had signed in August 1941. Poland was concerned that this statement of principles, including one barring territorial aggrandizement, might stand in the way of the realization of its centuries-old claim to East Prussia, but the Atlantic Charter proved to be no hindrance whatsoever to Poland taking over the southern two-thirds of the easternmost German province.

Thus the elimination of East Prussia from Germany can be seen as politically motivated—reflecting the desire of Russia and Poland to expand their territory and sphere of influence to the west. Yet they were able to achieve these goals only as a result of a world war instigated by Nazi Germany. Moreover, the manner in which this war was waged in the east strongly influenced the way in which the East Prussians were treated by Soviet troops and how they were expelled. The vicious war of annihilation also undercut the basis for ethnic Germans in Czechoslovakia, Hungary, Romania, Russia, and Yugoslavia to live side-by-side with their indigenous neighbors as they had done for centuries, and it led to the expulsion of millions of these Germans. Thus ethnic cleansing by Germany led to the cleansing of Germans from the eastern part of Germany and Europe. The underlying cause of the end of East Prussia and the misfortune of its inhabitants was therefore Hitler's Thousand Year Reich which was inaugurated in 1933. Thirteen years later, East Prussians paid the bitter price as victims of the storm Hitler unleashed. As the German saying goes, "Who sows the wind will reap the storm" ("*Wer Wind sät, wird Sturm ernten*").

Notes

1 Komarnicki, *Rebirth of the Polish Republic,* 326.
2 Polish Commission of Preparatory Work for the Conference of Peace, *East Prussia,* 22. Emphasis in the original.

3 Terry, *Poland's Place in Europe*, 23 n. 1. By contrast, Norman Davies has argued that while Lloyd George was in general sympathetic to the Poles, he did not favor their aims: "Thus, to be precise, Lloyd George's attitude to Poland, though not hostile, was ambivalent." But it is hard to see this ambivalence when Davies asserts without equivocation that Lloyd George thwarted Poland's objectives at the conference: "He was instrumental in withholding Danzig with its German majority and East Galicia with its Ukrainian majority from Poland, and in insisting on plebiscites in East Prussia and Upper Silesia.… Without exception, all his decisions concerning Polish frontiers flew in the face of Polish claims." Davies, "Lloyd George and Poland, 1919–20," *Journal of Contemporary History* 6, no. 3 (1971): 133 and 139.

4 Roos, *A History of Modern Poland*, 52–54.

5 Hansen, *Poland's Westward Trend*.

6 Ibid., 26.

7 Ibid., 29–30.

8 Ibid., 38.

9 Ibid., 52.

10 Ibid., 58–59.

11 This passage is quoted in Terry, *Poland's Place in Europe*, 32–33.

12 Ibid., 70.

13 This passage is quoted in ibid., 75–76.

14 Ibid., 76.

15 Salmon, *Poland, Czechoslovakia and Hungary*, 107–8.

16 Ibid., 227.

17 Wolfgang Benz makes this point emphatically: "Der nationalsozialistische Drang nach Osten und die Methoden, mit denen er für kurze Zeit verwirklicht wurde, zerstörten auch die Grundlagen des Zusammenlebens der deutschen Volksgruppen in Rumänian, in Ungarn, in der Tschechoslowakei, in Jugoslawien und in Rußland mit ihrer Umgebung. Die nationalsozialistische Politik war Ursache des Unglückes das am Ende des Zweiten Weltkrieges über die Opfer von Flucht und Vertreibung hereinbrach." (The Nazi drive toward the East and the methods with which for a short time it became reality, also destroyed the basis for the German groups in Romania, in Hungary, in Czechoslovakia, in Yugoslavia, and in Russia to live in peace with their neighbors. National-socialistic policy was the cause of the misfortune that descended upon the victims of flight and expulsion at the end of World War II.) Benz, *Die Vertreibung der Deutschen*, 55.

18 For an account of the background leading up to the declaration of the Charter, see Churchill, *The Grand Alliance*, 433–45. Terry provides a lengthy description

of the dilemma the charter posed for the Poles. See Terry, *Poland's Place in Europe*, 273–84.

19 Polonsky, *The Great Powers and the Polish Question*, 88.

20 Ibid., 89 n. 3.

21 There was concern in Great Britain, Poland, and the United States about whether the Soviet Union would adhere to the principles of the Atlantic Charter. These concerns are described in "The U.S.S.R. and the Principles of the Atlantic Charter and of the Four Freedoms," a memorandum prepared by the U.S.S.R. section of the British Foreign Office's research department, February 3, 1944, reprinted in Prazmowska, *The Soviet Union and Finland*, 168–75.

22 For an extensive account of the sources that describe what transpired between Sikorski and Roosevelt on these two trips, see Terry, *Poland's Place in Europe*, 92–107.

23 General Sikorski Historical Institute, *Documents on Polish-Soviet Relations*, 691.

24 The Poles made no secret of the fact that this was their intention. A pamphlet available to the general public reached a number of conclusions, including the following: "(1) The Germans have proved to be a disloyal minority in many countries. Nowhere was this more apparent than in Poland.... The Fifth Column work of the German citizens of Poland and their character as an outpost of Germany's *Drang nach Osten*, as well as the cruelty displayed by the Germans during their occupation of the country, will make it impossible for Poles and Germans to live side by side in Poland after the war. (2) The exchange of population between Greece and Turkey as carried out in accordance with the agreement of 1923, certainly removed the political tension between those two countries. A similar method will have to be used in order to reduce the tension between Germany and Poland. The Germans should be transferred from Poland, as well as from territories which will be incorporated into Poland after the war. (4) There is no doubt that a very large proportion of the German population of the Polish territories, including those to be incorporated into Poland, will voluntarily return to Germany with some haste. That is what happened in Western Poland after the First World War. After the present war, in which the Germans have surpassed all their previous records of brutality and ferocity, the flight of the Germans is likely to be even more universal. (7) The transfer of Germans to the Reich may have, to some extent, the character of an exchange of population, as there are in Germany proper some Poles who will have to be repatriated." Polish Ministry of Preparatory Work, Information Notes 6, "The German Minority in Poland and the Transfer of Population," 23–24.

25 Polish Ministry of Preparatory Work, Information Notes 1, "East Prussia and Danzig," 13–14.

26 For examples of such declarations, see Wagner, *The Genesis of the Oder-Neisse Line,* 13 n. 86.

27 Sherwood, *Roosevelt and Hopkins,* 696–97.

28 For a succinct description of Allied discussions of dismemberment, see Mosley, "Dismemberment of Germany—The Allied Negotiations from Yalta to Potsdam." Mosley himself was a participant in some of these discussions.

29 Hull, *The Memoirs of Cordell Hull,* 1265.

30 Ibid., 1287.

31 Rzheshevsky, *War and Diplomacy,* 23–24.

32 See Dallin, *Russia and Postwar Europe,* 169. Dallin's assertion that tsarist Russia had the territorial ambition of annexing East Prussia is made "[o]n the basis of the diplomatic (mostly secret) documents of the years 1914–1917 that have so far been made public, and on the basis of public statements of responsible political figures of that period...," 168. In this connection, it is worth recalling from Chapter I that in the eighteenth century Empress Maria Theresa of Austria promised Russia that it would receive East Prussia in return for its continued participation with Austria in their conflict with Prussia.

33 Rzheshevsky, *War and Diplomacy,* 11.

34 Ibid., 17.

35 Eden, *The Reckoning,* 338.

36 Ibid., 335.

37 Ibid., 345.

38 Rzheshevsky, *War and Diplomacy,* 60.

39 Ibid., 74.

40 Quotation taken from Terry, *Poland's Place in Europe,* 296 n. 116.

41 Ross, *The Foreign Office and the Kremlin,* 103.

42 Ibid., 95.

43 Ibid., 104. The Soviet account of this reference to the fate of Germans in East Prussia is more forceful: "He, Eden, would like to clarify the meaning of this Article. Suppose we agreed that East Prussia should be included in Poland. Then this Article would mean that we wished to take measures to remove the German population from East Prussia." Rzheshevsky, *War and Diplomacy,* 84. The British version of the text implies that the East Prussians would leave voluntarily, whereas the Soviet version conveys the sense of their forceful removal.

44 Ross, *The Foreign Office and the Kremlin,* 104 and 105.

45 Harvey, *The War Diaries of Oliver Harvey*, 130.

46 Eden, *The Reckoning*, 382.

47 Rzheshevsky, *War and Diplomacy*, 122.

48 Churchill, *The Hinge of Fate*, 301.

49 Prazmowska, *The Soviet Union and Finland*, 4: 57–58. For a complete account of this conference, see Document 17, "Secret Protocol," reproduced on pages 39–51 in this volume.

50 This document is reproduced in U.S. Department of State, *The Conferences at Cairo and Tehran*, 183–86.

51 Hull, *The Memoirs of Cordell Hull*, 1287.

52 Ibid., 1287.

53 U.S. Department of State, *The Conferences at Cairo and Tehran*, 154.

54 The following discussion is largely based on Masur, "Poland's Western Frontiers in the State Department's Concepts During World War II." For a more extensive discussion of the State Department's postwar planning for Germany, as well as a description of the personalities involved, see Pautsch, *Die territoriale Deutschlandplanung des amerikanischen Außenministeriums*.

55 The organization and functions of the Advisory Committee and its various subcommittees are described in Notter, *Postwar Foreign Policy Preparation*, 69–164. Notter served as the committee's executive secretary and provided input first as assistant chief of the Division of Special Research, then as director of the Division of Political Studies, and finally as an advisor in the Office of Special Political Affairs.

56 Mazur, "Poland's Western Frontiers," 278 n. 7.

57 Ibid., 280.

58 Ibid., 281.

59 Ibid., 283.

60 Sherwood, *Roosevelt and Hopkins*, 709–10.

61 This document is reprinted in U.S. Department of State, *The Conferences at Washington and Quebec*, 730–61. The part of this document that deals specifically with East Prussia is a memorandum prepared by the assistant chief of the Division of Political Studies; Philip E. Mosely, "Poland—Germany Territorial Problems: Polish-German Frontier From Silesia to the Baltic Sea," 731–36.

62 Ibid., 731.

63 Ibid., 732.

64 Ibid., 733.

65 Mazur, "Poland's Western Frontiers," 291.

66 Eubank, *Summit at Teheran*, 7.

67 U.S. Department of State, *The Conferences at Cairo and Tehran 1943*, 510. This volume is subsequently referred to as FRUS 1943. The minutes of these and other meetings of the Teheran Conference were taken by Charles Bohlen, first secretary at the American Embassy in Moscow, November 1943–January 1944.

68 FRUS 1943, 510.

69 FRUS 1943, 512.

70 Churchill, *Closing the Ring*, 362.

71 FRUS 1943, 512.

72 This account of how Churchill may have used the matches is taken from Wagner, *The Genesis of the Oder-Neisse Line*, 45.

73 FRUS 1943, 591.

74 FRUS 1943, 596–604.

75 FRUS 1943, 600.

76 Churchill, *Closing the Ring*, 400–401; FRUS 1943, 600.

77 This antipathy on the part of British political leaders (Churchill, Eden, Attlee, and Bevin) and Roosevelt is documented in Clark, *Iron Kingdom*, 673–74. For example, Clark quotes Roosevelt as telling Congress on September 17, 1943, that "When Hitler and the Nazis go out, the Prussian military clique must go with them. The war-breeding gangs of militarists must be rooted out of Germany [...] if we are to have any real assurances of future peace ...,'" 674.

78 Machray, *East Prussia*, 96.

79 Ibid., 102.

80 See Pautsch, *Die territoriale Deutschlandsplanung*, 263–69; and Kettenacker, *Krieg zur Friedenssicherung*, 448–49.

81 Clark, *Iron Kingdom*, xii.

82 Churchill, *Closing the Ring*, 403.

83 Ibid., 403. As Churchill points out in footnote 1 on page 403, the issue of whether the "Line of the Oder" should be the western or the eastern Neisse had not yet arisen.

84 FRUS 1943, 604. Churchill's rendition of what Stalin said conveys essentially the same quid pro quo demanded by Stalin: "Stalin then said that the Russians would like to have the warm-water port of Königsberg, and he sketched a possible line on the map. This would put Russia on the neck of Germany. If he got this, he would be ready enough to agree to my formula about Poland." Churchill, *Closing the Ring*, 403.

85 FRUS 1943, 604.

86 The text of this telegram is reprinted as Document 81 in Polonsky, *The Great Powers and the Polish Question*, 170–71.

87 The British conveyed the Soviet claim to the northern part of East Prussia to the Poles only on February 6, 1944. Churchill reported to Stalin the Poles' reaction when he informed them of this development: "For the first time on February 6th I told the Polish Government that the Soviet Government wished to have the frontier in East Prussia drawn to include, on the Russian side, Königsberg. The information came as a shock to the Polish Government, who see in such a decision a substantial reduction in the size and the economic importance of the German territory to be incorporated in Poland by way of compensation. But I stated that, in the opinion of His Majesty's Government, this was a rightful claim on the part of Russia. Regarding, as I do, this war against German aggression as one and as a thirty-years' war from 1914 onwards, I reminded M. Mikołajczyk [Polish Prime Minister in London] of the fact that the soil of this part of East Prussia was dyed with Russian blood expended freely in the common cause. Here the Russian armies advancing in August 1914 and winning the battle of Gumbinnen and other actions had...forced the Germans to recall two army corps from the advance of Paris which withdrawal was an essential part in the victory of the Marne. The disaster at Tannenberg did not in any way undo this great result. Therefore it seemed to me that the Russians had a historic and well-founded claim to this German territory." Richardson, *The Secret History of World War II*, 166. This is part of a letter entitled "Most Secret and Personal Message from Mr. Winston Churchill to Marshall Stalin," sent from London on February 20, 1944, and received in Moscow on February 27. Extracts of this same letter are reprinted in Polonsky, *The Great Powers and the Polish Question*, 182–85; Polonsky provides detailed footnotes describing the involved drafting process of this letter.

88 Polonsky, *The Great Powers and the Polish Question*, 171

89 Ibid., 171 n. 3.

90 Ibid., 171.

91 FRUS 1943, 565–68. See also Churchill, *Closing the Ring*, 381–82.

92 Churchill, *Closing the Ring*, 382.

93 FRUS 1943, 640–41.

94 FRUS 1943, 877.

95 The information about this map and the note Bohlen attached to it are given in FRUS 1943, 601, with the map itself reproduced on the facing page.

96 This agreement is described in Gornig, *Das nördliche Ostpreußen,* 89–90, and the text of the agreement is reproduced (in German) on pages 301–2. See also Terry, *Poland's Place in Europe,* 348–49, especially footnote 105, for a discussion of this secret agreement. The text is also reproduced in Böttcher, *Materalien zu Deutschlandfrangen,* 473–74. A brief commentary by Alexander Uschakov is given on page 475.

97 Gornig, *Das nördliche Ostpreußen,* 302. "Die Regierung der USSR hat auch anerkannt, daß die Grenze zwischen Polen und Deutschland entlang einer westlich von Swinemünde bis zum Fluß Oder verlaufenden Linie, wobei die Stadt Stettin auf polnischer Seite verbleibt, weiter aufwärts des Flußes Oder bis zur Neisse, und von hier entland des Flüßes Neisse bis zur tschechoslowakischen Grenze, festgelegt werden soll."

98 Raack, "Stalin Fixes the Oder-Neisse Line," *Journal of Contemporary History* 25, no. 4 (October 1990): 467–88.

99 Ibid., 473. Another writer, Vojtech Mastny, described these discussions in a similar vein: "The startling features of the talks are that they entailed some genuine bargaining rather than mere Soviet *Diktat,* and that the few non-Communist delegates present were the ones who dared to bargain—enough reason for Stalin to appear 'in the worst possible mood.'" See Mastny, *Russia's Road to the Cold War,* 178. According to Mastny, one of the topics that annoyed Stalin was the Polish demand for all of East Prussia, but "in the end Stalin angrily drew a straight line across the map, thus dividing East Prussia between the Soviet Union and Poland."

100 General Sikorski Historical Institute, *Documents on Polish—Soviet Relations,* 316.

101 Polonsky, *The Great Powers and the Polish Question,* 181.

102 Churchill's views are contained in a letter to Stalin dated February 21, 1944, quoted in ibid., 184.

103 General Sikorski Historical Institute, *Documents on Polish Soviet Relations,* Document no. 141, 251.

104 Ibid., 253.

105 Report by Mr. Stettinius to Mr. Cordell Hull on the conversation on June 12 between President Roosevelt and Premier Mikołajczyk concerning the territory and constitution of liberated Poland, Document no. 142, ibid., 257–58.

106 Ibid., 257.

107 Polonsky, *The Great Powers and the Polish Question,* 203 n. 5.

108 Mikołajczyk, *The Rape of Poland,* 93–97. It is relevant to note that Churchill devotes only one paragraph in his memoirs to this meeting, where he describes

how he pressed Mikołajczyk to correct the two flaws in his plan for postwar Poland, which Stalin insisted on. See Chruchill, *Triumph and Tragedy*, 235.

109 Ibid., 94–95.

110 Ibid., 96–97.

111 FRUS 1945, 204.

112 The primary U.S. source for the Yalta Conference is U.S. Department of State, *The Conferences at Malta and Yalta, 1945,* This source is referred to below as FRUS 1945.

113 FRUS 1945, 571.

114 FRUS 1945, 613–14.

115 FRUS 1945, 617.

116 Wagner, *The Genesis of the Oder–Neisse Line*, 108 n. 451.

117 FRUS 1945, 620–21.

118 FRUS 1945, 716.

119 Churchill, *Triumph and Tragedy*, 374; and FRUS 1945, 717.

120 For a description of the conflict between the Greeks and Turks after World War I, see Naimark, *Fires of Hatred*, 42–56. The Treaty of Lausanne, signed on July 24, 1923, mandated compulsory transfers of Greeks from Anatolia and Turks from Greece. The British delegation to this conference was led by none other than Lord Curzon, whose assessment of the outcome was the opposite of Churchill's. Curzon was highly critical of the forced exchange of Turkish and Greek populations and is quoted by Naimark as saying that it was "a thoroughly bad and vicious solution for which the world would pay a heavy penalty for a hundred years to come," 55. For a gripping account of one of the major battles in this conflict—the fall of Smyrna (modern Ismir) to the Turkish army in 1922—see Milton, *Paradise Lost: Smyrna, 1922*.

121 Byrnes, *Frankly Speaking*, 30.

122 Churchill, *Triumph and Tragedy*, 374.

123 Byrnes, *Frankly Speaking*, 30.

124 FRUS 1945, 792.

125 FRUS 1945, 898–906; Churchill, *Triumph and Tragedy*, 385–87; and Stettinius, *Roosevelt and the Russians*, 251–71.

126 FRUS 1945, 905. This paragraph, with two minor drafting changes, appeared at the end of Section VII, *Poland,* in the final Protocol of Proceedings of the Yalta Conference. See *Official Documents, Texts of Selected Documents on U.S. Foreign Policy 1918–1952* (New York: Woodrow Wilson Foundation, 1952), 10–19.

127 See Wagner, *The Genesis of the Oder-Neisse Line*, 124–27.

128 Truman, *Years of Decisions,* 341.

129 Leahy, *I Was There,* 396.

130 FRUS 1945, Potsdam, Vol. I, Document 177, 198–205.

131 FRUS 1945, Potsdam, Vol. I, Document 513, 751. The British government was fully in accord with this recommendation regarding East Prussia. See the British aide-mémoire on Poland's western frontiers, which was delivered to the State Department on July 13. See Document 518 in FRUS 1945, Potsdam, Vol. I, 777–81.

132 Molotov's remark was made at the Sixth Plenary Meeting on Sunday, July 22, at 5 p.m. See FRUS 1945, Potsdam, Vol. II, 259.

133 FRUS 1945, Potsdam, Vol. II, Document 1020, 988. The map referred to in the proposal was not found in the U.S. documentation of the Potsdam Conference.

134 FRUS 1945, Potsdam, Vol. II, 305–6.

135 This statement by Stalin was not included in the Soviet text of this plenary meeting. See Beitzell, *Teheran Yalta Potsdam,* vii.

136 FRUS 1945, Potsdam, Vol. II, 306.

137 FRUS 1945, Potsdam, Vol. II, 1597–99.

138 Ibid., 551–53. As noted on page 461, in the midst of the conference, an election was held in Great Britain in which the Conservatives lost to the Labor Party. As a result, Clement Attlee became head of the British delegation and was joined by his foreign secretary, Ernest Borin.

139 Ibid., 1489 and 1507.

140 Ibid., 88–98.

141 Ibid., 96.

142 Ibid., 203–21.

143 These protests are described in footnote 4 of Document no. 510 in FRUS 1945, Potsdam, Vol. I, 743–45. Harriman sent the first of these to Molotov on April 8, 1945, which noted that the press, including *Pravda* of April 3, had reported that part of pre-1937 German territory had been formally incorporated into Poland.

144 Truman, *Years of Decisions,* 367.

145 FRUS 1945, Potsdam, Vol. II, 209–10.

146 FRUS 1945, Potsdam, Vol. II, 211.

147 Truman, *Years of Decisions,* 369.

148 Ibid., 369.

149 Ibid., 369–70.

150 FRUS 1945, Potsdam, Vol. II, 215.

151 Ibid., 247–52.

152 Ibid., 249.

153 Ibid., 252.

154 Ibid., 331–36.

155 Leahy, *I Was there,* 406. Italics in the original.

156 Byrnes, *Speaking Frankly,* 81.

157 For a dramatic description of how Byrnes engineered this deal, see Mee, *Meeting at Potsdam.*

158 FRUS 1945, Potsdam, Vol. II, 390.

159 Ibid., 471–76. The U.S. proposal is Document no. 1151 in ibid., 1150.

160 See Document no. 1152 in ibid., 1150–51.

161 Ibid., 1151.

162 See Document no. 731 in ibid., 629–30.

163 See Document no. 961 in ibid., 921.

164 Cited in Kettenacker, *Germany since 1945,* 13.

165 Ibid., 13.

166 The extreme rapacity with which the Soviets removed everything of value from the territory occupied by the Red Army appears to have been an explicit policy agreed at the highest level of the Soviet government. A group was set up in 1943 to develop recommendations for reparations after the war and was called the "Commission on Compensation for the Losses Inflicted on the Soviet Union by Hitlerite Germany and its Allies." It was known as the Maisky Commission after its chairman, Ivan. M. Maisky, who was the Soviet ambassador to Great Britain from 1932 to 1943 and was subsequently deputy peoples commissar for foreign affairs from 1943 to 1946. On November 10, 1943, the outline for the commission's work was prepared, and according to Aleksei Filitov, who had access to the commission's files, "[i]ts fundamental principle was formulated quite unambiguously: 'To take from Germany and its allies everything which can be taken,' with the qualification 'allowing for the famine minimum.'" See his essay, "Problems of Post-War Construction in Soviet Foreign Policy Conceptions during World War II," in Francesca Gori and Silvio Pons, *The Soviet Union and Europe in the Cold War,* 6. The commission's report, which was sent to Molotov on January 11, 1944, ranged well beyond the subject of reparations. For example, with regard to Poland it recommended that "[i]n the West the whole of East Prussia can be included in Poland (or, perhaps, the greater part of it), plus a part of Silesia, but with resettlement elsewhere of the German inhabitants." Ibid., 9.

167 FRUS 1945, Potsdam, Vol. II, 519.

168 Byrnes, *Speaking Frankly,* 81.

169 Feis, *Between War and Peace,* 260

170 Sipols, *The Road to Great Victory,* 297.

171 This treaty is reproduced in U.S. Department of State, *Documents on Germany 1944–1985,* Department of State Publication 9446 (Washington, D.C., 1985), 319–21.

172 Ibid., 1125–27.

173 Treaty on the Final Settlement with Respect to Germany and a Related Agreed Minute. U.S. Senate, 101st Congress, 2nd Session, Treaty Doc., 101–20, U.S. Government Printing Office, Washington, 1990.

174 *International Legal Materials,* March 1991, Vol. 30, Issue 2, 504–14.

175 For a discussion of these two treaties, see Gornig, *Das nördliche Ostpreußen,* 161–63.

176 De Zayas, *Nemesis at Potsdam,* 86–87.

177 The primary source used here is Brandes, "Die Britische Regierung kommt zu einem Zwischenergebnis. Die Empfehlungen des Britischen Interdepartmental Committee on the Transfer of German Populations vom Mai 1944," in Pousta, Seifter, and Pešek, *Occursus, Setkání,* Begegnung, 45–68. A much more extensive treatment of the topic of the expulsion of Germans from Czechoslovakia and Poland after World War II is provided in Brandes, *Der Weg zur Vertreibung 1938–1945.*

178 Brandes, "Die Britische Regierung…," 49.

179 Ibid., 50.

180 Ibid, 67.

181 FRUS 1945, 189.

182 Ibid, 190.

183 FRUS 1945, Potsdam, Vol. 1, Document 435, 643.

184 Ibid., Document 439, 646–47.

185 Ibid., Documents. no. 440 and 441, 647–50.

186 FRUS 1945, Potsdam, Vol. II, 381–88.

187 Ibid., 383–84.

188 Ibid., 397–99.

189 Ibid., 523–24.

190 Ibid., 1511.

191 Ibid., 523.

192 Leahy, *I Was There,* 424.

193 Feis, *Between War and Peace,* 269–70.

194 Bohlen, *Witness to History,* 231.

BIBLIOGRAPHY

Anonymous. *A Woman in Berlin: Eight Weeks in a Captured City; A Diary*. New York: Metropolitan Books, Henry Holt, 2005.

Abraham, Waltraud. *Flucht aus Ostpreußen*. Willebadessen: Zwiebelzwerg Verlag, 1999.

Bamm, Peter. *Die unsichtbare Flagge*. Munich: Kösel Verlag, 1952.

Bartov, Omer. *The Eastern Front, 1941–1945: German Troops and the Barbarization of Warfare*. 2nd ed. Hampshire and New York: Palgrave of St. Martin's Press, 2001.

Beckherrn, Eberhard, and Alexej Dubatow. *Die Königsberg Papiere: Schicksal einer Deutschen Stadt; Neue Dokumente aus Russischen Archiven*. Munich: Langen Müller, 1994.

Beevor, Antony. *The Fall of Berlin 1945*. New York and London: Penguin Books, 2002.

Beitzell, Robert. *Teheran, Yalta, Potsdam: The Soviet Protocols*. Hattiesburg, Miss.: Academic Institute, 1970.

Benz, Wolfgang, ed. *Die Vertreibung der Deutschen aus dem Osten: Ursachen, Ereignisse, Folgen*. Frankfurt am Main: Fischer Taschenbuch Verlag, 1995.

Benz, Wolfgang, and Barbara Distel, eds. *Der Ort des Terrors: Geschichte der Nationalsozialistischen Konzentrationslager*, vol. 6. Munich: C. H. Beck, 2007.

Bergau, Martin. *Der Junge von der Bernsteinküste: Erlebte Zeitgeschichte 1938–1948.* Heidelberg: Heidelberger Verlagsanstalt, 1994.

———. *Todesmarsch zur Bernsteinküste: Das Massaker an Juden im ostpreußischen Palmnicken im Januar 1945: Zeitzeugen erinnern sich.* Heidelberg: Universitätsverlag Winter, 2006.

Blatman, Daniel. *The Death Marches: The Final Phase of Nazi Genocide.* Cambridge, Massachusetts, and London, England: The Belknap Press of Harvard University Press. 2011.

Blitz, Maria. *Endzeit in Ostpreußen: Ein beschwiegenes Kapitel des Holocaust.* Berlin: Stiftung Denkmal für die ermordeten Juden Europas, 2010.

Bohlen, Charles. *Witness to History 1929–1969.* New York: Norton, 1973.

Boockmann, Hartmut. *Ostpreußen und Westpreußen.* Berlin: Siedler Verlag, 1992.

Borodziej, Wlodzimierz, and Hans Lemberg, eds. *"Unsere Heimat ist uns ein fremdes Land geworden...." Die Deutschen östlich von Oder und Neiße 1945–1950; Dokumente aus polnischen Archiven.* vol. 1. Marburg: Herder Institut, 2000.

Böttcher, Hans Viktor, ed. *Materalien zu Deutschlandfragen: Politiker und Wissenschaftler nehmen Stellung 1989–91.* Bonn: Kulturstiftung der Deutschen Vertriebenen, 1989.

Brandes, Detlef. "Die Britische Regierung Kommt zu einem Zwischenergebnis: Die Empfehlungen des Britischen Interdepartmental Committee on the Transfer of German Populations vom Mai 1944," in Zdeněk Pousta, Pavel Seifter, and Jiří Pešek, eds. *Occursus, Setkání, Begegnung.* Prague: History Club, 1996.

———. *Der Weg zur Vertreibung 1938–1945: Pläne und Entscheidungen zum "Transfer" der Deutschen aus der Tschechoslowkai und aus Poland.* 2nd ed. Munich: R. Oldenbourg, 2005.

Browning, Christopher R. *The Origins of the Final Solution: The Evolution of Nazi Jewish Policy, September 1939–March 1942.* Lincoln: University of Nebraska Press, 2004.

Brownmiller, Susan. *Against Our Will: Men, Women and Rape.* New York: Fawcett Columbine, 1975.

Budnitskii, Oleg. "The Intelligentsia Meets the Enemy: Educated Soviet Officers in Defeated Germany, 1945," in *Kritika: Explorations in Russian and Eurasian History* 10, no. 3 (Summer 2009): 629–82.

Burleigh, Michael. *Death and Deliverance: "Euthanasia in Germany" 1900–1945*. Cambridge and New York: Cambridge University Press, 1994.

Buttar, Prit. *Battleground Prussia: The Assault on Germany's Eastern Front 1944 – 1945*. Oxford, U.K., and Long Island City, New York: Osprey Publishing, 2010.

Byrnes, James F. *Speaking Frankly*. New York: Harper and Brothers, 1947.

Christiansen, Eric. *The Northern Crusades*. London: Penguin Books, 1997.

Churchill, Winston. *The Grand Alliance: The Second World War*, vol. 3. Boston: Houghton Mifflin, 1950

———. *The Hinge of Fate: The Second World War*, vol. 4. Boston: Houghton Mifflin, 1950.

———. *Closing the Ring: The Second World War*, vol. 5. Boston: Houghton Mifflin, 1951.

———. *Triumph and Tragedy: The Second World War*, vol. 6. Boston: Houghton Mifflin, 1953.

Chuchin, Ivan. *Interned Youth: A History of the USSR NKVD Camp 517 for Interned German Women*. Moscow-Petrozavodsk: Memorial, 1995.

Clark, Alan. *Barbarossa: The Russian German Conflict 1941–1945*. New York: HarperCollins, 1985.

Clark, Christopher. *Iron Kingdom: The Rise and Downfall of Prussia 1600–1947*. Cambridge: The Belknap Press of Harvard University Press, 2006.

Clough, Patricia. *In langer Reihe über das Haff: Die Flucht der Trakehner aus Ostpreußen*. Munich: Deutscher Taschenbuch Verlag, 2006.

Dallin, David J. *Russia and Postwar Europe*. New Haven: Yale University Press, 1943.

Davies, Norman. "Lloyd George and Poland, 1919–20," *Journal of Contemporary History* 6, no. 3 (1971): 132–54.

———. *Heart of Europe: A Short History of Poland*. New York and Oxford: Oxford University Press, 2001.

Deichelmann, Hans. *Ich sah Königsberg sterben*. Schnellbach: Verlag Siegfried Bublies, 2000.

Denny, Isabel. *The Fall of Hitler's Fortress City: The Battle for Königsberg, 1945*. Philadelphia, Pennsylvania, and Newbury, U.K.: Casemate Publishers, 2007.

de Zayas, Alfred-Maurice. *Nemesis at Potsdam: The Anglo-Americans and the Expulsion of the Germans.* Rev. ed. London: Routledge and Kegan Paul, 1979.

————. *A Terrible Revenge: The Ethnic Cleansing of the East European Germans.* 2nd rev. ed. New York: Palgrave Macmillan, 2006.

Dieckert, Kurt, and Horst Großmann. *Der Kampf um Ostpreussen: Der umfassende Documentenbericht.* Stuttgart: Motorbuch Verlag, 2002.

Djilas, Milovan. *Conversations with Stalin.* New York: Harcourt, Brace and World, 1962.

Dobson, Christopher, John Miller, and Ronald Payne. *The Cruelest Night.* Boston: Little Brown and Company, 1979.

Domarus, Max. *Hitler: Speeches and Proclamations 1932–1945.* Vol. 3, *The Years 1939 to 1940.* Wauconda, Ill.: Bolchazy-Carducci, 1997.

Dönhoff, Gräfin Marion. *Namen die keiner mehr nennt: Ostpreußen; Menschen und Geschichte.* 23rd ed. Munich: Deutscher Taschenbuch Verlag, 1991.

Duffy, Christopher. *Red Storm on the Reich: The Soviet March on Germany, 1945.* New York: Da Capo Press, Atheneum Publishers, 1993.

Eckert-Möbius, Irene. *Flucht der Trömpauer: Das Ende des Gutes Trömpau, Kreis Königsberg, Land Ostpreußen.* Karlsruhe: Wulf Dietrich Wagner, 1993.

Eden, Anthony. *The Reckoning: The Memoirs of Anthony Eden, Earl of Avon.* Boston: Houghton Mifflin, 1965.

Egremont, Max. *Forgotten Land: Journeys Among the Ghosts of East Prussia.* New York: Farrar, Straus and Giroux, 2011.

Ehrenburg, Ilya, and Konstantin Simonov. *In One Newspaper: A Chronicle of Unforgettable Years.* New York: Sphinx Press, 1985.

Eisfeld, Alfred, and Victor Herdt, eds. *Deportation, Sondersiedlung, Arbeitsarmee: Deutsche in der Sowjetunion 1941–1956.* Cologne: Verlag Wissenschaft und Politik, 1996.

Erdelbrock, Georg, ed. *Verschleppt ins KZ Neuengamme: Lebensschicksale polnischer Jugendliche.* Bremen: Edition Temmen, 1999.

Eubank, Keith. *Summit at Teheran.* New York: William Morrrow, 1985.

Ewert, Erna, Marga Pollmann, and Hannelore Müller. *Frauen in Königsberg 1945–1948.* 7th ed. Bonn: Kulturstiftung der deutschen Vertriebenen, 2000.

Falk, Lucy. *Ich blieb in Königsberg.* Munich: Gräfe und Unzer, 1965.

Farca, Olga Katharina. *Allein die Hoffnung hielt uns am Leben,* part 2. Villingen-Schwenningen: Farca Verlag, 1999.

Feis, Herbert. *Between War and Peace: The Potsdam Conference.* Princeton, N.J.: Princeton University Press, 1960.

Filitov, Aleksei. "Problems of Post-War Construction in Soviet Foreign Policy Conceptions during World War II," in Francesca Gori and Silvio Pons, eds., *The Soviet Union and Europe in the Cold War, 1943–53.* New York: St. Martin's Press, 1997.

Fisch, Bernhard. *Nemmersdorf, Oktober 1944: Was in Ostpreußen wirklich geschah.* Berlin: Edition Ost, 1997.

Garbe, Detlef, and Carmen Lange, eds. *Häftlinge zwischen Vernichtung und Befreiung: Die Auflösung des KZ Neuengamme und seiner Außenlager durch die SS im Frühjahr 1945.* Bremen: Edition Temmen, 2005.

Garret, Stephen. *Ethics and Airpower in World War II: The British Bombing of German Cities.* London: Palgrave Macmillan, 1993.

Gause, Fritz. *Die Russen in Ostpreußen 1914/1915.* Königsberg in Preußen: Gräfe und Unzer, 1931.

———. *Die Geschichte der Stadt Königsberg in Preußen.* Vol. 3, *Vom Ersten Weltkrieg bis zum Untergang Königsbergs.* Cologne and Vienna: Böhlau Verlag, 1971.

General Sikorski Historical Institute. *Documents on Polish-Soviet Relations 1939–1945.* Vol. 2, *1943–1945.* London: Heinemann, 1967.

Gieszczyński, Witold. *The Role of the State Office for Repatriation in the Settlement of Warmia and Masuria (1945–1950).* (*Państwory Urzad Repatriacyjny w osadnictwie na Warmii i Mazurach,* 1945–1950. Publications and Materials of the Wojciech Ketrzynski Center of Scientific Research 183. Olsztyn: Osrodek Badan Naukowych, 1999.

Giordano, Ralph. *Ostpreußen ade: Reise durch ein melancholisches Land.* Munich: Deutscher Taschenbuch Verlag, 2003.

Glantz, David M. *Barbarossa: Hitler's Invasion of Russia 1941.* Stroud, Gloucestershire: Tempus Publishing, 2001.

Glantz, David M., and Jonathan House. *When Titans Clashed: How the Red Army Stopped Hitler.* Lawrence: University of Kansas Press, 1995.

Glass, Charles. *Americans in Paris: Life and Death under Nazi Occupation 1940–1944.* London: Harper Press, 2009.

Glass, Paul, and Fritz Bredenberg. *Der Kreis Sensberg.* Ostdeutsche Beiträge aus dem Göttinger Arbeitskreis 15. Würzburg: Holzner Verlag, 1960.

Goldberg, Anatol. *Ilya Ehrenburg: Revolutionary, Novelist, Poet, War Correspondent, Propagandist; The Extraordinary Epic of a Russian Survivor.* New York: Viking Penguin, 1984.

Gori, Francesca, and Silvio Pons, eds. *The Soviet Union and Europe in the Cold War, 1943 – 53.* New York: St Martin's Press, 1997.

Göttgen, Erich. *Der Wiederaufbau Ostpreußens, eine kulturelle, verwaltungstechnische und baukünstlerische Leistung.* Königsberg in Preußen: Gräfe und Unzer, 1928.

Gornig, Gilbert H. *Das nördliche Ostpreußen—gestern und heute: Eine historische und rechtliche Betrachtung.* 2nd ed. Bonn: Kulturstiftung der deutschen Vertriebenen, 1996.

Gottwaldt, Alfred, and Diana Schulle. *Die "Jundendeportationen" aus dem Deutschen Reich 1941–1945: Ein kommentierte Chronologie.* Wiesbaden: Matrix Verlag, 2005.

Gottwaldt, Alfred, Norbert Kampe, and Peter Klein, eds. *NS-Gewaltherrschaft: Beiträge zur historischen Forschung und juristischen Aufarbeitung.* Berlin: Edition Hentrich, 2005.

Graf, Jürgen, and Carlo Mattogno. *Concentration Camp Stutthof and its Function in National Socialist Jewish Policy.* Chicago: Theses and Dissertations Press, 2003.

Grass, Günter. *Crabwalk.* Orlando, Fla.: Harcourt, 2002.

———. *Peeling the Onion.* Orlando, Fla.: Harcourt, 2007.

Grossman, Vasily. *A Writer at War: Vasily Grossman with the Red Army 1941–1945.* Translated and edited by Antony Beevor and Luba Vinogradova. New York: Pantheon Books, 2005.

Guderian, Heinz. *Panzer Leader.* London: Michael Joseph, 1952.

Haagen, Paul H. "A Hamburg Childhood: The Early Years of Herbert Bernstein," *Duke Journal of Comparative and International Law* 12, no. 3 (2003): 7–59.

Haas, Michael. *International Human Rights: A Comprehensive Introduction*. New York: Routledge, 2008.

Hamburg Institute for Social Research. *The German Army and Genocide: Crimes Against War Prisoners, Jews, and Other Civilians in the East, 1941–1945*. Hamburg: The New Press, 1999.

Hansen, Ernst R. B. *Poland's Westward Trend*. London: George Annel and Unwin, 1928.

Harvey, John, ed. *The War Diaries of Oliver Harvey*. London: Collins, 1978.

Hastings, Max. *Armageddon: The Battle for Germany, 1944–1945*. New York: Alfred A. Knopf, 2004.

Hensel, Joachim, ed. *Medizin in und aus Ostpreußen*. Starnberg: Joseph Jägerhuber, 1990.

Herzog, Roman. *Remembrance and Perpetual Responsibility*. Bonn: Press and Information Office, 1995.

———. *Wahrheit und Klarheit: Reden zur deutschen Geschichte*. Manfred Bissinger, ed. Hamburg: Hoffman and Campe, 1995.

Hillmann, Jörg, and John Zimmermann. *Kriegsende 1945 in Deutschland*. Munich: R. Oldenbourg, 2002.

Horbach, Michael. *So überlebten sie den Holocaust: Zeugnisse der Menschlichkeit 1933–1945*. Munich: Schneekluth, 1995.

Hull, Cordell. *The Memoirs of Cordell Hull*, vol. 2. New York: Macmillan Co., 1948.

Jacobs, Benjamin, and Eugene Pool, *The 100-Year Secret: Britain's Hidden WWII Massacre*, Guilford, Connecticut: The Lyons Press, 2004.

Jacobs, Ingeborg. *Freiwild: Das Schicksal deutscher Frauen 1945*. Berlin: Propylaen, 2008.

James, Stephen. *Universal Human Rights: Origins and Development*. New York: LBF Scholarly Publishing, 2007.

Jänicke, Johannes. *Ich konnte dabeisein*. Berlin: Weichern-Verlag, 1984.

Karp, Hans-Jürgen and Robert Traba, eds. *Nachkriegsalltag in Ostpreußen: Erinnerungen von Deutschen, Polen und Ukrainern.* Münster: Aschendorff Verlag, 2004.

Katz, Joseph. *One Who Came Back: The Diary of a Jewish Survivor.* College Park, Md.: Dryad Press, 2006.

Kempowski, Walter. *Das Echolot,* vol. 2. Munich: Albrecht Knaus, 1999.

Kershaw, Ian. *The End: The Defiance and Destruction of Hitler's Germany, 1944–1945.* New York: The Penguin Press, 2011.

Kettenacker, Lothar. *Krieg zur Friedenssicherung: Die Deutschlandplanung der britischen Regierung wähend des Zweiten Weltkrieges.* Göttingen: Vandenhöck und Ruprecht, 1989.

———. *Germany since 1945.* Oxford: Oxford University Press, 1997.

Kibelka, Ruth. *Wolfskinder: Grenzgänger an der Memel.* 4th ed. Berlin: BasisDruck Verlag, 2003.

———. *Ostpreußens Schicksalsjahre 1944–1948.* Berlin: Aufbau-Verlag, 2001.

Kirstein, Emma. *Mein Tagebuch: Erinnerungen an schwere Zeiten vom 21. Oktober 1944 bis Neujahr 1946.* Bonn: Kulturstiftung der deutschen Vertriebenen, n.d.

Klee, Ernst. *Euthanasie im NS Staat: Die "Vernichtung lebensunwerten Lebens."* Frankfurt am Main: S. Fischer Verlag, 1983.

Klee, Ernst, and Willi Dressen. *"Gott mit uns": Der deutsche Vernichtungskrieg im Osten 1939–1945.* Frankfurt am Main: S. Fischer Verlag, 1989.

Klemperer, Victor. *I Will Bear Witness: A Diary of the Nazi Years, 1933–1941,* and *1942–1945.* New York: Modern Library, 1999 and 2001 paperback eds.

Klier, Freya. *Verschleppt ans Ende der Welt: Schicksale deutschen Frauen in Sowjetischen Arbeitslagern.* Frankfurt am Main and Berlin: Ullstein, 1996.

Knopp, Guido. *Die große Flucht: Das Schicksal der Vertriebenen.* Munich: Econ Verlag, 2001.

———. *Der Untergang der "Gustloff."* Munich: Econ Taschenbuch, 2002.

Kobylyanskiy, Isaak. *From Stalingrad to Pillau: A Red Army Artillery Officer Remembers the Great Patriotic War.* Lawrence: University Press of Kansas, 2008.

Koch, H. W. *A History of Prussia.* New York: Barnes and Noble, 1978.

Koenker, Diane P., and Ronald D. Bachman. *Revelations from the Russian Archives: Documents in English Translation.* Washington, D.C.: Library of Congress, 1997.

Königsberger Bürgerbrief 62 (Summer 2004), 63 (Winter 2004), and 64, special issue.

Komarnicki, Titus. *Rebirth of the Polish Republic: A Study in the Diplomatic History of Europe 1914–1920.* London: William Heinemann, 1957.

Kopelev, Lev. *To Be Preserved Forever.* Translated and edited by Anthony Austin. Philadelphia and New York: J. B. Lippincott, 1977.

Kossert, Andreas. *Preußen, Deutsche oder Polen? Die Masuren im Spannungsfeld des ethnischen Nationalismus 1870–1956.* Wiesbaden: Harrassowitz Verlag, 2001.

———. *Masuren: Ostpreußens vergessener Süden.* Berlin: Siedler, 2002.

———. *Ostpreußen: Geschichte und Mythos.* Munich: Siedler, 2005.

———. *Damals in Ostpreußen: Der Untergang einer deutschen Provinz.* Munich: Deutsche Verlags-Anstalt, 2008.

Kraft, Claudia. "Flucht, Vertreibung und Zwangsaussiedlung der Deutschen aus der Wojewodschaft Allenstein (Wojewodztwo Olsztynskie) in den Jahren 1945 bis 1950," in Borodziej and Lemberg, *"Unsere Heimat ist uns ein fremdes Land geworden...."*

———. "Who is a Pole, and Who a German? The Province of Olsztyn in 1945," in Ther and Siljak, *Redrawing Nations.*

Kuby, Erich. *The Russians and Berlin, 1945.* London: Heinemann, 1968.

Kuehn, Manfred. *Kant: A Biography.* Cambridge: Cambridge University Press, 2001.

Kurth, K. O., ed. *Documents of Humanity.* Göttingen: Göttingen Research Committee, 1952.

Lachauer, Ulla. *Die Brücke von Tilsit: Begegnungen mit Preußens Osten und Rußlands Westen.* 7th ed. Reinbek bei Hamburg: Rowohlt Taschenbuch Verlag, 2003.

Lasch, Otto. *So fiel Königsberg.* Stuttgart: Motorbuch Verlag, 2002.

Lass, Edgar Günther. *Die Flucht: Ostpreußen 1944/45.* Bad Nauheim: Podzum Verlag, 1964.

Leahy, William D. *I Was There.* New York: Whittlesey House, 1950.

Lehndorff, Hans Graf von. *Token of a Covenant: Diary of an East Prussian Surgeon 1945–1947.* Chicago: Henry Regenery, 1964.

Lieberman, Benjamin. *Terrible Fate: Ethnic Cleansing in the Making of Modern Europe.* Chicago: Ivan R. Dee, 2006.

Linck, Hugo. *Königsberg 1945–1948.* Leer: Gerhard Rautenberg, 1956.

———. *Im Feuer Geprüft.* Leer: Gerhard Rautenberg, 1973.

Lukowski, Jerzy, and Hubert Zawadzki. *A Concise History of Poland.* Cambridge: Cambridge University Press, 2001.

Luschnat, Gerhild. *Die Lage der Deutschen im Königsberger Gebeit 1945–1948.* 2nd ed. Frankfurt: Peter Lang, 1998.

Machray, Robert. *East Prussia: Menace to Poland and Peace.* Chicago: American Polish Council, District 20, 1943.

Manthey, Jürgen. *Königsberg: Geschichte einer Weltbürgerrepublik.* Munich: Carl Hanser Verlag, 2005.

Mastny, Vojtech. *Russia's Road to the Cold War: Diplomacy, Warfare, and the Politics of Communism.* New York: Columbia University Press, 1979.

Masur, Zbigniew. "Poland's Western Frontiers in the State Department's Concepts During World War II," *Polish Western Affairs* 21, no. 2 (1980): 274–96.

Matull, Wilhelm. *Vor 30 Jahren in Königsberg: Kaliningrad nach 30 Jahren.* Düsseldorf: private printing, 1976.

Mazower, Mark. *Hitler's Empire: How the Nazis Ruled Europe.* New York: The Penguin Press, 2008.

Mee, Charles L. Jr. *Meeting at Potsdam.* New York: Dell Publishing Co., 1976.

Megargee, Geoffrey. *Barbarossa 1941: Hitler's War of Annihilation.* Stroud, Gloucestershire: Tempus Publishing Ltd., 2007.

Meindl, Ralf. *Ostpreußens Gauleiter: Erich Koch; Eine politische Biographie.* Osnabrück: Fibre Verlag, 2007.

Merridale, Catherine. *Ivan's War: Life and Death in the Red Army, 1939–1945.* New York: Metropolitan Books, Henry Holt, 2006.

Middlebrook, Martin, and Chris Everitt. *The Bomber Command War Diaries: An Operational Reference Book, 1939–1945.* New York: Viking, 1985.

Mikołajczyk, Stanislaw. *The Rape of Poland: Pattern of Soviet Aggression.* New York: Whittlesey House, 1948.

Milton, Giles. *Paradise Lost: Smyrna, 1922; The Destruction of Islam's City of Tolerance.* New York: Basic Books, 2008.

Molotov, V. M. "New Facts about Nazi Atrocities," in *The Third Molotov Note On German Atrocities.* London: His Majesty's Stationery Office, April 27, 1942.

Montgomery, John Flournoy. *Hungary the Unwilling Satellite*. New York: Devin-Adair, 1947.

Morgenstern, Erika. *Überleben war schwerer als Sterben, Ostpreußen 1944–1945*. Munich: Herbig, 2004.

Morrow, Ian F. D. *The Peace Settlement in the German Polish Borderlands: A Study of Conditions To-day in the pre-War Prussian Provinces of East and West Prussia*. London: Oxford University Press, 1936.

Mosley, Philip E. "Dismemberment of Germany: The Allied Negotiations from Yalta to Potsdam," *Foreign Affairs* 28, no. 3 (April 1950): 487–98.

Müller, Wolfgang, and Reinhard Kramer. *Gesunken und Verschollen: Menschen und Schiffsschickale Ostsee 1945*. Herford: Köhlers Verlaggesellschaft, 1994.

Naimark, Norman M. *The Russians in Germany: A History of the Soviet Zone of Occupation, 1945–1949*. Cambridge: The Belknap Press of Harvard University, 1997.

———. *Fires of Hatred: Ethnic Cleansing in Twentieth-Century Europe*. Cambridge: Harvard University Press, 2002.

Nitschke, Bernadetta. *Wysiedlenie ludności niemieckiej z Polski w latach 1945–1949. The Expulsion of the German Population from Poland 1945–1949*. Zielona Gora: Wyzsza Szkola Pedagogiczna im. Tadeusza Kotarbińskiego, 1999.

Notter, Harley A. *Postwar Foreign Policy Preparation 1939–1945*. Publication 3580, General Foreign Policy Series 15, Part II. Washington, D.C.: Department of State, 1959.

Pautsch, Ilse Dorothee. *Die territoriale Deutschlandplanung des amerikanischen Außenministeriums 1941–1943*. Frankfurt: Peter Lang, 1990.

Peyinghaus, Marianne. *Stille Jahre in Gertlauken: Erinnerungen an Ostpreußen*. Berlin: Goldmann Verlag, 1985.

Polcz, Alaine. *One Woman in the War: Hungary 1944–1945*. Budapest and New York: Central European University Press, 1991.

Polian, Pavel. *Against Their Will: The History and Geography of Forced Migrations in the USSR*. Budapest and New York: Central European University Press, 2004.

Polish Commission of Preparatory Work for the Conference of Peace. *East Prussia*. Paris: April 1919.

Polish Ministry of Preparatory Work Concerning the Peace Conference. "The German Minority in Poland and the Problem of Transfer of Population." Information Notes 6. London: n.d.

———. "East Prussia and Danzig." Information Notes 1. London: April 1944.

Polonsky, Antony, ed. *The Great Powers and the Polish Question 1941–1945: A Documentary Study in Cold War Origins*. London: The London School of Economics and Political Science, 1976.

Power, Samantha. *"A Problem from Hell": America and the Age of Genocide*. New York: Perennial/HarperCollins, 2003.

Prazmowska, Anita, ed. *The Soviet Union and Finland, October 1943–March 1944*, vol. 4 of series A, *The Soviet Union and Finland*. Part III, From 1940–1945, Paul Preston and Michael Partridge, gen. eds., British Documents on Foreign Affairs: Reports and Papers from the Foreign Office Confidential Print. Bethesda, Md.: University Publications of America, 1997.

Raack, R. C. "Stalin Fixes the Oder-Neisse Line," *Journal of Contemporary History* 25, no. 4 (October 1990), 467–88.

Raus, Erhard. *Panzer Operations: The Eastern Front Memoirs of General Raus, 1941–1945*. Compiled and translated by Steven H. Newton. Cambridge, Mass.: Da Capo Press, 2005.

Reichling, Gerhard. *Die deutschen Vertriebenen in Zahlen*. Bonn: Kulturstiftung der Deutschen Vertriebenen,1986.

Reinoss, Herbert, ed. *Letzte Tage in Ostpreussen: Erinnerungen an Flucht und Vertreibung*. Munich: Langen Müller, 1983.

Richardson, Stewart, ed. *The Secret History of World War II: The Ultra-Secret Wartime Letters and Cables of Roosevelt, Stalin, and Churchill*. New York: Richardson and Steirman, 1986.

Richter, Friedrich. "Wirtschaftsprobleme Ostpreußens 1919 bis 1945: Ausgangslage, Politik, und Entwicklung," in Bernhart Jähnig and Silke Spieler, eds., *Das Königsberger Gebiet im Schnittpunkt deutscher Geschichte und in seinem Europäischen Bezüge*. Bonn: Kulturstiftung der deutschen Vertriebenen, 1993, pp. 45–71.

Roos, Hans. *A History of Modern Poland*. New York: Alfred A. Knopf, 1966.

Rörup, Iris. *Also sprach Vielliebchen: Stakkato gegen böse Zeiten*. Frankfurt: Ulrike Helmer Verlag, 1994.

Rosin, Hildegard. *Führt noch en Weg zurück?* Leer: Gerhard Rautenberg, 1983.

Ross, Graham, ed. *The Foreign Office and the Kremlin: British Documents on Anglo-Soviet Relations*. Cambridge: Cambridge University Press, 1984.

Roy, James Charles. *The Vanished Kingdom: Travels Through the History of Prussia*. Boulder, Colo.: Westview Press, 1999.

Rubenstein, Joshua. *Tangled Loyalties: The Life and Times of Ilya Ehrenburg*. New York: Basis Books, 1996.

Ryan, Cornelius. *The Last Battle*. New York: Simon and Schuster, Touchstone Edition, 1995.

Rzheshevsky, Oleg A., ed. *War and Diplomacy: The Making of the Grand Alliance; Documents from Stalin's Archives*. Amsterdam: Harwood Academic Publishers, 1996.

Salmon, Patrick, ed. *Poland, Czechoslovakia and Hungary, January 1940–December 1941*, volume 3 of Series F, Part III, Paul Preston and Michael Partridge, gen. eds., British Documents on Foreign Affairs: Reports and Papers from the Foreign Office Confidential Print. Bethesda, Md.: University Publications of America, 1997.

Sander, Heike, and Barbara Johr, eds., *BeFreier und Befreite: Krieg, Vergewaltigungen, Kinder*. Munich: Antje Kunstmann, 1992.

Schieder, Theodor, ed. *Dokumentation der Vertreibung der Deutschen aus Ost-Mitteleuropa*. Vol. 1, *Die Vertreibung der deutschen Bevölkerung aus den Gebieten Östlich der Oder-Neiße*. Part 1, *Die Flucht vor der roten Armee*; Part 2, *Die Zerstörung der Lebensgrundlagen der ostdeutschen Bevölkerung seit 1945*; Part 3, *Austreibung und Ausweisung der deutschen Bevölkerung aus den Gebieten östlich der Oder und Neiße*. Munich: Deutscher Taschenbuch Verlag, 2004. Originally published by the Bundesministerium für Vertriebene, Flüchtlinge und Kriegsgeschädigte, 1954–1961.

———, editor. *The Expulsion of the German Population from the Territories East of the Oder-Neisse-Line*. A selection and translation from *Dokumentation der Vertreibung der Deutschen aus Ost-Mitteleuropa*, vol. 1. Bonn: Federal Ministry for Expellees, Refugees and War Victims, 1956.

Schilling, Dr. Fritz. "Orkan in Ostpreusssen," In Hensel, *Medizin in und aus Ostpreußen.*

Schmidtke, Martin. *Rettungsaktion Ostsee 1944/1945: Eine Grosstat der Menschlichkeit.* Bonn: Bernard und Gräfe, 2006.

Schön, Heinz. *Die "Gustloff" Katastrophe: Bericht eines Überlebenden über die größte Schiffskatastrophe im Zweiten Weltkrieg.* Stuttgart: Motorbuch Verlag, 1984.

————. *Die Tragödie der Flüchtlingsschiffe Gesunken in der Ostsee 1944/45.* Stuttgart: Motorbuch Verlag, 2004.

Schüler-Springorum, Stefanie. *Die jüdische Minderheit in Königsberg/Preußen, 1871–1945.* Göttingen: Vanderhoeck und Ruprecht, 1996.

Scott-Clark, Catherine, and Adrian Levy. *The Amber Room: The Fate of the World's Greatest Lost Treasure.* New York: Walter Publishing, 2004.

Seaton, Albert. *The Russo-German War 1941–1945.* New York: Praeger Publishers, 1970.

Sherwood, Robert E. *Roosevelt and Hopkins: An Intimate History.* New York: Harper and Brothers, 1948.

Sipols, Vilnis. *The Road to Great Victory: Soviet Diplomacy 1941–1945.* Moscow: Progress Publishers, 1985.

Snyder, Timothy. *Bloodlands: Europe Between Hitler and Stalin.* New York: Basic Books, 2010.

Soine, Christel. *Vertrieben, geschunden, mißbraucht: Die Geschichte einer Verteibung aus Ostpreußen.* Völklingen: Verein für Heimatkunde Nonnweiler e. V., 1995.

Solzhenitsyn, Alexander. *Prussian Nights.* Translated from the Russian by Robert Conquest. New York: Farrar, Straus and Giroux, 1977.

Sommerfeld, Aloys. *Juden im Ermland: Ihr Schicksal nach 1933.* Zeitschrift für die Geschichte und Altertumskunde Ermlands 10. Osnabrück: Verlag A. Fromm, 1991.

Stamm, Hans-Ulrich. *Frag mich nach Ostpreußen: Ostpreußisches Mosaik.* Leer: Gerhard Rautenberg, 1974.

Starlinger, Dr. Wilhelm. *"Grenzen der Sowjetmacht,"* Beiheft zum Jahrbuch der Albertus-Universität Königsberg/Pr. IX (Der Göttinger Arbeitskreis Veröffentlichung Nr. 123). Würzburg: Holzner Verlag, 1954.

Steinert, Marlis G. *Hitler's War and the Germans: Public Mood and Attitude during the Second World War.* Edited and translated by Thomas E. J. de Witt. Athens, Ohio: Ohio University Press, 1977.

Stettinius, Edward. *Roosevelt and the Russians.* Garden City, N.Y.: Doubleday, 1949.

Terry, Sarah M. *Poland's Place in Europe: General Sikorski and the Origin of the Oder-Neisse Line.* Princeton: Princeton University Press, 1983.

Ther, Philipp, and Ana Siljak, eds. *Redrawing Nations: Ethnic Cleansing in East Central Europe 1944–1948.* Lanham, Md.: Rowman and Littlefield, 2001.

Thiel, Hans. *The Wolves of World War II: An East Prussian Soldier's Memoir of Combat and Captivity on the Eastern Front.* Jefferson, N.C. and London: McFarland, 2007.

Tilitzki, Christian. *Alltag in Ostpreußen 1940–1945: Die geheimen Lagerberichte der Königsberger Justiz.* Würzberg: Flechsig, 2003.

Truman, Harry S. *Years of Decisions: Memoirs,* vol. 1. Garden City, N.Y.: Doubleday, 1955.

Ungvary, Karisztian. *Battle for Budapest: 100 Days in World War II.* London and New York: I. B. Tauris, 2005.

U.S. Department of State, *Documents on Germany 1944–1985.* Department of State Publication 9446. Washington, D.C., 1985.

U.S. Department of State, Foreign Relations of the United States. *The Conferences at Cairo and Tehran.* Diplomatic Papers, Publication 7187. Washington, D.C.: Department of State, 1961. This volume is subsequently referred to as FRUS 1943.

―――. *The Conferences at Washington and Quebec, 1943.* Washington, D.C., 1970.

―――. *The Conferences at Malta and Yalta, 1945.* Department of State Publication 6199. Washington, D.C., 1955. The volume is subsequently referred to as FRUS 1945.

―――. *The Conference of Berlin (The Potsdam Conference) 1945.* Department of State Publication 7163, vols. I and II. Washington, D.C., 1960. This reference is subsequently referred to as FRUS 1945 Potsdam.

Vaughan, Hal. *Doctor to the Resistance: The Heroic True Story of an American Surgeon and his American Family in Occupied Paris.* Washington, D.C.: Brassey's, 2004.

Vertreibung und Vertreibungsverbrechen 1945–1948. Bericht des Bundesarchivs vom 28. Mai 1974. Archivalien und ausgewählte Erlebnisberichte. Bonn: Kulturstiftung der Deutschen Vertriebenen, 1989.

Wagner, Wolfgang. *The Genesis of the Oder-Neisse Line.* Stuttgart: Brentano-Verlag, 1957.

Weber, Mark. "Stutthof: An Important but Little-Known Wartime Camp." *The Journal of Historical Review* 16, no. 5 (September/October, 1997): 2–6.

Webster, Charles, and Noble Frankland. *The Strategic Air Offensive Against Germany, 1939–1945,* vol. III. London: H. M. Stationery Office, 1961.

Weinberg, Gerhard L. *A World at Arms: A Global History of World War II.* New York: Cambridge University Press, 1994.

Weissbrodt, David, and Connie de la Vega. *International Human Rights Law: An Introduction.* Philadelphia: University of Pennsylvania Press, 2007.

Wermter, Otto. "Flucht und Vertreibung der Familie Wermter aus Heinrikau in Ostpreußen, Januar 1945–Dezember 1946." Unpublished memoirs, 1995.

Werth, Alexander. *Russia at War 1941–1945.* New York: E. P. Dutton, 1964.

Wieck, Michael. *A Childhood under Stalin and Hitler: Memoirs of a "Certified Jew."* Madison, Wis.: The University of Wisconsin Press, 2003.

Wiesel, Elie. *Night.* New York: Hill and Wang, 2006.

Zaloga, Stephen J. *Bagration 1944: The Destruction of Army Group Center.* Westport, Conn., and London: Praeger Illustrated Military History Series, 2004.

Zeidler, Manfred. *Kriegsende im Osten: Die Rote Armee und die Besetzung Deutschlands östlich von Oder und Neiße, 1944/45.* Munich: Oldenburg Verlag, 1996.

Ziemke, Earl F. *Stalingrad to Berlin: The German Defeat in the East.* New York: Barnes and Noble, 1987.

MAP AND ILLUSTRATION CREDITS

Map 1. Germany before World War I. www.zum.de/whkmla/histatlas/germany/kaiser, copyright WHKMLA, reproduced with permission, Alexander Ganse

Map 2. Germany after World War I with Polish Corridor. www.zum.de/whkmla/histatlas/germany/weimar, copyright WHKMLA, reproduced with permission, Alexander Ganse

Map 3. Germany after World War II. www.zum.de/whkmla/histatlas/germany/194548, copyright WHKMLA, reproduced with permission, Alexander Ganse

Map 4. Union of the Duchy of Prussia and Brandenburg. Wikipedia Commons

Map 5. East Prussia 1923 – 1939. Wikipedia Commons: GNU Free Documentation License

Map 6. The Heiligenbeil Cauldron. Graefe and Unser

Map 7. Towns on the Bay of Danzig. Graefe and Unser

Map 8. Last Voyage of the *Wilhelm Gustloff*. Guido Knopp

Map 9. Westward Shift of Poland's Borders. Wikipedia Commons

Map 10. Poland: Eastern Frontier with Stalin's Red Line. U.S. Department of State

Map 11. The Oder-Neisse Line. Wikipedia Commons: GNU Free Documentation License

Illustration 1.   Marienburg Castle around 1944. Library of Congress, Prints and Photographs Division

Illustration 2.   Königsberg Castle around 1900. Library of Congress, Prints and Photographs Division

Illustration 3.   Damaged Königsberg Castle with Soviet Tanks. *Illustrations from the Front*, No. 8 (106) April 1945. Photo by G. Beliakin

Illustration 4.   Nemmersdorf Dead on Field. Wikipedia Commons: Bundesarchiv, Bild 1011-464-03831-26 / Kleiner / CC-BY-SA

Illustration 5.   Massacre at Metgethen. Library of Congress, Prints and Photographs Division

Illustration 6.   Flight on a Wagon. Wikpedia Commons: Bundesarchiv, Bild 175-S00-00326 / CC-BY-SA

Illustration 7.   Refugees Boarding Ship at Pillau. Wikipedia Commons: Bundesarchiv, Bild 146-1972-093-51 / CC-BY-SA

Illustration 8.   Abandoned Wagons on Trek. Art Resource, New York

Illustration 9.   Trek Crossing the Frisches Haff. Deutsches Historisches Museum, Berlin

Illustration 10.   Treks on the Ice – Photo by Soviet Plane. Archive Martin Schmidtke

Illustration 11.   *Wilhelm Gustloff.* Wikipedia Commons: Bundesarchiv, Bild 183-H27992/Sönnke, Hans / CC-BY-SA

Illustration 12.   Diagram of Where Torpedoes Hit the *Gustloff* . Archive Heinz Schön

Illustration 13.   Torpedo Boat *Löwe*. Archive Martin Schmidtke

Illustration 14.   Torpedo Boat *T 36*. Archive Heinz Schön

Illustration 15.   *Cap Arcona*. Wikipedia Commons

If not otherwise indicated, all translations from German to English were made by Heide Clark.

INDEX

ABOUT THE AUTHOR

Peter B. Clark is a Phi Beta Kappa graduate in philosophy from Reed College and received a PhD in economics from MIT. He taught economics at Duke University, worked at the Federal Reserve Board in Washington, and retired as a Senior Advisor from the International Monetary Fund. During his career as an economist, he published widely in his field. Married to a German who escaped from East Prussia in 1944, he became fluent in German and visited Germany many times, including the former capital of East Prussia, Königsberg (now Kaliningrad). This is his first non-economics book.

20184651R00336

Printed in Great Britain
by Amazon